משניות

ArtScroll Mishnah Series®

A rabbinic commentary to the Six Orders of the Mishnah

Rabbis Nosson Scherman / Meir Zlotowitz

General Editors

the mishnah

ARTSCROLL MISHNAH SERIES / A NEW TRANSLATION WITH A COMMENTARY **YAD AVRAHAM** ANTHOLOGIZED FROM TALMUDIC SOURCES AND CLASSIC COMMENTATORS.

Published by

Mesorah Publications, ltd

83-449

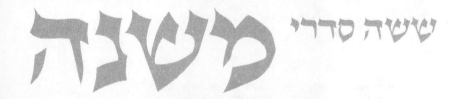

ששה סדרי **משנה**

FIRST EDITION
First Impression ... April, 1981

Published and Distributed by
MESORAH PUBLICATIONS, Ltd.
Brooklyn, New York 11223

Distributed in Israel by
MESORAH MAFITZIM / J. GROSSMAN
Rechov Bayit Vegan 90/5
Jerusalem, Israel

Distributed in Europe by
J. LEHMANN HEBREW BOOKSELLERS
20 Cambridge Terrace
Gateshead
Tyne and Wear
England NE8 1RP

THE ARTSCROLL MISHNAH SERIES®
SEDER MOED VOL. II: *PESACHIM / SHEKALIM*
© *Copyright 1981*
by MESORAH PUBLICATIONS, Ltd.
1969 Coney Island Avenue / Brooklyn, N.Y. 11223 / (212) 339-1700

ISBN
0-89906-254-7 (hard cover)
0-89906-255-5 (paperback)

ספר ממסכרת
חברת ארטסקרול בע״מ

Typography by Compuscribe at ArtScroll Studios, Ltd.
1969 Coney Island Avenue / Brooklyn, N.Y. 11223 / (212) 339-1700

Printed in the United States of America by Moriah Offset

﹂§ Seder Moed Vol. II

Pesachim / פסחים

Shekalim / שקלים

The Publishers are grateful to
YESHIVA TORAH VODAATH AND MESIVTA
for their efforts in the publication of the
ARTSCROLL MISHNAH SERIES

מסכת זו מוקדש

על ידי

ארי׳ ועליזה קסטנבאום
לזכר עולם לנשמת אביהם זצ״ל

ר׳ דוד ב״ר אליהו זצ״ל

עָנָיו בְּדַרְכּוֹ וְגָדוֹל בְּמַעֲשָׂיו וַחֲסָדָיו

Τhis tractate is reverently dedicated
   by
Mr. and Mrs. Leonard A. Kestenbaum
Lawrence, New York
in loving memory of their father
David Kestenbaum זצ״ל
Humble in manner, great in deeds and charity

His myriad good works for Klal Yisroel
included staunch support of
Torah Vodaath

נפטר לב״ע ט׳ אז׳ר ב׳ תשי״ז

ת נ צ ב ה

RABBI MOSES FEINSTEIN
455 F. D. R. DRIVE
NEW YORK, N. Y. 10002

OREGON 7-1222

משה פיינשטיין

ר"מ תפארת ירושלים

בנוא יארק

בע"ה

(handwritten letter in Hebrew)

נאם משה פיינשטיין

הנה ידידי הרב הגאון ר' אברהם יוסף ראזענבערג שליט"א אשר היה מתלמידי החשובים
ביותר וגם הרביץ תורה בכמה ישיבות ואצלינו בישיבתנו בסטעטן אייללנד, ובזמן האחרון
הוא מתעסק בתרגום ספרי קודש ללשון אנגלית המדוברת ומובנת לבני מדינה זו, וכבר
איתמחי גברא בענין תרגום לאנגלית וכעת תרגם משניות לשפת אנגלית וגם לקוטים מדברי
רבותינו מפרשי משניות על כל משנה ומשנה בערך, והוא לתועלת גדול להרבה אינשי
ממדינה זו שלא התרגלו מילדותם ללמוד המשנה וגם יש הרבה שבעזר השי"ת התקרבו
לתורה ויראת שמים כשכבר נתגדלו ורוצים ללמוד משניות בנקל בשפה
המורגלת להם, שהוא ממזכי הרבים בלמוד משניות וזכותו גדול. ואני מברכו שיצליחהו
השי"ת בחבורו זה. וגם אני מברך את חברת ארטסקרול אשר תחת הנהלת הרב הנכבד הרב ידידי
מוהר"ר מאיר יעקב בן ידידי הגאון ר' אהרן שליט"א זלאטאוויץ אשר הוציאו כבר הרבה
חבורים חשובים לזכות את הרבים וכעת הם מוציאים לאור את המשניות הנ"ל.

ועל זה באתי על החתום בז' אדר תשל"ט בנוא יארק.

נאום משה פיינשטיין

מכתב ברכה

יעקב קמנצקי

RABBI J. KAMENECKI

38 SADDLE RIVER ROAD

MONSEY, NEW YORK 10952

בע"ה

יום ה' ערב חג השבועות תשל"ס, פה מאנסי.

כבוד הרבני איש החסד שוע ונדיב מוקיר רבנן מר אלעזר נ"י גליק
שלו' וברכת כל טוב.

מה מאד שמחתי בהודעי כי כבודו רכש לעצמו הזכות שייקרא ע"ש
בנו המנוח הפירוש מבואר על כל ששת סדרי משנה ע"י "ארטסקראל"
והנה חברה זו יצאה לה מוניטין בפירושה על תנ"ך, והבה נקוה שכשם
שהצליחה בתורה שבכתב כן תצליח בתורה שבע"פ. ובהיות שאותיות
"משנה" הן כאותיות "נשמה" לפיכך טוב עשה בכוונתו לעשות זאת לעילוי
נשמת בנו המנוח אברהם יוסף ע"ה, ומאד מתאים השם "יד אברהם" לזה
הפירוש, כדמצינו במקרא (ש"ב י"ח) כי אמר אין לי בן בעבור הזכיר
שמי וגו'. ואין לך דבר גדול מזה להפיץ ידיעת תורה שבע"פ בקרב
אחינו שאינם רגילים בלשון הקדש. וד' הטוב יהי' בעזרו ויוכל לברך
על המוגמר. וירוה רוב נחת מכל אשר אתו כנפש מברכו.

יעקב קמנ...

מכתב ברכה

YESHIVAT TELSHE   ישיבת טלז
Kiryat Telshe Stone   קרית טלז־סטון
Jerusalem, Israel   ירושלים

בע"ה — ד' בהעלותך — לבני א"י, תשל"ט — פה קרית טלז, באה"ק

מע"כ ידידי האהובים הרב ר' מאיר והרב ר' נתן, נר"ו, שלום וברכה נצח!

אחדשה"ט באהבה ויקר,

לשמחה רבה היא לי להודע שהרחבתם גדול עבודתכם בקודש לתורה שבע"פ, בהוצאת המשנה בתרגום וביאור באנגלית, וראשית עבודתכם במס' מגילה.

אני תקוה שתשימו לב שיצאו הדברים מתוקנים מנקודת ההלכה, וחזקה עליכם שתוציאו דבר נאה ומתוקן.

בפנותכם לתורה שבע"פ יפתח אופק חדש בתורת ה' לאלה שקשה עליהם ללמוד הדברים במקורם, ואלה שבכר נתעשרו מעבודתכם במגילת אסתר יכנסו עתה לטרקלין חדש וישמשו להם הדברים דחף ללימוד המשנה, וגדול יהי' שכרכם.

יהא ה' בעזרכם בהוספת טבעת חדשה באותה שלשלת זהב של הפצת תורת ה' להמוני עם לקרב לב ישראל לאבינו שבשמים בתורה ואמונה טהורה.

אוהבכם מלונ"ח,
מרדכי

מכתב ברכה

RABBI SHNEUR KOTLER
BETH MEDRASH GOVOHA
LAKEWOOD, N. J.

בע"ה

שניאור קוטלר
בית מדרש גבוה
לייקוואוד, נ. דז.

[handwritten letter]

בשורת התרחבות עבודתם הגדולה של סגל חבורת "ארטסקרול", המעתיקים ומפרשים, לתחומי התורה בכל לשון שהם שומעים — מבשרת צבא רב לתורה
התושבע"פ, לשים אלה המשפטים לפני הציבור בצורה ולהשמיעם בכל לשון שהם שומעים — מבשרת צבא רב לתורה
בפיהם — לפתוח אוצרות בשנות בצורה ולהשמיעם בכל לשון שהם שומעים — מבשרת צבא רב לתורה
ולימודה [ע' תהלים ס"ח י"ב בתרגום יונתן], והיא מאוחות ההתעוררות ללימוד התורה, וזאת התעודה
על התנוצצות קיום ההבטחה "כי לא תשכח מפי זרעו". אשרי הזוכים להיות בין שלוחי ההשגחה לקיימה
וביצועה.

יה"ר כי תצליח מלאכת שמים בידם, ויזכו ללמוד וללמד ולשמור מסורת הקבלה כי בהרקת המים
החיים מכלי אל כלי תשתמר חיותם, יעמוד טעמם בם וריחם לא נמר. [וע' משאחז"ל בכ"מ ושמרתם זו
משנה — וע' חי' מרן רי"ז הלוי עה"ת בפ' ואתחנן] ותהי' משנתם שלמה וברורה, ישמחו בעבודתם חברים
ותלמידים, "שוטטו רבים ותרבה הדעת", עד יקויים "אז אהפוך אל העמים שפה ברורה וגו'" [צפני' ג'
ט', עי' פי' אבן עזרא ומצודת דוד שם].

ונזכה כולנו לראות בהתכנסות הגליות בזכות המשניות כל חז"ל עפ"י הכתוב "גם כי יתנו בגוים עתה
אקבצם", בגאולה השלמה בב"א.

הכו"ח לכבוד התורה, יום ו' עש"ק לס' "ויוצא פרח ויצץ ציץ ויגמול שקדים", ד' תמוז התשל"ט

יוסף חיים שניאור קוטלר
בלאאמו"ר הגר"א זצוק"ל

מכתב ברכה

ישיבה דפילאדעלפיא

(handwritten letter)

ב"ה

לכבוד ידידי וידיד ישיבתנו, מהראשונים לכל דבר שבקדושה

הרבני הנדיב המפורסם ר' אליעזר הכהן גליק נ"י

אחדשה"ט באהבה,

בשורה טובה שמעתי שכב' מצא את המקום המתאים לעשות יד ושם להנציח זכרו **של בנו אברהם יוסף ע"ה** שנקטף בנעוריו. "ונתתי להם בביתי ובחומתי יד ושם". אין לו להקב"ה אלא ד' אמות של הלכה בלבד. א"כ זהו בית ד' לימוד תורה שבע"פ וזהו המקום לעשות יד ושם לנשמת בנו ע"ה.

נר ד' נשמת אדם אמר הקב"ה נרי בידך ונרך בידי. נר מצוה ותורה אור, תורה זהו הנר של הקב"ה וכששומרים נר של הקב"ה שעל ידי הפירוש "יד אברהם" בשפה הלעוזית יתברבה ויתפשט לימוד ושקיעת התורה בבתי ישראל. ד' ישמור נשמת אדם.

בנו אברהם יוסף ע"ה נתברך בהמדה שבו נכללות כל המדות, לב טוב והיה אהוב לחבריו. בלמדו בישיבתנו היה לו הרצון לעלות במעלות התורה וכשעלה לארצנו הקדושה היתה היתה מבקשים להמשיך בלמודיו. ביקוש זה ימצא מלואו ועל ידי הרבים המבקשים דרך ד', שהפירוש "יד אברהם" יהא מפתח להם לים התלמוד.

התורה נקראת, "אש דתי" ונמשלה לאש שיש לה הכח לפעפע ברזל לפצוע כחות האדם, הניצוץ שהאיר בך רבנו הרב שרגא פייוועל מנדלוביץ זצ"ל שמרת עליו, ועשה חיל. עכשיו אתה מסייע להאיר נצוצות בנשמות בני ישראל שיעשה חיל ויהא לאור גדול.

תקותי עזה שכל התלמידי חכמים שנדבת רוחם להוציא מלאכה ענקית זו לפרש המשניות כולה, יצא עבודתם ברוח פאר והדר ויכוונו לאמיתה של תורה ויתקדש שם שמים יתירבה על ידי מלאכה זו.

יתברך כב' ובב"ב לראות ולרוות נחת רוח מצאצאיו.

הכו"ח לכבוד התורה ותומכיה עש"ק במדבר תשל"ט

אלי' סווי

מכתב ברכה

דוד קאהן

ביהמ"ד גבול יעבץ
ברוקלין, נוא יארק

[מכתב בכתב יד]

בס"ד   כ"ה למטמונים תשל"ט

כבוד רחימא דנפשאי, עושה ומעשה
ר' אלעזר הכהן גליק נטריה רחמנא ופרקיה

שמוע שמעתי שכבר תקעת כפיך לתמוך במפעל האדיר של חברת ארטסקרול — הידוע בכל קצווי תבל ע"י עבודתה הכבירה בהפצת תורה — לתרגם ולבאר ששה סדרי משנה באנגלית. כוונתך להנציח זכר בנך הנחמד אברהם יוסף ז"ל שנקטף באבו בזמן שעלה לארץ הקודש בתקופת התרוממות הנפש ושאיפה לקדושה, למטרה זו יכונה הפירוש בשם "יד אברהם"; וגם האיר ה' רוחך לגרום עילוי לנשמתו הטהורה שע"י יתרבה לימוד התורה שניתנה בשבעים לשון, על ידי כלי מפואר זה.

מכיוון שהנני מכיר היטב שני הצדדים, אוכל לומר לדבק טוב, והנני תקוה שיצלח המפעל הזה לתת יד ושם זכות לנשמת אברהם יוסף ז"ל. חזקה על חברת ארטסקרול שתוציא דבר נאה מתוקן ומתקבל מתחת ידה להגדיל תורה ולהאדירה.

והנני מברך אותך שתמצא נחם לנפשך, שהאבא זוכה לברא, ותשבע נחת — אתה עם רעיתך תחיה — מכל צאצאיכם היקרים אכי"ר.

ידידך עז
דוד קאהן

[xiii]   *Approbation*/מכתב ברכה

Preface

אָמַר ר׳ יוֹחָנָן: לֹא כָּרַת הקב״ה בְּרִית עִם יִשְׂרָאֵל אֶלָּא עַל־תּוֹרָה
שֶׁבְּעַל־פֶּה שֶׁנֶּאֱמַר ״כִּי עַל־פִּי הַדְּבָרִים הָאֵלֶּה כָּרַתִּי אִתְּךָ בְּרִית...״
R' Yochanan said: The Holy One, Blessed be He, sealed a covenant
with Israel only because of the Oral Torah, as it is said [Exodus
34:27]: For according to these words have I sealed a covenant with
you... (Gittin 60b).

In presenting the Torah public with this new volume of the
ARTSCROLL MISHNAH SERIES, we again extend a בִּרְכַּת הוֹדָיָה, a
blessing of thanksgiving, to Hashem Yisborach for endowing Mesorah
Publications with the awesome privilege of serving as His vehicle for
Torah dissemination. Simultaneous with the ongoing work on Tanach,
the Siddur, and other classics of Torah literature, the new Mishnah
Series has ב״ה become a major service to the English-speaking public
that has echoed the words of King David: גַּל־עֵינַי וְאַבִּיטָה נִפְלָאוֹת מִתּוֹרָתֶךָ,
Uncover my eyes that I may see wonders of Your Torah [Psalms
119:18].

Heretofore, there has been a serious lack of adequate English treatment of the Mishnah. In the view of roshei hayeshivah and Torah
scholars, there exists a need for a work that will treat he Mishnah with
depth and scope. Like the ARTSCROLL TANACH SERIES, this new series
draws upon large cross-sections of Talmudic, rabbinic, and halachic
sources. The purpose is to enable the reader to study each mishnah as
though he were sitting in a study hall, participating in the give and take
of Talmudic scholarship.

Nevertheless, we must again inject two words of caution.

First: Although the Mishnah, by definition, is a compendium of laws,
the final halachah does not necessarily follow the Mishnah. The
development of the final halachah proceeds through the Gemara, commentators, codifiers, responsa, and the acknowledged Torah poskim.
Even when our commentary cites the Shulchan Aruch, the intention is
to sharpen the reader's understanding of the Mishnah, but not to be a
basis for actual practice. In short, this work is meant as a study of the
first step of our recorded Oral Law — no more.

Second: As we have stressed in our other books, an ArtScroll commentary is not meant as a substitute for study of the sources. While this
commentary, like others in the various series, will be immensely useful
even to accomplished scholars and will often bring to light ideas and
sources they may have overlooked, we strongly urge those who are able
to study the classic seforim in the original to do so.

The pattern of the commentary and the style of transliteration follow those of the ARTSCROLL TANACH SERIES.

Hebrew terms connoting concepts for which there are no exact English translations are generally defined the first time they appear and transliterated thereafter.

For the reader's convenience, every word of the Mishnah has been included in the commentary headings. Therefore, the reader may study the commentary continuously without constantly referring back to the text, should he so desire.

The translation attempts to follow the text faithfully. Variations have been made when dictated by the need for clarity or English usage and syntax. Any words that have been added for the sake of flow and clarity are bracketed.

Some of the classic sources from which the commentary have been culled are: the GEMARA (abbreviated Gem.) with its commentaries, such as RASHI (1040-1105); TOSAFOS (Tos.) [Talmudic glosses by the school of scholars known collectively as Tosafists, who flourished after Rashi]; RITVA [R' Yom Tov Ishbili (1250-1330)]; RAN R' Nissim Gerondi (mid-14th cent.)]; NIMUKEI YOSEF [R' Yosef Chaviva (early 15th cent.)]; the classical Mishnah commentators; RAMBAM (1135-1204); R' MENACHEM MEIRI (1249-1306); RAV [R' Ovadiah of Bertinoro (end of 15th cent.)]; TOSEFOS YOM TOV (Tos. Yom Tov) [R' Yom Tov Lipmann Heller (1579-1659)]; and more recent commentators: TOSEFOS R' AKIVA [R' Akiva Eiger (1761-1837); TIFERES YISRAEL (Tif. Yis.) [R' Yisrael Lipschutz (1782-1860)], and many others who wrote on individual tractates. Some of them are listed below.

Generally, the commentary first offers the interpretation of Rav — Rabbeinu Ovadiah of Bertinoro — the premier commentator to Mishnah. We attempt to show Rav's sources for his comments, including the various discussions of the Gemara and the classic commentators. Where the preponderance of authorities compels us to deviate from Rav's interpretation, we attempt to show why. Other comments or more involved discussions are given in a smaller type size; the reader seeking only a basic understanding of the Mishnah may limit his study to the comments given in larger type.

We have placed major emphasis on Rambam's interpretation, as found in his Commentary to Mishnah and in Mishneh Torah, his halachic compendium. In referring to Rambam's commentary, we use R' Yosef Kafich's justly acclaimed translation of what is assumed to be Rambam's own manuscript.

Although most of the sources cited in the commentary will be familiar to scholars, some are less well-known. Among them are:

Rivevan to Shekalim by **R' Yehudah ben Binyamin HaRofeh of the family Anavim** (מִן הָעֲנָוִים; De Mansi), thirteenth century Italian commentator.

R' Shmuel — Commentary to Yerushalmi Shekalim attributed to anonymous disciple of the Tosafist **R' Shmuel ben Shneur** of Evreux.

R' Meshulam — Commentary to Yerushalmi by an unidentified Tosafist.

Rosh — Commentary to Shekalim by the famed commentator and Posek, published as *Perush Miksav Yad Kadmon.*

R' Shlomo Sirilio, a contemporary of **Yosef Karo,** a commentary on Yerushalmi Zeraim.

Taklin Chadatin and *Mishnas Eliyahu* to Yerushalmi Shekalim (in the Vilna ed. of the Talmud) by **R' Yisroel of Shklov,** a disciple of the Vilna Gaon.

Shoshanim L'David, by **R' David Pardo,** a commentary to Mishnah.

Lechem Shamayim by **R' Yaakov Emden,** a commentary to Mishnah, and the same author's *Mishneh Lechem,* glosses to Zeraim and Moed.

Kol HaRemez, by **R' Moshe Zacuto,** commentary to Mishnah.

Hon Ashir, by **R' Emanuel Chai Riki,** commentary to Mishnah.

N o such work can serve the need for which it is intended unless the author is a talmid chacham of a very high caliber. We are particularly gratified, therefore, to have engaged authors of high scholarship and accomplishment. Although anthologized from numerous sources each commentary is original in the sense that it reflects the author's own understanding, selection, and presentation.

This volume was written by RABBI HERSH GOLDWURM, a talmid chacham of unusual distinction. His earlier contributions to the ArtScroll Series, the commentaries to Daniel and Yoma, stamped him as a man of rare depth, breadth, and judgment. Self-effacing though he is, his work proclaims his stature. Mesorah Publications is proud to make his Torah knowledge available to Klal Yisrael.

A work of such magnitude is not done singlehandedly, though the scholarship is the author's. RABBI SHMUEL LICHTENSTEIN provided invaluable research and a first draft of Pesachim; and RABBI AVIE GOLD and RABBI NAFTALI KEMPLER assisted materially in producing a sefer worthy of the expectations of ArtScroll readers.

RABBI SHEAH BRANDER has displayed so consistently high a standard of graphic skill, that one runs the danger of taking his artistry for granted. We do not.

We are grateful to the staff of Mesorah Publications whose diligence and dedication finds expression in this sefer: MRS. SHIRLEY KIFFEL, MISS CHANEE FREIER, MISS EDEL STREICHER, MRS. SHEVI ASIA and MRS. FAIGIE WEINBAUM. STEPHEN BLITZ bears gracefully and skillfully the responsibility of disseminating the ArtScroll Series to the public.

We express our thanks to RABBI DAVID FEINSTEIN שליט״א and RABBI DAVID COHEN שליט״א whose constant concern and interest throughout the history of the ArtScroll Series have been in further evidence in the course of this work.

We are grateful to the officers and directors of YESHIVA TORAH VODAATH AND MESIVTA, whose assistance has done much to make the Mishnah Series possible. One of America's oldest and greatest Torah centers, Torah Vodaath now adds the printed word of Mishnah to its honor roll of distinguished service to Jewry.

Finally, we again express our deep appreciation to MR. AND MRS. LOUIS GLICK who have dedicated the commentary of the entire ARTSCROLL MISHNAH SERIES. It bears the name YAD AVRAHAM, in memory of their son AVRAHAM YOSEF ע״ה. An appreciation of the niftar will appear in Tractate Berachos. May this dissemination of the Mishnah in his memory be a source of merit for his soul. תנצב״ה.

Both in his role as an unassuming, but outstanding, patron of Torah and as a major figure in Torah Vodaath, Mr. Glick displays a constant and dedicated interest in our work. We are inspired by him and resolve to live up to his hopes for the ArtScroll Mishnah Series. May he and Mrs. Glick be blessed for their generous dedication to Torah, of which this project is but one instance.

Rabbi Nosson Scherman / Rabbi Meir Zlotowitz

כ״ז אדר ב תשמ״א / April, 1981
Brooklyn, New York

ﻼ מסכת פסחים ﻼ
ﻼ Tractate Pesachim

Translation and anthologized commentary by
Rabbi Hersh Goldwurm

Mesorah Publications, ltd

⅏§ Tractate Pesachim

The festival of Pesach, or *Chag HaMatzos* [literally, *Festival of Matzos*] celebrates the central event of Jewish history, the redemption of the Jewish people from Egypt. The significance of the redemption is best evidenced by the fact that the Ten Commandments begin with the declaration, *I am HASHEM, your God, who delivered you from the land of Egypt* (Exodus 20:2). The very fact that God introduces Himself as the Redeemer rather than the Creator serves to emphasize His role as the Mover of history, not merely its Initiator. The constant realization of His Divine Providence has sustained our people and given us the courage to withstand the cruelties of history and to imbue the Nation of Israel with the resilience to renew itself, notwithstanding the pogroms, massacres, and expulsions visited upon us throughout the ages.

In promulgating the commandments that mold our lives, the Torah devoted more *mitzvos* and rules to Pesach than to any other *mitzvah* or festival. *Rambam* enumerates three positive and five negative commandments relevant to the festival, in addition to the four positive and twelve negative commandments relating to the *Korban Pesach* (Pesach sacrifice), a total of twenty-four commandments related to the celebration of Pesach.

Our tractate is divided into two basic parts [and for this reason it is named in the plural *'Pesachim' (Meiri).*] The first four and the last chapters deal with the eight commandments that are unrelated to the Temple obligations relating to the Pesach sacrifice. They are (in *Rambam's* view):

1. To refrain from eating *chametz* (leaven) from midday of the fourteenth day of Nissan, Pesach eve (see *comm.* to 1:4);

2. to remove *chametz* on the fourteenth day;

3. to refrain from eating *chametz* during Pesach;

4. to refrain from eating a mixture containing *chametz*, during Pesach (see *comm.* to 3:1);

5. *chametz* shall not be 'seen' all seven days in a Jew's possession;

6. *chametz* shall not be 'found' all seven days in a Jew's possession;

7. to eat matzah on the Seder night; and

8. to relate the story of the redemption from Egypt on the Seder night.

With some tangential digressions, our tractate is arranged according to the sequence followed in the fulfillment of the *mitzvos* of the festival. The first three chapters discuss the obligation to 'search' for *chametz* on the night before Pesach (1:1-3), the exact time limits when it is still permitted to consume and derive benefit from *chametz* (1:4-2:1), the delineation of the forms of ownership of, and rights and interest in, *chametz* that obligate one to rid himself of it (2:2-2:3). The rest of the second chapter basically discuss the preparation of food for the festival, including a listing of what may and may not be used for the *mitzvos* of matzah and marror. The third chapter discusses miscellaneous laws, among others a listing of foods that may not be kept on the festival because of their *chametz* content, instructions on how to bake the matzos, and a definition of *chametz*. The fourth chapter deals with the prohibition against work on the afternoon before Pesach. Because the mishnah prefaces this chapter by mentioning the custom not to work even on the morning before Pesach, the Mishnah mentions various other customs not pertaining to the festival.

Chapters 5-9 deal with the laws of the regular Pesach offerings, on the fourteenth of Nissan, and *Pesach Sheni*, the Second Pesach, that is offered on the fourteenth of Iyar by those who could not offer the Pesach at its regular time. The final chapter discusses the laws of the seder service and meal.

אוֹר לְאַרְבָּעָה עָשָׂר בּוֹדְקִים אֶת הֶחָמֵץ לְאוֹר הַנֵּר. כָּל מָקוֹם שֶׁאֵין מַכְנִיסִין בּוֹ חָמֵץ אֵין צָרִיךְ בְּדִיקָה. וְלָמָה אָמְרוּ, ,,שְׁתֵּי שׁוּרוֹת בַּמַּרְתֵּף?'' —

יד אברהם

Chapter 1

1.

❧ The 'Search'

This tractate begins, appropriately, with the first *mitzvah* connected to the Pesach festival, בְּדִיקַת חָמֵץ, the *search for chametz*. This mitzvah is predicated upon the dual *mitzvos* of:

1. Eliminating *chametz* [הַשְׁבָּתָה] from Jewish possession, as stated in Scripture (*Exodus 12:15*): *But on the first day shall you eliminate leaven from your premises.* The Sages (*Gem. 4b-5b*) demonstrate exegetically that the Torah refers not to the first day of Pesach, but to the day *before* the festival (alternatively; to the 'first day' counting from the offering of the Pesach sacrifice). The Sages demonstrate further through Talmudic exegesis that this *mitzvah* applies only to the second half of the day — from noon — preceding the festival.

2. The prohibition against having or keeping *chametz* during Passover. This prohibition is expressed variously as (*Exodus 13:7*): לֹא יֵרָאֶה לְךָ חָמֵץ, *chametz shall not be seen with you*, and (*Exodus 12:1*): שִׁבְעַת יָמִים שְׂאֹר לֹא יִמָּצֵא בְּבָתֵּיכֶם, *[for] seven days leaven shall not be found in your houses.*
[For a full discussion of this topic see Appendix: **Search and Nullification** at the end of this tractate.]

אוֹר — *The evening*

In a departure from its usual meaning of *light*, the term אוֹר is used here to denote *evening*; the local idiom of the tanna who formulated this clause of the mishnah employed this word in this manner (*Gem.* 3a). Just as in Talmudic usage the appellation סַגֵּי נָהוֹר, lit. *much light*, describes a blind person, so is the word for light used here to denote darkness — i.e., night (*Rav; Rambam*).

Many reasons are advanced as to why the mishnah departs from form and uses אוֹר to denote night. *Rambam (Comm.)* suggests the tanna did not want to start with a word having the negative symbolism of 'darkness.' *Ba'al HaMaor* cites the verse (*Psalms* 119:130): *The opening of your words shall illuminate* ... [i.e., a statement of Torah should begin with an allusion to light] as the source of this usage. *Ravad* (glosses to *Ba'al HaMaor*) finds in it a halachic allusion. The 'search' should be commenced at the beginning of the night when some light is yet dis-

cernible (see *Hil. Chametz* 2:3 and *Orach Chaim* 431:1; *Chok Ya'akov* and *Mishnah Berurah* there).

לְאַרְבָּעָה עָשָׂר — *of the fourteenth [of Nissan]*

The *Gemara* (4a) explains that the evening was chosen for the 'search' (rather than early in the morning or in the sixth hour, when the *chametz* is to be burned) because people are usually home then and the darkness is conducive to searching with a candle [while candlelight is hardly noticeable in the daytime]. The use of a candle is a prerequisite for the performance of the search, as set forth further.

בּוֹדְקִים אֶת הֶחָמֵץ — *we must search for the chametz*

Rashi explains that בְּדִיקָה [*bedikah*], *search*, is necessary to ensure that one not transgress the prohibition against keeping *chametz* on the Pesach, but

1. The evening of the fourteenth [of Nissan] we must search for the *chametz* by the light of a candle. Any place into which *chametz* is not brought does not require a search.

So why have the Sages said, "Two rows of a [wine] cellar [must be searched]?" — [the Sages were refer-

YAD AVRAHAM

others (*Tos.* 2a, s.v. אור) say it is necessary only to ensure against inadvertent consumption of *chametz*, which could occur if the *chametz* were not searched out and destroyed (*Rav*). [The Scriptural requirement could be met by a declaration of בִּיטוּל, *nullification*.] (This is discussed at length in the Appendix: *Search and Nullification*.]

The Torah bans two substances on Passover. One is שְׂאוֹר, *se'or*, dough leavened to such a degree that it is used as a leavening agent in other doughs. We will refer to it as leavening. [Although it is frequently rendered *yeast*, this is incorrect. Modern yeast is a fungus that is not necessarily a grain product in its *pure* form, and would not be included in the Scriptural prohibition.] The other is חָמֵץ, *chametz*, a dough or dough product that leavened through any method, whether yeast or leavening was included in its ingredients, or it was left for a period of time considered sufficient for spontaneous leavening.

לְאוֹר הַנֵּר. — *by* [lit. *to*] *the light of a candle.*

Through an exegetical process involving several verses, the *Gemara* (7b) finds an allusion to the requirement of candle light for the search. Consequently, even if the 'search' was not performed at night and must be performed during the day a candle must be used (*Rav; see Orach Chaim* 433:1).

כָּל מָקוֹם שֶׁאֵין מַכְנִיסִין בּוֹ חָמֵץ אֵין צָרִיךְ בְּדִיקָה. — *Any place into which chametz is not* [usually] *brought does not require a search.*

We are not apprehensive that a ro-

dent or the like dragged *chametz* into such a place (*Rambam, Comm.* to mishnah 2).

Alternatively: The Sages did not categorically obligate one to search all chambers [לֹא פְּלוּג] without regard to the probability of *chametz* being there (*Rosh Yosef*).

The *Gemara* (8a) adds that this passage refers specifically to such places as wine cellars and storage places for oil, where *chametz* is not brought customarily. This accounts for the mishnah's question, 'So why have they said ...'

וְלָמָה אָמְרוּ, "שְׁתֵּי שׁוּרוֹת בְּמַרְתֵּף?" — *So why have the Sages* [lit. *they*] *said,* "*Two rows of a* [wine] *cellar* [must be searched]?"

In view of the law that no search is needed in such places, how do we account for the law given below that both Beis Shammai and Beis Hillel concur that two rows of a wine cellar must be searched? (*Rav*).

Sefer HaKerissus (R' Shimshon of Kinon) writes that before the time of R' Yehudah the Prince, the redactor of the Mishnah, there existed an organized codex of mishnah (see the last mishnah in Tractate *Keilim* and R' Akiva Eiger's gloss there). [R' Yehudah merely edited and standardized the text.] In this pre-Mishnaic codex there was a clause saying: שְׁתֵּי שׁוּרוֹת בְּמַרְתֵּף צְרִיכִים בְּדִיקָה — *Two rows in a* [wine] *cellar require a search* (R' Akiva Eiger). [The above explains the apparent paradox later in our mishnah, where Beis Shammai and Beis Hillel disagree about the extent of the 'search' in a wine cellar, but curiously agree that two — no more and no less — rows must be searched; they disagree only as to how to define these two rows. The authoritative pre-Mishnaic codex clearly stated that two rows required search. Beis Shammai and Beis Hillel disagreed, however, on the interpretation of the term 'two rows.'

מָקוֹם שֶׁמַּכְנִיסִין בּוֹ חָמֵץ.
בֵּית שַׁמַּאי אוֹמְרִים: שְׁתֵּי שׁוּרוֹת עַל פְּנֵי כָל
הַמַּרְתֵּף. וּבֵית הִלֵּל אוֹמְרִים: שְׁתֵּי שׁוּרוֹת
הַחִיצוֹנוֹת שֶׁהֵן הָעֶלְיוֹנוֹת.

יד אברהם

Sefer HaKerissus' basic premise concerning the early origin of the Mishnah was presented much earlier by *R' Sherira Gaon* in his famed *Igeres (letter;* see the full text in *Sefer Yuchasin* and other editions). *R' Isaac HaLevi* develops this theme at length in his magnum opum *Doros haRishonim* (v. 1 pp. 206-310, Israeli ed. see especially p. 218).]

Some versions (see *Gemara* and *Shinuyei Nuschaos*) have וּבַמֶּה אָמְרוּ, *And in what instance did they say* ...

מָקוֹם שֶׁמַּכְנִיסִין בּוֹ חָמֵץ. — [The sages were referring to] *a place into which they bring chametz.*

The *Gemara* (8a) explains that there are two types of winecellars. A cellar used for storing wine being held for sale does not require *bedikah,* because *chametz* is never brought there. The other type of cellar holds wine for domestic use. This type of cellar must be searched, because a servant may sometimes go there during a meal for more wine, and he may enter the cellar while holding a piece of bread. If so, he may very well inadvertently leave the *chametz* in the cellar.

בֵּית שַׁמַּאי אוֹמְרִים: שְׁתֵּי שׁוּרוֹת — *Beis Shammai say: Two rows*

[I.e., two rows of the aforementioned winecellar must be searched. Alternatively, Bais Shammai specifically refer to and define the two-row limitation placed upon the search for *chametz* in the pre-Mishnaic mishnah (see above s.v. וּבַמֶּה).]

עַל פְּנֵי כָל הַמַּרְתֵּף. — *over the entire front*

of the [wine] cellar [must be searched].

It was the practice of vinters to arrange the barrels so that each one rested upon the two barrels under it, very much as bricks are laid row upon row.

Beis Shammai require that two layers of barrels be searched. One is the entire vertical wall of barrels facing the front of the cellar, from floor to ceiling and from left to right. The other layer requiring *bedikah* is the horizontal layer of barrels facing the ceiling, from the front of the cellar to the back and from left to right (*Rav*).

The above is R' Yochanan's understanding of Beis Shammai's view. R' Yehudah interprets their words as meaning the two front, vertical walls from top to bottom (*Gem.* 8b).

וּבֵית הִלֵּל אוֹמְרִים: שְׁתֵּי שׁוּרוֹת הַחִיצוֹנוֹת שֶׁהֵן הָעֶלְיוֹנוֹת. — *But Beis Hillel say: The two outer rows which are the uppermost.*

[Beis Hillel disagree. They define שׁוּרָה, *row,* in our mishnah not as an entire wall of barrels, but rather as one of the many rows in each wall reaching from side to side.]

Of these rows only the two uppermost in the outer vertical wall must be searched (*Rav*).

The above is the amora Rav's opinion. Shmuel holds that Beis Hillel refers to the uppermost row of the outer wall and the row immediately behind it; the uppermost rows of the two outermost walls are meant (*Gem.* 8b).

2.

The following mishnah deals with the question of whether one need fear that weasels or other rodents — or any living thing, for that matter — carried *chametz* into an area after it had been searched. A careful reading of the mishnah reveals two underlying premises:

(a)   Though difficult, it would be possible to guard against the possibility that

1   ring to] a place into which we bring *chametz*.

1   Beis Shammai say: Two rows over the entire front of the [wine] cellar [must be searched].

But Beis Hillel say: The two outer rows which are the uppermost.

rodents had moved *chametz* from house to house in a courtyard or from place to place in a house.

(2) Theoretically, *chametz* could be dragged from courtyard to courtyard or even from city to city. Protection against such sweeping possibilities is simply impossible. For the Sages to require safeguards against the first fear and not against

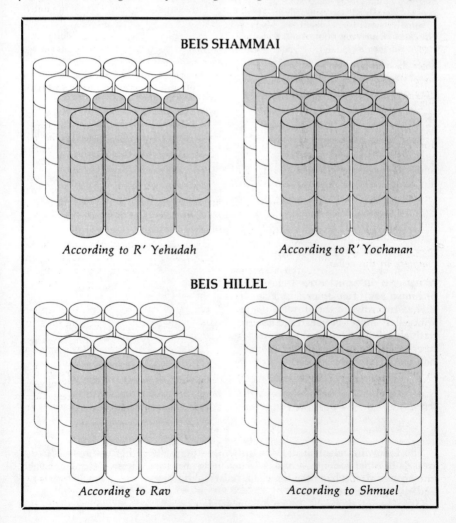

BEIS SHAMMAI

According to R' Yehudah   *According to R' Yochanan*

BEIS HILLEL

According to Rav   *According to Shmuel*

פסחים

א/ב **אֵין** [ב] חוֹשְׁשִׁין שֶׁמָּא גֵּרְרָה חֻלְדָּה מִבַּיִת
לְבַיִת, וּמִמָּקוֹם לְמָקוֹם. דְּאִם כֵּן,
מֵחָצֵר לְחָצֵר וּמֵעִיר לְעִיר. אֵין לַדָּבָר סוֹף.

יד אברהם

the second one would be inconsistent. Therefore, they ruled that neither possibility need be safeguarded against.

Various difficulties with approaches to these premises will be discussed at the end of the mishnah.

אֵין חוֹשְׁשִׁין שֶׁמָּא גֵּרְרָה חֻלְדָּה מִבַּיִת לְבַיִת, — *We need not be concerned that a weasel may have dragged* [chametz] *from house to house,*

[From a house (in the same court-yard) that has not yet been searched, to one that is already *chametz*-free.]

[The translation renders חֻלְדָּה as *weasel,* the meaning attributed to this word by tradition. Other translations are, *mole* and *rat.*]

וּמִמָּקוֹם לְמָקוֹם. — *or from place to place.*

Or from an unsearched corner of a house to one that has been searched already (*Rav; Rashi*).

By discounting fears that weasels may drag *chametz* to and fro behind the searcher's back, the mishnah indicates that one is not required to station guards in the entire courtyard or in his own house until the search has been completed, to insure against the possibility of weasels dragging *chametz* around (*R' Yehonasan; Meiri*). Alternatively, one need not search a second time after a previously unsearched place or house has been cleared of *chametz* (*Piskei HaRid*).

The *Gem.* (9a) infers from the phrasing of this clause that if no *chametz* was *known* to have entered the house, we have no 'fear' that nevertheless rodents had brought in *chametz.*

If, however, a weasel was seen bringing *chametz* into a house, the fear does exist that the *chametz* was not consumed by the

weasel, and a new search is required (*Gem.* 9a, Hil. Chametz 2:8; Orach Chaim 434:1)[1].

The above interpretation is that of *Rashi* and most commentators. *Rambam (Hil. Chametz 2:7, with Maggid Mishneh and comm.)* takes a different approach. The previous mishnah stated: Any place into which *chametz* is not brought does not require search. Our mishnah elaborates on that exemption and explains why we should not require a search in all places because of the fear that a rodent brought *chametz* to this area. The mishnah answers the question by stating that one need not fear that a weasel may have dragged [chametz] from [a house where *chametz* is used] to [a] house [where *chametz* is not brought] …

דְּאִם כֵּן, — *For if so,*

If we were to be concerned even with the possibility that a weasel may have brought *chametz* from one house to another after a search had been completed,

מֵחָצֵר לְחָצֵר וּמֵעִיר לְעִיר. אֵין לַדָּבָר סוֹף. — [then let us be concerned] *from court-yard to courtyard and from town to town. There is* [then] *no end to the matter.*

We must similarly be apprehensive that *chametz* had been dragged from the houses in one courtyard, or in one town where the search for *chametz* has not yet been conducted, to a house in a courtyard or town which has already been searched (*Rav; Rashi*).

It is impossible for all Jewry to con-

---

1. In this case the mishnah's logical argument *if so there is not end,* does not apply; we indeed do not require endless searches, but where we know *chametz* to be in the house it must be found. Furthermore, as explained below (see footnote to s.v. מחצר לחצר), the mishnah's argument suffices only to remove the obligation to be more apprehensive over the possible presence of *chametz* than is required by the Halachah with regard to other prohibitions. Since a forbidden substance is known to have been present, we must assume that it still is extant, therefore a new search must be made (see *S'fas Emes* and sources in the footnote).

1
2

2. We need not be concerned that a weasel may have dragged [*chametz*] from house to house, or from place to place. For if so, [then let us be concerned] from courtyard to courtyard and from town to town. There is [then] no end to the matter.

duct their search for *chametz* at the same time (*Ran, Yerushalmi*).

◄§ Doubtful Presence of Chametz

As noted above, our mishnah makes clear that — were it not for the impossibility of coping with the possible infiltration of *chametz* from distant places — precautions would be taken against the possibility that *chametz* was brought from corner to corner or house to house. The basis of this distinction is difficult, however, because the ordinary Torah rules for the resolution of uncertain situations [סְפֵיקוֹת] call for such a fear to be disregarded. The presence of *chametz* in the house is doubtful, and one can add to this the probability that even if it were present, it had been consumed by rodents. In a case of such compounded doubt [סְפֵק סְפֵיקָא], it should be ruled that no *chametz* exists in the house (*Gem.* 9a). In addition, because the obligation to search for *chametz* is not of Scriptural origin, it should not be required in instances of doubt [סְפֵיקָא דְרַבָּנָן לְקוּלָא].

One resolution of these questions is based on *Ravad's* contention (see *Hasagos* on *Ba'al HaMaor*; see also *Maggid Mishneh, Hil. Chametz* 2:10, *Turei Zahav* 439:1) that since the very obligation to search for *chametz* was instituted by the Rabbis for a doubtful situation — since one is required to search for *chametz* even when its presence in the household is doubtful the regular rules for deciding doubts cannot be applied (*R' David; Pnei Yehoshua*, s.v. בפירש״י; *S'fas Emes* and

others[1]). Alternatively: The *mitzvah* of searching, by definition, requires that the searcher assure himself beyond a reasonable doubt that no *chametz* is on his premises. Although the Halachah of Rabbinic decrees generally calls for leniency in case of doubt, such a ruling does not remove the underlying doubt; it merely permits one to proceed leniently. But in the case of the *chametz* search where the *mitzvah* is to *remove* doubt, a lenient ruling may be unacceptable (*S'fas Emes; Ha'amek Sh'eilah* 79:2).

Alternatively, the mishnah's conclusion is that some doubtfulness can be prevented (e.g., that *chametz* was brought from another corner or a nearby house) but that others cannot be (e.g., that chametz could conceivably come from far off). Because of the underlying similarity of both fears, for the sake of uniformity the Sages absolved people from concerning themselves with either one.

Here again the difficulty is obvious. Unless there is a halachic principle negating the apprehension that *chametz* may be present, the impossibility of safeguarding against the fear in *all* cases should not free people from dealing with the possibility whenever they can.

Ravad's postulate (see above) provides a solution to this problem, too. The case of the mishnah could be stated as follows: Should the apprehension that *chametz* had been dragged be subject to the extraordinary stringency of the rules dictated by the *mitzvah* of 'searching'? Or should it be decided only according to the rules in effect for

---

1. Based on this premise, *Mekor Chaim* (433:2) and *Bais Yisrael* conclude that only the extraordinary rules in effect for *chametz* are suspended for cases of doubtful dragging of *chametz*, but not the sort of general rules that govern the resolution of doubts in other areas of Torah law (see above footnote to s.v. וממקום למקום).

[ג] **רַבִּי** יְהוּדָה אוֹמֵר: בּוֹדְקִין אוֹר אַרְבָּעָה
עָשָׂר, וּבְאַרְבָּעָה עָשָׂר שַׁחֲרִית,
וּבִשְׁעַת הַבִּיעוּר.
וַחֲכָמִים אוֹמְרִים: לֹא בָדַק אוֹר אַרְבָּעָה
עָשָׂר, יִבְדֹּק בְּאַרְבָּעָה עָשָׂר, לֹא בָדַק בְּאַרְבָּעָה
עָשָׂר, יִבְדֹּק בְּתוֹךְ הַמּוֹעֵד; לֹא בָדַק בְּתוֹךְ

יד אברהם

other prohibitions? The mishnah teaches that the Sages decided to treat this apprehension like any other case of doubt, for if the more stringent course were chosen, it would create an obligation impossible to perform. Given this premise, it follows that even in the instance of 'from house to house and place to place,' the nature of the doubt (as articulated above) is such that it must be decided for leniency, according to the rules in effect for regular prohibitions (see *Mekor Chaim* 433:2 and 438, *Beis Yisrael*, and *S'fas Emes*).

Alternatively: The apprehensions about *chametz* from another house and that from another courtyard are not separate possibilities — in essence they are the same fear; *chametz* may have been introduced from the outside. By searching again to eliminate the possibility of *chametz* from another house, one would accomplish only a reduction of the chance that *chametz* had come in, not elimination of the apprehension. A search that will do nothing more than reduce the *probability* of *chametz* is not obligatory (cf. *S'fas Emes*).

3.

⊷§The 'Hour' in the Mishnah

Rambam (*Comm.* to *Berachos* 1:5) defines the 'hour' in Mishnaic usage as a twelfth of the daylight period, be it a long summer day or a short winter day. Hours of this sort are called שָׁעוֹת זְמַנִּיּוֹת, [lit. *temporary hours*], which can be defined loosely as *proportional hours*. This view is accepted almost unanimously as halachah (*Orach Chaim* 58:1; 89:1; 233:1)[1].

There is a controversy, however, as to how to measure the length of the day which forms the basis for these proportional hours. Some hold that the day is measured from daybreak (עֲמוּד הַשַּׁחַר) until nightfall (צֵאת הַכּוֹכָבִים), when three medium-sized stars became visible (*Magen Avraham* 233:2; 58:1; 443:2), while others (*Beur HaGra* to *Orach Chaim* 459:2) measure the day from sunrise (נֵץ הַחַמָּה) to sunset (שְׁקִיעַת הַחַמָּה). However, some authorities (*Terumas HaDeshen* 121) contend that since the hours mentioned in this mishnah are intended as a safeguard against people eating, using, or possessing *chametz* beyond the permissible times, it is logical to assume that the Sages did not measure these hours in fluctuating terms

---

1. Some authorities disagree and interpret the hour in the mishnah as the prevalent constant hour (שָׁעוֹת שָׁווֹת) consisting of sixty minutes. This opinion is held by *Shach* (*Nekudos HaKessef* to *Yoreh Deah* 184), *R' Ya'akov Emden* (*Lechem Shanayim Berachos* 1:2), *P'nei Yehoshua* (*Likutim* to *Berachos*), *Shulchan HaTahor, Teshuvos Mishknos Ya'akov Orach Chaim* and *Tos. HaRosh* to *Berachos* 3 (cited by *Da'as Torah*). According to this view the day always starts six sixty-minute hours before noon, no matter whether daybreak (the halachic start of the day) is earlier or later. *Terumas HaDeshen* (121) also seems to hold this view.

3. **R'** Yehudah says: We must search on the evening of the fourteenth, or on the morning of the fourteenth, or at the time of removal.

But the Sages say: If one did not search on the evening of the fourteenth, he must search on the [day of the] fourteenth; if he did not search on the [day of the] fourteenth, he must search during the festival; if

YAD AVRAHAM

that would be unfamiliar to the mass of people. Instead, the hours are constant, sixty-minute units. *Rama (Orach Chaim* 443:1) cites both views.

רַבִּי יְהוּדָה אוֹמֵר: בּוֹדְקִין אוֹר אַרְבָּעָה עָשָׂר, — *R' Yehudah says: We must search on the evening of the fourteenth [day of Nissan as set forth in mishnah 1],*

וּבְאַרְבָּעָה עָשָׂר שַׁחֲרִית, — *or on the morning of the fourteenth,*

If someone forgot or was unable to perform the 'search' at night as prescribed, he must do it the following morning (*Rav; Gem.* 10b).

וּבִשְׁעַת הַבִּיעוּר. — *or at the time of removal.*

[At the time when the left-over chametz and that found in the search must be removed, i.e., destroyed (see further 23:1). In the following mishnah the sixth hour (approximately the hour before noon) is designated as the hour when *chametz* is burned (see *Rashi* 10b, s.v. אלמא; *Tos.* 12b, s.v. אימתי).] R' Yehudah contends that the search may not be performed after midday, for there is an apprehension that someone may inadvertently eat whatever *chametz* he may find, thereby transgressing a Scriptural prohibition[1] (*Rav, Gem.* 10b).

Chametz may not be eaten even in the sixth hour, but since this prohibition is only Rabbinic in origin, the search obligation is not waived because of it (*R' David*).

However *Ba'al HaMaor* maintains that R' Yehudah means the end of the fifth hour (to 12b, s.v. אימתי; see *R' David* and *Maharam Chalavah*).

[The rationale for cancelling the *mitzvah* of search after the sixth hours is that consumption of *chametz* is a Scriptural prohibition, while searching for *chametz* is not. Therefore, the Sages prefer to withdraw their injunction to search rather than risk the chance that someone might eat *chametz*.][2]

וַחֲכָמִים אוֹמְרִים: לֹא בָדַק אוֹר אַרְבָּעָה עָשָׂר, יִבְדֹּק בְּאַרְבָּעָה עָשָׂר, — *But the Sages say: If one did not search on the evening of the fourteenth, he must search on the [day of the] fourteenth;*

I.e., all day (*Rav, Rambam, Tos.* 10b s.v. ואם). The sages are not concerned that the searcher may erroneously eat the *chametz* he finds during the search. They maintain that when one's whole purpose for searching is in order to destroy *chametz* it is illogical to fear an act that is diametrically opposed to his intention (*Rav; Gem.* 11a).

לֹא בָדַק בְּאַרְבָּעָה עָשָׂר, יִבְדֹּק בְּתוֹךְ הַמּוֹעֵד; — *if he did not search on the [day of the] fourteenth, he must search during the festival [lit. appointed time];*

During the seven days (or eight days in the diaspora) of the festival.

---

1. See preface to mishnah 4, which discusses the various views concerning the consumption of *chametz* on the afternoon of the fourteenth.

2. The commentators disagree as to why the mishnah considers the obligation to search a Rabbinic *mitzvah*. Some (*Maharshal*) contend that in the case of our mishnah the *chametz* had already been nullified, so that no Scriptural prohibition is involved. Others (*Maharsha*) argue that the obligation to search for unknown *chametz* is Rabbinic in every case. See Appendix, *Search and Nullification*.

פְּסָחִים הַמּוֹעֵד, יִבְדֹּק לְאַחַר הַמּוֹעֵד.
א/ד וּמַה שֶּׁמְּשַׁיֵּר, יַנִּיחֶנּוּ בְצִנְעָא, כְּדֵי שֶׁלֹּא יְהֵא
צָרִיךְ בְּדִיקָה אַחֲרָיו.

[ד] **רַבִּי** מֵאִיר אוֹמֵר: אוֹכְלִין כָּל חָמֵשׁ,
וְשׂוֹרְפִין בִּתְחִלַּת שֵׁשׁ.

יד אברהם

— לֹא בָדַק בְּתוֹךְ הַמּוֹעֵד, יִבְדֹּק לְאַחַר הַמּוֹעֵד.
*if he did not search during the festival
[lit. appointed time], he must search
after the festival.*

He must search for the *chametz* after
Pesach. Since *chametz* left in a Jew's
possession over Pesach is forbidden
both with regard to eating and benefit,
as stated in mishnah 2:5. There is the
apprehension that if left it may be eaten
inadvertently.

The foregoing interpretation is based on
Rambam, Tosafos and others who translate
מוֹעֵד in its usual rendition, *festival. Rashi*
takes a different approach to the mishnah.
In his view the term מוֹעֵד is used by the sages in
its literal sense: *the appointed time of
removal* — the sixth hour. According to
Rashi, the Sages' ruling would be rendered as
follows: *If one did not search on the evening
of the fourteenth he must search on [the
morning of] the fourteenth; if he did not
search on [the morning of] the fourteenth, he
must search during the time of removal [i.e.,
during the sixth hour]; if he did not search
during the time of removal he must search
after the time of removal [i.e., the rest of the
fourteenth day — but he must not search
during Pesach].* We do not fear that he will
eat it while searching during the fourteenth,
but it is forbidden to search during the
festival period proper.

Ran explains that there are two levels of
stringency in the Scriptural prohibition of
eating *chametz*. One is the simple prohibition
(לָאו) from midday of the fourteenth until the
evening of the fifteenth, when the festival
begins. The second, and more stringent, level
begins on Passover proper, when the punishment for eating *chametz* is כָּרֵת, *spiritual ex-*

cision. (see *Hil. Chametz U'Matzah* 1:1).
Therefore, *Ran* reasons, although the Sages
were lenient before Passover, using the
reasoning 'He himself is seeking to destroy it,
will he then eat it?', they refused to permit a
search when an offender could be subject to
the major punishment of *Kares*.

**וּמַה שֶּׁמְּשַׁיֵּר, — That which he leaves
over,**

Whatever *chametz* is purposely left
over after the evening search, for use in
the evening and morning meals (*Rashi*
19b, s.v. וּמה שמשייר).

The mishnah now reverts to a discussion of a normal, timely, *bedikah* and
expounds on the procedure following
the evening search.

**יַנִּיחֶנּוּ בְצִנְעָא, — He should place in
hiding,**

In a secure place, such as a dish or in
a corner so that it does not scatter (*Hil.
Chametz* 3:2). He should put it under
an overturned pot, or hang from the
ceiling. (*Orach Chaim* 434:1).

**כְּדֵי שֶׁלֹּא יְהֵא צָרִיךְ בְּדִיקָה אַחֲרָיו. — so that
it not be necessary to search for it
[again].**

For if one does not find the *chametz*
he put aside after the search or if he put
aside ten pieces and found only nine, it
is necessary to search again (see *Gem.*
9b).

However, if he overturned a pot on the
chametz or put it in a spot secure from rodents and animals, it is reasonable to assume
that it was taken by a person to eat and
another search is unnecessary. (*Orach Chaim*
434:1)

4.

◆§ **Chametz on the afternoon of the fourteenth of Nissan**

Although the dual prohibitions of consuming and keeping *chametz* are explicitly
referred to the time frame of Pesach itself (see *Exodus* 12:15, 13:7), the consensus is

מִשְׁנָיוֹת / פְּסָחִים **[12]**

1
4

he did not search during the festival, he must search after the festival.

That which he leaves over, he should place in hiding, so that it will not be necessary to search for it [again].

4. **R'** Meir says: We may eat [*chametz*] the entire fifth [hour], and we must burn [it] at the onset of the sixth [hour].

that in a less stringent form, both prohibitions obtain from the noon hour, even before the festival.

Regarding the prohibition against keeping *chametz*, the *Gemara* (4b) deduces from our mishnah that according to all the tannaim there is a Scriptural ban on keeping *chametz* before the festival. This is derived from the verse (*Exodus 12:15*): *However on the first day you shall eliminate leaven from your houses* ... The *Gemara* (4b-5b) demonstrates that *first day* refers to the day of the Pesach sacrifice — the fourteenth of Nissan, thus providing a basis for a Scriptural ban against keeping chametz after midday.

There are divergent opinions, however, concerning the permissibility of consuming *chametz* or deriving benefit from it during this time. R' Yehudah (*Gem.* 28b) holds that although the *kares* [excision] punishment applies only to the eating of *chametz* during Pesach, nevertheless there is a negative command prohibiting *chametz* consumption during the afternoon of the fourteenth. In this view, even deriving benefit from *chametz* during that time is forbidden. Scripturally (see mishnah 2:1; Tos. 23b, s.v. מאי). *Rambam* accepts this view as halachah (*Hil. Chametz* 1:8 see concurring views cited in *Magid Mihneh; Sefer HaMitzvos, Lo Sa'aseh* 199; see *Rosh* and *Tur* 443). Many authorities however (*Ramban, Sefer HaMitzvos loc. cit.* and *Milchamos* to 7a; *Ba'al HaMaor* there and 28a; *Ravad Hil. Chametz* 1:8 and others) accept R' Shimon's view that there is no explicit negative command. But there is a consensus that *chametz* may not be eaten or used in this time span, even according to R' Shimon[1].

Because the prohibition of *chametz* involves the entire populace, among whom are many who cannot accurately estimate the moment — midday — when the prohibition takes effect, the Sages decreed that the prohibition be observed before noon. This Rabbinic institution is the theme of mishnah 4.

רַבִּי מֵאִיר אוֹמֵר: אוֹכְלִין כָּל חָמֵשׁ. — *R'* *Meir says: We may eat [chametz] the entire fifth [hour],*
[For example, if the length of the day

is twelve hours, from 6 a.m. to 6 p.m., one may eat *chametz* until 11 a.m.]

וְשׂוֹרְפִין בִּתְחִלַּת שֵׁשׁ. — *and we must burn [it] at the onset of the sixth [hour].*

1. *Tos.* (28b s.v. רבי), *Ravad (Hasagos* on *Ba'al HaMaor* 7a), *Rambam (Sefer HaMitzvos, Lo Sa'aseh* 199; cf. *Milchamos* 7a) and others contend that the Scriptural obligation to 'remove' *chametz* also implies a prohibition against eating it. *Ba'al Halttur (Hil. Biur Chametz,* v.2, p. 248, cited in *Tur* 443) contends that the prohibition is only Rabbinic. *Ba'al HaMaor* (28b) goes even further and maintains that one may destroy the *chametz* by eating it (cf. *Maharam Chalavah* 4b).

Ran (Chiddushim to 6b; see also *Maharam Chalavah* to 7a) maintains that the prohibition against benefit is Scriptural, (in R' Shimon's view) but the majority of authorities hold this to be a Rabbinic prohibition.

וְרַבִּי יְהוּדָה אוֹמֵר: אוֹכְלִין כָּל אַרְבַּע,
וְתוֹלִין כָּל חָמֵשׁ, וְשׂוֹרְפִין בִּתְחִלַּת שֵׁשׁ.

[ה] **וְעוֹד** אָמַר רַבִּי יְהוּדָה: שְׁתֵּי חַלּוֹת שֶׁל
תּוֹדָה פְּסוּלוֹת מֻנָּחוֹת עַל גַּג
הָאִצְטַבָּא. כָּל זְמַן שֶׁמֻּנָּחוֹת כָּל הָעָם אוֹכְלִים.
נִטְּלָה אַחַת, תּוֹלִין — לֹא אוֹכְלִין וְלֹא שׂוֹרְפִין.

יד אברהם

I.e., no benefit may be derived from it — from the sixth hour on it is destined to be burned (*Rosh Yosef*)[1].

Although the *chametz* is Scripturally permitted in the sixth hour, the Sages forbade its use then, because one might miscalculate the time and think that the seventh hour is still the sixth. By extending the prohibition an extra hour, the Sages ensured that even if someone miscalculated, he would not transgress a Scriptural prohibition (*Rav, Rashi*; see *Gem.* 12b שית יומא בקרנתא קאי).

וְרַבִּי יְהוּדָה אוֹמֵר: אוֹכְלִין כָּל אַרְבַּע, וְתוֹלִין כָּל חָמֵשׁ, — *But R' Yehudah says: We may eat* [chametz] *the entire fourth* [hour], *but we suspend* [it] *the entire fifth* [hour],

I.e., we neither eat it nor destroy it but we may derive other benefit, such as feeding it to our animals (*Rav*).

R' Yehudah holds that the Sages restricted the consumption of *chametz* two hours before the Scriptural prohibition, because of the apprehension that

on a cloudy day, the usual margin of error is widened and a two hour mistake cannot be ruled out. (*Gem.* 12b).

Because this is a far fetched fear, the Sages did not go to the extent of prohibiting even derivation of benefit, for this would result in the total monetary loss of the *chametz* (*Pnei Yehoshua*; based on *Rashi*, s.v. ושורפין).

וְשׂוֹרְפִין בִּתְחִלַּת שֵׁשׁ. — *and we must burn it at the onset of the sixth* [hour].

I.e., from that time onward all benefits from *chametz* are forbidden (see above, s.v. ושורפין).

[In the sixth hour, because of the more likely possibility that one may miscalculate even on a sunny day (as explained above in R' Meir's view), the Sages enacted a more stringent ban and prohibited even deriving benefit (see *Rashi*, s.v. שורפין).]

As explained earlier the Sages were more lenient in regard to deriving benefit because they did not want their ban to cause the owner of the *chametz* a monetary loss. Only concerning the sixth hour did they feel that the all inclusive prohibition was warranted (*P'nei Yehoshua*; see *Rashash*; also *Hil. Chametz* 1:9 with *Chidushei HaGriz*).

5.

[R' Yehudah now relates how the commencement of the respective times of the prohibitions of *chametz* were made known in Jerusalem during the Temple era.]

וְעוֹד אָמַר רַבִּי יְהוּדָה: שְׁתֵּי חַלּוֹת — *R' Yehudah also said: Two loaves*

Two of the leavened loaves brought with the offering (*Rav, Rashi*).

Each loaf consisted of an *issaron* (עִשָּׂרוֹן Menachos 7:1), the equivalent in volume of 43.2 eggs.

שֶׁל תּוֹדָה — *of a thanksgiving offering*

1. According to most authorities one need not hurry to burn *chametz* immediately at the beginning of the sixth hour, but he may wait until the end of the hour to commence burning (*Rosh Yosef* here and 4b). *Rambam's* (*Hil. Chametz* 1:9) and *Shulchan Aruch's* (443:1) paraphrase of this ruling also suggests the above interpretation (see also *Mordechai* 533 and *Ohr Zarua* 2:256, p. 115). However it is customary to burn *chametz* before the fifth hour, in

1
5

But R' Yehudah says: We may eat [*chametz*] the entire fourth [hour], but we suspend [it] the entire fifth [hour], and we must burn it at the onset of the sixth [hour].

5. R' Yehudah also said: Two loaves of a thanksgiving offering [which had become] unfit were placed on the roof of the portico. As long as they lay [there] all the people would eat [*chametz*]. [When] one was removed, they suspended — they would neither eat nor burn [the *chametz*]. When both

YAD AVRAHAM

◆§The Thanksgiving offering

Scripture (*Leviticus* 7:11-15) provides for an offering to be brought when a person has been delivered from misfortune such as one who had recovered from a dangerous sickness, returned from a sea voyage, traversed a desert, or has been released from prison, as set forth in *Psalms* 107 (*Rashi* v. 12). This offering is called a *Todah* (תּוֹדָה), *thanksgiving offering*. Accompanying the animal sacrifice were forty loaves, four of which were given the *Kohanim*, and the rest eaten by the owner of the offering and his guests. Ten of these loaves were *chametz* while the rest were matzah (unleavened). [For an alternative understanding of this offering's purpose, see *Radak Shorashim, s.v.* ידה.]

פְּסוּלוֹת — [*which had become*] *unfit*

The Mishnah (*Zevachim* 5:6) notes that a thanksgiving offering may be eaten until the midnight after its sacrifice. The *Gemara* (13b) also states that one may not cause the likelihood that sacred food may become unfit [i.e., one may not offer a sacrifice if the time alloted by the Torah for its consumption will be curtailed (*Rashi*)]. Consequently it was forbidden to bring a thanksgiving offering on the fourteenth of Nissan, because the leavened loaves could be eaten only till midday due to the *chametz* prohibition; consequently, the likelihood would increase that the loaves would not be finished in time.

Therefore, whoever had reason to bring a thanksgiving offering brought it on the thirteenth, and since the number of people bringing thanksgiving offer-

ings then was so numerous, many loaves became unfit through being kept overnight. These unfit loaves were then used to signify the various stages of the status of *chametz* (*Rav; Gem.* 13b).

מְנָחוֹת עַל גַּג הָאִצְטְבָא. — *were placed on the roof of the portico* [lit *bench*].

There were a series of benches on the Temple Mount for people to sit upon (*Rashi*). The benches were covered with a roof so they could be used in inclement weather (*Rashi* 13b, s.v. גג). The loaves were placed on top of the roof so that they would be visible from afar (see *Gem.* 13b).

כָּל זְמַן שֶׁמְּנָחוֹת כָּל הָעָם אוֹכְלִים. — *As long as they* [the two loaves] *lay* [*there*] *all the people would eat* [*chametz*].

נִטְלָה אַחַת, תּוֹלִין — [*When*] *one* [*loaf*]

order to be able to nullify the *chametz* again after burning it as stated by *Rama* (434:2; see *Magen Avraham* and *Mishnah Berurah* there). If the nullification were delayed until the sixth hour began, it would be too late, because the *chametz* would have become worthless and could no longer be considered the legal property of its owner.

נִטְּלוּ שְׁתֵּיהֶן, הִתְחִילוּ כָל הָעָם שׂוֹרְפִין. רַבָּן גַּמְלִיאֵל אוֹמֵר: חוּלִּין נֶאֱכָלִים כָּל אַרְבַּע; וּתְרוּמָה כָּל חָמֵשׁ; וְשׂוֹרְפִין בִּתְחִלַּת שֵׁשׁ

יד אברהם

was removed, they suspended —

At the beginning of the fifth hour (10 a.m.) a messenger of the *Beis Din* [High Court] came and removed one loaf, and all knew that the fifth hour had arrived and they 'suspended' their chametz as explained further (*Rav; Rashi*).

לֹא אוֹכְלִין וְלֹא שׂוֹרְפִין. — *they would neither eat nor burn* [*the chametz*].

[This clause explains the term תּוֹלִין *they suspended*, i.e., the *chametz* is now no longer in a state of permissibility, nor is it yet under a total ban as it would be during the festival. It is in a state of suspension between these two extremes.]

Rambam (*Hil. Chametz* 1:9) uses the term *they suspended* to refer only to consecrated *chametz* such as *terumah* and the thanksgiving offering which may not yet be burned at this time. Regarding other *chametz*, it cannot be said *they do not burn* because one may burn these at any time he wishes (see *Chiddshei HaGriz*).

[See above mishnah 4 for an explanation of this law and the definition of the term 'they burn'.]

נִטְּלוּ שְׁתֵּיהֶן, הִתְחִילוּ כָל הָעָם שׂוֹרְפִין. — *When both were removed* [at the beginning of the sixth hour; 11 a.m.], *all the people would begin to burn* [*their chametz*].

The *Gemara* (14a) relates, 'Two cows used to plow on the Mount of Olives. As long as both were plowing all the people would eat; when one (cow) was removed they suspended, neither eating nor burning; when both were removed all the people would begin burning.'

רַבָּן גַּמְלִיאֵל אוֹמֵר: חוּלִּין נֶאֱכָלִים כָּל אַרְבַּע; — *Rabban Gamliel says: Nonconsecrated* [*chametz*] *may be eaten the entire fourth* [*hour*];

[Various tithes, having different degrees of sanctity, must be separated

from produce grown in *Eretz Yisrael* before it may be eaten (see below, *comm.* to 2:5, for a listing of all the necessary tithes).]

As long as any tithe has not been separated, the produce may not be consumed and is called טֶבֶל, *tevel*. After the tithes have been separated the remaining produce is called חוּלִּין [*chullin*], *secular* or nonconsecrated.

[Rabban Gamliel concurs with R' Yehudah's view concerning tithed *chametz*, and permits it to be eaten only up to the fifth hour. However regarding *terumah* Rabban Gamliel permits an extra hour of eating time.]

וּתְרוּמָה כָּל חָמֵשׁ; — *terumah* [*which is chametz may be eaten*] *the entire fifth* [*hour*];

[*Terumah*, the tithe given the *Kohen*, may be eaten only by *Kohanim* and their households, and must be safeguarded against contamination or destruction.] Because *terumah* should not be destroyed unless absolutely necessary, Rabban Gamliel allows its consumption for an additional hour (*Rav, Rashi*). [See above mishnah 4, s.v. תּוֹלִין and וְשׂורפין, for why the sixth hour is subject to more stringency than the fifth.]

Tosafos Chadashim notes that according to R' Yehudah loaves of thanksgiving offerings were chosen to indicate the various stages of prohibition in order to demonstrate, in opposition to Rabban Gamliel's view, that the *chametz* laws apply equally to consecrated *chametz* and to ordinary *chametz*.

וְשׂוֹרְפִין בִּתְחִלַּת שֵׁשׁ. — *and we must burn* [*all chametz*] *at the onset of the sixth* (*hour*).

[At the beginning of the sixth hour, consumption and derivation of benefit

were removed, all the people would begin to burn
[their *chametz*].

Rabban Gamliel says: Nonconsecrated [*chametz*]
may be eaten the entire fourth [hour]; *terumah*
[which is *chametz* may be eaten] the entire fifth
[hour]; and we must burn [all *chametz*] at the onset
of the sixth [hour].

YAD AVRAHAM

would be prohibited for both tithed and
terumah produce.]

Because most people are liable to mistake the seventh hour for the sixth, the
Sages advanced to the sixth hour all the

strictures obtaining in the seventh (*Rav;
Rashi*).

The halachah follows R' Yehudah (*Rambam, Comm., Hil. Chametz* 1:9, *Orach
Chaim* 443:1).

◆§ **Preface to Mishnayos 6-7**

A cardinal rule of *terumah* is that it must be safeguarded against contamination
(טֻמְאָה) and destruction (הֶפְסֵד), as God instructed Aaron (*Numbers* 18:8): ... *I have
assigned you the safeguarding of my terumos* ...

Pesach eve when *chametz* must be destroyed, a question arose. *Terumah*, too,
must be destroyed if it is *chametz* — must care be taken even during the burning
process to safeguard it from contamination? If so, two pyres would be required, one
for uncontaminated *terumah*, and a second for all other chametz, because if the two
came in contact with one another the *terumah* would become contaminated. It
might be, however, that since destruction of the *terumah* is imminent, the mandate
to safeguard it against *terumah* no longer applies. In order to resolve this question,
mishnah 6 introduces a parallel situation regarding the destruction of contaminated
sacrificial parts, followed by a dispute (mishnah 7) between R' Meir and R' Yose on
whether this situation is analogous to the pertinent question of burning *terumah*
that is *chametz*.

◆§ **Degrees of Tumah**

An understanding of the following mishnah requires knowledge of the basic
classifications of *tumah*. The severity of *tumah* and the ability of one contaminated
person or object to convey *tumah* to another are not uniform, but vary according to
the degree of *tumah* and the class of contaminated object.

The strictest level of tumah, אֲבִי אֲבוֹת הַטֻּמְאָה [lit. *father of fathers of tumah*], the
most severe origin of contamination, is a corpse. The next, and far more common
level, is known as אַב הַטֻּמְאָה [lit. *father*], *primary tumah*. This category includes:
one who touched a human corpse; the carcass of one of the eight species of שֶׁרֶץ, *rodent* or *reptile* listed in *Leviticus 1:30-31*; the carcass of an animal that died by some
means other than a valid ritual slaughter; or one who is a *zav, zavah,* or *niddah* (see
definitions of these terms in *comm.* to 8:5). [The various forms of this category are
listed in *Keilim* ch. 1, and elucidated by *Rambam* in his introduction to *Seder
Taharos.*]

A vessel or food that is contaminated by a [primary *tumah*] becomes a רִאשׁוֹן
לְטֻמְאָה [*rishon*], *first degree of contamination*. This degree of contamination is also
called וְלַד הַטֻּמְאָה [*vlad hatumah*], lit. *child* (as opposed to *av*, father) *of the tumah*],
secondary tumah. An object contracting *tumah* from a *rishon* is a שֵׁנִי לְטֻמְאָה
[*sheni*], *second degree of tumah* (or וְלַד וְלַד הַטֻּמְאָה, *child of child of the tumah*). In

[ו] **רַבִּי** חֲנִינָא סְגַן הַכֹּהֲנִים אוֹמֵר: מִימֵיהֶם
שֶׁל כֹּהֲנִים, לֹא נִמְנְעוּ מִלִּשְׂרֹף אֶת
הַבָּשָׂר שֶׁנִּטְמָא בִּוְלַד הַטֻּמְאָה עִם הַבָּשָׂר
שֶׁנִּטְמָא בְּאַב הַטֻּמְאָה, אַף עַל פִּי שֶׁמּוֹסִיפִין
טֻמְאָה עַל טֻמְאָתוֹ.

הוֹסִיף רַבִּי עֲקִיבָא וְאָמַר: מִימֵיהֶם שֶׁל
כֹּהֲנִים, לֹא נִמְנְעוּ מִלְּהַדְלִיק אֶת הַשֶּׁמֶן

יד אברהם

the case of חוּלִין, *unsanctified food*, contamination can go no further than a *sheni*; thus if a *sheni* touches unsanctified food, that food acquires no degree of contamination whatever.

Commensurate with the respectively greater degrees of stringency associated with *terumah* and sacrifices, their levels of contamination can go beyond that of *sheni*. Thus, if a *sheni* touches *terumah*, it becomes a שְׁלִישִׁי לְטֻמְאָה [*shelishi*], *third degree of contamination* — but the *tumah* of *terumah* goes no further than this degree. Sacrifices can go a step further, to רְבִיעִי לְטֻמְאָה [*revi'i*], *fourth degree of contamination*.

As a general rule, the word טָמֵא [*tamei*], *contaminated*, is applied only to an object which can convey its *tumah* to another object of its genre. An object which cannot convey its *tumah* in this way is called פָּסוּל [*pasul*], *invalid*, rather than *tamei*. Thus a third degree in the case of *terumah*, and a fourth degree in the case of sacrifices, are called *pasul* since they cannot convey their contamination to another object of their genre. It is true, for example, that a *sheni* of *chullin* can contaminate *terumah* and consecrated meat, making them *shelishi*, nevertheless, a *sheni* of *chullin* generally is *not* called *tamei*, because it cannot convey *tumah* to other *chullin*.

6.

רַבִּי חֲנִינָא סְגַן הַכֹּהֲנִים אוֹמֵר: — *R' Chanina, administrator of the Kohanim, says:*

[The term סְגָן [*s'gan*] is usually rendered 'Deputy Kohen Gadol' (e.g., 4:1). This translation is impossible in the context of R' Chanina's title, because הַכֹּהֲנִים the *priests*, is plural. But the *s'gan* was deputy only to the *Kohen Gadol* and held second highest rank in the Temple hierarchy. He was the *Kohen Gadol's* deputy and substitute, when necessary. See ArtScroll *comm.* to Yoma 3:1 for a discussion of the *s'gan's* duties.

Rambam (Hil. *Klei Hamikdash* 4:16), describes the *s'gan's* functions as follows: The administrator [or deputy] to the *Kohen Gadol* was appointed to be of service to the *Kohen Gadol* in his relations with the other *Kohanim*. He stood to the right of the *Kohen Gadol* constantly, and any directions trans-

mitted by the *Kohen Gadol* to the other *Kohanim* were executed by the *s'gan*. He also assisted the *Kohen Gadol* in his ritual duties. ''His relationship to the *Kohen Gadol* was that of a prime minister to a king.''

מִימֵיהֶם שֶׁל כֹּהֲנִים, — *In* [lit. *from*] *all the days of the Kohanim*,

[I.e., as long as the Temple stood, and the disposal of disqualified and contaminated sacrifices or their parts was the obligation of the *Kohanim*.]

לֹא נִמְנְעוּ מִלִּשְׂרֹף אֶת הַבָּשָׂר שֶׁנִּטְמָא בִּוְלַד הַטֻּמְאָה — *never did they refrain from burning* [*sacrificial*] *meat that had been contaminated by a secondary tumah*

Although the mishnah uses the term וְלַד, *vlad* [lit. *a child of tumah*] — a term

6. R' Chanina, administrator of the *Kohanim*, says: In all the days of the *Kohanim*, never did they refrain from burning [sacrificial] meat that had been contaminated by a secondary *tumah* together with [sacrificial] meat that had been contaminated by a primary *tumah*, although [by so doing] they added contamination to its contamination.

R' Akiva added, saying: In all the days of the *Kohanim*, never did they refrain from lighting oil

YAD AVRAHAM

that usually means a first degree of contamination — in our context the mishnah means *a second degree of contamination*, so that the sacrificial flesh contaminated by this *sheni* became a *shelishi* (שְׁלִישִׁי לַטֻּמְאָה) *(Rav; Gem. 14a)*.

[Technically the term *vlad*, *child*, is appropriate here, for all contaminations below the level of *av (father)* are included by the term *vlad hatumah*. Wherever the mishnah differentiates between the differing degrees of *vlad* it uses the numbers רִאשׁוֹן [*rishon*], *first*, שֵׁנִי [*sheni*], *second*, etc., to indicate the differing levels of contamination (see *Rambam, Comm.*).]

The *Gemara* reasons that were this *vlad* to be a *tumah* of the first degree the sacrificial meat touched by it would become only a *sheni*. If the meat were to be burned together with an *av* — a *rishon latumah* — the meat would not incur a heightening of *tumah*. The reason is that even uncontaminated meat coming in contact with a *rishon* becomes only a *sheni*, the same level already possessed by the meat in the situation of our mishnah.

עִם הַבָּשָׂר שֶׁנִּטְמָא בְּאַב הַטֻּמְאָה, — *together with [sacrificial] meat that had been contaminated by a primary tumah,*

Though this flesh had contracted a *tumah* of the first degree, it was burned together with the flesh containing a *tumah* of only the third degree.

אַף עַל פִּי שֶׁמּוֹסִיפִין טֻמְאָה עַל טֻמְאָתוֹ — *although [by so doing] they added contamination to its contamination.*

Since both are destined to be burned in any case, we are unconcerned with the addition of a new *tumah* *(Rav, Rashi)*.

Although according to Scriptural law foodstuffs do not contaminate other foodstuffs (according to some amoraim) and consequently no additional *tumah* is added when sacred flesh touches other sacred flesh, the Sages decreed that food *could* contaminate other food *(Rav; Gem. 14a)*.

הוֹסִיף רַבִּי עֲקִיבָא וְאָמַר: מִימֵיהֶם שֶׁל — *R' כֹּהֲנִים, לֹא נִמְנְעוּ מִלְּהַדְלִיק אֶת הַשֶּׁמֶן Akiva added* [to the words of R' Chanina], *saying: In all the days of the Kohanim never did they refrain from lighting oil*

Of *terumah*, which may be used by the *Kohanim* for fuel. *(Rav; Rashi)*.

Clearly, R' Akiva refers to oil of *terumah*, rather than of *kodesh* (sacred oil used in the Temple for meal offerings) for even *Kohanim* may not use *kodesh* for personal benefit, so it could not be burned in a lamp for illumination. Instead, contaminated oil of *kodesh* would be destroyed in the place in the Temple complex specially designated for burning disqualified and contaminated sacrifices [בֵּית הַדֶּשֶׁן] *(Rashi* 14b, s.v. נוקמה). [Besides, if R' Akiva's oil were *kodesh*, his case would offer no addition over that of R' Chanina (see below; cf *Tos.* 14b s.v. ואילו).

83-49

שֶׁנִּפְסַל בִּטְבוּל יוֹם בְּנֵר שֶׁנִּטְמָא בְּטְמֵא מֵת,
אַף עַל פִּי שֶׁמּוֹסִיפִין טֻמְאָה עַל טֻמְאָתוֹ.

[ז] **אָמַר** רַבִּי מֵאִיר: מִדִּבְרֵיהֶם לָמַדְנוּ
שֶׁשּׂוֹרְפִין תְּרוּמָה טְהוֹרָה עִם
הַטְּמֵאָה בַּפֶּסַח.

יד אברהם

שֶׁנִּפְסַל בִּטְבוּל יוֹם — *that had become unfit [through contact] with a t'vul yom* [lit. *one immersed that day*]

T'vul yom refers to one who had gone through a period of contamination. At the end of his period he immerses himself in a *mikveh* before sunset, but must wait until nightfall before he regains his ritual purity in regard to *terumah*. In the interim he is called a *t'vul yom*. His status is equivalent to one who is a second grade *tumah*, and by touching *terumah* he causes it to become a third degree *tumah*.

בְּנֵר שֶׁנִּטְמָא בְּטְמֵא מֵת, — *in a lamp that had been contaminated by one contaminated by a corpse,*

The lamp was contaminated by someone or something that had touched a corpse. Ordinarily, contact with a corpse makes something an *av* [primary *tumah*], so that anything it touches

would become a *rishon*. However there is an extraordinary exception to this rule. In the exclusive case of corpse contamination — an *avi avos hatumah* (the corpse itself) or an *av hatumah* (whatever touched the corpse) can convey its *own* level of *tumah* without it going down by one degree[1]. This exception, derived from Scriptural exegesis, provides that if any object except for one made of earthenware[2] touches an *avi avos* or an *av* of corpse contamination it receives the *same* degree of *tumah* as the object it touched. In other words, if a metal lamp touches a corpse, the lamp becomes an *avi avos*, a condition that could not exist in the case of any other *tumah*. The Gemara (14b) assumes that the lamp in our mishnah is, indeed, made of metal[3] and thus is an *avi avos*.

Consequently the oil burned in this lamp is changed from the degree of be-

1. This rule is derived from the expression בַּחֲלַל חֶרֶב, lit. *a corpse* [killed by] *a sword* (*Numbers* 19:16), the term with which the Torah describes the corpse that is a source of contamination. Because the mode of death and the murder weapon would seem to be irrelevant, the *Gemara* (14b) deduces that the Torah implies חֶרֶב הֲרֵי הוּא כֶּחָלָל, *the sword has the same status as the corpse itself*; just as the corpse is *avi avos*, so too a sword touching it becomes an *avi avos*.

2. In commenting that all utensils and clothing of whatever material (except earthenware) accept an equal degree of *tumah* in this case, *Rav* follows *Rambam* (Comm. here and *Ohalos* 1:2; *Hil. Tumas Mes* 5:3), *Ramban* (Comm. to Torah *Numbers* 19:16, *Bava Basra* 20a and *Shabbos* 101b), *R' Yitzchak of Simpont* (cited by *Rash Ohalos* 1:2 and *Rosh* there). Other commentators differ, however. *Rashi* (14b s.v., *Shabbas* 101b s.v. בדבר), *R' Tam* (cited by *Rash* to *Ohalos* 1:2), and *Ravad* (*Hil. Tumas Mes* 5:3) contend that this rule applies only to metal utensils.

3. The *Gemara* (14b) reasons that if the lamp were of earthenware (so that it would become only *rishon* after touching an *av* of whatever sort), there would be no reason for the mishnah to specify that the source of the contamination was a corpse [טְמֵא מֵת]. R' Akiva should have said simply בְּנֵר שֶׁנִּטְמָא, *in a lamp that had become contaminated*. It would have been understood that the source of the contamination was an *av*, for nothing below that level of *tumah* can confer *tumah* upon a utensil (*Rashi*).

that had become unfit [through contact] with a *t'vul yom* in a lamp that had been contaminated by one contaminated by a corpse, although [by so doing] they added contamination to its contamination.

7. **S**aid R' Meir: From their words we infer that we may burn uncontaminated *terumah* [which is *chametz*] with contaminated *terumah* on Pesach.

ing merely פָּסוּל, *unfit*, to that of a *rishon*, a first degree *tumah (Rav)*.

אַף עַל פִּי שֶׁמּוֹסִיפִין טֻמְאָה עַל טֻמְאָתוֹ. — *although [by so doing] they added contamination to its contamination.*

R' Akiva maintains that although the *tumah* increases by two degrees, rather than the one degree permitted by R' Chanina, it is still permissible to burn them together, being that both are *tamei*

in any case, and not merely *posul* [unfit] (*Rav; Gem.* 14b).

Additionally, R' Akiva even allowed a substance carrying only the name פָּסוּל, *unfit*, to be rendered *tamei* during the burning process. This is implicit in R' Akiva's statement because a *t'vul yom* cannot render *terumah*, *tamei*, only פָּסוּל, *unfit*. In R' Chanina's case, however, the flesh carried the appellation *tamei*, even though its *tumah* was only of the third degree (*Gem.* 14b).

7.

אָמַר רַבִּי מֵאִיר: מִדִּבְרֵיהֶם לָמַדְנוּ — *R' Meir said: From their words we infer* [lit. *leaven*]

From the previous statements of R' Chanina and R' Akiva (who added to R' Chanina's words; see *Tos. Yom Tov* s.v. שֶׁשּׂוֹרְפִין) who say that the *Kohanim* burned flesh that was a third degree *tumah* together with flesh that was a first degree *tumah. (Rav; cf Tos.* 15a, s.v. דמדאורייתא).

שֶׁשּׂוֹרְפִין תְּרוּמָה טְהוֹרָה עִם הַטְּמֵאָה בְּפֶסַח. — *that we may burn uncontaminated terumah [which is chametz] with contaminated terumah on Pesach.*

I.e., on the sixth hour of Pesach eve (*Rav, Rashi*; see *Rashi* and *Tos.* 15b s.v. נימא).

The *Gemara* (15b; according to R' Yochanan's view) explains that R' Meir (with R' Yose's concurrence) assumed that the *vlad* (second degree) of *tumah* mentioned by R' Chanina as the contaminator of the sacrificial flesh would include liquids contaminated by a utensil that was a *rishon* (a first degree of

tumah). R' Meir holds that Scriptural law does not give liquids the power to transmit *tumah* to others (see *Rashi* 16a, s.v. ספק and טהור, cf *Tos.* 15b, s.v. רבי) consequently the meat is uncontaminated according to Scriptural law (although it is *tamei* by Rabbinic decree). When it is later brought into contact with defiled meat during the burning, it is made Scripturally *tamei* (cf. *Tos.* 15a, s.v. דמדאורייתא), thereby proving the premise that even uncontaminated sacrificial parts destined to be burned need not be protected against *tumah*, as long as the meat is prohibited at least Rabbinically. By the same token, uncontaminated *terumah* in the sixth hour, when *chametz* is already Rabbinically prohibited and must be burned, need not be safeguarded against contamination.

The *Gemara* (15b) argues that, taken superficially (without the above assumption) R' Chanina's case can prove only that an *already* contaminated object may have a greater degree of contamination added to it, but not that one may contaminate a

83-49

אָמַר לוֹ רַבִּי יוֹסֵי: אֵינָהּ הִיא הַמִּדָּה. וּמוֹדִים
רַבִּי אֱלִיעֶזֶר וְרַבִּי יְהוֹשֻׁעַ שֶׁשּׂוֹרְפִין זוֹ לְעַצְמָהּ
וְזוֹ לְעַצְמָהּ. עַל מַה נֶּחְלְקוּ? — עַל הַתְּלוּיָה
וְעַל הַטְּמֵאָה. שֶׁרַבִּי אֱלִיעֶזֶר אוֹמֵר תִּשָּׂרֵף זוֹ
לְעַצְמָהּ וְזוֹ לְעַצְמָהּ, וְרַבִּי יְהוֹשֻׁעַ אוֹמֵר שְׁתֵּיהֶן
כְּאַחַת.

יד אברהם

previously uncontaminated object, even though it is destined for burning.

אָמַר לוֹ רַבִּי יוֹסֵי: אֵינָהּ הִיא הַמִּדָּה. — *R' Yose said to him: This is not analogous* [lit. *this is not the measure*].

R' Yose maintains that the power of liquids to contaminate other substances is Scriptural. Accordingly he refutes R' Meir's analogy to R' Chanina's case. In R' Chanina's case the flesh was already Scripturally *contaminated* to a degree, but the *terumah* of mishnah 6 had no contamination even though it must be burned as *chametz* in the sixth hour (*Rav*).

The halachah follows R' Yose (*Rav*; *Rambam, Comm.* and *Hil. Chametz* 3:4). However even R' Yose agrees that after midday when *chametz* is Scripturally prohibited, it may be contaminated (*Gem.* 15b; *Rambam, Hil. Chametz* 4:3).

וּמוֹדִים רַבִּי אֱלִיעֶזֶר וְרַבִּי יְהוֹשֻׁעַ שֶׁשּׂוֹרְפִין זוֹ לְעַצְמָה וְזוֹ לְעַצְמָה. — *[Even] R' Eliezer and R' Yehoshua concur that each is burned separately.*

R' Yose adds that although R' Eliezer and R' Yehoshua disagree (further in this mishnah) regarding the burning of 'suspended' (i.e. possibly contaminated) *terumah* together with definitely contaminated *terumah* at any time of the year,[1] they both concur that uncontaminated *terumah* may not be burned with contaminated *terumah*, even in the sixth hour when it is already Rabbinically prohibited (*Rav*).

[R' Yose maintains an analogy to the sixth hour cannot be drawn even from the fact that R' Yehoshua allows 'suspended' *terumah* to be contaminated. It could be argued that on the chance that suspended *terumah* is truly *not* contaminated, it is similar to *chametz-terumah* in the sixth hour in that it is not contaminated but still forbidden. If it is permitted to contaminate suspended *terumah* simply because its consumption is forbidden, why should one not be permitted to contaminate *terumah* in the sixth hour when it is likewise forbidden to be eaten, although it is not contaminated? Nevertheless R' Yose maintains that there is no analogy. For in the case of suspended *terumah*, there is at least the possibility that the *terumah* was *actually* contaminated, whereas *terumah* that is *chametz* is merely prohibited, but known to be uncontaminated.]

עַל מַה נֶּחְלְקוּ? — עַל הַתְּלוּיָה וְעַל הַטְּמֵאָה. — *Concerning what to do they differ? — Concerning suspended and contaminated [terumah].*

[*Terumah*, regarding which there is doubt whether it has been contaminated[2], is halachically in a state of

1. The interpretation given above — that R' Eliezer and R' Yehoshua disagree concerning 'suspended' *terumah* even year-round is from *Tosafos* (20b). *Meiri* maintains that their disagreement concerns only 'suspended' *terumah* when it is burned on Pesach eve. At other times, all agree that suspended *terumah* may not be burned nor contaminated.

2. As to the exact circumstances under which *terumah* may be put in a state of 'suspense'; see *Rashi* 15a, s.v. שנולד, *Tosafos* there, s.v. חבית, and *P'nei Yehoshua*.

R' Yose said to him: This is not analogous. [Even] R' Eliezer and R' Yehoshua concur that each is burned separately. Concerning what do they differ? — Concerning suspended and contaminated [*terumah*]. R' Eliezer says that each must be burned separately, but R' Yehoshua says that both [may be burned] together.

suspense: it may not be eaten and it is not burned[1], and is therefore called *teluyah* (תְּלוּיָה), *suspended*.]

שֶׁרַבִּי אֱלִיעֶזֶר אוֹמֵר תִּשָּׂרֵף זוֹ לְעַצְמָהּ וְזוֹ לְעַצְמָהּ, — *R' Eliezer says that each must be burned separately* [lit. *this by itself and this by itself*],

Their difference of opinion is based on the interpretation of the phrase: אֵת מִשְׁמֶרֶת תְּרוּמֹתָי, lit. *the safeguarding of my terumos* (Numbers 18:8). R' Eliezer says that אִם יֵשׁ לְמִקְרָא the text as traditionally vocalized is authoritative in Biblical interpretation, and the vocalization of the word תְּרוּמֹתָי presents the word *terumah* in the plural, *trumos*. The plural alludes to the presence of more than one kind of *terumah*, i.e. uncontaminated *terumah* and suspended *terumah*, too, so it is forbidden to add to the *tumah* status of any *terumah* by burning it with contaminated *terumah* (*Rav*, based on *Bechoros* 34a).

וְרַבִּי יְהוֹשֻׁעַ אוֹמֵר שְׁתֵּיהֶן כְּאֶחָת. — *but R' Yehoshua says that both* [may be burned] together.

R' Yehoshua holds יֵשׁ אִם לְמָסֹרֶת the text as it is spelled [lit. transmitted] is authoritative, and since the spelling תרומתי (without a *vav* between the *mem* and *tav*) would ordinarily be read תְּרוּמָתִי, *my terumah*, this indicates that only normal (uncontaminated) *terumah* is under a mandate to be *safeguarded*. If so, there is no prohibition against adding *tumah* to 'suspended' *terumah* (ibid.)

Alternatively, R' Yehoshua holds that the stress provided by the word, לְךָ, *to you*, in the verse (Numbers 18:8) *I have assigned* לְךָ, *to you, the safeguarding of my terumos* implies that only *terumah* that is given to you [לְךָ] for your permissible use and consumption, must be safeguarded, but not *terumah* that you are not permitted to enjoy, such as suspended *terumah*. R' Eliezer, however, refuses to categorize suspended *terumah* as not open to enjoyment because the possibility always exists that the prophet Elijah (who will herald the Messiah and resolve all unanswered halachic questions) will reveal that the suspended *terumah* was actually uncontaminated.

1. According to *Tosafos'* view (see above, s.v. וּמוֹדִים, with footnote) that R' Yehoshua permits the burning and contaminating of suspended *terumah* year-round, the appellation 'suspended' is puzzling, since the owner can dispose of the *terumah* immediately. *Tosafos* (20b, s.v. חא) explains that because this *terumah*, in contradistinction to unquestionably contaminated *terumah*, is not *required* to be burned, it is designated 'suspended'.

[א] כָּל שָׁעָה שֶׁמֻּתָּר לֶאֱכוֹל, מַאֲכִיל לִבְהֵמָה,
לְחַיָּה וּלְעוֹפוֹת, וּמוֹכְרוֹ לְנָכְרִי, וּמֻתָּר
בַּהֲנָאָתוֹ. עָבַר זְמַנּוֹ, אָסוּר בַּהֲנָאָתוֹ, וְלֹא יַסִּיק
בּוֹ תַנּוּר וְכִירַיִם.

יד אברהם

Chapter 2

1.

A discussion of the various time limits for the prohibitions against eating and
deriving benefit from *chametz* had begun in 1:4. The Mishnah now returns to this
topic and presents a slightly different version of the relevant laws.

כָּל שָׁעָה שֶׁמֻּתָּר לֶאֱכוֹל, — *As long as* [lit.
the whole time] *it is permitted to eat*
[*chametz*],

[The gist of the mishnah's statement lies in
its implication that when one may *not* eat
chametz he may not feed it to his livestock
(*Rashi*; see *Tos. Yom Tov, Tosafos
Chadoshim* and *Maharsha* to *Rashi*);
otherwise the mishnah's statement seems
self-evident, since one may surely feed
chametz to his animals while he is permitted
to eat it himself. However the *Gemara* (21a)
infers yet another law from the use of the apparently superfluous term שֶׁמֻּתָּר, *it is permitted*. The mishnah should have said: *As long
as one may eat* [*chametz*], *he may feed* ...
The insertion of the term *it is permitted*, suggests that the governing factor is whether
permission exists for *anyone* to eat *chametz*,
even if the individual in question is not
himself permitted to eat *chametz*. This
implication can be understood according to
Rabban Gamliel (mishnah 1:5) who rules
that an extra hour was allowed for the eating
of *terumah* after ordinary *chametz* was
prohibited. Thus our mishnah is explained as
follows:]

As long as it is permitted [for a *Kohen*] to
eat terumah, i.e., the fifth hour of the day,
one [even an Israelite] *may feed it* [any
chametz — even *chullin*] *to his livestock*,
even though *chullin* had been prohibited for
human consumption during this hour. [The
mishnah's point is that the Sages permitted
one to derive benefit from *chametz* for one
hour after its consumption became
prohibited.] The mishnah follows Rabban

Gamliel (above 1:5) who allows *terumah* to
be eaten for one hour — the fifth hour of the
day — after the prohibition of *chullin* (*Rav*;
Gem. 21a).

[The halachah does not follow Rabban
Gamliel's ruling concerning *terumah*, but the
basic premise of our mishnah — that *chametz*
may not be eaten in the fifth hour but benefit
may be derived from it — is halachically accepted (see *Orach Chaim* 443:1).]

מַאֲכִיל לִבְהֵמָה, לְחַיָּה וּלְעוֹפוֹת, — *one may
feed* [*it*] *to livestock, beasts and birds,*

The *Gemara* (21a) explains why it is
necessary to enumerate all three
categories. Had the mishnah mentioned
only domestic livestock, one could
speculate that only these may be fed
because their leftovers remain visible in
the barn or corral where the owner can
dispose of them in time, but perhaps it
is forbidden to feed *chametz* to beasts
near the deadline because they tend to
hide their leftovers, causing the owner
to transgress the prohibition against
possessing *chametz*. Once the mishnah
mentions both livestock and beasts, it
mentions birds to complete the listing of
all living things (*Rav*).

וּמוֹכְרוֹ לְנָכְרִי, — *and sell it to a Gentile*
The ruling follows *Beis Hillel*. Our
mishnah rejects the view of *Beis Shammai* (cited in *Gem.*), who maintain that a
Jew may not sell his *chametz* to a Gen-

1. As long as it is permitted to eat [*chametz*], one may feed [it] to livestock, beasts and birds, and sell it to a Gentile and [deriving] benefit from it is permitted. When its period has passed, [deriving] benefit from it is forbidden, and one may not fire an oven or a range with it.

YAD AVRAHAM

tile unless he knows that it will be consumed before Pesach (*Rav; Gem.* 21a).

וּמְתָּר בַּהֲנָאָתוֹ. — *and [deriving] benefit from it is permitted.*

The *Gemara* (21b) remarks that this passage of the Mishnah seems redundant in view of the mishnah's earlier ruling that *one may feed it to livestock.* The *Gemara* concludes that this clause alludes to the new rule that if someone takes *chametz* before it becomes forbidden and chars it to such an extent that it loses its taste and appearance[1] (*Rashi*), he is permitted to continue deriving benefit from it even after *chametz* becomes forbidden (*Rav*).

עָבַר זְמַנּוֹ, אָסוּר בַּהֲנָאָתוֹ, — *When its period has passed, [deriving] benefit from it is forbidden,*

The *period* under discussion is the fifth hour of the day, when benefits of the *chametz* may still be enjoyed. During the sixth hour, however, *chametz* is absolutely forbidden by Rabbinic injunction. Its status is now the same as if it were Scripturally forbidden (*Gem.* 21b). Consequently, the *Gemara* (ibid) adds, if someone betroths a woman with rabbinically forbidden *chametz*, his betrothal is invalid. The same is true of other Rabbinically forbidden *chametz* such as incomplete *chametz* (חָמֵץ נוּקְשָׁה: see prefatory comment to 3:1; *Rav;* see *Even HaEzer* 28:21).

The *Gemara* (21b) bases the restriction against deriving benefit from *chametz* on the Biblical phrase (*Ex.* 13:13): וְלֹא יֵאָכֵל חָמֵץ, *No*

chametz shall be eaten. Scripture does not use the more direct expression *one shall not eat chametz;* the passive term לֹא יֵאָכֵל חָמֵץ, *no chametz shall be eaten* implies the broader intimation that not only is a person forbidden to eat *chametz,* but it may not even be used as a source of any benefit that can contribute to the availability of any sort of food. Since the monetary value of benefits derived from *chametz* could be used to purchase food, or to free other assets to buy food, all benefits derived from *chametz* are forbidden on Pesach (*Tos. Yom Tov* based on *Rashi; Tos.* 21b, s.v. לא יאכל).

וְלֹא יַסִּיק בּוֹ תַּנּוּר וְכִירַיִם, — *and one may not fire an oven or a range with it.*

Firing an oven is, on surface, merely an example of deriving benefit and need not be mentioned specifically. The *Gemara* (21b) contends that the point here is that even according to R' Yehudah who holds that one may remove *chametz* only by burning it, one may not derive benefit from it during the process of burning (*Rav*).

Tosafos (21b, s.v. בהדי) explains that according to *Temurah* 7:6, it is permitted to use the ashes of forbidden substances that must be burned. Thus, according to R' Yehudah who requires that *chametz* be burned, the ashes may be used. Our mishnah now informs us that the benefit derived *while the chametz is burning* is not viewed as benefit from *ashes* and is prohibited (see *Gem.* 26b with *Tos.*, s.v. חדר; *Drush VeChidush* to 5a; cf. *Meharam Chalavah* who avers that the prohibition to fire an oven is Rabbinical; consequently any food prepared over the fire is not prohibited).

1. But it must be so charred that it is rendered inedible even for dogs (*Tos.* 21b, s.v. רכו). Even then it is permitted only to keep the ashes and to derive benefit from them, but not to eat them (*Rosh;* see *Mishnah Berurah* 442:43).

רַבִּי יְהוּדָה אוֹמֵר: אֵין בִּיעוּר חָמֵץ אֶלָּא
שְׂרֵפָה.
וַחֲכָמִים אוֹמְרִים: אַף מְפָרֵר וְזוֹרֶה לָרוּחַ אוֹ
מַטִּיל לַיָּם.

[ב] **חָמֵץ** שֶׁל נָכְרִי שֶׁעָבַר עָלָיו הַפֶּסַח, מֻתָּר
בַּהֲנָאָה; וְשֶׁל יִשְׂרָאֵל, אָסוּר
בַּהֲנָאָה — שֶׁנֶּאֱמַר ,,וְלֹא יֵרָאֶה לְךָ שְׂאֹר".

יד אברהם

רַבִּי יְהוּדָה אוֹמֵר: אֵין בִּיעוּר חָמֵץ אֶלָּא
שְׂרֵפָה. — *R' Yehudah says: There is no
removal of chametz except by burning.*

R' Yehudah arrives at this conclusion
by likening *chametz* to נוֹתָר, *leftover*,
portions of sacrificial meat that were not
eaten during their prescribed time.
Chametz and *leftover* are analogous
since both eating them and deriving
benefits from them are forbidden, also
the punishment for the willful eating of
either is *kares*, spiritual excision. R'
Yehudah assumes, therefore, that since
leftover meat must be burned (*Exodus
12:10*), *chametz*, too, must be burned
(*Rav; Gem. 28a; cf. Tos. R' Akiva*).

וַחֲכָמִים אוֹמְרִים: אַף מְפָרֵר וְזוֹרֶה לָרוּחַ —
*But the sages say: He may also crumble
and throw [it] to the wind*

The Sages refute R' Yehudah's analogy because not all forbidden substances share the requirement of burning (see *Rav*).

The language of the mishnah (he may *also*)

indicates that the Sages also agree that burning is preferable, but add that crumbling is
also sufficient. *Rif* and *Rosh* have a different
version: He crumbles, omitting the word אַף,
also. Their reading allows for the view that
only crumbling is permitted, but burning is
not[1]. The *Shulchan Aruch* prefers our version, which is also *Rambam's* reading
(*Magen Avraham 445:1*).

Although we decide in favor of the
Sages that crumbling is sufficient, it is
customary to burn the chometz (*Rama
in Orach Chaim 445:1*).

אוֹ מַטִּיל לַיָּם. — *or cast [it] into the sea.*

The *Gemara* (28a) discusses whether
casting into the sea is sufficient in itself,
or must be done in conjunction with
crumbling. The halachically accepted
view (*Orach Chaim 445:1*) holds that
only hard *chametz* or grain, which will
not disintegrate rapidly on its own, need
be crumbled before casting into the sea.
For all others casting into the sea in
itself is sufficient.

---

1. The reason for prohibiting burning as a method of removal is the rule in *Terumah 7:6* that
any substance whose prescribed means of removal is 'burying' (i.e., a means other than burning) may not be burned. This rule is based on a basic difference between a requirement to
burn and a requirement to dispose of something. When the commandment is to burn an object, we assume that there is a *mitzvah* to burn it. If so, the substance may not be used for
anything other than its *mitzvah*, but once the *mitzvah* is done [נַעֲשִׂית מִצְוָתוֹ], the remaining
ashes are no longer forbidden. In a case where burying — not burning — is required, it cannot
be said that burying is a *mitzvah*. Rather the Torah requires that the substance not be used in
any manner. In such cases, the Rabbis decreed that the forbidden substance *not be burned,
because they are permitted to use the ashes. See R' Akiva Eiger* in his glosses to *Magen
Avraham* and in *Derush VeChidush; Avnei Miluim, Teshuvos 9; Chidushei R' Chaim
HaLevi, Hil. Chametz 1:3* and many others.

R' Yehudah says: There is no removal of *chametz* except by burning. But the sages say: He may also crumble [it] and throw [it] to the wind or cast [it] into the sea.

2. Chametz of a Gentile over which Pesach has passed, [deriving] benefit from it is permitted; but [*chametz*] of a Jew, [deriving] benefit from it is forbidden — since it is said: *Nor shall leaven be seen with you (Exodus 13:7).*

YAD AVRAHAM

2.

חָמֵץ שֶׁל נָכְרִי שֶׁעָבַר עָלָיו הַפֶּסַח, — *Chametz of a Gentile over which Pesach has passed,*

[The Gentile kept his *chametz* until the end of Pesach.]

מֻתָּר בַּהֲנָאָה; — *[deriving] benefit from it is permitted;*

In fact, it may even be eaten, but the term 'deriving benefit' is employed, to correspond to the terminology of the second part of the mishnah, which states, *but [chametz] of a Jew, [deriving] benefit from it is forbidden,* to underscore the extent of the prohibition in a case where a Jew violates the precept to dispose of his *chametz.*

Alternatively (based on *Yerushalmi*): The mishnah avoids the statement that a Gentile's *chametz* may be eaten since some communities customarily refrain from eating a Gentile baker's bread (פַּת פַּלְטֵר: *Rav; Rambam*).

וְשֶׁל יִשְׂרָאֵל, אָסוּר בַּהֲנָאָה — שֶׁנֶּאֱמַר ,,לֹא יֵרָאֶה לְךָ שְׂאֹר". — *but [chametz] of a Jew, [deriving] benefit from it is forbidden — it is said: "Nor shall leaven be seen with you [Exodus 13:7].*

According to the *Gemara's* conclusion, the Scriptural prohibition against eating *chametz* does not extend to *chametz* 'which Pesach has passed

over,' meaning that a Jew kept it in his possession throughout the festival. Nevertheless, because he transgressed the injunction against keeping it, the Sages penalized the owner of the *chametz* and forbade him to derive any benefit from his transgression. The mishnah quotes this Scriptural verse not because it embodies the prohibition, but because it is the verse upon which the Sages based their decree that the transgressor may not benefit from his misdeed.

Some versions have here appropriately (*Exodus* 13:7): *Chametz shall not be seen with you* ... (see *Shinuyei Nuschaos, Rambam comm.* ed. R' Y. Kafich). See *Pnei Yehoshua* for an explanation for our version which oddly has שְׂאֹר, *leaven.*

If a Jew nullified his *chametz,* but after Passover he chances to find *chametz* that had inadvertently remained in his possession, there are two views in *Yerushalmi:* Reish Lakish permits its use, since no transgression was committed. R' Yochanan maintains that, the Sages banned the use of all Jewish-owned *chametz,* without exception, in order to prevent a scheming owner from claiming that he nullified his *chametz* when in fact he did not (*Rosh;* see *Orach Chaim* 448:5).

Rambam writes: '*Chametz* in a Jew's possession which was left over Pesach is forbidden forever even if *unintentionally* or *accidentally* left over' (*Hil. Chametz* 1:4; *Orach Chaim* 448:3).

[ג] **נָכְרִי** שֶׁהִלְוָה אֶת יִשְׂרָאֵל עַל חֲמֵצוֹ, אַחַר הַפֶּסַח מֻתָּר בַּהֲנָאָה; וְיִשְׂרָאֵל שֶׁהִלְוָה אֶת הַנָּכְרִי עַל חֲמֵצוֹ, אַחַר הַפֶּסַח אָסוּר בַּהֲנָאָה. חָמֵץ שֶׁנָּפְלָה עָלָיו מַפֹּלֶת, הֲרֵי הוּא כִמְבֹעָר. רַבָּן שִׁמְעוֹן בֶּן גַּמְלִיאֵל אוֹמֵר: כָּל שֶׁאֵין הַכֶּלֶב יָכוֹל לְחַפֵּשׂ אַחֲרָיו.

יד אברהם

3.

This mishnah continues the theme begun in mishnah 2 that the status of *chametz* depends on whether or not it was owned by a Jew. It will define the ownership of *Chametz* in an instance where legal possession is not self-evident.

נָכְרִי שֶׁהִלְוָה אֶת יִשְׂרָאֵל עַל חֲמֵצוֹ, — *If a Gentile lent [money] to a Jew* [before Pesach] *on his chametz,*

[The Jewish borrower pledged his *chametz* to the Gentile lender as collateral to assure the loan, then the Jew defaulted on the loan so that the collateral — the *chametz* — reverted to the Gentile.]

The *Gemara* (31a) adds that according to the halachically accepted view of Rava, the rule enunciated in the mishnah is true only if two conditions are met: (a) the terms of the loan agreement stipulated that in case of default the collateral becomes the lender's retroactively, from the moment the debt was incurred; (b) that the collateral was held in the lender's premises during Pesach.[1] Since the debt is in default

and the lender need not take any action to collect his debt, it is now established retroactively that the collateral was his property, not the Jew's throughout Pesach (*Rav*).

אַחַר הַפֶּסַח מֻתָּר בַּהֲנָאָה; — *[then] after Pesach [deriving] benefit from it is permitted;*

[If after Pesach a Jew purchased this *chametz* from the Gentile, he may use and eat it.]

There is a difference of opinion regarding the due date of the debt. *Rambam (Hil. Chametz 4:5)* maintains that the mishnah is concerned only with a debt that falls due before Pesach; in that case the *chametz* reverts to the Gentile before the festival and the Jew was never in violation, consequently its use is not forbidden after Pesach.[2] *Ravad* contends that even after Pesach, the *chametz*

1. Among the reasons for this provision are these: (a) Transference to the lender's premises is needed in order to effect formally the Gentile's legal acquisition (קִנְיָן) of the collateral (*Rosh*) since many authorities hold that a Gentile does not acquire possession simply with payment of money (see *Yoreh Deah* 320:6; *Chok Yaakov* 441:2 and *Mishnah Berurah* there par. 2). (b) To remove the borrower's liability. Were the Jewish borrower responsible for the safekeeping of the *chametz* during Pesach, it would be considered 'Jewish-owned *chametz*' for the purpose of falling under the decree forbidding its use after Pesach (*Gem.* 5b). In the absence of an agreement to the contrary, collateral held by a borrower is his responsibility and even if legal title to the collateral had been transferred to the lender, the borrower would remain obligated to remove it before Pesach (*Rosh*). But if the *chametz* is on the lender's premises, even if some liability is left to the borrower, he is not obligated in its 'removal' (*Magen Avraham* 441:3). [See also *P'ri Megadim, Eshel Avraham* 441:2; see *Mishnah Berurah* 441:2 with *Sha'ar HaTziyun* and *Be'ur Halachah*.]

2
3

3. If a Gentile lent [money] to a Jew on his *chametz*, [then] after Pesach [deriving] benefit from it is permitted; but if a Jew lent [money] to a Gentile on his *chametz*, [then] after Pesach [deriving] benefit from it is forbidden.

If a ruin collapsed over *chametz*, it is regarded as removed. Rabban Shimon ben Gamliel says: Provided a dog cannot search it out.

YAD AVRAHAM

is permissible if the aforementioned conditions are met, because the Gentile's ownership is retroactive. The *Shulchan Aruch* (*Orach Chaim* 441:1) decides in favor of *Ravad*.

וְיִשְׂרָאֵל שֶׁהִלְוָה אֶת הַנָּכְרִי עַל חֲמֵצוֹ, אַחַר הַפֶּסַח אָסוּר בַּהֲנָאָה. — *but if a Jew lent [money] to a Gentile on his (the Gentile's] chametz, [then] after Pesach [deriving] benefit from it is forbidden.*

[If the gentile defaulted on the debt, the *chametz* is considered the lender's and consequently forbidden since it had been 'kept' by a Jew over Pesach.]

[Here too (as in the obverse case), if two conditions are met the lender (in this case a Jew) is considered to be in legal possession of the *chametz*: (a) If default occurs, the collateral is the lender's retroactively, from the date of the transaction. (b) The collateral was held on the lender's premises. However even if the first condition is not met, it is possible for the lender to be responsible for the 'removal' of the *chametz* — if he has assumed any liability for the collateral. Then he is Scripturally prohibited to 'keep' the chametz even if it is not legally his (see footnote to s.v. נכרי) and as a result the Sages render it forbidden after Pesach (see *Orach Chaim* 441:2).]

חָמֵץ שֶׁנָּפְלָה עָלָיו מַפֹּלֶת, הֲרֵי הוּא כִמְבֹעָר. — *If a ruin collapsed over chametz, it is regarded as removed.*

It is not necessary to remove the

debris in order to find and destroy the *chametz* (*Tif. Yis.*). However, the owner must nullify it in his heart (בִּיטוּל), because it is conceivable that the debris will be removed during Pesach (*Rav* based on *Gem.* 31b with *Rashi*).

In *Rashi's* view, this requirement of nullification is only a Rabbinic measure to circumvent the possibility of his transgression. *Semak* (cited by *Magen Avraham* 433:17; *Bach* there) maintains that this nullification is needed to fulfil the Torah obligation to 'remove' the *chametz*. Once nullified, the *chametz* is regarded by our mishnah as removed with regard to the Rabbinic obligation to remove all *chametz* (even that already nullified). In the case of our mishnah, since the *chametz* is buried, the Sages did not require its owner to do more than nullify it. Consequently if nullification were no longer possible (after midday on the fourteenth of Nissan), the debris would have to be removed. *Mishnah Berurah* (433:25) cites both views without rendering a clear decision (see *Sha'ar HaTziyun* there 44-46). [See Appendix, *Search and Nullification*.]

רַבָּן שִׁמְעוֹן בֶּן גַּמְלִיאֵל אוֹמֵר: כָּל שֶׁאֵין הַכֶּלֶב יָכוֹל לְחַפֵּשׂ אַחֲרָיו. — *Rabban Shimon ben Gamliel says: Provided a dog cannot search it out.*

If the *chametz* is buried at a depth of at least three handbreaths (*Rav; Gem.* 31b). But if it is covered by less than this amount, he must remove the *chametz*

2. According to *Rambam*, as long as the borrower has the potential to retain the *chametz* — by paying the debt during or after Pesach — it is considered his under the terms of the prohibition not to keep *chametz*, even though it will later become the retroactive property of the Gentile lender. With regard to the prohibition against owning *chametz* during Pesach, the guidelines for defining 'ownership' allows for inclusion even of *chametz* that is not really 'owned' by the ordinary standards of legal ownership (see *Rosh* and *Ran*).

[29] THE MISHNAH / PESACHIM

פסחים
ד/ב
[ד] **הָאוֹכֵל** תְּרוּמַת חָמֵץ בַּפֶּסַח בְּשׁוֹגֵג,
מְשַׁלֵּם קֶרֶן וָחֹמֶשׁ. בְּמֵזִיד,
פָּטוּר מִתַּשְׁלוּמִים וּמִדְּמֵי עֵצִים.

ה/ב
[ה] **אֵלּוּ** דְבָרִים שֶׁאָדָם יוֹצֵא בָהֶן יְדֵי חוֹבָתוֹ
בַּפֶּסַח: בְּחִטִּים, בִּשְׂעוֹרִים, בְּכֻסְּמִין,
וּבְשִׁיפוֹן וּבְשִׁבֹּלֶת שׁוּעָל. וְיוֹצְאִין בִּדְמַאי,

יד אברהם

because of the possibility that a dog may drag it out on Passover (*Meiri, Tos. Yom Tov*; see *Rashi* s.v. משום ריחא: cf. *Aruch HaShulchan* 433:10). Rabban Shimon ben Gamliel does not dispute the first tanna, he only clarifies the dimensions of the debris (*Rambam; Tos. Yom Tov*).

4.

⊷§Terumah eaten by a non-Kohen

Terumah, the portion separated from produce and given a *Kohen*, may not be eaten by anyone except *Kohanim* and some members of their household (*Leviticus* 22:10). The Torah provides unique rules for repayment of the *terumah* when it is eaten בְּשׁוֹגֵג, *unwittingly*, by a non-*Kohen*. He must repay the principal plus a fifth. This payment must be made in produce (not money), which then is itself rendered *terumah* (*Leviticus* 22:14). This payment must be made even where there is no monetary loss to a *Kohen*, e.g., the *terumah* was eaten by a non-*Kohen* who had inherited it from his maternal grandfather — a *Kohen* — or where the aggrieved *Kohen* waives his claim or had given permission for the *terumah* to be eaten by a non-*Kohen* (see *Terumos* 6:1-2; *Rambam, Hil. Terumos* 10:22; *Gilyon HaShas* here; *Chazon Ish, Orach Chaim 118*). The additional payment is viewed by some as an atonement for the sin of eating (*Tos.* 29a, s.v. מאן). However for a non-*Kohen* who *knowingly* transgressed no special provisions are made. His only liability is that of restitution under the ordinary laws of damages; such restitution can be money, and even if it is produce it does not become *terumah*. In addition to his payment, he is liable to punishment for transgressing this negative mitzvah — premature death 'at the hands of Heaven' (מִיתָה בִּידֵי שָׁמַיִם): if he had been forewarned (הַתְרָאָה) by two witnesses he is liable to lashes (מַלְקוֹת).

הָאוֹכֵל תְּרוּמַת חָמֵץ בַּפֶּסַח — *One who eats terumah of chametz on Pesach*

The Mishnah discusses terumah that was separated before it leavened, or, that was separated in its leavened form before Pesach. In either case, it was valid *terumah* at the time of its designation because a *Kohen* could eat it. However, if it was already leavened and was separated during Pesach, its *chametz* status made it unfit for the *Kohen* to eat. Consequently, the designation, *terumah* cannot be applied to it for the Torah says: *"The first of*

your grain ... shall you give to him" (*Deuteronomy* 18:4) i.e., it must be *suitable* for him (*Meiri*; from *Gem.* 33a-b; see *Tos.* 32a, s.v. דבר).

בְּשׁוֹגֵג, — *inadvertently,*

He was unaware that he was eating *terumah*, although he may have known that it was *chametz* (*Rav; Rashi* based on one view in *Gem.* 32a).

מְשַׁלֵּם קֶרֶן וָחֹמֶשׁ. — *must repay [a Kohen] the principal plus a fifth.*

In terms of monetary value, the *terumah* he ate was completely worth-

2
4

4. **O**ne who eats *terumah* of *chametz* on Pesach inadvertently, must repay [a *Kohen*] the principal plus a fifth. If [he eats it] deliberately, he is free from payment and from [liability for] its value as fuel.

2
5

5. **T**hese are the species [of grain] with which a man fulfills his obligation [of *matzah*] on Pesach: with wheat, barley, spelt, rye and oats. And we can

YAD AVRAHAM

less, because *chametz* of a Jew is forbidden during and after Pesach; if so what principal is there to repay? In the case of ordinary *chametz* food, it is true that the *chametz* was worthless and therefore, no payment is possible, but *terumah* is unique. If it was eaten unwittingly by a non-*Kohen*, the amount to be repaid does not depend on its monetary value, but rather on the volume consumed, e.g., if someone ate a pound of fruit he must repay with a pound of that same species, even if the price at the time of repayment is much higher, and cannot absolve himself by paying money. Regarding the repayment of *terumah* eaten unwittingly, the Torah (*Leviticus* 22:14) says: ... *and he shall give the Kohen the holy*, meaning that he pays the *Kohen* with produce that becomes *terumah* ['holy'] thus replacing the *terumah* that was eaten. Consequently, *terumah* which is *chametz* must be replaced with an equal quantity regardless of the value of the eaten *terumah* (*Rav, Rashi*; based on one view in *Gem.* 32a).

בְּמֵזִיד, פָּטוּר מִתַּשְׁלוּמִים — *If* [*he eats it*] *deliberately, he is free from payment*
If he ate the *terumah*, knowing that it

was *terumah* and forbidden to him, even if he was not aware that it was *chametz*, he does not pay, since here the obligation to pay is not derived from the special provision designating payments for *terumah* (i.e., payment according to quantity), but upon the general laws of damages. Consequently, since *chametz* on Pesach has no monetary value, by definition there can be no obligation to pay, because no monetary loss was inflicted (*Rav, Rashi*; based on one view in *Gem.* 32a).

וּמִדְּמֵי עֵצִים. — *and from* [*liability for*] *its value as fuel* [lit. *value of wood*].
Even if the *terumah* in question was contaminated, in which case the *Kohen* could have used it as fuel, and by eating the *terumah* the offender deprived the *Kohen* of its use as fuel, he is free from payment.
[Uncontaminated *terumah* may not be used for fuel (*Sheviis* 8:2; *Tos. Yom Tov*).]
In this case, too, since the *terumah* was eaten deliberately, the offense falls into the category of common thievery where restitution is only made for the monetary loss; *chametz* on Pesach has no monetary value (*Rav; Rashi*).

5.

אֵלּוּ דְבָרִים שֶׁאָדָם יוֹצֵא בָהֶם יְדֵי חוֹבָתוֹ בְּפֶסַח: — *These are the species* [*of grain*; lit. *things*] *with which a man fulfills his obligation* [*of matzah*] *on Pesach.*

Only the flour of the grains listed below may be used to fulfill the *mitzvah* to eat matzah on the Seder night, the only time when there is a Scriptural

יד אברהם

commandment (*Exodus* 12:18) to do so: *In the evening you shall eat matzos* (*Rav, Rashi*).

בְּחִטִּים, בִּשְׂעוֹרִים, בְּכֻסְמִין, וּבְשִׁיפוֹן וּבְשִׁבֹּלֶת שׁוּעָל. — *with wheat, barley, spelt, rye and oats.*

However one does not discharge his obligation with millet, rice [or matzah made from any other crop but these five]. The Torah says, *You shall eat no leavened bread with it* [the Pesach of-fering] (*Exodus* 12:18). The proximity of the terms *leavened bread* and *matzah* indicates that one can fulfill his duty of eating matzah only with grains that can reach a state of leavening, but millet and rice are unacceptable because they do not leaven, rather they decay (*Gem.* 35a).

However it is customary to use only wheat (*Orach Chaim* 453:1) because this grain is the tastiest and the best liked by people (*Chok Ya'akov* 453:2).

◆§The Portions Separated from Produce

The discussion of the mishnah will now go into the various portions that must be separated from crops. They are the following:

תְּרוּמָה גְדוֹלָה — Terumah

The first portion separated is the *terumah* (usually between a fortieth and sixtieth of the total) which is given a *Kohen* and is forbidden to a non-*Kohen*. This portion is sometimes called תְּרוּמָה גְדוֹלָה, *the great terumah*, to differentiate it from תְּרוּמַת מַעֲשֵׂר, *from the [first] tithe*, which is given by Levites and which is also a form of *terumah* as described below, s.v. Tithe from the Tithe.

מַעֲשֵׂר רִאשׁוֹן — First Tithe

After the *terumah* has been separated, מַעֲשֵׂר רִאשׁוֹן, *the first tithe*, is taken from the remainder and presented to a Levite. This tithe is exactly a tenth of the crop.

מַעֲשֵׂר מִן הַמַּעֲשֵׂר — Tithe from the Tithe

From his first tithe, the Levite separates an additional *terumah* that he gives to a *Kohen*. The amount of his *terumah* is exactly one tenth of his first tithe. It is also called תְּרוּמַת מַעֲשֵׂר, the *terumah* of the *tithe* and has all the laws peculiar to *terumah*. Before separation, the first tithe is called *tevel*, and, like all produce before the separation of *terumah*, it may not be eaten. Thus before the first tithe may be eaten, two *terumahs* are taken from it: The regular *terumah*, which was separated from the entire crop, before the Levite's share was taken from it; the special tithe separated by the Levite. Consequently, if the original owner had neglected to separate the regular *terumah* from the produce before giving the first tithe to a Levite, the Levite must separate both the *terumah* and the tithe from the tithe. However, in some cases (see below, s.v. ובמעשר ראשון שנטלה) the obligation to separate the regular *terumah* from the first tithe is waived.

מַעֲשֵׂר שֵׁנִי — Second Tithe

In the first, second, fourth and fifth years of the seven-year Sabbatical cycle, a second tithe is separated from what remains of the produce after the *Kohen* and Levite's shares have been removed. This tithe must be brought to Jerusalem by the owner and eaten there by him, his household, and guests. If this is not convenient, the owner may redeem the produce for money, which he takes to Jerusalem and uses there for the purchase of food. The food assumes the sanctity previously resi-dent in the produce and redemption money.

מַעֲשֵׂר עָנִי — Tithe of the Poor

In the third and sixth years of the Sabbatical cycle, a tenth of the produce is

discharge it with *demai*, with first tithe whose
terumah has been separated, and with second tithe or

YAD AVRAHAM

separated for distribution to the poor. It has no sanctity or special requirements, but
the produce is *tevel* until this tithe is removed from it.

חַלָּה — Challah
Dough requires yet an additional *terumah*. This is called חַלָּה, *challah* [lit. *loaf*],
and has all of the laws of *terumah*.

טֶבֶל — Tevel
Tevel is the name given to every commodity that requires that one or more tithe
be removed from it. Prior to the separation of the particular tithe the food is called
tevel, a contraction of two words טַב לֹא, *not good*, meaning it lacks the process that
will make it fit for consumption (*Rav, Berachos* 7:1; *R' Manoach to Hil. Chametz*,
6:7). Alternatively, the word may be derived from the word טַבְלָא, *board* or *table*,
suggesting that this food is as inedible as a board (*Aruch, s.v.* טבלא: *ibid*).

דְּמַאי — Demai
With the passage of time, it became apparent to the Sages that many עַמֵּי הָאָרֶץ,
ignorant [and avaricious] *people*, were becoming less scrupulous in the separation
of the various tithes. Although they continued to separate *terumah* carefully and to
treat it with the proper seriousness, and most of them were just as careful with the
other tithes, significant numbers of them no longer separated any tithes except for
terumah. As a result, anyone who purchased produce from an ignorant person —
unless he was known to be fully observant — could not know whether or not the
produce was *tevel*, and the seller could not be trusted to give an honest answer even
if he were asked directly. Such a product was called דְּמַאי [*demai*], a contraction of
דָּא מַאי, *what is this?* In view of the possibility that the *demai* might be *tevel*, the
Sages forbade purchasers to eat it unless they separated the doubtful tithes.
However, they did *not* impose this burden upon poor people. In view of the compliance of *most* ignorant people with the laws of tithes and the great need of the
poor, the Sages allowed them to use *demai* without tithing.

וְיוֹצְאִין בִּדְמַאי, — *And we can discharge it*
[the obligation] *with demai,*
The reason one may fulfill his matzah
obligation with *demai* grain, although it
may not be eaten by an Israelite before
tithing, is that poor people *may* eat
demai (*Demai* 3:1); the Sages did not
impose their injunction on the destitute.
Technically, *anyone* cam avail himself
of the right to eat *demai* by declaring his
property ownerless and thus becoming
poor. Consequently, anyone who fulfills his matzah obligation with *demai*
does not have his performance of the
mitzvah disqualified on the grounds
that it is a *mitzvah* that came about as a
result of a transgression (Gem. 35b).
Ri (Tos. 35b, s.v. יוצאין) wonders whether
demai may be used for matzah without
hesitation for a first resort because [לְכַתְּחִילָה]

demai and matzah are both, in a sense לֶחֶם
עֹנִי, *food of the destitute.* Or perhaps it is
preferable not to use *demai* for the fulfillment of the mitzvah, and the prohibition
against initially eating *demai* is in effect even
where the *mitzvah* of matzah is concerned.
Only if it *has* been used [בְּדִיעֲבַד] is the eater
regarded as having discharged his obligation.

וּבְמַעֲשֵׂר רִאשׁוֹן שֶׁנִּטְּלָה תְרוּמָתוֹ — [*and*]
*with first tithe whose terumah has been
separated,*
If this statement were taken literally it
would be obvious; since *terumah* was
separated one may eat it. The *Gemara*
(35b), therefore, states that the mishnah
is concerned with a situation where only
its (the first tithe's) *terumah*, i.e., 'the
tithe from the tithe' which the Levite
gives the *Kohen* was separated, but not
the regular *terumah* (תְּרוּמָה גְדוֹלָה).

שֵׁנִי וְהֶקְדֵּשׁ שֶׁנִּפְדּוּ; וְהַכֹּהֲנִים — בְּחַלָּה
וּבִתְרוּמָה; אֲבָל לֹא בְטֶבֶל, וְלֹא בְמַעֲשֵׂר
רִאשׁוֹן שֶׁלֹּא נִטְּלָה תְרוּמָתוֹ, וְלֹא בְמַעֲשֵׂר שֵׁנִי
וְהֶקְדֵּשׁ שֶׁלֹּא נִפְדּוּ.
חַלּוֹת תּוֹדָה וּרְקִיקֵי נָזִיר — עֲשָׂאָן לְעַצְמוֹ,
אֵין יוֹצְאִין בָּהֶן; עֲשָׂאָן לִמְכֹּר בַּשּׁוּק, יוֹצְאִין
בָּהֶן.

יד אברהם

Under normal circumstances this would render the produce *tevel* (untithed) and forbidden, but the mishnah refers to a case where the first tithe has been separated before the grain has been threshed — before threshing, the obligation to separate *terumah* and the other tithes is not yet in effect. Therefore the Levite who receives his first tithe is obligated to give the *Kohen* only the tithe of the tithe, and not the regular *terumah*.

וּבְמַעֲשֵׂר שֵׁנִי וְהֶקְדֵּשׁ שֶׁנִּפְדּוּ; — *and with second tithe or consecrated produce that were redeemed;*

One may redeem his second tithe (מַעֲשֵׂר שֵׁנִי) or consecrated objects (הֶקְדֵּשׁ) with money. The redeemed produce loses its sacred status and may be consumed as *chullin* (non-sacred food), and the redemption money assumes the sacred status of the second tithe or consecrated substance. However, if the redeemer is the original owner, he must ask a fifth to the value of the item being redeemed. The mishnah speaks about a situation where the fifth was *not* added, and instructs us that though the fifth is an obligation, it is not indispensable to the redemption process. Therefore one can fulfill his matzah obligation even before paying the additional fifth *(Gem. 35b)*.

וְהַכֹּהֲנִים — בְּחַלָּה וּבִתְרוּמָה; — *Kohanim [can discharge their obligation] — with challah and with terumah;*

Although *challah* and *terumah* are not suitable food for non-*Kohanim*,

Kohanim may fulfill their obligation with them *(Rav; Gem. 35b)*.

אֲבָל לֹא בְטֶבֶל, — *but [one can] not [discharge his obligation] with untithed produce,*

Ordinary טֶבֶל [*tevel*], *untithed produce*, because it is prohibited, is obviously unfit for matzah. Our mishnah means to include even Rabbinically forbidden *tevel*, e.g., grain grown in an unperforated flower pot. By Scriptural law, such grain is not considered produce of the earth and need not be tithed, but the Sages imposed the tithe obligation on it. For matzah, however, they relaxed the *tevel* restriction *(Gem. 35b)*.

וְלֹא בְמַעֲשֵׂר רִאשׁוֹן שֶׁלֹּא נִטְּלָה תְרוּמָתוֹ, — *nor with first tithe whose terumah has not been separated,*

The circumstance referred to in the mishnah includes even a situation where he reversed the regular sequence and gave the first tithe to the Levite before separating the regular *terumah*. In this case, because the first tithe was taken off after threshing and storing, when the obligation to separate the regular *terumah* had taken effect, the Levite must separate both *terumah* and his own tithe, as opposed to the instance (above) where the first tithe has been separated before the *terumah* obligation took effect *(ibid)*.

וְלֹא בְמַעֲשֵׂר שֵׁנִי וְהֶקְדֵּשׁ שֶׁלֹּא נִפְדּוּ. — *nor with second tithe or consecrated produce that were not redeemed.*

Even if they were redeemed, but that

consecrated produce that were redeemed; *Kohanim* — with *challah* and with *terumah*; but not with untithed produce, nor with first tithe whose *terumah* has not been separated, nor with second tithe or consecrated produce that were not redeemed.

[Regarding] the [unleavened] loaves of the thanksgiving offering, and the nazirite's wafers — if he made them for himself, he cannot fulfill his obligation with them; but if he made them to sell in the market, he can fulfill his obligation with them.

YAD AVRAHAM

redemption was not performed properly, e.g. second tithe was redeemed with uncoined metal, or consecrated produce was redeemed with land (*ibid*).

The principle invalidating all the substances listed here for the fulfillment of the mitzvah of matzah is the invalidation of any, מִצְוָה הַבָּאָה בַּעֲבֵירָה, *mitzvah brought about by means of a transgression* (Ramban in *Likutim*, Ran and R' David).[1]

חַלּוֹת תּוֹדָה — [Regarding] the [unleavened] loaves of the thanksgiving offering,

With regard to the thanksgiving offering the Torah says: "If he offers it [a peace offering] *for thanksgiving, then he shall offer with the sacrifice of thanksgiving, unleavened loaves mixed with oil, and unleavened wafers smeared with oil"* (Lev. 7:12).

וּרְקִיקֵי נָזִיר — *and the nazirite's wafers —*

One who has vowed to be a nazirite must conform to the strictures spelled out in the Torah for such a vow. When his term is ended he brings the offerings prescribed for him by the Torah, among which is *a basket of unleavened bread,*

loaves *of fine flour mixed with oil, and unleavened wafers smeared with oil* (Numbers 6:15).

עֲשָׂאָן לְעַצְמוֹ, אֵין יוֹצְאִין בָּהֶן; — *if he made them for himself, he cannot fulfill his obligation with them;*

Although they are completely unleavened these loaves and wafers may not be used to fulfill the *mitzvah* of matzah. The Torah states: *and you shall guard the matzos* (Exodus 12:17), which the Sages understand as an injunction that during the preparation of matzah, it must be guarded for the sake of the *mitzvah* of eating matzah, not for any other purpose, such as a sacrifice (*Rav*, one view in *Gem.* 38b).

The mishnah refers to wafers and loaves which had merely been baked in the anticipation they would be used for a thanksgiving offering or a Nazirite. One may not offer a thanksgiving offering on Pesach eve as set forth in *Gem.* (13b; *Chiddushei R' Yoel Chassid*).

עֲשָׂאָן לִמְכֹּר בַּשּׁוּק, יוֹצְאִין בָּהֶן. — *but if he made them to sell in the market, he can fulfill his obligation with them.*

Anyone making loaves for sale considers beforehand: "If it is sold, well

---

1. The authorities cited above (see *Chidushei HaRan*) explain that the *Gem.* (35b) gives a different reason, one not concurred with by most tannaim or the halachah, in order to make the disqualification of the mishnah Scriptural. Nevertheless, even those disagreeing with the reason given by the *Gemara*, will disqualify the substances listed because the Rabbinic disqualification of 'mitzvah brought about by means of transgression' (cf. *Tos. Succah* 9a, s.v. ההוא and 30a, s.v. משום; *Sha'agas Aryeh* 96). This removes the difficulty raised by *Lechem Mishneh* (Hil. *Chametz* 6:7) concerning Rambam's disqualification of the substances listed in our mishnah.

[ו] וְאֵלּוּ יְרָקוֹת שֶׁאָדָם יוֹצֵא בָהֶן יְדֵי חוֹבָתוֹ בַּפֶּסַח, בְּחֲזֶרֶת וּבְעֻלְשִׁין וּבְתַמְכָא וּבְחַרְחֲבִינָה וּבְמָרוֹר. יוֹצְאִין בָּהֶן בֵּין לַחִין בֵּין יְבֵשִׁין, אֲבָל לֹא כְבוּשִׁין וְלֹא שְׁלוּקִין וְלֹא מְבֻשָּׁלִין. וּמִצְטָרְפִין לִכְזַיִת. וְיוֹצְאִין בְּקֶלַח

יד אברהם

and good; if not, I will fulfill the obligation of matzah with it" *(Rav; Gem.* 38b).

Although these matzahs have oil in them

and they should be invalid as *matzah ashirah* (rich matzah), nevertheless, since the amount of oil is miniscule — one quarter "log" for twenty large loaves, they do not fall into that category *(Gem.* 38b).

6.

וְאֵלּוּ יְרָקוֹת שֶׁאָדָם יוֹצֵא בָהֶן יְדֵי חוֹבָתוֹ בַּפֶּסַח, — **And these are the herbs with which one fulfills his obligation on Pesach,**

The Torah commands, *with bitter herbs they shall eat it [the Pesach offering] (Exodus* 12:8). The Biblical commandment to eat bitter herbs applies only when they are consumed with the Pesach sacrifice; otherwise, they are eaten only by Rabbinic commandment *(Rambam Hil. Chametz* 7:12). The *mitzvah* of eating matzah, on the other hand, is not dependent on the consumption of the sacrifice *(ibid.* 6:1).

בְּחֲזֶרֶת — **with lettuce,**

The translation follows *Rashi* (39a, s.v. חסא), *Aruch* (s.v. חזר 3) and many others (see at length in *Chok Yaakov* 473:18 and *Teshuvos Chacham Zvi* 119). [It is commonly accepted that this refers to romaine lettuce.] *Magen Avraham* (473:9) cites *Levush's* view that it is watercress, but *Chok Ya'akov* (ibid.) and *Eliyahu Rabbah* repudiate this opinion.

וּבְעֻלְשִׁין — **(and with) endives,**

The translation follows *Rav* and one view cited in *Shibolei HaLaket* (see *Chok Ya'akov* 473:18). Another view cited by *Shibolei HaLeket* (ibid). identifies עֻלְשִׁין as *escarole,*

while others *(Rambam, Comm.,* ed. *Kafich)* identify it as *chicory* (cf. *Aruch HaShalem).* Probably there is no real disagreement here, for both endive and escarole are considered to be types of chicory.

וּבְתַמְכָא — **(with) horseradish,**

The later authorities (אַחֲרוֹנִים) have confirmed that this is *chrein,* horseradish *(Tos. Yom Tov;* see *Magen Avraham* 473:10)[1]. See also *Meiri.*

וּבְחַרְחֲבִינָה — **(and with) charchavinah,**

The *Gemara* (39a) identifies this as a type of vine growing around palms. *Rambam* (according to R' Y. *Kafich)* identifies it as a type of thistle (קְרְצעינה, *Eryngium Creticum).* According to R' *Hai Gaon* (cited in *Aruch,* s.v. אצווא: see *Aruch HaShalem)* it is a type of acacia.

וּבְמָרוֹר. — **and (with) maror.**

According to *Rashi* (s.v. הירדופנין; see *HaMetargumeman)* this is wormwood (לַעֲנָה; see also *Chok Ya'akov* 473:18, cf. *Rama Orach Chaim* 473:5 and *Beur Halachah* there). *Rambam (Comm.*[2]) and *Aruch* (s.v. מר 6) identify it as a wild lettuce.

Meiri and R' *Aharon HaLevi* (cited in *Ritva)* and R' *David* maintain that מָרוֹר is a generic term embracing all bitter herbs with the characteristics listed in the *Gemara* (pale green color and containing sap). The premise that all bitter herbs, even those not listed

---

1. The comment found in standard editions of *Rambam's Commentary* contradicting this translation and identifying תַמְכָא as a type of עֻלְשִׁין is not found in his original commentary (see ed. *Kafich),* but is the addition of a translator or scribe.

2. *Rav* (see also *Meiri)* says: 'A type of bitter coriander,' but this is based on a misreading and a faulty translation in our versions of *Rambam's* commentary as pointed out by R' Y. *Kafich.*

6. **A**nd these are the herbs with which one fulfills his obligation on Pesach, with lettuce, endives, horseradish, *charchavinah*, and maror. One fulfills his obligation with them whether moist or dry, but not preserved, nor stewed, nor boiled. These combine to the size of an olive. One can fulfill his obligation with their stalk; with *demai*; with first tithe whose

YAD AVRAHAM

here, are acceptable seems also to be held by *Rashi Exodus* 12:8) and *Rama (Orach Chaim* 473:5). However later authorities rule that one must, if possible, use one of the species specified in the mishnah (lettuce, horseradish, endives), preferably lettuce. [As noted above, romaine lettuce is the commonly accepted variety.] Where these are not available, one may use any other bitter herb (preferably one having the characteristics listed above) but should not recite the benediction for the *mitzvah* of maror (see *Mishnah Berurah* 473:46-46 and *Beur Halachah* there).

יוֹצְאִין בָּהֶן בֵּין לַחִין בֵּין יְבֵשִׁין, — *One fulfills his obligation with them whether* [they are] *moist or dry,*

This refers only to the stalks, but the leaves must be fresh (*Rav; Gem.* 39b).

אֲבָל לֹא כְבוּשִׁין — *but not preserved,*

I.e., in vinegar (*Rav; Rashi*).

Magen Avraham (473:14) remarks that *Rashi's* view is not accepted halachically; even soaking in water is considered 'preserving' and disqualifies the herb (see *Mishnah Berurah* 473:38). There is however a distinction between preserving in water and in vinegar. Vinegar renders the herbs 'preserved' after a soaking period of (not more than) 18 minutes, while for water a 24 hour period is necessary (*Tif. Yis.* from *Yoreh Deah* 105:1).

וְלֹא שְׁלוּקִין — *nor stewed,*

I.e., cooked extensively until the herbs are reduced to a mush (*Rav, Rashi*).

וְלֹא מְבֻשָּׁלִין. — *nor boiled.*

I.e., nor even moderately cooked (*Rav, Rashi;* see *Tos.* 39b s.v. לא).

Boiling, stewing or preserving disqualifies herbs because it causes them to lose their bitter taste (*Berachos* 38b).

וּמִצְטָרְפִין לִכְזַיִת. — *(And) these combine to the size of an olive.*

The minimum required to fulfill the obligation of eating maror is a volume of herbs equal to that of an olive. Any combination of acceptable herbs may be used to achieve this requirement[1]. The same is true of matzah; one may use any combination of the grains enumerated to fulfill his obligation. This passage of the mishnah refers to the previous mishnah too (*Rav;* cf. *Ran*).

וְיוֹצְאִין בְּקֶלַח שֶׁלָּהֶן; וּבִדְמַאי; — *(And) one can fulfill his obligation with their stalk; with demai;*

[See above mishnah 5, s.v. בדמאי for an explanation of this law.]

Nevertheless one cannot discharge his obligation with vegetables that are known to be untithed, even though the tithing of vegetables is only a Rabbinic injunction. One cannot fulfill his obligation even with Rabbinically prohibited substances because it remains a מִצְוָה הַבָּאָה בַּעֲבֵירָה, *mitzvah which comes about by way of a transgression (Tos. Yom Tov, Rashi;* cf. above mishnah 5, s.v. ולא במעשר שני).

It may be that the main point of this clause is the implication that only *demai,* but not untithed vegetables, suffices. The explicitly stated law — that one can discharge his obligation with *demai* — can be deduced easily from the parallel passage concerning matzah (above mishnah 5). However one could

---

1. See *Rosh* 10:25, *Terumas HaDeshen* 245, *Sha'agas Aryeh* 100, *Teshuvos Chasam Sofer, Orach Chaim* 140, *Avnei Nezer Orach Chaim* 383.

שֶׁלָּהֶן; וּבְדְמַאי; וּבְמַעֲשֵׂר רִאשׁוֹן שֶׁנִּטְּלָה תְרוּמָתוֹ; וּבְמַעֲשֵׂר שֵׁנִי וְהֶקְדֵּשׁ שֶׁנִּפְדּוּ.

[ז] **אֵין** שׁוֹרִין אֶת הַמֻּרְסָן לַתַּרְנְגוֹלִים, אֲבָל חוֹלְטִין.

הָאִשָּׁה לֹא תִשְׁרֶה אֶת הַמֻּרְסָן שֶׁתּוֹלִיךְ בְּיָדָהּ לַמֶּרְחָץ, אֲבָל שָׁפָה הִיא בִּבְשָׂרָהּ יָבֵשׁ.

לֹא יִלְעַס אָדָם חִטִּין וְיַנִּיחַ עַל מַכָּתוֹ בַּפֶּסַח, מִפְּנֵי שֶׁהֵן מַחֲמִיצוֹת.

[ח] **אֵין** נוֹתְנִין קֶמַח לְתוֹךְ הַחֲרֹסֶת אוֹ לְתוֹךְ הַחַרְדָּל. וְאִם נָתַן, יֹאכַל מִיָּד. וְרַבִּי מֵאִיר אוֹסֵר.

יד אברהם

have argued that since the *mitzvah* of *maror* (in the post-Temple era) is required only Rabbinically, it can be discharged even with substances disqualified for the Scriptural *mitzvah* of matzah. Therefore, our mishnah makes clear that only *demai* — which is *probably* tithed as explained in commentary to mishnah 5 — is acceptable (*Meleches Shlomah*).

וּבְמַעֲשֵׂר רִאשׁוֹן שֶׁנִּטְּלָה תְרוּמָתוֹ; וּבְמַעֲשֵׂר שֵׁנִי
וְהֶקְדֵּשׁ שֶׁנִּפְדּוּ. — *(and) with first tithe*

whose terumah has been separated; and with consecrated substances and second tithe that were redeemed.

[See above mishnah 5, s.v. וּבְמַעֲשֵׂר רִאשׁוֹן, and s.v. וּבְמַעֲשֵׂר שֵׁנִי והקדש שנפדו, for commentary on these terms.]

[All of the disqualifications listed above (mishnah 5) for the *mitzvah* for matzah apply to maror as well (see *Rashi* cited above, s.v. ויוצאין בדמאי; cf. *Tos.* 114b, s.v. אכלן, *Sha'agas Aryeh* 94, 96).]

7.

אֵין שׁוֹרִין אֶת הַמֻּרְסָן לַתַּרְנְגוֹלִים, — *We may not soak bran for chickens,*

The bran may not be soaked at all, even in cold water (*Rav*), and even for less than eighteen minutes (*Tif. Yis.*) [because once soaked the leavening process has begun and it will continue to fulfillment].

[There is a question whether מֻרְסָן, *bran*, refers to the grain's husk or to the coarse part of the kernel. See *Rambam, Comm.* here (cf. ed. Kafich), *Aruch* (s.v. מרסן; cf. *Rashi*, *Shabbos* 76b, s.v. וסובן). According to the latter view, it may be that there is no possibility of leavening when only the husk is used. See *Magen Avraham* 454:1 with *P'ri Megadim*, *Chok Ya'akov* there. *Mishnah Berurah* (465:2) rules that even the husk is subject to leavening. Only the outer hay-like covering is exempt.

אֲבָל חוֹלְטִין. — *but we may scald it.*

Once scalded, grain will not leaven (just as baked matzah will not leaven).

However the *Geonim* (cited in *Rosh*) attest that 'we have never heard in the two yeshivos that they should permit this [scalding] …'. *Rambam* (*Comm.* here; *Hil. Chametz* 5:17) prohibits scalding for fear that people not be punctilious about the degree of heat the water is brought to. See *Orach Chaim* 454:3 and 465:1.

הָאִשָּׁה לֹא תִשְׁרֶה אֶת הַמֻּרְסָן שֶׁתּוֹלִיךְ בְּיָדָהּ
לַמֶּרְחָץ, — *A woman may not soak bran to take with her [lit. in her hand] to the baths,*

She may not make a bran paste to use as a cosmetic or a depilatory because it will leaven (*Rav; Rashi*).

terumah has been separated; and with consecrated property and second tithe that were redeemed.

7. **W**e may not soak bran for chickens, but we may scald it.

A woman may not soak bran to take with her to the baths, but she may rub it on her skin dry.

A man may not chew wheat and place it on his wound on Pesach, because it becomes *chametz*.

8. **F**lour may not be put into the *charoses* nor into the mustard. However, if one did put it [in], it must be eaten immediately. But R' Meir forbids [it].

YAD AVRAHAM

אֲבָל שָׁפָה הִיא בְּבְשָׂרָה יָבֵשׁ. — *but she may rub it on her skin dry.*

She may rub her skin with dry bran although she is dripping wet (*Rav; Rashi*).

Rosh defines the moisture in question as sweat.

Sweat (according to *Rosh*; see *Rama* in *Orach Chaim* 466:5) is not a leavening agent (cf. *Roke'ach* cited by *Rosh* 2:22).

Meiri (and *Maharam Chalavah*) maintain that even if the moisture is water she may rub the bran on her skin;

such a minute amount of moisture is not sufficient to trigger leavening.

Rosh states that it is advisable to refrain from rubbing bran on the skin in any case, for the woman may forget to remove the bran entirely before immersing herself in the water. This stricture is accepted by *Shulchan Aruch* (465:2).

לֹא יִלְעַס אָדָם חִטִּין וְיַנִּיחַ עַל מַכָּתוֹ בַּפֶּסַח מִפְּנֵי שֶׁהֵן מַחֲמִיצוֹת. — *A man may not chew wheat and put it on his wound on Pesach, because it becomes chametz.*

Saliva causes leavening (*Tos. Yom Tov; Orach Chaim* 466:1).

8.

אֵין נוֹתְנִין קֶמַח לְתוֹךְ הַחֲרֹסֶת — *Flour may not be put into the charoses*

Charoses is a dip used in Mishnaic times, made of fruit and spices with vinegar and some water[1]. It was customary to mix in some flour in order to blunt its sharpness (*Rav*; cf *Rashi*). It may not be made with flour on Pesach because after a while the flour will leaven (*Rashi*). However, if there is no water in the mix, the flour will not leaven, for fruit juice is not a leavening

agent[2] (*Rav* as explained by *Tos. Yom Tov*).

[The *charoses* of our mishnah should not be confused with the *charoses* of the Seder. They share the name because they have the characteristic described in footnote 1.]

אוֹ לְתוֹךְ הַחַרְדָּל. — *nor into the mustard.*

Which has been mixed with water (*Tos. Yom Tov* citing *Rosh* and *Ran*).

וְאִם נָתַן, יֵאָכֵל מִיָּד. — *However, if one did*

1. The name חֲרֹסֶת from חֶרֶס, *earthenware,* derives from the claylike consistency of the mixture (*Gem.* 116a; see *comm.* and *Tos. Yom Tov* to 10:3).

2. The view that fruit juice without water does not cause leavening is that of *Rosh, Ran* and *Rambam* (*Hil. Chametz* 5:2; see *Maggid Mishneh* there) and is the halachically accepted one

אֵין מְבַשְּׁלִין אֶת הַפֶּסַח לֹא בְמַשְׁקִין וְלֹא
בְמֵי פֵרוֹת. אֲבָל סָכִין וּמַטְבִּילִין אוֹתוֹ בָהֶן.
מֵי תַשְׁמִישׁוֹ שֶׁל נַחְתּוֹם יִשָּׁפְכוּ, מִפְּנֵי שֶׁהֵן
מַחְמִיצִין.

יד אברהם

put it [in], it must be eaten immediately.

[Although the flour is in danger of becoming *chametz* very quickly[1], nevertheless it can be assumed that it will not leaven in the very short time needed for consumption.]

The mustard should be eaten *immediately*, unlike ordinary mixtures of flour that may be eaten even later, provided no symptoms of leavening appear (see below 3:5), or within the 18-minute time span that is safe for doughs kneaded solely with water (see below 3:2; see *Chok Ya'akov* 462:4).

Only mustard may be eaten because its pungency delays the leavening of the inserted flour. In the case of *charoses*, however, even eating it immediately will not prevent the leavening of its flour (*Rav*; *R' Kahana* in *Gem.* 40b); therefore it must be burned without delay (*Gem.* 40b).

The halachic principle underlying this law is that juices, when mixed with water, not only cause leavening but also cause it to occur faster than would undiluted water (although the result is only incomplete *chametz*; see footnote to s.v. אין נותנין). Similarly the Sages (*Gem.* 36a; *Orach Chaim*

462:2) rule that dough kneaded with a mixture of water and juices must be baked immediately, according to most authorities[1].

וְרַבִּי מֵאִיר אוֹסֵר. — *But R' Meir forbids [it].*

He maintains that mustard is no different than *charoses*. The sharpness of the mustard will not retard the leavening process and consequently leavening will occur as speedily as it does in *charoses* (*Rav*).

[Thus we are concerned that the mustard, like *charoses*, (see footnote to s.v. ואם נתן) will leaven even during the short time elapsing during consumption.]

The halachah does not follow R' Meir (*Rav*; *Rambam comm.*; *Hil. Chametz* 5:19, *Orach Chaim* 464). However *Rama* (*loc. cit*) remarks that it is customary (among Ashkenazim) to refrain from eating mustard altogether.

אֵין מְבַשְּׁלִין אֶת הַפֶּסַח לֹא בְמַשְׁקִין — *We may not cook the Pesach offering either in liquids*

The term מַשְׁקִין, lit. *liquids*, as it is used throughout Mishnah, is a technical term denoting the seven liquids qualified to be rendered contaminated

(*Orach Chaim* 462:1; see at length in *Beis Yosef*). However, *Rashi* (35a, s.v. ביין ושמן: see *Ran* there) and *Ravad* (*Hil. Chametz* 5:2, see *Migdal Oz* there) hold that other liquids *can* initiate leavening even without water, although the resulting leavening process will not end in complete *chametz* (חָמֵץ גָּמוּר), but in incomplete *chametz* (חָמֵץ נוקְשֶׁה; see prefatory comment to 3:1). *Rama* (*Orach Chaim* 462:4) attests that it is the custom in 'these countries' (i.e., Ashkenazic communities) not to use juices and other liquids in dough, even with water. *Vilna Gaon* (*Beur HaGra* there) believes that one reason for this custom is the acceptance of *Rashi's* view.

The status of *chametz* leavened through water mixed with other liquids is also open to question. *Tosafos* (36b, s.v. מי) (ibid) and most authorities hold it to be 'incomplete *chametz*,' whereas *Rambam* seems to consider it complete *chametz*.

1. A difference exists between immediately baking, after which consumption is permitted even long after the baking is complete, and immediate consumption. In cases where the food must be eaten immediately, the leavening process is continuous, and in case of delay, the food may become *chametz*, but where baking takes place, the leavening process is arrested immediately (*P'ri Chadash Orach Chaim* 462; *Shulchan Aruch HaRav*; and *Aruch HaShulchan* to *Orach Chaim* 464).

We may not cook the Pesach offering neither in liquids nor in fruit juices. But we may baste and dip it in them.

The waters used by a baker must be poured out, because they become *chametz*.

YAD AVRAHAM

and which 'prepare' (מַכְשִׁיר) foodstuffs for contamination. These liquids are: wine, honey, oil, milk, dew, blood, and water as listed in *Machshirin* 6:4 (*Tif. Yis.: Kol HaRemez*).

וְלֹא בְמֵי פֵרוֹת. — *nor in fruit juices.*

This term includes any other fruit juices not included in the category of the seven מַשְׁקִין, *liquids* (ibid). In prohibiting the consumption of a cooked Pesach offering, the Torah mentions only cooking in water: *You shall not eat of it raw nor cooked in water* (Exodus 12:9), nevertheless the Sages found an allusion in this verse to prohibit cooking in any liquid. The verb used for cooking appears in a double form — וּבָשֵׁל מְבֻשָּׁל, that the prohibition embraces all kinds of cooking[1] (*Rav, Gem* 41a). [The reason the Torah specifies only water may be to indicate that even water, which does not lend any extraneous taste to the offering, is forbidden (see *Gem.* 41a; cf. *Maharsha* and *P'nei Yehoshua*).]

אֲבָל סָכִין — *But we may baste*
The offering while it is being roasted (*Rashi*; cf. *Rav*).

וּמַטְבִּילִין אוֹתוֹ בָּהֶן. — *and dip it* [the offering] *in them* [i.e. the liquids or juices].

After they are roasted, one may baste or dip the Pesach while eating it (*ibid*).

The language of the mishnah as well as that of *Rambam* (*Hil. Korban Pesach* 8:8) in-

dicate that during roasting only basting is permitted, whereas afterward, while eating, the offering may even be dipped into juices (*Shoshanim L'David*).

Tosafos (41a, s.v. אין) wonders why this mishnah is placed in this chapter [rather than the seventh, which deals with the roasting of the Pesach offering].

Maharam Chalavah (see also *Lechem Shamayim*; *P'nei Yehoshua*; *Tif. Yis*; and *Rashash*; cf *R' David* and *Meiri*) surmises that the phrase [the Pesach may be dipped] *in them* also permits the Pesach to be dipped in mustard and *charoses*. Thus after discussing the laws of these substances regarding the prohibition of *chametz*, the mishnah tangentially mentions their use for the Pesach offering.

מֵי תַשְׁמִישׁוֹ שֶׁל נַחְתּוֹם — *The waters used by a baker*
The water with which the baker cools his hands when moistening the dough. Some of the dough rinsed from his hands is retained in the water (*Rav*; *Rashi*).

Alternatively: the water in which the baker washes his hands and utensils (*Rambam*, *Hil. Chametz* 5:16).

יִשָּׁפְכוּ, — *must be poured out,*
If the amount of water is substantial, it should poured out on an incline so that the water is absorbed into the ground, and does not form a puddle, causing the particles to leaven on the ground (*Rav*; *Gem.* 42a; see *Orach Chaim* 459:4 with *Beur HaGRA*).

מִפְּנֵי שֶׁהֵן מַחְמִיצִין. — *because they* [the dough particles] *become chametz.*

---

1. The apparent meaning is that the extra limitation is contained in the otherwise superflous word. *Rambam* (*Comm.*) gleans an exegetical rule from this *Gemara*. One of the verbs used is in the gerund (מָקוֹר) form (i.e., the verb בָּשַׁל). This grammatical form always indicates a broad application.

יד אברהם

Chapter 3

1.

◆§ Chametz and its Various Forms

An understanding of the following mishnah requires a brief outline of the different categories of *chametz* and their relative degrees of stringency.

A. Pure *chametz*, unadulterated with other substances[1] (חָמֵץ גָּמוּר בְּעֵין).

B. Pure *chametz*, that was then mixed with other substances (חָמֵץ גָּמוּר עַל יְדֵי תַּעֲרוּבֶת). Such *chametz* is divided into two categories:

(1) If there is sufficient *chametz* in the mixture so that when a volume of three eggs[2] is eaten, one consumes *chametz* equal to the volume of an olive (כְּזַיִת בִּכְדֵי אֲכִילַת פְּרָס)[3], a negative commandment (מִצְוַת לֹא תַעֲשֶׂה) prohibits its eating. Pertaining to *kares*, *Rambam* (*Hil. Chametz* 1:6, *Sefer HaMitzvos*, *Lo Sa'asseh* 198) maintains that it does not apply, but *Ramban* (comments to *Sefer HaMitzvos* loc. cit.) argues that mixtures containing so great a proportion of *chametz* are in the same category as pure unadulterated *chametz*, and therefore subject to this punishment.

(2) If there is too little *chametz* in the mixture for an 'olive' to be consumed when one eats a volume of three eggs, R' Eliezer and the Sages disagree about its status (*Gem.* 42a). R' Eliezer maintains that it is included in the negative commandment against consumption of *chametz*, whereas the Sages hold that it us a mere prohibition[6].

C. חָמֵץ נוּקְשֶׁה, *chametz noksheh* (lit. *hardened chametz*), unfinished *chametz*, dough whose leavening process has not been completed (see mishnah 5), and *chametz* that was never fit for consumption. If, however the *chametz* had completed is leavening process and was fit to be eaten and then became unfit, it is considered complete *chametz* (חָמֵץ גמור).

Some tannaim hold *chametz noksheh* to be Scripturally prohibited by a negative commandment, while others contend that such substances are not included in the Scriptural prohibition (*Gem.* 43a)..

According to the latter view most authorities (*Tos.* 43a, s.v. מאן: *Ran*; *Meiri*; *Tur* 442; *Magen Avraham* 447:5 and others) assume there is only a rabbinic prohibition, but some later scholars (*Teshuvos Mishk'nos Ya'akov* 143; *Teshuvos*

---

1. *Aruch HaShulchan* (442:) asserts, citing *Yerushalmi* (3:1), that even if only most of the substance is composed of *chametz*, it is considered pure *chametz*. Substances in this category are subject to the prohibition against keeping *chametz* in one's possession (בַּל יֵרָאֶה) and one who eats them willfully is punishable with *kares*, spiritual excision.

2. The above is *Rambam's* view. Many authorities hold that the פְּרָס is the equivalent of four eggs. See *Eruvin* 8:2, 82b; *Hil. Chametz* 1:6; *Orach Chaim* 368:3, 409:7.

3. The בְּזַיִת, equivalent of an olive, is judged variously to be the equivalent of half or the third of an egg (see *Orach Chaim* 486 with *Beur HaGra* and *Mishnah Berurah*). Accordingly the percentage of *chametz* in this mixture ranges from 1/6 to 1/12 of the whole.

4. *Beis Yosef* (*Orach Chaim* 442) assumes that this is a Scriptural prohibition (also *Rav, Tos. Yom Tov* and *Ran* here; *Korban Nesanel* to *Rosh* pas. 40; cf. *Ravad's* gloss (3) on *Ba'al HaMaor, Meiri*). However, *Turei Zahav* (442:1) assumes that there is only a Rabbinic prohibition (see *Chok Ya'akov* 442:4).

1. [These must be removed on Pesach: Babylonian kutach, Median beer, Idumean vinegar, Egyp-

YAD AVRAHAM

Minchas Baruch 46; cf. *D'rush VeChidush R' Akiva Eiger*, p. 2., *Likkutim* to *Pesachim* 43a) develop the concept that unfinished *chametz* is not matzah and is prohibited by implication from the positive mitzvah to eat matzah for seven days! According to this view a grain product may not be eaten unless it can be classified as matzah.

The foregoing dealt with the status of the different categories of *chametz* regarding the prohibition of eating. Mishnah 1 (according to all views except that of *R' Tam*) discusses their status concerning the ban against possessing *chametz*. It should be pointed out that according to some authorities (*R' Moshe HaKohen* cited by *Maggid Mishnah* to Hil. *Chametz* 4:8; see *Kessef Mishneh* there; *Beur HaGra* to *Orach Chaim* 442:1) the Scriptural prohibitions against eating and possession do not necessarily go in tandem. According to the Sages, therefore, although there is no negative commandment against eating the substances in category 2b, these may still be subject to the negative commandment against keeping *chametz*.

אֵלּוּ עוֹבְרִין בְּפֶסַח: — *These* [substances] *must be removed* [lit. *these pass*] *on Pesach:*

The substances listed below must be 'removed' from the world, i.e., destroyed (*Riva* in *Tos.* 42a, s.v. וּאלו[1]). This requirement is of Rabbinic origin, for one is not mandated Scripturally to remove such substances from his premises, since the Torah prohibition applies only to substances comprised (almost) entirely of finished *chametz* (*Rav* based on *Ran*). The Rabbis introduced this ordinance because of their apprehension that one may forget himself and eat these foods, whose consumption is forbidden (*Ran* based on *Ba'al HaMaor*; see *Meiri* and *R' David*, *Tos.* 2a, s.v. אור).

Rashi and *Rambam* (*Comm.*; cf. the view presented in his code, *Hil. Chametz* 4:8; *Bais Yosef* and *Turei Zahav* to *Orach Chaim* 442) render עוֹבְרִין as *transgress*; one who keeps these substances in his possession on Pesach transgresses the Torah's command (*Exodus* 13:7): *And there shall not be seen with you* [*any*] *chametz, nor shall leavening be seen with you seven days.*

A third view, maintained by *R' Tam*, con-

tends that only finished, (almost) pure *chametz*, whose consumption carries the penalty of *kares* for eating must be destroyed. The substances listed here, although Scripturally forbidden for consumption, are not liable to this punishment, nor are they subject to either the Biblical interdiction against keeping *chametz*, or to a Rabbinic ordinance to that effect. According to this interpretation, the mishnah informs us that one who eats such *chametz* is in violation of the prohibition, and אֵלּוּ עוֹבְרִין would be rendered: [*For eating*] *these forms* [*of chametz*], *they are in violation* [*of the prohibition*].

כֻּתָּח הַבַּבְלִי, — *Babylonian kutach,*

A dipping-sauce composed of sour milk, moldy bread crusts and salt (*Gem.* 42a; cf. *Rav*).

וְשֵׁכָר הַמָּדִי, — *Median beer,*

In Talmudic times beer was commonly brewed from dates. Only in Media was barley used (*Rashi* 42b, s.v. שכר המדי).

The Median beer referred to here was prepared from dates and barley, and as such was in the category of 'mixed chametz' [see prefatory note, category B(2)]. By contrast, one who drinks modern beer, prepared ex-

1. Although he does not say so clearly, *Riva* seems to agree with *Rashi* that the substances listed here are included in the Scriptural prohibition against keeping *chametz* (see *Korban Nesanel* 3:2). However, most of the other authorities holding this interpretation (see at length in *Meiri* and *R' David*), believe that the provision for the removal of these substances is Rabbinic in origin.

הַמִּצְרִי, וְזוֹמָן שֶׁל צַבָּעִים, וַעֲמִילָן שֶׁל טַבָּחִים,
וְקוֹלָן שֶׁל סוֹפְרִים. רַבִּי אֱלִיעֶזֶר אוֹמֵר: אַף
תַּכְשִׁיטֵי נָשִׁים.
זֶה הַכְּלָל: כָּל שֶׁהוּא מִמִּין דָּגָן, הֲרֵי זֶה עוֹבֵר
בַּפֶּסַח. הֲרֵי אֵלּוּ בְּאַזְהָרָה, וְאֵין בָּהֶן מִשּׁוּם
כָּרֵת.

יד אברהם

clusively from barley, is subject to *kares* [i.e., it is in category B(1)], and it is surely included in the ban against keeping *chametz* (*R' Tam* cited in *Rosh* 3:1 and *Tos. HaRashba* 2a). However *Rashi* seems to indicate that even Median beer was prepared exclusively from barley, and yet it is still included among foods that are not considered pure *chametz* (see *P'nei Yehoshua*; cf *Aruch HaShulchan* 442:20).

וְחֹמֶץ הָאֲדוֹמִי, — *Idumean vinegar,*

This vinegar was made from wine fermented with barley (*Rav, Rashi*).

However, the barley was soaked in water before being mixed with the wine, for wine of itself, which is a fruit juice, is not a leavening agent (*Tos.* 35b, s.v. מי פירות). Alternatively: Water was mixed with the wine (*Tos. Yom Tov* citing *Rif* and *Yerushalmi*)[1].

וְזֵיתוֹם הַמִּצְרִי, — *Egyptian zisom,*

A concoction made from equal quantities of barley, saffron[1] and salt kneaded with water and used for medicinal purposes (*Rav, Rambam*). It helps to regulate the bowel movement; it acts as a laxative for the constipated and as a purgative for the diarrheic (*Gem.* 42b).

The four substances listed up to now all contain amounts of finished *chametz* (חָמֵץ גָּמוּר), i.e., *chametz* in an edible state. However, there is no *kares* punishment for their consumption because neutral ingredients are mixed with the *chametz*, putting them into category B(2). The next three substances to be listed in the mishnah are *chametz* found in a pure form, unadulterated with foreign ingredients. However, because they are not meant for consumption (though theoretically they can be eaten), they are relegated to the halachic status of חָמֵץ נוּקְשֶׁה, unfinished *chametz*, and there is no *kares* penalty for their consumption (see at length in *P'ri Megadim, Eshel Avraham* 442:1, *She'elos UTeshuvos Minchas Baruch* 44:1).

וְזוֹמָן שֶׁל צַבָּעִים, — *(and) dyers' broth,*

Bran was mixed with water to form a broth used in the preparation of certain red dyes (*Gem.* 42b with *Rashi*; *Rambam*; cf. *Mossaf HaAruch*, s.v. לכא).

וַעֲמִילָן שֶׁל טַבָּחִים, — *(and) cooks' dough,*

Grain that has not yet achieved one third of its ripeness is milled, and a dough is made from the flour. The dough is formed into a loaf the shape of a pot cover, which is then used to cover a cooking pot of meat to draw out the

---

1. The alternative interpretation depends on the resolution of an important halachic point. Pure fruit juice does not cause grain to leaven at all, but what of a fruit juice mixed with water — can such a mixture effect complete leavening (חָמֵץ גָּמוּר), or can it do not more than cause an unfinished leavening (חָמֵץ נוּקְשֶׁה)? If such a mixture cannot cause complete leavening, then Idumean vinegar — assuming it is made by placing barley in a mixture of vinegar and water — would be a mixture composed of a neutral (non-*chametz*) liquid and incomplete *chametz*, which is the subject of the argument between R' Eliezer and the first tanna (see below and *Meiri* to 35a). *Tosafos* (35b, s.v. ומי פירות) expresses the first opinion, that the barley had been soaked in water before being placed in pure vinegar, because *Tosafos* holds that a combination of vinegar and water would not cause even a slight degree of leavening. *Rambam* (see *Hil. Chametz* 5:2) and probably *Rif* hold that a mixture would cause an incomplete leavening.

1. According to R' Y. Kafich's rendering of *Rambam's Comm.* not saffron but safflower (i.e., false saffron) was used.

tian *zisom*, dyers' broth, cooks' dough and scribes'
paste. R' Eliezer says: also women's cosmetics.

This is the general rule, whatever is of a species of
grain must be removed on Pesach. These are in the
category of a prohibition but they are not subject to
kares.

YAD AVRAHAM

muck and bad smell (*Gem.* 42b with *Rambam*).

וְקוֹלָן שֶׁל סוֹפְרִים. — *and scribes' paste.*

A paste was made with rye flour which was kneaded with water, and used by tanners to paste several layers of leather together, and also by scribes in the preparation of paper (*Gem.* 42b with *Rashi*). *Rambam* (*comm.*; cf *Rav*) says this paste was made with fine flourdust from millstones. Scribes would use it for binding their books.

רַבִּי אֱלִיעֶזֶר אוֹמֵר: אַף תַּכְשִׁיטֵי נָשִׁים. — *R' Eliezer says: also women's cosmetics* [lit. *ornaments*].

The *tanna kamma* (first tanna) forbade only a mixture containing finished *chametz* or pure unfinished *chametz* [*chametz noksheh*], but he permitted the possession of *chametz noksheh* as part of a mixture. R' Eliezer disagrees. He holds that even a mixture containing *chametz noksheh* is forbidden. The cosmetics specified by him are such a mixture (*Rav; Ba'al HaMaor; Ran* and others).

The translation *cosmetics* is based on the *Gemara's* conclusion that the mishnah refers to a paste used as a depilatory (*Gem.* 43a).

Rambam (*comm.*) explains that cosmetics were not *chametz* because they were prepared without water; therefore they were permitted by the first tanna. R' Eliezer, however, is apprehensive that the cosmetic will be moistened during its application and become *chametz*. The halachah does not follow R' Eliezer.

A third approach is presented by *Ravad* (glosses to *Ba'al HaMaor*). He maintains that there is no halachic dispute here. R' Eliezer merely brings to our attention the fact that these cosmetics commonly contained *chametz*. *P'nei Yehoshua* contends that *Rashi* (43a, s.v. מאן) also holds this view.

זֶה הַכְּלָל: כָּל שֶׁהוּא מִמִּין דָּגָן, — *This is the general rule, whatever is* [made] *of a on Pesach.*

Anything made of one of the five species of grain (wheat, barley, spelt, rye and oats) and mixed with water (*Rashi*).

הֲרֵי זֶה עוֹבֵר בְּפֶסַח. — *must be removed on Passover,*

הֲרֵי אֵלּוּ בְּאַזְהָרָה, — *These* [i.e., the substances listed above] *are in the category of a prohibition* [lit. *warning*]

If he consumes them he transgresses a negative mitzvah (*Rav, Gem.* 42a)

Tosafos (43a s.v. למה) maintains that this passage of the mishnah is a continuation of R' Eliezer's view. According to the first tanna these are instances of sustances 'composed of a species of grain' that need not be removed, e.g., womens' cosmetics. According to the interpretations of *Rambam* and *Ravad* (see above), however, this part of the mishnah is unanimous.

The term אַזְהָרָה, *warning*, is applied to negative commandments, because most such commandments carry the punishment of מַלְקוּת, *lashes*, for their intentional violation in the face of a warning by witnesses. Like all corporal punishments, lashes cannot be given unless the Torah issues a Scriptural warning against committing the deed. The negative commandment is the 'warning' and is therefore referred to by that name.

וְאֵין בָּהֶן מִשּׁוּם כָּרֵת. — *but they are not subject to kares.*

[The Torah mandates כָּרֵת [*kares*], spiritual excision, as punishment for consumption of *chametz* (*Exodus* 12:19). The mishnah now informs us that this is so only for pure chametz in an unadulterated (see prefatory comments) state. The substances listed here, i.e., unfinished *chametz* (חָמֵץ נוּקְשֶׁה) and pure *chametz* mixed with other

[ב] **בָּצֵק** שֶׁבְּסִדְקֵי עֲרֵבָה, אִם יֵשׁ כְּזַיִת בְּמָקוֹם אֶחָד, חַיָּב לְבָעֵר; וְאִם לֹא, בָּטֵל בְּמִעוּטוֹ. וְכֵן לְעִנְיַן הַטֻּמְאָה. אִם מַקְפִּיד עָלָיו, חוֹצֵץ; וְאִם רוֹצֶה בְּקִיּוּמוֹ, הֲרֵי הוּא כָּעֲרֵבָה.

יד אברהם

substances are not subject to this punishment.

Our mishnah applies the Scriptural negative commandment against eating *chametz* even to incomplete *chametz* and to substances containing a lesser percentage of *chametz*[1] [category B(2); פָּחוֹת מִכְּדֵי אֲכִילַת פְּרָס]. This follows a minority opinion (see *Gem.* 43a). The consensus of sages however,

hold that these substances are not included in the negative commandment prohibiting the consumption of *chametz*; nevertheless these substances are 'prohibited'[2]. However all concur with the ruling set forth in the first passage of the mishnah and forbid both the consumption[3] and the keeping[4] of these substances (*Ran*; see also *Meiri*).

2.

בָּצֵק שֶׁבְּסִדְקֵי עֲרֵבָה, — *When dough remains in the grooves of a kneading through,*

And the dough serves to fortify cracks or holes in the trough (*Rav*; based on the halachically accepted view in *Gem.* 45a).

אִם יֵשׁ כְּזַיִת בְּמָקוֹם אֶחָד, חַיָּב לְבָעֵר; — *if there is as much as an olive's [volume] in one place, he must remove [it];*

[It must be removed from ones premises and destroyed.]

וְאִם לֹא, — *but if not,*

[I.e., if there is not as much as an olive in one place, even if the sum of the *chametz* in all the separate cracks adds up to the volume of an olive.]

בָּטֵל בְּמִעוּטוֹ. — *it is [considered] null because of its insignificance.*

[I.e., it is not considered to be *chametz* but an integral part of the utensil (see *R' Chananel* and *Meiri*).]

But if the dough does not serve to fortify the utensil, it must be 'removed' even if less than the size of an olive because the owner may detach the dough from the vessel. But if the dough is necessary to strengthen the vessel, its owner would not tamper with it lest he weaken the trough (*Rav*, based on the halachically accepted view in *Gem.* 42a; see *Orach Chaim* 442:7).

According to the *Geonim* (cited in *Meiri*), whenever the dough fills a groove it is considered as 'fortifying the utensil'. *Meiri* (see

---

1. *Rav* and *Rambam* comment that the mishnah's statement applies only where a greater percentage of *chametz* is present [category B(1); אֲבִילַת פְּרָס]. However, it is unlikely that they consider that to be the mishnah's intent, because the *Gemara* clearly interprets the mishnah to hold that even *chametz noksheh* and a mixture with a small degree of *chametz* is subject to the negative commandment. Rather *Rav* and *Rambam* mean to inform us that the mishnah's statement here is *halachically* true only if there is a substantial proportion of pure *chametz*.

2. See prefatory comments whether this prohibition is Scriptural or Rabbinic. It should be noted however that incomplete *chametz* (חָמֵץ נוּקְשֶׁה) is not Scripturally forbidden even according to those holding that all mixtures of true *chametz* are bound by Torah law.

3. See mishnah 5.

4. However *R' Tam* (see above, s.v. אלו עוברין) permits keeping of all of these substances even according to the tanna of our mishnah.

2. **W**hen dough remains in the grooves of a kneading trough, if there is as much as an olive's [volume] in one place, he must remove [it]; but if not, it is null because of its insignificance. And likewise regarding the [laws of] contamination. If he objects to it, it interposes; but if he desires it to remain then it is as the trough.

YAD AVRAHAM

also R' Chananel cited by Ran and R' David) believes this condition is fulfilled only when there is a crack or there is danger that a crack will form unless the utensil is strengthened (this seems to be also Rambam's view in Hil. Chametz 2:15). For Rashi's view see 42a, s.v. ה"ג; and 42b, s.v. אלא הא והא.

וְכֵן לְעִנְיַן הַטֻּמְאָה. — And likewise regarding [the laws of] contamination [tumah].

Where a contaminating agent, such as certain species of dead creeping things,[1] came in contact with the dough the size of an olive, its size is sufficient to lend it significance. Having an independent identity, the dough interposes itself between the contaminating agent and the trough; hence only the dough became tamei while the trough is protected.[2]

If the amount of dough was less than an olive sized piece, it is considered part of the utensil[3] (if the owner intends to leave it in the furrows), and any contaminating agent touching it is considered to have touched the utensil itself, thus conferring tumah upon it (Rav).

However, the above ruling that makes contamination conditional on an olive-sized particle of chametz, holds true only on Pesach, when the laws of the festival provide that the size of an olive is the key factor in whether or not chametz may be retained. At other times of the year, another factor determines whether or not the dough is considered part of the utensil or whether it is a separate entity capable of interposing against contamination. That factor will be set forth later in mishnah 4 (Rav based on Gem. 43a with Rashi).

Although the owner surely intends to remove this chametz to comply with the Halachah, it is not considered something to which he objects intrinsically, since he would not remove it were he not required to do so (See similar lines of reasoning in Kovetz HeAros to Yevamos 78a par. 514; Teshuvos Chazon Nachum 67:2, Avnei Nezer Yoreh Deah 253:7, cf. op. cit 265:3.).

אִם מַקְפִּיד עָלָיו. — If he objects to it,

If he intends to remove it eventually indicating that he objects to its presence in the vessel, the size of an olive or not (Rav).

חוֹצֵץ; — it interposes;

The Gemara (43a) explains that this

1. The carcasses of most small animals (e.g., frogs) do not confer tumah (in contradistinction to those of animals, and beasts). The exceptions to this rule are the carcasses of the eight creeping things' (שְׁרָצִים) listed in Leviticus 11:29-30. [The translations of the eight Hebrew words are the subject of much controversy.] Although in its literal sense, the term שֶׁרֶץ [sheretz], creeping thing, includes all creeping things — including frogs, which are not tamei — the Talmud uses it specifically for these eight contaminating species of sheretz.

2. Although the dough will contract tumah it cannot pass it to the utensil for it is a cardinal rule that foodstuffs can pass on their tumah only to other foods or liquids, but not to people and utensils (see Leviticus 12:33 with Rashi).

3. The mishnah omits mention of less than olive-sized amounts of chametz that are not needed to fortify the utensil. The Halachah requires that they be removed before Pesach — but do they interpose in the face of tumah by virtue of the fact that they are not regarded as part of

בָּצֵק הַחֵרֵשׁ, אִם יֵשׁ כַּיוֹצֵא בּוֹ שֶׁהֶחְמִיץ,
הֲרֵי זֶה אָסוּר.

[ג] **כֵּיצַד** מַפְרִישִׁין חַלָּה בְּטֻמְאָה בְּיוֹם טוֹב?
רַבִּי אֱלִיעֶזֶר אוֹמֵר: לֹא תִקְרָא
לָהּ שֵׁם עַד שֶׁתֵּאָפֶה.

יד אברהם

last passage refers to dough in the grooves of utensils all year round. Here, whether or not the dough is the size of an olive is of no concern, as it is on Pesach. The only thing that can give the dough the status of an outside object that interposes in the face of *tumah* is the owner's unwillingness to let it remain attached to the vessel.

[However it should be understood that the stipulations governing the status of the dough year round would apply on Pesach as well. Only the obverse is true; the olive-size rule stated for Pesach does not apply year round, i.e., the rule that dough the size of an olive interposes (even if the owner desires to keep it there) is irrelevant at other times of the year. But if he objects to a smaller amount, it would interpose on Pesach (even if it is of small size and the dough happens to fortify the utensil).]

וְאִם רוֹצֶה בְּקִיּוּמוֹ, הֲרֵי הוּא כָעֲרֵבָה. — *but if he desires it to remain then it is as the trough.*

בָּצֵק הַחֵרֵשׁ, — [Regarding] *"deaf" dough,*

[There is reason to suspect that a batch of dough has leavened, but it exhibits none of the symptoms of leavened dough outlined in mishnah 5.] When one smacks the dough, no sound is emitted, like a deaf person who, when addressed, shows no reaction. *(Rav; Rambam, Comm.)*

'As long as a person works with the dough — even an entire day — it does not leaven. But if he picked up his hand (i.e., he stopped working) and left it, so

that the dough remained until it reached [a point where it is able] to emit a sound when a person strikes upon it, then it has already leavened and must be burned. But if it does not emit a sound' *(Rambam, Hil. Chametz 5:13).*

Another version of the text is בָּצֵק הַחֵרֵס, *dough that is like a earthenware sherd,* i.e., not pliable, like normal dough, but hard and inflexible, and as a result one cannot ascertain whether it has leavened *(Rav; Rashi).*

Rashi adds that in addition the dough has preliminary symptoms of leavening; the dough's coloring has turned ashen, similar to that of a person who has turned pale from fright.

See mishnah 5, that according to the Sages, paleness of the dough is sufficient for the dough to be *chametz. According to Rashi,* therefore, our mishnah must follow R' Yehudah, which means that the established halachah does not adapt our mishnah.

אִם יֵשׁ כַּיוֹצֵא בּוֹ שֶׁהֶחְמִיץ, הֲרֵי זֶה אָסוּר. — *if there is [dough] similar to it that has already leavened, it is forbidden* [to eat or keep it].

If another specimen of similar dough that was kneaded at the same time is known to have become leavened during the interval, then the "deaf" dough is also forbidden *(Rav; Rashi).*

If there is no other dough by which to judge, then the factor to be considered is the length of time the dough was left without being kneaded. If this time span is long enough for an average person to walk a *mil,* 2,000 cubits, the dough is to be considered *chametz (Rav.; Gem. 46a).* Most commentators agree that this is 18 minutes (24 minutes according

the utensil? Or do we liken this case to the later rule of the mishnah, and say that only if the owner — in spite of the Halachah — objects to their presence, are they capable of interposing? The words of *Rashi* and *Rav* imply that the mere obligation to remove the *chametz* does not give it a separate identity.

[Regarding] "deaf" dough, if there is [dough] similar to it that has already leavened, it is forbidden.

3. How do we separate *challah* from contaminated dough on the festival?

R' Eliezer says: She should not designate it with the name [*challah*] until it is baked.

YAD AVRAHAM

to *Rambam* in *Comm.* here; see at length in *Tos. Yom Tov; Chok Ya'akov* and *Beur HaGra* to *Orach Chaim* 459:2). All the aforementioned refers only to an instance where the dough was left unkneaded. If however, it is constantly being kneaded (or worked upon), the process of leavening does not take place; even if it is kneaded all day

there is no suspicion of *chametz* (*Rambam* and *Shulchan Aruch* loc. cit. from *Baraisa* cited in 39b). However after the dough has been thoroughly worked over and has become warmed from the contact with the kneader's hands it may become *chametz* even in less than 18 minutes if it is left unattended (*Shulchan Aruch* loc. cit.).

3.

כֵּיצַד מַפְרִישִׁין חַלָּה בְּטֻמְאָה בְּיוֹם טוֹב? — *How do we separate challah from contaminated dough* [lit. *in contamination*] *on the festival* [*i.e., on Pesach*]?

[The Torah commands us to separate a portion from every batch of dough and give it to a *Kohen* (*Numbers* 15:18-21). This portion is called *challah*. The minimum amount of dough from which *challah* must be taken is a volume of 43.2 eggs. Challah is separated only from a dough made from one of the five species of grains; wheat, barley, spelt, rye and oats. The *challah*, like *terumah*, has a degree of holiness; it may only be eaten by a *Kohen* when both he and it are uncontaminated (see *Leviticus* 22:1-9, with *Rashi*).]

When baking on Pesach one separates the *challah* and bakes it immediately so that it will not have time to leaven. Then the baked *challah* is given to the *Kohen*. Where the dough has been contaminated we are faced with a problem, for contaminated *challah* may not be eaten; therefore, it may not be baked on *Yom Tov*, for cooking and baking on *Yom Tov* are permitted only for the purpose of אוֹכֶל נֶפֶשׁ, *human consumption* (see *Exodus* 12:16), which is impossible here. To lay the *challah* aside until evening when it can be burned is likewise forbidden because

the dough will leaven, causing the owner to be in possession of *chametz*. Nor can he use it as fuel for his cooking fire, since it is forbidden to burn or destroy sacred food on *Yom Tov* (*Shabbos* 24b), a prohibition that also prevents him from feeding it to his livestock (*Rav, Rashi*). Additionally, sacred food which is fit for human consumption may not be fed to animals even if it is *tamei* (*Meiri*; cf. *Tos. Yom Tov*). What then is the alternative?

רַבִּי אֱלִיעֶזֶר אוֹמֵר: לֹא תִקְרָא לָהּ שֵׁם עַד שֶׁתֵּאָפֶה. — *R' Eliezer says: She* [the woman doing the baking] *should not designate it with the name* [*challah*] [lit. *call for it a name*] *until it is baked.*

The entire dough should be baked before the *challah* is separated. Once baked, it can no longer become *chametz*, so she can later separate the *challah* and burn it when *Yom Tov* is over.

There are two options open for separating the *challah* after baking: (a) She may cut a piece from each individual loaf for *challah*. If this is done, no impermissible labor [מְלָאכָה] of 'baking' has taken place, because the act of placing each loaf in the oven was necessary whether or not the *challah* portion was attached to it. The (permitted) act needed to put the rest of the loaf into the oven suffices for the *challah* part as well (see *Beitzah* 21a עִיסָה חֲצִיָה שֶׁל נָכְרִי with *P'nei Yehoshua*; *Rashba* in *Tos.* here 46b s.v. הוֹאִיל: *Magen*

רַבִּי יְהוּדָה בֶּן בְּתֵירָא אוֹמֵר: תַּטִּיל בְּצוֹנֵן.
אָמַר רַבִּי יְהוֹשֻׁעַ: לֹא זֶה הוּא חָמֵץ
שֶׁמֻּזְהָרִים עָלָיו בְּבַל יֵרָאֶה וּבְבַל יִמָּצֵא. אֶלָּא
מַפְרִשָׁתָה וּמַנַּחְתָּה עַד הָעֶרֶב; וְאִם הֶחֱמִיצָה,
הֶחֱמִיצָה.

[ד] **רַבָּן** גַּמְלִיאֵל אוֹמֵר: שָׁלֹשׁ נָשִׁים לָשׁוֹת
כְּאַחַת וְאוֹפוֹת בְּתַנּוּר אֶחָד זוֹ אַחַר
זוֹ.
וַחֲכָמִים אוֹמְרִים: שָׁלֹשׁ נָשִׁים עוֹסְקוֹת

יד אברהם

Avraham 506:10). (b) Once the baking has
been done, it is adequate to place all the
loaves in a single basket and take one loaf as
challah for the entire batch; she need not actually go through the laborious process of
separating challah from each loaf individually. Even the baking of that particular loaf is
not regarded retroactively as having not been
for Yom Tov use; at the time it was baked its
owner was permitted to do so, because he
retained the option of using it for food had he
so desired. This is the option R' Eliezer ruled
permissible thus negating the need to utilize
the troublesome first option.

רַבִּי יְהוּדָה בֶּן בְּתֵירָא אוֹמֵר: תַּטִּיל בְּצוֹנֵן. —
R' Yehudah ben Beseira says: Let it be
cast into cold water.

[He should separate the challah and
put it into cold water. This will prevent
it from leavening so that he can leave it
in this state until after Yom Tov (during
the Intermediate Days) when he will
give it to the Kohen to dispose of. The
Kohen may then derive benefit from the
burning if it is done immediately after
removal from the water, before leavening takes place.]

However R' Eliezer rejects this option,
because he is apprehensive that the water
may not be cold enough to retard leavening
in every case. He holds that if at all possible
this method should not be considered (Rosh;
Tos. 46b, s.v. הואיל). However, both R'
Eliezer and R' Yehoshua agree that if he has
gone ahead and designated the challah while
it was still in dough form, he might then im-

merse it in cold water (Tos. 46a, s.v. תטיל).

אָמַר רַבִּי יְהוֹשֻׁעַ: לֹא זֶה הוּא חָמֵץ שֶׁמֻּזְהָרִים
עָלָיו בְּבַל יֵרָאֶה וּבְבַל יִמָּצֵא. — Said R'
Yehoshua: This is not the leaven concerning which we are warned "It shall
not be seen" [Exodus 13:9] and "It shall
not be found" [Exodus 12:19].

Once the challah designation is applied, that piece of dough becomes the
collective property of all the Kohanim
and does not belong to the original
owner of the dough any longer. The
Scriptural prohibition stresses: It [i.e.,
chametz] shall not be seen to you and it
shall not be found with you, implying
that one may see and possess someone
else's chametz. In this case the challah
dough need not be destroyed because it
is the property of neither the original
owners, nor of any specific Kohen
(Rav; Rashi).

אֶלָּא מַפְרִשָׁתָה וּמַנַּחְתָּה עַד הָעֶרֶב; וְאִם
הֶחֱמִיצָה, הֶחֱמִיצָה. — But he separates it
and leaves it until the evening; and if it
leavens, it leavens.

[Until the conclusion of the first or
last day of Yom Tov.]

[R' Eliezer and Ben Beseira disagree
with this argument, contending that the
original owner will transgress the
prohibition if the dough leavens.]

The Gemara (46b) suggests two approaches to understanding the divergent
views: Although the challah does not belong

3
4

R' Yehudah ben Beseira says: Let it be cast into cold water.

Said R' Yehoshua: This is not the leaven concerning which we are warned *"It shall not be seen"* [*Exodus* 13:7] and *"It shall not be found"* [*Exodus* 12:19]. But he separates it and leaves it until the evening; and if it leavens, it leavens.

4. **R**abban Gamliel says: Three women may knead at the same time and bake in the same oven, one after the other.

But the sages say: Three women may be occupied

YAD AVRAHAM

to him entirely once the designation has been made, the original owner nevertheless retains the power to give the *challah* to the *Kohen* of his choice. R' Eliezer and Ben Beseira contend that this power constitutes a certain degree of ownership [טוֹבַת הַנָאָה מָמוֹן] while R' Yehoshua disagrees, holding that this power is inconsequential.

Alternatively, they disagree regarding the rule of 'potential' [הוֹאִיל]. Under this rule, if someone has the power of bringing something about, it can be regarded as though it were factually in existence. Theoretically, therefore, if the original owner of *challah* had a means of removing it from

the collective ownership of the *Kohanim* and bringing it back into his possession, he could be held in violation of the prohibition against owning — or having the *potential* of owning — *chametz* on Pesach. In the case of *challah*, such a possibility *does* exist, because the designation of *challah* has the status of a vow, which can be annulled by an expert *rav* or a *beis din* under the proper conditions. Consequently, R' Eliezer views *challah* as still 'belonging' to the person who designated it, for it still has potential of becoming his, so if it became *chametz* he would transgress the prohibition[1]. R' Yehoshua does not accept this halachic principle.

רַבָּן גַמְלִיאֵל אוֹמֵר: שָׁלֹש נָשִׁים לָשׁוֹת כְּאַחַת — *Rabban Gamliel says: Three women may knead at the same time*

Three women are using an oven that has a capacity sufficient for only one dough at a time. If the three begin kneading at the same time and finish simultaneously, the second woman will have to wait until the first batch of dough has been baked, and the third will have to wait for the baking of two batches. Meanwhile, some dough will lay unkneaded (*Rambam*).

וְאוֹפוֹת בְּתַנּוּר אֶחָד זוֹ אַחַר זוֹ. — *and bake in the same oven, one after the other.*

Even though one dough will be left unattended while the other two are being baked, R' Gamliel is not concerned with the time lapse. He holds that dough does not leaven in so short a time span (*Rambam*).

וַחֲכָמִים אוֹמְרִים: שָׁלֹש נָשִׁים עוֹסְקוֹת בְּבָצֵק, — *But the Sages say: Three women may be occupied with dough [simultaneously],*

Although they may all be engaged in various parts of the work (as described below) simultaneously, they may not all start kneading at the same time because if they finish at the same time and have

---

1. The above version is found in our editions of the Talmud. *Rashi* (48a s.v. אבך ותא) emends the *Gemara* and presents this segment differently. See *Tos. Yom Tov.*

בְּבָצֵק, אַחַת לָשָׁה, וְאַחַת עוֹרֶכֶת, וְאַחַת
אוֹפָה.

רַבִּי עֲקִיבָא אוֹמֵר: לֹא כָל הַנָּשִׁים וְלֹא כָל
הָעֵצִים וְלֹא כָל הַתַּנוּרִים שָׁוִין.
זֶה הַכְּלָל: תָּפַח תִּלְטוֹשׁ בְּצוֹנֵן.

[ה] **שְׂאוֹר** יִשָּׂרֵף, וְהָאוֹכְלוֹ פָּטוּר. סָדוּק
יִשָּׂרֵף, וְהָאוֹכְלוֹ חַיָּב כָּרֵת.
אֵיזֶהוּ שְׂאוֹר? — כְּקַרְנֵי חֲגָבִים. סָדוּק? —
שֶׁנִּתְעָרְבוּ סְדָקָיו זֶה בָזֶה — דִּבְרֵי רַבִּי יְהוּדָה.

to wait for the oven, the time lapse may be too lengthy for the dough to remain unleavened (*Rav; Rashi*).

אַחַת לָשָׁה, וְאַחַת עוֹרֶכֶת, וְאַחַת אוֹפָה. — *one kneads, another shapes, and a third bakes.*

The Sages maintain that all must be involved with the dough at the same time so that none of it lays unattended. Therefore, while the third kneads, the second shapes or rolls the dough and bastes it with cold water, while the first bakes. Then the cycle repeats itself (*Rav; based on Gem. 48b*). [I.e., while the first one is kneading, the other two may not yet begin. When she starts to shape and baste, the second begins to knead. Only when the first one begins to bake and the second to shape, may the third one start to knead, so that the continuing cycle will not leave any dough unattended.]

Some commentators (see *Ritva* and the opinion cited by *Ran, Meiri, R' David* and *Teshuvos HaRashba* 1:124) hold that even when the dough is continually worked upon, no more than three women may use a single one-dough capacity oven. However, based on a *baraisa* cited on 48b, *Rambam, Hil. Chametz* 5:13 rules that as long as someone occupies himself with dough — even for an entire day — it does not reach the point of leavening. This opinion is accepted in *Shulchan Aruch* (459:2).

רַבִּי עֲקִיבָא אוֹמֵר: לֹא כָל הַנָּשִׁים וְלֹא כָל הָעֵצִים

וְלֹא כָל הַתַּנוּרִים שָׁוִין. — *R' Akiva says: Not all women and not all kinds of wood and not all ovens are alike.*

R' Akiva disputes R' Gamliel, who permits three women to knead at the same time. R' Akiva argues that one cannot generalize. Some women are less energetic than others, therefore the time lapse may be too extensive in their case. There are also ovens which do not heat rapidly, and there is wood which does not burn quickly. All these factors tend to retard the pace of the baking process, creating the possibility of leavening. R' Akiva, therefore, concurs with the sages that the dough should constantly be kept active (*Rav; Rambam*).

זֶה הַכְּלָל: תָּפַח תִּלְטוֹשׁ בְּצוֹנֵן. — *This is the general rule: If [the dough] rises let her wet it with cold water.*

When she notices, that the dough is about to rise let her baste the dough with cold water, by dipping her hand in water and running the wet hand over the dough. This process retards the leavening process (*Rav, Rashi*). This phrase is not part of R' Akiva's statement, it is rather an anonymous [and unanimous mishnah] (*Meleches Shlomo;* see above mishnah 3, ר' יְהוּדָה בֶּן בְּתֵירָא).

Rambam's (comm. ed. R' Y. Kafich) reads תָּפַח וְתִלְטֹשׁ בְּצוֹנֵן *let her moisten "and" baste* [it] *with cold water.* He explains that R'

with dough [simultaneously], one kneads, another shapes, and a third bakes.

R' Akiva says: Not all women and not all kinds of wood and not all ovens are alike.

This is the general rule: If [the dough] rises let her wet it with cold water.

5. **P**artly leavened dough must be burned, but one who eats it is exempt [from punishment]. Furrowed dough must be burned and one who eats it is liable to *kares*.

Which [dough] is [classified as] 'partly leavened'? — [When the furrows are] like locusts' horns. [Which is classified as] 'furrowed'? — When the furrows run into each other — [these are] the words of R' Yehudah.

YAD AVRAHAM

Akiva disagrees with the Sages too, contending that only when those occupied with the dough continually spray and baste it with cold water may three women use one oven (even in the manner outlined by the sage). תְּפַח is probably cognate to טוֹפֵחַ, *dripping*.

5.

שְׂאוֹר — *Partly leavened dough*

Dough that became leavened slightly, but did not complete the leavening process (Rav, Rashi)

יִשָּׂרֵף, — *must be burned,*

Although it is only חָמֵץ נוּקְשֶׁה, *unfinished chametz*, it must be destroyed (*Tif. Yis.*).

See above mishnah 1, s.v. וְאֵלּוּ עוֹבְרִין. Those who prohibit the possession of unfinished *chametz* support their view with this mishnah (see *Tos.* 2a, s.v. אוּר). See *Magen Avraham* (442:1) for a defense of the opposing view of *Tur* and *R' Tam*.

R' Yehudah holds that there is no negative commandment prohibiting the consumption of unfinished *chametz* (חָמֵץ נוּקְשֶׁה; see *Gem.* 431). Nevertheless it may not be eaten, and must be burned. See preface to mishnah 1 on whether this prohibition is Scriptural or Rabbinic. R' Meir (43a) disagrees, contending that although there is no *Kares* for consumption of unfinished *chametz*, one who eats it transgresses a negative *mitzvah*.

וְהָאוֹכְלוֹ פָּטוּר. — *but one who eats it is*

exempt [*from punishment*].

From both *malkos* [lashes] and *kares* (*Tos. Yom Tov; Rashi* 48b, s.v. והא אנן תנן).

The appearance of lines of furrows on dough is a symptom of fermentation.

סָדוּק יִשָּׂרֵף, וְהָאוֹכְלוֹ חַיָּב כָּרֵת.— *Furrowed dough must be burned and he who eats it is liable to kares.*

[The furrowsa positively indicate that the leavening process has been completed, rendering the dough finished *chametz*, חָמֵץ גָּמוּר.]

אֵיזֶהוּ שְׂאוֹר? — כְּקַרְנֵי חֲגָבִים. — *Which* [dough] *is* [classified as] 'partly leavened'? — [When the furrows are] like locusts' horns.

There are so few furrows on the surface of the dough that they do not meet (Rav, Rashi); also they are very thin (Rambam).

סָדוּק? — שֶׁנִּתְעָרְבוּ סְדָקָיו זֶה בָזֶה — [*Which is classified as*] '*furrowed'?* — *When the*

וַחֲכָמִים אוֹמְרִים: זֶה וָזֶה הָאוֹכְלוֹ חַיָּב כָּרֵת.
וְאֵיזֶהוּ שְׂאוֹר? — כָּל שֶׁהִכְסִיפוּ פָּנָיו כְּאָדָם
שֶׁעָמְדוּ שַׂעֲרוֹתָיו.

[ו] **אַרְבָּעָה** עָשָׂר שֶׁחָל לִהְיוֹת בַּשַּׁבָּת,
מְבַעֲרִין אֶת הַכֹּל מִלִּפְנֵי
הַשַּׁבָּת — דִּבְרֵי רַבִּי מֵאִיר.
וַחֲכָמִים אוֹמְרִים: בִּזְמַנָּן.
רַבִּי אֶלְעָזָר בַּר צָדוֹק אוֹמֵר: תְּרוּמָה מִלִּפְנֵי
הַשַּׁבָּת וְחוּלִין בִּזְמַנָּן.

יד אברהם

furrows run into [lit. *mingle with*] *each other.*

There are many furrows so that they run into each other (*Meiri*).

דִּבְרֵי רַבִּי יְהוּדָה. — [*these are*] *the words of R' Yehudah.*

וַחֲכָמִים אוֹמְרִים: זֶה וָזֶה הָאוֹכְלוֹ חַיָּב כָּרֵת. — *But the Sages say: If one eats either of these* [lit. *this or that, he who eats it*] *he is liable to kares.*

[The Sages maintain that furrows in any form, even if they do not run into each other, are an indication that the leavening process has been completed. As the *Gemara* (48b) puts it, 'There is no single furrow on the surface for which there are not many furrows below the surface' (*Gem.* 48b). Conse-

quently the dough classified as 'partly leavened' (חָמֵץ נוּקְשֶׁה) by R' Yehudah, is put by the Sages into the category of finished *chametz* [חָמֵץ גָּמוּר].

וְאֵיזֶהוּ שְׂאוֹר? — כָּל שֶׁהִכְסִיפוּ פָּנָיו כְּאָדָם שֶׁעָמְדוּ שַׂעֲרוֹתָיו. — [*If so,*] *which is 'partly leavened dough'? — Whenever its surface turns pallid, like* [*that of*] *a man whose hairs stand on end.*

Out of fright and terror his face turns pale (*Rav, Rashi*).

According to R' Yehudah, dough reaching this point of paleness is still classified as matzah (*Menachos* 53a; *Chullin* 23b). However it is prohibited rabbinically for consumption, although benefit (הֲנָאָה) may be derived from it (*Tos.* 43a, s.v. ונותנו: *Menachos* 53a, s.v. אי).

6.

אַרְבָּעָה עָשָׂר שֶׁחָל לִהְיוֹת בַּשַּׁבָּת, מְבַעֲרִין אֶת הַכֹּל מִלִּפְנֵי הַשַּׁבָּת—דִּבְרֵי רַבִּי מֵאִיר. *If the fourteenth* [*of Nissan*] *falls on the Sabbath, we remove everything* [*containing chametz*] *before the Sabbath —* [*these are*] *the words of R' Meir.*

The 'removal' of *chametz* means that it must be destroyed (see above 2:1). Obviously, this cannot be done on the

Sabbath, when burning and carrying things out of the home are forbidden, and if one cannot eat all the *chametz* in his possession he will be in violation of the negative commandment not to own *chametz* during Pesach. Accordingly, the *chametz* must be removed and destroyed on Friday. R' Meir rules that both *terumah* and *chullin* [i.e., non-

3
6

But the Sages say: If one eats either of these he is liable to *kares*. [If so,] which is 'partly leavened dough'? — Whenever its surface turns pallid, like [that of] a man whose hairs stand on end.

6. **I**f the fourteenth [of Nissan] falls on the Sabbath, we remove everything before the Sabbath — [these are] the words of R' Meir.

But the Sages say: [Everything is removed] at its [usual] time.

R' Eliezer bar Tzadok says; *Terumah* [must be removed] before the Sabbath and *chullin* at its [usual] time.

consecrated food] must be removed, except for what is needed for the two Sabbath meals when *chametz* may be eaten (*Rav*).[1]

וַחֲכָמִים אוֹמְרִים: בִּזְמַנָּן. — *But the Sages say: [Everything is removed] at its [usual] time.*

[The Sages disagree with R' Meir's ruling that *chametz* for only two meals may be left. They hold that one may leave as much *chametz* as he likes for the Sabbath on the assumption that there will be enough people to eat it. Any *chametz* that is not consumed will be 'removed' when the proper time comes (see above 1:4) in whatever manner is permissible on the Sabbath. See *Orach Chaim* 444:4-5 with *Mishnah Berurah* for the permissible methods of 'removal' for the Sabbath.]

רַבִּי אֶלְעָזָר בַּר צָדוֹק אוֹמֵר: תְּרוּמָה מִלִּפְנֵי הַשַּׁבָּת וְחוּלִּין בִּזְמַנָּן. — *R' Elazar bar Tzadok says: Terumah [must be removed] before the Sabbath and chullin at its*

[usual] time.

Terumah is the portion of the produce which must be separated and given to a *Kohen*; it may not be consumed by any non-*Kohen* (*Leviticus* 22:10). *Chullin* (lit. *secular* or *non-consecrated*) is the name given any item not consecrated in any manner; in our context it means non-*terumah*. R' Elazar makes a distinction between *terumah* which is forbidden for non-*Kohanim* and their animals, and is therefore likely to remain uneaten, and *chullin* which can easily be disposed of by human and animal consumption before the time of 'removal' (*Rashi*; cf *Rav*).

Rav and *Rambam*'s commentary state that the halachah follows R' Eliezer ben Tzadok, but in his code (*Hil. Chametz* 3:3; see *Ravad* and *comm.* there; *Rif* and *comm.* here and 13a) *Rambam* reverses himself and rules that both *chullin* and *terumah* must be removed before the Sabbath (following R' Eliezer ben Yehudah in *Gem.* 13a and R' Meir here). This is the view accepted by *Shulchan Aruch* (*Orach Chaim* 444:1).

1. Some commentators (*Ba'al HaMa'or* here, *R' Yitzchak ibn Gias* and *R' Efraim* cited in *Ran* and *Ravad* to 13a) interpret הכל, *everything*, literally: all *chametz* must be removed and only matzah may be eaten with the Sabbath meals.

[ז] **הַהוֹלֵךְ** לִשְׁחֹט אֶת פִּסְחוֹ, וְלָמוּל אֶת
בְּנוֹ, וְלֶאֱכוֹל סְעוּדַת אֵרוּסִין
בְּבֵית חָמָיו, וְנִזְכַּר שֶׁיֶּשׁ לוֹ חָמֵץ בְּתוֹךְ בֵּיתוֹ —
אִם יָכוֹל לַחֲזוֹר, וּלְבַעֵר, וְלַחֲזוֹר לְמִצְוָתוֹ,
יַחֲזֹר וִיבַעֵר; וְאִם לָאו, מְבַטְּלוֹ בְּלִבּוֹ.
לְהַצִּיל מִן הַגַּיִס, וּמִן הַנָּהָר, וּמִן הַלִּסְטִים,
וּמִן הַדְּלֵקָה, וּמִן הַמַּפֹּלֶת, יְבַטֵּל בְּלִבּוֹ. וְלִשְׁבֹּת

יד אברהם

7.

— הַהוֹלֵךְ לִשְׁחֹט אֶת פִּסְחוֹ, וְלָמוּל אֶת בְּנוֹ,
[If] someone is going to slaughter his
Pesach offering, (or) to circumcise his
son,

On the fourteenth day of Nissan
(Rav).

[All the actions enumerated here are
mitzvos.]

וְלֶאֱכוֹל סְעוּדַת אֵרוּסִין בְּבֵית חָמָיו, — or to
dine at a betrothal feast at the house of
his father-in-law,

[Although we have translated אֵרוּסִין as betrothal for the lack of an exact English equivalent, the word refers to a status much different than the simple 'engagement' implied
by the word betrothal. The feast under discussion is in celebration of קִדּוּשִׁין, kiddushin
(the Hebrew word for אֵרוּסִין), the ceremony
that is the first step in the process of marriage and that imposes many of the obligations of marriage. For example, after kiddushin the relationship can be dissolved only
by a גֵּט, bill of divorce, and an adultress is
liable to the death penalty like any married
woman. In contemporary times, this
ceremony — usually accomplished by the
giving of a ring — is performed in conjunction with the blessing and the chupah
ceremony that completes the marriage. In
Talmudic times, however, kiddushin was
customarily done independently, long before
the chupah and it was celebrated with a feast.

Since kiddushin is part of the process of
marriage, it is understandable that our mishnah describes it as a mitzvah. The consensus
of commentators, however, regards even today's engagement feast as sufficiently
significant to qualify as a mitzvah with
regard to the law given below in our mishnah

(see Mishna Berurah 444:24 with Sha'ar
HaTziyun.)]

וְנִזְכַּר שֶׁיֶּשׁ לוֹ חָמֵץ בְּתוֹךְ בֵּיתוֹ— — and he
remembers that he has chametz at
home—

[If he goes ahead to perform the mitzvah upon which he embarked, he may
not have time to return home and
'remove' the chametz before it is too
late.]

אִם יָכוֹל לַחֲזוֹר, וּלְבַעֵר, וְלַחֲזוֹר לְמִצְוָתוֹ,
יַחֲזֹר וִיבַעֵר; — if he is able to return,
remove [it], and [then] return to his
mitzvah, he must go back and remove
[it];

[If, by delaying the slaughter, circumcision, or feast, he will have time to
accomplish both it and the removal of
his chametz, he must do both.]

וְאִם לָאו, מְבַטְּלוֹ בְּלִבּוֹ. — but if not, he
nullifies it in his heart.

[As explained in the Appendix,
Search and Nullification, the Scriptural
requirement of removal is fulfilled
merely by בִּיטוּל בְּלֵב, conscious nullification.] With that accomplished, the
remaining requirement to remove
physically all chametz from one's
premises is only of Rabbinic origin.
This is superseded by the need to perform the mitzvah upon which he is embarked (Rav).

The mishnah seems to imply that permission to set aside the Rabbinic requirement is
extended only to one whose presence is
necessary for the performance of the respec-

7. [I f] someone is going to slaughter his Pesach offering, to circumcise his son, or to dine at a betrothal feast at the house of his father-in-law, and he remembers that he has *chametz* at home — if he is able to return, remove [it] and [then] return to his *mitzvah*, he must go back and remove [it]; but if not, he nullifies it in his heart.

[If he is on his way] to save [people] from a [marauding] troop, from a river, from bandits, from a fire, or from a collapsed building, he nullifies it in his

YAD AVRAHAM

tive *mitzvah*, such as the owner of a Pesach offering, father of the infant, or bridegroom. People who are merely guests at the feast, however, would not be permitted to content themselves with nullification. *Rambam (Hil. Chametz* 3:9) however, phrases this law as follows: 'One who left his house before the time of "removal" to perform a *mitzvah* or to attend a *mitzvah* feast, for example, a betrothal feast ...' *Rambam* would seem to imply that there is no difference between the host and the other guests; any one of them may nullify the *chametz* (*Tos. Akiva Eiger* citing *Magen Avraham* 444:10; cf. *Mishnah Berurah* 444:25).

If it is too late to nullify the *chametz* (e.g., after the onset of the sixth hour), which *mitzvah* takes precedence? Some hold that one should continue the *mitzvah* he is in the process of doing, while others hold that removal of the *chametz* must be done first, because one transgresses every minute he has it in his possession (see *Tos. R' Akiva Eiger* here; *Mishnah Berurah* 444:29 with *Sha'ar HaTziyun; Chidushei HaGrach al HaShas*).

לְהַצִּיל מִן הַגַּיִס, — [*If he is on his way*] *to save* [*people*] *from a* [*marauding*] *troop,*

Our text follows *Rav's* and *Rambam's* version (see *Hil. Chametz* 3:9; *Comm.* ed. Kafich). Some Jews were menaced by hostile troops and he went to rescue them. Other versions read that the danger was from עוֹבְדֵי כּוֹכָבִים, *idolators,* or נָכְרִים, *Gentiles* (see *Tos. Yom Tov* and *Shinuyei Nuschaos*).

וּמִן הַנָּהָר, — (*or*) *from a river,*
[To save people trapped by a flood.]

וּמִן הַלִסְטִים, וּמִן הַדְּלֵקָה, וּמִן הַמַּפֹּלֶת, — (*or*) *from bandits,* (*or*) *from a fire, or from a collapsed building,*
[A building collapsed, trapping people in the rubble. In each of the above cases peoples' lives are in jeopardy.]

יְבַטֵּל בְּלִבּוֹ. — *he nullifies it in his heart.*
Because human life is endangered in this group of cases, he should not go back to his house to 'remove' the *chametz* even if there is time to do so and still save the endangered people. He is to fulfill his Scriptural obligation through 'nullification' and not delay his mission (*Rav; Rashi*).

◆§ Designating a Sabbath Resting Place

On the Sabbath or the festivals, one may not go beyond an area extending 2000 cubits [תְּחוּם שַׁבָּת]in all directions from his domicile (see at length *Eruvin* ch. 5-6). If one must go beyond his permitted 2000 cubits — but less than 4000 — there is a device permitting him to do so. Before the Sabbath or festival commences, he may choose a spot within 2000 cubits of his abode and designate it as his 'rest station' [קוֹנֶה שְׁבִיתָה]. That place will be considered his 'home' for the Sabbath, meaning that the 2000 cubits limit will be measured in all directions from that spot, enabling him to walk 2000 cubits from his real home to his resting 'station' and then another 2000 cubits beyond it, a total of 4000 cubits from his home. This designation can be accomplished in two ways: Either by putting down the minimum amount of food

שְׁבִיתַת הָרְשׁוּת, יַחֲזֹר מִיָּד.

[ח] **וְכֵן** מִי שֶׁיָּצָא מִירוּשָׁלַיִם וְנִזְכַּר שֶׁיֵּשׁ בְּיָדוֹ
בְּשַׂר קֹדֶשׁ — אִם עָבַר צוֹפִים,
שׂוֹרְפוֹ בִּמְקוֹמוֹ; וְאִם לָאו, חוֹזֵר וְשׂוֹרְפוֹ לִפְנֵי
הַבִּירָה מֵעֲצֵי הַמַּעֲרָכָה.
וְעַד כַּמָּה הֵן חוֹזְרִין? — רַבִּי מֵאִיר אוֹמֵר:

יד אברהם

needed for two meals (see *Eruvin* 8:2; *Orach Chaim* 409:7) at the designated 'rest station,' and is assured that the food was still there on the onset of the Sabbath. This procedure is known as *Eruvei T'chumin*. Or, one may go to the designated 'rest station' and remain there at the beginning of the Sabbath (מֵעֶרֶב בְּרַגְלָיו: *Eruvin* 4:7-9, *Orach Chaim* loc. cit.).

וְלִשְׁבּוּת שְׁבִיתַת הָרְשׁוּת, יַחֲזֹר מִיָּד. — *If it was but to establish a voluntary resting place, he must return at once.*

The purpose of his trip was to be at his chosen resting place at the beginning of the festival so that he would be permitted to walk 2000 cubits beyond it on the Sabbath or the festival. If his need for the resting place was so that he could be free to walk for some purpose of his own choosing — but not for a *mitzvah* — then the need to remove his *chametz* created a conflict between a *mitzvah* (removal) and a personal wish. In that case he is forbidden to rely upon nullification, but must return home to dispose of his *chametz*. On the other hand, if his need for a resting place was so that he could pay a condolence call,

attend a *mitzvah* feast or the like, then he may rely on nullification (*Rav; Rashi*).

Tosafos (49a, s.v. לשבות) dispute this interpretation because one may never designate a Sabbath station unless he needs it to travel for a *mitzvah* purpose (*Eruvin* 31a). How then, could he designate a resting place for a personal need even if there *were* time to dispose of his *chametz* properly (see *Tos. R' Akiva Eiger*)? Therefore, *Tosafos* renders: *to observe the [festival] rest day in a voluntary manner.* According to this interpretation, our mishnah does not discuss the designation of a 'rest station'. Rather it speaks of someone who has made a decision of personal convenience to observe the Pesach festivities at a friend's or relative's home, and such a personal choice does not take precedence over the removal of *chametz*.[1]

8.

וְכֵן מִי שֶׁיָּצָא מִירוּשָׁלַיִם וְנִזְכַּר שֶׁיֵּשׁ בְּיָדוֹ בְּשַׂר קֹדֶשׁ — *Similarly, [if] someone left Jerusalem and remembered that he had sacrificial [lit. consecrated] meat in his hand —*

Flesh of offering becomes unfit if it is

removed from Jerusalem [and must be burned] (*Rav; Rashi*).

אִם עָבַר צוֹפִים, — *if he has passed Tzofim [lit. lookouts],*

Tzofim (or its Latin name, Scopus) is

1. *Rosh*, basing his comment on *Yerushalmi*, combines *Rashi's* and *Tosafos* interpretation. He designated a 'rest station' in order to celebrate the festival at his friend's house. This qualifies as a *mitzvah* regarding the laws of establishing a 'rest station,' but it is not sufficient to permit one to rely on mere nullification (see *Meiri*).

3
8

heart. If it was but to establish a voluntary resting place, he must return at once.

8. **S**imilarly, [if] someone left Jerusalem and remembered that he had sacrificial meat in his hand — if he has passed Tzofim, he burns it where he is; but if not, he [must] return and burn it before the Temple with the wood of the [altar] pyre.

And for how much [*chametz* or meat] must they return? — R' Meir says: In either case, [when there is]

YAD AVRAHAM

a place (or village) from which the Temple first becomes visible (*Rav; Rashi*).[1]

Tosafos (49a s.v. אם), however, argues that the mishnah's purpose is to designate points in all directions of Jerusalem beyond which one need not return. The language of *Tosefta* (3:10; cited by *Tos.*) indicated that *Tzofim* is not a specific spot, but rather any point (on all sides of Jerusalem) from which the Temple first becomes visible (cf. *Tos. Yom Tov*).

שׂוֹרְפוֹ בִּמְקוֹמוֹ; — *he burns it where he is* [lit. *in his place*];

The Sages did not burden him with the bother of returning to Jerusalem to burn the flesh (*Rav, Rashi*) [as should be done ideally].

וְאִם לָאו, חוֹזֵר וְשׂוֹרְפוֹ לִפְנֵי הַבִּירָה — *but if not, he [must] return and burn it before the Temple*

With reference to a sin offering that has become disqualified, the Torah states (*Leviticus* 6:23): *In the Holy … shall it be burned with fire*, from which we deduce (*Gem.* 24a) that also the flesh of offerings of lesser sanctity (קָדָשִׁים קַלִּים), which is eaten only within the walls of Jerusalem, must be burned within those same parameters, within the walls of Jerusalem — if it becomes disqualified (*Rashi; Rav; see further* 7:8).

The term בִּירָה is rendered *Temple*, according to Resh Lakish (*Zevachim* 104b). According to R' Yochanan (*ibid*), there was a particular place called *Birah* on the Temple Mount (outside the Temple Courtyard's walls; חוּץ לָעֲזָרָה), before which this flesh was burned.

מֵעֲצֵי הַמַּעֲרָכָה. — *with the wood of the [altar] pyre.*

Since he burns it 'before the Temple,' i.e., in the place designated for burning, he uses wood that was consecrated for use upon the altar (see *comm.* to 8:2).

The *Gemara* (82a) states that whenever one burns 'before the Temple' he may not use his own wood. Furthermore (*loc. cit*), one who wishes to burn the flesh with privately owned wood, should burn it within the walls of Jerusalem, but not before the Temple. Consequently, the mishnah's provision to 'burn it before the Temple' cannot be understood as a requirement. It is a dispensation: if one wishes to avoid the chore of obtaining wood for the burning, he is permitted to burn the flesh 'before the Temple' where he will be given 'wood of the pyre.'

וְעַד כַּמָּה הֵן חוֹזְרִין? — *And for how much [chametz or meat] must they return?*

Having stated that one who found himself before *Tzofim* with sacrificial meat, or one who remembered that he had *chametz* and is required to return

1. *R' Yaakov Emden* cites *Josephus Flavius* to the effect that seven 'stadia' (a stadia = 607 — 630 ft.) north of Jerusalem there was a special observation point (Scopus?). [In *Antiquities* (11, 8, 5) Josephus reports that Alexander the Great was met by the *Kohen Gadol* and his entourage at a place called *Sapha* (צוֹפֶה), because from it one could see the city and the Temple. In *Wars* (2, 19, 4) he mentions a military camp in the environs of Jerusalem called Scopus. I have not yet found the exact passage referred to by R' Ya'akov Emden.]

זֶה וָזֶה בִּכְבֵיצָה. רַבִּי יְהוּדָה אוֹמֵר: זֶה וָזֶה בִּכְזַיִת. וַחֲכָמִים אוֹמְרִים: בְּשַׂר קֹדֶשׁ בִּכְזַיִת, וְחָמֵץ בִּכְבֵיצָה.

יד אברהם

and 'remove' it (mishnah 7), the mishnah asks how much *chametz* or flesh must he have before he is required to do so *(Rav)*.

[In view of the fact that the obligation to return is a Rabbinic decree (see below), the volume for which they required this had to be decided by the Sages. All agree that they chose a volume that has significance in some halachic connection. R' Meir and R' Yehudah disagree regarding which halachah they chose to apply.]

רַבִּי מֵאִיר אוֹמֵר: זֶה וָזֶה — *R' Meir says: In either case* [lit. *this one and this one*],

[I.e., both in the case of *chametz* and the sacrificial meat.]

בִּכְבֵיצָה. — [*when there is*] *as much as an egg.*

R' Meir holds that the Sages pegged the obligation to return to the minimum quantity of food that is sufficient to pass contamination from itself to another substance, i.e., a volume the size of an egg *(Rav, Rambam; Gem. 48b).*

רַבִּי יְהוּדָה אוֹמֵר: זֶה וָזֶה בִּכְזַיִת. — *R' Yehudah says: In either case* [*when there is*] *as much as an olive.*

R' Yehudah maintains that the obligation to return was pegged to the maximum required amount needed to mandate punishment for transgression of the two relevant prohibitions (consuming *chametz* or offering such disqualified meat on the altar — as much as an olive [כְּזַיִת] *(Rav; Gem. 50a)*.

But if he has less than this amount of *chametz*, it suffices to nullify it (thus removing the Scriptural obligation), and in the case of sacred flesh, he burns it wherever he is[1] *(Rav; Rashi)*.

וַחֲכָמִים אוֹמְרִים: בְּשַׂר קֹדֶשׁ בִּכְזַיִת, וְחָמֵץ בִּכְבֵיצָה. — *But the Sages say: [For] sacrificial meat as much as an olive, but [for] chametz, as much as an egg.*

The Sages suggest that because of the stringency which the Torah regards leftover sacred flesh, we also take a stringent attitude, therefore demanding a return for an amount as small as the volume of an olive. For *chametz*, however, since nullification satisfies the Scriptural requirement, we take a more lenient approach and do not require the owner's return for any amount smaller that the volume of an egg *(Rav, Rambam)*.

---

1. According to *Tos.* (49a s.v. ושורפו), the Torah requires that flesh of greater sanctity [קָדְשֵׁי קָדָשִׁים] must be burned in the place where they could be eaten, i.e., the Courtyard. Flesh of lesser sanctity [קָדָשִׁים קַלִּים], however, can be burned anywhere by Torah law; the requirement to burn it in Jerusalem is of Rabbinic origin. Consequently, the mishnah's permission to burn the flesh anywhere can apply only to flesh of lesser sanctity, for which the Sages can relax their own restriction. But in the case of flesh for which the *Torah* ordains burning in the Courtyard, the flesh *must* be returned there no matter how great the inconvenience or distance (cf. *S'fas Emes*).

as much as an egg. R' Yehudah says: In either case [when there is] as much as an olive. But the Sages say: [For] sacrificial meat, as much as an olive, but [for] *chametz*, as much as an egg.

YAD AVRAHAM

Chapter 4

Chapter Four discusses a wide variety of customs, many of them unrelated to Pesach. The underlying premise of the chapter is the undisputed rule that people are obligated to follow the customs of their native towns, for a generally adopted custom has the force of halachah. This concept is introduced in mishnah 1 with a discussion about differing customs concerning work on the morning of the fourteenth of Nissan. The Talmud teaches (*Bava Metzia* 86b; cf. *Midrash Rabbah Bereishis* 48:14, *Shemos* 47:5): A person should never deviate from local custom, like Moses who did not eat when he was among the angels [during the forty days and forty nights when God taught him the Torah] and like the angels who *did* eat human food when they were Abraham's guests. Both cases — Moses behaving like angels and angels behaving like Abraham — demonstrate that one should conform to the practice of the place where he finds himself. As R' Meir puts it in the words of a proverb 'You have gone up to the town — follow its manners.'

R' *Achai Gaon (She'iltos* 67) cites: From where do we know that custom is an important matter? Said Rava bar Abba in the name of R' Yochanan in the name of Rav, for it is written (*Proverbs* 1:8): *Hear my son the reproof of your father, and forsake not the teaching of your mother.* R' *Sherira Gaon (Sha'arei Tzedek* part 4, 1:20; cited partially by *Tur, Choshen Mishpat* 368) states: From where do we know that custom is an important matter, for it written (*Deuteronomy* 19:14), *Do not move your neighbor's border — that which the ancients have partitioned ...* R' *Sherira* interprets this not only in its literal sense, but also with relation to generally accepted norms of behavior. Mishnah 1 deals with an additional element of this obligation. Where one has moved to a place whose customs differ from his own, 'Let no man deviate [from local custom], to avoid conflict,' for if he were to publicly flout local norms, strife could very well result.

Furthermore, *Rambam* (preface to *Mishneh Torah*; cf. *Hil. Mamrim* 1:2-3) rules that a custom instituted by the *Beis Din* of any generation is included in the Scriptural admonition (*Deuteronomy* 17:11) *You shall not deviate from the matter they* [the Rabbis] *impart to you ...* Indeed, some commentators argue that a blessing should be recited before the performance of (some) customs because they have the force of law (see *Tos. Succah* 44b, s.v. כאן; *Berachos* 14a, s.v. ימים and other commentators in both places; cf. *Shabbos* 23a והיכן ציוונו ...). An example of such a blessing is the one recited in most communities before the recitation of *Hallel* on *Rosh Chodesh*; unlike the obligatory *Hallel* of festivals, its recitation of Rosh Chodesh began in Talmudic times as a custom (see *Ta'anis* 28b; *Tos.* there, s.v. אמר, *Orach Chaim* 422:2, *Tur* and *Beis Yosef* there). A similar view, though not a generally adopted one, is R' *Saadyah Gaon's* ruling (*Siddur* p. 259; *Tur Orach Chaim* 606) that one should recite a blessing over the customary immersion in a *mikveh* on the eve of Yom Kippur (see also *Sefer HaMichtam* to *Pesachim* 116b; *Meiri's* preface to his responsa *Sefer HaYashar, Sheilos U'Teshuvos* 44:6, p. 99; A lengthy exposition on the halachic ramification of customs is found in *Pri Chadash* to *Orach Chaim* 468 and 496).

פְּסָחִים [א] **מָקוֹם** שֶׁנָּהֲגוּ לַעֲשׂוֹת מְלָאכָה בְּעַרְבֵי
ד/א פְּסָחִים עַד חֲצוֹת, עוֹשִׂין; מָקוֹם
שֶׁנָּהֲגוּ שֶׁלֹּא לַעֲשׂוֹת, אֵין עוֹשִׂין.
הַהוֹלֵךְ מִמָּקוֹם שֶׁעוֹשִׂין לְמָקוֹם שֶׁאֵין
עוֹשִׂין, אוֹ מִמָּקוֹם שֶׁאֵין עוֹשִׂין לְמָקוֹם
שֶׁעוֹשִׂין, נוֹתְנִין עָלָיו חֻמְרֵי מָקוֹם שֶׁיָּצָא מִשָּׁם,

יד אברהם

1.

מָקוֹם שֶׁנָּהֲגוּ לַעֲשׂוֹת מְלָאכָה בְּעַרְבֵי פְּסָחִים עַד חֲצוֹת, עוֹשִׂין; — *Where* [lit *A place*] *it is customary to do work on the eve of Pesach until midday, we may do* [*work*],

Abstention from labor before noon is only a custom, and is permitted where this custom was not adopted; after midday, however, labor is prohibited categorically. *Yerushalmi* (4:1) explains: It is not proper that a person go about his work while his Pesach offering is being sacrificed (i.e. after midday[11]). The day one offers sacrifice is regarded as a personal festival and labor is to be avoided (see *Hil. K'lei HaMikdash* 6:9 with *Mishneh LaMelech*). *Tosafos* (50a, s.v. מקום) holds that the prohibition is Scriptural, based on *Yerushalmi's* reason. However most authorities (*Rav, Ritva, Meiri*) hold it to be of Rabbinic origin. *Rambam*, too, (*Hil. Yom Tov* 8:18) rules that the Sages

forbade work on Pesach eve after midday although he states that abstention from labor on the day of sacrifice is nothing more than a custom (*Hil. Klei Hamikdash* 6:9) indicating that he does not rule like *Yerushalmi*.

According to *Yerushalmi's* reason, it would follow that nowadays, in the absence of the Pesach sacrifice, the prohibition does not apply (*Ba'al HaMaor*).

In fact, however, the halachah is that the prohibition remains in effect even when there is no Pesach offering (*Milchamos, Ravad, Hil. Yom Tov* 8:18 and others; *Orach Chaim* 468:1). *Yerushalmi* offers only one aspect of the impropriety of working past midday. The same reasoning applies contemporaneously too. One should not go about his personal business while there is much to do in anticipation of Passover, more so than for any other festival (*Ravad; Milchamos; Meiri*).[2]

In addition, since the restriction against labor was decreed by a convocation of Sages,

1. Many authorities (*Maggid Mishneh* to *Hil. Yom Tov* 8:18, *Ritva, R' David*) infer that in *Rashi's* view (50a, s.v. שלא לעשות) the prohibition after midday was instituted so that people would not forget to observe and prepare for the *mitzvos* of the day and evening. It may be, however, that *Rashi* refers only to the reason for the custom not to work even before midday, and not to the prohibition after midday (see *Meiri* and *Tzlach*).

See below that according to many authorities, *Rashi's* reason (that one not be distracted from making preparations) is indeed a contributory factor to the prohibition, even according to *Yerushalmi*.

2. As if to anticipate the objection that the Succos festival, too, requires extensive preparation (see *Maggid Mishneh, Hil. Yom Tov* 8:18), *Rashi* adds that Pesach is unique in that the *Gemara* (106a) exhorts us to begin the Seder as early as possible so that the children will be able to stay up. But on Succos, in the absence of a lengthy Seder requiring the participation of young children, many preparations may be done at night (see *Tos. Yom Tov*). There is however a Talmudic admonition not to work on every Sabbath and *Yom Tov* eve 'after *mincha*.' (According to some, this begins one half hour after midday, while others hold it to be

4
1

1. **W**here it is customary to do work on the eve of Pesach until midday, we may do [work], [but] where it is customary not to do [work], we may not do [work].

If one goes from where they do [work] to where they do not, or from where they do not to where they do, we lay upon him the stringencies of the place which he has left and the stringencies of the place to

YAD AVRAHAM

one would need another convocation of equal status to remove their prohibition (*Beitzah* 5a; *ibid.*).

A novel reason for this prohibition is advanced by *P'nei Yehoshua*. The Torah states (*Leviticus* 23:4); *These* (the following) *are the festivals* (מוֹעֲדֵי) *of HASHEM, holy convocations ...* (v. 5) *In the first month, on the fourteenth day of the month, in the afternoon is the Pesach* [offering] *for HASHEM*. The insertion of the fourteenth day among the festivals implies that the time of the Pesach sacrifice is also a 'festival', when at least some forms of work are prohibited.

This prohibition against labor, however, is not as stringent as that on the Yom Tov itself. In general it is similar to that in effect on *Chol HaMoed* (the Intermediate Days of the festival), but that it is milder in some respects (*Mishnah Berurah* 468:7).

מְקוֹם שֶׁנָּהֲגוּ שֶׁלֹּא לַעֲשׂוֹת, — [*but*] *where it is customary not to do* [*work*],

Such places instituted this custom as a precaution against forgetting to remove the *chometz*, sacrifice the Pesach offering, and bake the matzah (*Rav*,[1] *Rashi*).

In ancient days it was a universal custom to bake the matzos for the Seder on the eve of Pesach. This time-honored custom persists to this day in many (especially Chassidic) communities. Indeed many authorities maintain that one cannot fulfill his obligation of eating matzah at the Seder with matzos baked prior to midday. See *Tur Orach*

Chaim 498 with *Bais Yosef; Shulchan Aruch* there with *Beur HaGra* and *Pri Chadash*.

אֵין עוֹשִׂין. — *we may not do* [*work*].

In many of our communities it is the custom to do work (*Magen Avraham* 468:6; *Mishnah Berurah* sec. 12).

הַהוֹלֵךְ מִמְּקוֹם שֶׁעוֹשִׂין — *If one goes from where they do* [*work*]

[In his place of origin they work before midday.]

לִמְקוֹם שֶׁאֵין עוֹשִׂין, — *to where they do not,*

אוֹ מִמְּקוֹם שֶׁאֵין עוֹשִׂין לִמְקוֹם שֶׁעוֹשִׂין, — *or from where they do not to where they do,*

[Thus, a person who grew up with one custom finds himself in a place that observes a different custom. The question is, must one keep the customs of his home town even while he is not there?]

נוֹתְנִין עָלָיו חֻמְרֵי מָקוֹם שֶׁיָּצָא מִשָּׁם, — *we lay upon him the stringencies of the place which he has left*

[In the latter case, therefore, a person who originates in a place where work is not done must refrain from work even after his departure.]

[However if he has no intention of returning to his hometown, its customs are no longer binding on him (*Chullin* 18b; *Orach Chaim* 574:1; *Mishnah Berurah* 468:19).]

two and one half hours after midday.) According to *Rambam* (*Hil. Yom Tov* 8:17) this has the status of a prohibition (see *Gem.* 50b, *Orach Chaim* 251:1).

1. See note 1 to s.v. מקום שנהגו לעשות.

וְחֻמְרֵי מָקוֹם שֶׁהָלַךְ לְשָׁם. וְאַל יְשַׁנֶּה אָדָם,
מִפְּנֵי הַמַּחֲלֹקֶת.

[ב] **כַּיּוֹצֵא** בּוֹ, הַמּוֹלִיךְ פֵּרוֹת שְׁבִיעִית
מִמָּקוֹם שֶׁכָּלוּ לְמָקוֹם שֶׁלֹּא כָלוּ,

יד אברהם

וְחֻמְרֵי מָקוֹם שֶׁהָלַךְ לְשָׁם. — *and the stringencies of the place to which he has gone.*

[In the first case, therefore, one who has traveled to a place where work is not done is obligated to observe the customs of his new domicile.]

According to the consensus of authorities (see *Pri Chadash; Chok Ya'akov; Beur HaGra* and *Beur Halachah* to *Orach Chaim* 468:4) Here too, there is a distinction between a person who intends to remain in his new domicile and one who plans to return to his old home. In the former case, as a new permanent resident, he is intrinsically obligated to follow the customs of his newly adopted community — and he must keep them even when he is away temporarily. In the latter case, however, since he remains a citizen of his original home, his basic responsibility is to keep only the customs of his old hometown. However, he must keep the customs of his temporary abode as well 'lest it lead to conflict,' for a defiance of local custom would be considered a sign of contempt. In this case, therefore, he may work בַּמִּדְבָּר, (lit. *in the desert*) in forsaken areas outside of the perimeter (תְּחוּם) of the city, where he will not attract notice. He may not, however work at home even furtively (בְּצִנְעָא), because by its very nature work is hard to conceal (*Gem.* 51b-52a with *Tos., s.v.* ביישוב, *Ran* and others). Similarly, one who plans to return home may keep other customs secretively, as long as they will not cause conflict.

וְאַל יְשַׁנֶּה אָדָם, מִפְּנֵי הַמַּחֲלֹקֶת. — *But let no man deviate [from local custom], to avoid conflict.*

In its simple meaning, this clause seems to refer only to the case of one who went to a place where work is not done during the morning. Although the traveler's own custom allows him to work, he should not do so in order not to provoke conflict (*Gem.* 51b according to Abaye).

Rav, following Rava (*Gem.* 51b), comments that this clause refers (also) to the case of a non-worker who goes to a place where work *is* done. As the mishnah has just ruled, he must keep the 'restrictions of the place from which he has come,' even though this will contradict the more lenient custom of his present temporary domicile. The mishnah now explains that one must follow the prevailing custom only when doing so is necessary to avoid conflict; accordingly, for a stranger to perform labor in a non-working place would be a public demonstration of contempt for his neighbors. But for a non-working visitor to remain idle while his neighbors are working would antagonize no one — observers would assume simply that he has nothing to do. The rendition of the mishnah would be, *He who goes ... we lay upon him ... the restrictions of the place to which he has gone; although no man should deviate ...* Thus, our mishnah concludes by saying that the rule not to deviate applies only where a deviation would result in conflict.

2.

◄§ Sabbatical Year Produce and its Disposition

Just as the first six days of each week are designated for physical labor while the seventh day is the Sabbath, a day of rest (*Exodus* 20:8-11), so too are the first six years of each seven-year period designated for working the land while the seventh

which he has gone. But let no man behave deviate [from local custom], to avoid conflict.

2. **S**imilarly, one who transports crops of the Sabbatical year from a place where they have been exhausted to a place where they have not been

YAD AVRAHAM

year is Sabbath, a year of abstention from such work *(Leviticus 25:1-7)*. During that year — called שְׁבִיעִית *[Sheviis], seventh,* or שְׁמִיטָה *[Shemittah], release —* we are enjoined from cultivating and harvesting the fields, vineyards, and orchards of *Eretz Yisrael.*

Produce growing during the *Shemittah* year, either from seeds sown before the *Shemittah,* or from perennials, may be eaten. The סְפִיחִים, *aftergrowth,* i.e., the crops growing the seeds which fell inadvertently during the previous harvest and took root may, however, not be eaten; see *Pesachim* 51b; *Rambam, Hil. Shemittah* 4:2. However, as long as this permitted produce is growing, it must be maintained in a state of הֶפְקֵר *[hefker], abandonment,* accessible to all who wish to take it. Any display of ownership on the part of the farmer, such as fencing off the field or gathering large amounts of crops into his warehouse, is prohibited *(Rambam, Hil. Shemittah V'Yovel 4:24).* [See also ArtScroll *Shekalim* 2:2, s.v. *Shemittah.*]

Concerning produce of *Shemittah* (even if it was grown without cultivation; i.e., without transgressing the prohibition against field work) the Torah teaches: *And the Sabbath [produce] of the land shall be food for you ... and for your animals and for the beasts that are in your land (Leviticus 25:7).* From this the Sages *(Sifra* and *Rashi* loc. cit.; *Gem.* 52b) derive that 'only as long as the beasts can eat in the field, may you feed the animals in your house, [but] when there is no longer [food] available for the beasts in the field, you must make it unavailable for the animals in the house.'

The process of 'making the food unavailable' at home is called בִּיעוּר, lit. *disposal* or *removal.* There is disagreement as to the exact nature of this removal. *Rashi* (52b, s.v. משום שנאמר), *Rambam (Hil. Shemittah V'Yovel 7:3),* and *Ravad*[1] (loc. cit.) maintain that *removal* carries with it a prohibition against use by humans of the produce. *Tosafos* (52b, s.v. מתבערין) and *Ramban (Comm. to Torah, Lev. 25:7),* hold that it is sufficient merely that one *remove* the produce from his domicile and declare it *hefker* so that anyone can take it. That done, the former owner, as well, may take it for his own use, like anyone else. All agree that if the owner kept the produce and did not *remove* it, it may not be eaten.

כַּיּוֹצֵא בּוֹ, הַמּוֹלִיךְ פֵּרוֹת שְׁבִיעִית מִמָּקוֹם שֶׁכָּלוּ — *Similarly, one who transports crops of the Sabbatical year from a place where they have become exhausted*

This type of produce is no longer available for the beasts in the fields, and consequently the people of that area are obligated to remove it from their houses (Rav, Rashi).

לְמָקוֹם שֶׁלֹּא כָלוּ, — *to a place where they have not been exhausted,*

The traveler brought his produce to a place where there is still enough of this species in the fields for the beasts. Consequently the inhabitants of the new place still eat of the produce they had brought into their houses (Rav, Rashi).

1. *Ravad* maintains that the removal involves two stages. First when the supply of each particular kind of produce runs out in a town it must be removed from the houses and left ownerless for anyone to take; subsequently, when this supply runs out from the entire country, it may not be eaten at all and is buried.

פְּסָחִים אוֹ מִמָּקוֹם שֶׁלֹּא כָלוּ לְמָקוֹם שֶׁכָּלוּ, חַיָּב
ד/ג לְבַעֵר.
רַבִּי יְהוּדָה אוֹמֵר: אוֹמְרִים לוֹ, ,,צֵא וְהָבֵא
לָךְ אַף אַתָּה."

[ג] **מָקוֹם** שֶׁנָּהֲגוּ לִמְכֹּר בְּהֵמָה דַקָּה לְעוֹבֵד
כּוֹכָבִים, מוֹכְרִין; מָקוֹם שֶׁלֹּא נָהֲגוּ

יד אברהם

[As mentioned in the preface to this mishnah, the obligation of 'removal' goes into effect when a particular type of produce becomes exhausted in the fields. In this regard, *Eretz Yisrael* is divided into three parts, *Yehudah, Galil,* and Trans-Jordan (עֵבֶר לַיַּרְדֵּן: see *Gem.* 52b, *Shevi'is* 9:2). It is conceivable, therefore, that a certain type of produce may no longer be available in *Yehudah,* while it is still plentiful in the *Galil* so that 'removal' is not yet required there.]

אוֹ מִמָּקוֹם שֶׁלֹּא כָלוּ לְמָקוֹם שֶׁכָּלוּ, חַיָּב לְבַעֵר. — *or from a place where they have not been exhausted to a place where they have been exhausted, is required to remove [them].*

He is required to comply with the restrictions of both the place he left and the place to which he has come (*Rav, Rashi*).

It appears from *Rav* and *Rashi* (see also 52a, s.v. איפוך) that in the latter case, where supplies are exhausted in his present domicile, the requirement to 'remove' is based on two reasons: to conform with custom and to comply with the *mitzvah* of removal. In regard to this *mitzvah*, the determining factor is not the origin of the produce, but its whereabouts at the time of removal. In the mishnah's first case, where

supplies are exhausted only in the place of origin, the Scriptural *mitzvah* of 'removal' does not yet apply because supplies are still abundant where the produce is *now* located. Removal is mandated only because of the law requiring conformity with the custom in a person's place of origin. There, removal is required because supplies are not available, so that a citizen of that place is bound to comply wherever he is (see *Teshuvos Avnei Nezer, Orach Chaim* 124:19-26).

In summary, the Scriptural *mitzvah* of removal depends only on the whereabouts of the produce, but the place of origin must also be considered because of the obligation to maintain the custom of one's native place. (Consequently, if the place of origin was inhabited solely by Gentiles this would not apply.) However, if the obligation had already been in effect when the produce was moved to a different area, this cannot obviate the Scriptural obligation (*Chazon Ish, Shevi'is* 13:2; *op. cit. Orach Chaim* 124).

Maharam Chalavah remarks that in spite of the mishnah's comparison of produce to work on the eve of Pesach, the wording of the mishnah itself suggests that not all cases of produce are the same. The mishnah refers only to someone who travels with his produce, but someone who travels from a place where supplies are gone may surely eat any produce in his temporary abode — here the deciding factor is the produce, not the person.

⊷§ **Mixtures of Produce**

Ordinarily, if two or more different types of produce are mixed together, it would be possible to separate the one that required removal. Thus, if one had a barrel filled with corn, oranges, and apples, and the supply of oranges in the field became exhausted, he would simply remove his oranges from the barrel and be left with corn and apples. However, what if someone had three different species that were pickled or marinated together? Each type of produce had absorbed the taste of the other two. If one requires removal, may he eat the other two?

4
3

exhausted, or from a place where they have not been exhausted to a place where they have been exhausted, is required to remove [them].

R' Yehudah says: We say to him, "Go out and bring for yourself."

3. Where it is customary to sell small livestock to Gentiles, we may sell; where it is customary

YAD AVRAHAM

This is the subject of a tannaitic dispute in *Shevi'is* 9:5. R' Eliezer rules that if one species requires removal, all three must be made הֶפְקֵר, *ownerless*, because the other two contain the taste of the forbidden one. R' Yehoshua holds that all three *may* still be eaten, because he derives exegetically that only if *no part* of a food is still in the fields must it be removed. In our case, however, all three foods contain the taste of species that are still available, therefore none need be removed. Rabban Gamliel rules that each species is treated separately; we remove only the one whose supply has been exhausted, without regard to any of its taste that the others may have absorbed. In our mishnah, the first tanna is presumed to agree with R' Yehoshua's lenient view that a combination of pickled or marinated species is treated as a unit and that the mixture may be eaten despite the unavailability of one species. This ruling is inferred from the tanna's use of the plural from כָּלוּ, **they have been exhausted**, indicating that only if *all* of them are affected must removal be made.

Our mishnah now introduces the view of R' Yehudah who will agree with Rabban Gamliel, that the three foods are treated individually. *Shevi'is* 9:5 states that the halachah follows Rabban Gamliel; accordingly, it will follow R' Yehudah in our mishnah.

רַבִּי יְהוּדָה אוֹמֵר: אוֹמְרִים לוֹ, ,,צֵא וְהָבֵא לְךָ אַף אַתָּה״. — *R' Yehudah says: We say to him, 'Go out and bring for yourself'* We tell the owner of a barrel filled with three marinated species, one of which requires removal, 'Go out and see if you can find supplies of the one species in question.' In effect, R' Yehudah is saying that we are not concerned with the taste of the other two species. Since one of the three is no longer to be found, that variety must be removed, but the other two may still be retained. This ruling follows Rabban Gamliel as noted above, and is halachically adopted (*Rav*, based on Rav Ashi, *Gem.* 52a).

3.

Although the general principle obligating compliance with local custom has already been stated, the mishnah now lists a few examples, for not every popular usage is entitled to the status of an obligatory custom. The Sages felt that many customs were sufficiently rooted in reason to be incumbent upon everyone. The *Yerushalmi* (4:1; cited by *Tos.* 51b s.v. העושה, *Tur Orach Chaim* 299 and *Magen Avraham* there sec. 15) says concerning women who are accustomed not to do work on the night following the Sabbath — this is not a [legitimate] custom; [but not to work] until the end of the [*Ma'ariv*] prayer is a custom. *Yerushalmi* lists many other examples of such customs.

פְּסָחִים לִמְכּוֹר, אֵין מוֹכְרִין; וּבְכָל מָקוֹם אֵין מוֹכְרִין
ד/ד לָהֶם בְּהֵמָה גַסָּה, עֲגָלִים וּסְיָחִים, שְׁלֵמִין
וּשְׁבוּרִין.
רַבִּי יְהוּדָה מַתִּיר בִּשְׁבוּרָה.
בֶּן בְּתֵירָא מַתִּיר בְּסוּס.

[ד] **מָקוֹם** שֶׁנָּהֲגוּ לֶאֱכוֹל צָלִי בְּלֵילֵי פְסָחִים,
אוֹכְלִין; מָקוֹם שֶׁנָּהֲגוּ שֶׁלֹּא
לֶאֱכוֹל, אֵין אוֹכְלִין.

יד אברהם

מָקוֹם שֶׁנָּהֲגוּ לִמְכּוֹר בְּהֵמָה דַקָּה לְעוֹבֵד
כּוֹכָבִים, מוֹכְרִין; — *Where it is customay
to sell small livestock to Gentiles, we
may sell;*

[E.g., sheep, goats, etc. As stated further in the mishnah, the Sages prohibited the sale of large livestock to Gentiles.]

מָקוֹם שֶׁלֹּא נָהֲגוּ לִמְכּוֹר, אֵין מוֹכְרִין; —
*where it is customary not to sell, we
may not sell;*

Some towns instituted the practice
not to sell small livestock as a preven-
tive measure against selling large
animals (*Rav, Rashi*).

וּבְכָל מָקוֹם אֵין מוֹכְרִין לָהֶם בְּהֵמָה גַסָּה,
*but in all places we may not sell them
[Gentiles] large livestock,*

We are concerned that if selling were
allowed, a Jew may also rent or lend it to
a Gentile who will in turn work with the
animal on the Sabbath, thereby depriv-
ing it of rest on the Sabbath. The Torah
commands (*Exodus* 23:12) that an
animal owned by a Jew may not be
worked with on the Sabbath. Although
the animal has been leased or loaned, it
is still the Jew's animal (שְׂכִירוּת לֹא
קַנְיָא), and he is obligated not to allow it
to work on the Sabbath.

There is yet another reason for its
restriction. If such transactions were
permitted, a Jew might sell an ox on Friday just before sundown. The buyer
might then ask him to demonstrate the
animal's capacity to function when

laden. When the animal responds to the
Jew's prodding, he will have violated
the prohibition against causing an
animal to work on the Sabbath
[מְחַמֵּר] (*Rav*, based on *Avodah Zarah*
14b).

עֲגָלִים וּסְיָחִים, שְׁלֵמִין וּשְׁבוּרִין. — *calves or
foals, healthy* [lit. *whole*] *or maimed.*

Although young animals are not fit to
perform labor, and as such should not
fall under the prohibition of selling
large livestock, permission to sell them
could lead to the sale of large ones as
well. People would not realize that the
halachah varies between different
animals of the same species. The same is
true of maimed animals (*Rav; Rashi*).

ר׳ יְהוּדָה מַתִּיר בִּשְׁבוּרָה. — *R' Yehudah
permits* [selling] *in the case of a maimed
one.*

In contrast to calves or foals, maimed
animals will never be able to work, setting them apart from healthy animals;
they may therefore be sold. R' Yehudah
concurs with the first tanna's prohibition regarding calves and foals (*Rav*).

בֶּן בְּתֵירָא מַתִּיר בְּסוּס. — *Ben Beseira permits* [selling] *in the case of a horse.*

The mishnah refers to a riding horse,
which does no work when it is not
mounted by a person. In the case of
human beings being borne on the Sab-
bath, the rule is חַי נוֹשֵׂא אֶת עַצְמוֹ, *a living person carries himself* (*Shabbos
94a*), meaning that since live weight is

4
4

not to sell, we may not sell; but in all places we may not sell them large livestock, calves or foals, healthy or maimed.

R' Yehudah permits [selling] in the case of a maimed one.

Ben Beseira permits [selling] in the case of a horse.

4. Where it is customary to eat roast [meat] on the nights of Pesach, we may eat [it]; where it is customary not to eat [roast], we may not eat [it].

YAD AVRAHAM

easier to carry than dead weight, it is as if the bearer is not carrying the entire person. Such carrying is not similar to the sort done in the Tabernacle and, accordingly, is not in the category of Scripturally forbidden labor (*Rav; Rashi* see *Tos. Shabbos* 94a, s.v. שהחי, *Aruch HaShulchan, Orach Chaim* 301:34).

[According to this interpretation, the first tanna disagrees, because he feels that people will not grasp the distinction between horses and other animals, just as calves may not be sold for this reason. The *Talmud (Shabbos* 94a) concludes, that all agree that carrying humans is not Scripturally forbidden (*Tos. Yom Tov;* see *Tos., Shabbos* 94a, s.v. בסוס and *Avodah Zarah* 13b s.v. ובן).]

Rambam (also *Tos., Avodah Zarah* 13b, s.v. ובן) maintains, that the first tanna also allows the sale of a horse intended for riding.

The disagreement with Ben Beseira involves only a horse used to carry burdens (e.g., a horse used in hunting, which will be loaded with living animals that have been caught; see *Shabbos* 94a). The first tanna disallows the sale of such a horse on the premise that, unlike humans, animals bear down on the one carrying them; accordingly they are not in the category of living things that 'carry themselves' and it would be Scripturally forbidden to load them on a horse on the Sabbath. Ben Beseira holds that there is no fear that a hunting horse will be worked (in Scriptural terms) on the Sabbath.

The halachah does not follow Ben Beseira (*Rav; Rambam;* see *Hil. Shabbas* 20:4; cf. *Maggid Mishneh* there and *Tos. Yom Tov*).

Nowadays, however, the custom is to sell all kinds of animals to non-Jews. Various reasons for this are given by the *Poskim.* See *Yoreh Deah* 151:4.

4.

מָקוֹם שֶׁנָּהֲגוּ לֶאֱכוֹל צָלִי בְּלֵילֵי פְּסָחִים, אוֹכְלִין — *Where it is customary to eat roast [meat] on the night of Pesach, we may eat [it];*

[The Torah requires that the Pesach offering, eaten on the first night of Pesach, be roasted (*Exodus* 12:8). Some communities, therefore, instituted the custom not to eat any roast meat at the Seder meal, lest it be thought that the Pesach offering may be eaten outside of Jerusalem. However, this custom never attained the status of Rabbinic law binding upon everyone. *Sefer HaMichtam* explains that these places not only permitted roast meat to be eaten, but have a custom to *eat* roast meat in commemoration of the Pesach.

However meat used for the Seder may not be roasted in a manner resembling the offering, which was roasted as a whole, together with its entrails and legs. Todos of Rome accustomed the Roman Jews to eat goats roasted whole on the night of Passover. Thereupon the Sages sent him a message; 'If you were not Todos we would proclaim a ban upon you ...' (*Gem.* 53a see *Mishnah Berurah* 469:5).

מָקוֹם שֶׁנָּהֲגוּ שֶׁלֹּא לֶאֱכוֹל, אֵין אוֹכְלִין. — *where it is customary not to eat [roast], we may not eat [it].*

For it appears as if one were eating the Pesach sacrifice outside Jerusalem.

In Ashkenazic communities it is

מְקוֹם שֶׁנָּהֲגוּ לְהַדְלִיק אֶת הַנֵּר בְּלֵילֵי יוֹם הַכִּפּוּרִים, מַדְלִיקִין; מְקוֹם שֶׁנָּהֲגוּ שֶׁלֹּא לְהַדְלִיק, אֵין מַדְלִיקִין. וּמַדְלִיקִין בְּבָתֵּי כְנֵסִיּוֹת וּבְבָתֵּי מִדְרָשׁוֹת וּבִמְבוֹאוֹת הָאֲפֵלִים וְעַל גַּבֵּי הַחוֹלִים.

[ה] **מָקוֹם** שֶׁנָּהֲגוּ לַעֲשׂוֹת מְלָאכָה בְּתִשְׁעָה בְּאָב, עוֹשִׂין; מְקוֹם שֶׁנָּהֲגוּ שֶׁלֹּא לַעֲשׂוֹת מְלָאכָה, אֵין עוֹשִׂין; וּבְכָל מָקוֹם תַּלְמִידֵי חֲכָמִים בְּטֵלִים. רַבָּן שִׁמְעוֹן בֶּן גַּמְלִיאֵל אוֹמֵר: לְעוֹלָם יַעֲשֶׂה אָדָם עַצְמוֹ תַּלְמִיד חָכָם. וַחֲכָמִים אוֹמְרִים: בִּיהוּדָה הָיוּ עוֹשִׂין

יד אברהם

customary not to eat roast meat on Pesach eve (*Mishnah Berurah* 476:1 based on *Levush* and others).

מְקוֹם שֶׁנָּהֲגוּ לְהַדְלִיק אֶת הַנֵּר בְּלֵילֵי יוֹם הַכִּפּוּרִים, מַדְלִיקִין; — *Where it is customary to light [lamps] on the nights of Yom Kippur, we may light [them];*

Although lamps must be lit in Jewish homes on every Sabbath and festival, Yom Kippur is an exception. The reason for this is because one of the acts prohibited on Yom Kippur is cohabitation (*Yoma* 8:1), and it was feared that if a husband and wife could see one another they might feel a desire to cohabit. As a different safeguard against this occurring, some communities instituted that lamps *should* be lit in the homes, even in the bedrooms, on the assumption that people would thereby be discouraged from cohabitation, which is forbidden in an illuminated place [see *Niddah* 17a] (*Rav* from *Gem* 53b).

מְקוֹם שֶׁנָּהֲגוּ שֶׁלֹּא לְהַדְלִיק, אֵין מַדְלִיקִין. — *where it is customary not to light*

[them], *we may not light [them].*

These communities felt that the absence of lamps would serve better as a deterrent, for husbands would not see their wives (*ibid.*)

Wherever lamps are lit in the home, they must be lit in the bedroom too. This differs from the Sabbath and festival lamps (*Orach Chaim* 610:1, *Mishnah Berurah* sec. 4-5). The custom in Ashkenazic communities is to light lamps in the home on Yom Kippur (*Orach Chaim* 610:2).

וּמַדְלִיקִין בְּבָתֵּי כְנֵסִיּוֹת וּבְבָתֵּי מִדְרָשׁוֹת וּבִמְבוֹאוֹת הָאֲפֵלִים וְעַל גַּבֵּי הַחוֹלִים. — *But [in all places] we light [lamps] in synagogues, houses of study, dark alleys, and for the sick.*

For it is a mitzvah[1] to light lamps in honor of the festival and where the need for illumination exists, provided the apprehension noted above does not exist (*Tif. Yis.*).

The *Gemara* (53b) comments on the diverse customs regarding the kindling of lamps in the home, '*Your people are all righteous, they shall inherit the land forever*' (*Isaiah* 60:21). Whether they main-

1. *R' Eliezer Azkari* (cited in *Meleches Shlomo*) maintains that even in synagogues there is no mitzvah.

4
5

Where it is customary to light [lamps] on the
nights of Yom Kippur, we may light [them]; where it
is customary not to light [them], we may not light
[them]. But [in all places] we light [lamps] in synagogues, houses of study, dark alleys, and for the
sick.

5. Where it is customary to do work on the Ninth
of Av, we may do [it]; where it is customary
not to do work, we may not do [it]; but in all places
scholars are idle. Rabban Shimon Ben Gamliel says:
A man should always adopt the behavior of a scholar.
But the Sages say: In Judea they used to do work

YAD AVRAHAM

tained that we should light lamps or they
contended that we should not light them,

both were intended for the same purpose, i.e.
to preserve the sanctity of the holy day (53b).

5.

מְקוֹם שֶׁנָּהֲגוּ לַעֲשׂוֹת מְלָאכָה בְּתִשְׁעָה בְּאָב,
עוֹשִׂין; — *Where it is customary to do
work on the Ninth of Av, we may do*
[it];

The Ninth of Av (Tishah B'Av) is a
fast day commemorating the destruction of the Temple (see *Taanis* 4:6),
therefore *Tishah B' Av* invokes an at-
mosphere of אֲבֵלוּת *mourning*. With
respect to labor, however, its laws differ
from those of mourning in that there is
no prohibition against work. The reason
is that it is אֲבֵלוּת יְשָׁנָה, *an ancient
mourning*, that does not carry with it
the extreme restrictions of a recent loss,
the tragedy having taken place many
centuries ago (*Meiri*).

מְקוֹם שֶׁנָּהֲגוּ שֶׁלֹּא לַעֲשׂוֹת מְלָאכָה, אֵין
עוֹשִׂין; — *where it is customary not to do
work, we may not do* [it];

In order not to forget for a moment
the grief represented by this day (*Tif.
Yis.*).

וּבְכָל מָקוֹם תַּלְמִידֵי חֲכָמִים בְּטֵלִים. — *but in
all places scholars are idle.*

Scholars should feel the loss of the

Temple more than others (*Meiri*; cf.
Pnei Yehoshuah).

Alternatively, their abstention from
work is not so noticeable for they
refrain from work on many occasions
(*Bais Yosef, Orach Chaim* 554).

רַבָּן שִׁמְעוֹן בֶּן גַּמְלִיאֵל אוֹמֵר: לְעוֹלָם יַעֲשֶׂה
אָדָם עַצְמוֹ תַּלְמִיד חָכָם. — *Rabban Shimon
Ben Gamliel says: A man should always
adopt the behavior of* [lit. *make himself*]
a scholar.

Even an ordinary laymen should
refrain from work on the ninth of Av
without fear that he will appear to be
conceited. People will say that he is idle
because he has no work to do, not that
he considers himself to hold the rank of
scholar (*Rav; Rashi* from *Gem.* 55a).

But the first tanna maintains that if an ordinary person deports himself like a scholar
he gives the appearance of conceit (see *Gem.*
55a).

The halachah follows the first tanna
(*Rambam comm.* see *Hil. Taaniyos* 5:10 and
Tos. Yom Tov). However *Shulchan Aruch*
(*Orach Chaim* 554:22, based on R' Chananel
and *Tos., Berachos* 17b, s.v. רב שישא; see

מְלָאכָה בְּעַרְבֵי פְּסָחִים עַד חֲצוֹת, וּבַגָּלִיל לֹא הָיוּ עוֹשִׂין כָּל עִקָּר.

וְהַלַּיְלָה — בֵּית שַׁמַּאי אוֹסְרִין, וּבֵית הִלֵּל מַתִּירִין עַד הָנֵץ הַחַמָּה.

[ו] **רַבִּי** מֵאִיר אוֹמֵר: כָּל מְלָאכָה שֶׁהִתְחִיל בָּה קֹדֶם לְאַרְבָּעָה עָשָׂר, גּוֹמְרָהּ בְּאַרְבָּעָה עָשָׂר; אֲבָל לֹא יַתְחִיל בָּהּ בַּתְּחִלָּה בְּאַרְבָּעָה עָשָׂר, אַף עַל פִּי שֶׁיָּכוֹל לְגוֹמְרָהּ.

יד אברהם

Beis Yosef) rules that one may make himself a scholar. *Rama* adds that it is the Ashkenazic custom to refrain from work until noon on *Tishah B'Av.*

וַחֲכָמִים אוֹמְרִים: בִּיהוּדָה הָיוּ עוֹשִׂין מְלָאכָה בְּעַרְבֵי פְּסָחִים עַד חֲצוֹת, וּבַגָּלִיל לֹא הָיוּ עוֹשִׂין כָּל עִקָּר. — *But the Sages say: In Judea they used to work on the eve of Pesach until midday, while in Galilee they did no [work] at all.*

The mishnah now refers back to mishnah 1, which had described the abstention from work on the morning of the fourteenth of Nissan as a matter of custom, not halachah. That, however, is the opinion only of R' Meir (see *Gem.* 55a). Since the mishnah had set forth his view that it was a matter of custom, our chapter went on to list many other customs (see *Meleches Shlomo*). Our mishnah now informs us that the Sages (R' Yehudah) disagree. They hold that the status of Pesach eve was a matter of halachic dispute, not popular custom. The Sages of Judea rule that work was permitted, while the Sages in Galilee ruled that it is forbidden (*Rav* based on *Gem.* 55a).

However *Rambam* (*Comm.*) understands that the Sages of our mishnah concur with R' Meir that abstention from work is a custom; they merely listed the customs practiced in specific areas. In *Rambam's* view, only Beis Shammai's ruling later in the mishnah disagrees with R' Meir (see *Shoshanim l'David*).

The distinction between custom and law is illustrated in a situation where one left a place where work was forbidden and settled in a community where work is permitted. If the original prohibition was only a custom, becoming a member of the new community will remove the restriction. If, however, the prohibition was a halachic one, then it remains in effect (*Meiri; R' Yehonasan* cited by *Sefer HaMichtam*; see also *She'elos UTeshuvos Maharam al-Askar* and *Knesses HaGedolah* 496).

וְהַלַּיְלָה — בֵּית שַׁמַּאי אוֹסְרִין, — [*As for*] *the night, Beis Shammai forbid* [*work*],

[This passage continues the view presented by the Sages according to which the Galileans forbade work halachically on the morning of the fourteenth. The mishnah now discusses the status of the night preceding the fourteenth of Nissan, according to the Galileans.]

Beis Shammai forbade work on the evening preceding the fourteenth, similar to the festivals, when work is restricted from evening (*Rav*).

וּבֵית הִלֵּל מַתִּירִין עַד הָנֵץ הַחַמָּה. — *while Beis Hillel permit it until sunrise*

Beis Hillel compare the prohibition of work to that of eating on fast days,

4
6

on the eve of Pesach until midday, while in Galilee
they did no [work] at all.

[As for] the night, Beis Shammai forbid [work],
while Beis Hillel permit it until sunrise.

6. **R′** Meir says: Any work which one began
before the fourteenth, he may finish on the
fourteenth; but he may not begin it initially on the
fourteenth, even if he can finish it [before midday].

YAD AVRAHAM

when only the day is included,[1] not the
evening before (Rav; cf. Gem. 2b).

According to Yerushalmi (see commentary
to 4:1), the Galileans forbade work because
of the Pesach sacrifice, which is a form of
atonement. Fasting, too, is an act of expia-
tion. Therefore, it is logical that the day of
the Pesach sacrifice should have the laws of a

fast, because fasting and sacrifice are more
similar to one another than are festival
(which begins from the preceding night) and
sacrifice (Tos. Yom Tov).

Tosafos (2b, s.v. רבי) explains that sunrise
was chosen as the starting time for this
prohibition, for it is then that laborers leave
their homes for work.

6.

רַבִּי מֵאִיר אוֹמֵר: כָּל מְלָאכָה שֶׁהִתְחִיל בָּה
— קֹדֶם לְאַרְבָּעָה עָשָׂר, גּוֹמְרָהּ בְּאַרְבָּעָה עָשָׂר;
R′ Meir says: Any work which one be-
gan before the fourteenth [of Nissan], he
may finish on the fourteenth;

Even in places where it is customary
not to work before midday, it is permitted to complete tasks begun earlier,
provided the work is being done for the
sake of the festival. In the case of work
not related to the festival, it may be
done in the morning of the fourteenth
only if it is local custom to work (Rav
from Gem. 55a; Rashi 55b, s.v. גומרה).

אֲבָל לֹא יַתְחִיל בָּהּ בַּתְּחִלָּה בְּאַרְבָּעָה עָשָׂר,
אַף עַל פִּי שֶׁיָּכוֹל לְגוֹמְרָהּ. — but he may
not begin it initially on the fourteenth,
even if he can finish it [before midday].

The mishnah refers to places where
the custom is to refrain from work on
the fourteenth. As a result, one must
not work then, unless he started before

the fourteenth and his labor is for the
holiday's sake. Barring these circumstances, one must refrain even from
minor labors that can be completed
before midday (Meiri).

The above opinion is based on Rashi's
(and Rav's) interpretation and held by most
authorities (Rosh; Ran; Ravad and others).

Rambam (Comm., and Hil. Yom Tov 8:19)
maintains that R′ Meir refers even to places
where it is customary to work in such places.
The halachah — not custom — places limits
on what is permitted. New work, even if
needed for the festival, may not be started,
and previously started work may not be completed unless it is needed for the festival. The
only matter subject to custom is the completion of works begun before the fourteenth
and needed for Yom Tov.

In Shulchan Aruch the halachah is in dispute, R′ Yosef Karo ruling like Rambam, but
Rama dissenting and deciding for the more
lenient view of Rashi. Rama testifies that
Ashkenazic custom follows his view.

1. Although dawn is the halachic beginning of the day (see Megillah 2:4), here, because only
a Rabbinic prohibition is involved, the Sages deferred the prohibition until sunrise (Meiri,
Nimukei Yossef; cf. Rashash and Yesh Seder LaMishnah here).

וַחֲכָמִים אוֹמְרִים: שָׁלשׁ אֻמָּנִיּוֹת עוֹשִׂין
מְלָאכָה בְּעַרְבֵי פְסָחִים עַד חֲצוֹת; וְאֵלּוּ הֵן:
הַחַיָּטִים, הַסַּפָּרִים וְהַכּוֹבְסִין.
רַבִּי יוֹסֵי בַּר יְהוּדָה אוֹמֵר: אַף הָרַצְעָנִים.

[ז] **מוֹשִׁיבִין** שׁוֹבְכִין לְתַרְנְגוֹלִים בְּאַרְבָּעָה
עָשָׂר. וְתַרְנְגֹלֶת שֶׁבָּרְחָה
מַחֲזִירִין אוֹתָהּ לִמְקוֹמָהּ; וְאִם מֵתָה, מוֹשִׁיבִין
אַחֶרֶת תַּחְתֶּיהָ.

יד אברהם

וַחֲכָמִים אוֹמְרִים: שָׁלשׁ אֻמָּנִיּוֹת עוֹשִׂין
מְלָאכָה בְּעַרְבֵי פְסָחִים עַד חֲצוֹת; — But the
Sages say: [Practioners of] three crafts
may work on the eve of Pesach until
midday;

The Sages add another dimension to
the performance of labor in places
refraining from work. R' Meir permitted only the completion of work begun
prior to the fourteenth. The Sages contend however, that three crafts are in a
special category, and such work may be
commenced on the eve of Pesach even in
places accustomed to refraining from
other work (Rav, see above, s.v. אבל לא
יתחיל).

The above interpretation is Rav's. According to Rambam (see above, s.v. אבל לא
יתחיל), the Sages, too, refer to places accustomed not to refrain from work. There,
too, it was prohibited to commence any work
on the fourteenth. The Sages maintain that
the three crafts mentioned here may even be
commenced on the fourteenth.

וְאֵלּוּ הֵן: הַחַיָּטִים, — (and) they are tailors,
They are permitted to work because
we find a particular leniency with
regard to tailoring during the
Intermediate Days [חוֹל הַמּוֹעֵד], i.e., a
layman (not a professional tailor) may
sew in the usual way on the Inter-

mediate Days. Therefore, on the fourteenth, which is less restrictive than
the Intermediate Days, we permit all
tailoring, even by a craftsman (Rav,
Gem. 55b).

הַסַּפָּרִים וְהַכּוֹבְסִין. — barbers and
launderers.

Here, too, the dispensation is based
on the Intermediate Days, because one
who returns from overseas, and one
who is released from prison may cut his
hair and wash his garments on the
Intermediate Days (ibid.).

The Talmud (Mo'ed Katan 13a) adds
that even these three crafts are permitted only when needed for the festival
(see Hil. Yom Tov 8:19 and Mishnah
Berurah 468:23-24).

רַבִּי יוֹסֵי בַּר יְהוּדָה אוֹמֵר: אַף הָרַצְעָנִים. — R'
Yose bar Yehudah says: Also
shoemakers.

Because of the festival, pilgrims (עוֹלֵי
רְגָלִים) were permitted to repair shoes on
the Intermediate Days (ibid.).

The Sages maintain that the analogy
is not a proper one. The pilgrims were
allowed only to repair their shoes, not to
make shoes (ibid.).

The halachah follows the Sages (Rav;
Rambam, Hil. Yom Tov 8:19; Orach Chaim
468:5).

7.

מוֹשִׁיבִין שׁוֹבְכִין לְתַרְנְגוֹלִים — We may set
up coops for chickens
The translation is based on Ram-

bam's interpretation (Hil. Yom Tov
8:21; see Magid Mishneh).

Rashi's view is that the word שׁוֹבְכִין refers

4
7
But the Sages say: [Practitioners of] three crafts may work on the eve of Pesach until midday; they are tailors, barbers and launderers.

R' Yose bar Yehudah says: Also shoemakers.

7. **W**e may set up coops for chickens on the fourteenth.

If a [brooding] hen escaped, we may return her to her place; if she died, we may set another in her stead.

YAD AVRAHAM

to the eggs which are placed under the hens for brooding. Another opinion noted by *Rashi* is based on a version of the mishnah which reads: מוֹשִׁיבִין שׁוֹבָכִין וְתַרְנְגוֹלִים, 'we *may set up coops* [for doves] *and* [we may set up] *chicken coops*, i.e. hens [to brood]. *Rashi* remarks that the word שׁוֹבָךְ is customarily used in the Mishnah to refer to dove cotes (see *Beitzah* 1:3).

בְּאַרְבָּעָה עָשָׂר. — *on the fourteenth.*

According to some authorities this may be done all day (*Tur Orach Chaim* 468, *Tos. Yom Tov, Mishnah Berurah* 468:33; cf. *Meiri*) because this is not considered forbidden labor. Others maintain that the leniency concerning setting the coops extends only till midday. However it is permitted even where work is refrained from (*Meiri*).

וְתַרְנְגֹלֶת שֶׁבָּרְחָה מַחֲזִירִין אוֹתָהּ לִמְקוֹמָהּ; — *If a [brooding] hen escaped, we may return her to her place;*

This passage refers to the Intermediate Days, not the fourteenth. If a brooding hen left her fertilized eggs after sitting on them for three days, the embryo had started to form and the eggs are no longer fit for eating and can only be used for hatching. The hen may be returned to her place even in the Intermediate Days because the eggs would be a total loss [דָּבָר הָאָבֵד] otherwise. As the *Gemara* 55b argues, it is obvious that

this would be permitted on the fourteenth, inasmuch as one may even *set* the fowl for brooding,[1] can there even be a doubt that it is permitted to put her back?

According to *Rambam*, the mishnah never says that one may initially 'set' hens to brood on the fourteenth; indeed this is prohibited (in accordance with *Rambam's* view that most work is prohibited halachically). A hen may only be *returned* to brood, or if a brooding hen died another may be set in her place (see below).

Another condition for this dispensation is set by the *Gemara* 55b. Only if it is within three days of her flight from the eggs, so that her heat (i.e., the desire to brood) has not yet left her, may she be returned to the eggs. But if three days have elapsed since her 'rebellion' and she is no longer in heat [so that it is very difficult to get her to brood again (*Rashi*)], we may not put her back. *Vilna Gaon* (glosses to *Gem.* 55b) maintains that *Rif's* version did not include this condition (however see *R' Chananel* whose version is like ours). *Rambam* (*Hil. Yom Tov* 8:21) also omits this last condition (see *Kessef Mishneh; Beur HaGra* to *Orach Chaim* 468:16).

וְאִם מֵתָה, מוֹשִׁיבִין אַחֶרֶת תַּחְתֶּיהָ. — *if she died, we may set another in her stead.*

We may set another in her place since the eggs are already in the stage when they are good only for hatching (*Rav*).

1. The above is *Rashi's* construction of the *Gemara's* query. According to *Rambam*, the mishnah says that one may not initially 'set' a hen to brood on the fourteenth, but if she died 'he may set another in her place.' The *Gemara* argues 'if one may set another hen to replace the missing one, then surely the same hen may be returned to her place.'

גּוֹרְפִין מִתַּחַת רַגְלֵי בְהֵמָה בְּאַרְבָּעָה עָשָׂר,
וּבַמּוֹעֵד מְסַלְּקִין לַצְּדָדִין. מוֹלִיכִין וּמְבִיאִין כֵּלִים מִבֵּית הָאֻמָּן, אַף עַל
פִּי שֶׁאֵינָם לְצֹרֶךְ הַמּוֹעֵד.

[ח] **שִׁשָּׁה** דְבָרִים עָשׂוּ אַנְשֵׁי יְרִיחוֹ, עַל
שְׁלֹשָׁה מִחוּ בְיָדָם, וְעַל שְׁלֹשָׁה
לֹא מִחוּ בְיָדָם. וְאֵלּוּ הֵן שֶׁלֹּא מִחוּ בְיָדָם:
מַרְכִּיבִין דְּקָלִים כָּל הַיּוֹם; וְכוֹרְכִין אֶת שְׁמַע;

יד אברהם

Here, too, a new hen may be 'set' only if the eggs have already been sat upon at least three days, thereby spoiling them for consumption (*Rambam, Hil. Yom Tov* 8:21; *Orach Chaim* 468:7).

In this passage, the mishnah reverts to the general theme of this chapter — the day before Pesach. In the Intermediate Days this is prohibited[1] (*Rambam* loc. cit.; *Tur Orach Chaim* 536, see *Bais Yosef* there).

It is much harder to 'set' a hen on a brood that is not hers, than to return a hen to her own eggs. Because of the extra effort involved, this is prohibited on the Intermediate Days even though failure to do so will result in a loss (*Bais Yosef; Tos. Yom Tov*).

Meiri understands this dispensation of the mishnah to refer even to the Intermediate Days (see also authorities cited in *Beur Halachah* to 536:4).

גּוֹרְפִין מִתַּחַת רַגְלֵי בְהֵמָה בְּאַרְבָּעָה עָשָׂר, — **We may sweep away from under an animal's feet on the fourteenth,**

I.e., one may sweep dung aside and throw it away (*Rav; Rashi*).

Rambam (*Hil Yom Tov* 8:21), based on a baraisa (*Gem.* 55b), adds that one may take it out to the dungheap. This is permitted even after midday (*Meiri;* cf. above, s.v. בארבעה

עשר). The removal of dung is considered to be in preparation for the festival and is therefore permitted (*Meleches Shlomo*).

וּבַמּוֹעֵד מְסַלְּקִין לַצְּדָדִין. — **but on the festival we may [only] clear it away to the sides [of the stall].**

But on the Intermediate Days, we may not throw it outside on the dung heap. The law of *Chol HaMoed* is stricter than that of Pesach eve (*Rav; Rashi*).

מוֹלִיכִין וּמְבִיאִין כֵּלִים מִבֵּית הָאֻמָּן, אַף עַל פִּי שֶׁאֵינָם לְצֹרֶךְ הַמּוֹעֵד. — **We may take [lit. transport] utensils to, and bring them [back] from, the house of a craftsman, even though they are not needed for the festival.**

This passage again refers to the fourteenth. One may bring utensils to a craftsman and bring them back even if they are not needed for the festival (*Rav* based on *Gem.* 55b).

On *Chol HaMoed* however, one may bring home only utensils needed for the festival. If he does not trust the craftsman he may remove the utensils from his premises to the nearest safe place (*Hil. Yom Tov* 8:16, 21; *Orach Chaim* 468:10, 534:3).

1. Various arguments are advanced to bolster this view. Among them are these: Wherever there is no evidence to the contrary, this mishnah should be understood in context as referring to the fourteenth of Nissan. According to those who permit even the mother hen to be returned only within three days of its rebellion (see above, s.v. מחזירין), a new hen should always be excluded (*Bais Yosef; Tos. Yom Tov*).

Although one may initially 'set' a hen on the fourteenth to brood (*Gem.* 55b) the mishnah singles out for explicit mention the case of only replacing a dead hen, for it is harder to set a new hen upon strange eggs that have already been sat upon than to set one initially upon eggs. If this is permitted, then we know that it surely is permitted to set a hen initially (*Meiri*).

We may sweep away from under an animal's feet on the fourteenth, but on the festival we may [only] clear it away to the sides [of the stall].

We may take utensils to, and bring them back from, the house of a craftsman, even though they are not needed for the festival.

8. The citizens of Jericho did six things. For three they have reproved them and for three they have not reproved them. And these are the things for which they have not reproved them: They graft palms all day [of the fourteenth of Nissan]; they 'wrap' the *Shema*; and they reap and stack prior to

YAD AVRAHAM

8.

שִׁשָּׁה דְבָרִים עָשׂוּ אַנְשֵׁי יְרִיחוֹ, עַל שְׁלֹשָׁה מְחוּ בְיָדָם, וְעַל שְׁלֹשָׁה לֹא מִחוּ בְיָדָם. — *The citizens of Jericho did six things. For three they [the Sages] have reproved them and for three they have not reproved them.*

Although the Sages found all six things objectionable, they reproved the people for only three of them (*Rav* from *Gem.* 56a).

וְאֵלוּ הֵן שֶׁלֹא מִחוּ בְיָדָם: מַרְכִּיבִין דְּקָלִים כָּל הַיּוֹם; — *And these are the things for which they have not reproved them: They graft palms all day [on the fourteenth of Nissan];*

They would graft a branch of a (male) palm tree that bore poor fruits onto a barren (female) palm. In this manner they grafted many branches, and subsequently, the whole female tree bore good fruit (*Meiri, Aruch* s.v. נסך cited by *Tos. Yom Tov*).

Rav and *Rashi* say grafting was necessary because the 'female' trees would otherwise be barren.

[Grafting within the same species is permitted.]

[According to all interpretations of *mishnayos* 6 and 7, their actions were reprehensible, for they would graft even on the afternoon, when work is surely prohibited. Ac-

cording to *Rambam's* opinion, (above mishnah 6) grafting, which is not needed for the festival, is prohibited on the morning of the fourteenth even if started on the thirteenth.] The season for this grafting operation is a limited one, and it comes in Nissan. If the grafting is not done in season it will not succeed. Because of the loss involved, the Sages did not reprove the men of Jericho (*Tos. Yom Tov*).

Tzlach remarks that the people of Jericho must have judged this to be in the category of 'loss' (דְּבַר הָאָבֵד; i.e., if not done there would be damage to the tree), which may surely be done on the eve of Pesach (see above, mishnah 7, s.v. ותרנגולת שברחה), whereas the Sages did not agree with their evaluation.

וְכוֹרְכִין אֶת שְׁמַע; — *they 'wrap' the Shema;*

[I.e., they recited the *Shema* without the appropriate pauses (see below) as if it were one bundle that requires no separations to make it intelligible.]

R' Yehudah (*Gem.* 56a) explains that they did not pause when reciting *Hear O Israel, HASHEM our God, HASHEM is One.* Instead of drawing out the word אֶחָד, *One,* so that they could meditate and accept God's sovereignty upon themselves, they said the word quickly and went further. *Tosafos* explains that they ran the entire verse together: In

פסחים וְקוֹצְרִין וְגוֹדְשִׁין לִפְנֵי הָעֹמֶר, וְלֹא מִחוּ בְיָדָם.
ד/ח וְאֵלוּ שֶׁמִּחוּ בְיָדָם: מַתִּירִין גַּמְזִיּוֹת שֶׁל
הֶקְדֵּשׁ; וְאוֹכְלִין מִתַּחַת הַנְּשָׁרִים בַּשַּׁבָּת;

יד אברהם

order for its meaning to be clear, one must pause after שְׁמַע יִשְׂרָאֵל, *Hear O Israel,* [which calls upon the Jewish People to heed what follows], and then make the statement about God's Oneness. The people of Jericho made no such pause. Without it, the verse would sound like a plea to God that He listen to Israel's requests.

Rava says that they made the proper pause in the first verse, but failed to pause in a later verse. They ran together the words [*Those matters that I command you*] *today, shall be on your heart.* Without a pause after *today,* the Hebrew words could be understood to mean that only *today* must *these matters* be upon your heart, but not tomorrow. R' Yehudah says they omitted 'Blessed be the Name of, His glorious kingdom for ever and ever.' [They omitted it because Moshe did not inscribe this verse in the Torah.

Therefore, the Sages did not rebuke them for the omission.][1]

[See *Orach Chaim* 61:2, 6, 13, 15 for the proper mode of reciting the *Shema* in regard to the points raised here.]

וְקוֹצְרִין וְגוֹדְשִׁין לִפְנֵי הָעֹמֶר. — *and they reap*[2] *and stack prior to the Omer,*

[Grain from the new crop may not be eaten until the *Omer* offering has been offered on the second day of Passover (*Leviticus* 23:9-14).] The Sages decreed that one may not pile the new crop in the fields before the 'Omer' as asafeguard against inadvertent eating of the grain while working with it (*Menachos* 10:8, 71a; see *Gem.* 11a). The people of Jericho disregarded this Rabbinic safeguard (*Rav*). However the Sages did not reprove them for this because no violation of a Scriptural

---

1. Our custom is to recite *Blessed be,* etc. quietly. The reason, as stated in the *Gem.* (56a) is: R' Shimon ben Lakish said (*Genesis* 49:2): *And Jacob called to his sons and said: Gather together that I may tell you that which shall befall you in the End of Days.* Jacob wished to reveal to his sons the *End of Days* (i.e., the coming of the Messiah; see *Daniel* 12:13) whereupon the Heavenly Presence (שְׁכִינָה) departed from him. Said he: 'Perhaps, Heaven forbid, there is someone unfit among my children, like Abraham from whom there issued Ishmael or like my father Isaac from whom there issued Esau.' But his sons answered him, 'Hear O Israel [i.e., Jacob], *HASHEM our God, HASHEM is One.* Just as there is only One in your heart so is there only One in ours. At that moment Yaakov exclaimed, 'Blessed be the Name of His glorious kingdom for ever and ever.' Said the Rabbis, what should we do [in reciting *Shema*]? Shall we recite the verse Blessed be the Name … ? But our teacher Moshe did not say it [in the Torah]. Shall we not say it? But Jacob said it. They, therefore, enacted that it be recited quietly.

2. *Rashi* feels that the word וְקוֹצְרִין *and reaped,* is a scribe's error and should be deleted. The mention of reaping among the things that the people of Jericho did and were not reproved for implies that reaping before the Omer is prohibited, but this contradicts the unanimous statement of the tannaim (*Gem.* 56a; cf. *Yerushalmi*) to the contrary. Indeed the Gemara (there) deletes the mention of *reaping* from the list of things that the people of Jericho did against the will of the Sages. There is a Torah-based prohibition against reaping (see *Menachos* 71a) of choice grain of the quality from which the Omer is brought, but the crops of Jericho did not qualify for this honor. There is also no apprehension that a reaper may eat while working because people are sufficiently accustomed to avoid (בְּדִילֵי מִינָהּ) the eating of new grain (*Gem.* 11a). It is only in regard to stacking where no loss is incurred by waiting until after the Omer, that the Sages felt precaution was necessary (see *Rashi* 56a s.v. וגודשין; *Tos* 11a s.v. אבל). However, all of our versions and also *Rambam's* (see ed. *Kafich*) retain this word. Perhaps because even with its inclusion the statement of the mishnah is true — no one was reproved for reaping. The point of the statement, however, is that they did not reprove them for stacking even though it was forbidden; for reaping, which is permitted, no reproof is conceivable (*Lechem Shamayim*).

4   the Omer, but they have not reproved them.

8   And these are the things for which they have reproved them. They permit the branches which were sacred property [for personal use]; they eat the fallen fruit from beneath [the tree] on the Sab-

YAD AVRAHAM

prohibition was involved, and the fear that one may eat the grain is remote (see *Rashi* 56a, s.v. קוצרין and גודשין).

וְלֹא מְחוּ בְיָדָם. — *but they have not reproved them* [for those three acts].

וְאֵלוּ שֶׁמְחוּ בְיָדָם: מַתִּירִין גַּמְזִיּוֹת שֶׁל הֶקְדֵּשׁ; — *And these are the things for which they have reproved them. They permit the branches*[1] *which were sacred property* [for personal use];

Ordinarily, one who uses הֶקְדֵּשׁ, *consecrated property*, commits the sin of *me'ilah* and is liable to bring a guilt offering, and to pay the Temple treasury the value of the items used, plus a fifth extra *(Leviticus 5:14-16)*.

The people of Jericho held, correctly, that *me'ilah* applies only to objects that had *themselves* been consecrated, but not branches that grew later. The Sages held that nevertheless there is a prohibition[2], albeit without the consequences prescribed for *me'ilah* *(Gem 56b)*.

The *Gemara* (57a; cf. *Tosefta* 3:18) relates the circumstances in which these branches had been consecrated. There were sycamore trees in the vicinity of Jericho that thieves made a practice of chopping down for their own use, upon which the owners consecrated the trees.

וְאוֹכְלִין מִתַּחַת הַנְּשָׁרִים בַּשַּׁבָּת; — *(and) they eat the fallen fruit from beneath [the tree]* [lit. *from beneath the shedders*] *on the Sabbath;*

They ate fallen fruit that had not been removed from beneath the trees prior to the Sabbath. Any fruit that fell from a tree *on* the Sabbath may not be eaten on that Sabbath. However if one is sure that the fruit fell down before the Sabbath, it may be eaten even though it was removed from beneath the tree before the Sabbath. The dispute between the people of Jericho and the Sages involved a case where it was not known if the fruit had fallen before or on the Sabbath. In Jericho, they held that in a case of doubt, the fruit is not prohibited in accordance with the rule that Rabbinic prohibitions do not apply to doubtful cases (סְפֵיקָא דְּרַבָּנָן לְקוּלָא), but the Sages disagreed and reproved them for this *(Rambam, Comm.*, based on *Yerushalmi*; see other interpretations in *Tos.* 56b, s.v. מחלוקת; *HaMaor, Milchamos* and others).

The prohibition against fallen fruit is based on two Rabbinic laws (see *Gem.* 56b): (a) A special prohibition instituted because of the fear that one may forget himself and climb the tree to tear off attached fruit, which

---

1. The translation is based on *Rashi, R' Chananel* and the alternative rendering given by *Rav*. However *R' Chananel's* rendering is based on a different reading in the mishnah (גְּנָזְאָא) as pointed out by *Aruch* (s.v. גמז), as is *Rav's* (מַתְזִיר; see there and *Tos. Yom Tov*). *Rashi,* however, does have the word גְּמְזִיּוֹת and renders it *branches*. *Aruch* maintains that גְּמְזִיּוֹת are the flowers growing around the roots of trees. According to this view perhaps the people of Jericho argued that only the trees, not the earth around them, had been consecrated. The Sages however maintained that in accordance with *Bava Basra* 5:4 (81a) when three trees are sold, land is assumed to have been sold with them. Nevertheless, the people of Jericho may have felt that in view of the circumstances surrounding the consecration of these trees (see *comm.*), and taking into consideration that only a Rabbinic prohibition was involved (see *Gem.* 56b), we need not assume that in this case that land had been given with the trees.

2. The apparent meaning is that this is a Rabbinic restriction. See *R' Menachem Ziemba* in *Zera Avraham* 11:25 and *R' Yosef Engel, Asvon D'Oraysa* 3.

וְנוֹתְנִין פֵּאָה לְיָרָק, וּמִחוּ בְיָדָם חֲכָמִים.

[ט] שִׁשָּׁה דְבָרִים עָשָׂה חִזְקִיָּה הַמֶּלֶךְ, עַל שְׁלשָׁה הוֹדוּ לוֹ, וְעַל שְׁלשָׁה לֹא הוֹדוּ לוֹ. גֵּרַר עַצְמוֹת אָבִיו עַל מִטָּה שֶׁל חֲבָלִים וְהוֹדוּ לוֹ. כִּתַּת נְחַשׁ הַנְּחֹשֶׁת וְהוֹדוּ לוֹ.

יד אברהם

is Scripturally forbidden. (b) The general prohibition against *muktzah* (any object not in a state of מוּכָן *preparation* for use on the Sabbath). Since the fruit was still attached to the tree at the outset of the Sabbath, it was not fit for Sabbath use and is *muktzah*. Both laws prohibit even doubtful objects (סָפֵק), as postulated by the Sages (see *Beitzah* 3:2 with *Comm.*; *Gem.* there 3b-4a, *Mishnah Berurah* 322:5).

The *Gemara* 56a cites a *baraisa* giving a different version. In hunger years, the people of Jericho made openings in the fences around their orchards to allow the poor to take fallen fruit on Sabbaths and festivals. *Mishnah Berurah* (ibid) points out that although some Rabbinic restrictions are relaxed in favor of the poor, this restriction was not.

וְנוֹתְנִין פֵּאָה לְיָרָק, וּמִחוּ בְיָדָם חֲכָמִים. — *and they give pe'ah from vegetables, and the Sages have reproved them.*

Vegetables are exempt from *pe'ah* [the produce in a corner of the field, which one must leave for the poor (see *Leviticus* 23:22)] because whatever is

not gathered for storage [i.e., foods that must be eaten fresh] is exempt from *pe'ah*[1] (*Pe'ah* 1:4). The pitfall in giving *pe'ah* where there is no obligation to do so, is that *pe'ah* is exempt from tithes, while ordinary gifts are not. Thus the poor who will eat these vegetables under the mistaken assumption that they are *pe'ah*, will inadvertently be eating untithed food (*Rav; Rashi*).

The *Gemara* 56b explains that the dispute evolved regarding leaves that were put in storage together with roots. The roots can be preserved for long periods of time but the leaves will not keep. The people of Jericho held that since the leaves are kept in storage together with the roots, they fall into the category of produce gathered for storage and are obligated to have *pe'ah* left from them, although only the roots, not the leaves, can be preserved (מַכְנִיסוֹ לְקִיּוּם עַל יְדֵי דָבָר אַחֵר). The Sages, however did not accept this distinction.

9.

In our editions of the Talmud this passage is not printed as a mishnah but as a *baraisa*. It has however been incorporated into the printed editions of the Mishnah and is found in some of the manuscript versions as well (see *Shinuyei Nuschaos*). Already in *Rambam's* time some Mishnah's had it in their text (see the early version of *Rambam's Comm.* cited in the notes of R' Yosef Kafich). *Rambam* comments: 'This halachah is a *tosefta*, but I chose to comment on it because of the benefit (to be derived from its teachings).' It is included in this chapter because like the previous mishnah, it describes six acts done without the prior consent of the Sages, three of which they approved and three of which they disapproved.

שִׁשָּׁה דְבָרִים עָשָׂה חִזְקִיָּה הַמֶּלֶךְ, עַל שְׁלשָׁה הוֹדוּ לוֹ, — *King Chizkiah [Hezekiah] did six things. Concerning* [lit. *in*] *three*

they [the Sages] *agreed with him* [lit. *admitted to him*],

Tiferes Yisrael notes a fine point of

---

1. R' *Chananel* (see also *Tos. R' Peretz*) contends that the people considered certain vegetables in the category of crops gathered for storage.

bath; and they give *pe'ah* from vegetables, and the Sages have reproved them.

9. King Chizkiah did six things. Concerning three they agreed with him, and concerning three they did not agree with him. He dragged the bones of his father on a bier of ropes, and they agreed with him. He crushed the brazen serpent, and they agreed

YAD AVRAHAM

phraseology. Mishnah 8 uses the expression 'they did not *reprove* them.' The Sages did not consider any of the six acts of the people of Jericho to be praiseworthy, some were merely not reprehensible enough for reproach. Here the Sages concurred with Chizkiah in three cases and accepted his decision as the correct and commendable course of action (*Masgeres HaZahav*).

וְעַל שְׁלֹשָׁה לֹא הוֹדוּ לוֹ. — *and concerning three they did not agree with him.*

They did not *reprove* him (as they did Jerichotes) for each of these actions was a one-time occurrence and once done could not be corrected (the verb מָחוּ used earlier has the connotation, *to impede*), whereas the actions of the Jerichotes were ongoing and the Sages hindered them (*Hon Ashir, Shoshanim L'David*[1]).

גֵּרַר עַצְמוֹת אָבִיו עַל מִטָּה שֶׁל חֲבָלִים וְהוֹדוּ לוֹ. — *He dragged the bones of his father on a bier of ropes, and they agreed with him.*

[About Chizkiah's father, Achaz, it is told *(II Kings* 16:2-3): *... and he did not do what is right in the eyes of HASHEM his God as* [did] *David his* [fore]*father. And he went in the ways of the kings of Israel* (i.e., the idolators of the Ten Tribes; see there v. 2-20 and *II Chronicles* 20).] In order to expiate his father's sins, and to sanctify 'the Name' by demonstrating the repulsiveness of his evil so that others take heed, King Chizkiah dishonored the bones of his

father. The affront here was twofold. Instead of a royally appointed bier, a lowly 'bed of ropes' was used. And instead of being borne upon the shoulders of a mourning populace, his own son dragged (or caused to be dragged) the bier to its place of interment (*Rav; Rashi* to *Gem.* 56a).

Meiri and *R' Yehonasan* understand the verb גֵּרַר, *he dragged*, in an allegorical manner. He did not give him a royal burial, but rather buried him in a manner fitting the lowliest person.

An allusion to the dishonor done to Achaz's body can be found in *II Chronicles* (28:27) where it is related about him: *For they did not bring him to the burial ground of the kings of Israel*, implying that because of his wickedness he was not accorded the burial fit for a king (see *Metzudos* there).

Rashi (*Sanhedrin* 47a) explains that Chizkiah was not obliged to honor his father since he was a wicked person (see *Bava Kama* 94b, *Rama* in *Yoreh Deah* 240:18).

R' Yaakov Emden (*Lechem Mishneh*) explains that the term 'bones' is not literal; it refers to the entire body, which is destined to be reduced to bone. [This approach obviates the difficulties raised by *Tos. Yom Tov* (see also *Kol HaRemez* and *Shoshanim L'David*).]

כִּתַּת נְחַשׁ הַנְּחֹשֶׁת וְהוֹדוּ לוֹ. — *He crushed the brazen serpent, and they agreed with him.*

The Torah relates (*Numbers* 21:4-9) that as punishment for one of Israel's

1. *Shoshanim L'David* refutes *Kol HaRemez*'s (also *Tif. Yis.*) assertion that the Sages did not reprove Chizkiah because of their 'fear of the royal office' (מֵאֵימַת הַמַּלְכוּת). Surely Chizkiah, who was a scholar and saint, would not punish the Sanhedrin for reproving him when he erred.

גָּנַז סֵפֶר רְפוּאוֹת וְהוֹדוּ לוֹ.
עַל שְׁלֹשָׁה לֹא הוֹדוּ לוֹ. קִצֵּץ דְּלָתוֹת שֶׁל
הֵיכָל וְשִׁגְּרָן לְמֶלֶךְ אַשּׁוּר וְלֹא הוֹדוּ לוֹ. סָתַם
מֵי גִיחוֹן הָעֶלְיוֹן וְלֹא הוֹדוּ לוֹ. עִבֵּר נִיסָן בְּנִיסָן

יד אברהם

rebellions, God dispatched poisonous snakes to bite them. As an antidote, Moses fashioned a brazen serpent that cured every Jew who looked at it. This brazen serpent was later brought to Eretz Yisrael where it was kept until the days of Chizkiah. Scripture (II Kings 18:4) reports: "He (Chizkiah) removed the altars ... and crushed the brazen serpent that Moses had made, because until those days the children of Israel would burn incense to it ... They concurred with Chizkiah because his intentions was to destroy an object that had been converted to an idol (Rav, Rashi).

גָּנַז סֵפֶר רְפוּאוֹת וְהוֹדוּ לוֹ. — He hid the Book of Remedies, and they agreed with him

Ramban, in the foreword to his commentary on the Torah, (cf. Rambam Comm.) ascribes the authorship of this book to King Solomon. There are two schools of thought regarding the subject of this book. According to Rashi (56a) it contained direction for speedily curing all illnesses. Chizkiah concealed it because people were cured so quickly and effortlessly that illness failed to promote a spirit of contrition and humility.

Rambam (Comm.) demurs,[1] arguing that if seeking a cure for illness causes a diminution of faith, then carried to its logical conclusion, a hungry person should not eat lest he forget God after satisfying his hunger. The contrary is the result; a person satisfying his hunger pangs thanks God for sustaining him. The same is true concerning medical cures. Rambam therefore concludes one offers thanks to God for providing a cure for his illness.[2]

Rambam comments that this book contained types of remedies which are prohibited to a Jew, e.g., magical in-

1. Rambam's comments are directed at an interpretation 'which I have heard and they explained to me.' Although it is almost identical to Rashi's comment, Rashi's interpretation differs in one essential detail in that it stressed the speed with which healing was effected, leaving no room for contrition. In the interpretation refuted by Rambam, recovery is not attained with undue speed; the remedies offered merely insured healing. It could be argued that here even Rashi would concur.

2. This analogy of illness to hunger is challenged by Chazon Ish. The Talmud (Bava Kama 85a) says that the Biblical phrase, and he shall cause him to be thoroughly healed (Exodus 21:19), is a dispensation given to the physician to practice his profession. Similarly, the Talmud (Berachos 60a) states, "It is not the normal course of people [אֵין דַּרְכָּן שֶׁל בְּנֵי אָדָם ...] to engage in seeking medical help, but that has become the custom." Rashi there explains that it would be better to pray to God for salvation than seek a physician's help. Abaye disagrees and refers to the above cited passage giving a dispensation to physicians to heal. From all these sources it is clear that eating and healing are completely different. One does not need a dispensation to eat. The difference is that the need for food is not a punishment. To the contrary, the table of the righteous is compared to the Altar and eating is a sacred service, whereas illness is a punishment, which should cause one to repent and perform good deeds. Had the Torah not permitted us to use the physician's arts it could be argued that the patient is attempting to thwart God's will (Chazon Ish, Emunah Ubitachon 5:5).

A similar view is expressed by R' Yaakov Emden (Lechem Shamayim) who simultaneously draws a distinction between the cures in the Book of Remedies, which made recovery as commonplace as satisfying hunger with food, thus thwarting the Divine purpose of illness (contrition and repentance), and recovery affected through a physician. Here repentance and prayer

with him. He hid the Book of Remedies, and they agreed with him.

Concerning three they did not agree with him. He cut the doors of the Temple and sent them to the king of Assyria, but they did not agree with him. He stopped up the waters of the upper Gichon, but they

scriptions; these were set down in a book for study by judges who had to know which forms of magic are forbidden (see *Deuteronomy* 18:9 with *Rashi; Sanhedrin* 68a). Chizkiah hid this book because the people had begun using it for healing. Alternatively *Rambam* suggests that it contained instructions for the preparation of toxic substances, which could, if properly used, remedy certain sicknesses. When Chizkiah saw that people perverted the purpose of this book and began to use it as a primer for the preparation of poisons, he hid it.

עַל שְׁלֹשָׁה לֹא הוֹדוּ לוֹ. קִצֵּץ דְּלָתוֹת שֶׁל הֵיכָל וְשִׁגְּרָן לְמֶלֶךְ אַשּׁוּר — *Concerning three they did not agree with him. He cut* [off] *the doors of the Temple and sent them to the king of Assyria,*

When Sancheriv, King of Assyria, levied a heavy tribute upon King Chizkiah in return for the retreat of the

Assyrian armies from the land of Yehudah, Chizkiah's resources were strained. Scripture relates (*II Kings* 18:16): *At that time Chizkiah cut the doors of the Temple* [i.e., he pared off their gold covering (*Targum Yonasan, Radak*)] *and gave them to the King of Assyria.*

וְלֹא הוֹדוּ לוֹ. — *but they did not agree with him.*

He should have had faith that God would save him (*Tos. Yom Tov; Meiri*)

סָתַם מֵי גִיחוֹן הָעֶלְיוֹן — *He stopped up the waters of the upper Gichon,*

Scripture (*II Chronicles* 30:32) tells us that in order to prevent usage of the water by an enemy besieging Jerusalem, he, Chizkiah, stopped up the source of the upper Gichon (*Rashi*).

The river Gichon mentioned here is not identical with the Gichon in *Genesis* (2:13); rather it is the body of water near Jerusalem

is still necessary, for one cannot be sure he will find the right doctor, that he will diagnose the illness correctly, the medicine will be efficacious, and so on.

Rambam (*Leviticus* 26:11) states that when prophecy was still extant, *tzaddikim* would not resort to physicians; instead they would turn to the prophet who would teach them what sin caused the malady so that they could repent. Even in the post-prophetic era, if people would not resort to physicians, sickness could always be assumed to be the result of sin and could be remedied with repentance. However it can deduced from *Rambam's* words that because of the current general reliance upon physicians, a malady may be due to natural, not sin-related causes. It is also clear that *Ramban* does not consider reliance upon physicians a categorical sin, but something inconsistent with the philosophy expected of a true believer. According to *Ramban,* the dispensation to heal is directed solely at the physician: he must not desist from practicing his art upon one who is not strong enough in his convictions to rely upon God. See also *Teshuvos HaRashba* 1:419, 414; *Turei Zahav Yoreh Deah* 336:1, *Birkei Yosef* there, *Ibn Ezra* to *Exodus* 21:19; *Chovas HaLevavos Sha'ar HaBitachon* ch. 4; *Akeidas Yitzchak* to *Genesis Sha'ar* 26 (pp: 221-2). A unique distinction is advanced by *R' Yaakov ibn Chaviv* in his glosses to *Ein Yaakov.* Healing in the normal, prevalent fashion is permitted, but extraordinary, exotic, means should be shunned.

The regular editions of *Rambam's* comm. (see also *Meiri*) have it that these remedies were based upon astrological considerations (see *Hil. Avodah Zarah* 11:16, *Rambam's* letter to the community of Marseilles, for his view on astrology). However this is not found in the authoritative edition of R' Y. Kafich (see his notes there).

[א] **תָּמִיד** נִשְׁחָט בִּשְׁמוֹנֶה וּמֶחֱצָה וְקָרֵב
בְּתֵשַׁע וּמֶחֱצָה.

יד אברהם

known as the שִׁלוֹחַ, Shilo'ach (pool of Siloa) as evidenced from Targum Yonasan to I Kings 1:33 (Rashi, Berachos 10b s.v. סתם).

וְלֹא הוֹדוּ לוֹ. — but they did not agree with him.

For God, through the prophet Isaiah, had promised Chizkiah (II Kings 20:6, Isaiah 37:35) I will protect this city ... (Rashi). In addition, Chizkiah's tactic caused a diminution of Eretz Yisrael's resources, a forbidden act (Tif. Yis).

עִבֵּר נִיסָן בְּנִיסָן — He intercalated Nissan in Nissan,

Because the Torah mandates that Pesach always be in the spring (see Deuteronomy 16:1 with Rashi; Sanhedrin 13b), the months of the Jewish calendar year must correspond with the solar cycle. Since, however, a twelve-month lunar year is approximately 354 days — eleven and a quarter days less than a solar cycle — a thirteenth month has to be intercalated [i.e., inserted into the calendar] every few years. Since the institution of the standard calendar by Hillel the Prince (4118 / 358 B.C.E.; see appendices to ArtScroll Rosh Hashanah, p. 109), this is accomplished by automatically intercalating seven additional months every nineteen years according to a fixed schedule.

However in pre-Hillel days, other factors were also considered (see Hil. Kiddush HaChodesh 4:2-3) and the intercalation was not automatic. The Beis Din would deliberate as to whether or not to intercalate and would set the calendar accordingly.

In all cases, however, the intercalated month was always Adar; once Nissan began, a month could no longer be added. However Chizkiah (with his Beis Din) made the decision to intercalate after Nissan had already begun, so that

he could not add a second Adar, but had to designate a Second Nissan.

Scripture (II Chronicles 30:2,13,18; see Radak and Malbim there; Margalios HaYam to Sanhedrin 12b) relates regarding the beginning of Chizkiah's reign: And the king was advised ... to observe [lit. to perform], i.e., to sacrifice the Pesach offering] in the second month (i.e., Iyar). And a great multitude assembled in Jerusalem to celebrate [lit. to perform] the Festival of the Matzos in the second month (Iyar; i.e. the second Nissan) ... for they ate the Passover offering not as written, for Chizkiah prayed for them; May HASHEM the Good atone for [this].' The cause for this extraordinary intercalation was to enable the people to sacrifice in a cleansed state, for most of the people ... had not yet cleansed themselves (see Tos. Sanhedrin 12a, s.v. שעיבר).

וְלֹא הוֹדוּ לוֹ. — but they did not agree with him.

For it is written (Exodus 12:2): This month (Nissan) shall be for you ... from which we deduce (Sanhedrin 12b), 'this month is Nissan and none other', i.e. once the month has been designated the first month (Nissan) no other month (i.e., the following one) may be given this position of primacy, for if another month is added after Nissan, the true Nissan will be relegated retroactively to a Second Adar. The Talmud (ibid.) explains further that Chizkiah's error was due not to simple ignorance of the foregoing stipulation, but to his differing interpretation of it. Actually the intercalation took place on the thirtieth of Adar (which presumably consisted of thirty days that year). But since the thirtieth of any month is fit to be designated the first of the following month (a lunar month has either twenty-nine or thirty days), intercalation may not be performed on even that day. Chizkiah did not accept this distinction.[1]

1. Shoshanim L'David points out that apparently the nobles with whom Chizkiah conferred

did not agree with him. He intercalated Nissan in Nissan, but they did not agree with him.

1. The [afternoon] daily offering is [usually] slaughtered at eight and a half [hours], and offered at nine and a half [hours].

Chapter 5

1.

As set forth in the Torah *(Exodus 12:1-14, 43-49; 23:18; 34:25; Leviticus 23:5; Numbers 9:1-3; 28:16, Deuteronomy 16:2-3)* it is incumbent upon every Jew to sacrifice a Pesach offering on the afternoon before, and to partake of its flesh on the first night of, the festival. The major part of the next four chapters are devoted to a discussion of the laws pertaining to this offering. The Torah *(Numbers 9:9-12)* also provides an alternate date for someone who could not offer the Pesach on the fourteenth of Nissan. This second date, the fourteenth of Iyar, is known in the Talmud as פֶּסַח שֵׁנִי, *the Second Pesach*, the same name by which the offering is known. Part of the ninth chapter discusses the laws of *Pesach Sheni*.

תָּמִיד — *The [afternoon] daily offering*
[As part of the regular Temple service, two sheep were offered as burnt offerings every day without exception. Known as the קָרְבַּן תָּמִיד *[Tamid]*, literally *perpetual* or *continual sacrifice, one* of these sheep would commence the sacrificial service every morning, תָּמִיד שֶׁל שַׁחַר, *the morning daily offering*, and the second sheep would conclude the sacrificial service every afternoon — the תָּמִיד שֶׁל בֵּין הָעַרְבָּיִם, *afternoon daily offering* (see *Numbers 28:8*).

נִשְׁחָט בִּשְׁמוֹנָה וּמֶחֱצָה — *is [usually] slaughtered at eight and a half [hours]*,
[On a normal day, the afternoon *Tamid* was offered at approximately 2:30 p.m., eight and a half hours after a typical sunrise. See *comm.* above to 1:4

for an explanation of the time system used in Talmudic days.]

Although it was permissible to offer the daily afternoon offering as early as half an hour after midday (see further, s.v. נשחט בשש), the service was deferred for two hours on a regular day to allow the people more time for the offering of their donative and vow offerings (נְדָרִים וּנְדָבוֹת). With the exception of the Pesach and some unusual instances (see *Gem.* 59a), no offering could be slaughtered after the afternoon daily offering; thus this offering had to be slaughtered late in the day for the convenience of individuals bringing their private offerings *(Rav; Gem.* 58a).

Although the Torah provides that the offering be brought in the afternoon, the Sages instituted that it not be brought after eight

regarding this decision (see *II Chron.* 30:2 with *Radak* and *Malbim)* were not the members of the Sanhedrin, but his own advisers, his *nobles* (as they are termed in Scripture). Probably, because of his pre-eminence as a scholar and saint, an exception was made to allow Chizkiah — a king — to be a member of, and to preside over, the Sanhedrin. But why did Chizkiah not confer on this cardinal point of halachah with the rest of the Sanhedrin? The answer is provided in the assertion of the Talmud that the intercalation took place on the thirtieth of Adar and that the king would not have intercalated on the following day when Nissan had actually begun. Probably he reached his decision late in the day when there was not time enough to assemble the regular Sanhedrin. Therefore he hastily assembled an *ad hoc Beis Din* consisting of *his nobles*, i.e., those residing in his palace.

בְּעַרְבֵי פְסָחִים נִשְׁחָט בְּשֶׁבַע וּמֶחֱצָה וְקָרֵב
בִּשְׁמוֹנֶה וּמֶחֱצָה, בֵּין בַּחוֹל בֵּין בַּשַּׁבָּת.
חָל עֶרֶב פֶּסַח לִהְיוֹת בְּעֶרֶב שַׁבָּת, נִשְׁחָט
בְּשֵׁשׁ וּמֶחֱצָה וְקָרֵב בְּשֶׁבַע וּמֶחֱצָה. וְהַפֶּסַח
אַחֲרָיו.

יד אברהם

and a half hours. They felt that if the offering were deferred past this hour, there would
not be enough time for the rest of the service
to be performed in an unhurried manner
(Tos. 58a, s.v. תמיד).

Tosefos HaRashba elaborates further: As a
rule, one hour was allowed to elapse from the
time of the Tamid's slaughter to the offering
of its sacrificial parts (emurin) upon the altar
(see further, s.v. וקרב). Similarly, an hour
was allowed for each of the other required
afternoon services — burning of the incense
and the kindling of the menorah — that were
performed after the Tamid service and before
sunset. Consequently the slaughter of the
Tamid had to take place no later than three
hours before nightfall.

וְקָרֵב בְּתֵשַׁע וּמֶחֱצָה. — and offered at nine
and a half [hours].

The procedure of slaughter and the
blood service would consume an hour,
ending at nine and a half hours (Rav;
Rashi).

[The verb קָרֵב, offered, usually denotes
the offering up of the sacrificial parts onto
the pyre upon the altar — in the case of the
Tamid, which was a burnt offering, the entire animal would be offered. Within the
hour alloted for the service they slaughtered
the animal, received its blood, brought the
blood to the altar to be thrown upon its corners, flayed the carcass, dissected it, washed
and rinsed the entrails, brought the dissected
limbs to the altar ramp and laid them there,
and finally brought the parts to the top of the
altar to be tossed upon the pyre.]

בְּעַרְבֵי פְסָחִים נִשְׁחָט בְּשֶׁבַע וּמֶחֱצָה וְקָרֵב
בִּשְׁמוֹנֶה וּמֶחֱצָה, — On the eve of Pesach
it [the Tamid] is slaughtered at seven
and a half [hours], and offered at eight
and a half [hours],

Because the Pesach offering must be
slaughtered after the daily offering, the
latter's service had to be scheduled an
hour earlier to allow enough time for the
multitude of Pesach offerings which
had to be offered before sunset (Rav;
Rashi).

The time parameter allotted for the Pesach
differs drastically from that of all other offerings. Whereas all other offerings (with rare
exceptions) are offered exclusively before the
afternoon Tamid, the Pesach must be offered
only after the Tamid. The Gemara (59a)
derives this difference from terminology
used by the Torah to indicate the respective
times of these offerings. In the case of the
Tamid, the Torah always uses the expression
(Numbers 28:8, Ex. 29:39) בֵּין הָעַרְבָּיִם [lit.
between the evenings] to denote afternoon
(see further 5:3, s.v. משום שנאמר,for explanation of this term). In the case of the
Pesach, however, the Torah uses both the
term בֵּין הָעַרְבָּיִם (Exodus 12:6), and the term
עֶרֶב, evening (Deuteronomy 16:4). The latter
term, which usually denotes night (see
Genesis 1:5, Leviticus 23:32), implies that
the Pesach must be offered closer to evening
than the Tamid.

בֵּין בַּחוֹל בֵּין בַּשַּׁבָּת. — whether it is a
weekday or the Sabbath.

Since no personal sacrifices may be offered
on the Sabbath, it would have been logical to
offer the Tamid at its earliest permissible
time — six and a half hours (see below) — in
order to allow the maximum possible time for
the huge numbers of Pesach offerings. [On
an ordinary Sabbath, the Tamid is offered as
late as eight and a half hours only for reasons
of uniformity, but on the eve of Pesach it is
scheduled earlier in any case — why not
move it up two hours instead of only one?
(Rashi).] Nevertheless, even on the Sabbath
the time for the Tamid's slaughter is the same
as weekdays because of other services that
had to be performed on the Sabbath. The
Sabbath[1] Mussaf offerings were brought in

---

1. See Tosafos, Berachos 28a, s.v. ושל, that this schedule was followed only on the Sabbath.
See also P'nei Yehoshua and Tzlach there; Magen Avraham 291:2 with commentaries.

5
1

On the eve of Pesach it is slaughtered at seven and a half [hours], and offered at eight and a half [hours], whether it is a weekday or the Sabbath.

If the eve of Pesach fell on the eve of the Sabbath, it is slaughtered at six and a half [hours], and offered at seven and a half [hours]. The Pesach [sacrifice is offered] after it.

the sixth hour[2], and they were followed by the burning of the frankincense (שְׁנֵי בְזִיכֵי לְבוֹנָה) accompanying the *Panim* Breads (see *comm.* further 7:2, and *Yoma* 2:6, s.v. ובשבת, there 3:11). Thus the *Tamid* could not be offered before seven and a half hours (*Gem.* 58a)[3].

חָל עֶרֶב פֶּסַח לִהְיוֹת בְּעֶרֶב שַׁבָּת, — *If the eve of Pesach fell on* [lit. *fell to be*] *the eve of the Sabbath*,

In that event, more time was needed in the afternoon to allow the participants to roast their offerings before the beginning of the Sabbath. Although roasting is a necessary component of the *mitzvah*, it does not supersede the Sabbath (*Rav; Gem.* 58a; see further 6:1).

נִשְׁחָט בְּשֵׁשׁ וּמֶחֱצָה — *it is slaughtered at six and a half* [hours],

This is the earliest possible time for the slaughtering of the afternoon *Tamid*. Although technically the afternoon starts from the beginning of the seventh hour (at six hours, i.e. twelve

noon), nevertheless since the walls of the Temple were not perfectly perpendicular [they were wide at the bottom and tapered off at the top (*Rashi*)], the shade from the afternoon sun was not discernible until half an hour after midday (*Gem. Yoma* 28b).

וְקָרֵב בְּשֶׁבַע וּמֶחֱצָה. — *and offered at seven and a half* [hours].

[An hour was allotted for the whole procedure from slaughter until the limbs and *emurin* [i.e., sacrificial parts] were tossed onto the pyre of the altar (see above, s.v. וקרב).]

וְהַפֶּסַח אַחֲרָיו. — *The Pesach* [sacrifice is offered] *after it.*

[This clause refers to all the possible dates for the eve of Pesach listed above: The Pesach was *always* offered after the *Tamid*. Although the time fixed for the *Tamid* was predicated upon the need to provide time for the Pesach following it, the mishnah had heretofore never ex-

2. The fact that the term used to denote the time for the Sabbath *Mussafim* is, וּבְיוֹם הַשַּׁבָּת, *On the Sabbath day* (Numbers 28:9), and not, בַּבּוֹקֶר, *in the morning*, the term used for the *Tamid* (*op. cit.* 28:4), indicates that the *Mussaf* is offered later than the *Tamid*. The *Gemara* (34a) assumes (in a different context) that the term יוֹם, *day*, indicates a time later than the morning (*Rashi* 58a, s.v. ר׳ ישמעאל, as emended by *Levushei S'rad* to *Magen Avraham* 291:2). The term, *day*, implies the strong light of the day, and not early morning (*Rashi Yoma* 34a, s.v. ביום). Therefore the *Mussaf* was deferred to the latest possible time, the hour before midday. After that the sun begins to move lower in the sky and its light begins to diminish; that afternoon period is called בֵּין הָעַרְבַּיִם, lit. *between the evenings* (*Machatzis HaShekel* to *Magen Avraham* 291:2).

3. An hour was allowed to remove the old *Panim* Bread, arrange the fresh ones, burn the frankincense upon the altar, and distribute the breads among the *Kohanim*. Actually, they could have offered the afternoon *Tamid* at the beginning of the eighth hour, however it is possible that the distribution of the *Panim* Breads would require another half hour. Alternatively, the Sages did not want to make a special schedule for a Pesach eve falling on the Sabbath. Therefore since the *Tamid* could not be offered at the earliest possible time — half an hour after midday — it was deferred to seven and a half hours, the regular time on a weekday Pesach eve (*Rashi* 58a, s.v. בזיכין and בשבע and ובזביכיו בשבא).

פסחים [ב] הַפֶּסַח שֶׁשְּׁחָטוֹ שֶׁלֹּא לִשְׁמוֹ, וְקִבֵּל וְהִלֵּךְ וְזָרַק שֶׁלֹּא לִשְׁמוֹ, אוֹ

יד אברהם

plicitly stated this rule. Here the mishnah supplies the ruling, already implied
earlier, that the Pesach must be offered
after the *Tamid* (see also *Tzlach*).

Although it is permissible to merely put
the Pesach in the oven before sunset, and to

let it roast on the Sabbath (*Shabbos* 1:11),
this is a dispensation granted only as a last
resort[1]; ideally the roasting should be
finished before the onset of the Sabbath.
Consequently much time had to be allotted
for the roasting (*Tos. Yom Tov* with *Kol
HaRemez*).

2.

The following mishnah deals with an aspect of the Pesach offering that is part of
a larger area in the laws of sacrifices — the intention required during the performance of the sacrificial service. The discussion hinges on two elements of the
Torah-prescribed laws of sacrifices: (a) The עֲבוֹדַת הַדָּם, *service of the blood;* and (b)
the requirement of לִשְׁמָהּ, *the proper intention,* during the sacrificial service.

עֲבוֹדַת הַדָּם, Service of the Blood
In the laws of sacrifices special importance is attached to עֲבוֹדַת הַדָּם, *the service
of the blood,* which is divided into four parts, namely, שְׁחִיטָה, *slaughtering,* the offering; קַבָּלָה, *receiving* its blood in a specially designated vessel; הוֹלָכָה, *transporting* the blood to the altar; and finally זְרִיקָה, *throwing* the blood on the altar.
The service of the blood is the essential component of the offering, for it determines
the offering's halachic validity. If the blood service was properly done, the offering
is halachically valid and the owner has discharged his obligation, even though the
meat and fats were neither burned on the altar nor eaten.

לִשְׁמָהּ — Proper Intentions During the Sacrificial Service.
As outlined in *Zevachim* (4:6) every sacrifice must be offered with specific intentions on the part of the *Kohen* performing the sacrificial services. Although the
mishnah (*ad. loc.*) enumerates six distinct intentions the *Kohen* must bear in mind,
only two can effect the validity of the offering: לִשְׁמָהּ, *for its proper designation* [lit.
name] and לְשֵׁם הַבְּעָלִים, *for its owner*[2]. That is to say that the *Kohen* must perform
the four parts of the blood services with these two intentions: (a) He must offer the
sacrifice for its original designation, e.g., if it was a חַטָאת, *sin offering,* he must per-

---

1. Ordinarily it is prohibited to leave a roast in the oven on the Sabbath because of the fear
that one may forget and stir up the coals as he is accustomed to do on weekdays (see *Shabbos*
1:10). A special dispensation is granted for the roasting of the Pesach, on the assumption that
the roasting process is attended by the entire registered group. As a group, they will be careful
and remind anyone forgetting that it is the Sabbath, as set forth in the Talmud (Shabbos 20a).

2. The *Rishonim* (early commentators) disagree regarding the disqualification of שִׁנּוּי בְּעָלִים,
someone other than the owner. According to *Rashi* and *Tosafos,* such an intention disqualifies
only if, during one of the four blood services, someone intended to *throw the blood* for
someone other than the owner. For example, the one who slaughtered did so with the intention
that the blood would be thrown for Shimon instead of Reuben. Merely slaughtering for
someone else (without thought of throwing the blood), however, does not disqualify. This is
in contrast to an intent to perform the service for the wrong offering — if someone slaughtered
a sin offering as a burnt offering, it is disqualified, there is no need to include the throwing of
the blood in the wrong intention (*Zevachim* 4a, *Rashi* s.v. עבודות בד' וישנו, *Tos.,* s.v. מה;
Pesachim 61a, *Rashi,* s.v. בעלים שנוי אבל).
Rambam (Hil. Pesulei HaMukdashim 15:1) makes no such distinction. According to him an
intent for the wrong owner disqualifies even without reference to the throwing of blood (see
Mirkeves HaMishneh there; *Even HaEzel* op. cit. 13:1, *Keren Orah* to *Zevachim* 10a).

2. The Pesach offering that one slaughtered for some other designation, or [the *Kohen*] received, transported, or threw [its blood], for some

YAD AVRAHAM

form its service for the purpose of a sin offering, but he may not think that it is another kind of offering; (b) the *Kohen* must intend that he is sacrificing the offering for the purpose of its owner, e.g., Reuben's offering must be brought with the intention that it satisfy Reuben's obligation to offer a sacrifice.

❈ ❈ ❈

What if the *Kohen* performed the blood services without these two intentions? The halachah, as stated in *Zevachim* 1:1, draws the following distinction: A sin offering and a Pesach offering slaughtered with the intention that they are different sacrifices (e.g., the *Kohen* has in mind that the sin offering is a peace offering or that the Pesach is a burnt offering), or with the intention that they belong to someone other than the true owner, are entirely invalid. They may not be eaten nor may their fats be burned on the altar. All other sacrifices, by contrast, are valid in the sense that the offering may be eaten and burned. However, the owner has not satisfied his personal obligation. Had he, for example, made a vow to bring a peace offering, and it was slaughtered with a wrong intention, the offering is completed but the vow remains unfulfilled and the owner must bring another one.

However the *Talmud (Zevachim* 2b) demonstrates that no positive declaration — oral or conscious — of intent is ever necessary. In the absence of an intention to the contrary, it is assumed that the service was meant to be performed with whatever intention is needed [לִשְׁמָהּ קָאֵי סְתָמָא]. Moreover, according to one tanna, the Sages forbade the *Kohen* to make any oral statement of proper intentions lest he mistakenly make a negative comment and disqualify it (*Zevachim* 4:6, 46b). Only a negative intent can disqualify or render an offering unfit for the discharge of obligations.

Although the term מַחֲשָׁבָה, *intention*, is consistently used in connection with this law, some commentators conclude that only an oral negative declaration can invalidate the offering (*Rashi, Menachos* 2b, s.v. אבל, *Zevachim* 41b s.v., לא; *Tos. Pesachim* 63a, s.v. ר׳ מאיר, *Bava Metziah* 43b, s.v. החושב; see *Tos. Shantz* cited at length in *Shittah Mekubetzes ad. loc*). A sacrifice offered with no specific intention or even an unspoken improper intention is perfectly valid.

The discussion of the following mishnah focuses on the disqualification of the Pesach offering caused by improper intentions.

הַפֶּסַח שֶׁשְּׁחָטוֹ שֶׁלֹּא לִשְׁמוֹ, — *The Pesach offering that one slaughtered for some other* [lit. *not for its own*] *designation*,

[The *Kohen* slaughtered the Pesach with the intention that it be a different offering, e.g. a burnt or peace offering.]

וְקִבֵּל — *or* [*the Kohen*] *received*,

[This is the second of the services of the blood during which disqualification can occur. The *Kohen* receives the animal's blood in a sanctified basin [בְּלִי שָׁרֵת] directly from the incision in the sacrifice's neck.]

וְהִלֵּךְ — *transported*,

[After the blood is received, it must be brought to the altar for the ultimate service of the blood, throwing it upon the altar (זְרִיקָה). This transport of the blood from the point of sacrifice is considered a distinct service, and disqualification can occur during its performance.]

וְזָרַק — *or threw* [*its blood*],

This is the final step in the blood service — throwing it on the side of the altar.

שֶׁלֹּא לִשְׁמוֹ, — *for some other* [lit. *not for its own*] *designation*,

לִשְׁמוֹ וְשֶׁלֹא לִשְׁמוֹ, אוֹ שֶׁלֹא לִשְׁמוֹ וְלִשְׁמוֹ, פָּסוּל.

כֵּיצַד לִשְׁמוֹ וְשֶׁלֹא לִשְׁמוֹ? — לְשֵׁם פֶּסַח וּלְשֵׁם שְׁלָמִים. שֶׁלֹא לִשְׁמוֹ וְלִשְׁמוֹ? — לְשֵׁם שְׁלָמִים וּלְשֵׁם פֶּסַח.

[ג] **שְׁחָטוֹ** שֶׁלֹא לְאוֹכְלָיו, וְשֶׁלֹא לִמְנוּיָיו,

יד אברהם

[If the wrong intention was explicitly stated during only one of these services, the offering is disqualified, even if the other three services were performed properly. Each of these services is a separate unit, and need not be reinforced with wrong intentions during a companion service (Gemara 60a).]

אוֹ לִשְׁמוֹ וְשֶׁלֹא לִשְׁמוֹ, — or for its own designation and [then] for some other designation,

As the *Kohen* began one of these four services he intended the sacrifice for a Pesach offering, but later in the same service he intended it for another offering (*Tif. Yis.* based on one interpretation in *Gem.* 59b-60a). [The first expression of intent is not considered the primary one; consequently, the offering is disqualified by his second intention, even though he began it properly.][1]

אוֹ שֶׁלֹא לִשְׁמוֹ וְלִשְׁמוֹ, — or for some other designation and [then] for its own designation,

At first he performed the service for another offering and then during the same service, he intended it for the Pesach service. The mishnah holds that any intention, whether indicated first or second, is considered primary, and effects disqualification (ibid.).

פָּסוּל. — is invalid.

In brief, two laws are advanced here: The expressed intent to perform the service for another offering invalidates the offering. And such wrong inten-

1. This view is that of R' Yose (*Temurah* 25a), who holds that wherever two conflicting intentions are expressed, both the first and second intentions must be considered and either one can invalidate the offering.

Another view advanced in the *Gemara* 60a interprets the mishnah according to R' Meir who disagrees with R' Yose. R' Meir holds that whenever conflicting intentions are stated during the course of a single service, the first is paramount and the second is disregarded [בִּתְחִלַּת דְּבָרָיו אָדָם נִתְפַּס]. According to R' Meir the mishnah speaks about a situation where an entire service was performed for its proper designation, but with the simultaneous intent that a later service of the same offering would be done for a different designation. For example, while slaughtering an animal for the sake of Pesach, the *Kohen* states that he will receive its blood for the sake of a burnt offering. Such an intent is viewed as if the later service was actually performed with the stated wrong intention (מְחַשְּׁבִין מֵעֲבוֹדָה לַעֲבוֹדָה). According to this interpretation of the mishnah, the phrase, *for its own designation and for some other designation,* means that he performed one service (e.g. slaughtering) with the proper intention but intended to perform another service (e.g., throwing the blood) for another designation.

[According to this interpretation, the next passage of this mishnah, *for some other designation and for its own designation,* is superfluous, for in that case the very first service performed for an improper offering surely invalidates the offering; there is no reason to suppose that a simultaneous intention to perform a *later* service in the proper manner can redeem the improper performance of an earlier service. The mishnah includes this passage only to complete its listing of possible combinations.]

We have not presented *Rav's* view in the commentary because of the objections to it raised by *Tos. Yom Tov* (cf. *Kol HaRemez* and *Shoshanim L'David*).

other designation, or for its own designation and [then] for some other designation, or for some other designation and [then] for its own designation, is invalid.

What is an example of, 'For its own designation and [then] for some other designation'? — For the designation of a Pesach offering [first] and [then] for the designation of a peace offering. [What is an example of,] 'For some other designation and [then] for its own designation'?—For the designation of a peace offering and [then] for the designation of a Pesach offering.

3. [I f] he slaughtered it for other than those who can eat it, for other than its registrants, for un-

YAD AVRAHAM

tions invalidate the offering when stated during any one of the four blood services. Both of these laws are derived by the *Talmud (Zevachim* 7b; see there 4a) from the Torah.

בֵּיצַד לִשְׁמוֹ וְשֶׁלֹּא לִשְׁמוֹ? — לְשֵׁם פֶּסַח וּלְשֵׁם שְׁלָמִים. — *What is an example of, 'For its own designation and [then] for some other designation'? — For the designation of a Pesach offering [first] and [then] for the designation of a peace offering.*

The intention for a peace offering is merely an illustration of an invalidating purpose; the same would apply to an intention for any other offering. [The reason the mishnah chose to specify a peace offering may be to teach that although the Pesach is considered a form of peace offering (see below 9:6; *Gem.* 96b), nevertheless even this degree of improper intention invalidates the sacrifice *(Tif. Yis.; Kol HaRemez; Beis David).*

שֶׁלֹּא לִשְׁמוֹ וְלִשְׁמוֹ? — לְשֵׁם שְׁלָמִים וּלְשֵׁם פֶּסַח. — *[What is an example of,] 'For some other designation and [then] for its own designation'? — For the designation of a peace offering and [then] for the designation of a Pesach offering.*

[This mishnah is reproduced *verbatim* in *Zevachim* (1:4).]

3.

In addition to disqualifications of improper intentions (that the Pesach and sin offering have in common, as set forth in mishnah 2), the Pesach offering has some unique disqualifications of its own. These will be set forth in the following two mishnayos.

The four disqualifications listed in the beginning of our mishnah are all based on the stipulation that the Pesach offering must be eaten by those offering it, i.e., those registered on it before it is slaughtered. The law of other sacrifices, by contrast, requires only that they be eaten, without regard at the time of slaughter as to who will do the eating.

שְׁחָטוֹ שֶׁלֹּא לְאוֹכְלָיו, — *[If] he slaughtered it [the Pesach] for other than those who* can eat it,

He slaughtered the Pesach offering

פְּסָחִים לָעֲרֵלִים, וְלִטְמֵאִים, פָּסוּל. ה/ג
לְאוֹכְלָיו וְשֶׁלֹּא לְאוֹכְלָיו, לִמְנוּיָיו וְשֶׁלֹּא
לִמְנוּיָיו, לְמוּלִים וְלַעֲרֵלִים, לִטְמֵאִים
וְלִטְהוֹרִים, כָּשֵׁר.

יד אברהם

for an old man, a sick person, or a minor, whose physical condition does not permit him to eat the minimum required amount of the Pesach meat — the equivalent of an olive in volume [כְּזַיִת]. The offering is invalid because the Torah stipulates (*Exodus* 12:4): *Every man according to his eating* [*shall you slaughter* ...][1] thereby indicating that a minimum level of eating ability is required *(Rav; Gem.* 61a).

[The rule derived from this verse serves to disqualify the offering in two other instances listed here as well, *uncircumcised* and *contaminated*; they are merely different examples of the same condition — inability to eat (see *Tos.* 61a, s.v. לאוכליו). For each of these cases we must now only indicate the reason of this inability.] These cases all refer to a situation where only those unable to eat are registered on this offering *(Rav).* (Otherwise the offering would be valid as stated further in this mishnah: [*If he slaughtered it*] *for those who can eat it and for those who cannot eat it ...* [*it*] *is valid.*)

וְשֶׁלֹּא לִמְנוּיָיו, — *for other than its registrants,*
One of the requirements of the Pesach offering is that it may be eaten only by מְנוּיִים, literally *counted ones,* meaning the people who 'registered' on the offering prior to its slaughter by arranging to partake of its meat.[2]

The source for this requirement is the Scriptural phrase (*Exodus* 12:4): *Then let him and his neighbor take* [*the offering*] *... according to the number of the people (Rav; Gem.* 61a).

Therefore a Pesach slaughtered for an unregistered group is invalid, for it was in effect, slaughtered on behalf of people who cannot eat it, as outlined above.

[Three halachic provisions are contained in the above Scriptural passage: (a) An individual is not required to purchase and consecrate his own animal for the Pesach; it is sufficient for him to register on someone else's offering before its slaughter (see *Rashi* to *Exodus* 12:4 and *Pesachim* 8:3; 89a; *Mikdash David, Kuntres Lelnyaney Kodashim* 5:1); (b) only those who have registered on the Pesach may eat of it (*Zevachim* 5:8, 56b; see *Rashi* and *Rav* there); and (c) the slaughter must be performed on behalf of those registered on this offering. The final provision is the one discussed here.

Tosafos (61a s.v. ואתקש) points out that שֶׁלֹּא לִמְנוּיָיו, *for other than its registrants,* is not the same as the disqualifying intent of performing a service for someone other than the true owner [שִׁנּוּי בְּעָלִים; שֶׁלֹּא לְשֵׁם בְּעָלָיו], mentioned in the *preface* to mishnah 2 (see footnote there). The latter applies only to any of the four blood services done with the intention of *throwing blood* for someone other than the owner, e.g., a *Kohen* slaughtered Reuben's sacrifice with the expressed intention of throwing its blood on Shimon's behalf. But if someone *slaughtered* Reuben's offering with Shimon in mind, the offering is not disqualified. The requirement that one

---

1. The *Gemara* cites Rabbi's (רַבִּי יְהוּדָה הַנָּשִׂיא) contention that תָכֹסּוּ (translated *you shall count* by Onkelos and others) should be rendered, *shall you slaughter,* thus deducing the stipulation that not only must the Pesach be eaten, but even its slaughter must be performed for those fit to eat.

2. It is not clear whether registration requires an act of formal possession [קִנְיָן], making the registrant a legal partner in the offering, or whether verbal agreement to eat from the offering is sufficient; see *Zera Avraham* (6:9) for a discussion on this subject.

5
3

circumcised, or contaminated [persons], it is invalid.

[If he slaughtered it] for those who can eat it and for those who cannot eat it, for its registrants and for other than its registrants, for circumcised and for uncircumcised [persons], [or] for contaminated and for uncontaminated [persons], it is valid.

YAD AVRAHAM

has the registrants in mind, however, applies *only* to the slaughter, for that is the subject of the verse that states the requirement. Slaughter, performed for those other than the registrants, disqualifies the offering even if there was no intent to throw the blood in this manner.

Apparently *Rashi's* view (see 61a, s.v. אבל בשנוי בעלים; cf. *Riva* in *Tos.*, s.v. שחטו למולין) is that our mishnah's disqualification of a Pesach slaughtered for those who cannot eat it applies only if — during the slaughter — the *Kohen* expressed the intent to have the *flesh eaten* by people unable or ineligible to do so.

[However *Rambam* (*Hil. Korban Pesach* 2:1, 6) seems to disagree with both *Rashi* and *Tosafos*. According to him there is no difference between non-registrants and non-owners.]

לַעֲרֵלִים, — *for uncircumcised,*

With reference to the Pesach offering, the Torah states *and no uncircumcised one shall eat of it* (*Exodus* 12:48). Since uncircumcised people may not partake of the offering, a *Pesach* slaughtered exclusively for a group of uncircumcised people is invalid (*Rav*).

Rav, following *Rashi's* view (*Exodus* 12:48; *Yevamos* 70a, s.v. הערל; *Zevachim* 15b, s.v. ערל), adds that the term עָרֵל, *uncircumcised [person],* includes even someone who is excused from the obligation of *milah,* as in the case of a child whose two older brothers died from hemorrhaging caused by their circumcision. Although such a person need not be circumcised due to the possible danger that he will suffer the same consequences, he may not partake of the Pesach offering because he is uncircumcised, even though it is through no fault of his own.

Rabbeinu Tam (*Tos. Yeshanim Yevamos,* s.v. הערל; *Tos. Chagigah* 4b, s.v. דצרבה; *Zevachim* 27b, s.v. ערל) disagrees, arguing that a person who is absolved of the *mitzvah* of *milah,* cannot be termed an *uncircumcised*

person. The invalidation of *uncircumcised* refers only to someone who deliberately refrains from performing the *mitzvah* of *milah* from fear of pain.

In another dispute between *Rashi* and *Rabbeinu Tam, Rashi* holds that someone who deliberately refuses to let himself be circumcised is barred from eating the Pesach because he is בֶּן נֵכָר, *one who has estranged himself from God* [lit. *stranger*] (*Rashi* to *Exodus* 12:43; *Zevachim* 22b). *Rabbeinu Tam* holds that only a true apostate falls under that classification.

וְלַטְמֵאִים, פָּסוּל. — *or contaminated [persons], it is invalid.*

Persons contaminated by any *tumah* are forbidden to eat the flesh of offerings. Should one do so willfully the punishment is כָּרֵת, *spiritual excision* (*Leviticus* 7:20).

לְאוֹכְלָיו וְשֶׁלֹּא לְאוֹכְלָיו, לִמְנוּיָיו וְשֶׁלֹּא לִמְנוּיָיו, לְמוּלִים וְלַעֲרֵלִים, לִטְמֵאִים וְלִטְהוֹרִים, כָּשֵׁר. — *[If he slaughtered it] for those who can eat it and for those who cannot eat it, for its registrants and for other than its registrants, for circumcised and for uncircumcised [persons], [or] for contaminated and for uncontaminated [persons], it is valid.*

The *Kohen* performed the service with two categories of people in mind, those able and qualified to eat and those unqualified. The offering is valid because as the *Gemara* (61b) deduces from Scripture, intent disqualifies an offering only if it is entirely for the wrong people, i.e., those who cannot eat, but not if the intent is for a combination of some who can eat and some who cannot (מִקְצָת עָרְלָה לֹא שְׁמָהּ עָרְלָה).

The *Gemara* (62b) questions why mishnah 2 invalidates a Pesach sacrifice slaughtered

שְׁחָטוֹ קֹדֶם חֲצוֹת, פָּסוּל, — מִשּׁוּם שֶׁנֶּאֱמַר:
,,בֵּין הָעַרְבָּיִם". שְׁחָטוֹ קֹדֶם לַתָּמִיד, כָּשֵׁר,
וּבִלְבַד שֶׁיְּהֵא אֶחָד מְמָרֵס בְּדָמוֹ, עַד שֶׁיִּזָּרֵק דַּם
הַתָּמִיד; וְאִם נִזְרַק, כָּשֵׁר.

[ד] **הַשּׁוֹחֵט** אֶת הַפֶּסַח עַל הֶחָמֵץ עוֹבֵר
בְּלֹא תַעֲשֶׂה.
רַבִּי יְהוּדָה אוֹמֵר: אַף הַתָּמִיד.

יד אברהם

with a dual intention (for itself and a different offering) while our mishnah validates an offering sacrificed for a combination of eligible and ineligible people. One answer is that the case of mishnah 2 is more serious because it involves the offering itself. In our mishnah, however, everything relating to the animal itself is done properly — only the *people involved are in part not eligible (Rav)*.

שְׁחָטוֹ קֹדֶם חֲצוֹת, פָּסוּל — מִשּׁוּם שֶׁנֶּאֱמַר: ,,בֵּין הָעַרְבָּיִם". — *If he slaughtered it before noon it is invalid — because it is said: In the afternoon [Exodus 12:6].*

According to *Rashi (Exodus 12:6)* הָעַרְבָּיִם [in the plural] refers to the two darkenings (עֶרֶב) of the day: noontime when the day's brightness begins to end with the sun starting to drop toward the horizon, and the actual sunset. Thus בֵּין הָעַרְבָּיִם is the time, *between the [two] darkenings*.

Ramban (loc., cit.) is of the opinion that עַרְבָּיִם is the name given the time of day that commences at the sixth hour and concludes with the evening. Thus, בֵּין הָעַרְבָּיִם would be rendered *the midst of* עַרְבָּיִם. [The plural form עַרְבָּיִם is used because the period includes so many hours *(R' David Chiddushim to Pesachim 58a).*]

שְׁחָטוֹ קֹדֶם לַתָּמִיד, כָּשֵׁר, — *If he slaughtered it before the [afternoon] daily offering, it is valid,*

As explained in mishnah 1, the Pesach offering should follow the afternoon *Tamid.* This requirement applies to all aspects of the Pesach offering, requiring that both the slaughter and the throwing of the blood take place after those of the *Tamid.* The lesson of this mishnah is that if this rule was violated and the Pesach offering was slaughtered before the *Tamid,* the offering is valid despite the impropriety.

וּבִלְבַד שֶׁיְּהֵא אֶחָד מְמָרֵס בְּדָמוֹ, עַד שֶׁיִּזָּרֵק דַּם הַתָּמִיד; — *provided someone stirs its blood until the blood of the daily offering is thrown;*

If it happened that the Pesach offering was slaughtered before the afternoon *Tamid,* the throwing of the Pesach's blood must be delayed until after the throwing of the *Tamid's* blood. In this case, someone must continually stir the blood to prevent it from congealing and thereby become unfit for throwing.

וְאִם נִזְרַק, כָּשֵׁר. — *yet if it* [the *Pesach* blood] *was thrown [first], it is valid.*

If however, the Pesach offering's blood was thrown before that of the *Tamid,* it is fit nevertheless, because a failure to follow the prescribed sequence of the *Tamid* and the Pesach does not invalidate the offering if the violation has taken place [בְּדִיעֲבַד].

4.

The basis of the next mishnah is the verse לֹא תִשְׁחַט עַל חָמֵץ דַּם זִבְחִי, *You shall not slaughter with chametz the blood of My offering (Exodus 34:25).* As explained by the *Gemara (63b)* the sense of this admonition is to prohibit the possession of

If he slaughtered it before noon it is invalid — because it is said: *In the afternoon* [*Exodus* 12:6].

If he slaughtered it before the [afternoon] daily offering, it is valid, provided someone stirs its blood until the blood of the daily offering is thrown; yet if it was thrown, it is valid.

4. **O**ne who slaughters the Pesach offering with *chametz* [in his possession] is in violation of a negative command.

R' Yehudah says: Also the daily offering.

YAD AVRAHAM

chametz at the time of the Pesach's slaughter. Thus neither the slaughterer nor any member of those registered on the offering may have *chametz* in his possession at the time of slaughter *(loc. cit.).*[1]

הַשׁוֹחֵט אֶת הַפֶּסַח עַל הֶחָמֵץ — *One who slaughters the Pesach offering with chametz* [*in his possession*]

At the time of the slaughter, *chametz* is in the possession of either the slaughterer or one of the registrants, even though it was not in the Temple Courtyard *(Rav).*

Rav's commentary follows R' Yochanan (*Gem.* 63b) who interprets the Scriptural phrase עַל חָמֵץ to mean, *in possession of chametz.* Accordingly, it makes no difference where the chametz is located; we are concerned only with its owner. *Reish Lakish*, however, renders *near chametz.* In his view, the commandment is transgressed only if the *chametz* is actually in the Temple Courtyard at the time of slaughter. The halachah follows R' Yochanan (see *Hil. Korban Pesach* 1:5).

עוֹבֵר בְּלֹא תַעֲשֶׂה. — *is in violation of a negative command.*

He transgresses the prohibition of, *you shall not slaughter the blood of my sacrifice with chametz* (*Exodus* 34:25).[1] The offering however is valid (*Tos.* 63a, s.v. השוחט, from *Tosefta* 4:4; *Hil. Korban Pesach* 1:5).

There is a principle that if one committed an act in violation of the Torah, the act has no validity (*Temurah* 4b). Consequently,

why should a Pesach offering be valid if it was slaughtered in violation of the stricture against being in possession of *chametz*? In this case, however, the physical act of slaughter *was* performed properly. The *chametz* is an incidental factor not directly related to the slaughter; therefore its possession does not invalidate the slaughter (*Tif. Yis., Boaz*).

רַבִּי יְהוּדָה אוֹמֵר: אַף הַתָּמִיד. — *R' Yehudah says: Also the daily offering.*

According to R' Yehudah one who slaughters the afternoon daily offering of the fourteenth of Nissan while in possession of *chametz*, is also in violation of the same commandment. The commandment states '*You shall not slaughter with chametz the blood of* זִבְחִי, *My offering*' (*Exodus* 23:18). The *Gemara* 64a explains that the word זִבְחִי, **My** offering, implies the offering particularly assigned to Me [God], i.e. the *Tamid*, the only offering that God ever calls His own as it were: קָרְבָּנִי לַחְמִי, My offering, My sustenance ... (*Numbers* 28:2; see *Sifre* quoted in *Rashi* there; *Gemara* 64a).

If R' Yehudah's exegesis were to be taken absolutely literally, we would be forced to prohibit *chametz* all year round, because the *Tamid* is offered every single day. However

1. Ri (*Tos.* 63b, s.v. או) states that only the slaughterer transgresses when he or one of the group owns *chametz*. However *Minchas Chinuch* (mitzvah 89) maintains that *Chinuch* holds that the owner of the *chametz* transgresses as well.

רַבִּי שִׁמְעוֹן אוֹמֵר: הַפֶּסַח בְּאַרְבָּעָה עָשָׂר לִשְׁמוֹ חַיָּב, וְשֶׁלֹּא לִשְׁמוֹ פָּטוּר. וּשְׁאָר כָּל הַזְּבָחִים בֵּין לִשְׁמָן וּבֵין שֶׁלֹּא לִשְׁמָן, פָּטוּר. וּבַמּוֹעֵד לִשְׁמוֹ פָּטוּר, שֶׁלֹּא לִשְׁמוֹ חַיָּב. וּשְׁאָר כָּל הַזְּבָחִים בֵּין לִשְׁמָן בֵּין שֶׁלֹּא לִשְׁמָן, חַיָּב, חוּץ מִן הַחַטָּאת שֶׁשָּׁחַט שֶׁלֹּא לִשְׁמָהּ.

יד אברהם

logic dictates that the command applies only to a time when the possession of chametz is indeed prohibited, as on the afternoon of Pesach eve (see Gem. 5a and Tos., s.v. זמן).

In the case of the Tamid, in which every Jew is a partner, only the slaughterer's chametz is a factor in the prohibition, not that of any other Jew (see Tos. Menachos 78b, s.v. או; Tzlach and Sfas Emes here).]

רַבִּי שִׁמְעוֹן אוֹמֵר: הַפֶּסַח בְּאַרְבָּעָה עָשָׂר לִשְׁמוֹ חַיָּב, — R' Shimon says: [If one slaughters] the Pesach offering on the fourteenth under its own designation, he is liable.

Only if one slaughters the Pesach on the fourteenth while in possession of chametz is he liable to punishment for transgressing 'you shall not offering the blood of my slaughter, etc.', because then the sacrifice is in itself valid (Rav; Rashi).

וְשֶׁלֹּא לִשְׁמוֹ פָּטוּר. — But [if] under some other designation [lit. not its designation], he is not liable.

Since a Pesach slaughtered with the wrong intention is invalid (see mishnah 2), the invalidation of the sacrifice removes the transgression of offering while possessing chametz. R' Shimon (Chullin 81b, 85a) holds that the term שְׁחִיטָה, slaughter, applies only to a halachically valid slaughter that permits the animal to be eaten. A non-halachic killing, which does not render the animal fit for consumption, cannot be described by the term שְׁחִיטָה [halachic] slaughter [שְׁחִיטָה שֶׁאֵינָהּ רְאוּיָה לֹא שְׁמָהּ שְׁחִיטָה], and is therefore not included in the Torah's prohibition: לֹא תִשְׁחַט, You

shall not [perform שְׁחִיטָה] slaughter (Rav; Rashi).

וּשְׁאָר כָּל הַזְּבָחִים בֵּין לִשְׁמָן וּבֵין שֶׁלֹּא לִשְׁמָן, פָּטוּר. — And for all other sacrifices whether [slaughtered] for their own designation or under some other designation, he is exempt.

R' Shimon disagrees with the earlier tannaim in our mishnah who limit the prohibition of slaughtering with chametz to the Pesach offering and, according to R' Yehudah, the Tamid. In R' Shimon's view, the prohibition applies to all sacrifices. He deduces this from the fact that the Torah repeats the same phrase twice (Exodus 23:18 and 34:25) you shall not slaughter with chametz the blood of My offering. The repetition indicates that sacrifices other than the Pesach are included in this prohibition.

However, R' Shimon further notes, the Torah could have included all other offerings under a single prohibition simply by phrasing the admonition in the plural: you shall not slaughter ... My offerings. By choosing to repeat the prohibition, once for the Pesach and once for the other offerings, the Torah teaches that the two prohibitions are not identical; when it is forbidden to slaughter the Pesach with chametz — from noon till nightfall on Pesach eve — then the restriction against slaughtering other offerings is not in force, and conversely when it is forbidden to slaughter other sacrifices with chametz — during the seven days of Pesach — the prohibi-

5
4

R' Shimon says: [If one slaughters] the Pesach offering on the fourteenth under its own designation, he is liable. But [if] under some other designation, he is not liable. And for all other sacrifices whether [slaughtered] for their own designation or under some other designation, he is exempt. [And if one slaughters the Pesach] during the festival, under its own designation, he is exempt, under some other designation, he is liable.

While [if he slaughters] any other sacrifices whether under their own designations or under some other designations he is liable, except for a sin offering which he slaughtered under some other designation.

tion against slaughtering the Pesach does not apply.

Thus on the eve of Pesach, only the Pesach offering falls under this prohibition. In the case of other offerings, however, regardless of one's intention, he does not transgress the prohibition of slaughtering with *chametz*.

וּבַמּוֹעֵד לִשְׁמוֹ פָּטוּר, — [*And if one slaughters the Pesach*] *during the festival, under its own designation, he is exempt,*

Since he slaughtered the Pesach (while in possession of *chametz*) at a time inappropriate for it, the sacrifice is invalid and may not be eaten. As explained above, R' Shimon holds that any slaughter that does not make consumption permissible (שְׁחִיטָה שֶׁאֵינָה רְאוּיָה) is not considered a halachic slaughter (*Rav; Rashi*).

Rambam (Comm. see ed. *Kafich)* and *Meiri* hold that R' Shimon's rule applies not only, as stated, to one who slaughters a Pesach for the sake of a Pesach during the festival, but to one who does so the entire

year as well (cf. his *Comm.* to R' Yehudah's view in ed. *Kafich).*

שֶׁלֹא לִשְׁמוֹ חַיָּב. — *under some other designation, he is liable.*

[I.e., if he slaughtered the Pesach during the festival with the intention that it be a שְׁלָמִים, *peace offering,* because a Pesach offering which was not slaughtered on Pesach eve is automatically converted to a peace offering (see *Zevachim* 1:1). Accordingly, during the festival, one who slaughtered an erstwhile Pesach as a peace offering, has performed a valid slaughter. It is included, therefore, in the category of other valid offerings, which, if slaughtered with *chametz,* are in violation of the Torah commandment (*Rav; Rashi* based on *Gem.* 64a).[1]

וּשְׁאָר כָּל הַזְּבָחִים — *While [if he slaughters] any other sacrifices* [that were offered on the festival]

בֵּין לִשְׁמָן בֵּין שֶׁלֹא לִשְׁמָן, חַיָּב, — *whether under their own designations or under*

1. Although it is an undisputed rule that an unoffered Pesach becomes a peace offering (*Gem.* 64a), there is a Talmudic dispute whether this conversion is automatic. Some hold that the owner of the animal must consciously remove its designation as a Pesach [בְּעֵי עֲקִירָה] and intend that it become a peace offering. Consequently if the unoffered Pesach were slaughtered without any specific intent [סְתָמָא] the sacrifice would retain its Pesach classification. During the festival, of course, the slaughter of a Pesach is invalid and the slaughterer could not be

הַפֶּסַח [ה] נִשְׁחָט בְּשָׁלֹשׁ כִּתּוֹת, —
שֶׁנֶּאֱמַר: ,,וְשָׁחֲטוּ אֹתוֹ כֹּל קְהַל
עֲדַת יִשְׂרָאֵל'', קָהָל וְעֵדָה וְיִשְׂרָאֵל.
נִכְנְסָה כַּת הָרִאשׁוֹנָה, נִתְמַלֵּאת הָעֲזָרָה.
נָעֲלוּ דַלְתוֹת הָעֲזָרָה. תָּקְעוּ הֵרִיעוּ וְתָקְעוּ.

יד אברהם

some other designations, he is liable,

Since other sacrifices are valid even if slaughtered not for their own designation (see preface to mishnah 2), he is liable for slaughtering them with *chametz* regardless of his intention.

In this case, the slaughterer is in violation of two commandments: he slaughtered a valid offering while he was in possession of *chametz*, and he has violated the general commandment against possessing *chametz* during the

Pesach (*Rav; Rashi*).

חוּץ מִן הַחַטָּאת שֶׁשְּׁחָט שֶׁלֹּא לִשְׁמָהּ. — *ex-cept for a sin offering which he slaughtered under some other designation.*

A sin offering is invalid if it is offered under any designation but its own (*Zevachim* 1:1). In R' Shimon's view, therefore, the slaughterer has not performed a halachic slaughter while in possession of *chametz* (*Rav; Rashi*).

5.

הַפֶּסַח נִשְׁחָט בְּשָׁלֹשׁ כִּתּוֹת, — *The Pesach offering was slaughtered in three groups*

It is a *mitzvah* to form three separate groups even when there were few offerings and all the participants could fit into the Temple Courtyard at once (*Rav; Rashi*).

שֶׁנֶּאֱמַר ,,וְשָׁחֲטוּ אֹתוֹ כֹּל קְהַל עֲדַת יִשְׂרָאֵל'', קָהָל וְעֵדָה וְיִשְׂרָאֵל. — *for it is written: And the whole assembly of the con-gregation of Israel shall slaughter it [Ex-odus 12:6]. [The verse mentions] ''as-sembly,'' ''congregation,'' and ''Israel.''*

Each of these three terms — *assembly,*

congregation and Israel — is a word that connotes a group, thus the verse alludes to a total of three groups (*Rav*).

[The term עֵדָה, congregation, is not applied to less than ten people (*Sanhedrin* 2a; Numbers 14:27), and by transference the same is true of the terms קָהָל, assembly, and יִשְׂרָאֵל, Israel (*Malbim* to Exodus 12:6).]

The *Gemara* (64b) records an un-resolved question whether the Torah's intention was that three groups of ten offer the Pesach at separate times, or whether the converse is true, the Torah's intention was the Pesach be of-fered by one group consisting of thirty

liable. According to the other view, the conversion of a Pesach to a peace offering is automatic. If so, there is a difficulty in the law of our mishnah that exempts one who slaughtered a Pesach during the festival *as* a Pesach, on the grounds that the slaughter is invalid. In view of the automatic conversion to a peace offering, why is the slaughter invalid? It should be viewed as a peace offering slaughtered for another designation and valid (see *Tos.*, s.v. טעמא. The *Gemara* 64a explains that according to this view the mishnah must refer to a case where the owner of the offering had not yet discharged his obligation to sacrifice a Pesach, so that he would expect use of the unoffered animal as a *Pesach Sheni* [Second Pesach] on the fourteenth of Iyar, the make-up date for all who had not been able to perform this *mitzvah* on Pesach eve; see *Numbers* 9:1-14). This being so, the animal would not become a peace offering unless there is an expressed intention for it to be one.

5. The Pesach offering was slaughtered in three groups — for it is written: *And the whole assembly of the congregation of Israel shall slaughter it* [*Exodus* 12:6]. [The verse mentions] "assembly," "congregation" and "Israel."

The first group entered, the Temple Courtyard was filled. They closed the gates of the Temple Courtyard. They sounded a *tekiah*, a *teruah*, and again a

YAD AVRAHAM

people.

The ramifications of this question are clear. According to the first view, the *Pesach* requires the formation of three separate groups of at least ten people. According to the second view, there is no fixed number of groups, but the Pesach cannot be slaughtered by a group comprised of less than thirty individuals. To satisfy both sides of the question, ideally the Pesach should be offered in three separate groups of at least thirty people each. Our mishnah requires three groups but does not specify the number

But if this procedure is not feasible, the first group should be comprised of thirty people, thus satisfying the second view. After they have all slaughtered,[1] they may leave and another ten enter. Since twenty members of the first group remained behind, the total number of people remains thirty. On the hypothesis that the first view is correct, the ten newcomers may slaughter in any case (*Rashi*, 64b s.v. בני סגי; *Hil. Korban Pesach* 1:10).

Ohr Zorua 2:226, *R' Chananel* and *Meiri* suggest a different procedure: thirty enter the courtyard, but only ten of them slaughter; they exit and another ten enter and slaughter; they exit and the last ten enter making a total of thirty people in the Courtyard who have not yet slaughtered. Now all of them slaughter together.

נִכְנְסָה כַת הָרִאשׁוֹנָה, נִתְמַלֵּאת הָעֲזָרָה. נָעֲלוּ דַלְתוֹת הָעֲזָרָה. — *The first group entered, [when] the Temple Courtyard was filled. They closed the gates of the Temple Courtyard.*

[The Temple Court was aptly named עֲזָרָה because there they would assemble to pray to

God, who would help and succor (עוֹזֵר) them (*Aruch*, s.v. עזרה; *Radak Shorashim*, s.v. עזר; *Tos.Yom Tov Midos* 2:6).]

תָּקְעוּ הֵרִיעוּ וְתָקְעוּ. — *They sounded a tekiah, a teruah, and again a tekiah.*

Part of the service involved in the offering of public sacrifices is the sounding of trumpets at prescribed parts of the service. This ritual, based on *Numbers* 10:3, is described at length in *Succah* 5:5; and *Arachin* 10a (see also *Rambam, Hil. Klei HaMikdash* 7:6; and *Succah* 8:4, וּשְׁתֵּי חֲצוֹצְרוֹת בְּיָדָן). The sound and the sequence of the blast were parallel to those of the shofar on *Rosh HaShanah*. The *tekiah* is a long sustained blast, and the *teruah* a set of short, choppy blasts (see *Rosh Hashanah* 4:9).

During the service of other offerings the trumpets were sounded simultaneously with the wine libation, and preceding the שִׁיר, *song*, which was chanted in conjunction with the offering of every public sacrifice (see *Succah* 5:5, 53b with *Rashi*, s.v. חטש; *Tamid* 7:3). In the case of the Pesach offering, where no libation was appended to the service, the blasts were sounded during the slaughter (*Hil. Korban Pesach* 1:12; *Yerushalmi*).

As described in mishnah 7 the offering of the Pesach was accompanied by the recitation of *Hallel*. The trumpets were sounded preceding the recitation of the *Hallel* (ibid.; *Tos. HaRashba*). *Rambam* (ibid.) adds that each time the *Hallel* was begun, the blasts were sounded, indicating that the procedure of these trumpet blasts corresponded to that of other sacrifices; the trumpets were always sounded before the song of the day. In the case of the Pesach, *Hallel* can surely be considered the song of the Pesach offering (see *Gem.* 95b, 117a).

הַכֹּהֲנִים עוֹמְדִים שׁוּרוֹת שׁוּרוֹת, וּבִידֵיהֶם
בָּזִיכֵי כֶסֶף וּבָזִיכֵי זָהָב. שׁוּרָה שֶׁכֻּלָּהּ כֶּסֶף
כֶּסֶף, וְשׁוּרָה שֶׁכֻּלָּהּ זָהָב זָהָב. לֹא הָיוּ מְעֹרָבִין.
וְלֹא הָיוּ לַבָּזִיכִין שׁוּלַיִם, שֶׁמָּא יַנִּיחוּם וְיִקְרַשׁ
הַדָּם.

[ו] **שָׁחַט** יִשְׂרָאֵל וְקִבֵּל הַכֹּהֵן נוֹתְנוֹ לַחֲבֵרוֹ
וַחֲבֵרוֹ לַחֲבֵרוֹ, וּמְקַבֵּל אֶת הַמָּלֵא וּמַחֲזִיר אֶת

יד אברהם

הַכֹּהֲנִים עוֹמְדִים שׁוּרוֹת שׁוּרוֹת, — *The Kohanim stood rows upon rows,*

[The slaughter took place to the north of the altar and the *Kohanim* formed lines across the width of the Temple Courtyard, (from north to south) spanning the distance between the place of slaughter and the altar.]

וּבִידֵיהֶם בָּזִיכֵי כֶסֶף וּבָזִיכֵי זָהָב. — *and in their hands were silver bowls and golden bowls.*

These were consecrated vessels (כְּלֵי שָׁרֵת) designated to receive the blood (Rav).

שׁוּרָה שֶׁכֻּלָּהּ כֶּסֶף כֶּסֶף, וְשׁוּרָה שֶׁכֻּלָּהּ זָהָב זָהָב. — *One row was altogether of silver, the other row was altogether of gold.*

The uniform appearance of the rows enhanced their festive spectacle and was a נוֹי מִצְוָה, *beautification of the mitzvah* (Rav, Gem. 64b).

לֹא הָיוּ מְעֹרָבִין. — *They were not mixed up together.*

[As interpreted by *Tif. Yis., Sfas Emes* and others, this passage adds another detail to the previous one: not only is each row comprised entirely of gold or entirely of silver bowls, but even the rows themselves were not mixed

— all the gold rows were placed together in one section and all the silver rows in another. It appears to this writer, however, that the phrase 'a row of entirely silver and a row of entirely gold' conveys an opposite meaning. The rows alternated, first one of silver followed by one of gold (see *Meleches Shlomo*). The orderly and symmetric contrast created through this arrangement was also considered a נוֹי מִצְוָה, *beautification of the mitzvah*.]

וְלֹא הָיוּ לַבָּזִיכִין שׁוּלַיִם, — *Nor did the bowls have bases,*

They were wide at the top and pointy at the bottom (Rav; Rashi).

שֶׁמָּא יַנִּיחוּם — *lest they set them down*

The fear is that the *Kohanim* would set the bowls down, and in their preoccupation with the many offerings, forget to throw the blood immediately. The pointed bottoms of the bowls make it impossible to place them on the stone floor (Rav; Rashi).

וְיִקְרַשׁ הַדָּם. — *and the blood congeal.*

If the bowls could be put on the ground and remain there for any length of time, the blood would congeal. Congealed blood is unfit for the service of throwing (Rav; Rashi).

6.

שָׁחַט יִשְׂרָאֵל — *An Israelite slaughtered it,*

Anyone — Kohen, Levite, or Israelite — may perform the slaughter of an offering. This is the only blood service that need not be performed by a Kohen. Thus our mishnah means that even an

Israelite *may* slaughter if he wishes, but it does not mean that no one else is eligible (Rav; Rashi; Gem. 64b).

Although the language of *Rav* and *Rashi* suggests simply that an Israelite *may* slaughter the offering, *P'nei Yehoshua* and *Sefer HaMiknah* (to *Kiddushin* 41b) argue

tekiah. The *Kohanim* stood rows upon rows, and in their hands were silver bowls and golden bowls. One row was altogether of silver, the other row was altogether of gold. They were not mixed up together. Nor did the bowls have bases, lest they set them down and the blood congeal.

6. An Israelite slaughtered it, and the *Kohen* received it, and he would hand it to his fellow and he to his fellow. He would accept the full one and

YAD AVRAHAM

that slaughtering by the owner of the sacrifice is actually preferable to that of a *Kohen*, at least in the case of the Pesach offering (see *Minchas Chinuch* 5:8). See also *Ohr Zarua* 2:24, *Zera Avraham* 6:7, and *Sfas Emes* for a further discussion on this subject.

וְקִבֵּל הַכֹּהֵן — *and the Kohen received it* [i.e., the blood],

Receiving the blood in the bowl [קַבָּלָה] is the second blood service. In the words of the *Gemara,* from receiving and onwards the services must be performed by a *Kohen* (*Rav; Gemara* 64b; see *Zevachim* 2:1 and 3:1).

The blood had to be received in the bowl directly from the incision in the neck of the sacrifice (*Rashi* 64a, s.v. וקבל). If the blood spilled on the floor prior to being received in the bowl, the sacrifice is disqualified (*Zevachim* 2:1, 25a).

נוֹתְנוֹ לַחֲבֵרוֹ וַחֲבֵרוֹ לַחֲבֵרוֹ, — *and he would hand it to his fellow and he to his fellow.*

The *Kohanim* formed a line to pass the blood from one *Kohen* to the next until it reached the altar. The *Gemara* (64b) adds that the involvement of many *Kohanim* is in fulfillment of the principle, בְּרָב עָם הַדְרַת מֶלֶךְ, *the King's glory is in the multitude of people* (Proverbs 14:28). Accordingly the performance of this *mitzvah* is enhanced by including a large number of participants in its performance (*Rav* from *Gem.* 64b).

The *Gemara* (*Zevachim* 14b; *Hil. Pesulei HaMukdashim* 1:23) rules that הוֹלָכָה, *transport,* of the blood to the altar must be ac-

complished through walking. Thus, if a *Kohen* slaughtered near the altar, and performed the throwing of the blood merely by reaching over without walking, the offering is disqualified. In view of this premise the *Gemara* (ibid.; here 64b) requires that in addition to merely passing the bowls of blood to the altar in assembly line fashion, a *Kohen* must walk a little as he passes the bowl down the line. The commentators discuss whether every *Kohen* on the line must walk a little, or only the last one who throws the blood on the altar must do so (see *Meiri ad loc.; Mishnah LeMelech* to *Pesulei HaMikdoshim* 1:23; *Keren Orah Zevachim* 14b-15a).

וּמְקַבֵּל אֶת הַמָּלֵא וּמַחֲזִיר אֶת הָרֵיקָן. — *He would accept the full one and return the empty one.*

[The rows of *Kohanim* described above were engaged in two functions: Passing the full bowls of blood toward the altar where the blood was thrown upon it; and returning the empty bowls to be reused.]

The phraseology of the mishnah indicates that first the *Kohen* took the full bowl and then passed down the empty one. This is in conformity with the rule אֵין מַעֲבִירִין עַל הַמִּצְוֹת, *one does not pass over mitzvos* — i.e., when one has the opportunity to perform a *mitzvah* he must not ignore it. Since passing down the full bowl of blood is a fulfillment of the service of הוֹלָכָה, *transporting,* the blood, he first accepted the full one, thereby performing his share of the *mitzvah,* and only then did he pass down the empty bowl. Although the

הָרֵיקָן. כֹּהֵן הַקָּרוֹב אֵצֶל הַמִּזְבֵּחַ זוֹרְקוֹ זְרִיקָה אַחַת כְּנֶגֶד הַיְסוֹד.

[ז] **יָצְתָה** כַּת רִאשׁוֹנָה וְנִכְנְסָה כַּת שְׁנִיָּה. יָצְתָה שְׁנִיָּה, נִכְנְסָה שְׁלִישִׁית. כְּמַעֲשֵׂה הָרִאשׁוֹנָה כָּךְ מַעֲשֵׂה הַשְּׁנִיָּה וְהַשְּׁלִישִׁית.

קָרְאוּ אֶת הַהַלֵּל. אִם גָּמְרוּ שָׁנוּ, וְאִם שָׁנוּ שִׁלֵּשׁוּ, אַף עַל פִּי שֶׁלֹּא שִׁלְּשׁוּ מִימֵיהֶם. רַבִּי יְהוּדָה אוֹמֵר: מִימֵיהֶם שֶׁל כַּת הַשְּׁלִישִׁית לֹא

יד אברהם

return was necessary to prepare for a future *mitzvah*, it was not a *mitzvah* in itself (*Rav; Gem.* 64b).

כֹּהֵן הַקָּרוֹב אֵצֶל הַמִּזְבֵּחַ זוֹרְקוֹ זְרִיקָה אַחַת — *The Kohen nearest the altar would throw it with one toss*

The blood was thrown directly from the bowl to the altar. It was not sprinkled with the finger — a procedure that is required only for the חַטָּאת, *sin offering* (*Rav; Rashi*).

[In contrast to most other offerings, the blood of the Pesach was thrown only once. For most other offerings the blood was thrown upon two diagonal corners of the altar so that it would spread and cover portions of all four walls. See *Zevachim* ch. 5.]

כְּנֶגֶד הַיְסוֹד. — *opposite the base.*
The blood was thrown upon the lower half of the altar wall. By the

words *opposite the base*, our mishnah means that it may be thrown only upon a section of the wall above the protrusion of the base. The 'base' (see *Middos* 3:1) was a step-like protrusion, one cubit high and one cubit wide, which circled the bottom of the altar on the entire northern and western sides, and for one cubit along the eastern and southern sides (*Rav*).

The *Gem.* 64b, 87c, 121a, and *Zevachim* 37a cites the dissenting view of some tannaim who hold that the blood of the Pesach is not *thrown* as stated in our mishnah but poured gently from the bowl onto the wall of the altar (*Rashi* 89a, s.v. פסח בשפיכה).

Rambam (*Hil. Korban Pesach* 1:6) rules like this latter view (see *Kessef Mishneh* there). See also *Tosafos* (121a, s.v. כשתמצא) and *Riva* (cited in *Shittah MeKubetzes, Zevachim* 57a) for a different description of the spilling process.

7.

יָצְתָה כַּת רִאשׁוֹנָה וְנִכְנְסָה כַּת שְׁנִיָּה. יָצְתָה שְׁנִיָּה, נִכְנְסָה שְׁלִישִׁית. — *When the first group left, the second group entered. When the second left, the third entered.*

[As one group finished offering its Pesach, it would leave and the next group would enter.]

כְּמַעֲשֵׂה הָרִאשׁוֹנָה כָּךְ מַעֲשֵׂה הַשְּׁנִיָּה וְהַשְּׁלִישִׁית. — *Like the procedure of the*

first, so was the procedure of the second and the third.

[The procedure was identical for each group.]

קָרְאוּ אֶת הַהַלֵּל. — *They recited the Hallel.*

Standing upon the דוּכָן, *platform*, reserved for their singing, the Levites recited *Hallel* throughout the slaughter

return the empty one. The *Kohen* nearest the altar would throw it with one toss opposite the base.

7. **W**hen the first group left, the second group entered. When the second left, the third entered. Like the procedure of the first, so was the procedure of the second and the third.

They recited the Hallel. If they finished it, they repeated it, and if the repetition was completed they would recite it a third time, although they never did recite it a third time.

R' Yehudah says: The third group never reached

<hr>

YAD AVRAHAM

of the multitude of Pesach offerings (*Tosefta* 4:9 cited in *Tos.* 64a, s.v. קראו).

[*Rambam* (Hil. *Korban Pesach* 1:11) (ibid.) adds that the Levites sang, so long as they slaughtered *and offered* [i.e. threw the blood upon the altar].

Who recited the *Hallel? Rav* says, 'all the three groups,' indicating that the Hallel was said by those who brought the Pesach (cf. *Kol HaRemez* who suggests an emendation of *Rav's* words). Apparently his view is that the *Hallel* recited during the sacrifice of the Pesach is in the category of *Hallel* recited on Festivals and other occasions (see *Gem.* 117a), and is therefore obligatory for everyone, *Kohen, Levite* and Israelite (*Tos. Yom Tov*).

Tosafos (64a s.v. קראו) cites *Tosefta* (4:9) that this *Hallel* was recited by the Levites, standing on the platform reserved for singing. *Rambam* (*Korban Pesach* 1:11) concurs with this opinion. The explanation for this view is that this *Hallel* is in the category of *song* with which the Levites regularly accompany public offerings. Consequently it had to be recited by the Levites. [This view also explains why *Hallel* was recited again and again. Since it was a *mitzvah* to recite the song at the slaughtering of every offering, it had to be repeated as long as animals were still being slaughtered. Therefore, also, the recital would be interrupted in its midst when the third group was finished slaughtering, as R' Yehudah says later in the mishnah because it was not *Hallel per se* which was required, but the *song* to accompany the offer-

ing (cf. *Zhav Shva* to *Tos. HaRashba*; *Teshuvos Tzafnas Pane'ach* 2:8, *Michtevei Torah* 1-5; see also *Shoshanim L'David; Ohr Sameach*, Hil. *Korban Pesach* 1:13).

אָם גָּמְרוּ שָׁנוּ, — *If they finished it, they repeated it,*

When a large number of Pesachim were sacrificed, one recitation of the *Hallel* was not long enough to cover the entire slaughtering period, and they had to repeat the *Hallel* (*Rav; Rashi*).

וְאָם שָׁנוּ שִׁלֵּשׁוּ, — *and if the repetition was completed they would recite it a third time,*

If more time was taken up by the Pesach offering it was necessary to repeat the *Hallel* a third time.

אַף עַל פִּי שֶׁלֹּא שִׁלְּשׁוּ מִימֵיהֶם. — *although they never did recite it a third time.*

They never finished the third recitation because the *Kohanim* were numerous and performed the service with quickness and alacrity (*Rashi, Succah* 54b, s.v. ערב פסח cited by *Tos. Yom Tov*).

רַבִּי יְהוּדָה אוֹמֵר: מִימֵיהֶם שֶׁל כַּת שְׁלִישִׁית לֹא הִגִּיעוּ לְ,,אָהַבְתִּי כִּי-יִשְׁמַע ה' '' — *R' Yehudah says: The third group never reached as far as, I love, for HASHEM hears* [Psalms 116:1],

When the third group slaughtered, the Levites never got as far as the fourth

הִגִּיעוּ לְ„,אָהַבְתִּי כִּי־יִשְׁמַע ה' ''‚ מִפְּנֵי שֶׁעַמָּה מְעָטִין.

[ח] כְּמַעֲשֵׂהוּ בְחוֹל כָּךְ מַעֲשֵׂהוּ בַּשַּׁבָּת, אֶלָּא שֶׁהַכֹּהֲנִים מְדִיחִים אֶת הָעֲזָרָה שֶׁלֹּא בִרְצוֹן חֲכָמִים. רַבִּי יְהוּדָה אוֹמֵר: כּוֹס הָיָה מְמַלֵּא מִדַּם הַתַּעֲרֹבוֹת, זְרָקוֹ זְרִיקָה אַחַת עַל גַּבֵּי הַמִּזְבֵּחַ.

יד אברהם

chapter of *Hallel* starting with, *I love, for HASHEM hears*, because all the offerings had already been slaughtered by the time this passage was reached (*Rav; Rashi*).

מִפְּנֵי שֶׁעַמָּה מְעָטִין. — *because its people were few.*

Few people brought their offerings with the third group because most Jews were eager to perform the *mitzvah* as early as possible and did not tarry to this late hour (*Tif. Yis.*).[1]

8.

כְּמַעֲשֵׂהוּ בְחוֹל כָּךְ מַעֲשֵׂהוּ בַּשַּׁבָּת, — *Like its procedure on weekdays so was its procedure on the Sabbath*

If Pesach eve falls on the Sabbath the entire service described previously is performed without change or modification.

אֶלָּא שֶׁהַכֹּהֲנִים מְדִיחִים אֶת הָעֲזָרָה — *except that the Kohanim rinsed the Temple Courtyard*

The procedure followed by the Kohanim was identical on the Sabbath, including the rinsing of the Temple Courtyard, an activity that did not meet with the Rabbis' approval. Had their wishes been followed, the procedure on the Sabbath would have omitted the rinsing.

Accordingly the mishnah reads: The procedure was identical ... but this included the rinsing, which was done without sanction (*Rambam*).

A canal of running water went through the Temple Courtyard. When the *Kohanim* wanted to rinse away the accumulated blood from the floor, they closed the canal so that the water backed up and flooded the floor. Then they opened the canal allowing the water to run out, carrying with it the blood and refuse (*Rav; Rashi; Tosefta 4:10*).

שֶׁלֹּא בִרְצוֹן חֲכָמִים. — *without the consent of the Sages.*

The Rabbis did not condone the rinsing of the Temple Courtyard on the Sabbath because of their prohibition

---

1. The *Gemara* 65a cites a *Tosefta* 4:9 that this group was nicknamed the כַּת עַצְלָנִית, *lazy group*. The *Gemara* asks: Why so? [Was it not a requirement that there be three groups? (*Rashi*).] The answer utilizes a saying of *Rabbi Yehudah the Prince*: 'The world must have both perfume manufacturers and tanners [a trade that involves foul-smelling chemicals]. Happy is he whose trade is perfume manufacture; woe is to him who is a tanner', meaning that despite the requirement that there be a third group, meritorious people would not wait that long.

Kol HaRemez remarks that it was appropriate for them not to reach as far as '*I love*' for the true lovers of God are diligent and fervent in the performance of the *mitzvos* and would not be part of a group that delayed its *mitzvah* until just before the deadline (*Shoshanim L'David*).

as far as, *I love, for HASHEM hears,* [*Psalms* 116:1], because its people were few.

8. Like its procedure on weekdays so was its procedure on the Sabbath except that the *Kohanim* rinsed the Temple Courtyard without the consent of the Sages.

R' Yehudah says: He would fill a cup with the mixed blood [and] throw it once upon the altar. But

YAD AVRAHAM

against washing floors on the Sabbath. In Mishnaic times, most houses were built on the ground, so the earthen floor would often develop grooves and holes. Householders would smooth the floor in the process of rinsing, an act that constituted the forbidden Sabbath labor of בּוֹנֶה, *building*. To avoid the possibility of this happening, the Sages forbade the rinsing of floors in all cases. *Tosafos* (65a, s.v. המכבד) explains that ordinarily the decree would not apply to a marble floor like that of the Temple, but there were earthen spaces between the marble slabs; those spaces could develop holes that would be smoothed by the rinsing.

Although generally the rule is that Rabbinic prohibitions were not applied in the Temple (אֵין שְׁבוּת בַּמִּקְדָּשׁ), the Rabbis reasoned that rinsing the Temple Courtyard is not essential to the Temple service so they did not relax the prohibition in this case (*Gem.* 65a).

Rambam (*Hil. Korban Pesach* 1:16) rules that the *Kohanim* may rinse the floor because Rabbinical prohibitions, even when they do not interfere with the Temple service, do not apply in the Temple. Our mishnah reflects the opinion of only some tannaim and is not accepted as halachah (see comm. to *Rambam*; *Tzlach* here).

רַבִּי יְהוּדָה אוֹמֵר: כּוֹס הָיָה מְמַלֵּא מִדַּם הַתַּעֲרבוֹת, — *R' Yehudah says: He would fill a cup with the mixed blood* [Before it was rinsed away, the *Kohen* would fill a cup from the accumulated blood on the floor, which, in effect, was a mixture of the blood of all the

sacrifices offered that day.]

זְרָקוּ זְרִיקָה אַחַת עַל גַּבֵּי הַמִּזְבֵּחַ. — [*and*] *throw it once* [lit. *one toss*] *upon the altar.*

He would throw the blood from this cup upon the altar once. Consequently, even if all the blood of a particular sacrifice had spilled completely from its bowl with the result that no blood offering had been made, it could be assumed that at least a drop of it would appear in the cup of mixed blood. By throwing it upon the altar, the indispensible blood service would be performed and the offering validated.

The blood accumulated on the Courtyard floor can have three sources. First, it may have spilled from the bowl in which it was collected. Such spillage could have happened as a result of the extreme haste with which the service was done, and the blood remains valid for the blood service despite the mishap (*Zevachim* 3:1). A second possibility is that the blood was never collected in a bowl, but ran out directly from the incision in the slaughtered animal's neck. Such blood is invalid for service (*Zevachim* 2:1), but R' Yehudah maintains that the *Kohanim* are too reliable to have let this happen. The third possibility is that it is the blood that seeps from the incision [דַּם הַתַּמְצִית] after the initial gush of blood [דַּם הַנֶּפֶשׁ] had been collected for the service.

This third sort of blood would constitute by far most of the blood on the Courtyard floor. Although it is not forbidden to put such blood upon the altar, it is only the initial gush that is acceptable for the performance of the blood service. Consequently, a difficulty arises. The general principle of בִּיטוּל, *nullification,* means that a majority sub-

וְלֹא הוֹדוּ לוֹ חֲכָמִים.

[ט] **כֵּיצַד** תּוֹלִין וּמַפְשִׁיטִין? — אָנְקְלָיוֹת שֶׁל בַּרְזֶל הָיוּ קְבוּעִים בַּכְּתָלִים וּבָעַמּוּדִים, שֶׁבָּהֶן תּוֹלִין וּמַפְשִׁיטִין. וְכָל מִי שֶׁאֵין לוֹ מָקוֹם לִתְלוֹת וּלְהַפְשִׁיט, מַקְלוֹת דַּקִּים חֲלָקִים הָיוּ שָׁם, וּמַנִּיחַ עַל כְּתֵפוֹ וְעַל כֶּתֶף חֲבֵרוֹ, וְתוֹלֶה וּמַפְשִׁיט.

רַבִּי אֱלִיעֶזֶר אוֹמֵר: אַרְבָּעָה עָשָׂר שֶׁחָל לִהְיוֹת בַּשַּׁבָּת, מַנִּיחַ יָדוֹ עַל כֶּתֶף חֲבֵרוֹ, וְיַד

יד אברהם

stance nullifies a minority substance and renders it non-existent from a halachic standpoint. For example, if a non-kosher liquid falls into a larger volume of kosher liquid, the mixture is permitted because the minority liquid is nullified. If so, in our mishnah, the small amount of blood that may have spilled from the bowl should become nullified, with the result that no purpose would be served by collecting blood from the floor to place upon the altar. The *Gemara* replies that according to R' Yehudah the rule of nullification applies only where different substances become mixed, such as blood falling into wine. But in the case of two similar substances — such as the blood of our mishnah — halachic nullification does not take place, so that the blood from the bowl retains its identity [מִין בְּמִינוֹ לֹא בָּטִיל] (*Gem.* 64a-b; *Tos.* s.v. שמא).

[The Sages, however, maintain that the rule of nullification applies even to two similar substances. Consequently, the blood suitable for service would have become nullified by the other blood on the Courtyard floor.]

וְלֹא הוֹדוּ לוֹ חֲכָמִים. — *But the Sages did not agree with him.*

The Sages held that nothing could be accomplished by R' Yehudah's suggestion. In their view, even if it can be assumed that the blood of every sacrifice is represented in the cup of the mixed blood, it is nevertheless invalid for throwing upon the altar. Only the דַּם הַנֶּפֶשׁ, *life blood*, which flows out of the animal's neck in a steady stream is valid for throwing; the דַּם הַתַּמְצִית, *seeping blood*, which trickles out of the incision afterward is invalid for this service. Since the *mitzvah* is to receive all of the דַּם הַנֶּפֶשׁ, *life blood*, in the bowls during the service of קַבָּלָה, *receiving*, most of the blood on the Courtyard floor is of the דַּם הַתַּמְצִית, *seeping blood*, variety. Thus, the Rabbis reasoned, even if it can be assumed that the cup of mixed blood contains a small part of the spilled sacrificial blood it is nevertheless invalid.

9.

כֵּיצַד תּוֹלִין וּמַפְשִׁיטִין? — *How did they suspend and flay [them]?*

[The Pesach, like other offerings, had to be flayed prior to placing its sacrificial parts on the altar. To facilitate the flaying process, the animal was suspended, as described below.]

אָנְקְלָיוֹת שֶׁל בַּרְזֶל הָיוּ קְבוּעִים בַּכְּתָלִים — *Iron hooks were fixed into the walls*

The walls of the Temple Courtyard were equipped with hooks for this purpose (*Tif. Yis.*).

[According to the view (see *Tif. Yis.* to *Tamid* 3:5, *Boaz*) that the slaughterhouse

the Sages did not agree with him.

9. **H**ow did they suspend and flay [them]? — Iron hooks were fixed into the walls and into the pillars, on which they suspended and flayed [the Pesach]. Anyone for whom there was no room to suspend and flay [his animal], there were thin smooth stave there, which he placed upon his shoulder and upon the shoulder of his fellow and so hung and flayed [it].

R' Eliezer says: If the fourteenth fell on the Sabbath, he placed his hand on his fellow's shoulder, and

YAD AVRAHAM

was surrounded by a wall, the walls referred to are the walls of this area (cf. *Rashi* 64a, s.v. וקבועין).

וּבָעַמוּדִים, — *and into the pillars*

As recounted in *Middos* (3:5) the area immediately to the north of the altar was reserved for slaughter of sacrifices. Next to this area was the 'slaughter-house' (see *Hil. Bais HaBechirah* 5:13; *R' Shemayah* to *Middos* 3:5; cf. *Tif. Yis.* there; see diagram ArtScroll *Shekalim*, p. 107), which encompassed eight low pillars that supported blocks of wood. Each block had three rows of hooks affixed to it (*Rav; Rashi;* see also *Shekalim* 6:4). These are the pillars to which our mishnah refers.

שֶׁבָּהֶן תּוֹלִין וּמַפְשִׁיטִין. — *on which they suspended and flayed* [*the Pesach*].

[The carcass was suspended by its hind legs and skinned (see *Tamid* 4:2).]

וְכָל מִי שֶׁאֵין לוֹ מָקוֹם לִתְלוֹת וּלְהַפְשִׁיט, — *Anyone for whom there was no room* [lit. *whoever had no place*] *to suspend and flay* [*his animal*],

[If all the hooks were already occupied, leaving no room for suspending more animals]

מַקְלוֹת דַּקִּים חֲלָקִים הָיוּ שָׁם, — *there were thin smooth staves there,*

They used staves whose bark was peeled off (*Rav, Rashi*).

וּמַנִּיחַ עַל כְּתֵפוֹ וְעַל כֶּתֶף חֲבֵרוֹ, וְתוֹלֶה וּמַפְשִׁיט. — *which he placed upon his shoulder and upon the shoulder of his fellow and so hung and flayed* [*it*].

The carcass was suspended on the staves which were placed across the shoulders of two people.

רַבִּי אֱלִיעֶזֶר אוֹמֵר: אַרְבָּעָה עָשָׂר שֶׁחָל לִהְיוֹת בְּשַׁבָּת, — *R' Eliezer says: If the fourteenth fell on the Sabbath,*

R' Eliezer holds that the use of staves is forbidden on the Sabbath because of the *muktzah* [any object or substance whose use on the Sabbath was not anticipated may not be moved or used by Rabbinic decree. There are several varieties of *muktzah* with varying laws, discussed primarily in tractate *Beitzah*.]

R' Eliezer does not explain why the staves should be considered *muktzah*. In view of the fact that they are utensils needed for a permissible purpose, their use should be permitted.

However the Talmud (*Shabbos* 123b) explains R' Eliezer's rule in light of the fact that in Nechemiah's time a greater stringency was applied to the laws of *muktzah* to combat the prevailing flagrant desecration of of the Sabbath. As related in *Nechemiah* (13:15): *In those days I observed in Yehudah that they would press the wine-presses and bring in heaps of grain ...*

In the *Gemara's* words, 'At first [i.e. in Nechemiah's time] they (the Sages) said: [only] three utensils [directly connected to

חֲבֵרוֹ עַל כְּתֵפוֹ, וְתוֹלֶה וּמַפְשִׁיט.

[י] **קְרָעוֹ** וְהוֹצִיא אֵמוּרָיו, נְתָנוּ בְּמָגִיס וְהִקְטִירָן עַל גַּבֵּי הַמִּזְבֵּחַ. יָצְתָה כַת רִאשׁוֹנָה וְיָשְׁבָה לָהּ בְּהַר הַבַּיִת, שְׁנִיָּה בַּחֵיל, וְהַשְּׁלִישִׁית בִּמְקוֹמָהּ עוֹמֶדֶת. חָשֵׁכָה, יָצְאוּ וְצָלוּ אֶת פִּסְחֵיהֶן.

יד אברהם

וְיַד חֲבֵרוֹ עַל כְּתֵפוֹ, — *and the hand of his fellow [rested] upon his shoulder,*

The second individual similarly placed his left hand on the first one's shoulder, thus freeing the right hand for skinning the animal (*Tos. Yom Tov*).

וְתוֹלֶה וּמַפְשִׁיט. — *and thus he suspended and flayed [it].*

And thus he was able to flay the animal without using the staves. The Sages disagree with R' Eliezer and permitted the use of staves because of the principle of אֵין שְׁבוּת בְּמִקְדָּשׁ, *Rabbinic restrictions [concerning the Sabbath] do not [usually] apply in the Temple* (*Rav, Rambam*). Although, in principle R' Eliezer agrees with this rule, he holds that whenever possible this dispensation should be avoided (*Tos. Yom Tov*; cf. *Shabbos* 124a).

the preparation of food] may be moved on the Sabbath.' Gradually the Sages relaxed the stringency of the law of *muktzah* to the degree codified in the Halachah.

In other words, the rule cited by R' Eliezer was actually formulated and applied in the times of Nechemiah, and although the halachah of *muktzah* was altered subsequently, the mishnah recorded it in its original form [1]

Tosafos (loc. cit. s.v. לא) adds that the necessity to stem the tide of Sabbath desecration, led the Rabbis to ordain this stringent Rabbinic rule even in the Temple. This was a departure from the general rule that: אֵין שְׁבוּת בְּמִקְדָּשׁ, *Rabbinic restrictions do not (usually) apply in the Temple.*

מֵנִיחַ יָדוֹ עַל כְּתֵף חֲבֵרוֹ, — *he placed his hand on his fellow's shoulder,*

He placed his left hand on his fellow's right shoulder.

10.

קְרָעוֹ — *He tore it [open]*

[The *Kohen* opened the body cavity of the Pesach offering (cf. *Yoma* 6:7).]

וְהוֹצִיא אֵמוּרָיו, — *and removed its sacrificial parts,*

[The fats of every sacrifice and cer-

tain organs (the kidneys, parts of the liver, and the tail of sheep; see *Leviticus* 3:9-10, 14-15) had to be burned upon altar. Collectively, these parts are called אֵמוּרִין, *emurin*[1].]

נְתָנוּ בְּמָגִיס וְהִקְטִירָן עַל גַּבֵּי הַמִּזְבֵּחַ. — *put*

1. Although the mishnah was redacted and standardized by Rabbi (R' Yehudah the Prince, 2nd cent. C.E.), it had been formulized in the main at a much earlier date (probably by the 'Men of the Great Assembly' at the beginning of the Second Temple era; see *Yer. Shekalim* 5:1). With this passage of centuries, this body of law, which had been transmitted orally, developed into many versions that differed from each other on many points. Rabbi assumed the task of developing a standard text — the Mishnah. In many cases, however, he did not remove from the Mishnah earlier formulas that had become obsolete (מִשְׁנָה רִאשׁוֹנָה לֹא זָזָה מִמְּקוֹמָהּ). Striking examples of this practice are found in *Nedarim* (11:12) and *Kesubos* (5:2-3). (See *Tos. Bava Kama* 94a, s.v. בימי; *Keileim* 30:4 with *Tos. R' Akiva* and *Mishnah Acharonah*; *Iggeres R' Sherira Gaon.*) A lengthy and brilliant treatment of this theme is to be found in *Doros HaRishonim* (R' Isaac HaLevi Rabinowitz), v.1, pp. 204-311 (Israeli ed.).

the hand of his fellow [rested] upon his shoulder, and [thus] he suspended and flayed [it].

10. He tore it [open] and removed its sacrificial parts, put them in a plate and burned them upon the altar.

The first group went out and remained on the Temple Mount, the second [group] in the Chel, and the third [group] remained where they were. After dark, they went out and roasted their Pesach offerings.

YAD AVRAHAM

them [lit. it] in a plate and burned them upon the altar.

[Some versions (see *Shinuyei Nuschaos; Rambam, cd. Kafich*) have נְתָנָן, *he put them,* (plural). Whatever the version it is clear that the mishnah refers to all the sacrificial parts.]

Therefore the mishnah really means that whoever flayed and dissected the offering put the parts preparatory to their burning in a plate until a *Kohen* was available to burn them upon the altar (*Gem.* 65a). The *Gemara* (*ibid.*) explains that unlike the previously described flaying and dissection of the sacrifice, which may be performed by an Israelite, the burning of the sacrificial parts upon the altar may be done only by a *Kohen.*

יָצְתָה כַת רִאשׁוֹנָה וְיָשְׁבָה לָה בְּהַר הַבַּיִת, — *The first group went out and remained on the Temple Mount,*

When the eve of Pesach occurred on the Sabbath the first group carried its sacrifices no further than the Temple Mount (*Rav; Rashi*).

Although Jerusalem was enclosed by a wall, and thus had the status of a רְשׁוּת הַיָּחִיד, *private domain*[1], carrying was forbidden nevertheless, because the city streets were classifies as a חָצֵר שֶׁל רַבִּים, *public courtyard,* and an *eruv* (עֵרוּבֵי חֲצֵירוֹת)[2] would be needed in order to allow carrying (see *Eruvin* 10:9 with *Rambam* and *Tos. Yom Tov;* there 6b and 101a).

[The reason why no *eruv* was established in Jerusalem is discussed by various commentators, see *Tif. Yis. (Eruvin* 10:9) *Tos. Yom Tov (ibid.) Igros Moshe, Orach Chaim* (I) 139:5.]

Meleches Shlomo cites *Tosafos* in *Sotah* 40b (not in our versions) that they were permitted to take the offerings home, but the custom was not to do so lest their wives gather the mistaken impression that all prohibitions of the Sabbath are entirely overridden for the sake of the Pesach offering, and roast it before nightfall.

שְׁנִיָּה בַּחֵיל, — *the second [group] in the Chel.*

Rambam in his preface to *Kodashim* (cited by *Tos. Yom Tov*) traces the origin of the term *emurin* to the word אָמוּר, *it was said,* i.e., the parts the Torah has *said* are to be separated from the sacrifice and burned upon the altar. *Aruch* (s.v. מר 2, cited by *Rishon L'Tziyon* here) related the word to the Aramaic מר, *lord.* The parts which are offered upon the altar are considered the *lords* of the sacrifice. *Mishneh LaMelech* (Hil. Ma'aseh HaKorbanos 1:18) and *Tiferes Yisrael* define *emurin* as best parts, and cite a parallel usage: רֹאשׁ אָמִיר, *the uppermost growth* [of a tree] (*Isaiah* 17:6).

1. The sole physical specification for a רְשׁוּת הַיָּחִיד, *private domain,* is proper separation from surrounding areas. There is no requirement that the property be privately owned. As long as the area has a length and width of at least four handbreadths (טְפָחִים), and is surrounded by partitions at least 10 handbreadths high, it is a *private domain* (see *Shabbos* 6a-b).

2. A device through which many different units can be considered to be joined into one large unit, thereby removing the Rabbinic prohibition against carrying from one private domain to another.

אֵלּוּ [א] דְּבָרִים בְּפֶסַח דּוֹחִין אֶת הַשַּׁבָּת: שְׁחִיטָתוֹ, וּזְרִיקַת דָּמוֹ, וּמִחוּי

יד אברהם

[At a ten-cubit distance from the Temple Courtyard wall was a low wooden partition called סוֹרֵג, *Soreg*. The area between the *Soreg* and the Temple Courtyard was called the *Chel* (see *Middos* 2:3]. When the second group left the Temple Courtyard, they passed through the Women's Courtyard and stopped in the Chel *(Rav; Rashi)*.

וְהַשְּׁלִישִׁית בִּמְקוֹמָהּ עוֹמֶדֶת. — *and the third [group] remained where they were.*

I.e. the third group remained in the Temple Courtyard where they had slaughtered their offerings. *R' Akiva Eiger* notes that the term עוֹמֶדֶת, lit.

stood [as opposed to יָשְׁבָה, lit. *sat*, used in reference to the first group], is particularly appropriate, in view of the law that sitting in the Temple Courtyard was forbidden to all except for kings of the Davidic dynasty *(Yoma* 25a). Thus the third group, which remained in the Courtyard, had to stand until they left (see also *Ohr Sameach, Hil. Korban Pesach* 1:17).

חָשֵׁכָה, יָצְאוּ וְצָלוּ אֶת פִּסְחֵיהֶן. — *After dark* [lit. *it darkened*], *they went out and roasted their Pesach offerings.*

The roasting of the Pesach does not override the Sabbath *(Rav)*. Therefore they had to wait until nightfall *(Rav)*.

Chapter 6

1.

אֵלּוּ דְבָרִים בְּפֶסַח דּוֹחִין אֶת הַשַּׁבָּת: — *These* [i.e. the following] *things pertaining to the Pesach offering override the Sabbath:*

As mentioned previously (5:1), the Pesach offering may be brought on the Sabbath even though this involves acts which are in violation of the Sabbath. The source of this law is the word בְּמוֹעֲדוֹ, *in its appointed time*, which the Torah uses in connection with the obligation to bring the Pesach offering *(Numbers* 9:2). The same phrase is used in connection with the daily sacrifice,

teaching that just as the daily sacrifice is brought even on the Sabbath, the Pesach offering, too, must be brought in its appointed time even if it is the Sabbath *(Rav; Gem.* 66a).[1]

However, not everything involved in bringing the Pesach offering is permitted on the Sabbath. Anything that can be performed before or after the Sabbath does not override the Sabbath. Consequently the mishnah enumerates those services related to the Pesach offering that must be performed on the eve of Pesach, even if it falls on the Sabbath.

1. Historically the law of this mishnah has great significance for it gave rise to a dialogue that resulted in the ascendancy of Hillel the Elder (הִלֵּל הַזָּקֵן) as *Nassi* (lit. *prince*), the highest position of Jewish leadership in mishnaic times.

As related in the *Gemara* (66a), the fourteenth of Nissan once fell on the Sabbath and 'the sons of Beseira,' the heads of the *Beis Din* at the time, forgot whether or not the service of the Pesach offering overrides the Sabbath. Upon inquiring whether anyone knew the halachah, they were told that a certain man by the name of Hillel the Babylonian, who had arrived from Babylonia and studied under the two greatest men of the time, Shmaya and Avtalyon, knew the halachah. Hillel was summoned and convincingly expounded the halachah that the Pesach offering may be brought even on the Sabbath. Upon hearing his words, the sons of Beseira immediately proclaimed him *Nassi*. Hillel and his progeny, among whom was R' Yehudah HaNassi (the compiler of the Mishnah), ruled almost without interruption until the position was abolished by the Byzantine emperor in the first half of the fifth century.

1. **T**hese things pertaining to the Pesach offering override the Sabbath: Its slaughter; throwing of its blood; removal [of the offal] from its entrails;

YAD AVRAHAM

שְׁחִיטָתוֹ, — *Its slaughter;*

[Slaughter is one of the thirty-nine primary labors Scripturally prohibited on the Sabbath.]

The slaughter of the Pesach sacrifice cannot be postponed until nightfall since it is written *(Lev.* 7:38) **on the day** *that He commanded the children of Israel to present their offerings,* from which we learn that the slaughtering of a sacrifice, as well as any of the other עֲבוֹדוֹת, *sacrificial services,* must be done during the day *(Rav; Rashi).*[1]

וּזְרִיקַת דָּמוֹ, — *throwing of its blood;*

The throwing of blood upon the altar must also be performed during the day, and cannot be postponed until nightfall.

Tosafos (65b, s.v. אלו) comments that since *throwing* entails no desecration of the Sabbath, it need not be mentioned in connection with the actions that override the Sabbath. The mishnah notes it here because it is usually mentioned with *slaughter,* which was listed just previously as an act that does override the Sabbath.

Kol HaRemez (also *Lechem Shamayim Shoshanim L'David* and *Meromei HaSadeh)* suggests that since the offering is disqualified unless its blood is thrown, this service should be considered as תִּקּוּן, *perfecting* or *repairing,* which is Rabbinically prohibited. Indeed *Tosafos (Nazir* 28b, s.v. בבשי; see *Rosh* there) makes this categorization in a similar case *(Imrei Daas* in *Kevutzas M'forshei HaMishnah).*

וּמִחוּי קְרָבָיו, — *removal [of the of-*

fal] from its entrails;

The entrails are punctured to allow the offal to be removed. Although this is not an essential component of the sacrifical service, it is permitted on the Sabbath because leaving the entrails uncleaned until nightfall may cause them to putrefy *(Rav; Rashi).*

Additionally, *Yerushalmi* notes that the need for this process was 'so that it not appear as if the sacrificial parts come from a filthy offering.' Thus this service can be considered a necessary preparation for the sacrifice, and not merely a prelude to eating. *Meleches Shlomo* points out that this is indicated by the placement of this process in the mishnah between *throwing* and *burning of the fats* — both components of the sacrificial service.

Our translation and commentary follow one rendition in the *Gemara* 68a in interpreting the term מִחוּי קְרָבָיו. In an alternate rendition, the *Gemara* defines it as the removal of the mucus-like adhesions which must be scraped from the lining of the entrails. The reason for permitting this act is the same, to prevent putrefaction.

[*Rambam (Hil. Korban Pesach* 1:18) does not specify which of these interpretations he favors, indicating that the two renditions are not mutually exclusive.]

Which desecration of the Sabbath is involved in removing the offal? *Tiferes Yisrael* reasons this would be a Rabbinically prohibited form of דָּשׁ, *threshing,* because it involves the separation of the refuse [פְּסוֹלֶת] from the edible part [אוֹכָל]. It can also be said that this could be considered unnecessary bother [טִרְחָא] on the Sabbath.

1. [*Rav's* (and *Rashi)* choice of a Scriptural verse upon which to base the impossibility of deferring the slaughter until night is questioned by *Rashash:* Surely even if it were permitted in general to offer sacrifices at night this would not apply to the Pesach offering, which must be offered בְּמוֹעֲדוֹ, *in its appointed time (Numbers* 9:2), on the fourteenth of Nissan. Indeed the latter source is given by *Rambam (Comm.). Meiri* compounds the difficulty when he cites both sources, implying that both are needed. Perhaps these authorities assume that the term בֵּין הָעַרְבַּיִם, *in the afternoon* (lit. *between the evenings: Exodus* 12:6), giving the time when the Pesach must be offered, does not rule out the night in its literal translation. Because of the rule that the night is considered part of the preceding day with regard to the laws of the sacrificial service, the night of Pesach could be considered part of the fourteenth of Nissan, and fit for sacrifice in years when the eve of Pesach falls on a Sabbath — hence the need for the general prohibition against sacrifice at night.]

קָרְבָיו, וְהִקְטֵר חֲלָבָיו. אֲבָל צְלִיָתוֹ וַהֲדָחַת
קְרָבָיו אֵינָן דּוֹחִין אֶת הַשַּׁבָּת.
הַרְכָּבָתוֹ, וַהֲבָאָתוֹ מִחוּץ לַתְּחוּם, וַחֲתִיכַת
יַבַּלְתּוֹ אֵין דּוֹחִין אֶת הַשַּׁבָּת.
רַבִּי אֱלִיעֶזֶר אוֹמֵר: דּוֹחִין.

יד אברהם

וְהִקְטֵר חֲלָבָיו — *and the burning of its fats.*

The word 'fats' is used loosely. It includes everything included in the term אֵימוּרִין, *sacrificial parts that are burned on the altar (Tos. Yom Tov 5:10).*

The burning of the fats upon the altar, although not necessary for the fulfillment of the supplicant's obligation [לֹא מְעַכְּבֵי כַּפָּרָה], is nevertheless an essential part of the service performed with every offering, and should ideally be done on the day of sacrifice. Nevertheless, if delayed, the fats may be burned at night also.

Although halachically the fats may be burned at night, we nevertheless burn them on the Sabbath and do not wait until nightfall. This is because, in the *Gemara's* words (68b), חֲבִיבָה מִצְוָה בִשְׁעָתָה, *a mitzvah performed in its time* [i.e. as early as possible] *is precious,* and that is sufficient reason to override the Sabbath.

Tosafos (68b, s.v. אלו) remarks that yet another Scripturally forbidden labor — הֶפְשֵׁט, *flaying* — is permitted (see above 5:9). The mishnah need not mention this, because it is understood that removal of the sacrificial parts must be preceded by flaying.

אֲבָל צְלִיָתוֹ וַהֲדָחַת קְרָבָיו אֵינָן דּוֹחִין אֶת הַשַּׁבָּת. — *But its roasting and the rinsing of its entrails do not override the Sabbath.*

Roasting is classified under the primary labor מְבַשֵּׁל, *cooking,* and is Scripturally forbidden. Rinsing the entrails would be Rabbinically prohibited as a bother (טִרְחָא) unnecessary for the Sabbath (see above s.v. מחוץ). Since both these labors can be put off until evening, it is not necessary that

they override the Sabbath *(Rav; Rashi).*

[Rinsing the entrails can be deferred until nightfall without danger of putrefaction, since, in the main, the offal has already been removed.]

הַרְכָּבָתוֹ — *Carrying it* [lit. *its being made to ride*],

I.e. if the sacrificial animal had not been brought to the Temple Mount before the Sabbath, and it must be now carried through the public domain (רְשׁוּת הָרַבִּים) on the Sabbath in order to bring it to the Temple for sacrifice *(Rav; Rashi).*

וַהֲבָאָתוֹ מִחוּץ לַתְּחוּם, — *bringing it from outside the Sabbath limit.*

[One of the laws of the Sabbath forbids a person to walk outside an area that extends 2000 cubits on all sides of his residence (or city, see *Eruvin* ch. 5-6, *ArtScroll Beitzah* 5:3). This area is known as the *t'chum.* Consequently, if the animal was not brought to the Temple before the Sabbath and is now outside of the *t'chum,* bringing it would violate the Sabbath.]

וַחֲתִיכַת יַבַּלְתּוֹ — *and cutting off its wart*

A wart constitutes a מוּם, *blemish,* which disqualifies the animal as a sacrifice until it is removed. However, removal of a wart is classified under the primary labor גּוֹזֵז, *shearing,* and is Scripturally forbidden on the Sabbath *(Rashi, Eruvin* 103a, s.v. אם בכלי). This prohibition applies only to a moist wart that must be removed with an instrument. The removal of a dry wart, brittle enough to be crumbled by hand אִיפְרוּכֵי [מִיפְרִיךְ], is not considered shearing and may be done on the Sabbath even with an instrument, provided the animal is

and the burning of its fats. But its roasting and the rinsing of its entrails do not override the Sabbath.

Carrying it, bringing it from outside the Sabbath limit, and cutting off its wart do not override the Sabbath.

R' Eliezer says: They do override [it].

needed for the Temple service. Otherwise, the removal is Rabbinically forbidden (*Rashi* 68b, s.v. והא; *Eruvin* 103a).

אֵין דּוֹחִין אֶת הַשַּׁבָּת. — *do not override the Shabbos.*

I.e. these acts may not be performed on the Sabbath, even though as a result the sacrifice will not be brought. Since these preparations could have been accomplished before the Sabbath, the Sages forbade them on the Sabbath (*Rav; Rashi*).

Based on a reading in *Eruvin* 103a, *Rav* and *Rashi* explain that, in this tanna's view, one may not violate even Rabbinic injunctions for anything that could have been done before the Sabbath. Each of the three actions prohibited by the mishnah can be understood as Rabbinic in origin. Carrying the animal, because חַי נוֹשֵׂא אֶת עַצְמוֹ, *a live thing carries itself* (*Shabbos* 94b) and one who carries it violates only a Rabbinical prohibition[1], the restriction of *t'chum* according to most tannaim is not Scriptural, and removing a moist blemish is prohibited even if one does it with his teeth or his hand [i.e., without an instrument]; however when done in that unusual manner [כְּלְאַחַר יַד] it is prohibited only by Rabbinic decree, because the Scriptural definition of forbidden labor includes only work done in its normal manner.

רַבִּי אֱלִיעֶזֶר אוֹמֵר: דּוֹחִין. — *R' Eliezer says: They do override [it].*

R' Eliezer's opinion is that whatever is necessary for the performance of the *mitzvah* — even the preliminaries (מַכְשִׁירִין) — override the Sabbath.

R' Eliezer is consistent with his view regarding the *mitzvah* of circumcision (*Shabbos* 19:1), that whenever overriding the Sabbath is justified, even the preparatory actions (מַכְשִׁירִין) override the Sabbath (*Rav; Rashi* 68b, s.v. הא והא).

Consequently, in R' Eliezer's opinion, if the performance of a *mitzvah* overrides the Sabbath, the preparations, too, override it, even if a Scriptural transgression is involved (*Tos.* 68b s.v. ומה: *Tos. Yom Tov*).

Rambam (Comm.) comments that the dispute between the first tanna and R' Eliezer is whether the three activities listed in the mishnah are prohibited Scripturally, and therefore forbidden on the Sabbath, or probibited Rabbinically, and therefore permitted for the sake of the Pesach offering. In *Rambam's* view, both the first tanna and R' Eliezer agree that Rabbinic probibitions may be waived. In this, they disagree with R' Yeshoshua and R' Akiva in the next mishnah. Perhaps *Rambam* felt that because the first tanna here remains anonymous, he cannot be identified with the view of the tannaim whose names are mentioned explicitly in mishnah 2.

---

1. The concept of a living thing 'carrying itself' is based on the fact that live weight is easier to carry than dead weight, and living animals were not carried in the Tabernacle. However, only R' Nassan holds that this rule applies even to animals; the Sages apply it only to people because animals tend to 'push themselves downward,' thus causing their bearer to carry their full weight. In including the carrying of animals among Rabbinical prohibitions, the mishnah follows R' Nassan, even though the halachah does not accept his view (See *Shabbos* 94a; *Tos* there, s.v. שהחי; *Aruch HaShulchan, Hil. Shabbos* 301:27.)

אָמַר רַבִּי אֱלִיעֶזֶר, ,,וַהֲלֹא דִין הוּא! מָה [ב]
אִם שְׁחִיטָה שֶׁהִיא מִשׁוּם מְלָאכָה
דּוֹחָה אֶת הַשַּׁבָּת, אֵלּוּ שֶׁהֵן מִשׁוּם שְׁבוּת, לֹא
יִדְחוּ אֶת הַשַּׁבָּת!"
אָמַר לוֹ רַבִּי יְהוֹשֻׁעַ, ,,יוֹם טוֹב יוֹכִיחַ,
שֶׁהִתִּירוּ בּוֹ מִשׁוּם מְלָאכָה, וְאָסוּר בּוֹ מִשׁוּם
שְׁבוּת."
אָמַר לוֹ רַבִּי אֱלִיעֶזֶר, ,,מַה זֶּה, יְהוֹשֻׁעַ? מָה
רְאָיָה רְשׁוּת לְמִצְוָה?"

יד אברהם

2.

The following mishnah continues the theme of the previous one, as the disputants attempt to prove their respective points of view.

!אָמַר רַבִּי אֱלִיעֶזֶר, ,,וַהֲלֹא דִין הוּא — *Said R' Eliezer, "But is this not a logical argument!*

[The term דִין (lit. *judgment*) is very often used in Talmudic literature to denote the two deductive methods of reasoning קַל וָחוֹמֶר, *a fortiori*, and בִּנְיַן אָב or מַה מָּצִינוּ, *the drawing of parallels*, in which two similar cases are assumed to have the same law or characteristic.

R' Eliezer presented the following argument to support his position set forth above that one may violate the Sabbath even for מַכְשִׁירִין, *preliminary steps*, necessary for the Pesach, such as bringing the animal or removing a blemish. The theme of his reasoning is that Rabbinic prohibitions should be waived in favor of acts needed for the Pesach offering.]

Tosafos (68b, s.v. ומה) holds that R' Eliezer permits the overriding of even Scriptural prohibitions, as set forth in mishnah 1. Accordingly, the argument set forth here of R' Eliezer's opinion, which deals only with Rabbinic prohibitions, cannot be viewed as the sole basis of his opinion. Rather the intent of his argument is to force the first tanna to concede that at least Rabbinic prohibitions should be waived.

As mentioned above (comm. to mishnah 1, s.v. ר' אליעזר), *Rambam* holds that even R'

Eliezer permitted only Rabbinic prohibitions to be overridden. Thus his argument here can serve as the basis of his position.

מָה אִם שְׁחִיטָה שֶׁהִיא מִשׁוּם מְלָאכָה — *If slaughter [of the Pesach] which is [Scripturally prohibited as] a labor*

As one of the thirty-nine primary labors [אֲבוֹת מְלָאכוֹת] (listed in *Shabbos* 7:2), slaughter is Scripturally forbidden on the Sabbath (*Rav; Rashi*).

דּוֹחָה אֶת הַשַּׁבָּת, — *overrides the Sabbath,*

[The *mitzvah* of slaughtering the Pesach sacrifice overrides the prohibition against slaughter on the Sabbath.]

אֵלּוּ — [*then*] *these*

[I.e., the acts mentioned in connection with the dispute of R' Eliezer in the previous mishnah.]

שֶׁהֵן מִשׁוּם שְׁבוּת — *which are forbidden [merely] because of a Rabbinic prohibition,*

[The word שְׁבוּת (*shevus*), lit. *rest* or *abstention*, is a technical term used in the Talmud for actions Rabbinically prohibited on the Sabbath (see ArtScroll comm. to *Beitzah* 5:2).]

2. **S**aid R' Eliezer, "But is this not a logical argument! If slaughter [of the Pesach] which is [Scripturally prohibited as] a labor overrides the Sabbath, [then] these which are forbidden [merely] because of a Rabbinic prohibition, should certainly override the Sabbath!"

Said R' Yehoshua to him, "Let [the] festival [laws] prove [this], for on it they permitted labor, but forbade on it [what is proscribed] because of Rabbinic prohibitions."

R' Eliezer said to him, "What is this Yehoshua? What proof [can be adduced from] a permissible act to a *mitzvah?"*

YAD AVRAHAM

לֹא יְדְחוּ אֶת הַשַּׁבָּת! — *should certainly override the Sabbath!"*

[I.e., certainly Rabbinic prohibitions, which are less severe than slaughter, may be waived for the purpose of sacrifice.]

Tosafos (68b, s.v. ומה) notes that R' Eliezer surely acknowledges the distinction between the slaughter of the Pesach, which *must* be performed on the Sabbath, and the necessary preliminaries which could have been done prior to this day. Nevertheless, he felt that in view of the fact that even Scriptural prohibitions are waived in favor of this *mitzvah,* it is not logical that even non-mandated Rabbinic prohibitions should stand in its way for any reason.

אָמַר לוֹ רַבִּי יְהוֹשֻׁעַ, ,,יוֹם טוֹב יוֹכִיחַ, שֶׁהִתִּירוּ בּוֹ מִשׁוּם מְלָאכָה, — *Said R' Yehoshua to him, "Let* [the] *festival* [laws] *prove* [this]*, for on it they permitted* [certain Scriptural categories of] *labor,*

It is permissible to cook and bake on a festival *(Rav; Rashi)* [though these are primary labors (אֲבוֹת מְלָאכוֹת) that are prohibited on the Sabbath (or even on festivals when not needed for the sake of the festival)].

וְאָסוּר בּוֹ מִשׁוּם שְׁבוּת." — *but forbade on it* [what is proscribed] *because of Rabbinic prohibitions."*

It is prohibited to bring food from outside the Sabbath limit [תְּחוּם שַׁבָּת], even if it is needed for the festival *(Rav; Rashi;* see *Beitzah* 8:3-7).

Rambam (Comm.) offers another example: It is forbidden to play musical instruments on festivals even though this would enhance the festivities (see *Beitzah* 5:2 and *Succah* 5:1).

[These examples are selected by the commentators from hundreds of Rabbinic prohibitions, because they involve actions clearly necessary for the festival, thereby demonstrating R' Yehoshua's point: a valid basis for overriding a Scriptural prohibition would not necessarily justify waiving Rabbinic prohibitions.]

אָמַר לוֹ רַבִּי אֱלִיעֶזֶר, ,,מָה זֶה יְהוֹשֻׁעַ? מָה רְאָיָה רְשׁוּת לְמִצְוָה?" — *R' Eliezer said to him, "What is this Yehoshua? What proof* [can be adduced from] *a permissible act to a mitzvah?"*

I.e., the reason the Sages refused to waive Rabbinic prohibitions in favor of food preparation on the festivals is that it is not a need related to the fulfillment of a *mitzvah;* while one honors the festival by dining well, he is not *required* to do so. Feasting on the festivals, in R' Eliezer's view, is not a mitzvah. In the case of the Pesach offering on the Sabbath, the Torah obliges that it

הֵשִׁיב רַבִּי עֲקִיבָא וְאָמַר, ,,הַזָּאָה תּוֹכִיחַ,
שֶׁהִיא מִצְוָה, וְהִיא מִשּׁוּם שְׁבוּת, וְאֵינָהּ דּוֹחָה
אֶת הַשַּׁבָּת. אַף אַתָּה אַל תִּתְמַהּ עַל אֵלּוּ, שֶׁאַף
עַל פִּי שֶׁהֵן מִצְוָה, וְהֵן מִשּׁוּם שְׁבוּת, לֹא יִדְחוּ
אֶת הַשַּׁבָּת.''
אָמַר לוֹ רַבִּי אֱלִיעֶזֶר, ,,וְעָלֶיהָ אֲנִי דָן. וּמַה
אִם שְׁחִיטָה שֶׁהִיא מִשּׁוּם מְלָאכָה דּוֹחָה אֶת
הַשַּׁבָּת, הַזָּאָה שֶׁהִיא מִשּׁוּם שְׁבוּת אֵינוֹ דִין
שֶׁדּוֹחָה אֶת הַשַּׁבָּת.''
אָמַר לוֹ רַבִּי עֲקִיבָא, ,,אוֹ חִלּוּף? מָה אִם

יד אברהם

be offered, Therefore their refusal to waive restrictions for the sake of festival enjoyment cannot be used as proof that they would let these prohibitions stand in the way of a *mitzvah* (*Rav; Rashi*).

However, R' Yehoshua held that eating and drinking on the festivals is a *mitzvah*, and is therefore analogous to our situation (*Rav; Gem. 68b*).

הֵשִׁיב רַבִּי עֲקִיבָא וְאָמַר ,,הַזָּאָה תּוֹכִיחַ, —R' *Akiva responded and said, "Let 'sprinkling' prove [this]*,

[A person contaminated by contact with a corpse must undergo a cleansing process comprised of two sprinklings of *purification water* (one on the third and one on the seventh day of the cleansing period) followed by immersion in a *mikveh*. The מֵי חַטָּאת, *purification water*, is made of ashes of the 'Red Cow' (פָּרָה אֲדֻמָּה) mixed with spring water (מַיִם חַיִּים) (see *Numbers* 19:11-19).]

שֶׁהִיא מִצְוָה, — *for it is* [an action mandated by] *a mitzvah*,

If the seventh and final day of the

cleansing period fell on the Sabbath which is Pesach eve,[1] sprinkling is a *mitzvah*, for without it the contaminated person will not be permitted to partake of the Pesach offering at night, and thus be disqualified from fulfilling the *mitzvah* of the Pesach offering (*Rav; Rashi*).

וְהִיא מִשּׁוּם שְׁבוּת, — *and is forbidden*] *because of a Rabbinic prohibition,*

Because it sets the stage for immersion, the final step in the cleansing process, — sprinkling — is similar to מְתַקֵּן, *repairing*, which is Rabbinically prohibited on the Sabbath or festivals (*Rav; Rashi*; cf. *Beitzah* 18a). [The repair of utensils comes under the primary labor מַכֶּה בְּפַטִּישׁ, (lit. *hitting with a hammer*) applying the finishing touch to a product. Cleansing itself was prohibited by the Rabbis because it is similar to 'repairing the person,' by permitting him to enter the Temple and partake of offerings.]

The *Gemara* (69a) gives an additional reason for this prohibition: We are apprehensive that the person may forget and

---

1. There is question whether a person cleansed on Pesach eve from corpse contamination is in fact fit to discharge his obligation (see further 8:5 and *Hil. Korban Pesach* 5:2). Because of this, *Rambam* (*Comm.*) explains the problem of sprinkling discussed here as referring to an occasion when the *thirteenth* of Nissan is the seventh day of cleansing and falls on the Sabbath, so that if sprinkling were performed on the thirteenth the person would be fit to offer the sacrifice on the eve of Pesach.

6
2

R' Akiva responded and said, "Let 'sprinkling' prove [this], for it is a *mitzvah*, and is [forbidden] because of a Rabbinic prohibition, and does not override the Sabbath. So you should not wonder about these, that even though they are a *mitzvah*, and are [forbidden] because of a Rabbinic prohibition, they do not override the Sabbath."

Said R' Eliezer to him, "But about this do I apply my logic. If slaughter which is [forbidden] because it is [categorized as] a labor overrides the Sabbath, [then] sprinkling which is [forbidden only] by Rabbinic prohibition should surely override the Sabbath!"

Said R' Akiva to him, "Perhaps the opposite [is

carry the purification water in the public domain.

וְאֵינָה דוֹחָה אֶת הַשַּׁבָּת. — *and does not override the Sabbath.*

R' Akiva knew that sprinkling the water does not override the Sabbath, because he had so been taught by R' Eliezer himself *(Gem. 69a; cf. Rashi* and *Rav).*

אַף אַתָּה אַל תִּתְמַהּ עַל אֵלּוּ, — *So you should not wonder about these,*

[The actions prohibited Rabbinically in mishnah 1.]

שֶׁאַף עַל פִּי שֶׁהֵן מִצְוָה, — *that even though they are* [mandated by] *a mitzvah,*

[The command to offer a Pesach offering mandates that we transgress prohibitions preventing fulfillment of this *mitzvah*.]

וְהֵן מִשּׁוּם שְׁבוּת, לֹא יִדְחוּ אֶת הַשַּׁבָּת. — *and are* [forbidden] *because of a Rabbinic prohibition, they* [nevertheless] *do not override the Sabbath."*

The *Yerushalmi* relates that prior to this exchange, R' Akiva had studied under R' Eliezer for thirteen years without ever speaking up to contradict his mentor.

אָמַר לוֹ רַבִּי אֱלִיעֶזֶר, ,,וְעָלֶיהָ אֲנִי דָן. — *Said R' Eliezer to him, "But about this* [too]

do I apply my logic.

The same reasoning R' Eliezer used to permit the other activities, can be used to permit sprinkling as well *(Rav; Rashi).*

The *Gemara* (69a) comments that R' Eliezer had forgotten his own teaching that sprinkling was indeed forbidden.

וּמָה אִם שְׁחִיטָה שֶׁהִיא מִשּׁוּם מְלָאכָה דוֹחָה אֶת הַשַּׁבָּת, הַזָּאָה שֶׁהִיא מִשּׁוּם שְׁבוּת אֵינוֹ דִין שֶׁדּוֹחָה אֶת הַשַּׁבָּת!'' — *If slaughter which is* [forbidden] *because it is* [catergorized as] *a labor overrides the Sabbath,* [then] *sprinkling which is* [forbidden only] *by Rabbinic prohibition should surely override the Sabbath'."*

[This is the same reasoning R' Eliezer used to demonstrate the waiving of the other Rabbinic prohibitions.]

אָמַר לוֹ רַבִּי עֲקִיבָא, ,,אוֹ חִלּוּף? — *Said R' Akiva to him,' "Perhaps the opposite* [is more correct]?

Perhaps the reasoning should be applied in the opposite fashion: Instead of using slaughter as proof to permit Rabbinically prohibited actions, the prohibition against sprinkling should serve as proof that even slaughter should be forbidden. In other words, let us begin

הַזָּאָה שֶׁהִיא מִשּׁוּם שְׁבוּת אֵינָהּ דּוֹחָה אֶת
הַשַּׁבָּת, שְׁחִיטָה שֶׁהִיא מִשּׁוּם מְלָאכָה אֵינוֹ דִין
שֶׁלֹּא תִדְחֶה אֶת הַשַּׁבָּת!"

אָמַר לוֹ רַבִּי אֱלִיעֶזֶר, "עֲקִיבָא! עָקַרְתָּ מַה
שֶּׁכָּתוּב בַּתּוֹרָה: ,בֵּין הָעַרְבַּיִם ... בְּמֹעֲדוֹ׳, בֵּין
בְּחוֹל בֵּין בַּשַּׁבָּת."

אָמַר לוֹ, "רַבִּי, הָבֵא לִי מוֹעֵד לְאֵלּוּ כְּמוֹעֵד
לִשְׁחִיטָה."

כְּלָל אָמַר רַבִּי עֲקִיבָא: כָּל מְלָאכָה שֶׁאֶפְשָׁר
לַעֲשׂוֹתָהּ מֵעֶרֶב שַׁבָּת אֵינָהּ דּוֹחָה אֶת הַשַּׁבָּת.
שְׁחִיטָה שֶׁאִי אֶפְשָׁר לַעֲשׂוֹתָהּ מֵעֶרֶב שַׁבָּת,
דּוֹחָה אֶת הַשַּׁבָּת.

יד אברהם

with the fact that sprinkling is known to be forbidden — then let us deduce from it that even slaughter should be forbidden (Rav; Rashi).

מָה אִם הַזָּאָה שֶׁהִיא מִשּׁוּם שְׁבוּת אֵינָהּ דּוֹחָה אֶת הַשַּׁבָּת, שְׁחִיטָה שֶׁהִיא מִשּׁוּם — מְלָאכָה אֵינוֹ דִין שֶׁלֹּא תִדְחֶה אֶת הַשַּׁבָּת!" — If sprinkling which is [forbidden] by Rabbinic prohibition does not override the Sabbath, [then] slaughtering which is [forbidden] because it is [categorized as] a labor should [surely] not override the Sabbath!"

אָמַר לוֹ רַבִּי אֱלִיעֶזֶר, "עֲקִיבָא! עָקַרְתָּ מַה שֶּׁכָּתוּב בַּתּוֹרָה: בֵּין הָעַרְבַּיִם—בְּמֹעֲדוֹ, בֵּין בְּחוֹל בֵּין בַּשַּׁבָּת." — R' Eliezer said to him, "Akiva! You have [with your argument] uprooted what is written in the Torah: In the afternoon ... in its appointed time [Numbers 9:3], [which implies that the offering must be brought whenever the appointed time is] both on weekdays and on the Sabbath."

[Ostensibly, R' Eliezer felt that the language of the Torah itself suggests that the Pesach offering overrides the

Sabbath (probably because the admonition to offer in its time would be otherwise superfluous; cf. Malbim to Leviticus 16:21 s.v. עתי). As pointed out by Tosafos (66a, s.v. מה; see Tos. Ha-Rashba), there is disagreement on this point between the tannaim, with some holding the above view, while others resort to additional exegesis to deduce the undisputed rule that the Pesach offering overrides the Sabbath (see Mechilta Ex. 12:6 with Malbim).

The Gemara (69a) explains that R' Akiva surely realized that his argument was fallacious and its conclusion was untenable. He used this line of argument only to imply that he, as R' Eliezer's disciple, had it upon R' Eliezer's own authority that sprinkling indeed does not override the Sabbath, for if it did, logic would require the untenable conclusion that even slaughter is forbidden. The self-assurance with which R' Akiva projected his view was intended to serve as a reminder to R' Eliezer of his own teaching. R' Akiva felt that it would be disrespectful of him to remind R' Eliezer bluntly about his lapse of memory.

The version of the mishnah given above appears in all the old versions (see Shinuyei

more correct]? If sprinkling which is [forbidden] by Rabbinic prohibition does not override the Sabbath, [then] slaughtering which is [forbidden] because it is [categorized as] a labor should [surely] not override the Sabbath!''

R' Eliezer said to him,''Akiva! You have uprooted what is written in the Torah: *In the afternoon ... in its appointed time* [Numbers 9:3], [which implies] both on weekdays and on the Sabbath.''

Said he [R' Akiva] to him, ''My master! Give me an appointed time for these which is like the appointed time for slaughter.''

A general rule was stated by R' Akiva: Any labor that can be performed on the eve of the Sabbath does not override the Sabbath. Slaughtering which cannot be performed on the eve of the Sabbath, does override the Sabbath.

Nuschaos). However, *Tos. Yom Tov* notes that *Rashi* and *Rav* cite the preceding verse (*Numbers 9:2*) *Let the children of Israel perform the Pesach sacrifice in its appointed time,* indicating that this verse was the one meant. Because of this and other reasons he suggests the deletion of the words בֵּין הָעַרְבַּיִם *the afternoon* since this phrase is found only in v. 3.

אָמַר לוֹ, ״רַבִּי, הָבֵא לִי מוֹעֵד לְאֵלּוּ כְּמוֹעֵד לִשְׁחִיטָה״. — *Said he [R' Akiva] to him, ''My master! Give me an appointed time for these which is like the appointed time for slaughter.''*

I.e., R' Eliezer is incorrect in comparing the Scriptural prohibition against slaughter with the Rabbinic prohibitions under discussion in this and the previous mishnah. Since the source for the permission to override the Sabbath is the Scriptural phrase 'appointed time,' this precludes any analogy to the Rabbinically prohibited acts, since their performance is not mandated for a specific time. Even the act of sprinkling

— although it must be performed at a specific time — is also prohibited because, unlike the other Rabbinic prohibitions under discussion, it is not intrinsically related to the Pesach offering itself, and is therefore not included in the Scriptural dispensation that requires the overriding of the Sabbath (*Rav; Rashi*).

כְּלָל אָמַר רַבִּי עֲקִיבָא: כָּל מְלָאכָה שֶׁאֶפְשָׁר לַעֲשׂוֹתָהּ מֵעֶרֶב שַׁבָּת אֵינָהּ דּוֹחָה אֶת הַשַּׁבָּת. שְׁחִיטָה שֶׁאִי אֶפְשָׁר לַעֲשׂוֹתָהּ מֵעֶרֶב שַׁבָּת, דּוֹחָה אֶת הַשַּׁבָּת. — *A general rule was stated by R' Akiva: Any labor that can be performed on the eve of Sabbath does not override the Sabbath. Slaughtering, which cannot be performed on the eve of the Sabbath does override the Sabbath.*

[R' Akiva's rule also appears in *Shabbos* 19:1 along with its converse, 'That which cannot be done before the Sabbath overrides the Sabbath.']

[ג] **אֵימָתַי** מֵבִיא חֲגִיגָה עִמּוֹ? — בִּזְמַן
שֶׁהוּא בָא בְּחוֹל בְּטָהֳרָה
וּבְמֻעָט. וּבִזְמַן שֶׁהוּא בָא בַּשַּׁבָּת בִּמְרֻבֶּה
וּבְטֻמְאָה, אֵין מְבִיאִין עִמּוֹ חֲגִיגָה.

ו/ג

[ד] **חֲגִיגָה** הָיְתָה בָאָה מִן הַצֹּאן, מִן הַבָּקָר,
מִן הַכְּבָשִׂים, וּמִן הָעִזִּים; מִן

ו/ד

יד אברהם

3.

◄§ The Chagigah of the Fourteenth of Nissan

Simultaneous with the offering of the Pesach sacrifice, an additional offering was brought, known as the *Chagigah* [lit. *festival*] sacrifice. In contradistinction to the regular Chagigah that *must* be brought during the course of each of the three festivals [Pesach, Shavuos, and Succos], the Chagigah offered on the eve of Pesach is not absolutely obligatory. The basis of the practice to bring the Chagigah on Pesach is the Torah's commandment that the Pesach be eaten עַל הַשּׂוֹבַע, *when* [*one is*] *sated* (*Hil. Korban Pesach* 8:3), but the Torah does not *require* that flesh of Chagigah be eaten at the Seder. This offering is therefore only supplementary to the Pesach and is subject to certain restrictions, which are discussed in the following mishnah.

In a sense, this mishnah continues the laws of the previous one, because the Chagigah, like the acts discussed in mishnah 2, does not override the Sabbath (*Gem.* 69b).

אֵימָתַי מֵבִיא חֲגִיגָה עִמּוֹ? — *When does one bring a Chagigah with it?*

When is the Chagigah brought in conjunction with the Pesach sacrifice?

בִּזְמַן שֶׁהוּא בָא בְּחוֹל — *When it is offered on a weekday,*

When the eve of Pesach occurs on a weekday, it is permitted to offer personal sacrifices like the Chagigah, but it does not override the Sabbath.

בְּטָהֳרָה — *in purity,*

[When those participating in the sacrificial service and those who will partake of the offering are free of any *tumah* (contamination). In contrast to the Pesach offering which may sometimes be sacrificed and eaten while the people are *tamei* (see below), the Chagigah is subject to the laws normally governing sacrifices, and may not be

sacrificed or eaten if the people are contaminated.]

וּבְמֻעָט. — *and is insufficient* [lit. *with few*].

I.e., there are a large number of participants and relatively few Pesach sacrifices, necessitating that the offering be divided into small portions so that each will have a share. In order to ensure that they eat their portion of Pesach sacrifice 'while sated,' the participants partake first of the Chagigah to satisfy their hunger, and then eat the Pesach (*Rav; Rashi*).

וּבִזְמַן שֶׁהוּא בָא בַּשַּׁבָּת — *But when it is offered on the Sabbath,*

[When the eve of Pesach falls on a Sabbath, so that the service of the Pesach offering must override the Sabbath.]

6
3

3. When does one bring a *Chagigah* with it? — When it is offered on a weekday, in purity, and is insufficient. But when it is offered on the Sabbath, or is abundant, or in contamination, we do not bring a *Chagigah* with it.

6
4

4. A *Chagigah* may be brought from the flock, from cattle, from sheep or from goats; from

YAD AVRAHAM

בְּמְרֻבָּה — *or is abundant* [lit. *with many*],

When those 'registered' on a Pesach offering were few and subsequently the portions were large enough to satisfy the participants *(Rav; Rashi)*.

[Since the objective of satisfying the participants before they finish their Pesach meat can be fulfilled by the Pesach offering itself, the Chagigah offering would be unnecessary.]

וּבְטֻמְאָה, — *or in contamination,*

[When the majority of those obligated to offer the Pesach, or the *Kohanim* who were to perform the service, had been contaminated by contact with a corpse, the mitzvah of the Pesach offering overrides the restriction against partaking of an offering in a state of *tumah*. This provision, like the one for overriding the Sabbath, is derived through Scriptural exegesis (see further 7:4-5, *Gem.* 77a). The mishnah clarifies that this dispensation is not extended to the optional Chagigah, even though it customarily accompanies the Pesach.]

אֵין מְבִיאִין עִמּוֹ חֲגִיגָה. — *we do not bring a Chagigah with it.*

Since the Chagigah of the fourteenth is not obligatory, it does not qualify for any of the above dispensations *(Rav; Rambam)*.

[The *Gemara* (70a) gives the implication that were the Chagigah a Torah obligation it would have all the dispensations allotted the Pesach offering, and override the Sabbath and the laws of [corpse] contamination (see *Tos.* 70a, s.v. לאו).]

4.

Continuing the discussion of mishnah 4, the mishnah lists more difference between the Pesach and Chagigah offerings.

חֲגִיגָה הָיְתָה בָאָה מִן הַצֹּאן, — *A Chagigah may be brought* [lit. *would be brought*] *from the flock,*

The term צאן generally denotes small livestock, i.e., sheep and goats, the sense in which the word is used here. [However, depending on the context, sometimes it refers specifically to sheep *(I Samuel* 25:2) and occasionally even to all cattle and sheep (*I Samuel* 8:17). See *Radak Shorashim*, s.v. צון.]

מִן הַבָּקָר, מִן הַכְּבָשִׂים, וּמִן הָעִזִּים; — *from cattle, from sheep or from goats;*

[The phrase, *from sheep or goats*, is an elaboration on the term צאן, *flocks*. Perhaps, in view of *Radak's* comment that צאן may have various meanings, the mishnah felt it necessary to clarify this term.]

The first passage of the mishnah is probably patterned on the verse *(Deuteronomy* 16:2): *And you shall slaughter ... flocks and cattle*, which is taken by some tannaim (see *Rashi* and *Sifre* loc. cit., *Gem.* 70b, *Hil. Korban Pesach* 10:12; *Tzlach* and *S'fas Emes* to 70b) as a source for the bringing of the Pesach eve *Chagigah*. The *tanna* then proceeds to clarify the Scriptural term צאן.

Some versions (see *Shinuyei Nuschaos* and *Rambam, comm.* ed. Kafich) interchange the words הַצֹּאן, *the flock*, and הַבָּקָר, *the cat-*

פסחים
ו/ה
הַזְּכָרִים וּמִן הַנְּקֵבוֹת. וְנֶאֱכֶלֶת לִשְׁנֵי יָמִים
וְלַיְלָה אֶחָד.

[ה] **הַפֶּסַח** שֶׁשְּׁחָטוֹ שֶׁלֹּא לִשְׁמוֹ בַּשַּׁבָּת,
חַיָּב עָלָיו חַטָּאת. וּשְׁאָר כָּל
הַזְּבָחִים שֶׁשְּׁחָטָן לְשׁוּם פֶּסַח: אִם אֵינָן רְאוּיִין,

יד אברהם

tle, so that the clarifying phrase *from sheep or from goats* follows the word *flock* which it modifies (cf. *Rashash* and *Meleches Shlomo*).

מִן הַזְּכָרִים וּמִן הַנְּקֵבוֹת. — *from males or from females.*

These points are in contrast to the Pesach offering which must be male, and either a sheep or a goat *(Rav; Rashi; see Exodus 12:5).*

וְנֶאֱכֶלֶת לִשְׁנֵי יָמִים וְלַיְלָה אֶחָד. — *And it*

may be eaten for two days and one night.

In this case the two days are the fourteenth and fifteenth of Nissan, as well as the intervening night. Nevertheless, once the Chagigah is put on the table with the Pesach, it must be consumed before midnight, exactly like the Pesach, lest the meat of the Pesach become mixed with that of the Chagigah (*Rambam, Hil. Korban Pesach* 10:14).

5.

Returning to the initial topic of this chapter, the mishnah begins a discussion of a different aspect of bringing a Pesach offering on the Sabbath: the desecration of the Sabbath caused by invalidaion of the sacrifice. The act of slaughter is forbidden on the Sabbath, but the prohibition is superseded by the obligation to offer a Pesach sacrifice. In the event the sacrifice is invalidated, however, the slaugher would be considered a desecration of the Sabbath.

Ordinarily one is obliged to atone for a non-intentional [שׁוֹגֵג] desecration of the Sabbath by bringing a חַטָּאת, *sin offering*. In the view of some *tannaim*, however, desecration of the Sabbath caused by slaughtering an invalid or unauthorized offering is exempt from this obligation, because it was committed in the course of an intended *mitzvah*. The tannaitic controversy around this principle and the distinctions drawn between the various instances of its application, is the subject of the following mishnah.

הַפֶּסַח שֶׁשְּׁחָטוֹ שֶׁלֹּא לִשְׁמוֹ בַּשַּׁבָּת, — *If one slaughtered the Pesach offering for some other designation on the Sabbath,*

[We learned above (5:2) that a Pesach slaughtered with the designation of a different offering is invalid. Accordingly, if one *intentionally* slaughtered a Pesach with the intention that it be, for example, a burnt offering, he would be a willful desecrator of the Sabbath and be liable to כָּרֵת , *spiritual excision*. Our mishnah describes him as liable to bring a guilt offering, indicating that his desecration was caused by negligence,

not willfulness. The commentators explain what form this negligence took:] Instead of having in mind that he was slaughtering the animal for the sake of the Pesach offering, the slaughterer intended it to be some other offering. The *Kohen* mistakenly thought one may sacrifice the Pesach on the Sabbath even if his intention was to offer it as another sacrifice (*Rav; Rashi*), or he may have forgotten at the moment of sacrifice that it was the Sabbath and that a wrong intention would be a desecration of the day (*Tif. Yis.*).

males or from females. And it may be eaten for two days and one night.

5. If one slaughtered the Pesach offering for some other designation on the Sabbath, he is liable thereby for a sin offering. And all other sacrifices that he slaughtered with the designation of a Pesach offering: if they are not suitable, he is liable [for a sin

YAD AVRAHAM

חַיָּב עָלָיו חַטָּאת. — *he is liable thereby for a sin offering.*

Since the Pesach offering slaughtered for the sake of another sacrifice is invalid (5:2), its slaughter on the Sabbath constitutes unauthorized desecration of the day.

The *Gemara* (72a) cites the opinion of some (see *Menachos* 49a) that the offering is invalidated only if the slaughterer was aware that he was slaughtering a Pesach offering, but deliberately intended to uproot its Pesach designation and use it for some other offering. But if his wrong intention was due to an error, i.e. he mistakenly thought he was slaughtering another offering — then the sacrifice is a valid Pesach despite his intentions. In the case of our mishnah, therefore no actual desecration of the Sabbath would have taken place. This is the view accepted halachically (*Hil. Pessulei HaMukdashin* 15:1).

The *Gemara* (73a) also remarks that this clause of the mishnah is essentially self-evident: If the offering is invalid, then clearly its slaughter is an unauthorized desecration of the Sabbath, and a sin offering must be brought. This clause is given only to introduce the subsequent dispute between R' Eliezer and R' Yehoshua concerning the slaughter of other sacrifices with the designation of Pesach.

וּשְׁאָר כָּל הַזְּבָחִים שֶׁשְּׁחָטָן לְשׁוּם פֶּסַח: — *And all other sacrifices that he slaughtered with the designation of a Pesach offering:*

On the fourteenth which falls on the Sabbath, one slaughtered any sacrifice whose service does not override the Sabbath, with the intention of using it for the Pesach offering.

אִם אֵינָן רְאוּיִין, — *if they are not suitable,*

The Pesach offering must be a male sheep or goat, less than a year old (*Exodus* 12:5). Thus if the slaughtered animals were of a sort not eligible for the Pesach, e.g., goats or rams more than a year old, females, or cattle, the Sabbath has been desecrated. The slaughterer is liable for a sin offering if his desecration was inadvertent, either because he forgot it was the Sabbath or he thought it was permitted to sacrifice other offerings for the sake of Pesach (*Rav; Rashi*); or he mistakenly thought the animals enumerated by the mishnah were acceptable for a Pesach (*Tif. Yis.*).

חַיָּב; — *he is liable [for a sin offering];*

As noted in the prefatory remarks to this mishnah, some tannaim hold that if one desecrated the Sabbath under the erroneous impression that he was required to do so in the performance of a *mitzvah*, he is not liable to bring a sin offering. If so, our case would seem to fall under that category, because the slaughterer thought he was offering a Pesach. This is not so, however. To slaughter such animals for a Pesach offering is too obvious an error to rank as an instance of טוֹעֶה בִּדְבַר מִצְוָה, *one who errs in the commission of a mitzvah*, and all tannaim would agree that it should be considered as negligence that requires a sin offering (*Rav; Rashi*).

Aruch HaShulchan HaAssid (*Kodashim* 208:18) points out that an error in ascertaining the exact age of the offering *should* be classified as an error in the commission of a *mitzvah* and subject to the controversy

חַיָּב; וְאִם רְאוּיִין הֵן — רַבִּי אֱלִיעֶזֶר מְחַיֵּב
חַטָּאת, וְרַבִּי יְהוֹשֻׁעַ פּוֹטֵר.

אָמַר רַבִּי אֱלִיעֶזֶר, ,,מָה אִם הַפֶּסַח שֶׁהוּא
מֻתָּר לִשְׁמוֹ, כְּשֶׁשִּׁנָּה אֶת שְׁמוֹ חַיָּב, זְבָחִים
שֶׁהֵן אֲסוּרִין לִשְׁמָן, כְּשֶׁשִּׁנָּה אֶת שְׁמָן, אֵינוֹ דִין
שֶׁיְּהֵא חַיָּב?"

אָמַר לוֹ רַבִּי יְהוֹשֻׁעַ, ,,לֹא, אִם אָמַרְתָּ בְּפֶסַח
שֶׁשִּׁנָּהוּ לְדָבָר אָסוּר, תֹּאמַר בִּזְבָחִים שֶׁשִּׁנָּן
לְדָבָר מֻתָּר?"

אָמַר לוֹ רַבִּי אֱלִיעֶזֶר, ,,אֵמוּרֵי צִבּוּר יוֹכִיחוּ,

יד אברהם

between R' Eliezer and R' Yehoshua. [Accordingly the commentators who include over age animals in our mishnah would refer to animals that are obviously too old or whose age was known.]

וְאִם רְאוּיִין הֵן — **but if they are suitable**
The animal slaughtered for the Pesach was of the proper age, sex, and species, but it has previously been sanctified for a different offering. In his preoccupation with the service of the day, the slaughterer inadvertently used such animals for the Pesach instead of their true designation. This act, too, should constitute a desecration of the Sabbath, because an animal designated for one type of offering cannot be used for a different one (*Rav; Rashi*).

רַבִּי אֱלִיעֶזֶר מְחַיֵּב חַטָּאת, — R' Eliezer obligates him to bring a sin offering,
The slaughter of these sacrifices is an unintentional desecration of the Sabbath. That this mistake was committed as the result of an intention to perform a *mitzvah* is not a redeeming factor in R' Eliezer's opinion (*Rav; Rashi*).

וְרַבִּי יְהוֹשֻׁעַ פּוֹטֵר. — but R' Yehoshua absolves [him].
R' Yehoshua holds that his action does not require the atonement of a sin offering since it resulted from an intention to perform a *mitzvah* [the slaughter of a Pesach offering.] Furthermore, mistaken as it was, his action is considered a *mitzvah* in its own right, for the sacrifice that was slaughtered with the wrong intention is valid nonetheless (see *Zevachim* 1:1).[1]

It should be stressed that R' Yehoshua's ruling applies only to an instance where the slaughterer erred and thought he was discharging his obligation to sacrifice the Pesach offering, but if he knew it was a different offering and intended to divert it from its purpose, R' Yehoshua agrees that he must bring a sin offering (see *Gem.* 70a with *Rashi*, s.v. מה לו שאינן ראויין).

אָמַר רַבִּי אֱלִיעֶזֶר, ,,מָה אִם הַפֶּסַח שֶׁהוּא מֻתָּר לִשְׁמוֹ, — Said R' Eliezer, "If the Pesach which is permitted [on the Sabbath] for its own designation,

1. The need for this second factor — that a *mitzvah* is performed — in order to effect absolution from a sin offering is based on R' Shimon's view [טָעָה בִּדְבַר מִצְוָה וְעָשָׂה מִצְוָה] (*Gem.* 72a). R' Meir differs, maintaining that the intention to perform a *mitzvah* is sufficient reason to absolve one from the obligation of a sin offering, even if no *mitzvah* was actually performed (*ibid.*). Rambam's ruling on this question is unclear (see *Hil. Shegagos* 2:8 with *Kessef Mishneh* and *Lechem Mishneh*).

6
5
offering]; but if they are suitable — R' Eliezer obligates him to bring a sin offering, but R' Yehoshua absolves [him].

Said R' Eliezer, "If the Pesach, which is permitted [on the Sabbath] for its own designation, if he changed its designation he is liable, [then] other sacrifices, which are forbidden [on the Sabbath even] for their own designations, if he changed their designations he should surely be liable."

R' Yehoshua said to him, "Not so! If you say thus of the Pesach when he changed it to a forbidden matter, will you say thus of [other] sacrifices when he changed them to a permitted matter?"

Said R' Eliezer to him, "Let public offerings prove

YAD AVRAHAM

It is permitted to offer the Pesach when the fourteenth falls on the Sabbath (Rav; Rashi).

בְּשֶׁשִּׁנָּה אֶת שְׁמוֹ חַיָּב, — [nevertheless] if he changed its designation he is liable,

If he sacrificed it under some other name he is obligated to bring a sin offering, as set forth earlier (Rav; Rashi).

זְבָחִים שֶׁהֵן אֲסוּרִין לִשְׁמָן, — [then] other sacrifices, which are forbidden [on the Sabbath even] for their own designations,

Other personal offerings may not be sacrificed on the Sabbath.

בְּשֶׁשִּׁנָּה אֶת שְׁמָן, אֵינוֹ דִין שֶׁיְּהֵא חַיָּב?" — if he changed their designations, he should surely be liable."

R' Eliezer argues that if the slaughter of an invalidated Pesach offering can require the atonement of a sin offering, then the slaughter of a totally unauthorized offering certainly requires a sin offering.

אָמַר לוֹ רַבִּי יְהוֹשֻׁעַ, "לֹא, אִם אָמַרְתָּ בְּפֶסַח שֶׁשִּׁנָּהוּ לְדָבָר אָסוּר, — R' Yehoshua said to him, "Not so! If you say thus of the Pesach when he changed it to a forbidden matter,

[I.e., by slaughtering a Pesach for

another designation one becomes liable for a sin offering because he slaughtered it as an offering that may not be brought on the Sabbath (Rav; Rashi). In other words, his intention was for something that may not be slaughtered on the Sabbath.]

תֹּאמַר בִּזְבָחִים שֶׁשִּׁנָּן לְדָבָר מֻתָּר?" — will you say thus of [other] sacrifices when he changed them to a permitted matter?"

[I.e., by contrast, in the case of other sacrifices slaughtered erroneously as Pesach offerings, the slaughterer's intention — albeit erroneous — was to offer a Pesach, which is permissible on the Sabbath (ibid.). In other words, his intention was to do something that is not a desecration of the Sabbath.]

אָמַר לוֹ רַבִּי אֱלִיעֶזֶר, "אִמּוּרֵי צִבּוּר יוֹכִיחוּ, — Said R' Eliezer to him, "Let public offerings prove it,

The term public sacrifices refers to the sacrifices brought on behalf of the public as part of the daily or Sabbath and festival ritual, e.g. the daily offerings [תְּמִידִים] and mussaf offerings.

[Though the term אִמּוּרִין is usually used to denote the parts of the sacrifice offered upon the altar (see comm. above 5:10), here it

שֶׁהֵן מֻתָּרִין לִשְׁמָן, וְהַשּׁוֹחֵט לִשְׁמָן חַיָּב.״
אָמַר לוֹ רַבִּי יְהוֹשֻׁעַ, ״לֹא, אִם אָמַרְתָּ
בְּאֵמוּרֵי צִבּוּר שֶׁיֵּשׁ לָהֶן קִצְבָה, תֹּאמַר בַּפֶּסַח
שֶׁאֵין לוֹ קִצְבָה?״
רַבִּי מֵאִיר אוֹמֵר: אַף הַשּׁוֹחֵט לְשֵׁם אֵמוּרֵי
צִבּוּר, פָּטוּר.

[ו] **שְׁחָטוֹ** שֶׁלֹּא לְאוֹכְלָיו וְשֶׁלֹּא לִמְנוּיָיו,
לַעֲרֵלִין וְלִטְמֵאִין, חַיָּב. לְאוֹכְלָיו

יד אברהם

refers to the public offerings as a whole, lit. *those 'said'* [from אמר] or *mandated* for the public.

שֶׁהֵן מֻתָּרִין לִשְׁמָן, — *for they are permitted* [*to be offered*] *for their own designations,*

The public sacrifices are permitted to be offered on the Sabbath (*Rav; Rashi*).

וְהַשּׁוֹחֵט לִשְׁמָן חַיָּב.״ — *yet one who slaughters* [*other sacrifices*] *for their designations is liable.''*

For example, if someone slaughtered a personal burnt offering on the Sabbath for the communal burnt offering, the sacrifice is valid, but the slaughterer is liable for a sin offering.

This argument is intended to disprove R' Yehoshua's basic premise that one who errs in the commission of a *mitzvah* and actually performs a *mitzvah* is absolved from the obligation of a sin offering — even though he has committed an unauthorized desecration of the Sabbath.

[Apparently, R' Eliezer knew that R' Yehoshua concurred with this ruling.]

אָמַר לוֹ רַבִּי יְהוֹשֻׁעַ, ״לֹא. — *R' Yehoshua said to him, "Not so!*

R' Yehoshua agrees with R' Eliezer's ruling that one is liable for a sin offering if he slaughtered other sacrifices for the intention of public offering, but disagrees with the analogy to slaughtering a Pesach offering with the wrong intention.

אִם אָמַרְתָּ בְּאֵמוּרֵי צִבּוּר שֶׁיֵּשׁ לָהֶן קִצְבָה, — *If you say thus of public offerings which have a limit,*

On the Sabbath there are only two communal daily offerings and two *mussaf* offerings, and it is therefore easy to avoid a mistake. Consequently when a man mistakenly slaughters another offering as a public sacrifice, he cannot be regarded as having *erred* in the commission of a *mitzvah*, but must rather be regarded as having desecrated the Sabbath through negligence (*ibid*).

תֹּאמַר בַּפֶּסַח שֶׁאֵין לוֹ קִצְבָה?״ — *will you say thus of the Pesach which has no limit?''*

Since every individual must offer a Pesach, an enormous number of animals were slaughtered (see note to 5:5). Therefore it is quite possible for someone to err, and he is regarded as having erred in the commission of a *mitzvah* (*Rav; Rashi*).

רַבִּי מֵאִיר אוֹמֵר: אַף הַשּׁוֹחֵט לְשֵׁם אֵמוּרֵי צִבּוּר, פָּטוּר. — *R' Meir says: Even one who slaughters* [*other sacrifices*] *for the designation of public offerings, is not liable.*

R' Meir disagrees with both R' Eliezer and R' Yehoshua regarding the slaughter of other sacrifices for the purpose of public offerings. In his view, one who mistakenly offers any consecrated offering as one of the public of-

6
6

it, for they are permitted [to be offered] for their own designation, yet one who slaughters [other sacrifices] for their designations is liable."

R' Yehoshua said to him, "Not so! If you say thus of public offerings which have a limit, will you say thus of the Pesach which has no limit?"

R' Meir says: Even one who slaughters [other sacrifices] for the designation of public offerings, is not liable.

6. If one slaughtered it for those who cannot eat of it or for those not registered on it, for uncircumscribed or contaminated [people], he is liable.

YAD AVRAHAM

ferings mandated for that Sabbath, is not liable (Rav; Rashi).

R' Meir thus extends the concept that

erring in the commission of a *mitzvah* removes the obligation of a sin offering, even to *mitzvos* which have a limit.

6.

שְׁחָטוֹ שֶׁלֹּא לְאוֹכְלָיו — *If one slaughtered it* [the Pesach offering] *for those who cannot eat of it* [lit. *for not its eaters*]

We have learned previously (5:3) that a Pesach slaughtered exclusively for those who cannot partake of it is invalid. This would be the case if one slaughtered it for those who cannot consume even the minimum amount of meat (i.e., the volume of an olive; כְּזַיִת), such as the elderly, the sick, or small children (Tif. Yis.).

[The law of our mishnah holds true whether the group registered on this Pesach was in fact composed of both eaters and non-eaters, or the whole group consisted of non-eaters only. In both cases the offering is made invalid by the intention of the slaughterer, who had in mind that the offering would be for non-eaters. Although 5:3 taught that an intent that included both eaters and non-eaters does not invalidate the offering, an exclusive intent for non-eaters makes the offering invalid, despite the fact that the registrants include eaters.]

וְשֶׁלֹּא לִמְנוּיָיו — *or for those not registered on it,*

The slaughterer intended the slaugh-

ter for a group not registered on this Pesach (Tif. Yis.).

[As we learned previously (5:3), only those registered on the Pesach before the slaughter can fulfill their obligation through the service. However, even if a group had been registered upon a *Pesach*, the slaughterer's intention for another, unregistered group renders the offering invalid.]

לָעֲרֵלִין — *for uncircumcised*

[As noted previously (5:3), uncircumcised people may not partake of the Pesach offering, consequently they are in the category of non-eaters.]

וְלַטְמֵאִין — *or contaminated* [people],

Persons who have become contaminated in any manner whatsoever may not partake of the Pesach and are included in the category of non-eaters. According to *Rambam* (Hil. Korban Pesach 6:2), however, this disqualification extends even to those who will have completed their cleansing by nightfall and will then be qualified to partake of offerings. Nevertheless they are ex-

פסחים
ו/ו
וְשֶׁלֹּא לְאוֹכְלָיו, לִמְנוּיָיו וְשֶׁלֹּא לִמְנוּיָיו,
לְמוּלִין וְלַעֲרֵלִין, לִטְהוֹרִים וְלִטְמֵאִים, פָּטוּר.
שְׁחָטוֹ וְנִמְצָא בַעַל מוּם, חַיָּב.
שְׁחָטוֹ וְנִמְצָא טְרֵפָה בַסֵּתֶר, פָּטוּר.
שְׁחָטוֹ וְנוֹדַע שֶׁמָּשְׁכוּ הַבְּעָלִים אֶת יָדָם, אוֹ
שֶׁמֵּתוּ, אוֹ שֶׁנִּטְמְאוּ, פָּטוּר מִפְּנֵי שֶׁשָּׁחַט
בִּרְשׁוּת.

יד אברהם

cluded from the Pesach since at the time of the slaughter they were in a state of *tumah* (see footnote to 6:2, s.v. והיא, and *comm.* to 8:5).

חַיָּב. — *he is liable* [to bring a sin offering].

In the event the fourteenth of Nissan fell on a Sabbath, a *proper* Pesach service is ordained by the Torah, but an *improper* service constitutes a desecration of the Sabbath and is forbidden. In the cases given above, the Pesach is invalid and the Sabbath has been desecrated, thus obliging the slaughterer to atone for his action in the usual manner.

וְשֶׁלֹּא לְאוֹכְלָיו, לִמְנוּיָיו וְשֶׁלֹּא לִמְנוּיָיו, לְמוּלִין וְלַעֲרֵלִין, לִטְהוֹרִים וְלִטְמֵאִים, פָּטוּר. — [*However, if he slaughtered*] *for those who can eat of it and those who cannot eat of it, for those registered and those unregistered, for circumcised and uncircumcised, for those who are cleansed and those who are contaminated, he is not liable.*

[Since his intention included those who may eat for the *Pesach*, the offering is valid (see above 5:3), and the slaughtering was permitted even on the Sabbath.]

The *Gemara* (73a) remarks that both of these clauses are actually self-evident: if the offering is invalid, a desecration of the Sabbath has taken place; where it is valid none has occurred. These passages are mentioned in conjunction with the first clause in mishnah 5 (see there, s.v. חיב עליו), which mentioned the law concerning

the disqualification of 'for another designation', thus completing the entire list of invalidations which are classified under that disqualification in 5:2-3.

שְׁחָטוֹ וְנִמְצָא בַעַל מוּם, — *If one slaughtered it* [the Pesach offering] *and it was found to have a blemish.*

[And as a consequence the offering is invalid.]

חַיָּב. — *he is liable* [to bring a sin offering].

A blemish on the skin or external organs of the animal could have been discovered prior to the slaughter. The resulting desecration of the Sabbath is therefore not classified as unavoidable [אוֹנֶס], but as negligence [שׁוֹגֵג] (*Rav; Rashi*).

שְׁחָטוֹ וְנִמְצָא טְרֵפָה בַסֵּתֶר, — *If one slaughtered it and it was found to be trefah internally* [lit. in hiding],

[Certain physical defects (listed in *Chullin* 3:1) are considered by the Torah to be *trefah* (טְרֵפָה, lit. *torn off*), i.e., a defect that will cause death within a year. A *trefah* animal is forbidden by Torah law to be eaten (*Exodus* 22:30), or to be an offering (see *Zevachim* 9:3; *Temurah* 29a; *Leviticus* 1:2 with *Rashi*, s.v. ומן הצאן, and *Sifra; Rambam, Hil. Issurei Mizbe'ach* 2:11 with comm.). This is especially so for a Pesach offering, which must be eaten (see *Gem.* 78b). The common use of the term *trefah* to designate any non-kosher food is technically a misnomer. In its accurate meaning, *trefah* refers only to the sort of animal described here or to one that was 'torn' by a beast of prey.]

[However, if he slaughtered] for those who can eat of it and those who cannot eat of it, for those registered and those unregistered, for circumcised and uncircumcised, for those who are cleansed and those who are contaminated, he is not liable.

If one slaughtered it and it was found to have a blemish, he is liable.

If one slaughtered it and it was found to be trefah internally, he is not liable.

If one slaughtered it and then it became known that the owners had withdrawn from it, or had died, or had become contaminated, he is not liable, because he slaughtered with permission.

YAD AVRAHAM

[If after slaughtering the Pesach, one of its internal organs was found to be defective in a way that renders it *trefah*, the offering is, of course, invalid and the unauthorized slaughter on the Sabbath raises the question of desecration of the Sabbath and the liability of a sin offering.]

פָּטוּר. — *he is not liable.*
Though the Sabbath has been desecrated, there is no sin offering obligation because the internal *trefah* status of the animal is not something the slaughterer can detect in advance. Consequently the resulting Sabbath desecration is אוֹנֶס, *unavoidable,* and does not require a sacrificial atonement (*Tif. Yis.* based on *Rashi,* s.v. שחטו ונמצא בעל מום).

However, *Tosafos* (73a, s.v. שחטו) adduces proof from the *Gem.* that the absolution from the offering is based, not on the principle of unavoidability [it seems this is not considered unavoidable in all cases, see *Meromei Sadeh* and *Chidushei HaGri (Kanterowitz)*] but on the principle of erring in the commission of a *mitzvah.* Thus, *Tosafos* points out, R' Eliezer, who disagrees with this principle (above mishnah 5), will rule that he is liable in this case.

שָׁחֲטוּ וְנוֹדַע שֶׁמָּשְׁכוּ הַבְּעָלִים אֶת יָדָם, — *If one slaughtered it and then it became known that the owners had withdrawn*

from it,
[As long as the Pesach offering has not yet been slaughtered (see 8:3, 89a, *Exodus* 12:4 with *Rashi*) the registered owners may withdraw from one Pesach and register on another. If it happened that all the registrants withdrew, leaving the offering without owners, the slaughter would be invalidated, for it had been done for the sake of people not registered. Such a slaughter would be a desecration of the Sabbath, raising the question of the slaughterer's liability for a sin offering.]

אוֹ שֶׁמֵּתוּ, — *or had died,*
[The registrant died before the slaughter took place, leaving the Pesach offering ownerless and invalid as outlined above.]

אוֹ שֶׁנִּטְמְאוּ, — *or had become contaminated,*
[*Tumah* disqualifies the owner from eating, and precludes his fulfillment of the *mitzvah* of offering (see above, s.v. ולטמאין). In all of the above cases, if even one qualified owner remained, the offering is valid.]

פָּטוּר מִפְּנֵי שֶׁשָּׁחַט בִּרְשׁוּת. — *he is not liable because he slaughtered with permission.*
Since the slaughterer had no way of knowing about the changed circum-

פסחים [א] **כֵּיצַד** צוֹלִין אֶת הַפֶּסַח? — מְבִיאִין
א/ז שַׁפּוּד שֶׁל רִמּוֹן תּוֹחֲבוֹ מִתּוֹךְ פִּיו
עַד בֵּית נְקוּבָתוֹ, וְנוֹתֵן אֶת כְּרָעָיו וְאֶת בְּנֵי
מֵעָיו לְתוֹכוֹ — דִּבְרֵי רַבִּי יוֹסֵי הַגְּלִילִי.
רַבִּי עֲקִיבָא אוֹמֵר: כְּמִין בִּשּׁוּל הוּא זֶה; אֶלָּא
תּוֹלִין חוּצָה לוֹ.

יד אברהם

stances, nor had he any reason to in-quire about them, he is considered to have slaughtered with permission, and the Sabbath desecration is deemed an אוֹנֵס, *unavoidable act*, which does not carry the liability for a sin offering (*Rav; Rashi*).

The two categories of desecration that the mishnah considers unavoidable — the slaughter of an internally *trefah* animal and the slaughter of an offering that was revealed to be ownerless — are not identical. Where an animal was in-ternally *trefah*, prior knowledge was virtually impossible and the Sabbath

desecration was indeed unavoidable. But if the slaughter was invalid as a result of the condition or the non-existence of its owner, the Sabbath desecration could have been avoided had inquiry been made prior to the slaughter. However, since the slaugh-terer is not obliged to investigate the status of the owners, this desecration of the Sabbath is considered unavoidable. To underscore this reason, the mishnah adds here: *because he slaughtered with permission*, i.e., he was permitted to slaughter without previous inquiry (*Meromei Sadeh*).

Chapter 7

1.

כֵּיצַד צוֹלִין אֶת הַפֶּסַח? — *How do we roast the Pesach?*

[The Torah commands: *Do not eat of it raw or cooked at all in water, but rather fire-roasted* (Exodus 12:9). Consequently, the Pesach offering must be prepared in such manner that it can-not be considered cooked.]

מְבִיאִין שַׁפּוּד שֶׁל רִמּוֹן — *We bring a spit of pomegranate wood*

A metal spit will not do, because the metal will become hot and part of the Pesach will be roasted by the heat of the

spit, whereas the Torah states *fire-roast*, thus barring any roasting agent but fire (*Rav from Gem. 74a*)[1]. Likewise, the use of a spit of any wood other than pomegranate is forbidden because all other woods exude moisture, thereby causing the Pesach to be partially cooked rather then completely roasted (*ibid.*).

The language of *Rambam* (*Hil. Korban Pesach 8:10*) indicates that the preference of pomegranate over other woods is only a refinement of the *mitzvah* [מִצְוָה מִן הַמֻּבְחָר] and not essential (*Meleches Shlomo*).

1. The *Gemara* (74a) bases the disqualification of metal spits on it superior heat-conducting quality: 'If part of it is hot the whole is hot' (חַם מִקְצָתוֹ חַם כֻּלּוֹ). *Rashi* explains that the inner part of the spit (that covered by the carcass) becomes heated by the portion that is exposed to the fire, thus causing the portions of the Pesach touching the spit to be partly roasted by it, not by the fire [were it not for metal's capacity to conduct heat, we would assume that the carcass insulates the metal from getting hot, just as it does for wooden spits (see *Rashi*, s.v. שהשפוד אמרו לו and כשם).

7
1

1. **H**ow do we roast the Pesach? We bring a spit of pomegranate wood and thrust it [through] from its mouth to its anus and place its knees and its entrails inside it — [these are] the words of R' Yose HaGlili.

R' Akiva says: This is [considered] a form of cooking; rather they are hung outside it.

YAD AVRAHAM

תּוֹחֲבוֹ מִתּוֹךְ פִּיו עַד בֵּית נְקוּבָתוֹ, — *and thrust it [through] from its mouth to its anus*

The whole carcass must be suspended so that the head together with the incision in the neck faces downward, allowing the blood to flow off freely. The thicker end of the spit, must therefore be in the mouth, so that the carcass will not slip off (*Tos. 74a, s.v.* כיצד, cited by *Tos. Yom Tov*).

[This can be accomplished only by thrusting the point of the spit through the mouth and slipping it through the carcass until it reaches the anus.]

Kol HaRemez comments that the mode of thrusting described here specifies that the spit pass through the anus because a spit passing through other limbs, e.g. the thighs, runs the risk of breaking bones in its passage, and Scripture forbids the breaking of bones in the preparation and eating of the Pesach.

וְנוֹתֵן אֶת כְּרָעָיו וְאֶת בְּנֵי מֵעָיו לְתוֹכוֹ — דִּבְרֵי רַבִּי יוֹסֵי הַגְּלִילִי. — *and place its knees and its entrails inside it — [these are] the words of R' Yose HaGlili.*

R' Yose's opinion is that the knees and entrails must be placed inside the animal's body cavity in order to comply with the verse, *its head with its legs and with its innards (Exodus 12:19)*, indicating that these organs are to be roasted together with the body (*Rashi*).

Although the knees must be severed to fulfill this command, this is not a transgression of the command (regarding the Pesach); *and a bone shall you not break in it (Exodus 12:45)*. Only tendons are severed and they are not considered bones (*Meiri*).

רַבִּי עֲקִיבָא אוֹמֵר: כְּמִין בִּשּׁוּל הוּא זֶה; — *R' Akiva says: This is [considered] a form of cooking;*

For the entrails become cooked in the cavity, as if in a kettle (*Rav, Rashi*).

However R' Akiva's language suggests that this is regarded only as having the *appearance* of cooking, but is not prohibited Scripturally (see *S'fas Emes* and *Meiri*).

אֶלָּא תּוֹלִין חוּצָה לוֹ. — *rather they are hung outside it.*

The legs and entrails are placed directly on the same spit above the head (*Rav. Rashi*).

Tos. Yom Tov remarks that the innards had to be twisted around the head so that they would not fall off the spit which was slanted so that the head faced downward.

The *Gemara* (74a) relates, that because of the manner of its roasting, 'with the innards twisted above the head' R' Tarfon would, euphemistically, call the Pesach offering, גְּדִי מְקוּלָס, lit. *helmeted goat.*

Another view (*Rashi, Beitzah 22b, s.v.* גדי מקולס) is that the knees and innards were roasted beside the carcass, i.e. they were stuck anywhere along the spit. The euphemism *helmeted goat* arose because these organs hang next to the carcass just as a [helmeted, i.e., armed] soldier hangs his weapons beside him.

[Although the requirement to roast the knees and innards together with the carcass seems to be Scriptural *(its head together with its knees and innards, Exodus 12:9; see Tos. HaRashba)*, failure to do so would probably not disqualify the meat. Similarly *Tosafos* (74a, s.v. נחתך) remarks that if the *Pesach* is not roasted in one piece it is not disqualified.]

The halachah follows R' Akiva (*Rav; Rambam, Hil. Korban Pesach 8:10*).

[131]   THE MISHNAH / PESACHIM

אֵין [ב] צוֹלִין אֶת הַפֶּסַח לֹא עַל הַשַּׁפּוּד
וְלֹא עַל הָאַסְכְּלָא.
אָמַר רַבִּי צָדוֹק: מַעֲשֶׂה בְּרַבָּן גַּמְלִיאֵל
שֶׁאָמַר לְטָבִי עַבְדּוֹ, ,,צֵא וּצְלֵה לָנוּ אֶת הַפֶּסַח
עַל הָאַסְכְּלָא''.
נָגַע בְּחַרְסוֹ שֶׁל תַּנּוּר, יִקְלוֹף אֶת מְקוֹמוֹ.
נָטַף מֵרָטְבּוֹ עַל הַחֶרֶס וְחָזַר עָלָיו, יִטּוֹל אֶת
מְקוֹמוֹ. נָטַף מֵרָטְבּוֹ עַל הַסֹּלֶת, יִקְמוֹץ אֶת
מְקוֹמוֹ.

יד אברהם

2.

אֵין צוֹלִין אֶת הַפֶּסַח לֹא עַל הַשַּׁפּוּד וְלֹא עַל הָאַסְכְּלָא. — *We may not roast the Pesach offering either on a [metal] spit or on a roasting tray.*

[Metal may not be used in roasting as explained above (mishnah 1 s.v. שפוד).]

According to *Tzlach* (74a, s.v. אין צולין cited below, s.v. אמר ר' צדוק) a metal tray may not be used even if the carcass does not touch the metal at all, but is suspended above it on a wooden spit. The tray acting as a barrier between the fire and the offering is an instance of 'roasted by means of something other than the fire' [צְלִי מַחֲמַת דָּבָר אַחֵר], i.e., the heat is not transmitted directly from the fire to the roast (cf. *Lechem Shamayim*).

אָמַר רַבִּי צָדוֹק: מַעֲשֶׂה בְּרַבָּן גַּמְלִיאֵל שֶׁאָמַר לְטָבִי עַבְדּוֹ, ,,צֵא וּצְלֵה לָנוּ אֶת הַפֶּסַח עַל הָאַסְכְּלָא''. — *R' Tzadok said: It once happened* [lit. *a happening*] *that Rabban Gamliel said to Tavi, his slave, "Go out and roast for us the Pesach offering on the roasting tray."*

The *Gemara* (75a) explains that R' Tzadok's narrative implies a distinction not explicitly stated by the mishnah (חַסּוּרֵי מֵחַסְּרָא). The narrative cannot be taken literally, for it is not the style of the mishnah to relate a story refuting a position just stated unanimously by the mishnah. The distinction alluded to is that אַסְכְּלָה מְנוּקֶּבֶת, a *perforated roasting tray* (i.e., a grill), may be used. R' Tzadok's story was meant to support

this point. *Rashi* (there, s.v. מנוקבת) explains that the spaces between the bars of this tray are big enough so that the entire carcass can fit between them. The bars of the grill are used only to support the spit holding the offering. Clearly (as pointed out by *Tos. Yom Tov*) this spit must not be of metal. *Meiri* explains that one could have thought that the Sages would prohibit the use of a metal tray or grill in any manner, lest people come to use it in a forbidden manner.

Although the words of *Rambam* (Hil. Korban Pesach 8:9) suggest that one may place the offering directly on the metal bars of the grill (see *Ravad*), *Kessef Mishneh* questions whether this is indeed *Rambam's* view.

From this, *Tzlach* (74a, s.v. אין צולין) deduces that one may not roast over an unperforated roasting tray, even if the offering is suspended in such a way that it does not touch the metal.

נָגַע בְּחַרְסוֹ שֶׁל תַּנּוּר, — *If it* [the offering] *touched the earthenware of the oven,*

If the roasting carcass made contact with the oven, the meat that touched is not fire-roast, but roast through some intermediary substance (*Rav* and *Rashi* based on *Gem.* 76a).

יִקְלֹף אֶת מְקוֹמוֹ. — *he must pare off its place.*

[Only the meat exactly at the place of contact with the hot oven becomes dis-

2. We may not roast the Pesach offering either on a [metal] spit or on a roasting tray.

R' Tzadok said: It once happened that Rabban Gamliel said to Tavi, his slave, "Go out and roast for us the Pesach offering on the roasting tray."

If it touched the earthenware of the oven, he must pare off its place. If some of its juice dripped onto the earthenware and dripped back onto it, he must remove its place. If some of its juice dripped on the flour, he must remove a handful from its place.

YAD AVRAHAM

qualified; and this disqualification cannot spread to the adjoining areas (as it does in the cases listed further).]

נָטַף מֵרְטָבּוֹ עַל הַחֶרֶס וְחָזַר עָלָיו, — If some of its juice dripped onto the earthenware and back onto it [the offering],

The drippings which were heated by the hot earthenware and thereby disqualified for not being fire-roast were, in turn, absorbed into the flesh of the Pesach (Rav; Rashi).

יִטּוֹל אֶת מְקוֹמוֹ — he must remove its place.

[He must remove the meat at the place it is splattered by the juice.] Here 'paring,' which implies excision of only the thinnest sliver of meat, is insufficient. Rather, he must remove the meat, which suggests that an appropriate thickness of meat must be sliced away.]

A forbidden (hot) liquid which penetrates a (permitted hot) solid is assumed to be absorbed to some depth and consequently the entire section so affected must be removed (Rashi).

It must be assumed that in the preceding passage the part of the offering touching the oven did not contain a great amount of juice otherwise, there too, removal would have been necessary. However, a minute amount of liquid is of no consequence as set forth in mishnah 3 (Tos. 75b, s.v. יטול, cited by Tos. Yom Tov).

נָטַף מֵרְטָבּוֹ עַל הַסֹּלֶת, — If some of its juice dripped on the flour,

If the flour was already seething from the fire, dripping juices from the Pesach may be cooked by the heat of the flour, thus disqualifying the juice as roast by a means other than fire (Rav; Rashi).

יִקְמוֹץ אֶת מְקוֹמוֹ. — he must remove a handful from its [the juice's] place.

Since the disqualified juice is absorbed in the flour, he must remove a complete handful of flour and burn it just as he must do with any sacrificial meat that becomes unfit (Rav; Rashi).

The same burning process is required of the invalidated portions described in the preceding two passages (Tos. Yom Tov). Rambam (Hil. Korban Pesach 8:13) rules however, that it is sufficient to throw the flour away. To explain why the flour should not require burning like other invalidated sanctified substances, R' Avraham Te'umim (Chiddushim appended to Sheilos UTeshuvos Chessed L'Avrohom, v. II) suggests that juices absorbed in other substances cannot become disqualified to such a degree that they require burning. Tos. Yom Tov (here) implies that only disqualified meat, not juices and bones, must be burned.

Rambam (Hil. Korban Pesach 8:12; see also his Comm. ed. Kafich) gives a reason for the juice's disqualification which differs from that set forth above. Only roast meat of the Pesach may be eaten, but not non-meat portions that are separated from the body of

---

1. Rashi gives no approximation as to how much should be removed. However Rav states, 'a thickness as much as (the width of) a finger.' This figure is given as the halachah in Yoreh Deah 96:1 and 105:4 (see also Tur there).

סָכוֹ [ג] בְּשֶׁמֶן תְּרוּמָה, אִם חֲבוּרַת כֹּהֲנִים,
יֹאכֵלוּ. אִם יִשְׂרָאֵל: אִם חַי הוּא
יְדִיחֶנּוּ וְאִם צָלִי הוּא יִקְלוֹף אֶת הַחִיצוֹן.
סָכוֹ בְּשֶׁמֶן שֶׁל מַעֲשֵׂר שֵׁנִי, לֹא יַעֲשֶׂנּוּ דָמִים
עַל בְּנֵי חֲבוּרָה, שֶׁאֵין פּוֹדִין מַעֲשֵׂר שֵׁנִי
בִּירוּשָׁלָיִם.

יד אברהם

the animal. Juices that remain in the body of the offering are considered roast meat, but drippings from the animal are no longer regarded as *meat*, even though they are roasted over the fire. This view is supported by the manuscript version of the *Gemara* cited by R' *Kafich* (note 5 to his ed. of *Rambam's Comm.*), the old version cited in *Rashi* (76a, s.v. אקורי and יקמץ) and R' *Chananel* (in *Tos.* there, s.v. אלא).

3.

סָכוֹ בְּשֶׁמֶן תְּרוּמָה, — If he smeared it [the Pesach] with oil of terumah,

Smearing the offering with fruit juice during the roasting process does not constitute cooking and is permitted *(Rav; Rashi; see above 2:8).*

[*Terumah* is the portion of the produce which must be separated and given the *Kohen;* its consumption is forbidden to non-*Kohanim.* The mishnah will show where the presence of *terumah*-oil poses an obstacle to the consumption of the offering and how this problem can be resolved.]

אִם חֲבוּרַת כֹּהֲנִים, יֹאכֵלוּ. — if the group is composed of Kohanim, they may eat.

But only if it was merely *smeared* with oil before or while roasting; if it was dipped in liquids before roasting it may not be eaten [because this may be considered cooking (see above 2:8)] *(Yer.* cited by *Meleches Shlomo).*

אִם יִשְׂרָאֵל: אִם חַי הוּא יְדִיחֶנּוּ; — If [it is composed of] Israelites, [then:] if it [the offering] is raw, he must rinse it;

Cold uncooked meat is not absorbent *(Rav; Rashi).* In addition to being rinsed it must also be dried *(Rambam, Hil. Korban Pesach 8:14).* [This extra precaution of drying is probably necessary here because one may not dip the Pesach in liquids before roasting (see above).]

וְאִם צָלִי הוּא יִקְלוֹף אֶת הַחִיצוֹן. — but if it is roasted, he must pare the outside.

Cooked or roasted meat has a tendency to absorb liquids smeared on it *(Rav; Rashi).*

This situation differs from a similar case in the previous mishnah (juice splashed on earthenware and back onto the meat) where the ruling was that a finger-thickness of meat must be removed. There, where the meat's own juices are dripping, a more substantial amount of liquid is involved. In our mishnah, smearing involves only a minute amount of liquid and does not cause as deep a penetration of the meat as does dripping. Consequently paring away is sufficient *(Gem.* 76a).

There is a question whether the rule that roasted meat absorbs liquids applies only when the meat is still hot, or even when it is cold. *Tosafos* 75b, s.v. ואם, holds the latter view, but many authorities disagree. See R' *Yosef Karo* and *Rama, Yoreh Deah* 91:7 and sources cited there by *Shach* 21 and *Bais Yosef.*

סָכוֹ בְּשֶׁמֶן שֶׁל מַעֲשֵׂר שֵׁנִי, — If he smeared it [the Pesach] with oil of the second tithe,

[*Maaser sheni, the second tithe,* must be eaten in Jerusalem or, alternatively, redeemed for coins with which food-

3. **I**f he smeared it with oil of terumah, if the group is composed of Kohanim, they may eat. If [it is composed of] Israelites, [then:] if it is raw, he must rinse it; but if it is roasted, he must pare the outside.

If he smeared it with oil of the second tithe, its value may not be charged to the members of the company, since second tithe may not be redeemed in Jerusalem.

YAD AVRAHAM

stuffs must be bought in Jerusalem and eaten there.]

לֹא יַעֲשֶׂנּוּ דָמִים עַל בְּנֵי חֲבוּרָה, — *its value may not be charged to the members of the company,*

The value of the oil may not be charged to the group (*Tif. Yis.*).

שֶׁאֵין פּוֹדִין מַעֲשֵׂר שֵׁנִי בִירוּשָׁלָיִם. — *since second tithe may not be redeemed in Jerusalem.*

Redeemed in the context of our mishnah means *sold* (*Rav*).

The second tithe may not be redeemed or sold in Jerusalem for it is said

(*Deuteronomy* 14:25): *and you shall exchange* [*it*, i.e., second tithe] *for silver ... and go up to the place which HASHEM your God will choose,*[1] implying that redemption and sale are permitted only outside Jerusalem (*Rav; Rashi*).

Many versions (see *Rashi; Tos.* 75a, s.v. שאין; *Shinuyei Nuschaos*) have here שֶׁאֵין מוכרין, *for one may not sell* second tithe in Jerusalem.

[The term פּוֹדִין, *redeemed,* cannot be understood literally (to mean that the holiness is being removed from the food); since the *maaser sheni* oil will indeed be eaten in Jerusalem in a state of holiness the payment was surely not meant to change the oil from sacred to secular.]

4.

Although sacrifices may not be offered by contaminated individuals — indeed, if such a person performed the service the offering is invalid (*Zevachim* 2:1) — an exception is made for the regular public sacrifices and the *Pesach* offering. If the majority of the *Kohanim* in Jerusalem or, in the case of the Pesach, the majority of the assembled people are contaminated, the sacrifices may be offered despite the contamination of the participants. This is inferred from the verse regarding פֶּסַח שֵׁנִי, *the Second Pesach* (*Numbers* 9:10-11): *If any man ... be contaminated ... In the second month ... shall they perform it.* The singular form of the phrase *any man,*

---

1. *Tosafos* (75b, s.v. לפי) objects to this derivation, pointing out that the cited verse refers not to selling, but to redemption, i.e. transferring the sanctity of the second tithe from the produce to money. (In the case of selling, however, the produce retains its status after the transaction). *Tosafos* offers two other reasons for the prohibition against selling the second tithe: 1. It is a desecration of a *mitzvah* to barter it for money as if it were ordinary produce. 2. The Sages forbade selling second tithe in Jerusalem lest people fail to see the distinction between selling, which is permitted, and redemption, which is forbidden. According to this view, our mishnah's term פּוֹדִין, lit. *redeem,* need not be twisted to mean *selling,* but can be given its usual translation. The mishnah says it is forbidden to pay for the oil which is in effect selling, *because* it is forbidden to *redeem* the oil.

Also, according to the view (see *Kiddushin* 2:8, 53b, 54b) that maaser sheni is מָמוֹן גָּבוֹהַּ, *the property of HaShem,* no one has the authority to sell it (*Tos. HaRashba; Rosh* to Maaser Sheni 1:1, s.v. אין מוכרין).

חֲמִשָּׁה [ד] דְּבָרִים בָּאִין בְּטֻמְאָה, וְאֵינָן נֶאֱכָלִין בְּטֻמְאָה: הָעֹמֶר, וּשְׁתֵּי הַלֶּחֶם, וְלֶחֶם הַפָּנִים, וְזִבְחֵי שַׁלְמֵי צִבּוּר, וּשְׂעִירֵי רָאשֵׁי חֳדָשִׁים.

יד אברהם

implies that only contaminated individuals, not the public, are deferred to the next month to bring the Second Pesach; the *public* may offer a Pesach even while in a state of contamination. By means of a *gezerah shavah*[1] this concept is extended to all public offerings that are similar to the Pesach in that they must be sacrificed on a fixed date. However, this is true only of contamination arising from contact with corpses, for this is the subject of the cited verse, but no such dispensation applies to other types of contamination (from *Rav*). Mishnah 4 discusses the differences between the application of this dispensation to the Pesach to the other public sacrifices.

חֲמִשָּׁה דְּבָרִים בָּאִין בְּטֻמְאָה, וְאֵינָן נֶאֱכָלִין בְּטֻמְאָה:—*Five things* [offerings] *may be fered* [lit. come] *in a state of contamination, but may not be eaten in a state of contamination:*

The portions of the offerings that are usually eaten must be burned like all sacrificial flesh that has become contaminated (*Hil. Bias HaMikdosh* 4:11).

The *Gemara* (76b) comments that the mishnah's seemingly superfluous mention of the number *five* serves as an additional stress that only these offerings (and those exactly similar to them) may be offered in a state of contamination. Consequently, although the *Chagigah* offering (sacrificed on the festival) like the Pesach, must be brought by every individual it does not qualify for this dispensation, because — although its time is fixed — nevertheless, there is a degree of flexibility, because the *Chagigah* may be offered until seven days have passed.

[The following list is not meant to exclude other public offerings; *every*

public offering with a fixed date of offering may be offered in a state of contamination. Our mishnah specifies five offerings because of the characteristic they share: all are offered and also eaten, but a failure to eat them does not invalidate the offering. Consequently, the mishnah rules that the service of *offering* overrides the strictures of contamination, but the *mitzvah* of eating does not. Most other public offerings are either burnt offerings or sin offerings whose blood service takes place inside the Temple [חַטָאוֹת פְּנִימִיּוֹת], which are not eaten in any case.

הָעֹמֶר, — *the Omer,*

[The *Omer* is offered on the sixteenth of *Nissan*. It consists of an *omer*, a measure holding a volume equivalent to 43.2 eggs (or at least 86.4 fl. oz.) of crushed barley for a flour offering. A handful is removed from the *omer* and burnt upon the altar, and the rest is eaten by the *Kohanim* (see *Leviticus* 23:10-11).]

1. *Gezerah shavah* is one of the thirteen rules of exegesis handed down from Sinai in the Oral Torah. This rule provides that where the same word (or different forms of the same word) appears in two different passages of the Torah, one can apply the laws given in one passage to the subject of the other passage. However, this device can be used only where the word has been designated by the oral tradition for use as a *gezerah shavah*. Here the word בְּמוֹעֲדוֹ, *in its designated time*, appears in the passage about the Pesach offering (*Numbers* 9:3), and the similar word בְּמוֹעֲדֵכֶם, *in your festivals*, occurs with reference to the public festival offerings (*Numbers* 29:39). [In Hebrew, the same word, מוֹעֵד, serves for the concepts *designated time* and *festival*.]

4. **F**ive things may be offered in a state of contamination, but may not be eaten in a state of contamination: the Omer, the Two Loaves, the *Panim* Breads, the public peace offerings and the he-goats of the New Moons.

YAD AVRAHAM

וּשְׁתֵּי הַלֶּחֶם, — *the Two Loaves,*

On the *Shavuos* festival two leavened breads made of fine wheat flour were brought in conjunction with a complement of animal sacrifices (see *Leviticus* 23:16-19). Technically, these loaves were not an offering, since leaven cannot be offered upon the altar *(ibid.* 2:11); the slaughter of the attendant peace offerings conferred the status of an offering upon the loaves (*Menachos* 47a). The loaves were 'waved' [תְּנוּפָה] together with the live peace-offering lambs and also with the breasts and thighs [חָזֶה וָשׁוֹק] of the offerings (*Leviticus* 23:20). For the Two Loaves this *waving* is in lieu of offering upon the altar (*Tos. Menachos* 78b, s.v. לא, cited by *Gilyonei HaShas* here), and may not be done in a state of contaminated *Kohen* is available (see *Tos.* 77b, s.v. עומר).

וְלֶחֶם הַפָּנִים. — *(and) the Panim Breads,*

The *Panim* [lit. *face*] *Breads* were arranged on the golden table in the קֹדֶשׁ, *Holy,* in two tiers of six loaves each. There were two spoonfuls of frankincense [שְׁנֵי בְּזִכֵּי לְבוֹנָה], one near each tier. Every Sabbath the loaves were replaced and the frankincense burned upon the outer altar. These breads had

the status of meal offerings and were eaten by the *Kohanim* (see *Leviticus* 23:5-9).

וְזִבְחֵי שַׁלְמֵי צִבּוּר, — *(and) the public peace offerings,*

Among the sacrifices accompanying the *Two Loaves* brought on Shavuos were two yearling lambs designated as peace offerings (*Leviticus* 23:19). These were the only public peace offerings ever offered.

וּשְׂעִירֵי רָאשֵׁי חֳדָשִׁים. — *and the he-goats of the New Moons.*

Included in the Mussaf offerings for the New Moon was a he-goat sin offering. Like that of all sin offerings, its blood was offered upon the outer altar (חַטָּאות חִיצוֹנוֹת), and its flesh was eaten by the *Kohanim* (see *Numbers* 28:15).

The *Gemara* 76b notes that included in every festival *Mussaf* was a he-goat sin offering, but the mishnah saw no need to mention it because obviously it has the same status as public peace offerings, to which it is very similar in that it is a blood offering whose flesh is eaten by the *Kohanim.* Nevertheless the he-goats for the New Moons *are* mentioned lest it be thought that the New Moon is not significant enough to be considered a מוֹעֵד, *festival,*[1] on which offerings are brought even in a state of contamination.[2]

1. As mentioned above (footnote 1 to *prefatory remarks*), this dispensation is based on the word (*Numbers* 29:39) בְּמוֹעֲדֵכֶם, *in your festivals,* and thus applies only to days that have the status of 'festivals.'

2. [The *Gemara* does not explain why in light of this, three types of flour offerings must be mentioned even though they are so similar. The answer may be based on the premise that the typical style of the Mishnah teaches new laws in progressive stages of innovation [לֹא זוֹ אַף זוֹ], i.e., the first step is mentioned, then a second, more innovative case, then a third, and so on. Thus after the *Omer*, part of which is offered upon the altar, the *Two Loaves* must be mentioned even though no part of them goes upon the altar. These two flour offerings, however, have a special degree of importance, because both serve to lift prohibitions [לְהַתִּיר בָּאִין]: the *Omer* lifts the prohibition against eating of the new grain crop, and the Two Loaves

הַפֶּסַח שֶׁבָּא בְטֻמְאָה נֶאֱכָל בְּטֻמְאָה, שֶׁלֹּא
בָא מִתְּחִלָּתוֹ אֶלָּא לַאֲכִילָה.

[ה] נִטְמָא הַבָּשָׂר וְהַחֵלֶב קַיָּם, אֵינוֹ זוֹרֵק
אֶת הַדָּם. נִטְמָא הַחֵלֶב וְהַבָּשָׂר
קַיָּם, זוֹרֵק אֶת הַדָּם.
וּבַמֻּקְדָּשִׁין אֵינוֹ כֵן. אֶלָּא אַף עַל פִּי שֶׁנִּטְמָא
הַבָּשָׂר וְהַחֵלֶב קַיָּם, זוֹרֵק אֶת הַדָּם.

ז/ו
[ו] נִטְמָא הַקָּהָל אוֹ רֻבּוֹ, אוֹ שֶׁהָיוּ הַכֹּהֲנִים

יד אברהם

הַפֶּסַח שֶׁבָּא בְטֻמְאָה — [But] the Pesach of-
fering that is offered in contamination
[When a majority of the people or the
Kohanim were contaminated.]

נֶאֱכָל בְּטֻמְאָה, שֶׁלֹּא בָא מִתְּחִלָּתוֹ אֶלָּא
לַאֲכִילָה. — may be eaten in contamination, because its original purpose is only
for eating.
Concerning the Pesach, Scripture
states: Everyone according to his eating
(Exodus 12:4), indicating that the main
purpose of the Pesach service is to

qualify it for its subsequent consumption (Rav; Rashi).
However, even if the offering was not
eaten later, the participants have fulfilled
their obligation (Gem. 78b; Hil. Korban
Pesach 4:2). Thus if the public became contaminated after the service was performed,
the Pesach may not be consumed (Gem. 78b;
Hil. Korban Pesach 7:7-8). Consequently,
the terse language of the mishnah takes on
special significance. It is not the special mitzvah of eating the Pesach that puts it in a
special category, but the provision that its
service must be capable of qualifying it for
consumption.

5.

נִטְמָא הַבָּשָׂר וְהַחֵלֶב קַיָּם, — If the flesh [of
the Pesach offering] became con-
taminated but the fat remained [uncon-
taminated; lit. exists],
[Our mishnah discusses a situation
where the community was not in a state
of contamination. Only the flesh of a
particular Pesach became contaminated,
but the fats that would be offered on the
altar were unaffected.]
[The mishnah describes the uncontaminated state of the fats as הַחֵלֶב קַיָּם, lit.
the fat exists, because any part of the
sacrifice that becomes contaminated is, for all
practical purposes, non-existent.]

אֵינוֹ זוֹרֵק אֶת הַדָּם. — one may not throw
the blood.
The sole purpose of the Pesach
sacrifice is, as stated in the previous
mishnah, for its meat to be eaten at the
Seder feast, but in this case the contaminated meat will be burned. Failing
to achieve its purpose, the service would
have no validity and may not be performed (Rav; Rashi).
How is it possible for one part of the
animal to be fit while the other is contaminated, before the throwing of the blood
took place. Throwing usually takes place immediately after the blood has been received

lift the prohibition against offering of the new grain crop in the Temple. Therefore, the Panim
Breads are mentioned, to teach that even though they have none of the above characteristics
nevertheless they too are offered in a state of contamination. This distinction is made by the
Gemara 77a in a different context.]

[But] the Pesach offering that is offered in contamination may be eaten in contamination, because its original purpose is only for eating.

5. **I**f the flesh [of the Pesach offering] became contaminated but the fat remained [uncontaminated], one may not throw the blood. If the fat became contaminated but the flesh remained [uncontaminated] he throws the blood. But in the case of [other] consecrated animals it is not so. Rather even when the flesh became contaminated and the fat remained [uncontaminated] he throws the blood.

6. **I**f the community or its majority became contaminated, or if the *Kohanim* were con-

YAD AVRAHAM

so that it can be assumed to occur before the animal is opened. Does it not, therefore, follow that if the flesh is contaminated the fats within are similarly affected? The mishnah's case is possible only if the blood was not thrown immediately for some reason [e.g., if the Pesach was slaughtered before the *Tamid* (see 5:3)], but a *Kohen* kept stirring it to prevent coagulation. While this was happening the carcass was being flayed and dissected. In the interim the meat became contaminated; the fat which was already separated from the meat remained in its uncontaminated state (*Tif. Yis.*).

נִטְמָא הַחֵלֶב וְהַבָּשָׂר קַיָּם, זוֹרֵק אֶת הַדָּם. — *If the fat became contaminated but the flesh remained [uncontaminated] he throws the blood.*

[Here the essential purpose — eating— can be fulfilled. Failure to burn the sacrificial parts upon the altar does not affect the validity of any offering.]

וּבְמֻקְדָּשִׁין אֵינוֹ כֵן. אֶלָּא אַף עַל פִּי שֶׁנִּטְמָא הַבָּשָׂר וְחֵלֶב קַיָּם, זוֹרֵק אֶת הַדָּם. — *But in*

the case of [other] consecrated animals it is not so. Rather even when the flesh became contaminated and the fat remained [uncontaminated] he throws the blood.

[With respect to other sacrifices edibility is not essential to the fitness of the offering.]

The *Gemara* (77b) cites a disagreement between R' Eliezer and R' Yehoshua on whether it is essential for at least part of an offering to be in existence at the time of *throwing*. R' Yehoshua holds that throwing is valid only when it serves to lift a previously existing prohibition, i.e., it allows the flesh of the offering to be consumed. Nevertheless the existence of fats alone is sufficient to warrant throwing of the blood, for the blood service serves to permit the offering of the sacrificial parts upon the altar. R' Akiva Eiger deduces that the mishnah seems to agree with R' Yehoshua. Otherwise, it should have said that even when *both* the flesh *and* the fats became contaminated he throws the blood.

6.

נִטְמָא הַקָּהָל אוֹ רֻבּוֹ, — *If the community or its majority became contaminated,*

I.e., through corpse contamination. The abrogation of the laws of *tumah* for

the community comes into effect only with respect to a corpse contamination (*Rambam, Comm.*). The *Gemara* (79a) says that the mishnah applies even if

טְמֵאִים וְהַקָּהָל טְהוֹרִים, יֵעָשֶׂה בְטֻמְאָה.
נִטְמָא מְעוּט הַקָּהָל, הַטְּהוֹרִין עוֹשִׂין אֶת
הָרִאשׁוֹן, וְהַטְּמֵאִין עוֹשִׂין אֶת הַשֵּׁנִי.

[ז] **הַפֶּסַח** שֶׁנִּזְרַק דָּמוֹ וְאַחַר כָּךְ נוֹדַע
שֶׁהוּא טָמֵא, הַצִּיץ מְרַצֶּה.

יד אברהם

both the congregation and the Kohanim were fit, but the sacred vessels used for the preparation of the Pesach were contaminated.

In the situation posed by the mishnah, the minority of uncontaminated people may participate in the Pesach service even if in the process, they will become unfit through contact with the contaminated (i.e., they are not required to remain uncontaminated). The motive behind this extraordinary practice is 'because a public sacrifice is not divided', i.e., a public offering cannot be subject to two differing sets of rules, one requiring the uncontaminated to safeguard their pure status, and another for the contaminated, permitting them to offer despite their condition (*Gem.* 80a).

Meiri explains that it is an affront to the community for a minority to avoid contact with them.

אוֹ שֶׁהָיוּ הַכֹּהֲנִים טְמֵאִים וְהַקָּהָל טְהוֹרִים,
יֵעָשֶׂה בְטֻמְאָה. — *or if the Kohanim were contaminated but the community was uncontaminated, it* [the Pesach service] *is performed in contamination.*

[As outlined earlier (preface to mishnah 4) the source for this law is in the Scriptural narrative *And there were certain men who were contaminated by a dead human body* (Numbers 9:6). The Torah goes on to mandate that: *Any man* (אִישׁ אִישׁ) *who will be contaminated by the corpse of a dead person ... shall perform the Second Pesach.* The expression *Any man ...* implies that only an *individual* is deferred to the Second Pesach, but the community (defined as the majority or half of the community; *Gem.* 79b) offers on the first Pesach even when contaminated (from *Gem.* 67a).]

נִטְמָא מְעוּט הַקָּהָל, הַטְּהוֹרִין עוֹשִׂין אֶת
הָרִאשׁוֹן, וְהַטְּמֵאִין עוֹשִׂין אֶת הַשֵּׁנִי. — *If a minority of the community became contaminated, those uncontaminated observe the first* [Pesach offering], *and the contaminated observe the second* [Pesach offering].

[The First Pesach is the date designated for the initial sacrifice of the Pesach offering — the fourteenth of Nissan. The Second Pesach is the date reserved for those unable to perform the offering on the fourteenth of Nissan, because of contamination or other reasons (see 9:1-2). As set forth in the Torah *(Numbers 9:11),* the Second Pesach occurs on the fourteenth of the second month, Iyar.]

Upon close examination of the mishnah, a contradiction presents itself. In the first clause, the mishnah says, *If the community became contaminated or its* **majority** ... implying that if exactly *half* of the community became contaminated they would not qualify for this dispensation. However the second clause defines as individuals (and not qualifying for a dispensation) only the minority of the community, implying that exactly half of the community is entitled to the same dispensation granted the majority. The *Gemara* (79b; according to the amora Rav's view) finds middle ground between these two contradictory implications. If the majority of the community is contaminated, even the unaffected people do not have to be careful to perform the service in purity (see above, s.v. נטמא הקהל). But this lenient rule does not apply if only half of the community became contaminated; in this case even though the contaminated people observe the *First* Pesach, nevertheless the others must be careful to perform their offering in purity. If only a minority is contaminated those contaminated are deferred to the Second Pesach.

7
7

taminated but the community was uncontaminated, it is performed in contamination.

If a minority of the community became contaminated, those uncontaminated observe the first [Pesach offering], and the contaminated observe the second [Pesach offering].

7. **A**ny Pesach offering whose blood had been thrown and it was learned afterwards that it was contaminated, the *tzitz* effects acceptance. [But]

YAD AVRAHAM

⏵§ Preface to Mishnayos 7-9

The following three mishnayos discuss various ramifications of contamination as they affect a Pesach offering that was offered in a state of purity. Under discussion are cases where the people performing the service are not disqualified, but the flesh of the offering became *tamei*. The Sages expound that in cases where such contamination would disqualify an offering, the ציץ, *gold plate* [worn on the *Kohen Gadol's* forehead], propitiates the sin of *tumah* and lifts the disqualification (*Gem.* 16b; *Rashi* to *Exodus* 28:38). This atonement not only qualifies sacrifices whose flesh already has been offered in contamination, but even permits the continuance of their service once it was begun in a state of contamination. The Sages decreed, however, that if the contamination becomes known prior to the blood service, the blood should not be thrown. If this directive was disregarded willfully [בְּמֵזִיד] the offering is disqualified by Rabbinic decree (Ravina in *Gemara* 80b). However the *Kohen Gadol's tzitz* [gold plate] effects qualification to the extent that the owner's obligation is discharged, but it does not lift the prohibition against consumption of contaminated sacrificial meat (see *Rashi* to 16b, s.v. על הדם).

7.

הַפֶּסַח שֶׁנִּזְרַק דָּמוֹ וְאַחַר כָּךְ נוֹדַע שֶׁהוּא טָמֵא,
— *Any* [lit. *the*] *Pesach offering whose blood had been thrown and it was learned afterwards that it was contaminated,*

It was learned afterwards refers to either contamination of the flesh[1] or the blood *(Rav; Rashi).*

[If the blood was contaminated, the atonement of the *tzitz* validates the blood service that had been performed with disqualified blood. With the blood service validated, the Pesach may be eaten and the participants have discharged their obligation.] *Rambam (Comm.)* points out that the *Gemara*

1. The need for the *tzitz's* atonement in a case where only the flesh was contaminated must be dealt with from two aspects: (a) the requirements of sacrifices in general; (b) the peculiar requirements of the Pesach sacrifice that its owners must be permitted to eat it. Concerning the first aspect, as noted earlier (mishnah 5, s.v. ובמקדשין), R' Eliezer holds that the blood may be thrown even if the entire carcass has been burned. If so, the contamination of the offering would not require the atonement of the *tzitz*, since contamination is no different than the disappearance or destruction of the flesh and fats. However, according to the halachically accepted view of R' Yehoshua (see *Rambam, Hil. Pesulei HaMukdashin* 1:34 with comm.) the blood service may be performed only if at least some of the flesh or fats still exist. Thus if the entire offering became contaminated only the atonement of the *tzitz* prevents the offering

נִטְמָא הַגּוּף, אֵין הַצִּיץ מְרַצֶּה. מִפְּנֵי שֶׁאָמְרוּ:
הַנָּזִיר וְעוֹשֵׂה פֶסַח, הַצִּיץ מְרַצֶּה עַל טֻמְאַת
הַדָּם, וְאֵין הַצִּיץ מְרַצֶּה עַל טֻמְאַת הַגּוּף.
נִטְמָא טֻמְאַת הַתְּהוֹם, הַצִּיץ מְרַצֶּה.

יד אברהם

(17b) concludes that according to the halachic tradition attested to by Yose ben Yo'ezer (*Eduyos* 8:4) sacrificial blood cannot become contaminated,[2] so this mishnah, which runs counter to his tradition is not adopted as halachah.[3] In accord with this view, *Rambam's* formulation of the mishnah's halachah mentions only the law of contaminated meat.]

הַצִּיץ מְרַצֶּה — *the tzitz effects acceptance.*

On his head the *Kohen Gadol* wore a golden head-plate, צִיץ [tzitz], two fingers in width and reaching from ear to ear. On it were engraved the words קֹדֶשׁ ה', *holy to HASHEM (Exodus* 28:37; *Hil. Klei HaMikdash* 9:1).

The acceptance effected by the *tzitz* releases the participants in the Pesach group from the obligation of a second offering (*Rav; Rashi*).

The mishnah implies that if the con-

tamination were known *before* the throwing, the law would be different. However the Gemara (80b) concludes in Ravina's view, that even if the contamination *had* been known previously the *tzitz* would render the blood service valid if the *Kohen* did not intend to violate the prohibition against throwing it [שׁוֹגֵג]. If it were thrown בְּמֵזִיד, *willfully*, however, the *tzitz* does not atone. Even in this case, the *Talmud* (*Yevamos* 90a) explains that the offering is invalid only by Rabbinic law, and while they forbade the eating of the offering the participants have discharged their obligation. The view of *Rashi* and *Rambam* regarding this is beset with difficulties (see *Hil. Bias HaMikdash* 4:6-7; *Hil. Pesulei HaMukdashin* 1:34, *Hil. Korban Pesach* 4:2 with *comm.*, especially *Mirkeves HaMishneh* to *Hil. Korban Pesach*).

נִטְמָא הַגּוּף, — [But] *if the body* [*of the person*] *was contaminated,*

I.e., it later became known that the participant(s) had been in a state of contamination when the blood was thrown

from being disqualified. In this case, the effect of the *tzitz* is that it allows us to view the offering as if it were uncontaminated and still in existence (see *Gem.* 77a-b).

But this is not sufficient to satisfy the special requirement of the Pesach — that it be edible. As *Tosafos* (80b, s.v. נזרק) notes, the Pesach offering must be fit for consumption at the time of its service (see mishnah 5), but the *tzitz* cannot make permissible the eating of contaminated sacrificial meat!

Tosafos concludes that the mishnah discusses only contaminated blood. However *Rambam* (*Hil. Korban Pesach* 4:2) applies the mishnah's rule only to contaminated *flesh*, implying that the atoning power of the *tzitz* allows the offering to discharge the owners' obligation *as if* the flesh were edible, even though in fact it is halachically prohibited to eat it (see *Lechem Mishneh* and *Mirkeves HaMishneh*).

2. According to (the amora) Rav's view (*Gem.* 17a), Yose's testimony meant not only that blood cannot convey contamination to other materials, but that blood itself is impervious to contamination (טוּמְאַת עַצְמָן). R' Papa (*Gem.* 18b) explains that this was an oral tradition handed down to Moses on Sinai [הֲלָכָה לְמשֶׁה מִסִּינַי]. This view is adopted by *Rambam* (*Hil. Tumas Ochlin* 10:16).

3. *Rambam* (*Comm.* here and *Eduyos* 8:4) interprets this to mean that our mishnah (and others like it) was formulated prior to Yose's testimony (מִשְׁנָה רִאשׁוֹנָה). [The Sages did not amend the mishnah after Yose's testimony because the basic premise of the mishnah — the distinction between contamination known before throwing and contamination discovered afterwards — is valid as it applies to contaminated meat (see more about מִשְׁנָה רִאשׁוֹנָה above 1:1).]

7
7

if the body [of the person] was contaminated, [then] the *tzitz* does not effect acceptance. For they have said: [Concerning] the nazirite and for one who performs [the service of] the Pesach, the *tzitz* effects acceptance concerning contamination of the blood, but the *tzitz* does not effect acceptance for the contamination of the body.

If one became contaminated from a contamination of the deep, the *tzitz* effects acceptance.

YAD AVRAHAM

(*Tif. Yis.*). The same applies to the *Kohen* who performed the service (*Rambam*).

אֵין הַצִּיץ מְרַצֶּה. — [*then*] *the tzitz does not effect acceptance.*

The contaminated person must bring another offering on the Second Pesach, for his state of uncontamination during the throwing service disqualifies him from discharging his obligation (*Rav; Rashi*). [As noted the participants must be pure during the service; see *comm.* to 8:5.]

[The central point of this passage is that the *tzitz* does not atone for the contamination of people. The Talmud (*Zevachim* 23b) derives this rule exegetically from the verse describing the efficacy of the *tzitz: And Aaron shall bear ... the sin of the holy things* (*Exodus* 28:38), implying that the *tzitz's* effectiveness is limited to *the holy things*, and not for the people responsible for their sanctity (עֲוֹן הַקֳּדָשִׁים וְלֹא עֲוֹן הַמַּקְדִּישִׁין), i.e., the acceptability of the people performing the service or those essential to it.]

מִפְּנֵי שֶׁאָמְרוּ: הַנָּזִיר וְעוֹשֵׂה פֶסַח, הַצִּיץ מְרַצֶּה עַל טֻמְאַת הַדָּם, — *For they have said:* [Concerning] *the nazirite and for one who performs* [*the service of*] *the Pesach; the tzitz effects acceptance concerning contamination of the blood,*

[See ArtScroll *Comm.* to Shekalim 2:5, s.v. *Nazirite*, for a detailed exposition of the laws of the nazirite.]

The *nazirite* may, therefore, perform those acts that had been previously forbidden to him, such as drinking wine and coming in contact with corpses (*Rav; Rashi*). Regarding the Pesach, the offering is valid absolving him of the necessity of bringing the Pesach Sheni (*Tif. Yis.*). [In these cases the atonement of the *tzitz* has the further result that the offering may be eaten.]

וְאֵין הַצִּיץ מְרַצֶּה עַל טֻמְאַת הַגּוּף. — *but the tzitz does not effect acceptance for the contamination of the body* [i.e., the person].

If a nazirite becomes contaminated any time before termination of his vow he must start to observe his vow anew (*Numbers* 6:12). If he offered his sacrifices while contaminated (see *Tos. Yom Tov*), the *tzitz* cannot effect acceptance, thus his previous observance of the vow is void (*Rav; Rashi*).

נִטְמָא טֻמְאַת הַתְּהוֹם, הַצִּיץ מְרַצֶּה. — *If one became contaminated from a contamination of the deep, the tzitz effects acceptance.*

'Contamination of the deep' is a technical term denoting a *tumah* that was unknown to anyone and was discovered for the first time, e.g., one was in a house and it was subsequently discovered that a corpse had been buried beneath it. Thus, if *tumah* was discovered after the offering of the nazirite's sacrifices, or after the Pesach service had been completed, the *tzitz* atones for the sin of *tumah* even though here it concerns 'contamination of the body'. The ruling of 'contamination of the deep' applies only to corpse contamination, but to no other category of *tumah*.

[ח] **נִטְמָא** שָׁלֵם אוֹ רֻבּוֹ, שׂוֹרְפִין אוֹתוֹ
לִפְנֵי הַבִּירָה מֵעֲצֵי הַמַּעֲרָכָה.
נִטְמָא מְעוּטוֹ, וְהַנּוֹתָר, שׂוֹרְפִין אוֹתוֹ
בְּחַצְרוֹתֵיהֶן אוֹ עַל גַּגּוֹתֵיהֶן מֵעֲצֵי עַצְמָן.
הַצַּיְקָנִין שׂוֹרְפִין אוֹתוֹ לִפְנֵי הַבִּירָה, בִּשְׁבִיל
לֵהָנוֹת מֵעֲצֵי הַמַּעֲרָכָה.

[ט] **הַפֶּסַח** שֶׁיָּצָא אוֹ שֶׁנִּטְמָא יִשָּׂרֵף מִיָּד.

יד אברהם

This extraordinary form of 'atone-ment of the tzitz' is not based on Scrip-ture (which provides only for the sin of the holy *things*, not people) but upon

הֲלָכָה לְמֹשֶׁה מִסִּינַי, the oral tradition transmitted through Moses from Sinai (*Rav; Rashi* based on *Gem.* 80b and *Tosefta* 6:5).

8.

נִטְמָא שָׁלֵם אוֹ רֻבּוֹ, — *If the whole or the greater part of it* [the Pesach offering] *became contaminated,*

[The Torah (*Leviticus* 7:19) provides that flesh of sacrifices must be burned if it becomes contaminated.]

שׂוֹרְפִין אוֹתוֹ לִפְנֵי הַבִּירָה — *it must be burned before the Temple complex*

The name בִּירָה [*Birah*] is used to denote the entire Temple complex (*Rav; Rashi;* see *Tos. Yom Tov* to *Zevachim* 12:5).

[The site of the burning is probably the square facing the Temple Mount רְחָבָה שֶׁלִּפְנֵי הַר הַבַּיִת).]

Rav's interpretation of *Birah* is in ac-cord with that of *Resh Lakish* (*Yoma* 2a). R' *Yochanan* maintains that the reference is to a particular building on the Temple Mount [הַר הַבַּיִת] called 'Birah' (*Tos. Yom Tov*). Although the Pesach sacrifice may be burned throughout Jerusalem (see *comm.* to 3:8; and *Shekalim* 8:6-7), the Sages made an exception here [where most or all of the sacrifice is affected and it can be presumed that it happened due to gross negligence] in order to embarrass them so that they and the onlookers be more careful in the future (*Rav* from *Gem.* 81b).

מֵעֲצֵי הַמַּעֲרָכָה. — *with wood of the pyre.*

[I.e., wood intended for the pyre upon the altar.]

Permission was granted to use this wood so as not to embarrass someone who might not have his own wood (*Rav* from *Gem.* 82a).

[The *Gemara* cites this reason to explain a *baraisa's* ruling that even those who wanted to use their own wood were not permitted to do so.] Another reason — the one accepted by *Rambam* (*Hil. Korban Pesach* 4:3) — is that otherwise people would suspect those using pyre wood of theft, by taking home the left-over wood for their own use on the pretext that it was their own. But if every one were required to use pyre wood, no one could risk taking wood home from the Temple for he would surely be detected.

Tosafos (81b, s.v. נטמא) explains that the basis for this permission to use Temple wood is the rule that all property acquired by the Temple is bought on the condition that it be used as the *Beis Din* sees fit [see *Shevuos* 11a, לֵב בֵּית דִּין מַתְנֶה עֲלֵיהֶן).

The *Gemara* (81b) notes the apparent in-consistency with mishnah 3:8, which states that one who left Jerusalem and realizes that he has sacred flesh with him, must return to the city and burn it before the Temple com-plex with wood of the pyre. There, no dis-tinction is made between the greater or lesser part of the sacrifice. The *Gemara* explains that the earlier mishnah refers to a stranger

8. **I**f the whole or the greater part of it became contaminated, it must be burned before the Temple complex with wood of the pyre.

If the lesser part became contaminated, also the leftover [sacrificial meat], they burn it in their courtyards or on their rooftops with their own wood. The misers burn it before the Temple complex, in order to benefit from the wood of the pyre.

9. **A**ny Pesach offering that was taken out or became contaminated must be burned im-

YAD AVRAHAM

with no wood of his own who is, therefore, permitted use of the pyre wood under all conditions. Our mishnah discusses a city resident, who does not lack firewood.

נִטְמָא מְעוּטוֹ, וְהַנּוֹתָר, — *If the lesser part became contaminated, also the leftover [sacrificial meat],*

Sacrificial meat that was left over after the time prescribed for eating — even if not contaminated — must be burned as prescribed by *Leviticus 7:17* (*Tif. Yis.*)

שׂוֹרְפִין אוֹתוֹ בְּחַצְרוֹתֵיהֶן אוֹ עַל גַּגּוֹתֵיהֶן מֵעֲצֵי עַצְמָן.—*they burn it in their courtyards or on their rooftops with their own wood.*

As distinct from pyre wood, which may not be used on private property for fear that some wood will be unused and the owner may take it for his own purpose rather than for burning, thereby transgressing the prohibition against private use of consecrated property [מְעִילָה] (*Gem.* 82a).

הַפֶּסַח שֶׁיָּצָא — *Any* [lit. *the] Pesach offering that was taken out*

If the Pesach was removed for Jerusalem on the fourteenth [after its service, but before sundown] (*Rav, Rashi*).

[Like all other offerings of lesser sanctity (קָדָשִׁים קַלִּים), the Pesach may be eaten only within the walls of

הַצִּיקָנִין שׂוֹרְפִין אוֹתוֹ לִפְנֵי הַבִּירָה, בִּשְׁבִיל לֵהָנוֹת מֵעֲצֵי הַמַּעֲרָכָה. — *The misers burn it before the Temple complex, in order to benefit from the wood of the pyre.*

The *Yerushalmi* notes the strangeness of the word צִיקָנִין, a term found nowhere else. It suggests that this word is related to the root צעק, *shouting;* the people observing this individual's miserly behavior will taunt and deride him with shouts of: Miser! Miser! From this interpretation, *Yerushalmi* builds an alternative reason for the ban against using one's own wood when burning 'before the Temple complex' (see above, s.v. מֵעֲצֵי המערכה). Were it not for this ban, the person burning the lesser part of an offering would not be conspicuous as a miser. He could be assumed to be using his own wood.

The basis of the permission to use pyre wood in this case is the same as that mentioned above for a whole offering that became contaminated (s.v. מעצי המערכה). *Tosafos* (81b, s.v. נטמא) explains that we are apprehensive that, out of miserliness, they will refrain from burning these disqualified portions of offerings, and thereby cause unwitting transgression of the prohibitions against partaking of them.

9.

Jerusalem. If flesh of such offerings leaves these confines, it is disqualified and may not be eaten if later returned to Jerusalem.]

אוֹ שֶׁנִּטְמָא — *or became contaminated* [On the fourteenth of Nissan.]

יִשָּׂרֵף — *must be burned* [The Torah specifies that some dis-

נִטְמְאוּ הַבְּעָלִים אוֹ שֶׁמֵּתוּ תְּעֻבַּר צוּרָתוֹ,
וְיִשָׂרֵף בְּשִׁשָּׁה עָשָׂר.
רַבִּי יוֹחָנָן בֶּן בְּרוֹקָה אוֹמֵר: אַף זֶה יִשָׂרֵף
מִיָּד, לְפִי שֶׁאֵין לוֹ אוֹכְלִין.

[י] הָעֲצָמוֹת וְהַגִּידִין וְהַנּוֹתָר יִשָׂרְפוּ
בְּשִׁשָּׁה עָשָׂר. חָל שִׁשָּׁה

יד אברהם

qualified sacrificial parts, e.g., those contaminated and those left over after the time prescribed for their eating (see *Leviticus* 6:17,19), must be burned. Through Scriptural exegesis the Gemara (81b) extends this requirement to all disqualified parts of offerings of major sanctity [קָדְשֵׁי קָדָשִׁים], and to all offerings with regard to the sacrificial parts that should have been burned on the altar [אֵימוּרִין]. However even disqualified meat of lesser sanctity [קָדָשִׁים קַלִּים] must be burned because of the oral tradition from Sinai (הִלְכְתָא גְּמִירֵי לָהּ).

מִיָּד — *immediately.*
On the fourteenth of Nissan. They need not be left overnight to 'become disfigured' as in the parallel case discussed further. Were it left until the festival began, the burning would have to be postponed until the next day, because (see mishnah 10) disqualified sacrificial parts may not be burned on the *Yom Tov (Rav, Rashi).* [Nor may they be burned on the evening after *Yom Tov,* because such burning may not be done at night *(Gem 3a).*]

Rambam (Comm.) understands, שֶׁיָּצָא, *which was taken out,* as referring to the removal of the Pesach from the house where it is eaten, a violation of the precept *(Exodus* 12:46): It [the Pesach offering] *must be eaten in one house; you may not remove the meat.* Removal of any portion disqualifies it *(Hil. Korban Pesach* 9:1). Our mishnah now informs us that such meat must be burned immediately. *Tosafos Yom Tov* raises the difficulty that this removal is a disqualification on the night of the fifteenth when the Pesach is eaten; prior to that the Pesach may be car-

ried from place to place. Consequently, when this disqualification occurs the affected portion *cannot* be burned, because it is forbidden to burn disqualified sacrificial parts on *Yom Tov* (see next mishnah). Thus how can the mishnah say, 'it is burned immediately'?

נִטְמְאוּ הַבְּעָלִים אוֹ שֶׁמֵּתוּ, — *If the owners became contaminated or died,*
The offering itself is not disqualified, but since its registrants became disqualified, the Pesach cannot be eaten *(Rav, Rashi).* The same rule would apply if all the owners withdrew *(Meiri).*

תְּעֻבַּר צוּרָתוֹ, — *it must become disfigured*
The sacrifice must be left unburned until such time as it will be considered 'leftover' (נוֹתָר), i.e., after the time allowed for the consumption of the offering *(Rav).*

Mikdash David (Kodashim 17:4; see also *Tos.* 15a, s.v. ולד) establishes, that according to *Rashi,* 'disfigurement' does not require that the meat be considered 'leftover'; it is sufficient to wait until the morning after the disqualification, whether or not this would place the portion into category of נוֹתָר, leftover meat.

Rambam (Comm.; cf. *R' Chananel* 34b), maintains that צוּרָה עִיבּוּר, *disfiguration,* is meant literally: the meat must rot. At the same time, he states that in any case where the disqualification is in the animal itself — such as ' leftover' — it may be burned immediately. The implication is that if the disqualification was extraneous — such as contamination or death of the owners — disfiguration is required even after it becomes נוֹתָר, leftover meat, it may not be burned until it rots. This is highlighted by the fact that the Pesach becomes *leftover* on the morning of the fifteenth when it could hardly be rot-

mediately. If the owners became contaminated or died, it must become disfigured and be burned on the sixteenth.

R' Yochanan ben Berokah says: This too must be burned immediately, because there are none to eat it.

10. The bones, the sinews, and the leftover [meat] must be burned on the sixteenth. If the six-

YAD AVRAHAM

ten. It can be argued that the disqualification of 'leftover' — with the resultant requirement of immediate burning — applies only to edible sacrificial parts, not to parts disqualified before the limit is reached (see *She'eilos UTeshuvos Achiezer* 2:26, pp. 103-4; *Minchas Chinuch* 142; *Chazon Ish, Orach Chaim* 124), but meat affected by other disqualifications must wait for rotting. Thus these offerings may not be burned immediately after reaching the 'leftover' limit, and must wait until they rot.

וְיִשָּׂרֵף בְּשִׁשָּׁה עָשָׂר. — *and be burned on the sixteenth.*

But not on the fifteenth, because disqualified sacrificial parts may not be burned on the festival as set forth in the following mishnah (*Tif. Yis.*).

[As noted, the commentators distinguish between a disqualifying factor residual in the offering itself, and one imposed on it for external factors. *Tosafos* (82a, s.v. בשלמא) offers two approaches as to the source of this distinction: *Rashba* holds that it rests upon Scriptural exegesis. An alternative view (*ibid.*) is that it is dictated by Talmudic logic. The underlying reasoning for this distinction is probably based on the fact that the examples of burning specified by the Torah — contamination and 'leftover' — are due to disqualifications inherent in the parts themselves, therefore the law about such burning can be extended only to similar disqualifications (see Rashi 34b, s.v. ובבעלים). *Meiri* (see

also *Rashi* 73b, s.v. בדם), explains that where the disqualifying factor is external to the offering, the sacrifice is viewed as being essentially valid and therefore precluded from burning. The general rule is (*Gem.* 82b:) Whenever the disqualification is in its (the offering's) body it should be burned immediately; [but if the disqualification was] in the blood [e.g., the blood became disqualified or was spilled], or in the owners [e.g., in the case of a Pesach, they all became disqualified], it must become disfigured and [then] it goes to the place of burning.

רַבִּי יוֹחָנָן בֶּן בְּרוֹקָה אוֹמֵר: אַף זֶה יִשָּׂרֵף מִיָּד, לְפִי שֶׁאֵין לוֹ אוֹכְלִין. — *R' Yochanan ben Berokah says: This too must be burned immediately, because there are none to eat it* [lit. *it has no eaters*].

R' Yochanan maintains that the disqualification resulting from the contamination of the owners is in the same category as a disqualification of the sacrifice itself (*Meiri*).

Thus R' Yochanan agrees in principle with the first tanna — that only a disqualified offering may be burned immediately — but disagrees regarding the definition of a disqualification. This interpretation follows the view of R' Yoseif (*Gem.* 82b). According to the amora R' Yochanan (*ibid.*), however, R' Yochanan ben Beroka holds that no disqualification of the meat is needed. The offering may be burned immediately whenever it is clear that it cannot be eaten.

10.

הָעֲצָמוֹת — *The bones,*

The bones of the Pesach may not be broken (*Exodus* 12:46). As a result, their (edible) marrow which cannot be removed becomes 'leftover' (נוֹתָר) and must be burned [together with the

bones.]

The *Gemara* (831) points out that in the (halachically accepted) opinion of R' Yaakov, once consumption of the marrow had been permitted [שְׁעַת הֶבְשֵׁר], even if it had subsequently been con-

עֶשֶׂר לִהְיוֹת בַּשַׁבָּת, יִשָּׂרְפוּ בְּשִׁבְעָה עָשָׂר, לְפִי
שֶׁאֵינָן דּוֹחִין לֹא אֶת הַשַׁבָּת וְלֹא אֶת יוֹם טוֹב.

‏[יא] כָּל הַנֶּאֱכָל בְּשׁוֹר הַגָּדוֹל, יֵאָכֵל בִּגְדִי
הָרַךְ, וְרָאשֵׁי כְנָפַיִם וְהַסְּחוּסִים.

יד אברהם

taminated, the bones may not be broken. Accordingly they must be burned together with the marrow (see *Hil. Korban Pesach* 10:2, 6). But if consumption of the marrow had never been permitted (e.g., the offering had been contaminated before the blood service), the bones may be broken (see mishnah 11); consequently the bones may be cracked to remove the marrow for burning, but the bones, being inedible, need not be burned at all.

וְהַגִּידִין — *(and) the sinews*
[The term גידין includes such soft tissue as tendons, sinews, and nerves.]

The *Gemara* (83b) discusses the type of sinews meant by the mishnah. They cannot be the flesh sinews, since they must be eaten and become נוֹתָר, *leftover*, if they are not. Why, then, put them in a separate category? Neck sinews, on the other hand, are excluded because they are too tough and inedible to be considered flesh, obviating the necessity of burning them. The conclusion arrived at by the Sages is that the 'sinews' of the mishnah are either the fat of the thigh sinew, or the outer sinew of the thigh. The thigh sinew itself [גִּיד הַנָּשֶׁה] is Scripturally forbidden (*Genesis* 32:33), but its fat is technically permitted, although it is not eaten customarily. The outer sinew is forbidden only by Rabbinic law, and therefore requires burning as does edible meat.

וְהַנּוֹתָר יִשָּׂרְפוּ בְּשִׁשָׁה עָשָׂר. — *and the left-over [meat] must be burned on the six-*

teenth.

Although it became נוֹתָר, *leftover meat*, on the fifteenth, it may not be burned then because 'one may not burn disqualified sacrifice parts on the festival.' Therefore it must be set aside until the sixteenth, the first Intermediate Day.

חָל שִׁשָׁה עָשָׂר לִהְיוֹת בַּשַׁבָּת, יִשָּׂרְפוּ בְּשִׁבְעָה עָשָׂר, — *If the sixteenth falls on the Sabbath, they must be burned on the seventeenth,*

לְפִי שֶׁאֵינָן דּוֹחִין לֹא אֶת הַשַׁבָּת וְלֹא אֶת יוֹם טוֹב. — *because they do not override the Sabbath or a festival.*

The reason for not burning 'leftover' on Yom Tov is questioned by the Sages (83b). Why does the מִצְוַת עֲשֵׂה, *affirmative mitzvah*, of burning 'leftover', not override the לֹא תַעֲשֶׂה, *negative mitzvah*, forbidding work on *Yom Tov*, since there is a general rule that an affirmative command overrides a negative command? One of the replies is, that the Torah states (*Exodus* 12:10): *And you shall let nothing of it remain until morning, but that which remains of it until morning you shall burn with the fire.* The redundant phrase 'until the morning', implies that it is burned on the morning after it becomes 'leftover', i.e., on the sixteenth. The verse is understood to mean, *You shall let nothing of it remain until morning* [i.e., the morn of the fifteenth] *but that which remains of it* [shall be left] *until morning* [of the sixteenth — and then] *you shall burn with the fire* (see Rashi to *Exodus loc. cit.* and *Shabbos* 24b, s.v. שאין). Although the *Yom Tov* ends with nightfall, the burning must wait for morning because (*Gem.* 3a) 'one may not burn (disqualified) sacrificial parts at night' (*Tos. Shabbos* 24b, s.v. בקר).

11.

When a group registers on a Pesach offering, there must be sufficient meat for each one to receive a portion of *edible* meat equal in volume to an olive (בְּזַיִת).

teenth falls on the Sabbath, they must be burned on the seventeenth, because they do not override the Sabbath or a festival.

11. **A**nything edible in a large ox, must be eaten in a tender kid, including the ends of the shoulder blades and the cartilage. If one breaks the bone of an

YAD AVRAHAM

Consequently, the inedible parts of the animal cannot be included in the necessary portion. Also inedible portions are exempt from the prohibition against leaving over meat of the offering. Accordingly, the mishnah must define what is considered edible and what is not. Incidentally, the mishnah discusses the prohibition and punishment for breaking a bone of the Pesach offering.

כָּל הַנֶּאֱכָל בְּשׁוֹר הַגָּדוֹל, — *Anything edible in a large ox,*
All parts of a full-grown ox that are soft enough to be eaten, even after having become as hard and tough as they will ever become (Rav; Rashi).

יֵאָכֵל בִּגְדִי הָרַךְ, — *must be eaten in a tender kid,*
[The 'tender kid' is the Pesach offering, which must be a yearling of either goats or sheep (see Exodus 12:5).] With this statement, the mishnah excludes all parts of the Pesach that will harden and be inedible in an adult goat or sheep (as in a grown ox), even though they are still soft in a young kid. Such parts need not be eaten, and consequently may not be included in calculating the number of 'olive-sized' portions available to potential registrants (Rav; Rashi).

[Another probable ramification of this ruling is that one who eats these parts exclusively has not fulfilled the *mitzvah* of eating of the Pesach offering.]

וְרָאשֵׁי כְנָפַיִם וְהַסְחוּסִים. — *including the ends of the shoulder blades and the cartilage.*
This phrase clarifies the clause, *All that can be eaten of a large ox,* i.e.,

although the ends of the shoulder blades and cartilage of a large ox are edible only when boiled for a long period of time, these sinews of the broiled tender kid must be consumed (Rav based on Rava in Gem. 83a).

The translation given above is based on Rashi and Rav. Thus the mishnah has differing names for some formations of cartilage, for the ends of the shoulder blades are also cartilage. Rambam interprets רָאשֵׁי כְנָפַיִם as the *tendons* which connect the joints and סְחוּסִים as *cartilage* (Tos. Yom Tov).

Rambam (Hil. Korban Pesach 10:8) departs from the above interpretation and contends that the mishnah is concerned with the prohibition against breaking the bones of the Pesach offering (Exodus 12:46). The mishnah defines what is considered bone and what is considered flesh. Those parts of a large ox which are eaten when well cooked are not categorized as bones, and may be eaten — and broken — in the roast Pesach kid. Rambam's interpretation makes the clause about breaking bones (toward the end of our mishnah) germane to the issue being discussed. Ravad (ibid.) disagrees and maintains that the reference is to the prohibition, *you shall let nothing of it remain* (Exodus 12:10). In his view, the mishnah explains that any part of the large ox that can be eaten *must* be consumed, otherwise, its owner has transgressed the prohibition of leaving meat past the deadline.

◆§ **The penalty of lashes.**

As a general rule, anyone who transgresses a negative commandment after being warned not to do so by two witnesses, is punished by thirty-nine מַלְקוּת, *lashes.* [The mishnah refers to the exceptions to this rule, however. The penalty does not

הַשּׁוֹבֵר אֶת הָעֶצֶם בַּפֶּסַח הַטָּהוֹר, הֲרֵי זֶה
לוֹקֶה אַרְבָּעִים. אֲבָל הַמּוֹתִיר בְּטָהוֹר וְהַשּׁוֹבֵר
בְּטָמֵא, אֵינוֹ לוֹקֶה אֶת הָאַרְבָּעִים.

[יב] אֵבֶר שֶׁיָּצָא מִקְצָתוֹ, חוֹתֵךְ עַד שֶׁמַּגִּיעַ
לָעֶצֶם, וְקוֹלֵף עַד שֶׁמַּגִּיעַ לַפֶּרֶק,
וְחוֹתֵךְ.

יד אברהם

apply to a transgression that can conceivably involve the death penalty, nor does it apply to a case where monetary compensation is required, e.g., although one who assaults a fellow Jew has violated a negative commandment, he is obligated to pay damages instead of receiving lashes.]

The mishnah will now discuss another case where lashes are not inflicted for violation of a negative commandment. Although the Torah prohibits one to leave over sacrificial meat past the deadline designated for its eating (see below), one who does so is not punished by lashes. The *Gemara* (84a) offers two reasons for this: (a) Whenever a negative commandment is followed by a positive commandment that is designed to undo the transgression [לַאו הַנִּתָּק לַעֲשֵׂה] the logical assumption is that the Torah offers the positive commandment as the alternative to lashes. For example, the Torah forbids stealing, but commands a thief to return what he has stolen; therefore, restitution, not lashes, is the atonement for stealing. In the case of leaving over sacrificial meat, the Torah commands that leftover meat should be burned; thus the burning substitutes for lashes. (b) R' Yaakov (84a) rules that only for an active violation of a negative commandment is one liable to lashes. But leaving over sacrificial meat is a passive act — nothing is *done*, and lashes are not administered unless one has *committed* a wrong.

הַשּׁוֹבֵר אֶת הָעֶצֶם בַּפֶּסַח הַטָּהוֹר, הֲרֵי זֶה לוֹקֶה אַרְבָּעִים. — *If one breaks the bone of an uncontaminated Pesach, he incurs the penalty of forty [lashes].*

[He has transgressed the Scriptural command in reference to the Pesach, *neither shall you break a bone in it* (Exodus 12:10).]

Chinuch (Mitzvah 16) explains the reason for this prohibition by saying that it is not the custom of kings and princes to break and gnaw at bones. This is a habit only of the poor who lack sufficient food and gnaw at food to satisfy their hunger. Therefore, we, who proclaim that on this day we became, *a Kingdom of priests and a sanctified people* (Exodus 19:6), should deport ourselves in a manner befitting princes.

אֲבָל הַמּוֹתִיר בְּטָהוֹר, — *But one who leaves over [flesh] of an uncontaminated one* [i.e. of a Pesach],

Although it is forbidden to leave meat past the time when it must be eaten, one

who does so is not liable to lashes for doing so. This negative transgression, *you shall let nothing of it remain till morning* (Exodus 12:10), is followed by the compensatory commandment, *that which remains until morning you shall burn with fire* (ibid). The general rule is that when an affirmative command follows a negative command, (לַאו הַנִּתָּק לַעֲשֵׂה), it is regarded as the remedy for the transgression, and there is no punishment for the transgression. R' Yaakov is of the opinion that the reason he is absolved is because the prohibition was violated passively — not with a positive act — and there is a principle that one is not flogged for a passive transgression (*Rav* from *Gem.* 84a; see above, s.v. *The Penalty of Lashes*).

וְהַשּׁוֹבֵר בְּטָמֵא, אֵינוֹ לוֹקֶה אֶת הָאַרְבָּעִים. — *or one who breaks [a bone] of a contaminated one, does not incur the*

uncontaminated Pesach offering, he incurs the plenalty of forty [lashes]. But one who leaves over [flesh] of an uncontaminated one, or who breaks [a bone] of a contaminated one, does not incur the penalty of forty [lashes].

12. If part of a limb projected outside he cuts [it] until he reaches the bone, and pares [the meat] away until he reaches the joint and severs [the limb].

YAD AVRAHAM

penalty of forty [lashes].

The *Gemara* 84a infers this from *neither shall you break a bone* in it. The emphasis of the term *in it* teaches that only in *it*, a valid, uncontaminated offering, is one forbidden to break a bone, but one may do so with a contaminated Pesach (*Rav*).

Based on this derivation, the halachically accepted view (R' Yosef's) reasons that even when it is permitted to

offer and eat of a contaminated Pesach —where the public was *tameh* (see mishnah 5) — its bones *may* be broken (see *Hil. Korban Pesach* 10:1).

[We have already mentioned in the previous mishnah that according to the halachically accepted opinion even breaking the bones of a contaminated Pesach incurs punishment, if the contamination occurred after the offering had already been permitted for consumption, i.e., after the 'throwing' of the blood.]

12.

אֵבֶר שֶׁיָּצָא מִקְצָתוֹ, — *If part of a limb* [of an offering] *projected outside* [lit. *went out*].

Part of an offering projected beyond the boundary within which the Torah decreed that it must remain. There are three 'boundary' restrictions pertaining to various kinds of offerings.

Offerings of greater sanctity [קָדְשֵׁי קָדָשִׁים] are confined to the Temple Courtyard; offerings of lesser sanctity [קָדָשִׁים קַלִּים] are limited to within the walls of Jerusalem.

The Pesach offering has yet another boundary. In addition to its status as an offerings of lesser sanctity, it may not be removed from the group where it was designated to be eaten, to another group (see mishnah 13). If any part of an offering left the boundary applicable to it, that part is disqualified and must be separated from the rest of the offering

that remains 'inside' its boundary and is yet to be eaten. However, if part a Pesach offering was removed from Jerusalem or from its group,[1] there is a novel problem, for the Pesach carries with it the unique prohibition against breaking any bone. If so, how can the 'projecting' part of a limb be separated from the rest of the offering? Our mishnah now outlines the proper procedure (from *Rambam*).

חוֹתֵךְ — *he cuts* [it].

At the spot where the disqualified part meets the qualified part, he makes a circular cut all around the bone in order to separate the flesh that has 'gone out' and become forbidden, from the rest of the meat that must be eaten (*Rav*).

עַד שֶׁמַּגִּיעַ לָעֶצֶם, — *until he reaches the bone,*

[He may not cut *into* the bone,

---

1. The rule confining the Pesach to Jerusalem applies both on the fourteenth (after its slaughter) and the night of the fifteenth. However the prohibition not to take the Pesach out of the group applies only on the night of the fifteenth (*Tos. Yom Tov*). *Aruch HaShulchan*

וּבְמֻקְדָּשִׁין קוֹצֵץ בְּקוֹפִיץ, שֶׁאֵין בּוֹ מִשּׁוּם שְׁבִירַת הָעֶצֶם.
מִן הָאַגַּף וְלִפְנִים, כְּלִפְנִים; מִן הָאַגַּף וְלַחוּץ, כְּלַחוּץ. הַחַלּוֹנוֹת וְעָבִי הַחוֹמָה, כְּלִפְנִים.

[יג] שְׁתֵּי חֲבוּרוֹת שֶׁהָיוּ אוֹכְלוֹת בְּבַיִת אֶחָד, אֵלוּ הוֹפְכִין אֶת פְּנֵיהֶם הֵילָךְ וְאוֹכְלִין, וְאֵלוּ הוֹפְכִין אֶת פְּנֵיהֶם הֵילָךְ וְאוֹכְלִין, וְהַמֵּחַם בָּאֶמְצַע.

יד אברהם

because one may not break bones of the Pesach offering.]

וְקוֹלֵף — *and pares [the meat] away* [lit. *and peels*]

He slices the flesh still remaining 'inside' from the bone (*Rav; Rambam*) [since the entire bone must now be disposed of because of the section that protruded from the assigned boundary.]

עַד שֶׁמַּגִּיעַ לַפֶּרֶק, וְחוֹתֵךְ. — *until he reaches the joint and severs [the limb].*

[One may cut the tendons at the joint; they are not considered bone.]

The disqualified meat must be sliced off and burned, but the bone may be thrown away (*Hil. Korban Pesach* 9:2, *Tos. Yom Tov*).

However if the bone contained marrow, that is considered meat, and the entire bone must be burned (as outlined in mishnah 10; *Tos. Yom Tov*).

וּבְמֻקְדָּשִׁין קוֹצֵץ בְּקוֹפִיץ, שֶׁאֵין בּוֹ מִשּׁוּם שְׁבִירַת הָעֶצֶם. — *But with other offerings he may chop with a cleaver, for they are not subject to the [prohibition of] breaking a bone.*

Since other offerings do not share the prohibition against breaking a bone, the

precautions taken with regard to the Pesach do not apply, and the unfit portion is simply chopped off (*Rav*).

מִן הָאַגַּף וְלִפְנִים, כְּלִפְנִים; — *From the jamb inward is as inside;*

From the inner side of the jamb of Jerusalem's gates 'is as inside', and offerings of lesser sanctity (קָדָשִׁים קַלִּים) may be eaten there (*Rav; Rashi*).

Also if flesh of these offering projected from this boundary, it is disqualified (*Tif. Yis.*). *Rambam* understands that this clause refers to all three boundaries concerning offerings that have been described above (s.v. בשר שיצא). Whatever the type of meat, its boundary is defined by the inner jamb of whatever boundary it may not leave.

מִן הָאַגַּף וְלַחוּץ, כְּלַחוּץ. — *from the jamb outward is as outside.*

The mishnah first speaks of the *jamb inward.* From this we can infer that the area of the jamb proper should be considered to be *outside.* But then the mishnah speaks of the *jamb outward,* from which we may infer that the jamb itself is considered to be an extension of the *inside* area. The *Gemara* resolves the apparent contradiction by explaining that the former clause refers to the gateways

HaAssid (*Kodashim* 193:3-5) cites a *Tosefta* (6:9) that this prohibition takes effect only when the eating begins (cf. *Minchas Chinuch* 15:1, *Teshuvos Chazon Nachum* 133).

The general prohibition against eating flesh that has 'left its boundary' is derived exegetically from the apparently unrelated verse, וּבָשָׂר בַּשָּׂדֶה טְרֵפָה לֹא תֹאכֵלוּ, *flesh of torn beasts in the field, you may not eat* (Exodus 22:30). The phrase, *in the field,* seems superfluous, since the meat of a dead animal is forbidden no matter where it is found. Accordingly, the Sages (*Zevachim* 82b) derive the additional law that sanctified meat that is, for example, *in the field,* rather than in whatever boundary it belongs, becomes invalidated (*Rav*).

But with other offerings he may chop with a cleaver, for they are not subject to the [prohibition of] breaking a bone.

From the jamb inward is as inside; from the jamb outward is as outside. The windows and the thickness of the wall are as the inside.

13. If two groups were eating in the same house, one group may turn in one direction and eat, and the other group may turn in another direction and eat, with the kettle between them.

of the city, which were left unsanctified intentionally, so that the lepers — who are forbidden to enter Jerusalem — could enter the gateway to find shelter from the sun and rain. The latter clause refers to gates of the Temple Courtyard, which were sanctified, with the exception of the Nikanor gate.

הַחַלוֹנוֹת — *The windows*
[According to *Rambam*, this refers also to the windows in the Temple Courtyard wall (concerning offerings of greater sanctity), and to those in the house walls (regarding the Pesach offerings).]

וְעָבְיֵ הַחוֹמָה, כִּלְפָנִים. — *and the thickness of the wall are as the inside.*
The tops of Jerusalem's walls were thick enough for people to sit on them and eat (*Rav; Rashi*).
According to the amora Rav (*Gem* 85b), the roofs of Jerusalem's houses were not sanctified for the eating of offerings.

13.

שְׁתֵּי חֲבוּרוֹת שֶׁהָיוּ אוֹכְלוֹת — *If two groups were eating*
Of the same offering (*Rav; Rashi*).

בְּבַיִת אֶחָד, — *in the same house,*
The *Gemara* (86a) notes that this case follows R' Yehudah's ruling that many separate groups may eat one Pesach offering, but that each individual is limited to eating with one company. His view is determined by reconciling two verses. One verse (*Exodus* 12:7) states: *the houses* (plural) *wherein they* [the groups] *shall eat it* (the Pesach — singular), indicating that a number of companies may share one offering. A later verse 12:46 reads, בְּבַיִת אֶחָד יֵאָכֵל *''In one house shall it be eaten''* R' Yehudah interprets the second verse as a limitation on the individual eating from a Pesach; although the offering may serve many companies, each individual member is limited to a single group.

אֵלּוּ הוֹפְכִין אֶת פְּנֵיהֶם הֵילָךְ וְאוֹכְלִין, וְאֵלּוּ הוֹפְכִין אֶת פְּנֵיהֶם הֵילָךְ וְאוֹכְלִין, — *one group may turn in one direction and eat, and the other group may turn in another direction and eat,*
There is no reason for them to appear like one group by facing one another, because a Pesach may be eaten in two groups (*Rav; Rashi*).
Rambam (*Hil. Korban Pesach* 9:3) rejects this interpretation because if so, the mishnah should have stated simply that two companies may share one Pesach offering. He interprets that that mishnah *requires* the two groups to behave in a manner indicating that they are separate companies: *This group* [must] *turn to one side. Rambam* mentions a

וּכְשֶׁהַשַּׁמָּשׁ עוֹמֵד לִמְזוֹג, קוֹפֵץ אֶת פִּיו
וּמַחֲזִיר אֶת פָּנָיו עַד שֶׁמַּגִּיעַ אֵצֶל חֲבוּרָתוֹ,
וְאוֹכֵל.
וְהַכַּלָּה הוֹפֶכֶת אֶת פָּנֶיהָ וְאוֹכֶלֶת.

[א] **הָאִשָּׁה** בַּזְּמַן שֶׁהִיא בְּבֵית בַּעְלָהּ, שָׁחַט
עָלֶיהָ בַּעְלָהּ וְשָׁחַט עָלֶיהָ
אָבִיהָ, תֹּאכַל מִשֶּׁל בַּעְלָהּ. הָלְכָה רֶגֶל רִאשׁוֹן

יד אברהם

partition as a means of separation (see *Kessef Mishneh* loc. cit. and *Tos. Yom Tov*).

וְהַמֵּחַם בָּאֶמְצַע. — *with the kettle between them.*

In Talmudic times it was customary to dilute wine with warm water. Our mishnah now discusses the heater upon which the water kettle was placed. It may be placed between the two groups for the waiter's convenience. The fact that it may appear to be a partition separating the groups is immaterial since, as explained above, our mishnah rules that a Pesach may be eaten in two separate companies (*Rav; Rashi*).

Rambam (*Hil. Korban Pesach* 9:4) interprets this passage as an introductory clause to the following discussion of a waiter as if it had said ... אִם הַמֵּחַם בָּאֶמְצַע הַשַּׁמָּשׁ, *if the kettle is between them the waiter ... Tosafos* (119b, s.v. אמר; cf. *Maharsha* there) seems to view this clause as posing an obligation. The kettle *must* be placed between the groups to demonstrate that they are separate (in the spirit of *Rambam's* view).

וּכְשֶׁהַשַּׁמָּשׁ עוֹמֵד לִמְזוֹג, — *(And) when the waiter stands up to mix* [*the wine,*]

He too had registered upon this Pesach, and is part of the group with which he started to partake of it. When he gets up to serve the other group, he must leave his own company (*Rav; Rashi*).

קוֹפֵץ אֶת פִּיו וּמַחֲזִיר אֶת פָּנָיו — *he must close his mouth and turn his face*

To alleviate any suspicion that he is eating with the other group (*ibid*). [As mentioned above, although the offering

may be eaten by two groups, an individual may not eat with two groups; see *Shekalim* 4:2 where the mishnah teaches that one may not act in a manner that makes others suspicious of his actions.]

While away from his own group, the waiter must make it plain that he is complying with the law that he may not eat with the other group (*Rav; Rashi*).

Rambam (*Hil. Korban Pesach* 9:4) seems to interpret differently. If the waiter had food in his mouth when he was summoned to leave his group and serve the other one, he must close his mouth (and not chew), and keep his face turned toward his own group (see below, s.v. והכלה). Only upon returning to his group may he resume chewing the food in his mouth. The precautions prescribed by the mishnah (probably) serve to remind him not to swallow the meat he has in his mouth.

עַד שֶׁמַּגִּיעַ אֵצֶל חֲבוּרָתוֹ, וְאוֹכֵל. — *until he gets back to his own group,* [*then*] *he eats.*

Then he may swallow what he has in his mouth.

וְהַכַּלָּה הוֹפֶכֶת אֶת פָּנֶיהָ וְאוֹכֶלֶת. — *(And) the bride may turn away her face and eat*

Modesty and shyness may make a bride reluctant to face the company while eating. She may turn away from her colleagues, despite the appearance that she is not part of the group, because a Pesach may be eaten by two companies (*Rav; Rashi*).

Thus the main point of this passage — that

When the waiter stands up to mix [the wine], he must close his mouth and turn his face until he gets back to his own group, [then] he eats.

The bride may turn away her face and eat.

1. A woman, during the time she resides in her husband's house, [if] her husband slaughtered [a Pesach] on her behalf and her father slaughtered [a Pesach] on her behalf, she eats from [the Pesach] of her husband. If she went to spend the

YAD AVRAHAM

the Pesach may be eaten in two groups — is already known. *Tosafos* (86b, s.v. והכלה) suggests another interpretation: she may turn her face even if she started to eat facing the group; this is not considered eating in two places[1]. *Meiri* adds that this dispensation is given only to a bride; others may not turn away lest they come to eat in two places.

Chapter 8

1.

We learned previously (5:3, s.v. שלא למנוייו: see mishnah 3) that in order to discharge one's obligation he must be registered on the Pesach offering before its slaughter, and own a portion of its meat equivalent in volume to an olive. However one need not purchase and take possession of a Pesach portion himself. His portion may be assigned to him by a second party. Thus it may happen that an individual may have been registered upon more than one Pesach without his knowledge. But since one person may not bring more than one Pesach offering (*Baraisa* in *Gem.* 88b) a determination must be made as to which of the two registrations is valid. The following three mishnayos will deal with this topic.

הָאִשָּׁה בַּזְּמַן שֶׁהִיא בְּבֵית בַּעְלָהּ, — A woman, during the time she resides in her husband's house,

[The phrase 'resides in her husband's house' places two conditions on the law set forth here: (a) That she already has acquired the status of a *Nesuah* (נְשׂוּאָה), i.e., a woman whose marriage has been completed (see below 3:7, s.v. ולאכול סעודת ארוסין). As explained in *Kesubos* (4:5), *chupah*, the ceremony effecting this status, is basically the act of establishing the bride's residence in her

husband's domicile. (b) She plans to spend the Passover festival in her husband's house, rather than with her parents.]

שָׁחַט עָלֶיהָ בַּעְלָהּ וְשָׁחַט עָלֶיהָ אָבִיהָ, תֹּאכַל מִשֶּׁל בַּעְלָהּ. — [if] her husband slaughtered [a Pesach] on her behalf and her father slaughtered [a Pesach] on her behalf, she eats from [the Pesach] of her husband.

It is assumed that a married woman would prefer to be registered on her

---

1. *Kol HaRemez* notes, that according to the view that *Rambam* considers two groups facing away from each other as equivalent to having a partition between them it should be prohibited for a group-member to 'separate' himself from his group by facing away from the others. However a distinction may be drawn between two complete groups demonstrating their separateness by facing away from one another, and a single individual who is physically with the group, but faces away from it (see *Kiryas Sefer* to *Hil. Korban Pesach* 9:4; cf. *Chazon Ish Orach, Chaim* 124).

לַעֲשׂוֹת בְּבֵית אָבִיהָ, שָׁחַט עָלֶיהָ אָבִיהָ וְשָׁחַט
עָלֶיהָ בַּעֲלָה, תֹּאכַל בְּמָקוֹם שֶׁהִיא רוֹצָה.
יָתוֹם שֶׁשָּׁחֲטוּ עָלָיו אַפּטְרוֹפְּסִין יֹאכַל
בְּמָקוֹם שֶׁהוּא רוֹצֶה.
עֶבֶד שֶׁל שְׁנֵי שֻׁתָּפִין לֹא יֹאכַל מִשֶּׁל שְׁנֵיהֶן.
מִי שֶׁחֶצְיוֹ עֶבֶד וְחֶצְיוֹ בֶּן חוֹרִין, לֹא יֹאכַל מִשֶּׁל
רַבּוֹ.

יד אברהם

husband's offering (Rav, Rashi).[1]

A woman is obligated in the *mitzvah* of the
Pesach offering according to the halachically
accepted view of R' Yehudah (*Gem.* 91b; *Hil.
Korban Pesach* 1:1). Even according to the
view that she is not obligated, she may be
registered voluntarily on the offering and
partake of it (*ibid.*)

הָלְכָה רֶגֶל רִאשׁוֹן לַעֲשׂוֹת בְּבֵית אָבִיהָ, — *If
she went to spend the first festival in
her father's house,*

It was customary for a woman to
spend the first festival after her marriage at her father's house (*Rav; Rashi*).

שָׁחַט עָלֶיהָ אָבִיהָ וְשָׁחַט עָלֶיהָ בַּעֲלָה, תֹּאכַל
בְּמָקוֹם שֶׁהִיא רוֹצָה. — [*if*] *her father
slaughtered on her behalf and her husband slaughtered on her behalf, she
may eat in whichever place she desires.*

The *Gemara* (87a) says that this
mishnah deals with a woman who ordinarily does not frequent her parents'
house. We are, therefore, in doubt
regarding her intentions. The *Gemara*
further states that the intention must
have been verbalized by the time of
slaughter. Otherwise, we would be concerned with the matter of *bereirah* [lit.

choice], i.e., whether retroactive choice
has validity. The question would be
whether a desire expressed only after
the slaughter can be assumed to have
had legal standing retroactively to the
time of the slaughter. The halachah is
that we do not say *bereirah* where Torah
requirements are involved.

The inference is that if she does not ver-
balize her preference before slaughter, she
may eat of neither offering. Thus she may
eat [*only*] in the place she *had* desired [before
the slaughter]. But in the first case of the
mishnah — a woman who resides in her husband's house — she need not make her
preference known; it is assumed that she
prefers to have her husband act as her agent
(*Tos. Yom Tov*).

יָתוֹם שֶׁשָּׁחֲטוּ עָלָיו אַפּטְרוֹפְּסִין — *An
orphan for whom guardians slaugh-
tered*

He had more than one guardian and
each slaughtered a Pesach on his behalf.
(*Rav, Rashi*).

יֹאכַל בְּמָקוֹם שֶׁהוּא רוֹצֶה. — *may eat in
whichever place he desires.*

He may choose the Pesach in which
he will participate even after the
slaughter[2]. The problem of בְּרֵירָה,

1. Although the Talmud (*Nedarim* 36a) rules, 'if one designated a Pesach for his fellow, it is
unacceptable,' in our case the assumption that a wife wants her husband to act on her behalf is
so strong that it is as if she appointed him to be her agent (*Chazon Ish, Orach Chaim* 124).

2. *Tosafos* (88a, *s.v.* שמעת) notes the apparent inconsistency of our interpretations: in the
above case of a wife, the phrase, *the place she desires*, means that she must express her
preference by the time of slaughter, but in the case of an orphan, the identical phrase is taken
to mean that he may make his choice even at the Seder. *Tosafos* explains the basic difference
between the two cases. In the case of a wife, the mishnah informs us that she must make a
specific choice; we do not simply assume that she prefers her husband's Pesach. In the case of
an orphan, however, if he were required to express his desire before the slaughter like any
other Jew, there would be no point in mentioning the law. We *must* assume, therefore, that he
can make his choice even after the slaughter.

**8
1** first festival in her father's house, [if] her father slaughtered on her behalf and her husband slaughtered on her behalf, she may eat in whichever place she desires.

An orphan for whom guardians slaughtered may eat in whichever place he desires.

A slave belonging to two partners may not eat from either of them. One who is half slave and half free may not eat from his master's.

YAD AVRAHAM

retroactive choice, does not apply here because the Torah says (*Exodus* 12:3): *And they shall take ... a kid for a household*, implying that the head of the household has the power to purchase a Pesach for his minor children without their acquiescence (*Gem.* 88a with *Rashi*).

[I.e., the subsequent choice made by the orphan does not have to be effective retroactively, because the head of the household, in this case the legally appointed guardian, had the authority to slaughter on behalf of his ward.]

Tosafos (88a, s.v. שה) interprets the above passage as meaning that parents have no obligation to register their minor children. Thus the validity of the orphan's retroactive choice poses no difficulty (cf. *S'fas Emes*). However the question arises: How is it permitted to give Pesach meat to the technically unregistered children? It is forbidden to feed prohibited food to children, and one may not partake of a Pesach upon which he is not registered. *Tosafos* maintains that the Rabbinic prohibition against feeding children forbidden food is waived by the Rabbis in favor of the *mitzvah* of *chinuch* (חנוך), training the children in the observance of the *mitzvos* (cf. *Ran Nedarim* 36a, s.v. א״ר זירא, *Tos.* there).

עֶבֶד שֶׁל שְׁנֵי שֻׁתָּפִין לֹא יֹאכַל מִשֶּׁל שְׁנֵיהֶן. — *A slave belonging to two partners may not eat from either of them.*

Since half of the slave belongs to each partner, the registration is not valid for either half without permission from the other owner. Therefore, the slave may partake of a Pesach only when both owners had agreed to his registration (*Rav; Rashi*).

This rule applies only to cases where the partners are not cooperative about using each other's part of the slave (see *Tos., s.v.* מתניתין; cf. *Hil. Korban Pesach* 2:12 with *Kessef Mishneh*). Where they get along well, it can be assumed that each partner is satisfied with the other's registration, and the slave may choose to partake of whichever offering he wishes (*Gem.* 88a). [Probably here the slave must make his preference known before slaughter.]

The owner of a slave has the right to register his slave upon the offering of his choice, even against the wish of the slave. This right is based on the implication of the phrase (*Exodus* 12:3), *And he shall take ... a kid for a household* (*Gem.* 88a; cf. *Chazon Ish, Orach Chaim* 124).

The status of a Gentile slave owned by a Jew in regard to mitzvah observance is that of a Jewish woman, that is, after circumcision and immersion he is obligated in all the *mitzvos* incumbent upon women, among them the *mitzvah* of the Pesach offering (see above, s.v. שחט עליה).

מִי שֶׁחֶצְיוֹ עֶבֶד וְחֶצְיוֹ בֶן חוֹרִין, — *One who is half slave and half free*

[His owner freed half of him (see *Gittin* 41a) or he was a slave owned by two partners, one of whom freed him.]

לֹא יֹאכַל מִשֶּׁל רַבּוֹ. — *may not eat from his master's* [offering].

It is assumed that the master of half of him did not intend to register the free half upon his offering (*Rashi*). [Consequently the free, unregistered half may not partake of the offering just as any unregistered person may not do so.]

הָאוֹמֵר לְעַבְדּוֹ, „צֵא וּשְׁחֹט עָלַי אֶת
הַפֶּסַח," שָׁחַט גְּדִי יֹאכַל,
שָׁחַט טָלֶה יֹאכַל. שָׁחַט גְּדִי וְטָלֶה יֹאכַל מִן
הָרִאשׁוֹן.
שָׁכַח מָה אָמַר לוֹ רַבּוֹ, כֵּיצַד יַעֲשֶׂה? —
שָׁחַט טָלֶה וּגְדִי וְיֹאמַר, „אִם גְּדִי אָמַר לִי רַבִּי,
גְּדִי שֶׁלּוֹ וְטָלֶה שֶׁלִּי; וְאִם טָלֶה אָמַר לִי רַבִּי,

יד אברהם

The Gemara (88a) comments that the mishnah's statement 'he may not eat from his master's' implies that the half-slave may bring his own offering. This contradicts a baraisa, which states that he may not partake of any offering. This contradiction is resolved by assigning these two rulings to different time frames. The status of a half free slave was the subject of an ongoing dispute between Beis Shammai and Beis Hillel. Beis Shammai held that because of the slave's peculiar marital situation (he may marry neither a slave nor a free woman), his master should be forced to free him. In the earlier period (according to Beis Hillel's view that his master could retain him as a half-slave, despite the hardship this caused the part-slave), the master had the power to refuse the half-slave part the right to register on the Pesach of the half-free part (Rashi), just as a full slave is coerced to be registered upon the

offering his master prefers. At a later date Beis Hillel concurred with Beis Shammai. Our mishnah, which permits the slave to eat of his own offering, refers to the later period when Beis Hillel adopted the ruling that the owner is coerced to set the slave free. Thus, even in the interim, before the bill of manumission [גֵּט שִׁחְרוּר] is given to the half-slave, the owner has already lost his right to impose his will on the unfreed part, and cannot void the slave's registration on his own Pesach.

Rambam's interpretation (Comm.; see Hil. Korban Pesach 2:12) of this Gemara is the opposite of the above. Only in the earlier period was the slave permitted to eat of his own offering. After Beis Hillel's reversal he may eat of neither offering (see commentaries to Rambam for explanations of his view).

2.

הָאוֹמֵר לְעַבְדּוֹ, „צֵא וּשְׁחֹט עָלַי אֶת הַפֶּסַח," — One who says to his slave, "Go and slaughter the Pesach offering for me," [He did not specify whether he meant for the slave to slaughter a lamb (i.e., sheep) or a kid (i.e., goat), either of which is fit for the Pesach sacrifice (see Exodus 12:5).]

שָׁחַט גְּדִי יֹאכַל, שָׁחַט טָלֶה יֹאכַל. — [if] he slaughtered a kid he may eat [of it], if he slaughtered a lamb he may eat [of it].

This is so even where the slave's choice differs from the master's customary offering. Since the master did not specify what he desired, we assume that he depends completely on the slave's discretion (Rav; Gem.)

The mishnah chose to use a slave as a case

in point, rather than an agent who is a free man, to teach that even in the case of a slave, who would know his owner's usual preference, it is not assumed that the master expected the slave to slaughter only the type of animal that he was accustomed to use every year. Rather, since the master had expressed no preference, we presume that he left the choice completely to the slave's discretion (Tif. Yis., Kol HaRemez).

שָׁחַט גְּדִי וְטָלֶה יֹאכַל מִן הָרִאשׁוֹן. — If he slaughtered [both] a kid and a lamb he must eat of the first.

I.e., the first one slaughtered (see Rambam, Hil. Korban Pesach 2:11).

The second offering is invalid and must be burned (Rav; Rashi).

The Gemara (88b) demonstrates that, since one may not be registered upon

8
2

2. **O**ne who says to his slave, "Go out and slaughter the Pesach offering for me," [if] he slaughtered a kid he may eat [of it], if he slaughtered a lamb he may eat [of it]. If he slaughtered [both] a kid and a lamb he must eat of the first.

If he forgot what his master told him what should he do? — Let him slaughter a lamb and a kid and say: "If my master told me [to slaughter] a kid let the kid be his and the lamb mine; and if my master told me

YAD AVRAHAM

two sacrifices at the time of slaughter, both offerings are invalid and must be burned. The master's choice (after slaughter) cannot retroactively designate an offering as the intended one, for retroactive choice is not valid [אֵין בְּרִירָה] *(Rashi)*. The mishnah (which rules that the first animal slaughtered is the choice) speaks about a king who ordered his servants to slaughter for him. Because of the abundance of good food available to him *(Tos., s.v.* במלך) it is assumed that the king has no fixed preferences as far as the Pesach is concerned *(Rashi)*. Therefore the first offering slaughtered is valid. In a parallel situation, ordinary people (who can be assumed to have preferences as to the kind of meat they want for the Pesach) have both offerings judged invalid.

[The reasoning is (probably) that an ordinary person is assumed to reserve his decision as to his preference until the time of eating, by which time his choice cannot be effective retroactively. Because the choice of meat is so insignificant to a king, he is viewed as saying, in effect, that his only concern is the fulfillment of the *mitzvah*, thereby indicating a willingness to be registered upon the first offering, without regard to type (see *Aruch HaShulchan HaAssid* 186:1). *Rambam (Hil. Korban Pesach* 2:1) gives a different reason for this distinction. Regarding a king we must be concerned with the adverse reac-

tion a disqualification of his offering may bring forth (שְׁלוֹם מַלְכוּת). The king may be angry at the Sages for ruling his offering invalid *(Kessef Mishnah's* second interpretation there). [Obviously, this ruling is then applicable only to the later Hasmonean rulers and some of the Herodian dynasty who were notorious for their cruelty and persecution of the Sages.][1]

שָׁכַח מָה אָמַר לוֹ רַבּוֹ, בֵּיצַד יַעֲשֶׂה? — *If he forgot what his master told him, what should he do?*

The slave forgot whether his master told him to slaughter a lamb or kid *(Rav; Rashi)*.

שְׁחָט טָלֶה וּגְדִי וְיֹאמַר, ,,אִם גְּדִי אָמַר לִי רַבִּי, גְּדִי שֶׁלּוֹ וְטָלֶה שֶׁלִּי; — *Let him slaughter a lamb and a kid and say, "If my master told me [to slaughter] a kid, let the kid be his and the lamb mine;*

Although the course suggested by the mishnah seems simple enough, it cannot be followed under normal circumstances because of the general principle: 'Whatever a slave acquires is owned by his master'. If so, the slave cannot own a Pesach of his own. The advice of the mishnah can be carried out only if the slave enlists the cooperation of a shepherd with whom the master has extensive dealings. The shepherd gives the slave two animals, a kid and a

---

1. *Rambam's Commentary* (according to the more accurate Kafich edition) agrees with this view in *Mishneh Torah*. The commentary reads: 'All this is a result of the frivolousness of these rulers and the small degree of their subservience to the requirements of commandments.' However, the earlier commentators *(Kessef Mishneh; Tos. Yom Tov)* found difficulties with the earlier translation of *Rambam's Commentary* (found in the regular editions): 'Because of the ignorance of the *servants* and their small degree of involvement with commandments?'

פסחים טָלֶה שֶׁלוֹ וּגְדִי שֶׁלִי.״
ח/ג שָׁכַח רַבּוֹ מָה אָמַר לוֹ, שְׁנֵיהֶם יֵצְאוּ לְבֵית
הַשְׂרֵפָה. וּפְטוּרִין מִלַּעֲשׂוֹת פֶּסַח שֵׁנִי.

[ג] **הָאוֹמֵר** לְבָנָיו, ,,הֲרֵינִי שׁוֹחֵט אֶת
הַפֶּסַח עַל מִי שֶׁיַּעֲלֶה מִכֶּם
לִירוּשָׁלַיִם,״ כֵּיוָן שֶׁהִכְנִיס הָרִאשׁוֹן רֹאשׁוֹ
וְרֻבּוֹ, זָכָה בְּחֶלְקוֹ, וּמְזַכֶּה אֶת אֶחָיו עִמּוֹ.

יד אברהם

lamb, on the condition that one of them (he leaves the choice to the slave) will not become the property of the master [מַתָּנָה עַל מְנָת שֶׁאֵין לְרַבּוֹ רְשׁוּת בָּהּ]. Property given a slave with such a condition does not become the property of his master (see *Kiddushin* 23b). The slave now makes the choice of his personal offering conditional upon his master's choice saying, 'If the master told me a kid, let the kid be his and the lamb mine, i.e., since the kid is my master's, the lamb has been given me on the condition it not become my master's property (*Gem.* 88b).

וְאִם טָלֶה אָמַר לִי רַבִּי, טָלֶה שֶׁלוֹ וּגְדִי שֶׁלִי.״ — *and if my master told me* [*to slaughter*] *a lamb, let the lamb be his and the kid mine.''*

Retroactive selection [בְּרֵירָה] is of no concern here, because no new choice will be made by anyone after the slaughter. The master has *already* made his choice; it is the slave who will not know until later what he had been instructed (*Tif. Yis.*).

שָׁכַח רַבּוֹ מָה אָמַר לוֹ, — *If his master forgot what he had told him* [i.e., both the slave and the master forgot]

After the slave slaughtered the kid and the lamb with the aforementioned stipulation, he returned to his master, who in turn could not recall his own instructions to the slave (*Rav, Rashi*).

שְׁנֵיהֶם יוֹצְאִים לְבֵית הַשְׂרֵפָה. — *both* [i.e.,. the lamb and the kid] *go forth to the place of burning.*

After waiting for 'disfigurement' (עבור צוּרָה) they are burned on the sixteenth

of Nissan (*Meiri*).

It cannot now be clarified which offering is the master's and which the slave's. Thus they may not eat of either offering, for by doing so they would run the risk of transgressing the prohibition against eating of a Pesach without registration prior to slaughter (*Rav; Rashi*; see above 5:3, s.v. שלא למנויו).

[The expression בֵּית הַשְׂרֵפָה suggests that the mishnah refers to an area specifically designated for burning disqualified offerings. There was indeed such an area within the Temple Courtyard, known as בֵּית הַדֶּשֶׁן, the *Place of Ashes* (see *Zevachim* 104b). However it was used only for the burning of offerings that became disqualified while within the Temple Courtyard and were left there. But disqualified offerings that were removed from the Temple complex were burned wherever they were at the moment (see above 7:8).]

וּפְטוּרִין מִלַּעֲשׂוֹת פֶּסַח שֵׁנִי. — *And they* [the master and slave] *are exempt from participating* [lit. *doing*] *in* [the] *Second Pesach.*

Because 'it is revealed before Heaven' [כְּלַפֵּי שְׁמַיָא גַּלְיָא] that each one has truly offered a valid offering, although we do not know which offering belongs to whom (*Rav; Rashi*).

In the halachically accepted view, the *Gemara* (88b) qualifies this and says that only where the master still remembered his instructions during the slaughter and 'throwing' services, and forgot only subsequently are 'they' exempt. If, however, the master had

[to slaughter] a lamb, let the lamb be his and the kid mine."

If his master forgot what he had told him both go forth to the place of burning. And they are exempt from participating in [the] second Pesach.

3. **I**f one says to his sons, "I will slaughter the Pesach for the first among you to reach Jerusalem," [then] as soon as the first one has put his head the greater part of his body inside, he has acquired his portion, and he acquires his brothers' [portions] for them.

YAD AVRAHAM

already forgotten his instructions while 'throwing' was taking place or before, the offering is rendered inedible at the time of the service, and is disqualified; the Pesach offering may be offered only for those fit to eat of it (see above 5:3; Hil. Korban Pesach 3:1).

There is a general question pertaining to the Pesach of slaves. Tosafos (3b, s.v. ואנא) postulates that one who does not own land is exempt from bringing the Pesach (see Mishneh LaMelech, Hil. Korban Pesach 1:1). How then may a slave bring a Pesach, since he cannot own land for whatever a slave owns belongs to his master? It may be, however, that although he is not re-quired to bring the offering he may choose to do so voluntarily (Ohr Cha-dash, see Minchas Chinuch 5:7).

3.

הָאוֹמֵר לְבָנָיו, ,,הֲרֵינִי שׁוֹחֵט אֶת הַפֶּסַח עַל מִי שֶׁיַּעֲלֶה מִכֶּם רִאשׁוֹן לִירוּשָׁלָיִם,, — If one says to his sons, "I will slaughter the Pesach for the first among you to reach [lit. to go up to] Jerusalem,"

[The father leaves for Jerusalem to perform the sacrifice in the afternoon and allows the children to arrive after the service, in time to eat from the offer-ing at night. As an inducement to speed them on their way he offers to slaughter the Pesach for the one to reach Jerusa-lem first; he alone will be given a large portion in the Pesach, and the other brothers will be given portions by him from his portion.]

כֵּיוָן שֶׁהִכְנִיס הָרִאשׁוֹן רֹאשׁוֹ וְרֻבּוֹ, זָכָה בְּחֶלְקוֹ, וּמְזַכֶּה אֶת אֶחָיו עִמּוֹ. —[then] as soon as the first one has put his head and the greater part of his body inside [Jerusalem], he has acquired his portion,

and he acquires his brothers' [portions] for them.

The Gemara (89a) points out that the mishnah cannot be understood simply as stated, because it seems to be a case of retroactive choice [bereirah] as effected by the first son's arrival; such a case of bereirah is invalid [אֵין בְּרֵירָה]. Further-more the first son cannot register his brothers after slaughter has taken place. Rather, the Gemara explains, the mish-nah speaks of a case where the father had registered all his sons on this offer-ing, but in order to give his children an incentive not to delay, he spoke to them in the manner described in the mishnah (Rav).

Meiri (see also Rashi Gittin 25a, s.v. אמר) understands the Gemara to mean that only a father speaking to his children in such a manner, is assumed to register all of his children on the offering despite the implica-

לְעוֹלָם נִמְנִין עָלָיו עַד שֶׁיְּהֵא בּוֹ כְּזַיִת לְכָל אֶחָד וְאֶחָד.
נִמְנִין וּמוֹשְׁכִין אֶת יְדֵיהֶן מִמֶּנּוּ עַד שֶׁיִּשָׁחֵט.
רַבִּי שִׁמְעוֹן אוֹמֵר: עַד שֶׁיִּזְרֹק עָלָיו אֶת הַדָּם.

[ד] **הַמַּמְנֶה** עִמּוֹ אֲחֵרִים בְּחֶלְקוֹ, רַשָּׁאִין בְּנֵי חֲבוּרָה לִתֵּן לוֹ אֶת שֶׁלּוֹ, וְהוּא אוֹכֵל מִשֶּׁלּוֹ וְהֵן אוֹכְלִין מִשֶּׁלָּהֶן.

יד אברהם

tion of his words. Another person's similar statement — in the absence of an explicit verbal registration for all the brothers — would be taken as an indication of retroactive and post-slaughter registration, and would be invalid.

Ritva and *Maharam* (to *Gittin* 25a) hold that the father did register all the children, and *then* made the statement given in the mishnah. On the surface, he would seem to contradict his earlier intention and void his previous statement, but the mishnah makes the point that his later statement is meant only as an inducement to his tardy sons and not to void the original registration.

Others (*Tos. HaRashba, Chiddushei HaRamban* and *Rashba* to *Gittin* 25, and *Tos.* there, s.v. אי) interpret our *Gemara* to refer to children who are not yet *bar mitzvah*. The father has not actually registered his children prior to slaughter; because they are minors, registration is not necessary שֶׁה לְבַיִת אֲבֹות לַאו דְּאוֹרַיְיתָא). Consequently, such children are always considered to be 'registered.' This is clearly (according to all authorities) the interpretation of the *Talmud* in *Nedarim* (36a).[1]

לְעוֹלָם נִמְנִין עָלָיו עַד שֶׁיְּהֵא בּוֹ כְּזַיִת לְכָל אֶחָד וְאֶחָד. — *We may always be registered for it as long as there is* [at least] *an olive's volume for each one* [of the registrants].

[The requirement that the Pesach be sacrificed for registered eaters has been mentioned before (see above 5:3 and 6:4). The mishnah now defines the minimum portion that must be eaten by each registrant as equivalent to the volume of an olive. This minimum applies also to elderly and sick people. If they cannot consume that minimum, the Pesach may not be slaughtered for them.]

נִמְנִין וּמוֹשְׁכִין אֶת יְדֵיהֶן מִמֶּנּוּ עַד שֶׁיִּשָׁחֵט. — *They may be registered or withdraw* (*their hands*) *from it until it is slaughtered* [lit. *until he slaughters*].

[But after the slaughter, neither registration nor withdrawal is permitted. The *Gemara* (89a) demonstrates that these limitations are based on Scriptural exegesis.]

The mishnah's blanket authorization to register and withdraw up to the slaughter is taken to mean that even the entire group may withdraw, and a totally new group take its place on the same Pesach. This opposes the opinion of R' Yehudah (99a) that at least one of the original registrants must remain registered on the offering.

רַבִּי שִׁמְעוֹן אוֹמֵר: עַד שֶׁיִּזְרֹק עָלָיו אֶת הַדָּם. — *R' Shimon says: Until the blood is*

1. According to the first two interpretations, it is really the father, not the earliest arrival, who has given his sons possession. If so, the mishnah's expression that the son 'acquires for his brothers' is difficult. *Kol HaRemez* suggests that the father makes the other brothers' acquisition of their portions dependent upon the first brother. If he were to withdraw they too would lose their portions. *Shoshanim L'David* disagrees and offers, that in reality the first brother does nothing for the rest. He is only given the honor of being named as the one who gives possession to the others.

8
4

We may always be registered for it as long as there is [at least] an olive's volume for each one.

They may be registered or withdraw from it until it is slaughtered. R' Shimon says: Until the blood is thrown for it.

4. If one registers others upon his portion, [then] the members of the company are permitted to give him his [portion], and he eats his and they eat theirs.

thrown [lit. *until he throws the blood*] *for it.*

Although R' Shimon permits withdrawal even after the slaughter, as long as the blood has not been thrown, he concurs that registration must take place before the slaughter (*Rav; Gem.* 89a).

[R' Shimon and the first tanna base their views in the same verse, but disagree on exegetical grounds (*Gem.* 89a).]

The rule that registration must take place before slaughter is based on the verse (*Exodus* 12:4): ... [בְּמִכְסָת] *according to the number of people, every man according to his eating* [תָּכֹסּוּ] *shall you be numbered upon the kid.* The expression תָּכֹסּוּ, *shall you be numbered*, is redundant and is exegetically interpreted in its secondary, Aramaic, meaning of *slaughter.* Thus, ... *according to the number ... shall you slaughter,* i.e., registration must take place before slaughter (*Gem.* 89a).

4.

הַמְמַנֶּה עִמּוֹ אֲחֵרִים בְּחֶלְקוֹ, — *If one registers others (with him) upon his portion,*

E.g., there were ten registrants, entitling each man to a tenth of the offering. One of the men registered some additional people on his portion without consulting with the rest of the group (*Meiri*).

רַשָּׁאִין בְּנֵי חֲבוּרָה לִתֵּן לוֹ אֶת שֶׁלּוֹ, — [*then*] *the members of the company are permitted to give him his [portion],*

The other members of the group may bar the introduction of new members into their group. They may therefore give him his portion (e.g., his tenth) and tell him to eat separately with the people

he registered without their consent (*Rav, Rashi*).

The *Gemara* (89b) explains that the group's refusal of new members is not based upon the fear that they will eat more than the share (e.g., the tenth) alloted to the one member; even where there is assurance that this will not happen they may withhold consent. They can argue that they do not wish to spend their meal with strangers (see *Meiri* and *S'fas Emes*). The *Gemara* concludes that the group may decide to expel a member who is reputed to eat quickly. They may not however expel any member capriciously.

וְהוּא אוֹכֵל מִשֶּׁלּוֹ וְהֵן אוֹכְלִין מִשֶּׁלָּהֶן. — *and he eats his and they eat theirs.*

Our mishnah holds the view that one Pesach may be eaten in two groups (*Rav; Rashi; see above 7:13*).

יד אברהם

5.

The following mishnah discusses the status of the *zav* and *zavah* relative to the *mitzvah* of the Pesach offering. Some basic information about these forms of *tumah* [contamination] is necessary as background for the mishnah.

❧ Zav

The Torah teaches that a man having a seminal discharge [קֶרִי] becomes *tamei* [contaminated] *(Leviticus 15:16)*. Although he may immerse himself in a *mikveh* immediately after the occurrence, he is considered *tamei* until the next evening with regard to touching and eating sacrifices or *terumah*, and entering the Temple.

A different type of discharge, termed זִיבָה [*zivah*, lit. *seepage* or *flow*], (the person experiencing the omission is a זָב [*zav*]) is mentioned in the Torah *(ibid. 15:1-15)*. Though very similar to a seminal emission, it differs slightly in texture and color, and in the manner it is experienced *(Niddah 35b; Hil. Me'chussrei Kaparah 2:1-2; see Tos. Yom Tov to Zavim 2:1)*. However, the first emission of *zivah* is governed by the laws applicable to seminal discharges *(Zavim 1:1, Hil. Mechussrei Kaparah 2:6)*.

If one experiences two discharges of *zivah* in one day or on two consecutive days, his *tumah* is of a greater degree, and the cleansing process is more complex. He must count seven 'clean' days during which he experiences no discharges, immerses himself in a *mikveh* on the seventh day, and becomes cleansed on the following night. If, however, he experiences three discharges on one, two, or three consecutive days, the above process is sufficient to effect cleansing for *terumah*, but an additional step is necessary to effect cleansing with regard to sacrifices and the Temple. After counting the seven 'clean' days he must bring a sacrifice *(Leviticus 15:14)*. Until the sacrifice is brought, the *zav* carries the designation מְחוּסָּר כַּפָּרָה, *one who lacks atonement*, meaning that the process needed for total cleansing has not yet been completed.

❧ Zavah

The female *zavah* refers to an entirely different phenomenon involving a different set of laws.

The *zivah* discharge in the case of a woman is the same as menstruation, but the laws of *zivah* apply only during eleven days of the cycle that fall between her normal periods (see *Tur, Yoreh Deah* 183). If during those eleven days, she menstruates for only one day, she must make sure that the next day is free from discharge, immerse herself before sundown, and is totally purified with nightfall. She is called זָבָה קְטַנָּה, *minor zavah*, and this process is called שׁוֹמֶרֶת יוֹם כְּנֶגֶד יוֹם, *one who watches a day* [free from discharge] *against a day* [of discharge]. The same applies if she has discharges on two consecutive days; she 'watches' the third day, then immerses and is cleansed by evening. If however she discharged on three consecutive days she is a זָבָה גְדוֹלָה, *major zavah*, and must undergo a more stringent cleansing procedure. She must have seven consecutive 'clean days' free from discharge and immerse herself on the seventh day. She becomes cleansed with regard to *terumah* on the following evening, but she must offer a sacrifice on the eighth day *(ibid 15:25-30)*, until which she may not enter the Temple or touch or eat sacrifices.

5. **A** zav who experienced two discharges, they
may slaughter on his behalf on the seventh
[day]. If he experienced three, they may slaughter on
his behalf on his eighth [day].

YAD AVRAHAM

[The specific time limits of *niddah* and *zivah* are most complex and are beyond the scope of this work. The interested reader is directed to study *Niddah* 72-3; *Rambam, Hil. Issurei Biah* 6:1-3; and especially *Bais Yosef* to *Tur Yoreh Deah* 183.]

זָב שֶׁרָאָה שְׁתֵּי רְאִיּוֹת, — *A zav who experienced two discharges,*

After two discharges, a *zav* becomes contaminated for a seven-day period. He immerses himself on the seventh day and may eat sacrifices on the evening of the eighth, but he need not offer a sacrifice on the eighth day *(Rav)*. [Consequently, he will be fit to eat the Pesach the night following the seventh. See above, s.v. *Zav*.]

שׁוֹחֲטִין עָלָיו בַּשְּׁבִיעִי. — *they may slaughter on his behalf on the seventh [day].*

But only if he has performed immersion prior to slaughter. The offering is not sacrificed if he had not already immersed *(Rav from Gemara* 90b).

[The point of this passage is that a sacrifice may be offered even for one who is unfit at the time of the service. In our case, the *zav* is unfit to partake of sacrifices at the time of the Pesach service, but he may bring the Pesach and have the service performed because he *will* be fit to eat of it after nightfall.]

However, according to *Rambam*, the exception to this rule is someone whose *tumah* resulted from contact with a corpse [טָמֵא מֵת]. This is a special category and such a *tamei* may not offer the Pesach even though he will have completed the whole cleansing process (including immersion), and will be fit for eating sacrifices by nightfall. This is based on the passage in the Torah *(Numbers* 9:1-14) prohibiting sacrifice of the Pesach to people who were *contaminated because of a soul* [i.e., corpse contamination] and consequently could not *"perform the Pesach offering on 'that day'."* That they would have been fit at night is assumed because of two reasons: the phrase *'on that day'* implies that they would be fit after the day was over *(Gem.* 90b); also would they not be fit for

eating at night they would surely not have asked for permission to bring the Pesach *(Rambam, Comm.* to 7:6; *Rav* and *Meiri* here; *Hil. Korban Pesach* 6:2).

Many commentators *(Ravad,* loc. cit., *Tos.* 90b, s.v. שחל), based on the apparent meaning of the *Gemara* (90b), maintain that corpse contamination does not differ from other contamination: after completing the cleansing process and immersing, one may offer the Pesach. The passage in *Numbers* refers to individuals who had not yet immersed, and were prohibited from offering as long as they were still in that state. In this view, Moses did not bar them categorically from sacrificing; they had the option (and the obligation) to immerse themselves and be fit for the offering *(Tos.* 90b, s.v. שחל).

This discussion refers only to the Pesach offering. For other offerings, since eating is not an integral feature of the sacrifice (see above 7:4), the status of the supplicant is of no import; he may send his offering to the Temple to be offered even if his cleansing will not take place until a later date (see *Gem.* 62a). However, in this case, too, *Rambam (Hil. Bias Mikdash* 2:12) differentiates between corpse contamination and others. He rules that one made *tamei* by a corpse may not send his offerings to be sacrificed until he has cleansed himself.

רָאָה שָׁלֹשׁ, שׁוֹחֲטִין עָלָיו בַּשְּׁמִינִי שֶׁלּוֹ. — *If he experienced three* [discharges], *they may slaughter on his behalf on his eighth [day].*

If his eighth day, i.e., the day he brings his cleansing offering, is on the Pesach eve, they may offer the Pesach for him even before he brought his atonement offerings — provided the cleansing offering had already been handed over to the *Beis Din* of *Kohanim (Rav)*. If that was done, we may assume that *Beis Din* will yet offer his purification sacrifice that very day *(Gem.* 70b).

שׁוֹמֶרֶת יוֹם כְּנֶגֶד יוֹם, שׁוֹחֲטִין עָלֶיהָ בַּשֵּׁנִי שֶׁלָּה. רָאֲתָה שְׁנֵי יָמִים, שׁוֹחֲטִין עָלֶיהָ בַּשְּׁלִישִׁי.

וְהַזָּבָה, שׁוֹחֲטִין עָלֶיהָ בַּשְּׁמִינִי.

‏[ו] הָאוֹנֵן, וְהַמְפַקֵּחַ אֶת הַגַּל, וְכֵן מִי שֶׁהִבְטִיחוּהוּ לְהוֹצִיאוֹ מִבֵּית

יד אברהם

[But if he had not given his offering to the Beis Din we may not slaughter the Pesach on his behalf, lest he be negligent and not bring his cleansing sacrifices (Gem. 90b).]

The general rule is that no sacrifice is offered after the afternoon daily sacrifice except for the Pesach — thus effectively ruling out the performance of the cleansing offering after the Pesach service. An exception is made in the case of this cleansing offering, however, since the affected person could not bring his Pesach unless he were eligible to eat it at the Seder. Therefore, the mitzvah of Pesach, which carries כָּרֵת, spiritual excision, as punishment for its non-observance, causes the cleansing offering to override the prohibition against offering after the afternoon daily service (Rashi from Gem. 59a; cf. Tzlach).

שׁוֹמֶרֶת יוֹם כְּנֶגֶד יוֹם, שׁוֹחֲטִין עָלֶיהָ בַּשֵּׁנִי שֶׁלָּה. — A woman who observes a day against a day, they may slaughter on her behalf on her second [day].

As explained in the prefatory comments, if a woman menstruated for one day during the period when she is regarded as a zavah, she must 'observe' only one 'clean' day following the day of discharge, immerse herself on that day, and be fit to eat at night. If this second day fell on Pesach eve, she may

register on a Pesach offering, even though she is unfit at the time of the service, because she will be fit at night when the offering will be eaten (Rav). [Here, too, she must immerse herself in a mikveh prior to the slaughter of the Pesach offering.]

רָאֲתָה שְׁנֵי יָמִים, שׁוֹחֲטִין עָלֶיהָ בַּשְּׁלִישִׁי. — If she experienced discharges [lit. if she saw] for two days, they may slaughter on her behalf on the third [day.]

[Here the one 'clean' day necessary for cleansing is perforce the third day.]

וְהַזָּבָה, — And the zavah

[I.e., a זָבָה גְדוֹלָה, major zavah. This is a woman who menstruated for three consecutive days (during the eleven-day period reserved for zivah), and must observe seven consecutive 'clean' days, immerse herself on the seventh day, and offer cleansing sacrifices on the eighth.]

שׁוֹחֲטִין עָלֶיהָ בַּשְּׁמִינִי. — they may slaughter on her behalf on the eighth [day].

Even if she had not yet offered her cleansing sacrifices by the time of the Pesach slaughter, it is valid, so long as she had transferred her cleansing sacrifices to the Beis Din (Tos. Yom Tov).

6.

The mishnah will give a list of people who may be prevented from eating the Pesach for one reason or another. The mishnah rules that they should have the offering slaughtered on their behalf, but they should have, as partners, people whose participation in eating the Pesach is not in doubt.

⏤§ Onain

The Torah prescribes a period of mourning upon the death of the seven closest relatives (father, mother, brother, sister, son, daughter, and spouse), during which

A woman who observes a day against a day, they may slaughter on her behalf on her second [day]. If she experienced discharges for two days, they may slaughter on her behalf on the third [day].

And the zavah, they may slaughter on her behalf on the eighth [day].

6. **A**n *onain*, and one who clears away a pile of rubble, likewise one whom they have

YAD AVRAHAM

the mourner called an *onain*, [אוֹנֵן], is not permitted to partake of offerings (see *Leviticus* 10:19; *Deuteronomy* 26:14; *Zevachim* 101a).

This period extends only from the moment of death until nightfall of that day after which the ordinary laws of mourning (אֲבֵלוּת) go into effect. According to the opinion of R' Shimon, which is adopted by our mishnah (see *Zevachim* 100b), the *onain* laws apply after nightfall following the day of death only under Rabbinic law (אֲנִינוּת לַיְלָה מִדְּרַבָּנָן).[1]

הָאוֹנֵן, — *An* [lit. *the*] *onain,*

Since the Rabbinic prohibition prohibiting an *Onain* from sacrificial meat after nightfall, if enforced, would prevent an *onain* from fulfilling the *mitzvah* of eating the Pesach offering, it was waived by the Sages. As a general rule, the Sages did not insist on compliance with their law when it involves כָּרֵת, *spiritual excision*, the punishment for non-performance of the Pesach offering (*Gem.* 91a).

The above rule applies only if the death took place after the noon hour, meaning that the obligation to bring the Pesach went into effect before the person became an *onain*. If the *onain* period began before noon, the Rabbinic prohibition prevails and the *Onain* is deferred to the Second Pesach (*Tos.* 90b, s.v. האונן, from *Gem. Rambam*, 98a; *Hil. Korban Pesach* 6:9). [Naturally, in such a case no punishment is incurred; since the non-observance of the *mitzvah* is at the directive of the Sages, it is considered an involuntary act (אוֹנֶס).]

וְהַמְפַקֵּחַ אֶת הַגַּל, — *and one who clears away a pile of rubble,*

A building collapsed, trapping a person inside and the rubble is being searched. Although the searcher may find the victim dead and be contaminated by the body, and thus be forbidden to participate in the Pesach offering, the offering is slaughtered on his behalf. Since the victim may still be alive, we do not assume him to be dead in the absence of positive knowledge, because everyone is entitled to the presumption that he is uncontaminated [בְּחֶזְקַת טָהֳרָה] until his status is known to have changed *(Rav; Rashi).*

Rambam (Comm.; Hil. Korban Pesach 6:10) interprets this in a slightly different manner. There was no question that death had taken place; the only unknown factor is the location of the corpse. Thus, if no corpse is found on the site of the search, the searcher has discharged his obligation to bring the offering in an uncontaminated state, for it can be assumed that indeed there

---

1. Our use of the terms *onain* and 'mourner' are in reference to the prohibition against consuming (and sacrificing) offerings. The time limits applicable to various degrees of the אֲבֵלוּת, *mourning,* vary greatly according to the periods of seven days, thirty days, and a year. The term *onain,* is used for the full period until the burial of the deceased. That term is subject to other time limitations and refers (primarily) to the cessation of the *onain's* obligation to observe certain *mitzvos.*

הָאֲסוּרִים, וְהַחוֹלֶה וְהַזָּקֵן שֶׁהֵן יְכוֹלִין לֶאֱכוֹל
כַּזַּיִת, שׁוֹחֲטִין עֲלֵיהֶן.
עַל כֻּלָּן אֵין שׁוֹחֲטִין עֲלֵיהֶן בִּפְנֵי עַצְמָן, שֶׁמָּא
יָבִיאוּ אֶת הַפֶּסַח לִידֵי פְסוּל. לְפִיכָךְ, אִם אֵרַע
בָּהֶן פְּסוּל,פְּטוּרִין מִלַּעֲשׂוֹת פֶּסַח שֵׁנִי, חוּץ מִן

יד אברהם

is no body where he was searching.

וְכֵן מִי שֶׁהִבְטִיחוּהוּ לְהוֹצִיאוֹ מִבֵּית הָאֲסוּרִים,
— (and) likewise one whom they [his jailers] have promised to release him from prison,

In spite of this promise, the prisoner may not have a Pesach offered solely on his behalf. The Gemara 91a makes this rule conditional upon two facts: (a) The prison is under Gentile auspices and we cannot be sure that the promise will be kept; (b) it is outside the walls of Jerusalem; otherwise the prisoner may be able to partake of the Pesach even if he is not released. If, however, the jailors are Jewish, or the prison is in Jerusalem, the Pesach may be slaughtered on his behalf, even if no others are registered for it (Rav).

וְהַחוֹלֶה וְהַזָּקֵן שֶׁהֵן יְכוֹלִין לֶאֱכוֹל כַּזַּיִת, — and a sick or an aged person able to eat [flesh] the volume of an olive,

[As stated previously, a volume of meat equivalent to that of an olive is the minimum which must be eaten. Nevertheless their illness or frailty may make it impossible for them to eat sufficient meat.]

שׁוֹחֲטִין עֲלֵיהֶן. — they slaughter on their behalf.

[But only if other people are also registered on the same offering. Thus, even if the individuals listed here could not eat of the offering, it would not be disqualified, for a Pesach is valid if it was slaughtered for those fit to eat and for those not able (see above 5:3).]

עַל כֻּלָּן אֵין שׁוֹחֲטִין עֲלֵיהֶן בִּפְנֵי עַצְמָן, — For any of these they may not slaughter for them alone,

[If the company consists solely of people such as those enumerated by the mishnah.]

שֶׁמָּא יָבִיאוּ אֶת הַפֶּסַח לִידֵי פְסוּל. — lest they cause the Pesach offering to become invalid.

[It may be that those partners in the Pesach, all of whom have a real problem, will be unable to eat its meat as a consequence, though the service will have been valid and the participants will have fulfilled the mitzvah (and be absolved from participating in the Second Pesach as stated below), the flesh will remain unconsumed and become 'leftover' (נוֹתָר) and disqualified — a dishonor to the sacrifice.]

The grief-stricken mourners may come in contact with the corpse and become contaminated,[1] the rescuer

1. Thus, after the deceased has been buried and this fear no longer exists, they may slaughter a Pesach for the mourners themselves. This conclusion is indicated by Rashi (90b s.v. האונן), who defines onain as one whose 'dead is before him,' meaning while he is yet unburied. Although the law prohibiting a mourner from eating offerings clearly applies even after burial, Rashi held that in the context of the mishnah only a pre-burial mourner is meant, because the Rabbinical laws of mourner would not prevent him from eating of the Pesach at night, and after burial there is no longer a fear that he will become contaminated (Taharas HaKodesh to Zevachim 100b; cf. Tos. Yom Tov). However, Lechem Shamayim (and Tif. Yis.) understand that the apprehension is that he may have become contaminated during the burial and forgotten this as a result of his grief, thus causing the Pesach to be disqualified. Kol HaRemez suggests that in any case, they should not slaughter for a group made up exclusively of mourners so as not to differentiate between one case and the other (לֹא פְּלוּג).

8
6

promised to release him from prison, and a sick or an aged person able to eat the volume of an olive, they slaughter on their behalf.

For any of these they may not slaughter for them alone, lest they cause the Pesach offering to become invalid. Therefore, if any disqualification befall them they are exempt from participating in the Second Pesach, except for the one who was clearing a pile of

YAD AVRAHAM

may find the victim dead and become contaminated, the prisoner may remain incarcerated, the sick or elderly may find it difficult to consume an adequate portion of meat.

Rambam (Comm.) attributes our mishnah's apprehension regarding a mourner to the fear that because of his grief he may not be able to eat.

[*Rambam* has a different version of this mishnah (*Comm.*, ed. Kafich). *Meleches Shlomo* gives the same version in the name of *R' Yosef Ashkenazi.* Instead of our version, which speaks of a sick or aged person who *can* eat a sufficient quantity, their version reads: הָאוֹנֵן ... וְהַחוֹלֶה וְהַזָּקֵן **שֶׁאֵין** יְכוֹלִין לֶאֱכֹל כַּזַּיִת **אֵין** שׁוֹחֲטִין עֲלֵיהֶן ..., *the mourner ... and sick or elderly persons who* **cannot** *eat the volume of an olive — they may* **not** *slaughter on their behalf* ... Then, the next clause, beginning עַל בְּלָן *for any of these* ... rephrases the earlier law and adds the reason for the prohibition: for none of these may we slaughter because their possible inability to eat will cause the Pesach's meat to be leftover and become invalid. A careful reading of *Rambam's* commentary indicates this interpretation (see *Meleches Shlomo*). According to this version, the mishnah does not *explicitly* tell us that any of these people *may* participate in another group (as *Rashi* and *Rav* interpret the mishnah in the standard reading) — however, this law is true and is inferred from the phrase ... *they may not slaughter* **for them alone,** implying that they may join with others. This explains why *Rambam's* code omits mention of the permission for these people to slaughter in conjunction with others (*Hil. Korban Pesach* 5:9, 6:10), an omission that puzzles some of his commentators (see *Lechem Mishneh*). It is *Rambam's* practice to paraphrase cases

found in the mishnah, but not necessarily to mention cases *not* given by the mishnah.]

לְפִיכָךְ — *Therefore,*

Since they were considered fit for eating during the slaughter (*Rav; Rashi*) [otherwise the mishnah could not have permitted slaughter on their behalf].

According to *Rambam's* version (outlined s.v. שמא), the preposition, *therefore,* refers to the mishnah's explanation 'lest they cause the Pesach offering to become invalid.' If the only problem cited by the mishnah is the fear that Pesach meat may not be eaten in time, clearly the participants must have fulfilled their obligation (see his *Comm.*).

אִם אֵרַע בָּהֶן פְּסוּל, — *if any disqualification befall them* [these persons]

If any of the above fears are realized (*Tif. Yis.*), or any of the people were contaminated by a corpse (*Rambam*).

פְּטוּרִין מִלַּעֲשׂוֹת פֶּסַח שֵׁנִי, — *they are exempt from participating in the Second Pesach,*

[Though they were unfit to eat the offering, they must not offer another sacrifice on the fourteenth of Iyar, when those who did not offer on Pesach eve must sacrifice.] Since they were fit to eat it during the slaughter and the blood throwing service, the sacrificial service was valid and the people have discharged their obligation (*Rav; Rashi*). [As we have already learned previously (7:4) only *fitness* to eat is a prerequisite for the fulfillment of one's obligation, not the actual eating.]

הַמְפַקֵחַ בַּגַּל, שֶׁהוּא טָמֵא מִתְּחִלָּתוֹ.

‏[ז] **אֵין** שׁוֹחֲטִין אֶת הַפֶּסַח עַל הַיָּחִיד —
דִּבְרֵי רַבִּי יְהוּדָה. וְרַבִּי יוֹסֵי מַתִּיר.
אֲפִלּוּ חֲבוּרָה שֶׁל מֵאָה שֶׁאֵין יְכוֹלִין לֶאֱכוֹל
כְּזַיִת, אֵין שׁוֹחֲטִין עֲלֵיהֶן.
וְאֵין עוֹשִׂין חֲבוּרַת נָשִׁים וַעֲבָדִים וּקְטַנִּים.

יד אברהם

חוּץ מִן הַמְפַקֵחַ בַּגַּל, — *except for the one who was clearing a pile of rubble,*
[One who had been clearing a ruin in search of a survivor and, after the offering had already been slaughtered and the blood 'thrown', found the victim dead under the rubble, must offer again at the time of the Second Pesach. Although he had been *assumed* to be fit for eating at the time of the service, he had not discharged his obligation because in actual fact, he had become contaminated unwittingly.]

שֶׁהוּא טָמֵא מִתְּחִלָּתוֹ. — *for he was [found to be] contaminated retroactively.*
Now that the corpse was in fact dis-

covered, we assume him to have become contaminated from when he started to clear the ruin, before the service took place. A corpse causes contamination not only to one who touches it, but even to one who passes over it (מַאֲהִיל). The *Gemara* (91a) qualifies this by stating that the mishnah refers only to a circular (*Rambam, Comm.* says a triangular[1]) pile of rubble, about which it can be assumed that whoever searches it must have covered all parts of it with his body from the beginning of his search. But where the pile is long and rectangular, we cannot assume that he became contaminated prior to the service, and he is exempt from observing the Second Pesach (*Rav; Rashi*).

7.

אֵין שׁוֹחֲטִין אֶת הַפֶּסַח עַל הַיָּחִיד — דִּבְרֵי רַבִּי יְהוּדָה. — *They may not slaughter the Pesach offering for an individual — [these are] the words of R' Yehudah.*
R' Yehudah bases his law on the verse לֹא תוּכַל לִזְבֹּחַ אֶת הַפֶּסַח בְּאַחַד שְׁעָרֶיךָ *You may not slaughter the Pesach offering in one of your cities* [except for Jerusalem] (*Deuteronomy* 16:5). R' Yehudah reads the verse as if the pause came after בְּאַחַד, which can be rendered *for one*; thus the verse states, *you may not slaughter the Pesach for one*, i.e., *on behalf of a single person* (*Rav, Gem.* 91a).
[The reason R' Yehudah takes the

verse out of context is because the word בְּאַחַד, *in one*, is superfluous. If the sole purpose of the verse was to forbid the Pesach's slaughter outside Jerusalem it could have said, *You may not slaughter in your cities.*]

וְרַבִּי יוֹסֵי מַתִּיר. — *[But] R' Yose permits [this].*
R' Yose proves his point from the singular form used in the verse (*Exodus* 12:4): ... *every man according to* אָכְלוֹ, *his eating* ...
The halachah follows R' Yose (*Rambam Comm.*). 'But we make an effort (מִשְׁתַּדְּלִין) not to slaughter a Pesach for an individual for it is said (*Exodus* 12:47) ... *they* (plural),

1. Probably *Rambam* means that a circular pile would tend to peak in the middle (forming a conical or triangular shaped pile) so that anyone clearing it would, starting from the top, have 'hovered' over the corpse (as explained in *Tos. HaRashba*).

8
7

rubble, for he was [found to be] contaminated retroactively.

7. **T**hey may not slaughter the Pesach offering for an individual — [these are] the words of R' Yehudah. [But] R' Yose permits [this].

Even [if] a group [consists of] a hundred [people], if they are unable to eat the volume of an olive, we may not slaughter on their behalf.

We may not form a group [solely] of women, slaves and minors.

YAD AVRAHAM

shall observe it' (Hil. Korban Pesach 2:2; see Kessef Mishneh).

אֲפִלּוּ חֲבוּרָה שֶׁל מֵאָה שֶׁאֵין יְכוֹלִין לֶאֱכוֹל כְּזַיִת, אֵין שׁוֹחֲטִין עֲלֵיהֶן. — *Even [if] a group [consists of] a hundred [people], if they are unable to eat the volume of an olive, we may not slaughter on their behalf.*

This passage is a continuation of R' Yose's statement (*Rav* from *Baraisa* 91a). The amount of people registered on a Pesach is of no account; the only thing which matters is whether those registered are able to eat a sufficient quantity *(Rav; Rashi)*. However, even R' Yehudah agrees that even a hundred people who are unable to eat it may not have a Pesach offered for them *(Tos.* 91a, s.v. עשרה).

According to *Rashi* (as understood by *Sfas Emes)*, if there is even one person among the group of a hundred who is able to eat the equivalent of an olive, the Pesach may be offered for them.

Rav, however, follows *Rambam*, *(Hil. Korban Pesach 2:2)*, who rules that one may not slaughter the Pesach for a group among whom there is even *one* individual who is not fit to eat. The mishnah's ruling (5:3) that such a Pesach is valid is only after the fact, but it does not mean to say that it is proper to sacrifice such an offering initially [לְכַתְּחִילָה]. The impropriety of such an offering is not based on an apprehension that part of the offering may not be eaten and become נוֹתָר, *leftover,* for surely the remaining ninety-nine

people can eat the extra meat. Rather it is due to the prohibition against having an improper intention during the service of offerings (see *Hil. Pesulei HaMukdashin* 18:1-2 and *Even HaAzel* there); this prohibition includes an intention to slaughter for the sake of one unfit to eat. Though the *Kohen's* simultaneous intent to slaughter for the ninety-nine fit people prevents the offering from being disqualified, it is nevertheless prohibited to include an unfit person in his intentions for the full group *(Chiddushim* to *Hil. Korban Pesach* 2:2 appended to Responsa *Chessed L'Avraham Mahadura Tinyana). Rav* follows *Rambam's* rendition. *Sfas Emes (Chuddishim* to *Hil. Korban Pesach)* believes that *Rashi's* view can be reconciled with *Rambam.*

וְאֵין עוֹשִׂין חֲבוּרַת נָשִׁים וַעֲבָדִים וּקְטַנִּים. — *We may not form [lit. make] a group [solely] of women, slaves and minors.*

The mishnah does *not* forbid a group comprised exclusively of women, or of slaves; it forbids only a combination of women and slaves or a combination of children and slaves. The basis of this prohibition is the fact that heathen slaves were generally of low moral quality and suspect of licentious behavior. Groups composed exclusively of women and slaves are frowned upon because of the possibility of licentiousness and groups of minors and slaves to prevent degenerate influence on the children.

אונן [ח] טוֹבֵל וְאוֹכֵל אֶת פִּסְחוֹ לָעֶרֶב,
אֲבָל לֹא בְּקֳדָשִׁים.
הַשּׁוֹמֵעַ עַל מֵתוֹ, וְהַמְלַקֵּט לוֹ עֲצָמוֹת, טוֹבֵל
וְאוֹכֵל בְּקֳדָשִׁים.

יד אברהם

However, a group consisting exclusively of minors may not be formed for they lack 'sufficient intelligence' (Hil. Korban Pesach 2:4 cited by Rav).[1]

8.

אוֹנֵן טוֹבֵל וְאוֹכֵל אֶת פִּסְחוֹ לָעֶרֶב, — An onain immerses [himself in a mikveh] and eats his Pesach offering in the evening,

The Scriptural law forbidding mourners to eat offerings applies only to the day of death. The following night, he is proscribed to eat of sacrifices by Rabbinic law. Throughout these periods the mourner is called an onain. Here the Sages lifted the Rabbinic prohibition [even if the deceased has not yet been buried (Rashi)] in order to avoid deferral of the mitzvah of Pesach, which carries the punishment of כָּרֵת, spiritual excision, for non-observance (Rav from Gem. 92a).

However the onain must immerse himself in a mikveh before partaking of offerings for there is a (Rabbinic) rule (see Chagigah 3:3) requiring immersion for anyone who has been prohibited to partake of offerings (Rav; Rashi). Alternatively, the Sages were concerned he had not been careful to avoid tumah [contamination] during his period of mourning, and may have incurred a contamination applicable only to offerings (Hil. Avos HaTumah 12:15 cited in Tos. Yom Tov; see also Shoshanim L'David).

Rambam (Comm. here; Hil. Korban Pesach 6:9) offers another reason for the onain's immersion (see Lechem Mishneh there). The immersion serves to alert him to pause in his mourning, so that he not become distracted [שֶׁלֹא יַסִּיחַ דַּעְתּוֹ]; distraction in

itself — i.e., a period when one is not vigilant against contact with contaminating objects — can disqualify one from eating offerings.

Although mishnah 6 has already permitted the slaughter of a Pesach for an onain, Hon Ashir suggests that the primary point of our mishnah is that the onain needs immersion (although this too is stated elsewhere, in Chagigah 3:3). Rambam (in Comm. to mishnah 6; see also Shoshanim L'David) points out that mishnah 6 refers only to slaughtering and our mishnah to eating. This is better understood in light of Rambam's version of mishnah 6 (comm. there s.v. שמא), which rules that a Pesach may not be slaughtered for a mourner. Thus, referring to an instance where the Pesach had been slaughtered in violation of the prohibition, our mishnah rules that the mourner may partake of it at night. It may also be that the main point of our mishnah is that a mourner may not partake of other offerings even at night, as set forth below. Our mishnah is this only source of the law, as can be seen from Zevachim 99b.

אֲבָל לֹא בְּקֳדָשִׁים. — but [may] not [eat other] offerings.

A mourner is prohibited by Rabbinic law from partaking of offerings on the night after the death. The provision that the supplicant partake of his offering is only a mitzvah (i.e., it does not carry a punishment), and does not merit a waiver of a Rabbinic prohibition (Rambam; cf. Rav here).

The Talmud (Zevachim 99b), however, proves, contrary to our mishnah, that the prohibition against eating other offerings was also waived on Pesach night in order not

1. See the differing interpretations of 'sufficient intelligence' in Kessef Mishneh (there), Mishneh LaMelech (there 2:13, s.v. וראיתי), Sfas Emes (Chiddushim to Hil. Korban Pesach), Aruch HaAssid HaShulchan 184:15, Ohr Gadol in Mishnayos ed. Vilna.

8. **A**n *onain* immerses [himself] and eats his Pesach offering in the evening, but [may] not [eat other] offerings.

One who hears about the death of his relative, or one who has arranged for bones [of a close relative] to be gathered on his behalf, immerses [himself] and eats of offerings.

to differentiate between one offering (the Pesach) and others (see *Hil. Korban Pesach* 6:9).

הַשּׁוֹמֵעַ עַל מֵתוֹ, — *One who hears about the death of his relative* [lit. *one who hears about his deceased*],

He learned about the death of one of the seven relatives [see *comm.* to 8:6, s.v. הָאוֹנֵן) for whom one must observe the laws of mourning. Having heard the news after the day of death, he is an *onain* only by Rabbinic decree *(Rav; Rashi).*

וְהַמְלַקֵּט לוֹ עֲצָמוֹת, — *or one who has arranged for bones [of a close relative] to be gathered on his behalf,*

[I.e., he re-inters the remains of a relative for whom one must mourn. If the deceased has been interred temporarily in a grave not his, he may later be moved to his own grave. It is also permissible to exhume the deceased to be buried near his parents or in *Eretz Yisrael* (*Yoreh Deah* 363:1).] Also it was customary in some places to bury the dead temporarily in moist earth (without a coffin), so that the body would decompose speedily. Later they would re-inter the bones in a coffin *(Yer. Mo'ed Kattan* 1:4; *Yoreh Deah* 363:4; cf. *Tif. Yis.*). At the time of reburial, here described as 'gathering the bones', all the relatives are obliged to observe a period of mourning until nightfall (*Mo'ed Kattan* 8a; see *Yoreh Deah* 403:1; cf. there 375:6 with *Shach*). During the mourning period, the prohibition against mourners eating of

offerings also applies (by Rabbinic law). The night after the mourning period is not under this ban, however, since it does not follow the day of death. The same rule applies to mourners when the burial takes place on the day after death; the following night they are not under any ban against eating sacrifices (see *Zevachim* 101b, *Hil. Bias HaMikdash* 2:10).

[Perhaps the example of gathering the bones was chosen by the mishnah in order to teach that in this case, too, immersion is necessary. For one who buried a relative this need not be stated; it is included in the ruling requiring immersion for a mourner (above and in *Chagigah* 3:3). As explained by *Rashi*, one is termed a 'mourner' with regard to the consumption of offerings as long as the deceased is not buried (cf. *Tosefos Rid*).]

The *Gemara* (93a) comments that the person who physically gathered the bones incurs corpse contamination and requires a full seven-day cleansing period. The mishnah speaks about one who has arranged to have the bones collected, but did not come into contact with them.

טוֹבֵל וְאוֹכֵל בְּקָדָשִׁים. — *immerses [himself] and eats of offerings.*

Since there is only a Rabbinic ban even during the day, the night is under no ban whatsoever, and all offerings may be eaten *(Rav; Rashi).*

[Although the night is not under the Rabbinic ban against eating of offerings, he must nevertheless immerse himself, like anyone who has been a mourner during the day (see above s.v. אוֹנֵן).]

פסחים
ט/א

גֵּר שֶׁנִּתְגַּיֵּיר בְּעֶרֶב פֶּסַח — בֵּית שַׁמַּאי
אוֹמְרִים: טוֹבֵל וְאוֹכֵל אֶת פִּסְחוֹ לָעֶרֶב.
וּבֵית הִלֵּל אוֹמְרִים: הַפּוֹרֵשׁ מִן הָעָרְלָה
כְּפוֹרֵשׁ מִן הַקֶּבֶר.

[א] **מִי** שֶׁהָיָה טָמֵא אוֹ בְדֶרֶךְ רְחוֹקָה, וְלֹא
עָשָׂה אֶת הָרִאשׁוֹן, יַעֲשֶׂה אֶת הַשֵּׁנִי.

יד אברהם

גֵּר שֶׁנִּתְגַּיֵּיר בְּעֶרֶב פֶּסַח — *If a proselyte had been converted on the eve of Pesach*
[The process of conversion consists of three essential procedures: (a) circumcision, (b) immersion, (c) acceptance of the *mitzvos*. In the case of a conversion that became final on the fourteenth of Nissan, our mishnah deals with the question of whether the proselyte may offer the Pesach on that day.]

בֵּית שַׁמַּאי אוֹמְרִים: טוֹבֵל וְאוֹכֵל אֶת פִּסְחוֹ לָעֶרֶב. — *Beis Shammai say he immerses [himself] and eats of his Pesach offering in the evening.*
The additional immersion is necessary to permit eating of offerings (similar to the immersion required of a mourner).

וּבֵית הִלֵּל אוֹמְרִים: הַפּוֹרֵשׁ מִן הָעָרְלָה כְּפוֹרֵשׁ מִן הַקֶּבֶר. — *But Beis Hillel say: One who separates [himself] from an uncircumcised state is like one who separates himself from the grave.*
[The expression 'an uncircumcised state' refers to a Gentile. The case of a Jew who had been uncircumcised for health reasons is discussed below.]
Beis Hillel likens a proselyte to one who has been contaminated by a grave. Such contamination requires a seven-day cleansing process, which includes sprinkling with מֵי חַטָּאת, *cleansing water* — a mixture of ashes from the פָּרָה אֲדוּמָה, *Red Cow*, and spring water.
The *Gemara* (92a) explains that Beis

Shammai and Beis Hillel both agree that the proselyte does not truly have corpse contamination — because Scripture subjects only Jews to such contamination — and would be eligible to eat the Pesach offering under Torah law. This explains why Bais Shammai imposes no restriction on him. Beis Hillel, however, maintains that the Rabbis decreed the seven-day cleansing on the proselyte in order to prevent the possibility of future error. A proselyte would surely not be learned enough in Jewish law to know that he had not been subject to corpse contamination. Knowing that he had come into contact with bodies as a Gentile, and remembering that he had been permitted to eat Pesach meat right after his conversion, he would assume that even corpse contamination does not prevent someone from offering the Pesach. Consequently, in some future year when, as a Jew, he may truly become contaminated with a corpse, he may erroneously assume — based on the day of his conversion — that he may go ahead and offer his Pesach after nothing more than a simple immersion.
Obviously, the above fear would not apply to an uncircumcised Jew. Therefore, if a Jew had not been circumcised because his brothers had died as a result of circumcision, and then has himself circumcised as an adult on the day before Pesach, he may eat the Pesach that night *(Rav from Gem.* 92a).
Sfas Emes asks why do Beis Hillel fear only for the following Pesach. Why do they not entertain the same fear pertaining to

משניות / פסחים   [174]

9
1

If a proselyte had been converted on the eve of Pesach — Beis Shammai say he immerses [himself] and eats of his Pesach offering in the evening.

But Beis Hillel say: One who separates [himself] from an uncircumcised state is like one who separates himself from the grave.

1. One who was contaminated or was on a distant journey, and had not observed the First [Pesach], must observe the Second. If he erred or was

YAD AVRAHAM

other offerings all through the year? He therefore maintains that Beis Shammai agree with Beis Hillel that during the rest of the year a proselyte must undergo the seven-day purification process in order to eat of offerings. But where the Pesach is concerned, Beis Shammai hold that the Sages did not maintain this stricture in order not to defei this *mitzvah*. On the other hand, Beis Hillel say that although through the year, the proselyte may realize that corpse contamination requires a seven-day cleansing process, he may assume that for the Pesach this is not necessary. He will offer as proof the fact that on the Pesach eve of his conversion, a cleansing period was not required.

Alternatively, *Aruch HaShulchan HaAssid* (190:4) maintains, that even according to Beis Hillel, the stricture requiring a seven-day cleansing for a proselyte, applies only to the Pesach offering. Year-round no such period is required. Moreover *Yerushalmi* (here) rules that if the Pesach had been slaughtered for him he may partake of it.

The *Gemara* (93a) comments that according to Beis Hillel, this is one of three instances where the Sages insisted upon compliance with their strictures, even where this interferes with a *mitzvah* that carries spiritual excision (כָּרֵת) as a punishment. *Rambam (Hil. Korban Pesach* 6:7) explains that this insistence is due to the fact that the proselyte was not obligated in the *mitzvah* until his conversion became final, which in turn could have been deferred until after the eve of Pesach.

Chapter 9

Because the period of time allowed for the sacrifice of the Pesach offering was so brief — the afternoon of Erev Pesach — there would always be many who could not participate in the service. For their benefit, the Torah (*Numbers* 9:9-13) provided a second date when the Pesach could be offered — the fourteenth of Iyar — a full month after the First Pesach. The alternate date is called פֶּסַח שֵׁנִי [*Pesach Sheni*], *Second Pesach*. As examples of people who could not sacrifice on the First Pesach, Scripture (*Numbers* 9:10) uses, *one was contaminated by a dead* [human] *body* or who was *on a distant journey*. The first three mishnayos of this chapter detail the laws pertaining to *Pesach Sheni*. The rest of the chapter is devoted to miscellaneous general laws concerning the Pesach offering.

1.

מִי שֶׁהָיָה טָמֵא אוֹ בְדֶרֶךְ רְחוֹקָה וְלֹא עָשָׂה אֶת הָרִאשׁוֹן, — *One who was contaminated or was on a distant journey and had not observed* [lit. *made*] *the First* [Pesach],

[A contaminated person is not permitted to bring an offering to the Tem-

ple while someone on a distant journey is physically incapable of doing so.]

יַעֲשֶׂה אֶת הַשֵּׁנִי. — *must observe the Second.*

[I.e., on the fourteenth of Iyar (*Numbers* 9:11).]

פסחים שָׁגַג אוֹ נֶאֱנַס, וְלֹא עָשָׂה אֶת הָרִאשׁוֹן, יַעֲשֶׂה
ט/א אֶת הַשֵּׁנִי. אִם כֵּן, לָמָּה נֶאֱמַר ,,טָמֵא'' אוֹ
שֶׁהָיָה ,,בְדֶרֶךְ רְחֹקָה''? — שֶׁאֵלּוּ פְּטוּרִין
מֵהִכָּרֵת, וְאֵלּוּ חַיָּבִין בְּהִכָּרֵת.

יד אברהם

שָׁגַג — [Likewise] *if he erred*
[E.g. he forgot it was Erev Pesach or
that one is obligated to bring a Pesach
offering at that time.]

אוֹ נֶאֱנַס, — *or was prevented,*
[An unforeseen circumstance prevented him from bringing the sacrifice.]

וְלֹא עָשָׂה אֶת הָרִאשׁוֹן, יַעֲשֶׂה אֶת הַשֵּׁנִי. —
*and [therefore] did not observe the First
[Pesach], he must observe the Second.*
[The provision for a *Pesach Sheni*
was meant not only for someone who
was contaminated or on a distant
journey, but for anyone who neglected
to bring his Pesach offering, for
whatever reason. As the Gemara (93a)
states, even one who willfully neglected
(מֵזִיד) to offer on the First Pesach,
observes the Second Pesach. An allusion to this is found (92b) in the mishnah's expression וְלֹא עָשָׂה, *and did not
observe*, implying that the subject is
someone who *could have*, but did not,
bring the offering in time.
Accordingly, the mishnah refers to
three cases: one did not bring his offering because (a) he erred, (b) was
prevented, or (c) וְלֹא עָשָׂה, or [willfully]
did not observe ...

אִם כֵּן, — *If so,*
If so a *Sheni Pesach* must be brought
even by people who inadvertently, accidentally, or even intentionally failed
to offer the required First Pesach ...

לָמָּה נֶאֱמַר ,,טָמֵא'' אוֹ שֶׁהָיָה ,,בְדֶרֶךְ רְחֹקָה''?
— *why is it said: One who was con-
taminated or was on a distant journey*
(Numbers 9:10)?
[Why does Scripture specify only
these two cases, since the requirement
of *Pesach Sheni* applies in all cases
where the first one was omitted?]

The *Gem.* (93a) comments that the
Torah had to specify *one who was contaminated* in order to make clear that
such individuals cannot have the Pesach
offered for them, even by an agent.
Indeed it was the inquiry of *the people
who were contaminated by a corpse*
(Numbers 9:6) that prompted the
revelation by Moses that a *Pesach Sheni*
could be offered. The *Gemara* concludes
that the mishnah's question is directed
at one who was on a far journey — *why
was it necessary for the Torah to specify
that case, in view of the law that anyone
may bring a Pesach Sheni?*

שֶׁאֵלּוּ פְּטוּרִין מֵהִכָּרֵת, — *Because these
[two cases] are exempt from kares,*
In the specified cases of contaminated
individuals or people on a far journey
on Erev Pesach, they are exempt from
spiritual excision [*kares*] even if they
willfully (בְּמֵזִיד) neglect to offer a
Pesach Sheni. Since they could not offer
the originally required Pesach, they remain exempt (*Rambam, Comm.* and
Hil., Korban Pesach 5:2; *Rav*).
Someone who willfully neglected to offer
the *Pesach Sheni* as well as the First Pesach is
unquestionably liable to the punishment of
kares. However, what if he *did* offer the
Pesach Sheni, is he still liable to *kares* for his
transgression in having failed to bring the
First Pesach? In *Rashi's* view (see 93a, s.v.
תשלומין) he is liable according to Rabbi [R'
Yehudah HaNassi] and R' Nassan, and he is
exempt according to R' Chaninah. *Rambam*
(*Hil. Korban Pesach* 5:2) holds that all tannaim agree that spiritual excision is due only
to one who offers neither the First nor the
Second Pesach. *Ravad* does not disagree on
this point. If, however, the neglect to offer
the *Pesach Sheni* was not willfull, there is
disagreement amont the tannaim. *Rambam*
(ibid.) rules like Rabbi that he is punishable
by *kares* for the intentional sin of having ignored the requirement of the First Pesach.

prevented, and [therefore] did not observe the First [Pesach], he must observe the Second. If so, why is it said: *One who was contaminated* or was *on a distant journey [Numbers 9:10]?* — Because these are exempt from *kares,* but those are liable to *kares.*

YAD AVRAHAM

וְאֵלוּ חַיָּבִין בְּהִכָּרֵת. — *but those* [the latter] *are liable to kares.*

Individuals who omit the First Pesach (whether בְּמֵזִיד, *willfully,* or even בְּאוֹנֵס[1] due to circumstances beyond their control) for reasons other than those specified by Scripture, are liable to *kares* if they fail to offer a *Pesach Sheni*[2] (*ibid*).

The explanation of the above is as follows:

In the opinion of Rabbi (according to whom our mishnah rules), the Second Pesach can have either of two functions: (a) It is a second opportunity to bring a Pesach that was not brought in its proper time. In this aspect of the *Pesach Sheni,* it is not regarded as an independent *mitzvah,* but as a 'make-up date' for the First Pesach. (b) *Pesach Sheni* can also be regarded as an independent *mitzvah,* which is incumbent upon those who were not obligated to bring the First Pesach.[3]

In the case of people who did not offer the First Pesach due to miscalculation [שֹׁגֵג] or circumstances beyond their control [אוֹנֵס], the obligation to offer the First Pesach did indeed lay upon them, but they are not punishable by *kares* for their failure to do so, because they did not engage in an intentional violation. The possibility of 'making up' their neglect by offering a *Pesach Sheni* means

that the obligation of the First Pesach remains in effect; it is comparable to one who was prevented from bringing his offering during the first hour, but still has the opportunity to bring it during the rest of the day. If he intentionally fails to bring it later, he bears the liability of a willful offender, despite his valid excuse during the first hour. Similarly, failure to bring a *Pesach Sheni* renders one liable to *kares* for not having offered the Pesach that was required on Erev Pesach.

Regarding individuals who were 'contaminated' or 'on a far journey' during the First Pesach, the situation is different. Their status in regard to the First Pesach is viewed, not as one of unintentional or accidental non-observance they cannot be held responsible for, but as exemption from the very obligation of the offering. The Second Pesach is not an extension of the earlier obligation, but a new, independent obligation — and one which does not carry the punishment of spiritual excision. This dual conceptualization is derived from the singling out of these two conditions in the verse in *Numbers* (9:13): *And a man who is pure and was not on a journey and refrains from observing the Pesach offering — that soul shall be excised from its people.* The implication of the verse is that non-observance because of those conditions is not punishable.

1. In *Rav* and *Rambam's* interpretation the mishnah holds like Rabbi, cited above (*Gem.* 93a).

2. There is, however, an obvious difference between willfull neglect and other types of non-observance. In the former case he is liable even if his subsequent non-observance of the Second Pesach is unintentional; the liability is due to his neglect of the First Pesach. However, if the omission of the First Pesach was unintentional, *kares* can be imposed only if neglect of the Second Pesach was intentional.

3. The above is *Rambam's* interpretation and is followed by *Rav.* However *Rashi* [following the apparent meaning of the *Gem.* 92a) and most authorities (see *Ravad*) make no distinction between failure to bring the First Pesach because of the two reasons given by Scripture and any other valid reason. Consequently, when the last phrase of our mishnah says 'those are liable to *kares*', it refers to those who willfully violated the commandment of the *First Pesach,* while the phrase 'these are exempt ... ' covers all other situations (i.e., accident and miscalculation as well as contamination and being far away).

[ב] אֵיזוֹ הִיא ,,דֶּרֶךְ רְחֹקָה"? — מִן הַמּוֹדִיעִים וְלַחוּץ, וּכְמִדָּתָהּ לְכָל רוּחַ — דִּבְרֵי רַבִּי עֲקִיבָא. רַבִּי אֱלִיעֶזֶר אוֹמֵר: מֵאִסְקֻפַּת הָעֲזָרָה וְלַחוּץ. אָמַר רַבִּי יוֹסֵי: לְפִיכָךְ נָקוּד עַל ה' לוֹמַר, לֹא מִפְּנֵי שֶׁרְחוֹקָה וַדַּאי, אֶלָּא מֵאִסְקֻפַּת הָעֲזָרָה וְלַחוּץ.

[ג] מַה בֵּין פֶּסַח הָרִאשׁוֹן לַשֵּׁנִי? — הָרִאשׁוֹן אָסוּר בְּבַל יֵרָאֶה וּבַל יִמָּצֵא, וְהַשֵּׁנִי,

יד אברהם

2.

אֵיזוֹ הִיא ,,דֶּרֶךְ רְחֹקָה"? — *What is a distant journey* [Numbers 9:10]?

[What does the Torah mean when it uses the term *on a distant journey*, to describe an individual who is exempt from the First Pesach? How far is *distant*?]

מִן הַמּוֹדִיעִים וְלַחוּץ, וּכְמִדָּתָהּ לְכָל רוּחַ, דִּבְרֵי רַבִּי עֲקִיבָא. — *From Modi'in and beyond, or a like distance in any direction* — [these are] the words of R' Akiva.

Modi'in, the native town of the Hasmoneans, was about fifteen *mil*[1] (each *mil* is comprised of two thousand cubits) from Jerusalem. Fifteen *mil* is regarded as the distance one can travel at a normal pace from noontime to sunset on Erev Pesach. During that time of the year, the day and night are roughly twelve hours each. Thus, if one began walking from Modi'in at noon, when the Pesach service was about to

begin, he could not walk to Jerusalem in time to bring the Pesach offering before the day was over. Since he was too far away to make the offering possible for himself, he is regarded as being on a 'distant journey' (*Rashi* 93a).

Rambam (*Hil. Korban Pesach* 5:9, see *Comm.* here) and (probably) *Rav* maintain that the beginning point used to establish one as being on a *distant journey* is sunrise, not noontime. Thus if one is, at sunrise, too distant from Jerusalem to reach the Temple by the *beginning* of the Pesach service — noontime — he is judged to be on a *distant journey*.

רַבִּי אֱלִיעֶזֶר אוֹמֵר מֵאִסְקֻפַּת הָעֲזָרָה וְלַחוּץ — *R' Eliezer says: From the threshold of the Temple Courtyard and beyond*.

R' Eliezer maintains that even if he was in Jerusalem, but was prevented by uncontrollable circumstances, such as illness, from reaching the Temple Courtyard before the conclusion of the service, he is considered to have been on

1. The exact distance is the subject of controversy among the amoraim (93b-94a). *Rambam* (*Comm.*; *Hil. Korban Pesach* 5:15) adopts the figure fifteen *mil*. Most other authorities adopt sixteen *mil* as the correct figure. However *Kol HaRemez* and *Shoshanim L'David* comment that the controversy concerns only the average distance walked in six hours — 16 *mil* according to most authorities. Nevertheless, with regard to exemption from the Pesach offering, a 'distant journey' is only fifteen *mil*, since that is clearly the distance from Modi'in to Jerusalem. Although a person who left Modi'in at noon would reach Jerusalem just before nightfall, he would not have enough time to go up to the Temple and sacrifice the offering.

9
2

2. **W**hat is *a distant journey?* — From Modi'in and beyond, or a like distance in any direction — [these are] the words of R' Akiva.

R' Eliezer says: From the threshold of the Temple Courtyard and beyond.

Said R' Yose: Therefore there is a dot over the letter "Hei", as if to say, not because it is literally distant, but rather from the threshold of the Temple Courtyard and beyond.

9
3

3. **W**hat are the differences between the First Pesach and the Second? — The First [Pesach] comes under the prohibition of, *It shall not be seen and is shall not be found* [*Exodus* 12:19], whereas at

YAD AVRAHAM

a *distant journey.* R' Akiva, however, holds that anyone within a fifteen *mil* radius of Jerusalem cannot be considered at a 'distance.' For such a person to be delayed by illness falls under the category of אוֹנֶס, *accidental delay (Rav).*

אָמַר רַבִּי יוֹסֵי לְפִיכָךְ נָקוּד עַל ה' — *Said R' Yose: Therefore, there is a dot over the letter "Hei"*

[In the Torah scroll a dot is placed above certain letters indicating a hidden meaning. The last letter of the word רְחוֹקָה, *distant (Numbers 9:10),* has a dot placed above it. R' Yose expounds on the significance of that letter.]

לוֹמַר, לֹא מִפְּנֵי שֶׁרְחוֹקָה וַדַּאי, אֶלָּא מֵאִסְקֻפַּת הָעֲזָרָה וְלַחוּץ — *as if to say, not because it is literally distant, but rather from the threshold of the Temple Courtyard and beyond.*

R' Yose concurs with R' Eliezer, but adds that the Torah lends credence to

his view. Whenever a dot is placed over a letter it indicates that the word be interpreted as if the letter were deleted. Thus, instead of the feminine word רְחוֹקָה, which would be interpreted as the adjective, *distant,* modifying the feminine דֶּרֶךְ, *journey,* the word becomes the masculine רָחוֹק. As such it can be rendered, *a distant one,* referring to anyone who is removed from the Temple, no matter what the distance, thus, *Any man ... on a journey, is distant,* indicating that the main consideration is that the person is removed from the Temple *(Yerushalmi* here, cited by *Tos. Yom Tov).*

Rav offers another explanation. The dot over the *Hei* indicates that it is read as a separate word. The numerical value of *Hei* is five, implying that if one is רָחֹק ה', as little as *five cubits distant* from the threshold when the final Pesach slaughter is under way, he is judged to be on a *distant journey.*

3.

מַה בֵּין פֶּסַח הָרִאשׁוֹן לַשֵּׁנִי? — *What are the differences between the First Pesach and the Second?*

[What are the differences between the laws surrounding the two Pesach sacrifices?]

הָרִאשׁוֹן אָסוּר בְּבַל יֵרָאֶה וּבַל יִמָּצֵא, — *The First [Pesach] comes under the prohibition of, It [chametz] shall not be seen and it shall not be found [Exodus 12:9],*

This verse forbids a Jew to possess any *chametz* from nightfall of the first

[179]   **THE MISHNAH / PESACHIM**

פסחים מַצָּה וְחָמֵץ עִמּוֹ בַּבָּיִת; הָרִאשׁוֹן טָעוּן הַלֵּל
ט/ד בַּאֲכִילָתוֹ, וְהַשֵּׁנִי אֵינוֹ טָעוּן הַלֵּל בַּאֲכִילָתוֹ.
זֶה וָזֶה טְעוּנִין הַלֵּל בַּעֲשִׂיָּתָן, וְנֶאֱכָלִין צְלִי
עַל מַצָּה וּמְרוֹרִים, וְדוֹחִין אֶת הַשַּׁבָּת.

[ד] הַפֶּסַח שֶׁבָּא בְטֻמְאָה, לֹא יֹאכְלוּ מִמֶּנּוּ
זָבִין וְזָבוֹת נִדּוֹת וְיוֹלְדוֹת; וְאִם

יד אברהם

day of Passover, and the Torah specifies that the sacrifice may not be offered while one has *chametz* in his possession. This prohibition does not apply to *Pesach Sheni.*]

וְהַשֵּׁנִי, מַצָּה וְחָמֵץ עִמּוֹ בַּבָּיִת; — *whereas at the Second [Pesach], both matzah and chametz are with him in the house;*

The *Gemara* (95a) infers from the verse (*Numbers 9:12*): *According to all the statutes of the Pesach offering shall they observe it [the second Pesach],* that only with respect to those statutes involving *it,* i.e., the sacrifice itself, must the two Pesach offerings be similar. Both must be an unblemished yearling sheep or goat, the service must be the same for each, and each must be roasted, etc. But laws that are not directly related to the sacrifice, such as the prohibitions against having *chametz* on the Pesach festival, and not slaughtering the Pesach while in possession of *chametz* do not apply.

הָרִאשׁוֹן טָעוּן הַלֵּל בַּאֲכִילָתוֹ, — *the First [Pesach] requires the recitation of Hallel during [the Pesach's] eating,*

Referring to the song to be recited at the fall of Sennacherib, Isaiah exclaimed: *"You shall have a song as in הַלַּיְלָה הִתְקַדֶּשׁ חַג the night when a festival is hallowed"* (*Isaiah 30:29*). The Sages explain that *the night* alludes to the night of Pesach, indicating that the night hallowed for a festival requires the recital of song, i.e., *Hallel (Rav; Gem. 95b).*

וְהַשֵּׁנִי אֵינוֹ טָעוּן הַלֵּל בַּאֲכִילָתוֹ. — *but the Second does not require Hallel during its eating [i.e., of the Pesach].*

Since the night of the Second Pesach is not a festival, *Hallel* is not required (ibid).

S'fas Emes adds that the Haggadah is not recited on the Second Pesach even if one had not observed this *mitzvah* on the First Pesach, for the verse from which this *mitzvah* is derived, (*Rambam, Hil. Chametz Matzah 7:1*) *Remember this day on which you came out from Egypt* (*Exodus 13:3*) — refers explicitly to the First Pesach. [Besides, this *mitzvah* is in the category of *mitzvos* only incidental to the Pesach offering; as noted above (s.v. וְהַשֵּׁנִי חָמֵץ), such *mitzvos* are Scripturally excluded from the service of *Pesach Sheni.* Only for the recital of *Hallel* need a new source be cited, for it could be thought that this *mitzvah* is connected to th e eating of the Pesach, as are the eating of matzah and bitter herbs with it.]

Tosefta (8:3) cited partially in *Tosafos* (95a, s.v. מה) lists many more differences. The first Pesach: is offered in three groups (see 5:5); is offered even if the community is contaminated[1] (see above 7:4-6); carries the punishment of spiritual excision for nonobservance (see above 9:1); is accompanied by a *Chagigah* offering (see above 6:3) and is seven days in duration. All these are absent in the Second Pesach.

Tosafos (ibid.) adds to this the provision (*Gem.* 96a) that the kid used for the First must be inspected four days for blemishes, and not the Second. *Rambam (Hil. Korban Pesach 10:15)* rules that only the First Pesach may not be taken out of the group (see above 7:13), but the Second may.

זֶה וָזֶה — *Both [lit. this and that]*

1. This point is the subject of a dispute among tannaim [*Yoma* 51a] but the opinion given here is the one accepted by halachah (see *Rambam, Hil. Korban Pesach 10:15*).

the Second [Pesach], [both] matzah and chametz are with him in the house; the First requires the recitation of *Hallel* during [the Pesach's] eating, but the Second does not require *Hallel* during its eating.

Both require the recitation of *Hallel* when they are offered; [both] are eaten roasted, together with matzah and bitter herbs; and [both] override the Sabbath.

4. If the Pesach was offered in a state of contamination, *zavin*, *zavos*, menstruants, or women after childbirth may not eat of it; but if they

<hr>

YAD AVRAHAM

[The First and Second Pesach.]

טְעוּנִין הַלֵּל בַּעֲשִׂיָתָן, — *require the recitation of Hallel when they are offered* [lit. *done*];

The verse excluding the Second Pesach from the recital of *Hallel* (see above, s.v. הראשון טעון) refers to the night only (*as in the night ...*), but not to the time of slaughter. Concerning the *Hallel* said in the daytime during the service of the sacrifice, there is no Scriptural exclusion, so the obligation to recite it remains in effect (*Rav; Gem.* 95b).

[Here the recital of *Hallel* is connected to the sacrifice of the Pesach, and is required because of its similarity to the mitzvah of eating the Pesach with matzah and bitter herbs.]

הַפֶּסַח שֶׁבָּא בְטֻמְאָה, — *If the Pesach was offered in a state of contamination,*

In the event a majority of the nation was contaminated on 14 Nissan when the Pesach must be offered, the *mitzvah* of Pesach supersedes the prohibitions forbidding contaminated individuals to eat from, or perform the service for, an offering (see above 7:4).

— לֹא יֹאכְלוּ מִמֶּנּוּ זָבִין וְזָבוֹת נִדּוֹת וְיוֹלְדוֹת; *zavim, zavos, menstruants and women after childbirth may not eat of it;*

וְנֶאֱכָלִין צָלִי — *[both] are eaten roasted,*

For this is a *mitzvah* pertaining to the body of the offering (see above, s.v. והשני מצה; cf. *Tos.* 95a, s.v. בכלליה).

עַל מַצָּה וּמְרוֹרִים, — *together with matzah and bitter herbs;*

Here the Torah explicitly commands (*Numbers* 9:11): *together with matzos and bitter herbs shall they eat it.*

וְדוֹחִין אֶת הַשַּׁבָּת. — *and [both] override the Sabbath.*

Meleches Shlomah infers from *Yoma* 51a that *Pesach Sheni* does not override the prohibition against offering sacrifices in a state of contamination. Only the First Pesach may be offered if the majority of the community is contaminated.

4.

[For a description of the contaminations of *zav* (plural *zavim*) and *zavah* (plural *zavos*) see comm. above 7:5 (s.v. *Zav* and *Zavah*). The denomination *zav* in our mishnah refers also to a *zav* who had only one emission (who is governed by the laws applicable to בַּעַל קֶרִי, *one who had a seminal emission*) as well as one who has had a seminal emission (בַּעַל קֶרִי), and had not immersed himself in a *mikveh* before sundown. In the instance of *zavos*, our mishnah uses the term to include both זָבָה גְדוֹלָה, *a major*

[ה] **מַה** בֵּין פֶּסַח מִצְרַיִם לְפֶסַח דּוֹרוֹת? —
פֶּסַח מִצְרַיִם מִקְחוֹ מִבֶּעָשׂוֹר, וְטָעוּן

יד אברהם

zavah, who has had three discharges and שׁוֹמֶרֶת יוֹם כְּנֶגֶד יוֹם, lit. *one who observes a day against a day*, i.e., a woman who has had only one or two discharges.]

Niddos [singular *niddah*] are women who have menstruated on any day other than those designated for *zivah* (see above 7:5, s.v. *Zavah*), i.e. most menstruations. They are *tamei* for seven days, and may immerse themselves on the night following the seventh day and be eligible to partake of offerings the following night (see footnotes to 7:5).

A *woman after childbirth* has the status of a *niddah*, with all the attendant laws, for a period of one week for the birth of a male, and two weeks for a female, after which she can purify herself through immersion in a *mikveh*. Ordinarily one who is eligible to eat *terumah* may do so in the evening after immersion (הַעֲרֵב שֶׁמֶשׁ). The same holds true for the meat of offerings, unless a cleansing sacrifice is required.

In the case of a mother after childbirth, however, there is an exception. Although her contamination was removed with immersion, she may not eat *terumah* or the meat of offerings for forty days after the birth of a male infant, and eighty days after that of a female. With the conclusion of these respective periods she may eat *terumah* after nightfall. On the day after those periods are over, she brings her cleansing offerings, and only then may she partake of sacrificial meat.

[In excluding these types of contaminated people, the mishnah points out that, although the Pesach may be offered if the majority of the people are contaminated, this dispensation applies only to such forms of contamination as

result from contact with a corpse or some other form of corpse contamination (see below, s.v. פְּטוּרִים מכרת). But the dispensation does not apply to טֻמְאָה יוֹצֵא עָלָיו מִגּוּפוֹ, *contamination resulting from a bodily emission of the affected person*. People so affected are not counted in forming the majority, nor may they partake of the offering even when it is offered in a state of contamination. The reason for excluding these people is based on the Scriptural passage that introduces the *mitzvah* of *Pesach Sheni* (Numbers 9:10). The verse specifies *a man ... who shall be contaminated because of a dead body*. From this we infer that only *a man* — i.e. an *individual* — can be relegated to bring *Pesach Sheni*, but not the entire community. Furthermore, we infer that the dispensation that the community should not delay its Pesach offering applies only if the contamination was corpse related. Other forms of contamination would require the affected person — or community — to wait for *Pesach Sheni* (*Rav; Rashi* from *Gem.* 67a).

וְאִם אָכְלוּ, — *but if they did eat,*
[If individuals possessing one of the aforementioned state of contamination transgressed, and did partake of the Pesach offering.]

פְּטוּרִים מִכָּרֵת. — *they are exempt from* [the penalty of] *kares,*
This penalty applies only to one who eats flesh of offerings that will be consumed by purified individuals, but not when the offering will be consumed by others who are also in a state of contamination. In the case of our mishnah, however, since the offering will be eaten by individuals who have contracted

9
5
did eat, they are exempt from [the penalty of] *kares.*
R' Eliezer exempts [them] even [from the *kares*
due] for entering the Temple.

5. **W**hat are the differences between the Pesach
[offered] in Egypt and the Pesach offering of
[succeeding] generations? — The purchase of the
Egyptian Pesach was on the tenth [of Nissan], it re-

YAD AVRAHAM

corpse contamination, even individuals
not accorded a dispensation to eat are
nevertheless exempted from the penalty
for doing so *(Rav; Gem.* 95a).

The mishnah omits a whole class of contaminated individuals — those who come in
contact with contaminating agents, such as
carcasses of animals that died without benefit
of *shechitah (נְבֵילוֹת)*, or of certain specific
smaller animals *(שְׁרָצִים)* that contaminate
one who touches them, etc. *Rambam (Hil.
Korban Pesach* 7:8) rules that they are accorded the same dispensation to partake of
the offering as are those defiled by a corpse
(Tos. Yom Tov). However, they may not
enter the Temple Courtyard and participate
in the service *(Hil. Bias HaMikdash* 4:12),
nor are they included in the census determining that a majority of those assembled are
contaminated. For this, only corpse contamination is of concern *(Hil. Korban Pesach
7:1,8; see Lechem Mishneh* there; cf. *Kol
HaRemez* and *Shoshanim L'David* who suggest a different interpretation of *Rambam's*
view).

R' — רַבִּי אֱלִיעֶזֶר פּוֹטֵר אַף עַל בִּיאַת מִקְדָּשׁ.
*Eliezer exempts [them] even [from the
kares due] for entering the Temple.*

[The penalty for entering the Temple
while in a state of defilation is *kares,
spiritual excision (Numbers* 19:13).
However, R' Eliezer maintains that this
penalty does not apply when the Pesach
is being offered by individuals in a state
of corpse contamination; then even
those contaminated individuals who are
not allotted a special dispensation are
n e v e r t h e l e s s n o t g i v e n t h i s
punishment.]

R' Eliezer derives his opinion from
the verse *(Numbers 5:2): Command the
children of Israel that they send out
from the camp every metzora, every
zav, and whoever is contaminated
because [a] dead [body].* This juxtaposition of *zav* and other contaminations,
with that of corpses, teaches (according
to R' Eliezer), that all these varieties of
contaminated people have the same
status with regard to entering the Temple; either all are excluded or, as in the
case of the Pesach, all are included *(Rav;
Gem.* 95b).

The halachah does not follow R' Eliezer
(Rav; Rambam).

5.

מַה בֵּין פֶּסַח מִצְרַיִם לְפֶסַח דוֹרוֹת? — פֶּסַח
מִצְרַיִם מִקְחוֹ מִבֶּעָשׂוֹר, *— What are the differences between the Pesach [offered] in
Egypt [lit. the Pesach of Egypt] and the
Pesach offering of [succeeding] generations? — The purchase of the Egyptian
Pesach was on the tenth [of Nissan],*
Scripture states *(Exodus 12:3): On
the tenth of this month, they shall take
(i.e. purchase) each man a kid.* From the
special stress given by the phrase, *this*

month, the Sages infer that only on *this*
Nissan — i.e., that of the actual Exodus,
— is acquisition prescribed for the tenth
of the month but not for Pesach offerings of succeeding generations. For
those offerings, one may hold any
number of animals in reserve until the
last minute, before choosing one for the
offering.

The law requiring that an animal intended for a Pesach be inspected for

[183]   THE MISHNAH / PESACHIM

הַזָּאָה בַּאֲגֻדַּת אֵזוֹב עַל הַמַּשְׁקוֹף וְעַל שְׁתֵּי הַמְּזוּזוֹת, וְנֶאֱכָל בְּחִפָּזוֹן, בְּלַיְלָה אֶחָד. וּפֶסַח דּוֹרוֹת נוֹהֵג כָּל שִׁבְעָה.

[ו] אָמַר רַבִּי יְהוֹשֻׁעַ, ״שָׁמַעְתִּי שֶׁתְּמוּרַת הַפֶּסַח קְרֵבָה, וּתְמוּרַת הַפֶּסַח אֵינָהּ קְרֵבָה, וְאֵין לִי לְפָרֵשׁ.״

יד אברהם

blemishes for a four-day period is based on the same phrase, *and they shall take on the tenth* ..., and that four-day requirement still applies to Pesach. Only concerning the requirement of purchase (or designation) on the tenth is the Pesach of generations excluded from the provisions of this verse (*Gem.* 96a; *Tos. Yom Tov*).

וְטָעוּן הַזָּאָה בַּאֲגֻדַּת אֵזוֹב עַל הַמַּשְׁקוֹף וְעַל שְׁתֵּי הַמְּזוּזוֹת, — *(and) it required sprinkling [of its blood] with a bundle of hyssop upon the lintel and upon the two doorposts,*

The Torah explains that the reason for this sprinkling was, to distinguish Jewish homes from Egyptian homes where the firstborn would be killed (*Exodus* 12:13).

Obviously, since this reason does not apply to the Pesach of generations, the logical conclusion is that the law of sprinkling, too, does not apply to it (*Tos. Yom Tov*). [Besides, since the Pesach is offered in the Temple, its blood has the greatest degree of sanctity (קָדְשֵׁי קָדָשִׁים), and may not be removed from the Temple Courtyard. Were it removed the blood would be disqualified.]

וְנֶאֱכָל בְּחִפָּזוֹן, — *and was eaten in haste*

The verse providing that the Egyptian Pesach be eaten in haste stresses (*Exodus* 12:11): *And thus shall you eat*

'it' ... and you shall eat 'it' in haste ... implying that only *it*, i.e., the Pesach under discussion in this verse — the Egyptian one, — must be eaten in haste, not the 'Pesach of generations' (*Gem.* 96a).

בְּלַיְלָה אֶחָד. — *during one night.*[1]

The *Gemara* (96a-b) notes that this clause cannot refer to the difference between the time alloted for eating the Pesach of Egypt and that of future generations, because every Pesach is eaten for only one night. Rather, it must be understood relative to the last clause of the mishnah (see below).

Although the time limitation of the Egyptian Pesach is not unique, it is mentioned so that we not draw the mistaken inference, that because the Egyptian Pesach was eaten in 'haste', less time was allotted for its eating (*Hon Ashir*).

וּפֶסַח דּוֹרוֹת נוֹהֵג כָּל שִׁבְעָה. — *but the Pesach of [succeeding] generations is observed all seven [days].*

The *Gemara* (96b) points out that this clause cannot refer to the offering, which is never brought on any day other than 14 Nissan. Rather, it refers to the prohibition against eating *chametz*. The mishnah implies that for the Pesach celebration in Egypt, the prohibition against consumption of *chametz* was in effect for only one day — the fifteenth of Nissan. [The verses specifying seven

1. *Tosefos Yom Tov* points out that this mishnah which allows the Pesach to be eaten all night, contradicts mishnah 10:9 which cites a Scriptural prohibition to eat it after midnight. The exact time allotted for the eating of the Pesach is the subject of a disagreement between R' Akiva and R' Elazar ben Azaryah (*Gem.* 120b). Our mishnah holds with R' Akiva who allows a full night while 10:9 holds with R' Elazar ben Azaryah who limits the eating until midnight.

quired sprinkling [of its blood] with a bundle of hyssop upon the lintel and upon the two doorposts, and was eaten in haste during one night. But the Pesach of [succeeding] generations is observed all seven days.

6. **S**aid R' Yehoshua, "I have heard that the substitute of a Pesach is offered, and that the substitute of a Pesach is not offered, but I cannot explain [it]."

YAD AVRAHAM

days for this prohibition (*Exodus* 12:15, 18-20) are prefaced with: (*v.* 14) ... *and you shall celebrate it as a festival for HASHEM*, *'for your generations' shall you celebrate it as 'an eternal decree' (v. 14)*, implying that the following verses refer to the 'Pesach of generations'.] The prohibition against *chametz* during Pesach in Egypt is contained in the verse (*Exodus* 13:3), *Remember this day* ... *and chametz shall not be eaten*, which is followed by (*v.* 4): *Today you exit in the month of spring*, implying that on the day of exodus *chametz* was banned.[1]

Rambam (Comm.) understands the previous clause as well — 'the Pesach of Egypt is for one night' — to refer to the prohibition

against *chametz*. In Egypt the prohibition against *chametz* was for only one night (i.e., the first night of Pesach in addition to the following day) whereas the prohibition against *chametz* in future 'generations' applies for seven days. However, it is hard to reconcile this interpretation with the *Gemara*.

The Pesach was slaughtered in three groups (5:7). How was this accomplished for the Pesach of Egypt, which was slaughtered by every individual near his house (see *Tosefta* 8:8)? *Yerushalmi* (5:5 cited by *Tos. Yom Tov*) relates, 'Power was given to the voice of Moses so that his voice carried over the whole land of Egypt. And what did he say? "From this place to that place is one group ..." '

6.

The Torah (*Leviticus* 27:10) prohibits the exchange of a sacrifice for even a choice animal. If an exchange was made in violation of the Torah, it does not remove the sanctity of the first animal, but the exchange *does* serve to consecrate the second animal, with the result that both animals are sacred. This substitute is called a *temurah*, literally *exchange*. The following mishnah discusses the ramifications of such an exchange when performed upon a Pesach offering.

אָמַר רַבִּי יְהוֹשֻעַ, ״שָׁמַעְתִּי שֶׁתְּמוּרַת הַפֶּסַח קְרֵבָה, — *Said R' Yehoshua, "I have heard that the substitute of a Pesach is offered,*

R' Yehoshua heard from his mentors that the 'substitute' Pesach is offered as a peace offering.

Whenever an animal consecrated as a Pesach cannot be offered for that purpose, it becomes transformed into a peace offering (see above 5:4). The substitute of any offering assumes the status of the sacrifice for which it was substituted, e.g., an animal substituted for a burnt offering becomes a burnt offering, and is sacrificed as such. R'

1. There is a question whether only the prohibition against eating *chametz* was kept in Egypt, or whether the laws regarding labor and the possession of *chametz* were also in effect on that day. *Ran* (116b, s.v. מצה) states that all the prohibitions as well as that against having *chametz* applied in Egypt (see *R' M. Kasher, Haggadah Sheleimah* pp. 195-8).

אָמַר רַבִּי עֲקִיבָא, ,,אֲנִי אֲפָרֵשׁ'': הַפֶּסַח
שֶׁנִּמְצָא קֹדֶם שְׁחִיטַת הַפֶּסַח, יִרְעֶה עַד
שֶׁיִּסְתָּאֵב, וְיִמָּכֵר, וְיִקַּח בְּדָמָיו שְׁלָמִים, וְכֵן
תְּמוּרָתוֹ. אַחַר שְׁחִיטַת הַפֶּסַח, קָרֵב שְׁלָמִים,
וְכֵן תְּמוּרָתוֹ.

יד אברהם

Yehoshua had it from his teachers that the substitute of a Pesach is a peace offering, since the Pesach itself is a variety of peace offering.

Rashi and Rav add, that it is offered as a peace offering אַחַר הַפֶּסַח, *after the Pesach*. *Tos. Yom Tov* points out that the *temurah* may offered even during the Pesach festival; consequently the phrase, *after the Pesach*, can only mean that the *temurah* is offered after 14 Nissan, the time of the Pesach offering. However, *Tosefos Yom Tov* wonders why it cannot be offered as a peace offering on the fourteenth. Later commentators (*Ohr Chadash; Rashash; Shoshanim L'David*) respond, that there is a technical reason why the offering must wait until after 14 Nissan. Since the Pesach is sacrificed after the daily offering, it is too late to offer the *temurah* on that day, because no offering except for the Pesach may be sacrificed after the daily offering (see *Gem.* 59a).

וּתְמוּרַת הַפֶּסַח אֵינָה קְרֵבָה, — *and that the substitute of a Pesach is not offered up,*
R' Yehoshua had also heard an opposing statement from his teachers that a Pesach substitute is not offered. If so, it must be left to pasture until it develops a blemish, is sold, and a peace offering bought with the money (*Rav; Rashi*).

וְאֵין לִי לְפָרֵשׁ''. — *but I cannot explain [it]."*
Obviously the contradicting statement must refer to differing circumstances, but R' Yehoshua did not know to which circumstances the different rules should be applied (*Rav; Rashi*).

אָמַר רַבִּי עֲקִיבָא, ,,אֲנִי אֲפָרֵשׁ'': — *Said R' Akiva, "I will explain":*

הַפֶּסַח שֶׁנִּמְצָא קֹדֶם שְׁחִיטַת הַפֶּסַח, — *If the [original] Pesach offering was found before the slaughtering of the [substitute] Pesach,*
The situation is that the original Pesach had been lost and another animal designated as a Pesach in its place, and the original Pesach was recovered before the slaughter of the substitute Pesach (according to *Rabbah* in *Gem.* 96b; see *Hil. Korban Pesach* 4:7 with commentaries and *Tzlach* here).[1] Consequently, two animals are now available for sacrifice as a Pesach, both of them acceptable. If the original Pesach is bypassed despite its halachic acceptability, it cannot subsequently be offered as a peace offering because it had been explicitly rejected [דְּחוּי], and a rejected sacrifice cannot become qualified again (*Rav; Rashi*).

יִרְעֶה עַד שֶׁיִּסְתָּאֵב, — *it must be left to pasture until it develops a blemish,*
Only upon suffering a blemish that would disqualify it as an offering may it be redeemed, but not before, even though, as in our case, the animal may not be sacrificed because of its 'rejection'; (see *Tos.* to 97b s.v. ויביא).

וְיִמָּכֵר, — *is [then] sold,*
[The sale serves as, פִּדְיוֹן, *redemption*, by means of which the animal reverts to חוּלִין, *unconsecrated property*, and the

1. There is disagreement among the tannaim as to which offering should (ideally) be sacrificed; R' Yose holding that the first should be chosen, while the Sages maintain that the owner may offer whichever he wishes. *Rambam (Hil. Korban Pesach* 4:6) rules like the Sages. However, this disagreement has no effect on our mishnah, for all agree that if the substitute Pesach was offered it is valid.

9
6

Said R' Akiva, "I will explain": If the [original] Pesach offering was found before the slaughtering of the [substitute] Pesach, it must be left to pasture until it develops a blemish, is [then] sold, and a peace offering is bought with its proceeds, and so is [the rule regarding] its substitute. [But if it was found] after the slaughtering of the [substitute] Pesach, it is offered as a peace offering, and so is [the rule regarding] its substitute.

YAD AVRAHAM

money given for it assumes its former sanctity. In this case it has the designation of דְּמֵי שְׁלָמִים, *money for the purchase of peace offerings.*

וְיִקַּח בְּדָמָיו שְׁלָמִים, — *and a peace offering is bought with its proceeds,*

[The animal purchased with the redemption fund automatically acquires the designation attached to the money — peace offering — and is offered up as such.]

וְכֵן תְּמוּרָתוֹ. — *and so is [the rule regarding] its substitute.*

Even after the 'rejected' original Pesach was put out to pasture, it retains its sanctity, to the extent that any animal designated as its substitute assumes its holiness. However it, too, must be put out to pasture, etc., and its redemption funds used to purchase a peace offering *(Rav; Rashi).*

[A *temurah* (substitute) always assumes the status of the animal for which it was substituted. Accordingly, if the original Pesach has become a 'rejected' offering because the substitute was offered in its place, the new *temurah* is a 'reject' from the moment of its consecration. If, however, the substitution was made before any animal was slaughtered as a Pesach, both the original Pesach and the *temurah* do not assume the status of 'rejects' until after the substitute animal was slaughtered as the Pesach *(Gem. 96b-97a).*

אַחַר שְׁחִיטַת הַפֶּסַח, — *[But if it was found] after the slaughter of the [substitute] Pesach,*

If on the other hand, the lost Pesach was recovered only after the replacement had been sacrificed.

קָרֵב שְׁלָמִים, — *it is offered as a peace offering,*

The recovered Pesach may itself be offered as a peace offering; there is no need to wait for a blemish and sell it. Since the lost Pesach had not been recovered by the time of the Pesach sacrifice, it is not considered having been explicitly 'rejected' and therefore remains acceptable as a peace offering

וְכֵן תְּמוּרָתוֹ. — *and so is [the rule regarding] its substitute.*

Since the original Pesach is acceptable as a peace offering, the same would apply to an animal substituted for it, because it was substituted for a valid peace offering. It was about this case that R' Yehoshua heard that 'the substitute of a Pesach is offered.'

The *Gemara* 96b comments that R' Yehoshua's teachers could have applied their rulings to the *original* Pesach rather than the substitutes — if the original Pesach becomes 'rejected', it may not be offered; otherwise it may. It is obvious that the *temurah* assumes the status of the offering for which it was substituted.[1]

1. The *Gemara* explains that R' Yehoshua's teachers specified 'substitute' rather than Pesach, because they wanted to prevent a mistaken notion that another substitute designated before the slaughter of the substitute Pesach could be offered as a peace offering even though the original Pesach (for it had been substituted) is considered 'rejected'. We might have reasoned that the substitute had the broad designation of a peace offering because it was never truly in-

[ז] הַמַּפְרִישׁ נְקֵבָה לְפִסְחוֹ, אוֹ זָכָר בֶּן שְׁתֵּי שָׁנִים, יִרְעֶה עַד שֶׁיִּסְתָּאֵב, וְיִמָּכֵר, וְיִפְּלוּ דָמָיו לִנְדָבָה. הַמַּפְרִישׁ פִּסְחוֹ וָמֵת, לֹא יְבִיאֶנּוּ בְּנוֹ אַחֲרָיו לְשֵׁם פֶּסַח, אֶלָּא לְשֵׁם שְׁלָמִים.

[ח] הַפֶּסַח שֶׁנִּתְעָרֵב בִּזְבָחִים, כֻּלָּן יִרְעוּ עַד שֶׁיִּסְתָּאֲבוּ, וְיִמָּכְרוּ, וְיָבִיא בִדְמֵי

יד אברהם

7.

הַמַּפְרִישׁ נְקֵבָה לְפִסְחוֹ, אוֹ זָכָר בֶּן שְׁתֵּי שָׁנִים, — *If someone designates* [lit. *sets aside*] *a female* [*animal*] *for his Pesach offering, or a male in its second year,*

[Neither of these are fit for a Pesach offering because the Torah specifies, *an unblemished kid, a yearling male* (Exodus 12:5).]

יִרְעֶה עַד שֶׁיִּסְתָּאֵב, וְיִמָּכֵר, — *it must be left to pasture until it develops a blemish, and is sold,*

[A disqualifying blemish renders an offering redeemable (see above 9:6, s.v. ירעה).]

וְיִפְּלוּ דָמָיו לִנְדָבָה. — *and its money is* [*placed in*] *a donative offering* [*chest*].

The money is deposited in one of the six chests in the Temple marked, נדבה, *donative offering* (see *Shekalim* 6:5), and is used for burnt offerings (*Rav; Rambam, Comm.*).

The version given above is that of our editions of Mishnah and Talmud and is that of *Rambam (Comm.), R' Chananel,* and *Rav.* However, the version of *Rashi* and *Tosafos* has, וְיָבִיא בִדְמֵי שְׁלָמִים, *and brings from its money peace offerings.* Thus the rule here is the same as that of 9:6 which states that a substitute of a Pesach that cannot itself be of-

fered becomes a peace offering. It should be noted that in his code, *Rambam (Hil. Korban Pesach* 4:4) rules that peace offerings are brought with the money, thus contradicting his commentary where he rules that burnt offerings are brought.

According to our version, which *Rambam* interprets as requiring that the money be used for burnt offerings, an explanation is needed to differentiate between our case and that of the previous mishnah.[1] *R' Chananel* understands the *Gemara* (98a) as a reference to this problem. The *Gemara* derives that יֵשׁ דִּחוּי בְּדָמִים, *the rule of rejection applies to money,* i.e. (as interpreted by *R' Chananel*), whenever an offering has been 'rejected' the rejection extends even to the funds for which it is redeemed, with the result that even the funds are disqualified for that type of offering. Since a female cannot be used for a Pesach — and every Pesach is a variation of a peace offering — the rejected female and the proceeds of the redemption cannot be used for peace offerings. It may be conjectured that the previous mishnah disagrees with this broad application of the principle of rejection and rules that 'there is no rejection for money'. [This interpretation of *R' Chananel* is cited partly in *Tos. Zevachim* 12b, s.v. ושמע). Indeed as noted above, *Rambam* rules *(Hil. Korban Pesach* 4:4) that the money should

tended to be a Pesach and nothing else. Consequently, it cannot be judged a 'rejected' Pesach.

To negate this view R' Yehoshua's teachers specified the *temurah,* thus giving it the status of a 'rejected' offering (*Rashi* 96b, s.v. דאיכא; but see *Tos.,* s.v. קמ"ל).

1. *Tos. Yom Tov's* explanation links this to the quesiton of whether, בְּעֲלֵי חַיִּים נִדָּחִין, *live offerings can be* [disqualified because they have been] *rejected.* But this is difficult to reconcile with the general understanding of this question. See *Lechem Mishneh's* rebuttal of a similar opinion held by *Kessef Mishneh (Hil. Korban Pesach* 4:4).

7. **I**f someone designates a female [animal] for his Pesach offering, or a male in its second year, it must be left to pasture until it develops a blemish, [then] is sold, and its money is [placed in] a donative offering [chest].

If one had designated his Pesach offering and [then] died, his son who inherits it may not bring it as a Pesach offering, but rather as a peace offering.

8. **I**f the Pesach offering was confused with [other] offerings, they must all be left to pasture until they develop blemishes, and are sold. Then he should

YAD AVRAHAM

be used for the purchase of peace offerings, thus clearly disagreeing with R' Chananel's broad principle of rejection. Most other interpretations of 98a (see Rashi and Tos., s.v. ושמע, Tos. Kiddushin 7a, s.v. שמע and Zevachim 12a, s.v. ושמע), however, do not extend the principle of rejection to money, thus making impossible the version in our mishnah that requires the use of the funds for burnt offerings.

Tosafos (97b, s.v. המפריש) points out, that when a blemish is developed before the offering of the Pesach, the money realized from the sale of the offering is reserved for the purchase of Pesach offerings (דְמֵי פֶּסַח). Only after the Pesach has been offered, when any leftover Pesach animal is transformed into a peace offering does the redemption money also acquire the same denomination (see also Hil. Korban Pesach 4:4).

הַמַּפְרִישׁ פִּסְחוֹ וָמֵת, — *If one had designated* [lit. *set aside*] *his Pesach offering and* [then] *died*,

The mishnah refers only to a case where there were no other partners in the Pesach, so that his death left it ownerless and without any registrants (Rav; Rashi). [A Pesach without registered eaters is invalid; see above 5:3.]

לֹא יְבִיאֶנּוּ בְּנוֹ אַחֲרָיו לְשֵׁם פֶּסַח, — *his son*

who inherits it [lit. after him] may not bring it as a Pesach offering,

Although people may register upon an offering until its slaughter (8:3), this can be done only if there is no instant when the Pesach is completely ownerless. As soon as a Pesach becomes ownerless it is disqualified as a Pesach; see below mishnayos 10-11 (Tos. Yom Tov).

אֶלָּא לְשֵׁם שְׁלָמִים. — *but rather as a peace offering.*

[It is subject to the law which renders any Pesach a peace offering if it cannot be offered as a Pesach (see 9:6).]

The mishnah refers to a situation where the son of the deceased was not registered with his father on the offering. Otherwise it would not have been ownerless and could be offered up as a Pesach offering (Tos. Yom Tov; Gem. 98a).

However, a distinction is drawn between a death occurring before noon and after noon. If the death occurred before noon the son would be an *onain* and deferred to the Second Pesach (see above 8:6). However if it happened after noontime so that being an *onain* does not defer him (see *ibid.*), the Pesach is offered now (Gem. 98a).

8.

הַפֶּסַח שֶׁנִּתְעָרֵב בִּזְבָחִים, — *If the Pesach offering was confused with* [other] *offerings,*

ferings,

E.g., if one designated three lambs for

הַיָּפֶה שֶׁבָּהֶן מִמִּין זֶה, וּבִדְמֵי הַיָּפֶה שֶׁבָּהֶן מִמִּין
זֶה, וְיַפְסִיד הַמּוֹתָר מִבֵּיתוֹ.

נִתְעָרֵב בִּבְכוֹרוֹת — רַבִּי שִׁמְעוֹן אוֹמֵר: אִם
חֲבוּרַת כֹּהֲנִים יֹאכֵלוּ.

יד אברהם

offerings; one for a Pesach, one for a peace offering, and one for a burnt offering (Rav; Rashi).

[If the Temple service for each of these three offerings were the same, there would be no problem: the Kohanim would simply perform the standard service and have in mind that it is intended for whatever category of offering the particular animal happens to belong to. In our case, however, the services are different: the Pesach's blood is thrown once upon the altar wall, opposite the 'base' (see above 5:6), whereas the blood of burnt and peace offerings is thrown upon the two diagonal corners of the altar. Furthermore, the meat of the Pesach is eaten for a night, of a peace offering for two days and the included night, and a burnt offering is burned completely on the altar.]

כֻּלָּן יִרְעוּ עַד שֶׁיִּסְתָּאֲבוּ, — they must all be left to pasture until they develop blemishes,

[A permanent blemish that disqualifies the animal to be sacrificed renders it redeemable (see above mishnah 6, s.v. ירעה).]

וְיִמָּכְרוּ. — and are sold.

[Once sold, the animal loses its consecration, and its former sanctity (קדושה) is transferred to the proceeds of the sale.]

וְיָבִיא בִדְמֵי הַיָּפֶה שֶׁבָּהֶן מִמִּין זֶה, וּבִדְמֵי הַיָּפֶה שֶׁבָּהֶן מִמִּין זֶה, — Then he should bring this type of offering equivalent in value to the best of them [lit. and he should bring with the value of the best of them from this type], and he should bring the other type of offering

equivalent in value to the best of them,

The owners' obligation is not only to ultimately sacrifice the required type of offering, but also to use the entire value of the designated offering for its specified purpose. In the event the offering is redeemed, the entire sum of the redemption money is rendered consecrated to be used for purchasing that particular type of sacrifice. Thus, for example, the entire sum realized from the sale of a burnt offering is designated דְּמֵי עוֹלָה, money [reserved for the purchase] of burnt offerings. In the case of our mishnah, we do not know which type of offering the most expensive lamb was. In order to remove any possibility of doubt, the owner must buy a lamb worth as much as the most expensive of the three unidentified lambs for each type of offering. For example, if one of the lambs was worth a sela and the two other lambs half a sela each, three lambs worth at least a sela each must be purchased for each of the three offerings (Rav; Rashi).

Since each coin contains the sanctity of its respective offering, it would be forbidden to spend the Pesach coin for a burnt offering, and so on. If so, how can the new offerings be purchased? This problem is avoided through the following method redeeming the animals:

The owner brings an amount of money three times the value of the dearest of the lambs, e.g., if its price was one sela he brings three sela. He sets aside one sela and says, 'with this sela, I redeem the burnt offering, whichever it is.' He repeats this procedure for the peace offering and the Pesach (Rav; Rashi).

וְיַפְסִיד הַמּוֹתָר מִבֵּיתוֹ. — and he must cover the added cost from his own purse [lit. he loses the additional from his

9
8

bring this type of offering equivalent in value to the best of them, and he should bring the other type of offering equivalent in value to the best of them, and he must cover the added cost from his own purse.

If it was confused with firstborn offerings — R' Shimon says: If the group is composed of *Kohanim*, they may be eaten.

house].

A loss must be absorbed for the purchase of only two offerings, since the third was worth the full value of the required expenditure *(Tif. Yis.)*.

נִתְעָרֵב בִּבְכוֹרוֹת — *If it* [the Pesach] *was confused with firstborn offerings*
[The firstborn offspring of cattle, sheep, and goats is automatically consecrated and must be given to a *Kohen*, who in turn offers it and, together with his household and other *Kohanim*, eats the meat. The throwing of the blood is identical for the Pesach and firstlings (see *Zevachim* 5:8), so that the confusion of identity poses no problems regarding the service, which may be performed though the identity of each individual offering is left unclarified. However, there are differences between the offerings regarding their consumption. Firstlings may be consumed only by *Kohanim* (or members of their households). Also the time allotted for consumption differs. Firstlings may be eaten for two days and a night whereas Pesach may only be eaten till midnight following the sacrifice.]

רַבִּי שִׁמְעוֹן אוֹמֵר: אִם חֲבוּרַת כֹּהֲנִים יֹאכֵלוּ. — *R' Shimon says: If the group is composed of Kohanim, they* [*the offerings*] *may be eaten.*
I.e., they should all be slaughtered and eaten on Pesach night. Since the members of the group are all *Kohanim*,

they may all eat even the firstlings. The service also poses no problem for as already mentioned, the procedure is the same. The only difference is in the length of time allowed for eating. R' Shimon maintains that this too poses no problem, for it is possible to consume all the offerings in the time allowed for the Pesach.

However, the Sages disagree with R' Shimon's ruling. They contend that it is forbidden to create a condition that will require an offering to be consumed in a period a time shorter than that allowed by the Torah, because that may result in the meat becoming 'leftover' and forbidden. In our case, by slaughtering all the animals for use at the Seder, the firstlings meat will lose a day and a night of its allotted period of eating *(Gem. 98b)*.

R' Shimon obviously, does not share the Sages' apprehensions on this matter *(Rav; Rashi)*.

The procedure followed according to the Sages differs slightly from that described in the first clause of the mishnah. Here too, the offerings will be left to graze until disqualified. However, firstlings need not be redeemed even after developing a blemish; instead, they are eaten as soon as they become disqualified [נֶאֱכָלִין בְּמוּמָן]. Upon disqualification of the offerings, the owner redeems whichever is the Pesach, whichever it is, for the value of the best one, and then all the animals must be eaten according to the restrictions applicable to blemished firstlings *(Gem. 98; Rambam, Hil. Korban Pesach 4:8)*.

[ט] חֲבוּרָה שֶׁאָבְדָה פִּסְחָהּ, וְאָמְרָה לְאֶחָד, ,,צֵא וּבַקֵּשׁ וּשְׁחֹט עָלֵינוּ''; וְהָלַךְ וּמָצָא וְשָׁחַט; וְהֵם לָקְחוּ וְשָׁחֲטוּ. אִם שֶׁלּוֹ נִשְׁחַט רִאשׁוֹן, הוּא אוֹכֵל מִשֶּׁלּוֹ, וְהֵם אוֹכְלִים עִמּוֹ מִשֶּׁלּוֹ. וְאִם שֶׁלָּהֶן נִשְׁחַט רִאשׁוֹן, הֵם אוֹכְלִין מִשֶּׁלָּהֶן, וְהוּא אוֹכֵל מִשֶּׁלּוֹ. וְאִם אֵינוֹ יָדוּעַ אֵיזֶה מֵהֶן נִשְׁחַט רִאשׁוֹן, אוֹ שֶׁשָּׁחֲטוּ שְׁנֵיהֶן כְּאֶחָד, הוּא אוֹכֵל מִשֶּׁלּוֹ, וְהֵם אֵינָם אוֹכְלִים עִמּוֹ; וְשֶׁלָּהֶן יֵצֵא לְבֵית הַשְּׂרֵפָה; וּפְטוּרִין מִלַּעֲשׂוֹת פֶּסַח שֵׁנִי.

יד אברהם

9.

חֲבוּרָה שֶׁאָבְדָה פִּסְחָהּ, וְאָמְרָה לְאֶחָד, ,,צֵא וּבַקֵּשׁ וּשְׁחֹט עָלֵינוּ'' — A group that lost its Pesach offering and said to one [of their company], "Go out, seek [it] [the lost offering], and slaughter [it] for us;"

וְהָלַךְ וּמָצָא וְשָׁחַט; — and he went out, found [the missing animal], and slaughtered

[He found the animal and slaughtered it on behalf of the company.]

וְהֵם לָקְחוּ — Meanwhile they bought

[Because of their apprehension that the lost animal would not be recovered in time for the sacrifice, they bought another animal to offer as a Pesach.

וְשָׁחֲטוּ. — and slaughtered [another].

[They slaughtered the newly acquired Pesach for their group.]

אִם שֶׁלּוֹ נִשְׁחַט רִאשׁוֹן, — If his was slaughtered first,

[I.e., the lost and recovered Pesach was slaughtered first.]

הוּא אוֹכֵל מִשֶּׁלּוֹ, וְהֵם אוֹכְלִים עִמּוֹ מִשֶּׁלּוֹ. — he eats of his and they eat of his with him.

Since they appointed him to act as

their agent to slaughter the first animal, they were all registered on his offering at the time of its slaughter, so they could not be numbered on another Pesach offering. Accordingly, the second animal had no owners eligible to eat from it and could not be offered as a Pesach. Instead it must be left and offered later as a peace offering (as are all Pesach offerings which have not been offered).

וְאִם שֶׁלָּהֶן נִשְׁחַט רִאשׁוֹן, הֵם אוֹכְלִין מִשֶּׁלָּהֶן, — But if theirs was slaughtered first, they eat of theirs

Their slaughter of the subsequently purchased offering demonstrates that they have withdrawn their registration from the first (lost) offering. As taught previously (8:4), one may withdraw his registration from a Pesach before it was slaughtered (Rav; Rashi).[1]

וְהוּא אוֹכֵל מִשֶּׁלּוֹ. — and he eats of his.

For he never participated in the purchase and registration on the second offering (Rav; Rashi).

וְאִם אֵינוֹ יָדוּעַ אֵיזֶה מֵהֶן נִשְׁחַט רִאשׁוֹן, — If it is not known which of them was slaughtered first,

---

1. The mere purchase of another offering offers no such demonstration. It could be interpreted as a precautionary move to assure the group of a Pesach in case the first offering was not found (see Teshuvos Maharik 76:1).

9. **A** group that lost its Pesach offering and said to one, "Go out, seek [it], and slaughter [it] for us;" and he went out, found [it] and slaughtered [it]. Meanwhile they bought and slaughtered [another]. If his was slaughtered first, he eats of his and they eat of his with him. But if theirs was slaughtered first, they eat of theirs and he eats of his. If it is not known which of them was slaughtered first, or if both were slaughtered at the same time, [then] he eats of his but they do not eat with him; and theirs must be burned; but they are exempt from observing the Second Pesach.

YAD AVRAHAM

אוֹ שֶׁשָּׁחֲטוּ שְׁנֵיהֶן כְּאֶחָד, הוּא אוֹכֵל מִשֶּׁלּוֹ וְהֵם אֵינָם אוֹכְלִים עִמּוֹ; — *or if both were slaughtered at the same time, [then] he eats of his but they do not eat with him;*

The possibility exists that theirs was slaughtered an instant before his[1], with the result that the second offering is their Pesach, in which case they could not eat of the first, not being registered on it (*Rav; Rashi*).

וְשֶׁלָּהֶן יֵצֵא לְבֵית הַשְּׂרֵפָה — *and theirs must be burned* [lit. *exits to the house of burning*];

They are forbidden to eat theirs because of the possibility that his was slaughtered first, thus effectively invalidating their registration on the newly selected offering.

[In the Temple complex there was an area reserved for the burning of invalidated offerings; it was named the 'house of burning' (see above 8:2, s.v. ויצאו).]

וּפְטוּרִין מִלַּעֲשׂוֹת פֶּסַח שֵׁנִי. — *but they are exempt from observing the Second Pesach.*

The Second Pesach is incumbent only upon those who had not participated in the offering of the First Pesach sacrifice. In our situation, however, they *were*

participants in the first of the two offerings; what was lacking was only definite knowledge of which Pesach came first. Though their doubt restricts them from eating of their Pesach, this does not nullify their fulfillment of the *mitzvah* of offering. Though a *mitzvah* in its own right, eating is not a prerequisite for this *mitzvah* (אֲכִילָה לֹא מְעַכְּבָא) (*Rav; Rashi*).

Nevertheless the offering must be fit for consumption at the time of the service. In a very similar case where a slave had forgotten his master's instructions and as a result offered two offerings (see 8:2), the master is exempt from the Second Pesach only if at the time of the 'throwing' he, the master, still remembered his own original instructions, in which case a valid Pesach had been offered in his behalf. Here, however, when both are offered simultaneously it cannot be known at the time of the blood service which Pesach is the right one, thus rendering the flesh, de facto, unfit for consumption and consequently invalidating the entire offering process. *Tosafos* (98b s.v. ופטורין) notes this difficulty but does not articulate the difference between the two cases. *Tzlach* suggests that the exemption is due to the possibility that the lost Pesach was slaughtered first. This offering, which is eaten by the messenger is surely valid in any case. The

---

1. Where both offerings were offered at the same time it is assumed that the two offerings only *seemed* to be simultaneous (אִי אֶפְשָׁר לְצַמְצֵם), but in reality one was offered before the other. Consequently, this must be regarded as a case where it is not known which offering was slaughtered first (*Tos. Yom Tov; Maharsha; see Teshuvos Maharik* 76:1).

אָמַר לָהֶן אָמַר לָהֶן, ,,אִם אֲחַרְתִּי, צְאוּ וְשַׁחֲטוּ עָלַיי'';
הָלַךְ וּמָצָא וְשָׁחַט, וְהֵן לָקְחוּ וְשָׁחֲטוּ; אִם
שֶׁלָּהֶן נִשְׁחַט רִאשׁוֹן, הֵן אוֹכְלִין מִשֶּׁלָּהֶן, וְהוּא
אוֹכֵל עִמָּהֶן. וְאִם שֶׁלּוֹ נִשְׁחַט רִאשׁוֹן, הוּא
אוֹכֵל מִשֶּׁלּוֹ, וְהֵן אוֹכְלִין מִשֶּׁלָּהֶן. וְאִם אֵינוֹ
יָדוּעַ אֵיזֶה מֵהֶם נִשְׁחַט רִאשׁוֹן, אוֹ שֶׁשָּׁחֲטוּ
שְׁנֵיהֶם כְּאֶחָד, הֵן אוֹכְלִין מִשֶּׁלָּהֶן, וְהוּא אֵינוֹ
אוֹכֵל עִמָּהֶן; וְשֶׁלּוֹ יֵצֵא לְבֵית הַשְּׂרֵפָה; וּפָטוּר
מִלַּעֲשׂוֹת פֶּסַח שֵׁנִי.
אָמַר לָהֶן וְאָמְרוּ לוֹ, אוֹכְלִין כֻּלָּם מִן
הָרִאשׁוֹן. וְאִם אֵין יָדוּעַ אֵיזֶה מֵהֶן נִשְׁחַט
רִאשׁוֹן, שְׁנֵיהֶן יוֹצְאִין לְבֵית הַשְּׂרֵפָה.

יד אברהם

stipulation that the person be fit is not a condition for the fulfillment of his *mitzvah*;
rather it is a prerequisite for the validity of
the offering. Consequently, since in this case
this requirement is filled by the messenger,
the others too, have fulfilled their *mitzvah*
with the lost Pesach in the eventuality that is
was slaughtered first (see another explanation in *Lechem Mishneh* to *Hil. Korban
Pesach* 3:4).

אָמַר לָהֶן, — *If he said to them,*
[If the member of the company who
went to seek out the lost offering said to
the other members.]

,,אִם אֲחַרְתִּי, צְאוּ וְשַׁחֲטוּ עָלַיי''; — *"If I
delay, go out and slaughter for me;"*
In this case the group members did
not instruct him: "Slaughter for us"
(Rav).

הָלַךְ וּמָצָא וְשָׁחַט, — [and] he went out,
found [it], and slaughtered [it].
[I.e., the previously lost Pesach.]

וְהֵן לָקְחוּ וְשָׁחֲטוּ; — *Meanwhile they
bought and slaughtered* [another];
[I.e. they bought another offering.]

אִם שֶׁלָּהֶן נִשְׁחַט רִאשׁוֹן, הֵן אוֹכְלִין מִשֶּׁלָּהֶן, —
*If theirs was slaughtered first, they eat
of theirs*

[When they purchased the second offering, they effectively detached themselves from the first offering. In the
absence of any instruction to their agent
to the contrary, purchase alone effects
detachment.]

וְהוּא אוֹכֵל עִמָּהֶן — *and he eats with them.*
His instruction to them, "Slaughter
for me," effectively registers him with
the group's Pesach. Thus, once their offering has been slaughtered he cannot
detach himself from it. *His* offering
then becomes a Pesach without owner
and is disqualified and burned (Rav;
Rashi).

וְאִם שֶׁלּוֹ נִשְׁחַט רִאשׁוֹן, הוּא אוֹכֵל מִשֶּׁלּוֹ —
*But if his was slaughtered first, he eats
of his*
[Since the slaughter of his offering
took place before that of the group, he
in effect disassociated himself from
their Pesach.]

וְהֵן אוֹכְלִין מִשֶּׁלָּהֶן. — *and they eat of
theirs.*
[They had not appointed him to be
their representative and had already
withdrawn from the lost Pesach.]

9
9

If he said to them, "If I delay, go and slaughter for me," and he went out, found [it] and slaughtered [it]. Meanwhile they bought and slaughtered [another]. If theirs was slaughtered first, they eat of theirs and he eats with them. But if his was slaughtered first, he eats of his and they eat of theirs. If it is not known which was slaughtered first, or if both were slaughtered at the same time, [then] they eat of theirs, but he does not eat with them; and his is burned; but he is exempt from observing the Second Pesach.

If he said to them and they said to him, all [of them] eat of the first. But if it is not known which of them was slaughtered first, both are burned.

YAD AVRAHAM

וְאִם אֵינוֹ יָדוּעַ אֵיזֶה מֵהֶם נִשְׁחַט רִאשׁוֹן, אוֹ שֶׁשֶּׁחֲטוּ שְׁנֵיהֶם כְּאֶחָד, הֵן אוֹכְלִין מִשֶּׁלָּהֶן, — *If it is not known which was slaughtered first, or if both were slaughtered* [lit. *they slaughtered*] *at the same time,* [then] *they eat of theirs,*

[Since they did not appoint him to slaughter for them.]

וְהוּא אֵינוֹ אוֹכֵל עִמָּהֶן; — *but he does not eat with them;*

[For it is possible that his was the first offering slaughtered.]

וְשֶׁלּוֹ יֵצֵא לְבֵית הַשְּׂרֵפָה; — *and his is burned* [lit. *exits to the house of burning*]*;*

The possibility exists that their offering was the first to be slaughtered. He, having appointed them his agents to offer the Pesach, would have become disassociated from his own Pesach. Because of this doubt, it needs to be burned (Rav; Rashi).

וּפָטוּר מִלַּעֲשׂוֹת פֶּסַח שֵׁנִי. — *but he is exempt from observing the Second Pesach.*

[Because in either case, he was registered on a Pesach.]

אָמַר לָהֶן — *If he said to them* "If I delay go and slaughter for me."

וְאָמְרוּ לוֹ, — *and they said to him,* "Go out, seek, and slaughter [it] for us."

אוֹכְלִין כֻּלָּם מִן הָרִאשׁוֹן. — *all* [of them] *eat of the first.*

For here the messengers are agents of the group and vice versa, so that all of them are in effect registered on the first Pesach slaughtered (Rav; Rashi).

וְאִם אֵין יָדוּעַ אֵיזֶה מֵהֶן נִשְׁחַט רִאשׁוֹן, — *But if it is not known which of them was slaughtered first,*

[Or if the two offerings seemed to be slaughtered simultaenously.]

שְׁנֵיהֶן יוֹצְאִין לְבֵית הַשְּׂרֵפָה. — *both are burned* [lit. *both exit to the house of burning*].

However, all the people are exempt from the Second Pesach as in the previous cases (Rav; Rambam, Hil. Korban Pesach 3:6; see Tzlach and Lechem Mishneh).

לֹא אָמַר לָהֶן וְלֹא אָמְרוּ לוֹ, אֵינָן אַחֲרָאִין
זֶה לָזֶה.

[י] שְׁתֵּי חֲבוּרוֹת שֶׁנִּתְעָרְבוּ פִּסְחֵיהֶן, אֵלּוּ
מוֹשְׁכִין לָהֶן אֶחָד, וְאֵלּוּ מוֹשְׁכִין
לָהֶן אֶחָד. אֶחָד מֵאֵלּוּ בָּא לוֹ אֵצֶל אֵלּוּ, וְאֶחָד
מֵאֵלּוּ בָּא לוֹ אֵצֶל אֵלּוּ. וְכָךְ הֵם אוֹמְרִים, ,,אִם
שֶׁלָּנוּ הוּא הַפֶּסַח הַזֶּה, יָדֶיךָ מְשׁוּכוֹת מִשֶּׁלָּךְ
וְנִמְנֵיתָ עַל שֶׁלָּנוּ. וְאִם שֶׁלָּךְ הוּא הַפֶּסַח הַזֶּה,
יָדֵינוּ מְשׁוּכוֹת מִשֶּׁלָּנוּ וְנִמְנֵינוּ עַל שֶׁלָּךְ.''

יד אברהם

לֹא אָמַר לָהֶן וְלֹא אָמְרוּ לוֹ, — *If he said
nothing to them and they said nothing
to him,*

And of their own volition, one went
to seek the lost Pesach and subsequently
found and slaughtered it, while the
others bought and slaughtered another.[1]

Although there were indications that
their intentions were to slaughter the

Pesach for each other, since there were
no explicit instructions, they are not
responsible for one another (*Rambam
Comm. and Hil. Korban Pesach* 3:6).

אֵינָן אַחֲרָאִין זֶה לָזֶה. — *they are not
responsible for each other.*

Neither party has any claim on the
other and each party eats of its own
Pesach whatever the order of slaughtering is.

10.

שְׁתֵּי חֲבוּרוֹת שֶׁנִּתְעָרְבוּ פִּסְחֵיהֶן, — *If the
Pesach offerings of two groups were
confused.*

Their offerings were mixed up before
slaughtering (*Rambam*). [Before the
slaughter, people may still withdraw
from their previously selected Pesach
and register on another offering (see
above 8:3).]

אֵלּוּ מוֹשְׁכִין לָהֶן אֶחָד, — *these take* [lit.
draw] *one* [*a Pesach*] *for themselves.*

[One group chooses one of the offerings of uncertain ownership.]

וְאֵלּוּ מוֹשְׁכִין לָהֶן אֶחָד. — *and the others
take* [lit. *draw*] *one* [Pesach] *for themselves.*

[The other company takes the

remaining offering.]

אֶחָד מֵאֵלּוּ בָּא לוֹ אֵצֶל אֵלּוּ, וְאֶחָד מֵאֵלּוּ בָּא
לוֹ אֵצֶל אֵלּוּ.— [Then] *a member of one
group* [lit. *these*] *comes to the other
group, and a member of the other group
comes to this group,*

[Each group chooses a member of the
opposite group to be included in their
own group, registered on its offering.]

Although any individual may
withdraw his registration any time
before the slaughter and re-register on
another offering, this course may not be
taken by *all* members of the group; one
of the original members must remain
registered on the offering so that it will
never be in an ownerless state (see *Gem.*
99a). Therefore it is necessary to form

1. The *Gemara* (99a) remarks of the last instance 'Silence is better for the wise, and how much
more so for fools' as it is said (*Proverbs* 17:28): '*Even a fool, when he holds his peace is
regarded wise'.*

9
10
If he said nothing to them and they said nothing to him, they are not responsible for each other.

10. If the Pesach offerings of two groups were confused, these take one for themselves, and the others take one for themselves. [Then] a member of one group comes to the other group, and a member of the other group comes to this group, and they declare the following, "If this Pesach is ours, [then] you are withdrawn from your own [Pesach] and you are registered on ours. But if this Pesach is yours, then we withdraw from ours and we are registered on yours."

YAD AVRAHAM

new groups, each containing at least one member of each of the original groups. Accordingly, if we call the original groups A and B, and the subsequently formed groups C and D; group C will consist of the members of group A plus one member of group B, and group D will include the members of group B plus one member of group A. Group C chooses one of the offerings. If this had been the offering of group A, only the single new member from group B need re-register. If, however, this was the offering that had been owned by group B whose members are now in group D, a single member of the original remains and he is joined by the new members who come from the other group.

When they withdraw from their old offering to re-register on the new one, their previous offering is not left ownerless because one member of the original company remains with it, thus the offering is still valid *(Rav; Rashi).*

וְכָךְ הֵם אוֹמְרִים, — *and they declare the following,*
The members of each company declare to their newly appointed member *(Rav; Rashi).* [This declaration is necessary to effect the re-registration needed to normalize the situation.]

אִם שֶׁלָּנוּ הַפֶּסַח הַזֶּה,, — *"If this Pesach is ours,*

If the animal we have presently chosen is the Pesach we had originally designated, so that our registration need not be changed but yours does *(Rav; Rashi).*

יָדֶיךָ מְשׁוּכוֹת מִשֶּׁלְּךָ וְנִמְנֵית עַל שֶׁלָּנוּ. — [*then] you are withdrawn* [lit. *your hands are withdrawn] from your own* [*Pesach] and you are registered on ours.*
[We instruct you to withdraw your previous registration in order to join with us. The new member's explicit assent is not needed, for he has already assented to be a member of this group.]

וְאִם שֶׁלְּךָ הוּא הַפֶּסַח הַזֶּה, — *But if this Pesach is yours,*
[If the Pesach we have now chosen was originally the one picked by your previous group, and is consequently still yours.]

יָדֵינוּ מְשׁוּכוֹת מִשֶּׁלָּנוּ — *then we withdraw* [lit. *our hands are withdrawn] from ours*
We relinquish our ownership in the offering originally owned by us and bestow it upon the other group *(Rav).*

וְנִמְנֵינוּ עַל שֶׁלְּךָ.,, — *and we are registered on yours."*
[We register on the Pesach originally owned by you and your previous group. It is assumed that the owners of the Pesach assent to this registration.]

וְכֵן, חָמֵשׁ חֲבוּרוֹת שֶׁל חֲמִשָּׁה וְשֶׁל עֲשָׂרָה עֲשָׂרָה, מוֹשְׁכִין לָהֶן אֶחָד מִכָּל חֲבוּרָה וַחֲבוּרָה, וְכֵן הֵם אוֹמְרִים.

[יא] **שְׁנַיִם** שֶׁנִּתְעָרְבוּ פִּסְחֵיהֶם, זֶה מוֹשֵׁךְ לוֹ אֶחָד וְזֶה מוֹשֵׁךְ לוֹ אֶחָד; זֶה מְמַנֶּה עִמּוֹ אֶחָד מִן הַשּׁוּק, וְזֶה מְמַנֶּה עִמּוֹ אֶחָד מִן הַשּׁוּק; זֶה בָּא אֵצֶל זֶה, וְזֶה בָּא אֵצֶל זֶה, וְכָךְ הֵם אוֹמְרִים, ,,אִם שֶׁלִּי הוּא פֶּסַח זֶה, יָדֶיךָ מְשׁוּכוֹת מִשֶּׁלָּךְ וְנִמְנֵיתָ עַל שֶׁלִּי; וְאִם שֶׁלָּךְ הוּא פֶּסַח זֶה, יָדַי מְשׁוּכוֹת מִשֶּׁלִּי וְנִמְנֵיתִי עַל שֶׁלָּךְ.''

יד אברהם

וְכֵן, חָמֵשׁ חֲבוּרוֹת שֶׁל חֲמִשָּׁה וְשֶׁל עֲשָׂרָה עֲשָׂרָה, — *Similarly, if there were five groups, each comprising five or ten [members lit. fiv groups of five five or of ten ten],*

I.e., the offerings of these groups became confused.

Also, if ten groups each consisting of ten members had their offerings mixed up the procedure would be identical (*Tif. Yis.*).

מוֹשְׁכִין לָהֶן אֶחָד מִכָּל חֲבוּרָה וַחֲבוּרָה, — *they take to themselves one person from each group*

If, as in the first example, there were five groups of five members each, five new groups are formed, each comprised of one member from each of the original groups, thereby ensuring that at least one of the original owners retained his original registration (*Rav; Rashi*).

However if the amount of offerings exceeds the number of members in each group, so that each group cannot have

one of its members registered on each of the offerings in doubt (e.g., each of five groups has only four members), this procedure cannot be followed. See below (9:11, s.v. ונמניתו על שלך) for possible arrangments to rectify this situation.

וְכֵן הֵם אוֹמְרִים. — *and declare the same.*

Four of the new group say to the fifth member: If the Pesach we have chosen was originally yours, the four of us withdraw from our four respective offerings and are registered upon yours.

Then the fifth member (to whom this declaration had been directed) joins with three of the other members and forms a new foursome (e.g., members 1, 2, 3, 5) who will now direct this formula to another member (e.g., member 4). So they continue until each member has had this declaration made to himself by the other four. This must be repeated in all the groups (*Rav; Rashi*).

11.

שְׁנַיִם שֶׁנִּתְעָרְבוּ פִּסְחֵיהֶם, — *Two [individuals] whose Pesach offerings were confused,*

[Reuben and Simon had each desig-

nated an animal for his own Pesach, and had not yet registered a group upon it (see 8:7). The animals now became mixed up before the slaughter.]

9
11
Similarly, if there were five groups, each comprising five or ten [members], they take to themselves one person from each group and declare the same.

11. Two [individuals] whose Pesach offerings were confused, this one takes one [Pesach] for himself, and that one takes one for himself; this one registers some stranger with himself, and that one registers some stranger with himself; this one comes to that [Pesach], and that one comes to this [Pesach], and they say thus, "If this Pesach offering is mine, [then] you are withdrawn from yours and are registered upon mine; and if that Pesach offering is yours, I am withdrawn from mine and am registered upon yours."

YAD AVRAHAM

זֶה מוֹשֵׁךְ לוֹ אֶחָד וְזֶה מוֹשֵׁךְ לוֹ אֶחָד; — *this one takes one Pesach for himself, and that one takes one for himself;*

[Reuben and Simon each takes one of the offerings.]

זֶה מְמַנֶּה עִמּוֹ אֶחָד מִן הַשּׁוּק, וְזֶה מְמַנֶּה עִמּוֹ אֶחָד מִן הַשּׁוּק; — *this one registers some stranger* [lit. *one from the market*] *with himself, and that one registers some stranger with himself;*

Each individual now registers on his original Pesach, whichever it happens to be [but not upon the Pesach he has *now* chosen; to simplify the explanation of the mishnah, we will say that Reuben chooses Levi and Simon chooses Judah] *(Rav; Rashi).*

By having two people registered on each Pesach, this arrangement will make it possible for them to switch registrations, as outlined below, without leaving either offering ownerless for any period of time. Without such registration, they would be unable to offer their newly chosen animals because the animal Reuben now holds may really be Simon's (and vice versa), in which case neither is registered on the animal he is using for his offering. Furthermore, each may not simply register on the

other person's offering without withdrawing from his own because an individual cannot be registered on two different Pesach offerings at the same time *(Gem. 88b).*

זֶה בָּא אֵצֶל זֶה, וְזֶה בָּא אֵצֶל זֶה, — *this one comes to that [Pesach], and that one comes to this [Pesach],*

[Each original owner comes to the Pesach chosen by the other. Each Pesach is now in the custody of a newly registered stranger, thus Reuben's Pesach is held by Levi and Simon's is held by Judah.]

וְכָךְ הֵם אוֹמְרִים, — *and they say thus,*

[To the stranger who is now in charge of the Pesach.]

„אִם שֶׁלִּי הוּא פֶּסַח זֶה, — *If this Pesach offering is mine,*

Reuben declares to Judah, "If this Pesach chosen by Simon (and now held by you, as his partner) is actually mine, then Simon had no power to accept you as his partner on *this* animal, and you are his partner in the other Pesach."

יָדֶיךָ מְשׁוּכוֹת מִשֶּׁלָּךְ — *[then] you* [lit. *your hands] are withdrawn from yours*

"I ask you to remove yourself from your share in Simon's Pesach."

[א] עַרְבֵי פְּסָחִים סָמוּךְ לַמִּנְחָה לֹא יֹאכַל אָדָם עַד שֶׁתֶּחְשָׁךְ. וַאֲפִלּוּ עָנִי שֶׁבְּיִשְׂרָאֵל לֹא יֹאכַל עַד שֶׁיָּסֵב.

יד אברהם

וְנִמְנֵיתָ עַל שֶׁלִּי — *and are registered upon mine;*
[I.e., the Pesach you are holding which is actually mine.]

וְאִם שֶׁלָּךְ הוּא פֶּסַח זֶה, — *and if that Pesach offering is yours,*
"Both Simon and I happened to pick the animals that were truly ours, with the consequence that you are Simon's partner in the Pesach you are holding."

יָדַי מְשׁוּכוֹת מִשֶּׁלִּי — *I am withdrawn from mine*
"I withdraw from my Pesach."

וְנִמְנֵיתִי עַל שֶׁלָּךְ." — *and am registered upon yours."*
The *Gem.* (99a) cites a disagreement between R' Yehudah and R' Yose as to whether it is required that at least one of the *original* group of registrants retains his registration throughout. R' Yehudah maintains that as long as the offering is never left ownerless, it does not matter who are the registrants at the time of slaughter. The *Gemara* notes that our mishnah seems to

contradict R' Yehudah's view, for assuming that the choice made by the original owners was correct, the process set forth by our mishnah would leave each owner registered upon an offering other than their original one, leaving their original offerings in the possession of Levi and Judah.
The *Gemara* responds, that since each offering had had only one registrant originally — a situation not to be tolerated during the slaughter service (see 8:7) — it was taken for granted that additional members would be added. Therefore, the subsequent registered stranger is regarded as one of the original group. It is further pointed out (according to this view), that in a parallel case where more than one person had originally been registered, an additional member would not be so regarded. Thus, the previous mishnah which indicates no procedure for a case where the number of members in each group is less than the amount of offerings, follows R' Yehudah's view.
Rambam (*Hil. Korban Pesach* 3:7) does not clarify the halachah on this point (see *Lechem Mishneh* there; *Aruch HaShulchan HaAssid* 185:17).

Chapter 10

After concluding the discussion of the Pesach sacrifice, the Mishnah turns to the final section of the Passover ritual — the Seder. In the Temple era this included the *mitzvah* of eating of the Pesach at the end of the meal. Appropriately, this chapter closes with a discussion about the consumption of the sacrifice.

The Seder, literally *order*, is given that name because of the strictly ordered structure it requires to assure the fulfillment of the many Scriptural and Rabbinical *mitzvos* of the evening. The exact year when the present form of the Seder was instituted is hidden in antiquity, but we find in this chapter that the service was already known and being practiced by the people in Mishnaic times. Our chapter is involved with clarifying the order and illuminating various aspects of the Seder.

1.

עַרְבֵי פְּסָחִים — *On the eve* [lit. *eves*] of *Pesach*
Our version of the mishnah is in the plural, עַרְבֵי פְּסָחִים, *on the eves of Passovers*, i.e., on all the eves of the Passover festival. *Tosafos* (99b s.v., ערבי) quotes another version, עֶרֶב פְּסָחִים, which is rendered, *On the afternoon of Pesachs*, i.e. the afternoon on

which [many] Pesach offerings are sacrificed, or alternatively, on the afternoon of both the First and Second Pesach offerings.

[For those who offer the Second Pesach, there is a *mitzvah* to eat *matzah* and *marror* together with it (*Numbers* 9:11). Thus, those who had neglected to offer a Pesach on the fourteenth of Nissan, may not eat on the

10
1

1. **O**n the eve of Passover close to the Minchah [period], a person may not eat until it becomes dark.

Even the poorest man in Israel may not eat unless

YAD AVRAHAM

afternoon of Iyar the fourteenth 'close to the Minchah ... ' so that they will have a hearty appetite for the prescribed foods of the night.]

סָמוּךְ לַמִּנְחָה — close to the Minchah [period],

The regular afternoon offering was called the Minchah [lit. gift or offering] as in II Kings (16:15), the morning burnt offering and מִנְחַת הָעֶרֶב, the afternoon offering, and in Psalms 141:2 (see Radak, Shorashim s.v. נחה). By association, the time period in which the afternoon sacrifice was offered also acquired the name Minchah, as did the afernoon prayer. [See ArtScroll comm. to Daniel 9:21 for reasons why the afternoon offering and prayer are specifically called Minchah].

Ramban (Exodus 12:6) holds that the name Minchah is not connected to the sacrifice, but refers to the gradual setting of the sun beginning at noon. The term minchah is thus derived from נחה, to rest.

Though the entire afternoon is referred to as Minchah, it is divided into two specific periods.

The first is called מִנְחָה גְדוֹלָה, greater Minchah, starting from one half hour after midday. This is the earliest that the afternoon offering is ever slaughtered. The seond period, מִנְחָה קְטַנָה, lesser Minchah, beginning 3½ hours after midday; this was the usual time for the afternoon offering to be offered upon the altar (see above 5:1). It was followed immediately by the rest of the service, including the libation and the singing of the daily hymn (see Yoma 33a, אַבָּיֵי הֲוָה מְסַדֵּר).

The Gemara (107b) concludes that the mishnah refers to the lesser Minchah. Close to the Minchah, i.e. half an hour prior to it (Rashbam; Cf. Rambam Comm. and Hil. Chametz 6:12) in the

beginning of the tenth hour [appr. 3 P.M.] (Rav).

לֹא יֹאכַל אָדָם — a person may not eat

He should refrain from eating in this period so that he will have a good appetite to eat the matzah that will be eaten for the mitzvah of the evening. It is a הִידוּר מִצְוָה, beautification of the mitzvah, that it be done with gusto (Rav from Gem. 107b).

This prohibition must refer to foods other than leavened bread, since chametz is forbidden at least from the beginning of the sixth hour (see 1:3). Nor does the mishnah refer to matzah, since matzah may not be eaten all day. Yerushalmi (here) compares eating matzah on the eve of Pesach to one who lives with his betrothed (אֲרוּסָתוֹ) before the chuppah ceremony has taken place. Consequently the mishnah must refer to other foods, which are permitted on Pesach Eve (Rav; Rambam). [As explained in the Gem. 107b, one may eat small amounts of vegetables and fruits. The mishnah means that one may not gorge himself on these foods.]

Tosafos (99b, s.v. לא) says the mishnah refers to מַצָּה עֲשִׁירָה, rich matzah, made of flour and eggs or fruit juices. Since such matzah is not accceptable for the mitzvah, it may be eaten on Pesach eve. Nonetheless, such matzah should not be eaten from 'close to the Minchah' and further.

עַד שֶׁתֶּחְשַׁךְ. — until it becomes dark.

[When he will perform the mitzvah of eating matzah.]

All mitzvos of the Seder can be accomplished only after dark. Tosefta (2:14) says, the mitzvos of eating the Pesach, matzah, and marror may be performed only after dark, for the Torah proclaims regarding the Pesach: And they shall eat the meat [of the Pesach] on this night (Exodus 12:8) — and matzah and marror are compared to Pesach (Tos. 99b, s.v. עד).

וַאֲפִלּוּ עָנִי שֶׁבְּיִשְׂרָאֵל לֹא יֹאכַל עַד שֶׁיָּסֵב. — Even the poorest man in Israel may not eat unless he reclines.

Reclining during a meal was regarded

פסחים ‏ וְלֹא יִפְחֲתוּ לוֹ מֵאַרְבָּעָה כוֹסוֹת שֶׁל יַיִן, וַאֲפִלּוּ
י/א ‏ מִן הַתַּמְחוּי.

יד אברהם

as the stamp of a free-man, and the celebration of the festival of freedom requires that one's action conform to the habits of the liberated. It is incumbent upon every Jew, therefore, no matter what his station or his usual custom, to act in the manner of liberated people *(Rashi).*

'They required him to eat while reclining, in the manner of royalty and nobility, so that it (the meal) be in the mode of freedom' *(Rambam, Comm.).*

Even a poverty-stricken person, who lacks pillows for comfortable reclining, and who does not customarily recline, must do so at the Seder, even if he must recline on a hard bench *(Mordechai* here; see *Rama, Orach Chaim* 472:2 with *Magen Avraham).*

The *Gemara* (108a) clarifies, that only while eating the matzah and drinking 'the four cups' is reclining essential. However *Rambam (Comm.; Hil. Chametz* 7:7-8) apparently understands the mishnah to refer to the entire Seder meal. Though it is not essential to recline throughout the meal, one who does so is 'praiseworthy' (see *Orach Chaim* 472:7 with comm.).

Tosafos (99b, s.v. ואפילו) quotes an opinion that the phrase, *even the poorest man in Israel,* is linked with the previous phrase. Thus: *A person may not eat until it becomes dark — even [if he is] the poorest man in Israel,* i.e., even a poor man who is famished, having had very little food during the day, must wait until dark to observe the *mitzvah* properly.

In this vein, *R' Akiva Eiger* quotes an interesting interpretation based on *Berachos* 2b. A poor man, the *Gemara* says, eats before it becomes dark in order to spare himself the expense of oil for a lamp. Our mishnah warns, therefore, that on Pesach eve, even the indigent must not eat before dark.

‏ וְלֹא יִפְחֲתוּ לוֹ מֵאַרְבָּעָה כוֹסוֹת שֶׁל יַיִן, *—and* they [the administrators of the public

charity fund *(Rav)]* must give him [the poor man] *not less that four cups of wine,*

[The Sages instituted that every Jew drink four cups of wine during the course of the Seder, as outlined in the following mishnayos. It is incumbent upon the community, through its charity funds, to provide the poorest people with sufficient wine to perform even this Rabbinic *mitzvah.* It goes without saying that poor people must be provided with such necessities as matzah and food.]

Our translation *they* [the administrators …] follows *Rav, Rashbam,* and *Tos.* 99b, s.v. לא.

Alternatively this clause is rendered literally, *and they* [the cups of wine given him] *should be not less to him* [the poor man] *than four cups of wine (Meiri; Ritva).*

‏ וַאֲפִלּוּ מִן הַתַּמְחוּי. *— even though he is supported from the [charity] plate.*

Those eligible to take food from the *tamchuy* (see explanation of *tamchuy* below) are the poorest of the poor; they lack even enough food for two meals. Even such people are obligated in the *mitzvah* of Four Cups. If the administrators of the charities neglected to give them wine, the paupers must do their utmost to fulfill the *mitzvah,* event to the point of selling clothing, borrowing, or hiring themselves out *(Rashbam).*

Alternatively, even if the expense of fulfilling the *mitzvah* will force one to accept support from the *tamchuy,* he must do so. For example, if one has enough money to buy food for the day, he must use it for wine even though that will force him to resort to the *tamchuy* for bare subsistance *(R' Yechiel* in *Tos.* printed in *Mordechai;* see also briefly in *Tos.* 99b s.v. לא).

⤟§ **The Charity Plate**

In Talmudic times there were two types of charity collections.

The תַּמְחוּי *tamchuy* [literally *a large bowl*] with partitions for different types of food [see *Aruch,* s.v. תמחוי, *Rashi* 12b, s.v. תמחוי] — was a collection of food for the

10
1

he reclines. And they must give him not less than four cups of wine, even though he is supported from the [charity] plate.

very needy. Food was collected every day to be distributed on that very evening to the neediest, but poor people who had food enough for two meals were not permitted to take from the 'collection plate'.

The קוּפָּה, *Kupah* — literally the [*collection*] *chest* or *box* — consisted basically of monies collected to be distributed on a weekly basis. For the most part, the *tamchuy* was distributed among wandering beggars, whereas the local poor received their weekly portion in money from the *kupah*. There were also other collections earmarked for specific needs such as בְּסוּת, *clothing*, and the like (from *Peah* 8:7 with *Rambam's Comm.* and *Hil. Matnos Aniyim* 9:1-13).

אַרְבַּע כּוֹסוֹת — The Four Cups

A number of reasons are given for drinking four cups of wine at the Seder. The most frequently mentioned reason is that they correspond to the four expressions of redemption used by God with regard to the Exodus from Egypt: וְהוֹצֵאתִי, *I will bring out;* וְהִצַּלְתִּי, *I will rescue;* וְגָאַלְתִּי, *I will redeem;* and וְלָקַחְתִּי, *I will take* [*you to Myself as a nation*] (*Exodus* 6:6-7; *Rav; Rashi; Rashbam* based on *Yerushalmi* 10:1, *Bereishis Rabbah* 88:5, and *Shemos Rabbah* 6:4).

Maharal MiPrague (*Gevuros Hashem* ch. 60; see also *Meiri and Sefer HaMichtam*) elaborates on the significance of these different expressions, and explains that they correspond to the different types of bondage foretold to Abraham in the 'Covenant between the Parts' (בְּרִית בֵּין הַבְּתָרִים). There (*Genesis* 15:13), God revealed to Abraham ... *your offspring shall be aliens in a land not their own, they will serve them, and they will oppress them* ... This prophecy includes a loss of independence, a state of slavery, and a degree of oppression and brutalization beyond anything usually associated with mere slavery.

When the time for redemption arrived, these facets of the bondage were removed in the reverse order of their severity. First the excessive oppression and tyranny were mitigated (*Exodus* 6:6): *I will* **take you out** *from* סִבְלוֹת, *the sufferings of Egypt*. Then the bonds of slavery were loosened entirely (*ibid.*), *and* **I will deliver you** *from their bondage*. Finally the Jews were granted their total independence (*ibid.*): *and* **I will redeem you** *with an outstretched arm and great judgments* — the Exodus. However, complete freedom was not the ultimate purpose of God's intervention in the history of Israel. His goal was for Israel to become eternally and indelibly identified as God's Chosen People. Therefore He promised (*Exodus* 6:7): *And* **I will take you** *to Myself for a nation and I shall be a God unto you* ... For each of these levels of redemption we thank and praise God with a litany of song and blessing, and drink a cup of wine in gratitude.

Various other symbolisms are attributed to these four cups. They correspond to:

The four times the term כּוֹס, *cup*, is mentioned in Pharaoh's recitation of his dream, and Joseph's subsequent interpretation of it (*Genesis* 40:11, 13). This event was one of the occurrences leading to the bondage and the ultimate redemption (*Meiri*).

The four kingdoms destined to rule the world, as revealed to Daniel (*Daniel* 2:31-43, ch. 7-8).

The allegorical four 'cups' of wrath and vengeance that will be 'poured' upon the evildoers of the world. These 'cups of vengeance' are found in Scripture four times (*Jeremiah* 25:15, 51:7 and *Psalms* 75:9 and 11:6), where the term כּוֹס, *cup*, is a

[ב] מָזְגוּ לוֹ כוֹס רִאשׁוֹן. בֵּית שַׁמַּאי
אוֹמְרִים: מְבָרֵךְ עַל הַיּוֹם, וְאַחַר
כָּךְ מְבָרֵךְ עַל הַיָּיִן.
וּבֵית הִלֵּל אוֹמְרִים: מְבָרֵךְ עַל הַיָּיִן, וְאַחַר
כָּךְ מְבָרֵךְ עַל הַיּוֹם.

[ג] הֵבִיאוּ לְפָנָיו; מְטַבֵּל בְּחַזֶרֶת עַד שֶׁמַּגִּיעַ

יד אברהם

metaphor for the full measure of Divine wrath and punishment. Corresponding to the four cups of punishment are four 'cups of consolation' that God will offer His people in the 'time to come'. See *Maharal* (loc. cit.) for the significance of these symbols.

In general, however, the abundance of wine drunk at the Seder signifies the theme of freedom, which is dominant in the entire Pesach ritual (see *Gem.* 108b: (ארבעה כסי תקינו רבנן דרך חירות; ידי יין יצא ידי חירות לא יצא).

2.

מָזְגוּ לוֹ — *They pour* [lit. *mixed*] *for him* [for the individual conducting the Seder service; i.e., the master of the house].

In Talmudic times it was customary (and obligatory for wine used in the fulfillment of *mitzvos*; see *Tos., Shabbos* 76b s.v. כדי) to mix one part of wine with two parts of water (see *Shabbos* 77a) because of the thickness of the wine.

The phrase מָזְגוּ, *they poured*, is also the source for the custom that the head of the family not pour for himself; instead others pour his wine for him as a symbol of freedom (*Tif. Yis.*; see *Rama, Orach Chaim* 473:1, *Chok Yaakov* and *Beur HaGra* there).

כוֹס רִאשׁוֹן — *the first cup.*
[Over which the *Kiddush* will be recited.]

בֵּית שַׁמַּאי אוֹמְרִים: מְבָרֵךְ עַל הַיּוֹם, — *Beis Shammai say: He recites the benediction over the day,*
[The structure of the *Kiddush* includes two blessings, one for the wine and a second for the holiness of Israel and the particular festival day. Beis Shammai maintain that the *Kiddush* should begin with the blessing of the day: *Blessed ... Who has chosen us from among all nations ... Blessed ... Who sanctifies Israel and the festive seasons.*]

וְאַחַר כָּךְ מְבָרֵךְ עַל הַיָּיִן. — *and then he recites the benediction over the wine.*

The blessing 'Blessed ... Who creates the fruit of the vine' is recited after the benediction of the day. Beis Shammai reason that because the holiness of the festival had begun with nightfall, long before the wine to be drunk for the *Kiddush* was brought to the table, it follows that the blessing over the day takes precedence over that of the wine (*Rav; Gem.* 114a). In addition, the sanctity of the day *causes* the *Kiddush* to be recited with its blessings over the wine. It is fitting, therefore, that the cause be acknowledged before the consequence (*Gem.* 114a with *Rashbam*).

וּבֵית הִלֵּל אוֹמְרִים: מְבָרֵךְ עַל הַיָּיִן, וְאַחַר כָּךְ מְבָרֵךְ עַל הַיּוֹם. — *But Beis Hillel say: [First] he recites the benediction over the wine, and then he recites the benediction over the day.*

Beis Hillel reason that the wine is the cause for the recitation of *Kiddush*, because if one has no wine (or bread) no *Kiddush* is recited (*Rav; Gem.* 114b). Another contention of Beis Hillel is that the benediction over wine, which is pronounced whenever someone drinks wine, is more frequent than the *Kid-*

10
2

2. **T**hey pour for him the first cup. Beis Shammai say: he recites the benediction over the day, and then he recites the benediction over the wine.

But Beis Hillel say: he recites the benediction over the wine, and then recites the benediction over the day.

10
3

3. [**T**hen] they bring [it] before him; he eats [dipped] lettuce before he reaches the course

dush, which is pronounced only on Sabbaths and festivals. The general rule is תָּדִיר וְשֶׁאֵינוֹ תָּדִיר תָּדִיר קוֹדֵם, *a constantly performed mitzvah or blessing takes precedence over a non-constant one (Gem. 114a).*

This dispute concerning precedence of *Kiddush* or wine-blessing applies to the *Kiddush* benedictions any time of the year,

whether on the Sabbath or the festivals (*Berachos* 8:1).

This dispute (and the reasoning behind it) applies also to a *Kiddush* recited over bread (or on Pesach, matzah) in the absence of wine. Beis Shammai hold that the benediction *HaMotzi* is said after the *Kiddush*, and Beis Hillel maintain that it be said before the *Kiddush* benediction.

3.

הֵבִיאוּ לְפָנָיו — [*Then*] *they bring* [it] *before him;*

I.e. they bring him vegetables (*Rav; Rashi*).

Alternatively, they brought the table bedecked with food, and placed it before the person conducting the Seder (*R' Chananel*). It was customary in Talmudic times to place a small, traylike table before each participant in the meal. On the Sabbath or festival it would be brought after *Kiddush* (*Tos.* 114a, s.v. הביאו).

מְטַבֵּל בְּחֲזֶרֶת — *he eats dipped lettuce* [lit. *he dips in lettuce*]

Because the mode of eating in Talmudic times consisted of dipping the food into a dressing, the mishnah uses the verb טבל [lit. *to immerse*] to connote eating (*Rav; Rashi; Rashbam, Tos.* 114a, s.v. מטבל; *Aruch*, s.v. טבל).[1]

Although the cited authorities all assume that the lettuce is dipped before being eaten, there is disagreement regarding the substance into which it is dipped. *Rashi, Rambam (Hil. Chametz* 8:2), and others (see a listing of sources in *Hagaddah Shlemah* p. 101) hold that *charoses* is used for this dipping too, while *Rashbam, R' Tam (Tos.* 114a, s.v. מטבל), *Rav*, and others maintain that (fruit) vinegar or salt water suffices at this point in the Seder. The prevalent custom follows the latter view (see *Orach Chaim* 473:6).

Obviously the lettuce eaten at this point is not meant to fulfill the *mitzvah* of eating *marror*. That *mitzvah* is performed after the consumption of matzah, in accordance with the sequence of their mention in the Torah (*Ex.* 12:11): *... with matzos and bitter herbs shall you eat it* [the Pesach]. According to *Rashi, Rashbam* and many others, the

1. *Rambam (Comm.* see ed. Kafich) explains the phrase, מְטַבֵּל בְּחֲזֶרֶת, as if the verb were מְטַפֵּל *he occupies himself.* If so, the phrase would be rendered *he occupies himself with lettuce,* and there would be *no* requirement, to dip the lettuce into anything. *Ran, Meiri, Maharam Chalavah,* and *R' David* variously attribute this view to *Rashi* and *Rashbam,* but this is inconsistent with our versions. The cited versions, however, repudiate this view vigorously, adducing proof for their stand from the *Gemara* 114b. Our versions of *Rashi* and *Rashbam* explicitly mention 'dipping.' In his Code (*Hil. Chametz* 8:2), however, *Rambam* rules that the lettuce is dipped in charoses.

פסחים י/ג
לְפַרְפֶּרֶת יֵיפַת.
הֵבִיאוּ לְפָנָיו מַצָּה וְחַזֶּרֶת וַחֲרֹסֶת וּשְׁנֵי

יד אברהם

mishnah intends to make this point in the next phrase, as will be explained in the *comm.* to עַד שֶׁמַּגִּיעַ לְפַרְפֶּרֶת הַפַּת. That the *mitzvah* of *marror* is performed later is indicated by our mishnah, which says (below) that after the dipped lettuce had been eaten, *they brought before him matzah, 'lettuce', and charoses* ... If so, the Talmud asks, why is it necessary to eat vegetables at this point? — So that the children will [be provoked to] ask *(Gem. 114b).*

The well-known premise that many things are done at the Seder to arouse the curiosity of the children is based on the verse (*Exodus* 13:14): *And it shall come to pass when your son will ask you* ... Surely, the value of an impression made upon the young, uncluttered mind of a child is inestimable. However two questions arise: Firstly, what is so extraordinary about the eating of lettuce or other vegetables that it should rouse the child's interest? Surely, nothing was unusual about the dipping, for that was the common manner of eating in Talmudic times.[1] *Rashi, Rashbam,* and *Rav* explain that it was not customary to eat vegetables before the meal [especially when one will eat vegetables — bitter herbs — with the meal.]

Additionally, what does one tell the child if he is successful in provoking the child to ask the desired question?[2] Surely, merely arousing the child's interest without the means to satisfy his curiosity may even be counter-productive.

Maharil (Hil. Pesach) suggests, that having vegetables before the meal in addition to those that would be eaten later, is a sign of freedom and well-being (see also *Rosh* here, *ArtScroll Haggadah* p. 63; *Turei Zahav*

473:7 with *Pri Magadim, Gevuros Hashem* ch. 50; the summary of the views by *R' Ch. L. Katz* in *VaYaged Moshe,* p. 101).

This ritual of eating a vegetable is popularly known as *karpas* (see in *R' Yosef Tuv Alom's* liturgy for *Shabbos HaGadol* שָׁקֵל גַּרְגִּירָא אוֹ כַּרְפְּסָא; *Orach Chaim* 473:4), probably because some authorities prefer the vegetable named *karpas* for this part of the Seder (see footnote above).

Why does the Mishnah single out Lettuce?

As mentioned above, any vegetable may be used for the ritual, but a special teaching can be gleaned from our mishnah's mention of lettuce. Even if someone had no other vegetable but lettuce, and as a consequence would have fulfilled his obligation to eat bitter herbs by eating lettuce at the outset of the Seder — since lettuce is one of the *bitter herbs* enumerated in 2:6—he must still eat lettuce *again* after eating matzah, in order to fulfill the Rabbinic requirement that a vegetable be eaten in addition to the bitter herbs eaten for the *mitzvah* of *marror (Gem. 114b).*

The view presented above is predicated on the premise that מִצְוֹת אֵין צְרִיכוֹת כַּוָּנָה *[the fulfillment of] mitzvos does not require intent.* If such intent were indeed required for fulfillment of a *mitzvah,* then a person eating lettuce for the first dipping would obviously be required to eat *marror* again later, for he would not have intended to fulfill his obligation to eat *marror* at this point. According to the opinion that 'intent' is required for the fulfillment of a *mitzvah,* the mishnah must be explained differently (see *Gem. 114b).*

עַד שֶׁמַּגִּיעַ לְפַרְפֶּרֶת הַפַּת. — *before he reaches the course that is secondary to the matzah* [lit. *loaf*].

The translation follows *Rashi* and

1. The second question in the *Mah Nishtanah (*מַה נִּשְׁתַּנָה*)* deals with the unusual practice of dipping two times on the Seder night. The question is commonly understood to treat dipping as an anomaly, but this was obviously not the intent of this question at the time it was framed, for then dipping was the common practice. Furthermore, unless the child had been coached previously, how could he know that two dippings would take place? See *comm.* mishnah 4 for an understanding of this question.

2. The various popular reasons given for the use of בַּרְפַּס, *karpas,* at this point in the Seder explain only why the vegetable *karpas* (translated variously as celery and parsley) is preferred over other vegetables for the first dipping, as suggested by *Maharil (Magen Avraham* 473:4; see *Chok Yaakov)* and *Arizal.* The reasons given for the preference of *karpas* do not apply to the basic requirement that a vegetable be eaten. (See the summary of reasons for *karpas* in *VaYaged Moshe* pp. 102-3).

10
3

that is secondary to the matzah. [Now] they brought
before him matzah, lettuce and charoses, and two

YAD AVRAHAM

Rashbam who interpret this term
(פְּרֶפֶרֶת הַפַּת) a part of the meal not eaten
with the matzah, but after it. In this
case, it is the vegetable eaten as *marror*,
which follows matzah in the Seder. [See
Berachos 6:2 where this word פַּרְפֶּרֶת is
used in a similar way.]

I.e., the eating of the abovementioned
dipped lettuce takes place before the
eating of *marror*, which follows the
matzah bread as it is written *(Numbers
9:11): with matzos and* [then] *bitter
herbs shall they eat it.* Aside from the
bitter herb, a vegetable is eaten before
the Seder meal, so that the children dis-
cern the different mode of eating this
night and are induced to ask *(Rashi;
Rashbam).*

Ramban (cited by *Ran* and *R' David*
also *R' Chananel, Meiri,* and *Maharam
Chalavah*) maintains that פַּרְפֶּרֶת in
general refers to wafer-like pastries.
The matzah is so called because it, too,
is generally similar to a thin wafer.

Rav, too, interprets this phrase as
referring to matzah, basing his comment on a version that reads עַד שֶׁמַּגִּיעַ
לְפַרְפֵּר הַפַּת, *until he reaches* [the time]
to crumble the bread, i.e., when the matzah is broken prior to the recitation of
the blessing over it. According to these
interpretations, the mishnah is stating
that the dipped lettuce mentioned earlier
is the only food eaten before the matzah.

A novel interpretation is suggested by
Shoshanim L'David (cf. *Tif. Yis.*). The mishnah refers to the requirement to break one of
the matzos used at the Seder *(Berachos* 39b;
Pesachim 115b-116a). The mishnah now informs us that the breaking of the matzah *(the
crumbling of the bread,* as in *Rav*) takes
place immediately after the first dipping — *he
eats lettuce until the crumbling of the bread.*
The mishnah appropriately follows up this
comment with *they brought before him matzah* ... We thus have a Mishnaic basis for
the prevalent custom to break the matzah
before beginning the recital of the *Haggadah.
Shulchan Aruch HaRav* 473:36 (see also *R'
Manoach* to *Hil. Chametz* 8:6) justifies this

custom on the following halachic grounds:
The *Haggadah* should be recited over matzah
fit for fulfillment of the *mitzvah (Gem.*
115b). Since that matzah should be a broken
piece *(ibid.),* it follows that it be broken prior
to the recital of the *Haggadah* (cf. *Machzor
Vitri* sec. 61 for an interesting reason for
breaking the matzah). The first one known
to this writer to mention the custom is *Rashi*
(Machzor Vitri sec. 65, 68). Later it is mentioned by *Rosh, Mordechai* and many others.
It is not found in the Siddurim of the Geonim
R' Amram and *R' Saadiah,* nor does *Rambam
(Hil. Chametz* 8:67) mention it.

הֵבִיאוּ לְפָנָיו — [Now] *they brought
before him*
After the first dipping *(Rashi;
Rashbam)* [i.e., after the 'dipped' lettuce
has been consumed.]

[According to *Rav, Rashi,* and *Rashbam*
(see above, s.v. הביאו), these items had not
been brought as yet, and were now set in
front of him.

According to *R' Chananel* and *Tosafos
(ibid.),* however, the entire table, ostensibly
containing all the essentials of the meal, had
been before him previously (with the lettuce). *Tosafos* (114a s.v. הביאו) explains that
after the dipped lettuce had been eaten, the
table with the foodstuffs on it was removed
(as set forth in *Gem.* 115b), in order to draw
the childrens' attention to the proceedings,
and to cause them to ask the obvious question: Why is the table removed before we
start the meal? This gives the father an opportunity to respond with, 'We will return
the table again to eat dipped herbs,' thus
prompting the question (from the *Mah
Nishtanah* formula; see mishnah 4): 'On all
the nights we do not dip ... but on this night
two times.' [However, it is evident from
Rambam's paraphrase of our mishnah *(Hil.
Chametz* 8:1) that the phrase *they brought
before him ...* in this part of our mishnah
refers to the action already mentioned at the
beginning of the mishnah. It is also evident
that *Rambam* anticipates the view of some
commentators *(Meiri)* that this clause recap-
itulates the first clause of the mishnah. The
mishnah now returns to list which articles
were brought.]

The matzah and bitter herbs had to be
brought before the *Haggadah* was

[207] **THE MISHNAH / PESACHIM**

תַּבְשִׁילִין, אַף עַל פִּי שֶׁאֵין חֲרֹסֶת מִצְוָה.
רַבִּי אֶלְעָזָר בְּרַבִּי צָדוֹק אוֹמֵר: מִצְוָה.
וּבַמִּקְדָּשׁ הָיוּ מְבִיאִין לְפָנָיו גּוּפוֹ שֶׁל פֶּסַח.
[ד] **מָזְגוּ** לוֹ כוֹס שֵׁנִי. וְכָאן הַבֵּן שׁוֹאֵל אָבִיו.
וְאִם אֵין דַּעַת בַּבֵּן, אָבִיו מְלַמְּדוֹ:

יד אברהם

recited, in line with one of the implications of the term used to describe matzah in *Deuteronomy* 16:3. There it is described as לֶחֶם עֹנִי which is usually translated *bread of affliction*, from the root ענה, *to afflict* or *oppress*. *Homiletically, the word* עֹנִי *is rendered* by the other meaning of the root ענה. *to answer* or *speak out*, as *bread upon which many matters are recited* [i.e., the *Haggadah*] (as set forth in the *Gem.* 36a). Also when we say (in the Haggadah; cf. mishnah 5): *this matzah* ... *this marror* ... these substances should be present.

Rambam (*Hil. Chametz* 8:4) maintains that the matzah and bitter herbs [and in Temple times, the meat of the Pesach sacrifice] were not returned to the table until it was time to recite, 'Rabban Gamliel says', which contains the statements: This Pesach ... This matzah ... This marror ...

מַצָּה — *matzah,*
Three matzos, one of which would be broken to symbolize לֶחֶם עֹנִי, *bread of affliction*. The two whole matzos were needed for the *HaMotzi* blessing as on every Sabbath and festival (*Tif. Yis.*).

וַחֲזֶרֶת — *(and) lettuce,*
With which to fulfill the *mitzvah* of *marror*, bitter herbs. Above (2:6) five vegetables are mentioned as valid for fulfillment of the *marror* obligation. Perhaps the mishnah singles out only lettuce because, as stated in the Gemara 39a, lettuce is the first choice for this *mitzvah*.

וַחֲרוֹסֶת — *and charoses,*
[To be used as a dipping sauce for the marror.]
[*Rav* (above 2:8; see *Rashi* there) defines חֲרוֹסֶת as a vinegary mixture in which foods were dipped. *Rambam* (*Comm.* there), defines it simply as the mixture described in

our mishnah (see below), indicating that *charoses* is not a generic term, but a name given the specific mixture referred to here, probably because of its similarity to cement (from חֶרֶס, *earthenware*; see *Tos. Yom Tov* here).]

⸕ᔥ **What is Charoses?**
Rav describes *charoses* as follows: It is made from figs (see *Tos.* 116a s.v. צריך), filberts, pistachios [I have found no previous source for this], almonds (*Tos.* loc. cit.), and many types of fruit. Apples are placed in it (see *Gem.* 116a אָמַר אַבַּיֵי ... לִקְהוּיֵיהּ זֶכֶר לְתַפּוּחַ; cf. *Tos. Yom Tov* and *Kol HaRemez*). All these ingredients are placed in a mortar and pounded to a pulp, and [fruit] vinegar (see *Rashi* 116a s.v. לסמוכיה) is mixed in. Then thin spice fibers, e.g., cinnamon, resembling straw [which was mixed into the mortar in Egypt; see *Exodus* 5:7-18] are placed upon it (*Gem.* 116a). It [the charoses] should have a thick texture as a remembrance of the טיט, *mortar* [made by the Jews in Egypt] (*ibid.*).
Rambam gives a similar recipe (*Comm.*; see also *Hil. Chametz* 7:11): 'This is how we make it. We soak figs or dates, cook and pound them until they are soft. [Then] we knead them with vinegar and put into them something strawlike (see ed. Kafich) without grinding it.'
See also *Rama* in *Orach Chaim* 473:6. Many other recipes may be found in *Haggadah Shleimah* (pp. 62-64) and *VaYaged Moshe* (pp. 29-33).

וּשְׁנֵי תַבְשִׁילִין, — *and two cooked dishes;*
To commemorate the Pesach and Chagigah (see above 6:3-4) sacrifices that were consumed in Temple times as part of the Seder ritual (*Gem.* 114b).
It is customary nowadays to take a roasted shank bone [to commemorate the Pesach] and a boiled egg [to commemorate the Chagigah] (*Orach Chaim* 473:4; see *R' Chananel* cited in *Tos.* 114b s.v. שני). There was no requirement to eat these; they may be

cooked dishes; although the charoses is not a mitz-vah.

R' Eliezer bar R' Tzadok says: [The dipping is] a mitzvah.

And in the Temple they would bring before him the body of the Pesach [offering].

4. They pour him a second cup [of wine]; and here the son asks of his father. (And) if the son has not [enough] understanding, his father instructs him

YAD AVRAHAM

left on the plate throughout the Seder. Moreover the roasted shank bone may not be eaten, for it is forbidden to eat roasted meat at the Seder in the absence of a Pesach offering (see 4:4). However, *Maharshal* (*Teshuvos* 88; cited by *Turei Zahav* and *Magen Avraham* to *Orach Chaim* 473:4) maintains that it is an obligation to commemorate the offerings by eating the cooked dishes. (According to this view, the shank bone must be cooked, not roasted). Some (*Beur HaGra, Orach Chaim* 476:6) say that at least the egg should be eaten at the beginning of the meal.

אַף עַל פִּי שֶׁאֵין חֲרוֹסֶת מִצְוָה. — *although charoses is not a mitzvah.*

The *Gemara* (116a) explains that although there is no *mitzvah* to dip the *marror* into *charoses*, it is nevertheless done because the *charoses* acts as an antidote to קְפָּא, *kaffa*. *Rashi* and *Rashbam* define this as the sharpness (אֶרֶס, lit. *poison*) residual in the sap of the lettuce.

Similarly *R' Hai Gaon* (cited in *Aruch*, s.v. קפא) explains that *kaffa*(=swelling) is the bloating caused by the gastric gases which result from eating lettuce.

Alternatively, *R' Chananel* (see *Tos.* 115b, s.v. קפא) defines *kaffa* as a [undetectable] worm that dies from the fumes of the *charoses*.

רַבִּי אֱלִיעֶזֶר בְּרַבִּי צָדוֹק אוֹמֵר: מִצְוָה. — *R' Eliezer bar R' Tzadok says: [The dipping is] a mitzvah.*

R' Eliezer holds that dipping into charoses was a *mitzvah* because of its symbolism. Because it contains apples, it commemorates the תַּפּוּחַ, *apple tree* (*Shir HaShirim* 8:5), that was instrumental in the Jewish nation's fertility in Egypt (see *Sotah* 11b; *Rashi* and *Rashbam* here); or it symbolizes the mortar produced by the slave labor of the Jews in Egypt (*Gem.* 116a).

The halachah follows R' Eliezer bar Tzadok (*Hil. Chametz* 7:11; *Orach Chaim* 475:1). *Rambam's* Commentary, however, rules against R' Eliezer (see *Meromei HaSadeh* here for resolutions of the contradictions. Also see *Bigdei Yesha* to *Mordechai* note 19 for a novel approach to the conflicting views of the mishnah).

וּבַמִּקְדָּשׁ הָיוּ מְבִיאִין לְפָנָיו גּוּפוֹ שֶׁל פֶּסַח. — *And in the Temple they would* [also] *bring before him the body of the Pesach [offering].*

This was done during the Temple era (*Tif. Yis.*) [probably because they would say פֶּסַח זֶה, *this Pesach* ... during the recital of the *Haggadah*.]

4.

מָזְגוּ לוֹ כוֹס שֵׁנִי — *They pour him a second cup [of wine].*

So that he can recite the Haggadah over wine (*Meiri*).

Alternatively, the wine is poured in order to arouse the child's curiosity and provoke him to ask: Why are we drinking again before the meal has begun (*Rashi; Rashbam; Tur Orach Chaim* 473; *Rosh* in responsa cited by *Bais*

,,מַה נִּשְׁתַּנָּה הַלַּיְלָה הַזֶּה מִכָּל הַלֵּילוֹת? —
שֶׁבְּכָל הַלֵּילוֹת אָנוּ אוֹכְלִין חָמֵץ וּמַצָּה, הַלַּיְלָה
הַזֶּה כֻּלּוֹ מַצָּה. שֶׁבְּכָל הַלֵּילוֹת אָנוּ אוֹכְלִין
שְׁאָר יְרָקוֹת, הַלַּיְלָה הַזֶּה מָרוֹר. שֶׁבְּכָל
הַלֵּילוֹת אָנוּ אוֹכְלִין בָּשָׂר צָלִי שָׁלוּק וּמְבֻשָּׁל,
הַלַּיְלָה הַזֶּה כֻּלּוֹ צָלִי. שֶׁבְּכָל הַלֵּילוֹת אָנוּ
מַטְבִּילִין פַּעַם אַחַת, הַלַּיְלָה הַזֶּה שְׁתֵּי
פְּעָמִים.''

יד אברהם

Yosef there; Shulchan Aruch there sec. 7.)

וְכָאן הַבֵּן שׁוֹאֵל אָבִיו. — And here the son asks of his father.

[The asking of the question is a necessary prelude to the recital of the Haggadah. Scripture's first mention of the recital of the Exodus story is in response to a son's question (Exodus 12:26). As mentioned earlier (mishnah 3 s.v. הביא) much care is taken to impress the children with the story of the Exodus and the lessons to be gleaned from it.]

This point in the Seder is most appropriate for the questions, for the pouring of the second cup serves to arouse the child's curiosity (see above s.v. מזגו) [and lead him to ask the other questions as well] (Rashi; Rashbam).

Alternatively, because by now the table carrying the food had been removed (Gemara 115b) and subsequently brought back (see mishnah 3 s.v. הביאו), the curiosity of the child is aroused (Ran; Meiri).

The version given above (וְכָאן) is that given in our editions of the Talmud, and that of Rashi, Rashbam, R' Chananel and Rambam (ed. Kafich).

Others have the version וְכֵן, it is correct [as in בְּנוֹת צְלָפְחָד דּוֹבְרוֹת, the daughters Tzelafchad speak correctly (Numbers 27:7).] I.e. it is correct and timely to ask now.

וְאִם אֵין דַּעַת בַּבֵּן, — (And) if the son has not [enough] understanding

[To notice and question on his own.]

אָבִיו מְלַמְּדוֹ — his father instructs him [to ask]:

[Even if the son is intelligent enough to formulate his own questions, there is an obligation to ask the four questions listed here (see Rashbam s.v. פטרתן and Tos. s.v. כדי to Gem. 115b, Meiri, Rama in Orach Chaim 473:7). Thus these four questions refer not only to the clause, 'If the son has not enough ...' but also to, 'Here the son, asks his father ... : Why is this night ...', meaning that every child must ask these questions, even though an intelligent child is free to ask as many other questions as he likes.[1]

However our versions of Rambam's code (Hil. Chametz 8:2) suggests a different approach to this mishnah. 'Here the son asks, and the reader says: 'Why is this night ... Since Rambam differentiates between the questions of the son and the formula of our mishnah, clearly the son's questions and the four questions listed here are separate matters. Accordingly, the mishnah would be rendered as follows: The son asks [miscellaneous questions according to his level of intelligence]; if the son has no understanding the father teaches him [to ask assorted questions]. [Then the reader recites]: 'Why is this night ...' (see Hagahos Chasam Sofer to Orach Chaim 473:7; Shinuyei Nuschaos in Rambam ed. Frankel).

1. However R' Yeshayah DiTrani (cited in Shibolei HaLeket 218) maintains (based on Gem. 115b, פָּטְרָתָן מִלּוֹמַר מַה נִּשְׁתַּנָּה), that when the son asks questions on his own there is no obligation to recite these four questions. This seems also to have been Maharil's opinion. But Rama (473:7) rules that only when the son has asked these four questions are the participants exempt from reciting this formula.

**10
4**   [to ask]. "Why is this night different from all nights?
— On all nights we eat *chametz* and matzah, but this
night only matzah. On all nights we eat other greens,
but on this night bitter herbs. On all nights we eat
meat, roasted, stewed, or cooked, but on this night
only roasted. On all nights we might eat dipped
vegetables once, but on this night twice.

YAD AVRAHAM

מַה נִּשְׁתַּנָה הַלַּיְלָה הַזֶּה מִכָּל הַלֵּילוֹת? — *Why is this night different* [lit. changed] *from all* [other] *nights?*

[This clause introduces all the questions.]

Aruch HaShulchan 473:21 renders it as an exclamation. Thus: How different is this night ...!

[This rendition fits the interpretation attributed to *Rambam* (above, s.v. אביו מלמדו) that this formula is unrelated to the son's questions, but is recited by the reader. Since he knows the reason for the 'difference,' he is expected to exclaim with feeling: How different is this night! If these questions are asked by an inquiring child, ostensibly not aware of the answers, he could hardly be expected to exclaim, but rather to ask for an explanation of why the customs of this night are so unusual.]

שֶׁבְּכָל הַלֵּילוֹת אָנוּ אוֹכְלִין חָמֵץ וּמַצָּה, הַלַּיְלָה הַזֶּה כֻּלּוֹ מַצָּה. — *On all* [other] *nights we eat chametz and matzah, but this night only matzah.*

— שֶׁבְּכָל הַלֵּילוֹת אָנוּ אוֹכְלִין שְׁאָר יְרָקוֹת, *On all* [other] *nights we eat other greens,*

שְׁאָר, lit. *the rest*, is rendered *other*, i.e. on the other nights we usually eat greens other than *marror* — bitter herbs; these are usually shunned because of their bitterness. Although the bitter herbs have not been eaten up to this point, the child can realize that they will be eaten for they have already been brought to the table (see *Ritva comm.* to *Haggadah*; cf. *Rashbatz* in *Yavin Shemuah, Maamar Afikoman*).

הַלַּיְלָה הַזֶּה מָרוֹר. — *but on this night bitter herbs.*

Tosafos (116a, s.v. הלילה) remarks that here, as distinct from the first question (כֻּלּוֹ מַצָּה, *only matzah*), we do not say כֻּלּוֹ מָרוֹר, *over bitter herbs*, for we *do* eat other vegetables — e.g., for the first dipping.

שֶׁבְּכָל הַלֵּילוֹת אָנוּ אוֹכְלִין בָּשָׂר צָלִי שָׁלוּק וּמְבֻשָּׁל — *On all* [other] *nights we eat meat, roasted, stewed, or cooked,*

[I.e., שָׁלוּק, *stewed* for a lengthy time, or, מְבֻשָּׁל, *cooked briefly*. See *comm.* above 2:6.]

הַלַּיְלָה הַזֶּה כֻּלּוֹ צָלִי. — *but on this night only roasted.*

The mishnah agrees with the tanna (ben Teima) who maintains that the Chagigah that is eaten with the Pesach (see above 6:3-4) must also be roasted. Therefore it is correct to say *only* (כֻּלּוֹ) roasted (*Tos.* 116a s.v. כולו; *Gem.* 70a). [Obviously this question was posed only when the Temple stood. In our days the question about reclining is substituted for it (see *Haggadah Shleimah* p. 115).]

שֶׁבְּכָל הַלֵּילוֹת אָנוּ מַטְבִּילִין פַּעַם אֶחָת. — *On all* [other] *nights we might eat dipped vegetables once,*

[I.e., we eat dipped greens only once.]

The *Gemara* (116a) emends the text to read, אֵין אָנוּ מַטְבִּילִין אֲפִלּוּ פַּעַם אֶחָת — *We do not dip* [greens] *even one time,* i.e., it is not customary to eat even one course of greens before the meal (*Meiri; Ritva; R' Yeshayah* iln *Shibolei HaLeket* 218 and many other *comm.* to the *Haggadah*, see *Haggadah Shleimah*).[1]

---

1. It cannot be that the question is about the act of dipping, for this was the regular mode of eating in Talmudic times, as stated by *Rashi* and others to mishnah 3. (See *comm.* there, s.v. מטבל).

וּלְפִי דַעְתּוֹ שֶׁל בֶּן אָבִיו מְלַמְּדוֹ. מַתְחִיל
בִּגְנוּת וּמְסַיֵּם בַּשֶּׁבַח. וְדוֹרֵשׁ מֵ,,אֲרַמִּי אוֹבֵד
אָבִי'' עַד שֶׁיִּגְמֹר כָּל הַפָּרָשָׁה כֻּלָּהּ.

[ה] **רַבָּן** גַּמְלִיאֵל הָיָה אוֹמֵר: כָּל שֶׁלֹּא אָמַר
שְׁלֹשָׁה דְבָרִים אֵלּוּ בַּפֶּסַח, לֹא יָצָא

יד אברהם

"הַלַּיְלָה הַזֶּה שְׁתֵּי פְעָמִים." — but on this night twice.

I.e., two courses of greens are eaten before the meal; the *marror*, too, is eaten before the meal proper *(ibid)*.

Alternatively: *On all other nights we do not exert ourselves greatly to eat dipped vegetables even once, but on this night we make a great effort to eat two dipped greens* (Nimukei Yosef; see Haggadah Shleimah).

וּלְפִי דַעְתּוֹ שֶׁל בֶּן אָבִיו מְלַמְּדוֹ. — *and according to the intelligence of the son his father instructs him.*

[The father's response should be geared to the mental capacity of the child.]

Rambam (Hil. Chametz 8:2) puts it as follows: 'It is a *mitzvah* to inform the children even if they do not ask, as it is said *(Exodus 13:8)*: *And you shall tell your son. And according to the son's intelligence his father instructs him. How so?* If he was young or foolish he says to him, "My son! all of us were slaves in Egypt like that maid or that slave, and on this night, the Holy One, Blessed is He, redeemed us and took us out to freedom." If the son was grown up and intelligent, he informs him [about] what transpired with us in Egypt, and the miracles which were performed for us by Moses our teacher — everything according to the intelligence of the child.'

מַתְחִיל בִּגְנוּת. — *He begins* [the recitation of the Haggadah] *with the disgrace.*

He commences with a narrative of Israel's disgraceful origins. The *Gemara* (116a) presents two views as to what is considered 'the disgrace.' The amora *Rav* says it is the recital of the formula, עֲבָדִים הָיִינוּ, *We were slaves to Pharaoh in Egypt ...*; Shmuel holds the disgrace

to be, מִתְּחִילָה עוֹבְדֵי עֲבוֹדָה זָרָה הָיוּ אֲבוֹתֵינוּ, *In the beginning our ancestors were idol worshipers ...*

Our version of the Haggadah includes both views (see *Rambam, Hil. Chametz 7:4*), and is probably predicated on the premise that there is no halachic disagreement here; Rav and Shmuel concur that both formulas are referred to as 'the disgrace' (see ArtScroll Haggadah pp. 90-1; Haggadah Shleimah pp. 19-26). R' Manoach (Hil. Chametz 7:4) points out that Rav's view is actually the answer given in the Torah *(Deut. 6:20)* to the question asked by the son. He finds a Scriptural basis for Shmuel's view as well.

וּמְסַיֵּם בַּשֶּׁבַח. — *and concludes with the glory.*

He contrasts the 'the disgrace' with a recital of the glory with which God has blessed us; for He brought us close to His service, and took our ancestors from Egypt *(Rav)*.

[I.e., corresponding to the disgrace of, *In the beginning our ancestors were idol worshipers*, God brought us close to His service, and the climax of, *We were slaves ...* is that HASHEM has taken us out from there (see *Hil. Chametz 7:4*).]

וְדוֹרֵשׁ מֵאֲרַמִּי אוֹבֵד אָבִי — *And he expounds upon* [lit. *from*]: *(Deut. 26:5) The Aramean* [Laban] *sought to destroy my father* [Deut. 6:5].

[We have translated this verse according to the exposition of it in the Haggadah. The Sages interpret אֲרַמִּי אוֹבֵד as a reference to *Laban* the Aramean who *sought to destroy* the posterity of Jacob. In the simple meaning of the verse, however, *Ibn Ezra* and *Sforno* render the phrase as a reference to Jacob who wandered for a time like *a lost Aramean*, while *Rashbam*, translating similarly, interprets it as a

And according to the intelligence of the son his father instructs him. He begins with the disgrace and concludes with the glory. And he expounds upon (Deut. 26:5): *The Aramean sought to destroy my father* until he ends the whole portion.

5. Rabban Gamliel used to say: Whoever has not said these three things on Passover has not fulfilled his obligation. And they are the following:

YAD AVRAHAM

reference to Abraham who once lived in Aram and later wandered, as if lost, through Canaan.]

The exposition required by the mishnah as part of the *Haggadah* is taken from *Mechilta (Kol Bo).*[1]

The *Haggadah's* method of presenting the exposition is as follows: First a complete verse is recited, then the midrashic exposition is given phrase by phrase. The next verse is then recited and expounded phrase by phrase, and so on until the portion is concluded.

עַד שֶׁיִּגְמוֹר כָּל הַפָּרָשָׁה כֻּלָּהּ. — *until he ends the whole portion.*

[I. e., until … *with wonders (Deut. 26:8)*, which ends the last verse concerned with the Exodus. (The exposition of this verse in the *Haggadah* reaches until רַבִּי יוֹסֵי הַגְּלִילִי אוֹמֵר).

Alternatively, the verse: *And He has brought us to this place* [the Temple] *and given us this land …* is also included in the mishnah's requirement to recite *the portion.* In this view, the sections of the *Haggadah* that deal with Israel being brought to *Eretz Yisrael* and being given a Temple [עַל אַחַת כַּמָּה וְכַמָּה and בָּמָה מַעֲלוֹת טוֹבוֹת] are expositions of verse 9.

5.

רַבָּן גַּמְלִיאֵל הָיָה אוֹמֵר: כָּל שֶׁלֹּא אָמַר שְׁלֹשָׁה דְבָרִים אֵלּוּ בְּפֶסַח—*Rabban Gamliel used to say: Whoever has not said these three things on Pesach* [i.e. during the night of the *Seder*]

In the context of our mishnah, *said,* means to explain the reasons for these three *mitzvos* (Rav; Rashbam).

The source of Rabban Gamliel's ruling is the verse (*Exodus 12:27*): *And you shall say this is a Pesach offering …* which contains an explanation for the offering (see below). Just as one must

explain the Pesach concept, one must similarly expound upon the concepts of matzah and *marror* for the Torah compares these *mitzvos* to the Pesach *(Tos. Yom Tov; Tos. 116a, s.v.* וַאֲמַרְתֶּם).

לֹא יָצָא יְדֵי חוֹבָתוֹ. — *has not fulfilled his obligation.*

One who fails to explain the three *mitzvos* has not fulfilled his obligation in an *ideal* manner; however, the basic obligation has been discharged even without the explanation[2] *(Ran; Ritva*

---

1. This exegesis has been omitted from our versions of the *Mechilta*. *Meiri* attributes this exposition to *Sifre* where it is found in our versions in an abbreviated form, probably because it was so well known from the *Haggadah* (however see *Yalkut Shimoni*).

Malbim has included the *Haggadah* text in his version of *Sifre*.

2. Significantly, *Abudraham* cites the view of *Rif*, that a blessing is not recited before the *Haggadah* (as is commonly done before the performance of a *mitzvah*) because the obligation has already been satisfied with the mere *mention* of the Exodus in the *Kiddush*. Similarly he gives *Rashba's* opinion that a blessing is not appropriate in this instance, since 'one has discharged his duty with a mere statement,' [דִּיבּוּר בְּעָלְמָא] and the further elaboration on this

יְדֵי חוֹבָתוֹ. וְאֵלּוּ הֵן: פֶּסַח, מַצָּה וּמָרוֹר.
פֶּסַח — עַל שׁוּם שֶׁפָּסַח הַמָּקוֹם עַל בָּתֵּי
אֲבוֹתֵינוּ בְּמִצְרָיִם.
מַצָּה — עַל שׁוּם שֶׁנִּגְאֲלוּ אֲבוֹתֵינוּ בְּמִצְרָיִם.
מָרוֹר — עַל שׁוּם שֶׁמֵּרְרוּ הַמִּצְרִיִּים אֶת חַיֵּי
אֲבוֹתֵינוּ בְּמִצְרָיִם.
בְּכָל דּוֹר וָדוֹר חַיָּב אָדָם לִרְאוֹת אֶת עַצְמוֹ
כְּאִלּוּ הוּא יָצָא מִמִּצְרָיִם — שֶׁנֶּאֱמַר: ,,וְהִגַּדְתָּ

יד אברהם

comm. to *Haggadah; see Darkei Moshe Tur; Orach Chaim* 473:19).

However, *Rambam* (Hil. *Chametz* 7:5), who cites this mishnah without qualification, seems to take Rabban Gamliel's statement at face value. (See *Pri Megadim* in *Eshel Avraham* 479:1 and 485, who implies that even according to *Ran*, one who omits the explanations has not discharged his Rabbinic obligation).

◆§ Which Obligation has not been Discharged?

On the surface, it seems that Rabban Gamliel refers to the obligation to recount the details of the Exodus (סִפּוּר יְצִיאַת מִצְרַיִם); in order to recount the narrative properly, he must include an explanation of these three *mitzvos*. This is implicit in *Rambam (Hil. Chametz* 7:5) who says (as part of his elaboration on the *mitzvah* to 'recount the miracles ...'; see there 7:1-6): 'Whoever has not said these three things ... And these things — all of them — are denominated *Haggadah*.'

Some commentators (see *Chiddushei Aggados Maharsha; Abudraham; Kol Bo*) understand, that without explanation of these *mitzvos*, one has not fulfilled even his obligation to eat them. Even if one ate these three things he has not fulfilled his obligation unless he also explains the reasons for them (see at length in *Teshuvos Binyan Tziyon* 1:30; *Haggadah Moadim U'Zemanim; Vayaged Moshe* p. 156). A similar requirement is found regarding the *mitzvah* of

succah (see *Bach Orach Chaim* 625, *Magen Avraham* with *Eshel Avraham* and *Mishnah Berurah* there).

Another approach is suggested by *Shibbolei Haleket's* (218) comment that Rabban Gamliel refers to the obligation upon a father to respond to his child's four questions. In this view, the narrative includes two *mitzvos*: one to recount the details of the Exodus, and the other to respond to the questions of the children. Rabban Gamliel teaches that although the Exodus story has been recounted up to this point, if one does not explain these three *mitzvos* he has not fulfilled his obligation to answer his child's questions. The four questions had been basically about these three *mitzvos* (according to some even the question about the two dipped greens is related to the *mitzvah* of marror).]

וְאֵלּוּ הֵן: פֶּסַח, מַצָּה וּמָרוֹר. — *and they are the following:* [The] *Pesach* [offering], *matzah, and marror.*

פֶּסַח — [the] *Pesach offering* [is offered]

[I.e. the reason for the Pesach offering is as follows]:

עַל שׁוּם שֶׁפָּסַח הַמָּקוֹם עַל בָּתֵּי אֲבוֹתֵינוּ בְּמִצְרָיִם — *because the Omnipresent One passed over the houses of our ancestors in Egypt.*

[Some versions (see editions of the Talmud; *Shinuyei Nuschaos, Haggadah Shleimah* pp. 127-129) include the

theme is merely laudatory, but not obligatory. See the preface to *Maaseh Nissim* on the *Haggadah* (by the author of *Nesivos HaMishpat*) who objects strongly to this view (see also *Pri Megadim* in *Eshel Avraham* 489:2 and 485:1).

10

5

[the] Pesach [offering], matzah, and marror.

[The] Pesach offering [is offered] — because the Omnipresent One passed over the houses of our ancestors in Egypt.

Matzah [is eaten] — because our ancestors were redeemed in Egypt.

Marror [is eaten] — because the Egyptians embittered the lives of our ancestors in Egypt.

In every generation a man must regard himself as if he himself had gone out of Egypt — for it is said:

YAD AVRAHAM

verses inserted in the *Haggadah's* version of Rabban Gamliel's statement, as follows: 'As is written: *And you shall say it is a Pesach for HASHEM, because He passed over the houses of the children of Israel in Egypt when He smote the Egyptians, and He saved our households'* (Exodus 12:27).

Rambam's (Hil. Chametz 7:5, 8:4) version of the mishnah (see *comm.* ed. Kafich), like ours, does not include verses. Nevertheless, his rendition of Rabban Gamliel's statement in the *Yad* (Hil. Chametz 8:4) does include the relevant verses.

Interestingly, *Nimukei Yosef* comments on this mishnah: 'Whoever has not said these three things with the verses which demonstrate the significance of these *mitzvos* has not fulfilled his obligation.'

[הַמָּקוֹם] lit. *the Place*, is an appellation often used to denote the Deity, for as the Sages put it, 'He is the place of the world, but the world is not His place.' This title expresses the concept that God, Who 'contains' the world, cannot be constrained by the limitations of space.]

מַצָּה—עַל שׁוּם שֶׁנִּגְאֲלוּ אֲבוֹתֵינוּ בְּמִצְרָיִם. — *Matzah [is eaten]—because our ancestors were redeemed in Egypt.*

The text of this clause as rendered in the *Haggadah* (see also *Hil. Chametz* 8:4; cf. there 7:5) contains the following elaboration on the theme of גְּאֻלָּה, *deliverance (see Shinuyei Nuschaos; Haggadah Shleimah* pp. 127-129): 'Matzah ... Because the dough of our ancestors had no time to become *chametz* before the King of Kings, the Holy One, Blessed is He, revealed Himself to them and redeemed them; as it is said (Exodus 12:39): *And they baked the dough which they had taken out of Egypt as circular matzos, for it had not leavened, because they were driven out of Egypt and could not delay, nor had they prepared themselves any provisions for the way.'*

The *mitzvah* to eat matzah had already been commanded in Egypt, before the baking of matzah described in the cited verse took place. It was in anticipation of this event that God had commanded the eating of matzah (*Ran; R' Yeshayah* in *Shibbolei HaLeket* 218; and many of the *Haggadah* comm.).

מָרוֹר—עַל שׁוּם שֶׁמֵּרְרוּ הַמִּצְרִיִּים אֶת חַיֵּי אֲבוֹתֵינוּ בְּמִצְרָיִם. — *Marror [is eaten]— because the Egyptians embittered the lives of our ancestors in Egypt.*

[Here, too, the aforementioned versions have the following addition: As it is said (*Exodus* 1:14): *And they embittered their lives with hard labor, with mortar and bricks, and through every sort of labor in the field; all their work at which they enslaved them was rigorous.*

בְּכָל דּוֹר וָדוֹר חַיָּב אָדָם לִרְאוֹת אֶת עַצְמוֹ, כְּאִלּוּ הוּא יָצָא מִמִּצְרַיִם — *In every generation a man must regard himself as if he himself had gone out of Egypt*

As if he was redeemed this very night (*Rambam, Hil. Chametz* 7:6).

לְבִנְךְ בַּיּוֹם הַהוּא לֵאמֹר, בַּעֲבוּר זֶה עָשָׂה ה׳ לִי
בְּצֵאתִי מִמִּצְרָיִם.״ לְפִיכָךְ אֲנַחְנוּ חַיָּבִין
לְהוֹדוֹת, לְהַלֵּל, לְשַׁבֵּחַ, לְפָאֵר, לְרוֹמֵם, לְהַדֵּר,
לְבָרֵךְ, לְעַלֵּה וּלְקַלֵּס לְמִי שֶׁעָשָׂה לַאֲבוֹתֵינוּ
וְלָנוּ אֶת כָּל הַנִּסִּים הָאֵלּוּ: הוֹצִיאָנוּ מֵעַבְדוּת
לְחֵרוּת, מִיָּגוֹן לְשִׂמְחָה, וּמֵאֵבֶל לְיוֹם טוֹב,
וּמֵאֲפֵלָה לְאוֹר גָּדוֹל, וּמִשִּׁעְבּוּד לִגְאֻלָּה.
וְנֹאמַר לְפָנָיו, ״הַלְלוּיָהּ!״

[ו] עַד הֵיכָן הוּא אוֹמֵר? — בֵּית שַׁמַּאי
אוֹמְרִים: עַד ״אֵם הַבָּנִים שְׂמֵחָה.״

יד אברהם

שֶׁנֶּאֱמַר: וְהִגַּדְתָּ לְבִנְךָ בַּיּוֹם הַהוּא לֵאמֹר, בַּעֲבוּר
זֶה עָשָׂה ה׳ לִי בְּצֵאתִי מִמִּצְרָיִם״ — for it is
said[Exodus 13:8]: *And you shall tell
your son on that day saying: 'For the
sake of this* [i.e., the fulfillment of His
mitzvos, such as Pesach, matzah and
marror (Rashi there)] *HASHEM did for
me when I went out of Egypt.*

In the context of the chapter in which
it appears, the phrase *on that day* refers
to an unspecified future day in generations to come, when parents who have
not personally experienced the Exodus
will relate the Exodus story to the
children. When the family celebrates
Pesach, parents will tell their children
what *HASHEM did for 'me.'*

In addition to the verse given here, the
Haggadah cites the verse (*Deut.* 6:23): *And
us He has brought out from there* as the basis
for the premise that every person should
regard the Exodus as a personal redemption.
Rambam (Hil. *Chametz* 7:6 and in his text of
the Haggadah) cites only the latter verse (see
Gem. 116b). He adds however (7:6): 'Concerning this, the Holy One, Blessed is He,
commands in the Torah (*Deut.* 5:15): *And
you shall remember that you were a slave ...*
as if to say [you should think of the Exodus]
as if you yourself had been a slave, been
redeemed, and gone out to freedom.'

לְפִיכָךְ אֲנַחְנוּ חַיָּבִין לְהוֹדוֹת, לְהַלֵּל, לְשַׁבֵּחַ,
לְפָאֵר, לְרוֹמֵם, לְהַדֵּר, לְבָרֵךְ, לְעַלֵּה, וּלְקַלֵּס, לְמִי
שֶׁעָשָׂה לַאֲבוֹתֵינוּ וְלָנוּ אֶת כָּל הַנִּסִּים הָאֵלּוּ

הוֹצִיאָנוּ מֵעַבְדוּת לְחֵרוּת מִיָּגוֹן לְשִׂמְחָה
וּמֵאֵבֶל לְיוֹם טוֹב וּמֵאֲפֵלָה לְאוֹר גָּדוֹל
וּמִשִּׁעְבּוּד לִגְאֻלָּה — *Therefore we are
obliged to give thanks, to praise, to
laud, to glorify, to exalt, to honor, to
bless, to extol, and to shower acclaim
upon Him, Who performed all these
miracles for our ancestors and for us.
He brought us forth from slavery to
freedom, from sorrow to joy, from
mourning to festivity, from darkness to
great light, and from servitude to
redemption!*

Our versions have nine expressions of
praise. Together with the *Halleluyah* with
which we conclude this passage, there is a
total of ten, corresponding to the ten syn-
onyms for praise that are found in *Psalms*, as
stated in the Gemara (117a). Thus we praise
God in nine diverse ways as a prelude to the
ultimate in praise — *Halleluyah* (*Maharal,
Gevuros Hashem* ch. 61).

Similarly, *Vilna Gaon* (comm. to *Haggadah*) offers, that the ten praises correspond
to the ten plagues. Thus *Halleluyah* —
representing *Hallel*, which is said only for
complete deliverance — corresponds to the
tenth plague which resulted in complete
freedom.

[Alternatively, it should be noted that the
Exodus is characterized in five different ways
(from slavery to freedom, etc.). Since we owe
God (at least) a two-fold thanks [טוֹבָה כְּפוּלָה,
lit. *a doubled favor*] we arrive at a total of ten
types of praise (adapted from *Rashbatz,
Maamar Afikoman*).]

And you shall tell your son on that day saying, For the sake of this HASHEM did for me when I went out from Egypt (Exodus 13:8). Therefore we are obliged to give thanks, to praise, to laud, to glorify, to exalt, to honor, to bless, to extol, and to shower acclaim upon Him Who performed all these miracles for our ancestors and for us: He brought us forth from slavery to freedom, from sorrow to joy, from mourning to festivity, from darkness to great light, and from servitude to redemption! So let us say before him — Halleluyah!

6. Until where does he recite? — Beis Shammai say: Until, *A joyful mother of children* [*Psalms*

הַלְלוּיָה!,,—לְפָנָיו וְנאמַר — *So let us say before Him, "Halleluyah!"*

[I.e., let us recite before Him the ultimate praise — *Hallel* — which starts with *Halleluyah*.]

[Alternatively, in Talmudic times the reader (חַזָּן) would recite the *Hallel* loudly, and those unable to recite it themselves would fulfill their obligation by listening to his recital and responding with *Halleluyah* at the end of each sentence (*Succah* 38b). Accordingly, in this passage of the *Haggadah*

we declare, 'Let us acclaim God with outcries of *Halleluyah.'*]

The *Gemara* (117a) states: 'Who recited (i.e., instituted) this *Hallel*? The prophets among them [i.e., the Jews departing from Egypt] instituted that Israel should recite it for every festival and at every misfortune — may it not come upon them! — from which they are redeemed, they recite it [as thanks] for their redemption.'

6.

אומֵר? הוא הֵיכָן עַד — *Until where does he recite?*

Although the previous mishnah concluded by saying that *Hallel* is to be recited (see *comm.* s.v. וְנאמַר), all agree that only a small part of *Hallel* is recited before the meal. The question of our mishnah is how much of *Hallel* is recited at this point? The reason *Hallel* is cut short before the meal is because the tannaim were anxious to finish the *Haggadah* rather quickly so that the children would not fall asleep before eating matzah (*Gem.* 109a). To avoid delay, only the section of *Hallel* that alluded to the Exodus was attached to the *Haggadah*; the rest, which alludes to the future Redemption, was left for after the meal (*Tos. Yom Tov*).

The above comment of *Tosefos Yom Tov* is based on his interpretation of R' Eliezer's statement (*Gem.* 109a) בְּלֵילֵי מַצּוֹת חוֹטְפִין, יִשְׁנוּ שֶׁלּא תִּנוֹקוֹת בִּשְׁבִיל סָחִים, *we rush* [to eat (*Rashbam*)] *matzos on the night of Pesach for the sake of children, so that they will not fall asleep*. According to this interpretation, it is logical that only the necessary portion of *Hallel* should be recited before the meal. However, *Rashbam* cites another interpretation: חוֹטְפִין, [*the matzos are*] *snatched away* ... i.e., the table bearing the matzos is taken out of the room so that the surprised children will become wide awake and ask questions. According to this interpretation, our concern is that the children stay awake to ask the four questions, not that they remain awake until matzos are eaten. If so, *Hallel* would not be abbreviated for their sake (*Kol HaRemez, Shoshanim L'David*).

Maharal (*Gevuras Hashem* ch. 62) ex-

וּבֵית הִלֵּל אוֹמְרִים: עַד ,,חַלָּמִישׁ לְמַעְיְנוֹ מָיִם.''

וְחוֹתֵם בִּגְאֻלָּה. רַבִּי טַרְפוֹן אוֹמֵר: ,,אֲשֶׁר גְּאָלָנוּ וְגָאַל אֶת אֲבוֹתֵינוּ מִמִּצְרַיִם,'' וְלֹא הָיָה חוֹתֵם.

רַבִּי עֲקִיבָא אוֹמֵר ,,כֵּן ה' אֱלֹהֵינוּ וֵאלֹהֵי אֲבוֹתֵינוּ יַגִּיעֵנוּ לְמוֹעֲדִים וְלִרְגָלִים אֲחֵרִים הַבָּאִים לִקְרָאתֵנוּ לְשָׁלוֹם, שְׂמֵחִים בְּבִנְיַן עִירֶךָ

יד אברהם

plains that the purpose of the dividing the Hallel, part before the Pesach offering is eaten and part afterwards, is to demonstrate that the praises are being said in conjunction with the feast of redemption. Indeeed, by inserting the feast in the midst of Hallel, the Sages symbolized that the very feast of Pesach is a form of praise. In the absence of the offering, matzah, which complemented the consumption of the Pesach, serves as its replacement as 'tart' of Hallel (see comm. to mishnah 8, s.v. Afikoman matzah).

בֵּית שַׁמַּאי אוֹמְרִים: עַד ,,אֵם הַבָּנִים שְׂמֵחָה.''. — Beis Shammai say: Until "A joyful mother of children" [Psalms 113:8].

[The first paragraph of Hallel.]

Tosefta (10:6); also Yerushalmi) cites Beis Shammai's justification of the view. 'Have they already exited Egypt that we mention the Exodus from Egypt?' Since the redemption did not occur until midnight — when the first-born died and Pharaoh beseeched Israel to leave — it behooves us to recite the chapter of Hallel referring specifically to the Exodus — When Israel went out of Egypt ... (Psalms 114:1) — as near to midnight as possible, hence after the meal.

The first paragraph alludes to the Exodus, because it speaks of raising up the destitute and needy and it describes Israel as servants of HASHEM implying that they were no longer slaves of Pharaoh (Kol HaRemez).

וּבֵית הִלֵּל אוֹמְרִים: עַד ,,חַלָּמִישׁ לְמַעְיְנוֹ מָיִם.''. — Beis Hillel say: Until "The flint

into a spring of water" [Psalms 114:8].

[Beis Hillel hold that the first two paragraphs of Hallel are recited.]

In view of the fact that this section of the Seder is concluded by blessing God for redeeming Israel, it is logical that we recite the portion of Hallel that speaks of the miracle at the Sea of Reeds. The true climax of the Exodus was the Splitting of the Sea and the swamping of the Egyptian army. Of that event, Scripture states that God saved Israel (Exodus 14:30), after which Israel fully believed in God and Moses (ibid. v. 31). Beis Hillel maintain that it would be incongruous to recite a blessing for redemption without mentioning its climactic event (Tos. Yom Tov).

וְחוֹתֵם בִּגְאֻלָּה — He concludes [the Haggadah] with [a blessing about] redemption.

This dictum is shared by all tannaim, but this tanna does not give the text or the extent of the blessing. That is the subject of a dispute between R' Tarfon and R' Akiva, who disagree regarding the text and nature of the blessing (Rav; Rashbam).

We must assume that this tanna expresses the unanimous view that such a blessing must be recited, but that the text of the blessing is left for R' Tarfon and R' Akiva to define. Otherwise, this unnamed tanna kamma would be assumed to be a majority, based on the general rule that an unattributed opinion is that of several tannaim. If so, the halachah would have to follow this majority view, but the accepted halachah goes ac-

10
6

113:8] Beis Hillel say: Until, *The flint into a spring of water* [*Psalms* 114:8].

He concludes [the Haggadah] with [a blessing about] redemption. R' Tarfon says: 'Who redeemed us and redeemed our ancestors from Egypt,' and he does not conclude [with a final blessing].

R' Akiva says: '... so may HASHEM our God and the God of our ancestors bring us to future festivals and pilgrimages, which approach us, in peace, gladdened in the rebuilding of Your city and joyful at

YAD AVRAHAM

cording to R' Akiva's opinion below. Consequently it is clear that there are only two opinions regarding this blessing, not three (*Rashbam*).

ר׳ טַרְפוֹן אוֹמֵר: „אֲשֶׁר גְּאָלָנוּ וְגָאַל אֶת אֲבוֹתֵינוּ מִמִּצְרַיִם — *R' Tarfon says: "Who redeemed us and redeemed our ancestors from Egypt,"*

[R' Tarfon has no need to say the obvious: that the blessing begins בָּרוּךְ אַתָּה ה׳ אֱלֹקֵינוּ מֶלֶךְ הָעוֹלָם, *Blessed are You, HASHEM, our God, King of the universe.*]

[The text of the blessing reiterates the point made above in mishnah 5, that every Jew must identify with the Exodus as though he, himself, had been redeemed from Egypt. Therefore, this text thanks God for saving *us*, as well as our ancestors.]

Rif, Rambam (Hil. Chametz 8:5), and *Rosh* add a phrase to the blessing: וְהִגִּיעָנוּ הַלַּיְלָה הַזֶּה לֶאֱכוֹל בּוֹ מַצָּה וּמָרוֹר, *and brought us on this night to eat matzah and marror.* This addition is also part of R' Akiva's blessing below and is in our text of the *Haggadah*.

וְאֵינוֹ חוֹתֵם — *and he does not conclude* [*with a final blessing*].

[The general rule is that a בְּרָכָה אֲרִיכְתָּא, *lengthy blessing*, begins with mention of God and His majesty, and concludes with a בְּרָכָה קְצָרָה, *brief blessing*, that says בָּרוּךְ אַתָּה ה׳, *Blessed are You, HASHEM*, and concludes with a very brief recapitulation of the theme of the blessing. For example, the first

blessing of *Bircas HaMazon* contains a lengthy blessing of God as the Giver of food and sustenance. In conclusion, it sums up briefly: *Blessed ...* הַזָּן אֶת הַכֹּל, *Who nourishes all*. Such a concluding blessing is unnecessary, however, if the entire blessing is brief in itself, and devoted to a single theme.]

In the case of R' Tarfon's text, the entire text of the blessing is a brief thanksgiving for redemption, consequently, there is no need to summarize it with a final blessing (*Rav; Rashbam; Tos.*).

ר׳ עֲקִיבָא אוֹמֵר: — *R' Akiva says:*

[R' Akiva adopts R' Tarfon's text as the beginning of his own blessing, but he adds to it.]

„כֵּן ה׳ אֱלֹקֵינוּ וֵאלֹקֵי אֲבוֹתֵינוּ יַגִּיעֵנוּ לְמוֹעֲדִים וְלִרְגָלִים אֲחֵרִים הַבָּאִים לִקְרָאתֵנוּ לְשָׁלוֹם, *"...so may HASHEM our God and the God of our ancestors bring us to future festivals and pilgrimages, which approach us, in peace,*

Festivals refers to Rosh Hashanah and Yom Kippur, while *pilgrimages* refers to Pesach, Shavuos, and Succos, which Jews are commanded to celebrate in Jerusalem when the Temple stands (*Abarbanel*).

Just as we have been privileged to observe the commandments of this night to eat matzah and *marror* (according to the version of *Rif, Rambam*, and *Rosh* cited above), so may we be privileged to observe the *mitzvos* of all

פסחים וְשָׂשִׂים בַּעֲבוֹדָתֶיךָ. וְנֹאכַל שָׁם מִן הַזְּבָחִים וּמִן
י/ז הַפְּסָחִים,'' כו' עַד ,,בָּרוּךְ אַתָּה ה' גָּאַל
יִשְׂרָאֵל.''

[ז] **מָזְגוּ** לוֹ כוֹס שְׁלִישִׁי, מְבָרֵךְ עַל מְזוֹנוֹ.
רְבִיעִי, גּוֹמֵר עָלָיו אֶת הַהַלֵּל,
וְאוֹמֵר עָלָיו בִּרְכַּת הַשִּׁיר.

festivals in their appointed times
(Chukas HaPesach).

שְׂמֵחִים בְּבִנְיַן עִירְךָ וְשָׂשִׂים בַּעֲבוֹדָתֶךָ. —
gladdened in the rebuilding of Your city
and joyful at Your service.

Gladdened [שִׂמְחָה] refers to public
expressions of joy, while joyful [שָׂשׂוֹן]
refers to inner happiness (Etz Chaim).

[Malbim defines שִׂמְחָה, gladness, as
happiness that may be short term, while
שָׂשׂוֹן refers to lasting joy. If so, this
phrase may imply that while we will
celebrate the rebuilding of the Temple,
it is only by serving God through performance of the commandments that we
can assure the permanence of our joy.]

וְנֹאכַל שָׁם מִן הַזְּבָחִים וּמִן הַפְּסָחִים...'' —May
we eat there [i.e., in Jerusalem] of the
[Chagigah] offerings and Pesach sacrifices...'

Ordinarily, the flesh of two sacrifices,
Chagigah and Pesach, is eaten at the
Seder feast. In compliance with the requirement that the Pesach be eaten
when one is no longer hungry, the meat
of the Chagigah is eaten first (Gem.
119b). For that reason, the Chagigah is

listed before the Pesach in the blessing
(Tos. 116b, s.v. ונאמר; Maharil).

According to Maharil and Mahari
Weil, if Pesach Eve fell on a Sabbath,
the order of this phrase is changed to
read מִן הַפְּסָחִים וּמִן הַזְּבָחִים, from the
Pesach and the Chagigah sacrifices. The
reason for the change is that a Chagigah
may not be slaughtered on the Sabbath.
On such days, only the Pesach will be
eaten at the Seder and the Chagigah will
wait until the Intermediate Days, consequently the order of the blessing should
reflect the change. The consensus of
commentators, however, oppose this
alteration, ruling that the formula of the
Sages may not be tampered with.

עַד ,,בָּרוּךְ אַתָּה ה' גָּאַל יִשְׂרָאֵל.'' — until
"Blessed are You, HASHEM, Who has
redeemed Israel."

R' Akiva's, text of the blessing is
quite lengthy. Furthermore, it includes
prayers for future good fortune in addition to its expression of thanks. Because
of its' length and the addition of new requests, it requires a brief concluding
blessing to summarize its major point
(Rav; Tos.; Rashbam).

7.

מָזְגוּ לוֹ כוֹס שְׁלִישִׁי, מְבָרֵךְ עַל מְזוֹנוֹ. — They
pour him a third cup, [and] he blesses
for his food.

The 'blessing' in this case is the Bircas
HaMazon that is recited after meals.
There is a halachic question whether a
cup of wine must always be poured for
the recitation of Bircas HaMazon, just
as the Sages ordained that many other

mitzvos — such as Kiddush, Havdalah,
and the marriage ceremony — be
honored with a cup of wine (see Gem.
105b, Tos., s.v. ש"מ ברכה; Orach
Chaim 181:1). R' Chanan (Gem. 117b)
sought to infer from our mishnah that a
cup was indeed required for the recitation of Bircas HaMazon. Rava rejected
this proof, maintaining that the Sages

משניות / פסחים [220]

Your service. May we eat there of the offerings and Pesach sacrifices ...' until 'Blessed are You HASHEM Who has redeemed Israel.

7. They pour him a third cup, [and] he blesses for his food.

A fourth [cup, and] he completes the *Hallel* over it and recites the 'Blessing of the Song' over it.

ordained four cups for the Seder in commemoration of the freedom awarded Israel at the Exodus [דֶּרֶךְ חֵרוּת]. Having provided that the cups be drunk, the Sages wished to attach each one to the performance of a *mitzvah*.

רְבִיעִי, גּוֹמֵר עָלָיו אֶת הַהַלֵּל, — *A fourth* [*cup, and*] *he completes the Hallel over it*

As noted in mishnah 6, one or two chapters of *Hallel* were recited before the feast; now the rest of *Hallel* is recited. This portion of *Hallel* alludes to Israel's exile among and servitude to the nations, the Messianic era, the resuscitation of the dead, and the World to Come; therefore it is appropriate to the second half of the Seder, which looks ahead to the future Redemption (*Gem.* 118a;).

R' Tarfon (cited in *Gem.* 118a) adds, that after the recitation of the regular *Hallel* has been completed, one should recite the הַלֵּל הַגָּדוֹל, *Great Hallel*, the title given to *Psalm* 136. That psalm is composed of twenty-six verses describing God's goodness, each of which ends with the refrain כִּי לְעוֹלָם חַסְדּוֹ, *for His kindness endures forever*. R' Yochanan explains that it is called the 'Great Hallel' because it relates that God, Who sits at the zenith of the universe, mercifully provides nourishment to every living thing. R' Yehoshua ben Levi adds that the psalm's twenty-six verses allude to the twenty-six generations from the Creation until the giving of the Torah [which lacked the merit of fulfilling *mitzvos*] but were sustained through God's mercy (*Gem.* 118a).

וְאוֹמֵר עָלָיו בִּרְכַּת הַשִּׁיר. — *and recites the*

'Blessing of the Song' over it.

What is the 'Blessing of the Song'? R' Yehudah says it is יְהַלְלוּךְ, *Let* [all your works] *praise You*, the blessing with which *Hallel* is always concluded. [It is the *blessing* of the *Hallel song* (*Rashbam*).] R' Yochanan says that the 'Blessing of the Song' is נִשְׁמַת כָּל חַי, *The soul of every living thing*, the long and beautiful song of praise — concluding with the blessing יִשְׁתַּבַּח, *Lauded ... Blessed ... God, Great king* (see *Derishah* to *Orach Chaim* 480:1). — with which the first section of the morning service is concluded on the Sabbath and festivals. [It is called 'Blessing of the Song' because it climaxes the part of *Shacharis* that is known as פְּסוּקֵי דְזִמְרָה, *Verses of Praise* (*Rashbam*).]

Rav comments that the interpretation of R' Yehudah and R' Yochanan are mutually exclusive — the blessing is either one or the other, but not both. The common custom, he adds, is to comply with both opinions by reciting both blessings.

Rashbam and *Tosafos* (118a, s.v. ר' יוחנן) maintain that R' Yochanan agrees with R' Yehudah that יְהַלְלוּךְ [*Yehalelucha*] is recited, but R' Yochanan holds that נִשְׁמַת [*Nishmas*] is recited in addition to *Yehalelucha*. As explained by *Maharsha*, this view is that two separate blessings are recited: *Yehalelucha* in its entirety, and *Nishmas* including the blessing at the end of *Yishtabach*, the prayer that concludes the section of praise beginning with *Nishmas*. According to *Rashbam*, R' Yochanan bases his contention on

בֵּין הַכּוֹסוֹת הַלָּלוּ אִם רוֹצֶה לִשְׁתּוֹת יִשְׁתֶּה.
בֵּין שְׁלִישִׁי לִרְבִיעִי לֹא יִשְׁתֶּה.

[ח] **וְאֵין** מַפְטִירִין אַחַר הַפֶּסַח אֲפִיקוֹמָן.

יד אברהם

the argument that *Yehalelucha* is always a part of *Hallel*, so there would be no need for the mishnah to single out this part of *Hallel*.

Rosh conjectures that it might indeed be necessary for the mishnah to specify *Yehalelucha*, even if no additional blessing is intended. The fact that the *Hallel* of the Seder is not preceded by a blessing could have led us to the conclusion that no final blessing is said, either. To avoid this error, the mishnah tells us that *Yehalelucha* is not omitted from the standard *Hallel* text. See *Ran*, however, for a lengthy discussion of whether or not a blessing is indeed required to introduce the *Hallel* of the Seder.

Tosafos (ibid) contends, that only if R' Yochanan holds that two separate blessings are recited can we justify the custom (current in *Tosafos'* time) of reciting two blessings. If such a double blessing were not required by either R' Yehudah or R' Yochanan, it would be forbidden to recite them, since one of the blessings would be a בְּרָכָה לְבַטָּלָה, *purposeless blessing*.

In a similar vein, *Shoshanim L'David* argues that we must maintain that R' Yochanan calls for *Nishmas* in addition to *Yehalelucha*. If we were to assume, as does *Rav*, that both amoraim hold that only one of the texts is recited, then it would be forbidden to follow *Rav's* course of reciting all the praises anyway, because the recitation of R' Yehudah's paragraphs would be a הֶפְסֵק, *interruption*, between *Hallel* and the blessing according to R' Yochanan, and vice versa.

The halachah follows the opinion of R' Chaim Kohen (118a Tos., s.v. ר׳ יוחנן) who infers from the mishnah's use of the singular form — בְּרְכַּת הַשִּׁיר, the **Blessing** of the Song — that only one blessing is recited, notwithstanding that (in his view) R' Yochanan holds that *Yehalelucha* and *Nishmas* are combined.

There are three customs regarding the exact order of the praises and the concluding blessing (see *Orach Chaim* 480 and commentaries). They are:

(a) After concluding *Hallel* and the *Great Hallel* (Psalm 136), *Nishmas* is recited until,

but not including, the blessing in *Yishtabach*. Then *Yehalelucha* and its blessing are recited.

(b) After *Hallel*, *Yehalelucha* is said without its blessing. Then the *Great Hallel* and *Nishmas* are recited up to the blessing of *Yishtabach*. Then, the blessing of *Yehalelucha* [בָּרוּךְ ... מֶלֶךְ מְהֻלָּל בַּתִּשְׁבָּחוֹת, *Blessed ... King Who is extolled with praises*] is recited.

(c) This custom is the same as number 2, except that *Yishtabach* is said to completion as the concluding blessing.

בֵּין הַכּוֹסוֹת הַלָּלוּ אִם רוֹצֶה לִשְׁתּוֹת יִשְׁתֶּה. — *Between these cups, if one wishes to drink, he may drink;*

I.e., between the first two cups and the last two cups *(Rashbam)*.

[*Rashbam's* commment seems to imply that it is forbidden to drink between the first and second cups, but see below where he seems to contradict himself.]

בֵּין שְׁלִישִׁי לִרְבִיעִי לֹא יִשְׁתֶּה. — *between the third and fourth [cups] he may not drink.*

Yerushalmi explains that if someone were to drink more wine after the third cup, he might become drunk and be unable to finish the *Haggadah*. However, we do not fear that drunkenness will result from drinking during the feast — between the second and third cups — because wine does not have so intoxicating an effect when it is taken with food *(Rav; Rashbam)*.

Rashbam adds that it is likewise permitted to drink between the first and second cups, without fear of intoxication [possibly because one is still wide awake and alert, whereas after a heavy meal and at least three cups of wine, more drink will tend to have a greater effect]. However, this is an apparent contradiction of *Rashbam* cited above that only between the second and third cups may one drink at will *(Kol HaRemez)*.

Rif cites *Yerushalmi* that it may be forbid-

Between these cups, if one wishes to drink, he may drink; between the third and fourth [cups] he may not drink.

8. **O**ne may not conclude [the feast] after the Pesach with dessert.

YAD AVRAHAM

den to drink between the first two cups as well, for fear of intoxication. The mishnah omits this law because people do not habitually drink much before the meal in any case *(Tos. Yom Tov; Orach Chaim 473:3).*

Eliyah Rabbah and *Chok Yaakov (*loc. cit.) infer that since the reason for not drinking involves possible intoxication there is no objection to drinking non-alcoholic beverages.

Ramban holds that once the second cup has been poured and the recitation of the *Haggadah* begun (see *Orach Chaim* 473:1; cf. *Beur Halachah* 473, s.v. הרשות) it is forbidden to drink. *Ran* goes a step further and forbids random drinking as soon as the second cup has been poured for the purpose of beginning the *Haggadah,* even before the recitation has begun.[1]

8.

וְאֵין מַפְטִירִין אַחַר הַפֶּסַח אֲפִיקוֹמָן. — *One may not conclude [the feast] after [eating] the Pesach with dessert.*

It was customary in the Talmudic era that after a meal was completed, various refreshments and delicacies were brought to the participants, much like the dessert of modern times. Those desserts were known as *afikoman* and were of many varieties, based on the taste of the individual eater. As examples, the *Gemara* (119b) says that *Rav* would eat fowl, *Shmuel* a mushroom dish, and R' *Yochanan* sweets *(Rav; Rashbam; Gem.* 119b).

The prohibition against eating anything after the Pesach is part of a general Rabbinic requirement (based on a Scriptural support) that all sacrificial meat be eaten כְּדֶרֶךְ שֶׁהַמְּלָכִים אוֹכְלִין, *in the manner in which kings eat.* Royalty does not eat ravenously, on an empty stomach. Therefore, sacrificial meat should be eaten preferably late in the meal, after one is no longer hungry *(Sotah* 15a; *Menachos* 21b. See *Rambam, Hil. Maaseh HaKorbanos* 10:11, and *Hil. Korban Pesach* 8:3). Were one to eat after the Pesach, his appetite would suggest that the Pesach meat left him hungry, therefore, the Sages ordained that the last taste remaining in his mouth should be that of the Pesach *(Rashbam).*

Yerushalmi offers a reason that applies only to the Pesach. Since it is forbidden to break a bone of the Pesach offering *(Exodus* 12:46; *Numbers* 9:12), the Sages forbade one to eat the Pesach while he was still hungry, lest he break a bone in his desire to get at meat or marrow.

Tosafos (119b, s.v. לא) and *Rambam (Hil. Chametz* 8:10), maintain that the reason (applying to both the matzah and the Pesach; see below) is so that 'the taste of the Pesach and the matzah remain in his mouth' (cf. *Baal HaMaor, Milchamos* and *Meiri).*

1. *Mishnah Berurah* (473:13) contends that according to the practice cited by *Rama* (474) that a blessing must be made over each of the four cups, any random drinking would automatically require a blessing, because it is taken for granted that the wine-blessing of *Kiddush* was not meant to apply to all drinking during the Seder. If so, it would be forbidden to drink even between the first two cups because a blessing would be required and that would make it appear as though the drinker was adding to the ordained number of four cups. If no blessing were necessary — e.g., if he had in mind during *Kiddush* that he would drink more wine later — then the question of drinking between the first two cups would depend on the views cited in the commentary.

יָשְׁנוּ מִקְצָתָן, יֹאכֵלוּ; כֻּלָּן, לֹא יֹאכֵלוּ.
רַבִּי יוֹסֵי אוֹמֵר: נִתְנַמְנְמוּ, יֹאכֵלוּ; נִרְדְּמוּ,
לֹא יֹאכֵלוּ.

יד אברהם

⏴§ The Afikoman Matzah

One of the most popular features of the Seder ritual is the portion of matzah known as the *Afikoman*. As used in our mishnah, however, the word *afikoman* refers to various delicacies eaten as dessert — why is it applied to matzah?

The *Gemara* (119b) cites the view of Shmuel (according to the version accepted as halachah), that just as one does not eat an [*Afikoman*] dessert after the flesh of the Pesach, so, too, in the absence of the sacrifice, one does not conclude the matzah feast, i.e. *Seder*, with dessert. Since the Sages ordained that the *Seder* meal must be concluded with the final portion of matzah, it came to be called *Afikoman*, 'dessert.'

Although the rule forbidding food after the Pesach applies equally to matzah, the mishnah specifies only Pesach in this regard, despite the possibility of an erroneous inference that one may eat other foods after matzah. The *Gemara* (119b) explains that Pesach had to be specified because of its novelty. We would have reasoned that one surely may not eat after matzah, for the eating will obliterate the insubstantial taste of the matzah from his mouth (see above. s.v. אין מפטירין), but one should be permitted to eat after the Pesach, for the strong, pungent taste of roast meat will not fade as a result. Therefore the Mishnah teaches that *even* after the Pesach, one may not 'conclude with dessert.'

⏴§ What is the Reason for Eating the Matzah Last?

In the commentary to the mishnah we have outlined three reasons for the ruling not to eat after the Pesach. The reason cited there as the view of *Tosafos* and *Rambam* — that the taste of Pesach should remain in his mouth — applies equally to matzah, or is even *more* pertinent to matzah, as argued by the above cited *Gemara*. However according to the two other views — that a sacrifice should be eaten in a 'royal' manner or that the Sages wanted to avoid the possibility of hungry eaters breaking a bone of the Pesach — a rationale is needed to justify the application of this rule to matzah.

There are two approaches to this problem. One view (*Tos.* 120a, s.v. באחרונה, *Rashi* and *Rashbam* 119b, s.v. אין מפטירין אחר מצה) contends that the matzah always was eaten with the Pesach in Temple days, consequently it was eaten at the end of the meal. We imitiate this practice in our time as a memorial to the Temple practice (זֵכֶר לַמִּקְדָּשׁ). A very similar, though essentially different, approach is taken by some (*Ramban* in *Milchamos*; *Meiri*; *Baal HaMaor*; cf. *Hasagos* of *Ravad* there). In lieu of the Pesach offering, we eat an olive's volume of matzah to commemorate the Pesach. This consumption of matzah should therefore conform to all the strictures of the Pesach it commemorates (cf. *R' David*).

Interestingly, *Bach* (to *Orach Chaim* 471; also *Maharil* cited by *Magen Avraham* 471:1) combines both of these approaches. He rules that one should eat the volume of two olives, one in commemoration of the Pesach, and the second to remember the matzah eaten with the Pesach at the end of the meal.

יָשְׁנוּ מִקְצָתָן, יֹאכֵלוּ; — *If some fell asleep, they may eat;*

The mishnah (7:13) taught earlier, that it is forbidden for members of a group to begin eating their Pesach offer- ing in one location, and then take it somewhere else to finish eating. Although a Pesach may be divided among two groups, each group may eat it in only one place.[1] Our mishnah teaches

10
8

If some fell asleep, they may eat; if all, they may not eat.

R' Yose says: If they dozed, they may eat; if they fell into deep sleep, they may not eat.

YAD AVRAHAM

that under certain circumstances, the Rabbis decreed that the group is considered to have ceased to exist as a unit. For its members to reconstitute themselves even in the same place is forbidden Rabbinically, because it appears similar to a case of the same group moving elsewhere to continue its eating.

The Rabbis consider sleep equivalent to having concluded the meal and left the place, because when someone sleeps he cannot be considered as yet intending to resume the meal. If the meal is subsequently resumed, it is viewed as a different meal, distinct from the previous one. As such it would be considered as if the Pesach was eaten in two places. The mishnah teaches, however, that if only one person fell asleep, this is not viewed as a dissolution of the group for even that individual (because the group is still intact), and all — even the individual who had slept — may eat (Rav; Rashbam).

Ravad (Hasagos on Baal HaMaor here; Hil Chametz 8:14), has a different approach to this mishnah. In his view the Pesach becomes disqualified if the entire group fell asleep. The Torah requires that terumah and sacrificial meat must be safeguarded at all times, and that הֶיסַח הַדַּעַת, removal of attention, is a disqualification (see Gem. 34a-b). If everyone fell asleep, no one is caring for the Pesach and it is disqualified.

Ravad bases this view on Yerushalmi, but it cannot be reconciled with our versions of Yerushalmi.

Yet another view is presented in Kessef

Mishneh (loc. cit.). The rule discussed here is based on the first law of the mishnah that one may not conclude after the Pesach with dessert. If the group has slept, the meal is considered concluded, and they may not eat again, even from their own Pesach (see Tur Orach Chaim 478).

כֻּלָּן, לֹא יֹאכֵלוּ. — if all [of them fell asleep], they may not eat.

For this would be considered eating the Pesach in two places, as explained above.

In view of the Gemara's ruling that the law not to 'conclude...the Pesach with dessert' applies equally to the Afikoman matzah with which we conclude our Seder feast, does the rule regarding sleep during the consumption of the Pesach apply to the Afikoman matzah? If so, one who falls asleep after eating part of the Afikoman would not be permitted to eat matzah afterward. Rambam and Rashbam (Hil. Chametz 8:14) hold that it does apply (see also Rif and Rosh), while Ravad (loc. cit., Hasagos to Baal HaMaor) and Baal HaMaor disagree, arguing that the requirement upon which this law is based does not apply to the Afikoman matzah. Shulchan Aruch (Orach Chaim 478:2) rules according to the former view that one may not eat after falling asleep. Rama (there sec. 1) adds that the Afikoman, like the Pesach, may not be eaten in two places.[2]

רַבִּי יוֹסֵי אוֹמֵר נִתְנַמְנְמוּ, יֹאכֵלוּ; — R' Yose says: If they [merely] dozed, they may eat;

Dozing is not in the category of 'sleep' in terms of this law.

The Gemara (120b) defines dozing as

1. As noted, this mishnah has been explained according to the opinion accepted earlier (7:13). According to the divergent opinion of R' Shimon (Gemara 86a), an individual may eat his portion of the Pesach in two places, but a Pesach offering may not be divided among two different groups. Thus, the law propounded here is a logical extension of his ruling: after falling asleep the group is considered dissolved, and for them to resume the meal later is equivalent to eating the Pesach in two groups (cf. R' David).

2. Although they agree that matzah is not similar to Pesach, Ravad and Baal HaMaor disagree on the reason for the distinction between the two. Ravad, following his view (see footnote to s.v. ישנו מקצתן) that sleeping is analogous to the disqualification of הֶיסַח הַדַּעַת, removal of at-

[ט] הַפֶּסַח אַחַר חֲצוֹת מְטַמֵּא אֶת הַיָּדַיִם. הַפִּגּוּל וְהַנּוֹתָר מְטַמְּאִין אֶת הַיָּדַיִם.

בֵּרַךְ בִּרְכַּת הַפֶּסַח, פָּטַר אֶת שֶׁל זֶבַח; בֵּרַךְ

יד אברהם

'sleeping yet not sleeping, awake yet not awake', e.g., if someone calls him he answers, yet he cannot respond coherently; however, if he is reminded [of something] he recalls.'

נִרְדְּמוּ, לֹא יֹאכֵלוּ — *if they fell into a deep sleep, they may not eat.*

R' Yose refers to the clause in the first tanna's words permitting them to eat if only 'some of them slept.' R' Yose modifies this and maintains that this is so only if they merely dozed. But if any individual members of the group fell into a deep sleep, those people may not eat, even if part of the group remained awake. If the entire group dozed, even if they did not sleep deeply, they may also not eat *(Rav; Rashbam).*

Rambam (*Comm.; Hil Chametz* 8:14) holds a view diametrically opposed to Rav's. R' Yose refers to the clause forbidding them to eat if they all fell asleep. To this R' Yose adds a distinction. They are forbidden to eat only if they had fallen into a dead sleep. But if they, i.e., the entire group, merely dozed, they may nevertheless eat.

The halachah follows R' Yose *(Rav; Rambam, Comm., Hil. Chametz* 8:14).

9.

הַפֶּסַח אַחַר חֲצוֹת מְטַמֵּא אֶת הַיָּדַיִם. — *The Pesach offering contaminates one's hands after midnight.*

Like all other offerings on the last night allotted for their consumption, the Pesach offering may be eaten only until midnight. According to the view followed by our mishnah, however, the Pesach differs from other offerings. While they are prohibited only *Rabbinically* in the second half of the night — 'to keep a man distant from transgression' *(Berachos* 1:1) — the Pesach's permissible term of eating expires at midnight by *Scriptural* law. Consequently, at midnight it is not only forbidden for consumption, it becomes נוֹתָר, *leftover (Gemara* 20b). The Rabbis decreed contamination upon the hands of anyone touching 'leftover' sacrificial meat. Though other sacrifices become 'leftover' only in the morning, the Pesach becomes 'leftover' at mid-

night. Accordingly, it contaminates hands from midnight, while this decree of contamination applies to other offerings only in the morning.

The *Gemara* (120b) points out that this is the opinion of R' Elazar ben Azaryah. In R' Akiva's view, the Pesach does not differ from other offerings; it, too, may be eaten until dawn under Scriptural law. According to R' Akiva, since the prohibition of the Pesach after midnight is only Rabbinical, its flesh is not subject to the stricture of contamination until dawn.

Rashbam (120b, s.v. ר' אלעזר) comments that according to R' Elazar ben Azaryah (our mishnah), the phrase, in *Exodus* (12:10): *You shall not leave over of it until the morning and whatever is left over of it in the morning you shall burn with fire,* refers only to the time of burning the leftover, which may not be burned at night (see *Gem.* 3a). The verse must be construed as follows: *You shall not* [cause anyone to] *leave over of it*

tention, maintains that this disqualification is not applicable to matzah. Baal HaMaor argues that the analogy of matzah to Pesach surely should not extend to the rule mandating that the Pesach be eaten in one place (see *Rashbam* 120a, s.v. ישנו כולן, *Tos.* 119b, s.v. אמר, *Rama* in *Orach Chaim* 478:1). According to the interpretation given above in *Kessef Mishneh's* name (s.v. ישנו מקצתן), it is logical to assume that the rule regarding sleeping applies to matzah.

9. The Pesach offering contaminates one's hands after midnight. *Piggul* and leftover [sacrificial meat] contaminate the hands.

If he recited the blessing for the Pesach offering he exempts the blessing of the [*Chagigah*] offering —

YAD AVRAHAM

[i.e., by failing to consume the meat before midnight], *until the morning* [but] *whatever is left over of it,* [only] *in the morning shall you burn it with fire* (see *Tos. Berachos* 9a, s.v. ר' אליעזר; *Tzlach* here and *Berachos*).

Though the disagreement involves the Pesach meat, it has implications for current practice. The *Afikoman* that is eaten at the conclusion of the Seder meal commemorates the Pesach, and is subject to the same laws. Also, the *mitzvah* of matzah is exegetically linked to that of Pesach, and is subject to the same time limitations (*Gem.* 120b; see *Tos.* 99b, s.v. עד שתחשך and *comm.* to 10:1). *Rambam* (Hil. *Korban Pesach* 8:15) rules according to R' Akiva, while *Tosafos* (120b, s.v. אמר) adopts R' Elazar ben Azaryah's view. *Rosh* (here) comments that even in R' Akiva's view one should, ideally, eat the matzah before midnight 'in order to keep distant from a transgression,' consequently the question becomes academic since all agree that one *should* eat the *Afikoman* before midnight. *Shulchan Aruch* (477:1) rules that even the *afikoman* should be eaten before midnight. However, if one did not eat any matzah at all before midnight, there is a question among the authorities as to whether the eater may recite the blessing (*Blessed ... and has commanded us concerning the eating of matzah;* see *Mishnah Berurah* there).

הַפִּגּוּל — *Piggul* [lit. *abomination*]

Although the word *piggul* has the general meaning of abomination, it is most often used to denote a sacrificial animal if disqualified in the following manner: during his performance of any of the four blood services (slaughter, receiving the blood, transporting it to the altar, and throwing it upon the altar), the *Kohen* had the intent[1] of eating its meat or burning its sacrificial parts on the altar after the time allotted by the Torah. For example, if someone received the blood of a peace offering with the intention that the meat would be eaten for three full days, instead of the permissible two days and a night, the offering is disqualified immediately and its consumption is prohibited even though the intention was not carried out. The punishment for eating the meat at any time is *kares,* spiritual excision. The name given this disqualification by the Torah (*Leviticus* 7:18) is *Piggul.*

וְהַנּוֹתָר —*and 'leftover'* [sacrificial meat]

Flesh of sacrifices that had actually been left beyond the time alotted for its consumption, is thereby disqualified and must be burned.

מְטַמְּאִין אֶת הַיָּדַיִם. — *contaminate the hands.*

If one's hands come in contact with the above substances, they — i.e., the hands only — acquire a Rabbinic contamination (of the degree of *sheni;* see Hil. *Avos HaTumah* 8:3 and preface to 1:6).

[For other cases where the Rabbis decreed contamination of hands, see *Zavin* 5:12, 3:2-5, *Shabbos* 14a).]

בֵּרַךְ בִּרְכַּת הַפֶּסַח — *If he recited the blessing for the Pesach offering*

Before partaking of the Pesach, one recites a blessing just as one does before

---

1. The *Gemara* (120b-121a) gives differing reasons for the Sages' decree regarding *piggul* and leftover. In the latter case their ruling was intended to spur 'the lazy among the *Kohanim*' to make sure the entire offering was consumed. The knowledge that they might be contaminated, and thereby disqualified to perform the service and to eat sacrifices, would spur them to eat their meat in time. For *piggul* the reason is concern that the *Kohen* performing the service [perhaps because of a personal antipathy to the owner of the offering (*Tif. Yis.*)] may intentionally disqualify an offering with illicit intent. The fear of ensuing contamination might prevent such behavior.

פְּסָחִים אֶת שֶׁל זֶבַח, לֹא פָּטַר אֶת שֶׁל פֶּסַח — דִּבְרֵי ט/י רַבִּי יִשְׁמָעֵאל.
רַבִּי עֲקִיבָא אוֹמֵר: לֹא זוֹ פוֹטֶרֶת זוֹ, וְלֹא זוֹ פוֹטֶרֶת זוֹ.

יד אברהם

the performance of most *mitzvos*. *Tosefta* (10:8) gives the formula for this blessing as: *Blessed ... Who has sanctified us by His commandments, and has commanded us to eat the Pesach (Rashbam).*

פָּטַר אֶת שֶׁל זֶבַח. — *he exempts [the blessing] of the offering.*

As mentioned above 6:3-4, a *Chagigah* offering was sometimes brought in conjunction with the Pesach, to ensure that the participants in the feast would not be hungry when they ate the Pesach. If eaten before the Pesach offering, a blessing would be said over the *Chagigah* too: *Blessed ... Who has sanctified us by His commandments, and commanded us to eat the offering (Rashbam; Rambam).* Or, alternatively if he brought vow or donative offerings on Pesach eve and eats of them at the Seder meal, the Pesach blessing exempts him from reciting a blessing before partaking of them *(Rashbam).*

The commentators wonder how it is possible that he ate of the Pesach first, in view of the law postulated earlier (mishnah 8) that nothing be eaten after the Pesach offering.

Tzlach resolves this by demonstrating from *Rambam's* account of the Seder procedure in the Temple era *(Hil. Chametz* 8:7, 9), that the Pesach was eaten twice during the meal. It was eaten at the *beginning* of the meal, immediately after matzah and *marror* and a blessing was recited over it. At the conclusion of the meal, at least an olive's volume of Pesach meat was eaten again, and after that, no other food may be eaten.

Tzlach also wonders how the blessing that specifies Pesach meat can be considered to include other offerings? Why should it be different from a wine blessing made for cake? He resolves this by referring to the view of the amora Rav *(Gemara* 70b), who finds Scriptural support for the offering of a *Chagigah* on the eve of Pesach in the verse *(Deuteronomy* 16:2), *And you shall slaughter a Pesach to HASHEM, flocks and cattle.* Since cattle are not fit for the Pesach offering, it is inferred that the reference to cattle implies the *Chagigah* offering. It follows, therefore, that this *Chagigah* is, by extension, also included in the term Pesach, and can be included in the blessing under that name. [*T'zlach's* answer, however, does not resolve this question according to the view (see *Rashbam* above) that the word *offering* in the mishnah may refer to offerings other than the *Chagigah.*]

10
9
[but] if he recited that of the [*Chagigah*] offering,
he does not exempt that of the Pesach offering —
these are the words of R' Yishmael.

R' Akiva says: This one does not exempt that one,
nor does that one exempt this one.

בֵּרַךְ אֶת שֶׁל זֶבַח, — [*but*] *if he recited that*
[i.e. the blessing] *of the offering,*
[I.e., he ate first of the other offering.]

לֹא פָּטַר אֶת שֶׁל פֶּסַח — דִּבְרֵי רַבִּי יִשְׁמָעֵאל.
— *he does not exempt that* [i.e. the bles-
sing] *of the Pesach offering — these are
the words of R' Yishmael*
[The Pesach is not included by the
term *offering* used in that blessing.]

The *Gemara* (121a with *Rashbam*)
explains that since all offerings other
than Pesach have their blood 'thrown'
toward the altar from a distance, the
generic term, זֶבַח, *offering,* connotes an
offering of this type. The Pesach, which
has its blood 'poured' downward[1], i.e.
in a nearly perpendicular direction, is
therefore not included under this term
זֶבַח, *offering,* nor can the blessing, *to eat
the offering,* exempt the consumption

of the Pesach. Despite this difference in
the manner of offering blood, the term
Pesach can include the *Chagigah,* for, in
R' Yishmael's view, even offerings
whose blood service should be done
through 'throwing', are nonetheless
valid if their blood was poured in the
fashion of the Pesach.

רַבִּי עֲקִיבָא אוֹמֵר: לֹא זוֹ פוֹטֶרֶת זוֹ, וְלֹא זוֹ
פוֹטֶרֶת זוֹ. — *R' Akiva says: This one* [the
offering] *does not exempt that one* [the
Pesach], *nor does that one* [the Pesach]
exempt this one [the offering].

R' Akiva holds that other offerings
cannot be validated by 'pouring' their
blood upon the altar. Since the two ir-
reconcilable, different blood services are
other offerings cannot be included under the term Pesach, just as Pesach cannot be included under the term זֶבַח, *offering* (*Gemara* 121a with *Rashbam*).

1. That the blood of the Pesach is 'poured' and not 'thrown' is assumed to be the view of R'
Akiva and R' Yishmael (*Gem.* 121a; see *Rashbam,* s.v. כשתימצי לומר). However, as pointed
out by the *Gemara* (63b), the mishnah (5:6), in describing the blood service of the Pesach, uses
the term 'throws'. The *Gemara* (*ibid.*) comments that mishnah follows the divergent opinion
of R' Yose HaGlili who holds 'throwing' to be the mode mandated by the Torah even for the
Pesach's blood.

Appendix: Search and Nullification

◈§ The בְּדִיקָה — 'Search'

This tractate begins, appropriately, with the first *mitzvah* connected with the Pesach festival, בְּדִיקַת חָמֵץ, the *search for chametz*. This mitzvah is predicated upon the dual *mitzvos* of:

1. Eliminating *chametz* [הַשְׁבָּתָה] from Jewish possession, as stated in Scripture (*Exodus 12:15*): *But on the first day shall you eliminate leaven from your premises.* The Sages (*Gem.* 4b-5b) demonstrate exegetically that the Torah refers not to the first day of Pesach, but to the day *before* the festival (alternatively; to the 'first day' counting from the offering of the Pesach sacrifice.) The Sages demonstrate further through Talmudic exegesis that this *mitzvah* applies only to the second half of the day — from noon — preceding the festival[1].

2. The prohibition against having or keeping *chametz* during Passover. This prohibition is expressed variously as (*Exodus 13:7*): לֹא יֵרָאֶה לְךָ חָמֵץ, *chametz shall not be seen with you*, and (*Exodus 12:1*): שִׁבְעַת יָמִים שְׂאוֹר לֹא יִמָּצֵא בְּבָתֵּיכֶם, [*for*] *seven days leaven shall not be found in your houses.*

There is much discussion among the commentators as to whether the 'search' for *chametz* is a Torah obligation, or only a Rabbinic *mitzvah*. The discussion centers on two questions: (a) Is the presumption that *chametz* is present founded on the rules of evidence and probability that are generally used to decide such questions under Torah law? and (b) even if we are to *assume* — without *positive* knowledge — that *chametz* is present, does the Torah's prohibition against possession extend even to *chametz* whose existence is in doubt or whose whereabouts is unknown? Both these questions are discussed at length by the later commentators (see *Pri Chadash* to *Orach Chaim* 431; *Pnei Yehoshua* and *Ohr Chadash* at the beginning of *Pesachim, Mekor Chaim* in preface to chapter 431 and many others; see also *Maharsha* and *Maharshal*, 6a s.v. ואם לא בדק: *Tos.* 21a, s.v. ואי; *Ran* 2a, s.v. אלא).

However, the text of the *Gemara* (4b: בְּדִיקַת חָמֵץ מִדְּרַבָּנָן דְּמִדְאוֹרַיְיתָא בְּבִיטוּל בְּעָלְמָא סַגִּי) suggests, that the obligation to search for *chametz* is of Scriptural origin (see also *Tur Orach Chaim* 434) — unless בִּיטוּל, *nullification*, has been made. 'Nullification' is a declaration of conscious intent by the owner that he considers his *chametz* to be 'null', i.e., valueless, in his eyes. By doing so he divests himself of the obligation to search for and destroy this *chametz* (see further, s.v. בִּיטוּל, *nullification*)

Based on the above cited *Gemara*, it is the unanimous consensus of the authorities that nullification removes the obligation to search. It is equally clear, however, from the first mishnah of our tractate that one *must* perform the search, even if he has chosen to nullify the *chametz*. There are various solutions to this apparent contradiction.

Rashi (2a, s.v. בודקין), as explained by *Ran*, says the search is necessary to avoid [a possible] transgression of the prohibition against keeping *chametz*, because the Sages refused to rely solely on the device of nullification. By definition, nullification is a wholehearted declaration of the nullity and valuelessness of the *chametz* — and it is possible that an owner may not have meant his nullification sincerely, in which case it would have no validity. In a similar vein, *Rav* and *Nimukei Yosef* suggest that after nullification, one may find an appetizing cookie and — forgetting that it is Pesach — intend to eat it, thereby retroactively voiding his nullification, because he will have demonstrated that the *chametz* in question was not truly worthless to him. *Tosafos* (2a, s.v. אור) maintains that nullification would indeed suffice for the Scriptural requirement, but the Rabbinic obligation to search is based

on an apprehension that the continued presence of *chametz* in the house may lead to inadvertent consumption. [*Tosafos* does not share the fear that the nullification will prove retroactively invalid.]

The *Gemara* (6b) adds that merely searching for *chametz* is insufficient, unless it is followed by nullification. The Sages were apprehensive that some *chametz* would be overlooked during the search and subsequently found; whereupon the owner would transgress the prohibition against keeping *chametz*, unless he destroyed it immediately. Having nullified it, however, nothing is transgressed if the *chametz* is later found, even though it must be destroyed by Rabbinic law.

◆§ בִּיטוּל — Nullification

As noted above, nullification is sufficient to comply with the Scriptural prohibition against keeping *chametz*. Although mentioned only once in the mishnah (3:7), nullification plays an important role in the laws of *chametz* and is a required part in the halachic process of *chametz*-removal. As many commentators note, nullification [*bitul*] is a unique concept, one that is virtually without parallel in Halachah.

Performance of Nullification

Yerushalmi gives the following formula to be recited for nullification: כָּל חָמֵץ שֶׁיֵּשׁ לִי בְּתוֹךְ בֵּיתִי וְאֵינִי יוֹדֵעַ יִבָּטֵל, *Let all chametz that I have in my possession, about which I am unaware, be nullified. Rashi* (4a, s.v. חובת הדר) cites part of an Aramaic version similar to *Yerushalmi's* text. The formula now used (with slight variations) is: 'Let all *chametz* that is in my possession, which I have not seen and have not destroyed, be nullified and be considered like the soil of the earth.' Mishnah 3:7 states clearly that one may 'nullify in his heart,' but some commentators (*Ritva* 7a, to *Kiddushin* 42b) maintain that the *bitul* must be enunciated; the above mishnah means only that it need not be recited loudly. At any rate, *Shulchan Aruch* (*Orach Chaim* 434:2) rules one should *say* the nullification formula (at least preferably).

The Scriptural Sources

Some authorities (*Rashi* 4b, s.v. בביטול: *Rambam Hil. Chametz* 2:2) believe that the *elimination* of *chametz* mandated by the Torah *(Exodus* 12:15): *And on the first day shall you eliminate leaven from your houses,* refers to mental and verbal elimination through nullification. Others hold that no Scriptural source is necessary, for nullification is merely the process of removing ownership from the *chametz,* thereby relieving the erstwhile owner of responsibility for it, since one is not held culpable for *chametz* that is not his own *(Gem.* 5b). In this vein, *Sifre* (to *Deuteronomy* 16:4, cited by *Ran* 2a) comments on the verse *(Exodus* 13:7): *And leaven shall not be seen with you* [i.e. in your possession] the following: 'Nullify [the *chametz*] in your heart' [because then the *chametz* is not longer yours].

Legal Basis of Nullification

We have seen that *bitul* frees one from the transgression of owning *chametz* on

---

1. There is much discussion among Talmudic scholars about whether this *mitzvah* mandates that one must actively eliminate and destroy any *chametz* in his possession, or whether it is merely a passive requirement that one not *have* any *chametz*, and that destruction of the *chametz* is the *means* to achieve that *mitzvah* rather than the *mitzvah* itself (see *Minchas Chinuch* 9, *Chidushei R' Chaim HaLevi* to *Hil. Chametz; Teshuvos Maharik* 174; *Teshuvos Avnei Nezer, Orach Chaim* 318 and others). A related question (according to the first view that destruction *per se* is the *mitzvah*) is whether the *chametz* must be destroyed before noon of the fourteenth or that Scripturally one can (or should) wait until after noon (see *R' Isser Z. Meltzer's* glosses to *Ramban Pesachim; Mordechai* 533).

Pesach, but how does this process operate? This question is closely related to the problem of the sources. According to one view, the mental nullification of the *chametz* puts it in the category of a non-food, and as such not classifiable as *chametz (Ramban Likutim,* see *Teshuvos Avnei Nezer, Orach Chaim* 317; *Meiri* 6b, cf. his *Magen Avos* 18; at length in *Maharam Chalavah* 6b). Those espousing this view must hold that nullification has a specific Scriptural basis, otherwise a mere declaration could not transform an edible food into a non-food. *Tosafos* (4b, s.v. מדאורייתא) maintains that nullification is no different than the familiar forfeiture of ownership (הֶפְקֵר). But others *(Ran, Ramban)* object that the text of the *bitul* formula employed does not suggest forfeiture; rather the *chametz* is rendered ownerless for a different reason. The *Gemara* (6b) states that because no benefit may be derived from *chametz* on Pesach, it is intrinsically ownerless, since 'ownership' implies the possession of an object's monetary value. If *chametz* has no utility or value because the Torah prohibits its use, it is worthless and hence ownerless. That someone is held in violation of the Torah's injunction against possessing *chametz* is because the Torah imposes the responsibility on the 'owner' as if it were really his. Thus a formal declaration that the *chametz* is null and worthless in one's eyes suffices to remove this technical, 'imposed' ownership, consequently rendering the worthless *chametz* truly ownerless, a condition that it had as a practical matter in any case.

What Nullification Accomplishes

Nullification removes the Scriptural prohibition against keeping *chametz*, yet Rabbinic law mandates that nonetheless, the *chametz* must be searched out and destroyed (see *comm.* to 1:1). In certain circumstances, where destruction of the *chametz* would present undue difficulty, nulllification suffices (see 3:7; 2:3; with *comm.*). The Sages also ruled that one not rely on the 'search' itself, but rather that as a matter of course, everyone nullify his unknown and unfound *chametz (Gem.* 6b).

⊷§ מסכת שקלים §⊷

⊷§ Tractate Shekalim

Translation and anthologized commentary by
Rabbi Hersh Goldwurm

Mesorah Publications, ltd

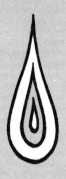

⇜§ Tractate Shekalim

כִּי תִשָּׂא אֶת־רֹאשׁ בְּנֵי־יִשְׂרָאֵל לִפְקֻדֵיהֶם וְנָתְנוּ אִישׁ כֹּפֶר נַפְשׁוֹ לַה׳ בִּפְקֹד אֹתָם
וְלֹא־יִהְיֶה בָהֶם נֶגֶף בִּפְקֹד אֹתָם: זֶה יִתְּנוּ כָּל־הָעֹבֵר עַל־הַפְּקֻדִים מַחֲצִית הַשֶּׁקֶל
בְּשֶׁקֶל הַקֹּדֶשׁ עֶשְׂרִים גֵּרָה הַשֶּׁקֶל מַחֲצִית הַשֶּׁקֶל תְּרוּמָה לַה׳: כֹּל הָעֹבֵר עַל־
הַפְּקֻדִים מִבֶּן עֶשְׂרִים שָׁנָה וָמָעְלָה יִתֵּן תְּרוּמַת ה׳: הֶעָשִׁיר לֹא־יַרְבֶּה וְהַדַּל לֹא
יַמְעִיט מִמַּחֲצִית הַשֶּׁקֶל לָתֵת אֶת־תְּרוּמַת ה׳ לְכַפֵּר עַל־נַפְשֹׁתֵיכֶם: וְלָקַחְתָּ אֶת־
כֶּסֶף הַכִּפֻּרִים מֵאֵת בְּנֵי יִשְׂרָאֵל וְנָתַתָּ אֹתוֹ עַל־עֲבֹדַת אֹהֶל מוֹעֵד וְהָיָה לִבְנֵי
יִשְׂרָאֵל לְזִכָּרוֹן לִפְנֵי ה׳ לְכַפֵּר עַל־נַפְשֹׁתֵיכֶם:

When you will count the heads of the Children of Israel to determine their numbers, let each man give the redemption of his soul to HASHEM, when you number them. Thus there shall be no plague when you number them. This shall they give, all who pass among the numbered, half a shekel in the shekel of the Sanctuary — twenty gerah to the shekel — half a shekel, a Terumah to HASHEM. All who pass among the numbered, from twenty years and older, shall give the Terumah of HASHEM. The wealthy may not increase nor may the indigent decrease from half a shekel, to give the Terumah of HASHEM, to atone for your souls. And you shall take the redemption money from the Children of Israel and give it for the service of the Tent of Meeting; then it shall be a memorial for the Children of Israel before HASHEM, to atone for your souls (Exodus 30:12-16).

Although the above verses seem to refer only to the contribution of a half shekel to facilitate a census, the Sages understood them also as a command to contribute yearly to a Temple fund for the purchase of the communal sacrifices ordained by the Torah (see *Sefer HaChinuch* 105; *Semag, asseh* 45; *Sefer HaMitzvos* of *R' Saadyah Gaon, asseh* 20; cf. *Ibn Ezra* and *Perush R' Avraham ben HaRambam* to *Exodus* 30:13).

As the Scriptural source of the annual half shekel head tax, *Rambam (Comm.* and *Sefer HaMitzvos, asseh* 172) adduces without explanation זֶה יִתְּנוּ ... מַחֲצִית הַשֶּׁקֶל בְּשֶׁקֶל הַקֹּדֶשׁ, *This shall they give ... half a shekel in the shekel of the Sanctuary.*

Rashi (to *Exodus* 30:15, based on *Yerushalmi* and *Megillah* 29b), understands the verse, הֶעָשִׁיר לֹא־יַרְבֶּה ... לְכַפֵּר עַל־נַפְשֹׁתֵיכֶם, *the wealthy may not increase ... to atone for your souls,* as an allusion to the communal sacrifices. Since they serve as an atonement, all Jews must have an equal share.

A third opinion derives the annual contribution from the concluding passage of this section (*v.* 16): וְהָיָה לִבְנֵי יִשְׂרָאֵל לְזִכָּרוֹן לִפְנֵי ה׳ לְכַפֵּר עַל־נַפְשֹׁתֵיכֶם, *Then it shall be a memorial for the Children of Israel before HASHEM, to atone for your souls* (*Abarbanel; Malbim*). According to this opinion, the final phrase refers to the proceeds from the census as well as to the contributions for building the Tabernacle. That the census, too, is described as coming *to atone* indicates that the funds are used for the regular offering. The entire section in *Exodus* (30:12-16) is modified by this last phrase and refers both to the half shekel given for the census *and* to the yearly payment to the Temple. This explains *Rambam's* view (cited

משניות / שקלים [2]

above) that even those verses clearly referring to the census are taken to refer also to the yearly half shekel.

R' Saadyah Gaon (cited by Ibn Ezra, cf. Perush R' Avraham ben HaRambam) adduces proof from II Chronicles (24:6) that the half shekel was meant to be given yearly to the Temple. There, King Yoash complains to the Kohen Gadol Yehoyada, 'Why have you not required the Levites to bring in ... the tax of Moses ... ?'

Although the mitzvah of shekel was mandatory only as long as the Temple stood (Mishnah 8:8; Rambam, Hil. Shekalim 1:8), its observance is still commemorated in the custom of contributing half of the current currency unit — i.e. half a dollar, half a pound — to charity on Purim eve before the reading of the Megillah (Rama, Orach Chaim 694:1; see Darkei Moshe to Tur there).

The first half of Tractate Shekalim discusses the collection of the annual half shekel head tax (chaps. 1-2) and how this money was disbursed (chaps. 3-4). The latter half (chaps. 5-8) discusses the administrative structure of the Temple, the different types of donations given, and other tangential subjects related to the Temple.

Logically, the subject matter of this tractate belongs in Seder Kodashim which discusses the sacrifices and other procedures of the Temple. However, because the time allotted for the giving of the shekel — the month of Adar — closely precedes the festival of Pesach and is thus considered germane to that festival, it was placed here (cf. R' Sherira Gaon cited by Tos. Yom Tov).

Shekalim is the only tractate in Seder Moed which has no corresponding Gemara in the Babylonian Talmud. For this reason, most editions of the Babylonian Talmud contain the version of Yerushalmi. Thus, the commentary will use the abbreviation Yer. (for Yerushalmi) rather than Gem. (for Gemara) which is used in the other tractates.

שקלים [א] **בְּאֶחָד** בַּאֲדָר מַשְׁמִיעִין עַל־הַשְּׁקָלִים
א/א
וְעַל־הַכִּלְאָיִם.
בַּחֲמִשָּׁה עָשָׂר בּוֹ קוֹרִין אֶת־הַמְּגִלָּה בַּכְּרַכִּין;

יד אברהם

Chapter 1

1.

בְּאֶחָד בַּאֲדָר מַשְׁמִיעִין עַל־הַשְּׁקָלִים — On the first of Adar they [the Sanhedrin] proclaim about [the payment of] the shekalim,

This proclamation was to remind everyone to have his half shekel in readiness to be paid at the proper time (Rambam, Comm. and Hil. Shekalim 1:9).

In addition to the proclamation of Beis Din there was an additional reminder: the portion

of Shekalim (Exodus 30:11-16) would be read in the synagogues on the Sabbath that fell on or before the first of Adar (Megillah 3:4 with Rashi and Rav). Although shekel contributions for the Temple service are not applicable in the absence of the Temple, the synagogue reading is still observed in commemoration of the Temple period [זֵכֶר לַמְּקְדָּשׁ] (Chinuch 105; Mishnah Berurah 685:1). [Although the mishnah uses the word shekel, the actual amount contributed by each individual was only a half shekel, as specified by the portion in Exodus.]

◄§ Kilayim.

The Torah forbids the planting together of kilayim, mixtures of diverse species. There are two categories of such mixtures: (a) כִּלְאֵי זְרָעִים, mixtures of seeds; and (b) כִּלְאֵי הַכֶּרֶם, mixtures of the vineyard.

The first category, mixtures of seeds, is based on Leviticus 19:19: לֹא תִזְרַע כַּרְמְךָ כִּלְאָיִם, do not seed your field with a mixture. This applies to mixtures of various species of vegetable, grain, or fruit. Not only is it forbidden to plant such species together, it is forbidden to allow the mixture to remain in the ground ϵven if it was planted by a non-Jew, or if the seeds became implanted through natural causes. If a mixture grew together all the species except one must be uprooted. If such produce has grown to maturity, however, it may be eaten. Furthermore, this prohibition applies only in Eretz Yisrael (Kiddushin 39a; Yoreh Deah 296:69).

The second category, mixtures of seed planted in a vineyard, is more stringent. Produce grown of such a mixture may neither be eaten nor used; it must be burned (Deuteronomy 22:9). Moreover this prohibition is extended (by Rabbinic law) to the Diaspora (Orlah 3:9; Kiddushin 1:9; Yoreh Deah 296:1, 69).

Our mishnah teaches that on Rosh Chodesh Adar, Beis Din proclaimed that farmers must take care to rid themselves of kilayim. Since the mishnah does not specify either type of kilayim, it refers to both, for it is forbidden to keep any type of kilayim (Makkos 21b; Yoreh Deah 297:2).

וְעַל־הַכִּלְאָיִם. — and about kilayim.
'On the first of Adar they proclaim about the forbidden mixtures, and every person goes out to his garden and field, and cleans out the forbidden mixture' (Rambam, Hil. Kilayim 2:15).

Around the time of Rosh Chodesh Adar the fresh produce starts to sprout,

and the presence of kilayim will become evident (Megillah 29b with Rashi and Tos., s.v. ועל הכלאים: cf. Yer. here 2a).

The Mishnah (Kilayim 2:10) exempts most mixtures (see Yoreh Deah 297:5-6) of seed in which the dominant species is more than twenty-four times as much as the other species or combination of species. Though

1. On the first of Adar they proclaim about [the payment of] the shekalim, and about *kilayim*. On the fifteenth of Adar they read the *Megillah* in the walled cities; they [commence] to repair the

that mishnah mentions only seeds, it can be inferred from *Moed Katan* (6a) that this rule holds true even when the seeds have already taken root and sprouted. Such sprouts need not be uprooted if the minority comprises less than one twenty-fourth of the total yield of that particular field. Thus if one finds that his field has sprouted other species, he need uproot only enough to bring their proportion to below one twenty-fourth of the total output (*Rav; Rambam, Comm.* and *Hil. Kilayim* 2:7; *Meiri; Yoreh Deah* 297:8).

Rav, citing his teachers (see *Rosh*), differentiates between a mixture of seeds, which may be planted if the lesser species is below a twenty-fourth of the total, and the plants that grow from the seeds. Because all the seeds are intermingled in a single mixture, the minority is regarded as בָּטֵל, *nullified*, by the majority, with the result that the total mixture is not a forbidden entity. Once the plants have grown and become identifiable, however, the principle of בִּיטוּל, *nullification*, no longer applies. This principle rules only where one substance is forbidden, such as *trefah* meat, and the other is permitted. Only in such a case, do we say that the lesser substance loses its identity when mixed with the greater one. In the case of *kilayim*, however, both substances are permitted so long as they remain *separate*; it is only when they grow together that they are forbidden. Therefore, one of the species must be uprooted completely, whereupon the remaining species is permissible.

[Besides, once the seeds sprout, the different species can be recognized, thus negating the applicability of בִּיטוּל, *nullification*. This principle is used only where the minority substance cannot be identified. However, the point made by *Rav* may be applied to כִּלְאֵי בְּגָדִים, *a prohibited mixture of wool and linen in clothing.* There too, even a minute, undetectable amount of linen thread present in a wool garment (or vice versa) renders the whole garment unfit for wearing (see *Rama* in *Yoreh Deah* 299:1; sources cited in *Shach* and *Beur HaGra* there). As *Rav* submits, the dominant species cannot nullify the lesser one, because neither wool nor linen is intrinsically forbidden.]

בַּחֲמִשָּׁה עָשָׂר בּוֹ קוֹרִין אֶת־הַמְּגִלָּה בַּכְּרַכִּין; — *On the fifteenth of Adar* [lit. of it] *they read the Megillah in the walled cities;*

The word כְּרַךְ denotes a city surrounded by a wall, in contrast to עִיר which refers to any city, whether walled or not (see *Mosaf HeAruch*).

Since the spontaneous celebration of victory over Haman throughout the Persian Empire originally took place on the fourteenth of Adar — the day the Jews gained relief from their enemies after having battled and defeated them on the thirteenth — Mordechai proclaimed that day as an annual festival (*Esther* 9:19). The Jews of Shushan, however, had a miracle all their own because they fought their enemies on the fourteenth day as well. Hence, its original celebration was on the *fifteenth* of Adar (*Esther* 9:18). In commemoration of that miracle, the fifteenth was proclaimed as the Purim of Shushan.

Rather than limit that celebration to Shushan, the Sages ordained that, on the fifteenth of Adar, Shushan Purim be celebrated in all cities which, like Shushan, had walls around them. To accord honor to the cities of *Eretz Yisrael* which were desolate at the time of the miracle, and to attach the remembrance of *Eretz Yisrael* to the miracle in some way, the Rabbis extended the celebration of Purim on the fifteenth to all cities that were walled from the days of Joshua son of Nun (who led the conquest of *Eretz Yisrael*), thus including the towns of *Eretz Yisrael* in the category of the world's celebrated cities. Shushan itself was unwalled in the time of Joshua, but it was accorded a privileged status because the miracle [being celebrated] took place there (see *Megillah* 2b; *Rambam, Hil. Megillah* 1:5; *Yer.*).

שקלים ומתקנין אֶת־הַדְּרָכִים וְאֶת־הָרְחוֹבוֹת וְאֶת־
א/א מִקְוָאוֹת הַמַּיִם; וְעוֹשִׂין כָּל־צָרְכֵי הָרַבִּים;
וּמְצַיְּנִין אֶת־הַקְּבָרוֹת; וְיוֹצְאִין אַף עַל־
הַכִּלְאָיִם.

יד אברהם

Although in the list of events that took place on the fifteenth of Adar, only one is relevant to our tractate — that money changers began to sit regularly to facilitate payment of the half shekalim (mishnah 3) — once the date is mentioned, the tanna gives a complete list of things that were done at the same time. This type of insertion is common in the Mishnah (Rav; Tosafos, Moed Katan 6a, s.v. וט'י; cf. Tos. Yom Tov).

The above explains why the almost universal reading of the Megillah on the fourteenth is omitted by our mishnah. Its purpose was not to give the laws of the Megillah, but to mention all the items relating to the fifteenth (Tos. Yom Tov).

וּמְתַקְּנִין אֶת־הַדְּרָכִים — (and) they [commence] to repair the roads,

Scripture obligates the Beis Din to keep the roads of Eretz Yisrael in good repair. Regarding the עָרֵי מִקְלָט, cities of refuge, provided as a haven for the inadvertent murderer, the Torah states: תָּכִין לְךָ הַדֶּרֶךְ, Prepare yourself the way [lit. road] (Deuteronomy 19:3). Included in this obligation is routine maintenance of the roads, broadening major roads to thirty-two cubits, and erection of bridges (Sifre to Deuteronomy 19:3; Makkos 10b; Rambam, Comm. and Hil. Rotze'ach 8:5; Meiri; see also Bava Basra 100b).

The obligation to repair the roads is not inherently related to the fifteenth of Adar. The Sages ordained this date, however, since the rainy season had inevitably damaged the roads severely (Rav; Tosefta 1:1).

וְאֶת־הָרְחוֹבוֹת — (and) the town squares

[Each town had an open area where people would gather on fast days for prayer (see Taanis 2:1).]

Rambam (Comm.) and Rav apparently do not have this phrase in their Mishnah texts. In their respective explanations, Rambam and Rav mention the need to repair the squares as part of the explanation of the previous phrase.

Alternatively, דְּרָכִים are roads used for inter-city travel, while רְחוֹבוֹת are streets within the city itself (R' Meshullam; see also Meleches Shlomo).

וְאֶת־מִקְוָאוֹת הַמַּיִם — and the accumulations of water;

[One who has contracted טוּמְאָה (tumah), contamination, must immerse in a מִקְוֶה, mikveh (lit. accumulation), containing a minimum of forty se'ah of water. In Mishnaic times, natural accumulations of rain water, e.g., in ditches or caves, were used for this immersion.] Mud and other debris which may have fallen into these mikvaos during the winter rains are now removed (Rav; R' Meshullam; Rashi, Moed Katan 6a).

Additionally, the volume of water in each mikveh is measured. Mikvaos that needed no repair or cleaning but that lacked a sufficient volume of water, were replenished and revalidated (Rav; Rambam; cf. Moed Katan 5a).

וְעוֹשִׂין כָּל־צָרְכֵי הָרַבִּים — (and) they attend to [lit. do] all of the public needs;

They [the courts] adjudicate capital, corporal, and civil cases; attend to the redeeming of arachin[1], charamim[2], and consecrated objects[3]; investigate

1. עֲרָכִין, Arachin — Someone who vows to contribute to the Temple treasury an amount equal to his own 'worth', or that of any other person, must give an amount fixed by the Torah, according to age and sex; (see Leviticus 27:1-8). This is called עֵרֶךְ, lit. assessment (plural, arachin). The court now turns its attention to the collection of these vows.

1
1

roads, the town squares and the accumulations of water; they attend to all of the public needs; they mark the graves; and they also go out [to inspect the fields] for *kilayim.*

YAD AVRAHAM

the circumstances of a wife suspected of adultery[4] (see *Rambam, Hil. Sotah* 4:1; *Tos. Yom Tov);* attend to the burning of the Red Cow[5], boring the ear of the Jewish slave[6], the cleansing of the מְצוֹרָע, *metzora*[7]; and see to it that reservoirs are made accessible to the public for the rainless summer months (*Yer.* 3a cited by *Rav* and *Rambam;* see *Yer. Moed Katan* 1:2; *Rambam, Hil. Arachin* 8:1 and *Hil. Yom Tov* 7:1).

Most of these matters are unrelated to the fifteenth of Adar. Nevertheless, since *Beis Din* contracts road repairs at this date, it is an appropriate time to attend to other public needs (*Tos. Yom Tov*).

Meiri explains: (a) the adjudication of these matters symbolizes that the year and its 'curses' have come to an end. [For the order

of counting the months. Nissan is the first month of the year, although the new calendar year begins on the first of *Tishrei* (see *Exodus* 12:2 and *Rosh Hashanah* 1:1 with *comm.*)]; (b) The different types of property donated to the Temple treasury were appropriately collected together with the shekalim which went for the upkeep of the Temple service.

וּמְצַיְּינִין אֶת־הַקְּבָרוֹת; — *they mark the graves;*

Lest an unsuspecting passerby become contaminated (טָמֵא) by stepping on a grave or by coming under the canopy of a tree simultaneously covering both him and the grave, it was customary to mark the graves with lime (see *Ma'asar Sheni* 5:1; *Bava Kama* 69a). During the winter rains, many

2. חֲרָמִים, *Charamim* — Objects consecrated to the Temple treasury are called חֵרֶם (plural, *charamim*), literally *banned,* in consecrating them. The uniqueness of this type of consecration is discussed in *Arachin* (8:4-7). The Temple administrators must ensure that these pledges are sold or redeemed so that the treasury can use the proceeds as needed.

3. הֶקְדֵּשׁוֹת, *Consecrated objects* — This refers to objects consecrated in an ordinary manner. These too are sold by the Temple administrators and the proceeds are used for the Temple.

4. סוֹטָה, *Sotah* — A woman who, after being duly warned by her husband that he suspected her of adultery, was found secluded with the alleged adulterer, is called a סוֹטָה, *sotah.* The Torah *(Numbers* 5:11-31) requires a detailed ritual of which the drinking of מַיִם הַמְאָרְרִים, *waters which cause curse* (specially prepared consecrated water), is a prominent feature. If the woman is guilty, it causes her death; if not, she becomes miraculously pregnant thus establishing her innocence.

5. פָּרָה אֲדֻמָּה, *Red Cow* — A red cow was burned and its ashes gathered and preserved. Anyone wishing to purge himself of טוּמְאָה, *contamination,* stemming from contact with a corpse, had to have a mixture of these ashes and spring water sprinkled upon himself at two prescribed intervals, after which he would immerse himself in a *mikveh* (see *Numbers* 19:1-22). Of course they did not burn a cow every fifteenth of Adar. During the entire period from the giving of the Torah till the destruction of the Second Temple, only eight red cows were burned *(Parah* 3:5), so unusual was it to find an animal fitting all the specifications. What is probably meant is that the court or the *Kohanim* checked on the supply of ash every fifteenth of Adar.

6. עֶבֶד נִרְצָע, *Bored servant* — If a Jewish indentured servant [עֶבֶד עִבְרִי] wished to remain in bondage under his master past the allotted six years his ear was bored, as set forth in *Exodus* (21:5-6) and he served until the Jubilee Year.

7. מְצוֹרָע, *Metzora* — Tzara'as is a disease characterized by skin lesions called *nega'im.* One contracting this disease is called a *metzora* (see *Leviticus* 14:1-32; *Mishnah Megillah* 1:7, ArtScroll ed.).

[7]   THE MISHNAH / SHEKALIM

שקלים **[ב] אָמַר** רַבִּי יְהוּדָה: בָּרִאשׁוֹנָה הָיוּ
א/ב עוֹקְרִין וּמַשְׁלִיכִין לִפְנֵיהֶם;
מִשֶּׁרַבּוּ עוֹבְרֵי עֲבֵירָה, הָיוּ עוֹקְרִין וּמַשְׁלִיכִין
עַל־הַדְּרָכִים. הִתְקִינוּ שֶׁיְּהוּ מַפְקִירִין כָּל־
הַשָּׂדֶה כֻּלָּהּ.

א/ג **[ג] בַּחֲמִשָּׁה** עָשָׂר בּוֹ שֻׁלְחָנוֹת הָיוּ יוֹשְׁבִין
בַּמְּדִינָה. בְּעֶשְׂרִים וַחֲמִשָּׁה

יד אברהם

grave markers would be obliterated *(Rav; Rambam;* see *Rashi, Moed Katan* 6a, s.v. ואת מקוואות המים and *Yer.* here 3a).

The Talmud *(Moed Katan 5a)* cites eight verses each of which supports the halachic obligation of marking graves.

וְיוֹצְאִין אַף עַל־הַכִּלְאָיִם — *and they* [the emissaries of the court *(Rav)]* also *go out* [*to inspect the fields*] *for*

kilayim.

On the first of Adar they had issued a proclamation warning everyone to weed out the forbidden admixtures. Now they sent out emissaries to investigate whether this admonition had been heeded *(Rambam),* and to uproot the forbidden plant shoots as related in the next mishnah *(Rav).* [See *comm.* to *Moed Katan* 1:2.]

2.

אָמַר רַבִּי יְהוּדָה: בָּרִאשׁוֹנָה הָיוּ עוֹקְרִין
וּמַשְׁלִיכִין לִפְנֵיהֶם; — *Said R' Yehudah: At first they* [the court's emissaries] *would uproot and throw* [*the kilayim*] *before them;*

In earlier times it was sufficient for the emissaries to throw the uprooted plants at the feet of the transgressors. This was sufficient to shame them into obeying the halachah *(Rav).*

[Subsequently, the transgressors became bolder, and more stringent methods were needed (see below).]

R' Yehudah does not contradict the first tanna. Rather, he elaborates on the comment, 'and they also go out to inspect the fields for *kilayim*' at the end of mishnah 1 *(Meleches Shlomo).*

מִשֶּׁרַבּוּ עוֹבְרֵי עֲבֵירָה, — *when the number of transgressors increased,*

The transgressors actually benefited from the court's policy of uprooting [and, as a result, ridiculed the emissaries who were supposedly 'punishing'

them]: (a) they were spared the tedious chore of weeding out unwanted mixtures; and (b) they were able to use the uprooted shoots for fodder *(Rav; Baraisa* cited in *Yer.* and *Moed Katan* 6b).

הָיוּ עוֹקְרִין וּמַשְׁלִיכִין עַל־הַדְּרָכִים. — *they would uproot and throw* [*the kilayim*] *upon the roads.*

This precluded the use of the uprooted shoots as fodder. But the transgressors still felt that they had profited in that they need not weed out the unwanted species themselves. Therefore ... (ibid.).

הִתְקִינוּ שֶׁיְּהוּ מַפְקִירִין כָּל־הַשָּׂדֶה כֻּלָּהּ. — [*Finally,*] *they* [i.e., the Sages] *instituted that they declare the entire field ownerless.*

They would render all the produce of that field ownerless, thus allowing anyone else to claim the produce as his own *(Tur, Choshen Mishpat* 273).

Scripture empowered the *Beis Din* to strip

1
2 2. Said R' Yehudah: At first they would uproot and throw [the *kilayim*] before them; when the number of transgressors increased, they would uproot and throw [the *kilayim*] upon the roads. [Finally,] they instituted that they declare the entire field ownerless.

1
3 3. On the fifteenth of Adar money-changers would sit in the province. On the twenty-fifth

owners of their title and confiscate property if necessary. When Ezra and the leaders of the people wanted to ensure the attendance of all the people at a gathering designed to combat the evil of intermarriage, they proclaimed *(Ezra 10:8): Whoever would not come within three days ... his fortune be confiscated (Rav* from *Yer.* 3a and *Yevamos* 89b; *Gittin* 36b).

Tur *(Choshen Mishpat* 273) understands that this disentitlement is automatic. Accordingly, the phrase 'and they declared

ownerless' refers not to an act of confiscation by the emissaries, but to the proclamation about *kilayim* mentioned in the previous mishnah. In its proclamation that the people remove these 'mixtures', *Beis Din* included the warning that anyone not complying with this directive by the fifteenth would be automatically disentitled *(Derishah* to *Tur; Turei Zahav* to *Shulchan Aruch). Beis Yosef* disagrees and rules *(Choshen Mishpat* 273:8) that an official declaration of disentitlement is required for each individual abuse.

3.

In mishnah 1 the tanna had informed us that on the first of Adar the *Beis Din* issued a proclamation to ready the people for the *mitzvah* of the half shekel. Having digressed to mention other matters on *Beis Din's* agenda during Adar, the Mishnah now returns to the main theme of this tractate, the shekalim.

בַּחֲמִשָּׁה עָשָׂר בּוֹ שֻׁלְחָנוֹת הָיוּ יוֹשְׁבִין — *On the fifteenth of Adar* [lit. *in it] money-changers* [lit. *tables] would sit*

So as to be easily accessible to anyone who wished to exchange his currency into half shekel pieces *(Meiri).*

Because the people came from different countries and many did not know the value of their currency with respect to the local money used in the Temple, they would need the services of a money-changer *(Rav; Rosh).*[1]

The standard practice was for a moneychanger to conduct his business over a simple שֻׁלְחָן, literally *table-person (Rambam).*

These money-changers also served a more basic function — that of collecting the half shekels. It was their duty to 'demand softly' that the half shekel be paid; but they were not empowered to coerce anyone into paying. The money-changing role was but incidental to this major assignment; it was a service that enabled one who had only larger coins to discharge his obligation *(Rambam, Hil. Shekalim* 1:9).

[They *began* sitting on the fifteenth and continued to do so for the duration of the shekel collection (see *R' Shmuel* cited below, s.v. בחמשה).]

בַּמְּדִינָה. — *in the province.*

The words מְדִינָה, *province*, and

1. Those who knew the exchange rate could negotiate an exchange into local currency without the services of a Temple appointed money-changer. If their foreign coins were freely accepted in Jerusalem, a half shekel worth of such coins could be used to discharge the obligation of the foreign currency (see *Bava Kama* 97b; *Tos.* there, s.v. שיהו; the *Yerushalmi* cited there is not found in our version; see *Yer. Ma'asar Sheni* 1:1).

[9]   THE MISHNAH / SHEKALIM

שְׁקָלִים יָשְׁבוּ בַּמִּקְדָּשׁ. מִשֶּׁיָּשְׁבוּ בַּמִּקְדָּשׁ הִתְחִילוּ א/ג לְמַשְׁכֵּן.

אֶת־מִי מְמַשְׁכְּנִין? לְוִיִּם וְיִשְׂרְאֵלִים, גֵּרִים וַעֲבָדִים מְשֻׁחְרָרִים, אֲבָל לֹא נָשִׁים וַעֲבָדִים

יד אברהם

מִקְדָּשׁ, Sanctuary, appear in conjunction with each other in many mishnayos (e.g., *Succah* 3:12 and *Rosh Hashanah* 4:1). According to *Rambam (Comm.)*, the term מְדִינָה, *province*, includes all cities of *Eretz Yisrael* except Jerusalem, while מִקְדָּשׁ, *Sanctuary*, refers to Jerusalem. *Rav* (following *Rashi*) understands מִקְדָּשׁ, *Sanctuary*, to mean the Temple itself, and מְדִינָה, *province*, to refer to the city of Jerusalem.[1]

Alternatively, the term מְדִינָה may be translated *(large) city*. Thus: *On the fifteenth money-changers would sit in the large cities.* (See *Perush HaGra, Esther* 1:1; *Aruch HaShulchan HeAssid* 83:8). *Radak (Shorashim, s.v. מדין)* allows מְדִינָה, *province*, to be translated either *city* or *province*, depending on the context (cf. *Daniel* 8:2).

בְּעֶשְׂרִים וַחֲמִשָּׁה יָשְׁבוּ בַּמִּקְדָּשׁ. — *On the twenty-fifth they [the money-changers] sat in the Temple.*

The translation follows *Rashi*.

According to *Rambam*, the term מִקְדָּשׁ, *Mikdash*, refers to Jerusalem (based on *Rav*).[2] [But according to *Rashi's* view above, מִקְדָּשׁ refers to the Temple itself.]

The money-changers sat neither in the Temple itself nor in the Courtyard, but within the area known as הַר הַבַּיִת, *the Temple Mount*, adjacent to the Courtyard (*R' Shmuel*).[3]

The appointment of money-changers to sit in the Temple area emphasized that only four days remained until the first of Nissan — the date when all half shekalim were due in the Temple treasury (see preface to mishnah 1). Because of the resulting heightened awareness people would be spurred to hurry their payment of the half shekel (*Rashi* to *Megillah* 29b, s.v. יושבים במקדש; *Rav*).

The seemingly arbitrary choice of the

1. Although a casual reading of *Rav* gives the impression that only Jerusalem is referred to in the term מְדִינָה, in other mishnayos (*Succah* 3:12 and *Rosh Hashanah* 4:1) this term clearly includes all areas outside the Temple, whether inside or outside of Jerusalem. It should be so construed here too; *Rav* specifies Jerusalem only to accentuate the difference between *Rashi's* interpretation, in which Jerusalem is included in this term, and *Rambam's* where the term refers only to areas outside of Jerusalem (based on *Tos. Yom Tov*; cf. *Tif. Yis.*).

2. [Alternatively, *Rambam* may concur that these money-changers sat in the Temple; though the term מִקְדָּשׁ, lit. *Sanctuary*, includes Jerusalem, it surely does not exclude the Temple. This is suggested by *Rambam's* choice of words (*Hil. Shekalim* 1:9): 'On the twenty-fifth of the month the money-changers sat in the מִקְדָּשׁ.' In those instances where *Rambam* understands the term מִקְדָּשׁ in the Mishnah to include the entire city (e.g., *Rosh Hashanah* 4:1), he uses the word Jerusalem in formulating the halachah (e.g., *Hil. Shofar* 2:8; concerning *Succah* 3:12, see comm. there; *R' Manoach* to *Hil. Lulav* 7:13 and *Aruch LaNer* to *Succah* 41a; cf. *Vilna Gaon* cited by *Taklin Chadatin* and *Mishnas Eliyahu* to 2:1). Accordingly, his use of מִקְדָּשׁ in the case of shekalim suggests that he means the Sanctuary itself. If this is a correct analysis of *Rambam's* view, we need not assume that the money-changers in the province quit their positions from the twenty-fifth on. The only thing that changed at this date was that money-changers were assigned in the Temple in addition to those in the provinces and Jerusalem.]

3. [*R' Shmuel* considers it inconceivable that the Courtyard, where most of the Temple service took place, was utilized for the purpose of money changing. For one, it is prohibited for anyone to sit in the Courtyard (*Sotah* 40b). Moreover, even if the expression they *sat* is not taken literally, the traffic generated by the collection of the half shekalim would surely hinder the performance of the Temple service.]

1
3
they sat in the Temple. From the time they sat in the Temple, they would commence to seize collateral. From whom did they seize collateral? — [From] Levites and Israelites, proselytes and freed slaves, but

YAD AVRAHAM

twenty-fifth has a halachic symbolism. The daily offerings (תְּמִידִים) sacrificed on the first of Nissan had to be purchased with the new half shekalim. But the animals used for the daily offering had to be inspected for any possible invalidating blemish (מום) for a four-day period prior to their sacrifice (Menachos 49b). Thus it was customary that the animals to be offered on the first of Nissan were chosen on the twenty-fifth of Adar [the Adar preceding Nissan never has more than 29 days; Rosh Hashanah 19b] (R' Meshullam).

מִשֶּׁיָּשְׁבוּ בַּמִּקְדָּשׁ הִתְחִילוּ לְמַשְׁכֵּן. — From the time they sat in the Temple, they would commence to seize collateral [from those tardy in paying].

I.e., they would seize valuables as collateral to assure eventual payment of the debt (Rambam, Comm.).[1]

From when the money-exchanges were set up in the Temple, the emissaries in the provinces, [who had heretofore only 'demanded softly' (Rambam cited above, s.v. בחמשה עשר, commenced to seize collateral (R' Shmuel).

The Tosefta (1:2) explains the act of seizure with a parable. A surgeon may order a patient to be strapped (often against his will) to the operating table to allow the doctor to perform a curative procedure. So too, God's decree that public offerings (קָרְבְּנוֹת צִבּוּר) be brought to cure (i.e., atone for) the spiritual maladies of the nation must be enforced even against the will of an individual donor.

The Tosefta goes on to infer from Scripture the rule of distrainment (seizing collateral) regarding the half shekel tax. And you shall take (i.e, even by force, if neces-

sary) the atonement money from the Children of Israel (Exodus 30:16).

אֶת־מִי מְמַשְׁכְּנִין? לְוִיִם וְיִשְׂרְאֵלִים, — From whom did they seize collateral? — [From] Levites and Israelites,

But not from Kohanim, as set forth further (mishnah 4). The clause including Levites is necessary to overrule the opinion maintaining that only those included in the general census are obligated in the half shekel. This would exclude Levites (Rav; see comm. to mishnah 4, s.v. אלא).

גֵּרִים וַעֲבָדִים מְשֻׁחְרָרִים, — proselytes and freed slaves,

A heathen slave could be retained by his Jewish master only if he agreed to undergo circumcision and accept the mitzvos (Yevamos 48b; Yoreh Deah 267:4). Upon doing so, he is required to perform only those mitzvos incumbent upon women (Chagigah 4a). Such a slave is known in Mishnaic terminology as עֶבֶד כְּנַעֲנִי, a Canaanite slave, or as עֶבֶד שֶׁאֵינוֹ מְשֻׁחְרָר, an unfreed slave. In the event he is subsequently freed, he automatically attains the status of a proselyte, and becomes obligated in the performance of all mitzvos (see Yevamos 47b; Rambam, Hil. Issurei Bi'ah 13:2 with Maggid Mishneh; Hagahos R' Akiva Eiger to Yoreh Deah 267:7).

אֲבָל לֹא נָשִׁים — but not from women,

In reference to the half shekalim, the Torah states (Exodus 30:12): And every 'man' shall give ... (Rav; Rosh; R' Shmuel).

1. There are two varying bases for such seizures: (a) Any payment mandated by the Torah is viewed as a financial obligation, that subjects the estate of the debtor to a lien; such seizure may be made in the person's absence and even after his death; and (b) the court is empowered to coerce a recalcitrant person to perform a mitzvah. If so, this seizure is a means of coercion rather than collection (see Chiddushei HaRamban to Bava Basra 176a) and may only be done in the presence of the owner (Minchas Chinuch 105:1).

שְׁקָלִים וּקְטַנִּים.

א/ג   כָּל־קָטָן שֶׁהִתְחִיל אָבִיו לִשְׁקוֹל עַל־יָדוֹ, שׁוּב
אֵינוֹ פּוֹסֵק.
וְאֵין מְמַשְׁכְּנִין אֶת־הַכֹּהֲנִים, מִפְּנֵי דַרְכֵי
שָׁלוֹם.

יד אברהם

Meiri suggests that women are exempted because this is a '*mitzvah* whose performance is limited to a specific time (מִצְוַת עֲשֵׂה שֶׁהַזְּמַן גְּרָמָא)' and such *mitzvos* are not incumbent upon women (*Kiddushin* 1:7).[1]

וַעֲבָדִים — *slaves*

Non-Jewish slaves are required to perform only those *mitzvos* incumbent upon women (*Rav;* see above, s.v. <div dir="rtl">עֲבָדִים מְשֻׁחְרָרִים</div>).

וּקְטַנִּים. — *nor minors.*

With regard to seizing collateral, a boy is considered a minor as long as he has not yet exhibited the physical manifestations of adulthood, i.e., pubic hair (*Rambam, Comm.*). [However, anyone below the age of thirteen is considered a minor for all purposes even if he already has this sign of maturity (*Niddah* 46a; *Rambam, Hil. Ishus* 2:10-11).]

Without explaining why, *Rav* (also *Chinuch* 105; see also *Roke'ach* 233) explains that 'minor' in our mishnah refers to one under twenty years of age. *Tosefos Yom Tov* conjectures that *Rav* bases his opinion on the

verse (*Exodus* 30:14; see preface to this tractate) that sets the minimum age of those counted in a census at twenty. However, *Tosefos Yom Tov* rejects *Rav's* view, and cites *Rambam* (see above) and *Ramban* (to *Exodus*) to the contrary.

כָּל־קָטָן שֶׁהִתְחִיל אָבִיו לִשְׁקוֹל עַל־יָדוֹ, שׁוּב אֵינוֹ פּוֹסֵק. — [*In the case of*] *a minor whose father has commenced to contribute the half shekel on his behalf, [the father] may not cease to do so.*

I.e., having voluntarily assumed this *mitzvah*, the father should not cease until the son reaches majority whereupon the son becomes obligated on his own (*Rambam Comm.; Rav*).

R' Shmuel asserts that *Rav's* ruling is based on a special enactment (תַּקָּנָה) by the Sages.

Meiri asserts that here too, the father's assets may be seized if he fails to give in succeeding years. However, *R' Meshullam* disagrees and maintains that the duty of the father not to cease is only a meritorious act, not an absolute duty.[1]

1. [Surely, *Meiri* cannot mean to suggest that the Adar date limits this *mitzvah* to a specific time; the choice of the month Adar is a mere convenience and if one gave the half shekel earlier or later, he has discharged his duty.

Perhaps *Meiri* means that the *mitzvah* of shekel is not completed in the mere act of giving. The cardinal feature of the *mitzvah* is that everyone's half shekel should be available for the purchase of the public offerings of that year. Thus the *mitzvah* has a 'specific time' in that each half shekel had a specific twelve month period during which it served its purpose in the treasury. Thereafter, the obligation was to bring the offerings of the following year (see *Berachos* 20b ... מהו דתימא הואיל וכתיב בה ערב ובקר).]

1. *R' A. Sofer* (glosses to *Meiri*) asks why the same ruling does not apply to women and others exempted from giving as well.

Perhaps the answer lies in the explanation given by *R' Elazar ben Yehudah* (*Sefer HaRokeach* 233). The father's giving for his minor son is a performance of the *mitzvah* of חִינּוּךְ, *training his son in future performance of mitzvos*; accordingly once he commences to

מִשְׁנָיוֹת / שְׁקָלִים   [12]

1
3 not from women, slaves nor minors.

[In the case of] a minor whose father has commenced to contribute the half shekel on his behalf, [the father] may not cease to do so.

For the sake of peace, they do not seize collateral from the *Kohanim*.

YAD AVRAHAM

Rav (based on *Rosh*) maintains that if the father dies before the son achieves his majority, the half shekel must be paid by the son. *Tosefos Yom Tov* questions how the father's commitment can become binding upon the son. He also points out that *Rambam's* wording *(Comm; Hil. Shekalim* 1:7) seems to contradict *Rav's* view.

וְאֵין מְמַשְׁכְּנִין אֶת־הַכֹּהֲנִים, מִפְּנֵי דַרְכֵי שָׁלוֹם.
— *For the sake of peace, they do not seize collateral from the Kohanim.*

Although *Kohanim* are obliged to pay the half shekel (see next mishnah), they are only *asked* to pay, but not coerced *(Rambam, Hil. Shekalim* 1:10; *Meiri).*

Since *Kohanim* are not paid a salary for their performance of the sacrificial services, we show our appreciation by not coercing them; we assume that all (or most) of them will pay their share voluntarily. To the few recalcitrant *Kohanim, Beis Din* grants a share in the

public offering in exchange for their Temple service. In this respect they are no worse than other laborers who perform work for the Temple and are paid with Temple funds. *Beis Din* has the jurisdiction to disburse Temple funds for salaries (see 4:1; *Rav* elaborating on *Yer.).*

Obviously the *Kohanim* would feel affronted if this courtesy were not extended them, and the coercion of even a single *Kohen* would cause friction *(Tos. Yom Tov).*

As set forth in the next mishnah, the *Kohanim* maintained that they were exempt from payment of the half shekel. Though the Sages felt that the *Kohanim* were wrong, they could not offer conclusive proof. Thus, in accordance with the dictum, הַמּוֹצִיא מֵחֲבֵירוֹ עָלָיו הָרְאָיָה, *the burden of proof lies with the claimant (Bava Kama* 3:11), the court could not collect the money *(R' Shmuel;* cf. *R' Yehudah;* and *Tos. Rid).*

train his child in the performance of any *mitzvah*, he may not desist from doing so in the future. Viewed from this perspective, one cannot be considered as having accomplished the *mitzvah* of *training his son* unless he has persevered at that *mitzvah* until the child reaches his maturity and performs the *mitzvah* on his own. If, however, the father desists from the *mitzvah* before the son comes of age, he is considered only to have started a *mitzvah* — that of 'training' — but not having completed it. Thus the principle set forth in our mishnah is that a voluntary initiation of a *mitzvah* is considered a vow to complete that *mitzvah* (cf. *Teshuvos Tashbatz* 3:45). In the case of women and other exempt people who give voluntarily, that giving is a complete *mitzvah* in and of itself wholly independent of next year's collection.

Meiri's view concurs with *Rokeach's* that the father's duty is based on the *mitzvah* of training which, not having a monetary character, is not subject to seizure. Also, there is no precedent for coercing a parent to train his child. However, if the father's act is construed to be a vow to contribute, seizure may be in order. A case for viewing a monetary vow as a financial obligation to be collected from the vower's estate (even if he is deceased) is made by many authorities (see *R' Yosef Karo* in *Teshuvos HaRama* 47-8; *Machaneh Efraim, Hil. Nedarim; Ketzos HaChoshen* 290:3). Besides, the *mitzvah* to fulfill the vow would in itself be grounds for seizure of assets. (See footnote to s.v. משישבו במקדש above.)

שקלים [ד] **אָמַר** רַבִּי יְהוּדָה: הֵעִיד בֶּן־בּוּכְרִי
א/ד בְּיַבְנֶה, כָּל־כֹּהֵן שֶׁשּׁוֹקֵל אֵינוֹ
חוֹטֵא.

אָמַר לוֹ רַבָּן יוֹחָנָן בֶּן־זַכַּאי: לֹא כִי. אֶלָּא כָּל־
כֹּהֵן שֶׁאֵינוּ שׁוֹקֵל חוֹטֵא. אֶלָּא שֶׁהַכֹּהֲנִים
דּוֹרְשִׁים מִקְרָא זֶה לְעַצְמָן: ,,וְכָל־מִנְחַת כֹּהֵן

יד אברהם

4.

Having stated the *Kohanim* are not coerced to contribute half shekels, the mishnah now discusses whether they are obligated to pay the half shekel at all. Thus *Rivevan* understands this mishnah as a continuation (or, at least, an explanation) of the previous one. [Indeed, in our versions of *Yerushalmi* these two mishnayos appear as one.]

אָמַר רַבִּי יְהוּדָה: הֵעִיד בֶּן־בּוּכְרִי בְּיַבְנֶה, — *Said R' Yehudah: Ben Buchri testified in Yavneh*

The Talmud (*Rosh HaShanah* 31a-b) relates that forty years before the destruction of the Temple (*Sanhedrin* 41a and *Avodah Zarah* 8a), the Sanhedrin moved from the Hewn-Stone Chamber (לִשְׁכַּת הַלְּבֵּזִית) in the Temple Courtyard to *Chanus* (חָנוּת, a site on the Temple Mount; *Rashi* to *Sanhedrin* 41a and *Avodah Zarah* 8b, s.v. חנות; cf. *Rosh HaShanah* 31, s.v. מלשכת), from there to Jerusalem (i.e. the city proper), and from Jerusalem to Yavneh. The move to Yavneh took place while R' Yochanan ben Zakkai was נָשִׂיא, *president,* of the Sanhedrin, immediately after the destruction of Jerusalem and the Temple (cf. *Gittin* 56a-b).

Ben Buchri spoke during Rabban Yochanan ben Zakkai's term as president. He probably *testified* to an old tradition.

כָּל־כֹּהֵן שֶׁשּׁוֹקֵל אֵינוּ חוֹטֵא. — *that any Kohen who contributes [the half shekel] has not sinned.*

Ben Buchri holds Kohanim to be exempt from the half shekel. Consequently, it could be argued that their contributions remain unconsecrated. If so, animals purchased with such funds would likewise remain unconsecrated, and it would be sinful to offer them in the Temple ((חֻלִּין בַּעֲזָרָה). To dispel this notion, Ben Buchri testified that there was no objection to such contributions

because it could be assumed that the donor has wholeheartedly transferred his ownership of the half shekel to the public (*Rav; Menachos* 21b).

אָמַר לוֹ רַבָּן יוֹחָנָן בֶּן־זַכַּאי: לֹא כִי. — *Rabban Yochanan ben Zakkai replied to Ben Buchri* [lit. *to him*]: *It is not so.*

[I.e. the tradition you cite has been corrupted. The correct version is as follows:]

אֶלָּא כָּל־כֹּהֵן שֶׁאֵינוּ שׁוֹקֵל חוֹטֵא. — *Rather, any Kohen who does not contribute [the half shekel] has sinned.*

Rabban Yochanan holds that Kohanim are obligated to give the half shekel just as Israelites are.

The disagreement between Ben Buchri and Rabban Yochanan centers around the interpretation of the verse (*Exodus* 30:3) which refers to the half shekel: כָּל־הָעֹבֵר עַל־הַפְּקֻדִים, *this shall they give, all who pass among the numbered.*

Ben Buchri renders this verse in its literal sense, i.e., all those included in the census. This excludes the entire tribe of Levi (i.e., both *Kohanim* and Levites) who were not included in the regular census (see *Numbers* 1:48-9).[1] Rabban Yochanan, on the other hand, understands the verb הָעֹבֵר, *who pass,* to refer to those who passed through the

1
4

4. Said R' Yehudah: Ben Buchri testified in Yavneh that any *Kohen* who contributes [the half shekel] has not sinned.

Rabban Yochanan ben Zakkai replied to Ben Buchri: It is not so. Rather, any *Kohen* who does not contribute [the half shekel] has sinned. But the *Kohanim* interpret the following verse for their own benefit: *Every meal offering of a Kohen shall be en-*

YAD AVRAHAM

Sea of Reeds — Kohanim, Levites and Israelites. The verse is to be rendered, *'All those who passed* [through the sea shall be] *among the counted* [for the half shekel] *(Rav, Meiri* and *Tosafos, Menachos* 21b, s.v. כל, based on *Yer.;* see also *R' Shlomo Sirilio).*

Yerushalmi adds that the verse commanding the contribution of a half shekel: *This (זֶה) shall they give ... a half shekel ... (Exodus* 30:13), hints at the *Kohanim's* obligation. The numerical value of the word זֶה *(this)* is twelve, i.e., *twelve* (tribes) *shall give,* implying that the obligation also falls on the tribe of Levi (see *Shoshanim L'David).*

The commentators cited above hold that Ben Buchri and Rabban Yochanan disagree regarding Levites as well as *Kohanim.* Perhaps the mishnah speaks exclusively about *Kohanim* because the statement about not coercing (mishnah 3), which introduces this argument, refers to *Kohanim* only (see *comm.* there; cf. *R' Shlomo Sirilio).* In light of this, the Scriptural proof attributed to the *Kohanim* by Rabban Yochanan ben Zakkai (below) — which seems to exempt only *Kohanim* — was viewed by them as an argument refuting those who held that *all who passed the sea* were obligated. However, the *Kohanim* also had a source that exempted the Levites in addition to themselves.[1]

Rambam (also *R' Shmuel* p. 11, s.v. מסייע

לבן בוכרי and *P'nei Moshe;* see footnote above) understands that the controversy in the mishnah is about *Kohanim* only. Ben Buchri exempted them for the reason cited by Rabban Yochanan. The exemption derived in *Yerushalmi* from the verse *'all who pass among the numbered'* (explained above) is attributed by *R' Shmuel* to a third view (not mentioned in the mishnah) which exempts Levites as well (see below, s.v. אלא שהכהנים).

אֶלָּא שֶׁהַכֹּהֲנִים דּוֹרְשִׁים מִקְרָא זֶה לְעַצְמָן: — *But the Kohanim interpret the following verse for their own benefit* [lit., *for themselves*]:

[This is a continuation of Rabban Yochanan's statement. Presumably, Rabban Yochanan explains how the tradition cited by Ben Buchri happened to become corrupted.]

וְכָל־מִנְחַת כֹּהֵן כָּלִיל תִּהְיֶה לֹא תֵאָכֵל.'' — *Every meal offering of a Kohen shall be entirely burnt; it may not be eaten [Leviticus* 6:16].

Unlike an Israelite's meal offering of which only a fistful (קוֹמֶץ) is burnt upon the altar — the rest eaten by the *Kohanim* — a *Kohen's* entire meal offering is burned. Using this precept as their premise, the *Kohanim* adduced the

---

1. Although the Levites were later counted in a separate census (*Numbers* 3:14-39), they did not *pass* in front of Moses, Aaron, and the heads of the tribes, as did those counted in the regular census (*Numbers* 1:3-4 see *Ramban* there to v. 28). In the Levitic census, Moses stood in front of the Levite domiciles and asked for the number of inhabitants in each (see *Rashi* to *Numbers* 3:16). Thus the expression *who pass among the numbered* does not refer to the Levites (*Korban HaEdah; Taklin Chadatin).*

Yerushalmi (above) apparently contradicts *Ramban* (*Exodus* 30:12) who holds that the dispute in our mishnah refers only to *Kohanim,* but that all concur that the Levites were required to contribute in the census mentioned in *Exodus* 30:13 and 38:26 (*Shaar HaMelech, Hil. Shekalim* 1:1; and others).

שקלים כָּלִיל תִּהְיֶה לֹא תֵאָכֵל״. הוֹאִיל וְעֹמֶר וּשְׁתֵּי

א/ה הַלֶּחֶם וְלֶחֶם הַפָּנִים שֶׁלָּנוּ, הֵיאַךְ נֶאֱכָלִים?

[ה] אַף עַל־פִּי שֶׁאָמְרוּ: אֵין מְמַשְׁכְּנִין

נָשִׁים וַעֲבָדִים וּקְטַנִּים —

אִם שָׁקְלוּ, מְקַבְּלִין מִיָּדָן.

הָעוֹבֵד כּוֹכָבִים וְהַכּוּתִי שֶׁשָּׁקְלוּ, אֵין

יד אברהם

following argument in favor of their position.

הוֹאִיל וְעֹמֶר וּשְׁתֵּי הַלֶּחֶם וְלֶחֶם הַפָּנִים שֶׁלָּנוּ, — If [lit. since] the Omer offering, the Two Loaves and the Panim Bread are ours,

[The Kohanim argued that if they were required to pay the half shekel, they would have a portion in all the public sacrifices, including the meal offerings listed here. (For descriptions and details about these three offerings see comm. to 4:1.)]

הֵיאַךְ נֶאֱכָלִים? — how may they be eaten? Scripture states: Every meal offering of a Kohen shall be entirely burnt (Leviticus 6:16). The Kohanim argued that if they had to contribute toward communal offerings, the above-named meal offerings would have to be burned as are all such offerings that are given by a Kohen. Since we know that these offerings are in fact eaten by the Kohanim, they must be exempt from the mitzvah of the half shekel.

However, Rabban Yochanan ruled, this argument is built upon an erroneous premise. The provision that a Kohen's meal offering be burnt concerns only a private, and not a public, meal offering (Rav; Yer.).

Although the Two Loaves are not מְנָחוֹת, meal offerings, in the usual sense — since they are not burnt upon the altar — they are, nevertheless, referred to as מִנְחָה חֲדָשָׁה, a new meal offering (Leviticus 23:15), by the Torah (R' Shmuel).

[Although Panim Breads, are never called מִנְחָה, meal offering, in a sense they can be viewed as a meal offering. This offering comprised two parts: the breads and the accompanying frankincense. Because the frankincense is burned on the altar, it assumes the role played by the fistful (קוֹמֶץ) that is separated from other meal offerings. The Torah (Leviticus 24:7) refers to the frankincense as: אַזְכָּרָה, a memorial, a term usually applied to the fistful (see e.g., Leviticus 2:2, 9, 16 and Rashi to 24:7). Scripture is even more explicit when it says (there v. 9): and they should eat it (the Panim Bread) in a holy place, for it is for him holy of the holies from the fire offerings of HASHEM.]

5.

אַף עַל־פִּי שֶׁאָמְרוּ: אֵין מְמַשְׁכְּנִין נָשִׁים וַעֲבָדִים וּקְטַנִּים — Though they [the Sages] have said [mishnah 3]: "They do not seize collateral from women, slaves, or minors,"

These persons usually have access to monies which are not theirs (but their husband's, master's, or father's respectively), and it is reasonable to suspect

that money contributed by them may be given without the consent of the true owner. Accordingly, the law of mishnah 3 that such people are not forced to contribute, could be misconstrued to mean that even their voluntary offerings are refused for fear that they may be contributing money that is not truly theirs. Our tanna now corrects this mis-

tirely burnt; it may not be eaten [Leviticus 6:16]. If the Omer offering, the Two Loaves and the Panim Bread are ours, how may they be eaten?

5. **T**hough they have said: "They do not seize collateral from women, slaves, or minors" — [nevertheless,] if they contributed [the half shekel] we accept it from them.

[However,] if a Gentile or a Cuthean contributed,

interpretation *(R' Shmuel; commentator cited by R' Meshullam).*

אִם שְׁקָלוּ, מְקַבְּלִין מִיָּדָן. — *[nevertheless,] if they contributed [the half shekel] we accept it from them* [lit. *from their hands*].

Because, as ruled in *Bava Kama* (119a), we may accept small contributions from women *(ibid.).*

[The reason for this ruling is that it would not matter even if our suspicion were correct that the money was given without permission. Since only small amounts are involved we may reasonably assume that the owners do not mind.]

הָעוֹבֵד כּוֹכָבִים — *[However,] if a Gentile* [Although the literal translation of עוֹבֵד כּוֹכָבִים is a *star-worshiper,* the expression generally refers to all non-Jews regardless of their religious persuasions. Originally the terms נָכְרִי, *stranger,* and גּוֹי, *nation,* were used in Mishnah and *Gemara* to refer to non-Jews in general, while the early Judeo-Christians were called מִינִים, *heretics.* However, due to medieval censorship of the Talmud and other Jewish works, considerable confusion exists whenever these and similar terms are mentioned. Because of the whims of individual censors, the following terms (when not altogether omitted) are used interchangeably: נָכְרִי, גּוֹי, כּוּתִי, נוֹצְרִי, מִין, עוֹבֵד גִּילוּלִים, עוֹבֵד כּוֹכָבִים וּמַזָּלוֹת=עַכּוּ"ם, אֶפִּיקוֹרוֹס, and many more. Some modern editions of the Talmud have attempted to correct the texts, but it is doubtful whether the confusion caused by the censors will ever be cleared up completely.]

וְהַכּוּתִי שֶׁשָּׁקַל, — *or a Cuthean contributed,*

The coming of the כּוּתִים, *Cutheans,* to *Eretz Yisrael* is described in *II Kings* (17:24-41).The Assyrian king brought non-Jewish citizens of various countries [probably mostly from Cutha, hence the generic term Cutheans] to settle the cities of Samaria left desolate by the exile of the Ten Tribes. Although they ostensibly converted to Judaism, this conversion was not due to an honest conviction. Rather, they saw conversion as a protective measure to end a plague of wild lions which overtook Samaria. Because their basis for conversion was not a true commitment to Judaism, considerable dispute arose among the Sages regarding the validity of such conversion (see *Kiddushin* 75b). Whatever their status, they remained a sect unto themselves — known as Samaritans because they lived in Samaria — and exhibited great animosity toward the Jews (see *Ezra* 4 for a description of their effort to prevent the construction of the Second Temple and *Yoma* 69a for their attempt to have the Temple destroyed). Later, in Talmudic times, the Cutheans were discovered worshiping the image of a dove upon Mount Gerizim, whereupon the Rabbis designated them totally Gentile [עוֹבְדֵי כּוֹכָבִים גְּמוּרִין] (*Chullin* 6a). [This designation, however, had not yet been assigned during the Temple era and cannot thus be considered the reason for the injunction against accepting Cuthean shekalim.]

מְקַבְּלִין מִיָּדָן. וְאֵין מְקַבְּלִין מִיָּדָן קִנֵּי זָבִין וְקִנֵּי
זָבוֹת וְקִנֵּי יוֹלְדוֹת; וְחַטָאוֹת וַאֲשָׁמוֹת. אֲבָל
נְדָרִים וּנְדָבוֹת מְקַבְּלִין מִיָּדָן.

יד אברהם

אֵין מְקַבְּלִין מִיָּדָן — *we do not accept [it] from them* [lit., *The Gentile or the Cuthean who contributed — we do not accept from their hands*].

Sifra (to *Leviticus* 22:25) understands that the injunction, *and from the hand of a stranger shall you not offer the sacrifice of your God out of any of these*, refers to acceptance of half shekels from Gentiles.

R' Shmuel (see also *Taklin Chadatin*) understands that the quote from *Ezra* (4:3; see below), *It is not for you and us to build a house to our God*, is adduced here to serve as a source for rejecting the half shekel contributions of Gentiles.

He adds that the exclusion of Gentiles from sharing in *building* the Temple, excludes them from the half shekel as well, since the remainder of this money (שְׁיָרֵי הַלִּשְׁכָּה) is used to repair the Temple (see below, s.v. וכן הוא מפורש, and 4:2).

Yerushalmi attributes the statement in our mishnah disqualifying the Cutheans to the tanna who invalidates their conversion (see above, s.v. והכותי) and thereby renders them Gentiles. Consequently, according to the opinion that their conversion was valid, we may accept their half shekels (cf. *Taklin Chadatin*).

◆§ Zav and Zavah

The law of זָב, *zav*, is found in *Leviticus* 15:1-15: אִישׁ אִישׁ כִּי יִהְיֶה זָב מִבְּשָׂרוֹ זוֹבוֹ טָמֵא הוּא ... וְאִישׁ אֲשֶׁר יִגַּע בְּמִשְׁכָּבוֹ יְכַבֵּס בְּגָדָיו וְרָחַץ בַּמַּיִם ... וְכִי־יִטְהַר הַזָּב מִזּוֹבוֹ וְסָפַר לוֹ שִׁבְעַת יָמִים לְטָהֳרָתוֹ ... וּבַיּוֹם הַשְּׁמִינִי יִקַּח־לוֹ שְׁתֵּי תֹרִים אוֹ שְׁנֵי בְּנֵי יוֹנָה ... אֶחָד חַטָּאת וְהָאֶחָד עֹלָה, *Any man who will have an issue from his flesh, his issue is contaminated ... And any man who will touch his bed shall wash his clothes and bathe himself in water ... And when one is cleansed of his issue, he shall count for himself seven days of his cleansing ... On the eighth day he shall take for himself two turtledoves or two young pigeons ... one as a sin offering and one as a burnt offering ...*

Scripture teaches that a male who has experienced a seminal issue becomes טָמֵא, *contaminated*. If such issue was repeated, with no apparent cause, he becomes contaminated to the extent that even a bed or chair upon which he lies or sits becomes contaminated. He transmits this contamination even though his flesh does not come in direct contact with his seat. For example, if a number of cushions are on a chair, and the *zav* sits on them, even the bottom cushion becomes contaminated. When the issue stops, he must count seven 'clean' days during which he experiences no issue. Then he must immerse himself in spring water. If there had been a third issue, then in addition to the above counting he must also bring two bird sacrifices, one a sin offering, the second a burnt offering.

A זָבָה, *zavah*, is אִשָּׁה כִּי־יָזוּב זוֹב דָּמָהּ יָמִים רַבִּים בְּלֹא עֶת־נִדָּתָהּ, *a woman whose blood flowed many days but it was not the time of her menses* (*Leviticus* 15:25). The verses go on to describe her cleansing process. If the flow continues three days or more, then when it stops *she shall count for herself seven days and then be cleansed. On the eighth day she shall take for herself two turtledoves or two young pigeons ...* (*Leviticus* 15:28-29). This pair of birds is referred to as a קַן, *nest*, hence the terms קִנֵּי זָבִים וְקִנֵּי זָבוֹת, *nests of zavim and nests of zavos.*

For a more complete description of *zavah*, see *Niddah* 35b and *Rashi* to *Leviticus* 15:25; *Tur Yoreh Deah* 283 with *Beis Yosef*.

we do not accept [it] from them. Nor do we accept from them bird offerings of *zavim, zavos* and women after childbirth; nor sin offerings and guilt offerings. But we accept vow offerings and gift offerings from them.

YAD AVRAHAM

◁§ A Woman After Childbirth

אִשָּׁה כִּי תַזְרִיעַ וְיָלְדָה זָכָר וְטָמְאָה שִׁבְעַת יָמִים ... וּשְׁלֹשִׁים יוֹם וּשְׁלֹשֶׁת יָמִים תֵּשֵׁב בִּדְמֵי טָהֳרָה ... וְאִם־נְקֵבָה תֵלֵד וְטָמְאָה שְׁבֻעַיִם ... וְשִׁשִּׁים יוֹם וְשֵׁשֶׁת יָמִים תֵּשֵׁב עַל־דְּמֵי טָהֳרָה וּבִמְלֹאת יְמֵי טָהֳרָה לְבֵן אוֹ לְבַת תָּבִיא כֶּבֶשׂ בֶּן־שְׁנָתוֹ לְעֹלָה וּבֶן־יוֹנָה אוֹ תֹר לְחַטָּאת ... וְאִם־לֹא תִמְצָא יָדָהּ דֵּי שֶׂה וְלָקְחָה שְׁתֵּי־תֹרִים אוֹ שְׁנֵי בְּנֵי יוֹנָה אֶחָד לְעֹלָה וְאֶחָד לְחַטָּאת ... — *If a woman gives birth and delivers a male she shall be* tamei [contaminated] *for a seven day period ... and for a thirty-three day period she shall wait, although her blood is pure* [see Ramban]. *But if she delivers a female she shall be* tamei *for twice seven days ... and for a sixty-six day period she shall wait, although her blood is pure. When her pure days have been completed for a male child or a female child, she shall bring a yearling lamb as a burnt offering and a young pigeon or a turtledove as a sin offering ... But if she cannot afford* [lit. *if her hand cannot find*] *enough for a lamb, she shall take either two turtledoves or two young pigeons, one as a burnt offering and one as a sin offering ... (Leviticus 12:2-8)*

For a seven day period in the case of a boy, or a fourteen day period in the case of a girl, the יוֹלֶדֶת [yoledes], *woman who has recently given birth*, remains in a con- taminated state as if she were a *niddah* (menstruant). When this time elapses she cleanses herself of her contamination by immersing in a *mikveh*. However, for an additional period of thirty-three days for a male child and sixty-six for a female, she is forbidden to enter the Temple environs or partake of sacrificial meat. Forty (33+7) or eighty (66+14) days after she has delivered, the *yoledes* brings the prescribed offerings and is thenceforth permitted to enter the Temple environs and to eat sacrificial meat.

The prescribed sacrifice comprises a yearling lamb as a burnt offering and a bird as a sin offering, if the woman can afford the cost. If not, she is permitted to bring a pair of birds, one of them replacing the lamb. Such pairs of birds are called קִנֵּי יוֹלֶדֶת, lit. *nests of a woman after childbirth. Though the mishnah speaks of a* קֵן, literally *a nest*, implying at least two birds, this is not intended to imply that this law applies only to a poor woman's offering.

וְאֵין מְקַבְּלִין מִיָּדָן קִנֵּי זָבִין וְקִנֵּי זָבוֹת וְקִנֵּי יוֹלְדוֹת; — *Nor do we accept from them* [lit. *from their hands*]; i.e., *from Gentiles and Cutheans*] *bird offerings* [lit. *nests*] *of zavim, zavos, and women after child- birth;*

Even according to *Rambam's* opinion (below) that, according to the tanna of this mishnah, חַטָּאת, *sin offerings*, of Gentiles may be offered in the Temple, this would not extend to the offering of a *yoledes*, which is not offered to atone for any specific or known sin.

וַחֲטָאוֹת וַאֲשָׁמוֹת. — *nor sin offerings and guilt offerings.*

Sin offerings (חַטָּאוֹת) are sacrificed to atone for inadvertent (שׁוֹגֵג) transgres- sion of certain sins. They are negative transgressions for which an intentional violation is punished with כָּרֵת, *spiritual excision* (see *Rashi* to *Lev.* 4:2; *Shabbos* 69a).

Sin offerings are also offered for the sins enumerated in *Leviticus* 5:1-4, and as part of every *mussaf* service (except that of Shabbos).

שקלים
א/ה

זֶה הַכְּלָל: כָּל־שֶׁנִּידָר וְנִידָב, מְקַבְּלִין מִיָּדָן;
כָּל־שֶׁאֵין נִידָר וְנִידָב, אֵין מְקַבְּלִין מִיָּדָן. וְכֵן
הוּא מְפֹרָשׁ עַל־יְדֵי עֶזְרָא — שֶׁנֶּאֱמַר: „לֹא־
לָכֶם וָלָנוּ לִבְנוֹת בַּיִת לֵאלֹהֵינוּ."

יד אברהם

Guilt offerings (אֲשָׁמוֹת) are offered for a various array of different transgressions and occasions (see *Leviticus* 5:14-26; 14:12; 19:21; *Numbers* 6:12; *Zevachim* 5:5).

All the types of sacrifices listed above are categorized as offerings which 'cannot be vowed nor donated'; these offerings may be brought only to atone for a specific transgression, or where warranted by the occasion (e.g., the nazirite's guilt offering). According to the rule laid down further in this mishnah, we do not accept these from Gentiles or Cutheans.

אֲבָל נְדָרִים וּנְדָבוֹת מְקַבְּלִין מִיָּדָן — *But we accept vow offerings* [lit. *vows*] *and gift offerings from them.*

נְדָרִים [*nedarim*], *vow offerings*, are sacrifices that were consecrated in fulfillment of a vow to bring the offering. In making such a vow one says: הֲרֵי עָלַי ... , *I take upon myself* to bring a sacrifice. At a later time an animal is consecrated in fulfillment of this vow.

נְדָבוֹת [*nedavos*], *gift offerings*, are sacrifices that are voluntarily consecrated without any prior personal obligation on the part of the donor (*Kinnim* 1:1; see *Megillah* 1:6 with *comm.*). In this case the donor says: הֲרֵי זֶה, *this is*, i.e., this animal is consecrated as a sacrifice. Only עוֹלוֹת, *burnt offerings*, and שְׁלָמִים, *peace offerings*, may be brought as either *nedarim* or *nedavos*.

The Talmud (*Menachos* 73b) derives from the verse in *Leviticus* (22:18): אִישׁ אִישׁ ... אֲשֶׁר יַקְרִיב קָרְבָּנוֹ לְכָל־נִדְרֵיהֶם וּלְכָל־נִדְבוֹתָם — *Anyone* [lit. *A man, a man*] ... *who brings his offering, whether they are vow offerings or gift offerings* ... the double expression אִישׁ אִישׁ, *a man, a man*, is interpreted as referring to any person, whether Jew or Gentile. Thus, Scripture teaches that Gentiles may offer vow and gift offerings in the Temple (*Rashi; Sifra*).

— זֶה הַכְּלָל: כָּל־שֶׁנִּידָר וְנִידָב, מְקַבְּלִין מִיָּדָן; *This is the general rule: Whatever may be vowed or donated, we accept from them* [lit. *from their hands*]; — as explained above.

— כָּל־שֶׁאֵין נִידָר וְנִידָב, אֵין מְקַבְּלִין מִיָּדָן. *whatever may not be vowed nor donated, we do not accept from them* [lit. *from their hands*].

[Such offerings may not be accepted from Gentiles, since the verse (*Leviticus* 22:18) adduced to permit their sacrifices to be offered in the Temple (see above) refers specifically to vows and donations.]

Yerushalmi comments that this passage of the mishnah surely includes Cutheans for it is inconceivable that a Gentile, who would be foreign to the concepts of the Torah (*Rambam, Comm.*), would endeavor to bring bird offerings of *zavim* and the like. [Moreover, since the contaminations (טוּמְאוֹת) of *zav* and *zavah* do not apply to non-Jews, a bird offering brought by a Gentile could not be termed a 'bird offering of *zavim'*.]

Rambam's version of the mishnah reads slightly differently (see *Tos. Yom Tov* and *R' Y. Kafich's* ed. of the *Comm.*; cf. *Kessef Mishneh, Ma'aseh HaKarbanos* 3:2): אֵין מְקַבְּלִין מִיָּדָם קִנֵּי זָבִים וְזָבוֹת קִנֵּי יוֹלְדוֹת, חַטָּאוֹת וַאֲשָׁמוֹת מְקַבְּלִין מֵהֶם. זֶה הַכְּלָל ... , *We do not accept from them bird offerings of a zav or zavah, or bird offerings of a child-bearing woman; but we accept sin offerings and guilt offerings from them. This is the general rule* ...

According to this version the two seemingly redundant clauses of the mishnah have separate subjects. The first clause ('we do not accept ... from them') lists which offerings a Cuthean may or may not offer. The second clause ('This is the general ... ') elaborates on the same topic as it pertains to a Gentile. A

1
5

This is the general rule: Whatever may be vowed or donated, we accept from them; whatever may not be vowed nor donated, we do not accept from them. And so has it been made clear by Ezra — as it is said: *It is not for you and for us to build a house for our God [Ezra 4:3].*

Cuthean's sin offering, however, is accepted for 'since his intent is for atonement he may repent' [and accept the true faith in its entirety].

Rambam comments that in our days, after the Rabbinical proclamation which rendered the Cutheans Gentiles for all purposes *(Chullin* 6a; עֲשָׂאוּם בְּגוֹיִם גְּמוּרִים), all these distinctions between them and Gentiles do not apply.

Even as it pertains to a Gentile, *Rambam (Comm.; Hil. Ma'aseh HaKarbanos* 3:2, based on *Menachos* 73b) rules that the halachah does not follow our mishnah. He rules according to the opinion of *R' Akiva (Menachos* 73b) that we accept only burnt offerings from a Gentile. Moreover, he rules *(loc. cit.* 3:3) that even a Gentile's peace offering (שְׁלָמִים) is sacrificed as a burnt offering (based on *R' Huna, Menachos* 73b).

וְכֵן הוּא מְפֹרָשׁ עַל־יְדֵי עֶזְרָא — שֶׁנֶּאֱמַר: "לֹא־לָכֶם וָלָנוּ לִבְנוֹת בַּיִת לֵאלֹהֵינוּ." — *And so has it been made clear by Ezra — as it is said: It is not for you and for us to build a house for our God [Ezra 4:3].*

[Our text follows the emendation of *Yesh Seder LaMishnah;* see also *Shnuyei Nuschaos.*]

Ezra relates the story of the construction of the Second Temple. Cyrus issued a proclamation allowing all Jews to return to *Eretz Yisrael* and to rebuild the *Beis HaMikdash* (1:1-3). When the enemies of Judah and Benjamin heard that the [returned] exiles were building a palace for *HASHEM*, God of Israel, they approached Zerubavel and the [other] leaders saying, "Let us build with you, for [we do] as you do. We pray to your God and sacrifice to Him since the days of Essar Chadon, king of Assyria, who has brought us up here" (4:1-2).

But Zerubavel and Yeshua, the

Kohen Gadol, did not agree: *"It is not for you and for us* [together] *to build a house for our God"* (4:3).

The enemies proceeded to intimidate the Jews and otherwise hamper their reconstruction efforts (4:4-5) until a conglomeration of nationalities and ethnic groups succeeded in halting the rebuilding through a petition to King Artachshasta [variously identified as Cyrus, who had undergone a change of heart in the latter days of his reign *(Rashi)* or Ahasuerus who ascended the Persian throne two years after Cyrus' initial proclamation *(Ibn Ezra)]* (4:7-24).

Since the 'enemies of Judah and Benjamin' persisted so strongly and spared no avenue in their attempt to stop the Temple's construction, it is clear that their original offer of assistance was a devious plot to sabotage the project from within. Failing in their subterfuge, they advanced to less subtle methods and waged a no holds barred campaign to achieve their end.

But who were these unspecified enemies? Their identity is to be found in their own words to Zerubavel, *"We pray to your God ... since the days of Essar Chadon* [son of Sennacherib *(Rashi)], king of Assyria, who has brought us up to here"* (4:2), and in the letter they addressed to Artachshasta, *" ... and the other peoples exiled by Asnapar* [Sennacherib *(Rashi)] whom he settled into the cities of Samaria"* (4:10). The 'enemies of Judah and Benjamin' are clearly the Cutheans.

Thus, the mishnah adduces the verse from *Ezra,* which disqualifies Gentiles and Cutheans from any role in the building of the Temple, as proof that

יד אברהם

their shekalim, the excess of which is used for Temple repair, are unacceptable (R' Shmuel). [Though this interpretation is strongly suggested by the context, it contains many difficulties[1], leading us to offer the alternative interpretation that the mishnah does not cite this verse to prove its previous statements, but to demonstrate that the barring of Gentile and Cuthean contributions to the half shekel fund is not unique since there is precedent for rejecting their contributions.]

R' Yochanan (Arachin 6a and Yer. here) derives from this verse the rule that we should not accept contributions for the building of the Temple (בְּדֶק הַבַּיִת) from Gentiles (and Cutheans). However, a distinction is drawn between בַּתְּחִלָּה, lit. in the beginning, and בַּסּוֹף, the end. Rashi understands that בַּתְּחִלָּה refers only to the initial building, when sabotage was a legitimate fear. After the edifice has been erected, however, we may accept such contributions. Rambam (Hil. Matnos Aniyim 8:8) renders

בַּתְּחִלָּה like לְכַתְּחִלָּה, initially, and בַּסּוֹף like בְּדִיעֲבַד, after the fact. Thus we may not accept contributions for the initial building or the later upkeep of the Temple, but if this rule has been disregarded and the contribution has been accepted, we do not have to return the money. However, if a Gentile contributed an object (e.g., a beam), the use of which will be conspicuous in the edifice, it may not be used (Arachin 6a). We may, however, accept Gentile contributions for a synagogue, but only if we are certain that the donor has no idolatrous intentions (see Arachin 6a; Rambam, ibid.; Yoreh Deah 259:4).

Yerushalmi derives yet another rule from this verse. We may not even accept contributions for the erection of walls around Jerusalem or even the digging of aqueducts for in a further exchange between Nehemiah and the enemies of the Jews concerning the erection of the wall around Jerusalem, Nehemiah retorted, "But you have no portion, nor right, nor memorial, in Jerusalem" (Nechemiah 2:20). This rule is accepted by Rambam (ibid.).

6.

◄§ Kalbon

Under certain conditions an additional payment called a *kalbon*, must accompany the half shekel. The amount of this premium is discussed at the end of mishnah 7. Before giving its amount, the mishnah delineates who must pay the *kalbon* and who is exempt. The exact circumstance under which the *kalbon* is required is the subject of a dispute between *Rambam* and *Rashi*.

Rambam (Comm. and Hil. Shekalim 3:1) explains that because large numbers of people needed half shekel coins during the month of Adar, half shekel pieces were very much in demand, pushing the price of two half shekalim above that of one full shekel. Consequently, someone wishing to exchange a *sela* (full shekel) for two half

1. The following difficulties are inherent in R' Shmuel's view: (a) Cuthean donations are barred by Scripture. How then can Yerushalmi attribute this rule only to the opinion which invalidates Cuthean conversion? (b) Surely a distinction must be drawn between the verse in Ezra where the Cutheans wanted to contribute directly to the building of the Temple, and our mishnah where only monies left over after the purchase of sacrifices were used for Temple building, but the contribution's main purpose is for public sacrifices. Yerushalmi clearly makes this distinction and allows indirect contribution. (c) Zerubavel barred the Cutheans because he suspected sabotage, as suggested by Scripture (see above). This surely does not prove that a Cuthean's half shekel should be refused when the Temple is already built and this suspicion is no longer present. The Talmud (Arachin 5b) clearly draws this distinction (see also Rashi there 6a, s.v. בתחילה and Yer. here with commentaries).

YAD AVRAHAM

shekel pieces would have to pay the money-changer a surcharge for the exchange. When a full shekel was given in payment for two people, the money-changer would be bypassed and his surcharge avoided. This caused a discrepancy in the value of half shekel payments since those who paid in half shekels were giving coins of greater value than two people sharing in a whole shekel. To eliminate this discrepancy, the Rabbis required that people sharing in a shekel should contribute an extra *kalbon*, the amount they would avoid paying the money-changer. Accordingly, one paying with a half shekel piece is exempt from this *kalbon*.

Rashi (Beitzah 39b, s.v. כשחייבין) reasons that because half shekel pieces were thin and therefore prone to loss, it was common to exchange them for coins of larger denominations; since such transactions were subject to a money-changer's service charge, the donor of a half shekel, in effect, would be giving the Temple treasury a slightly lower value since it would have to bear the money-changing expense. To compensate the Temple for this cost, the donor was required to add a *kalbon* to his half shekel contribution. This reason applies only to people who gave half shekels, but in order to prevent discrepancies and complications (משום לא פְלוג), the Sages required the *kalbon* premium even when a *sela* coin is given for two people.

— In an alternative interpretation, *Rashi (Bechoros 56b, s.v.* האחין) suggests that the giving of the *kalbon* was instituted as a precaution in case an individual's half shekel coin was slightly lighter than the silver content prescribed by law.

The above discussion is based on the *tanna kamma's* view that the *kalbon* premium is Rabbinically ordained. However, the mishnah below cites the opinion of R' Meir, who, according to *Yerushalmi*, bases the *kalbon* on the Scriptural requirement that the half shekel payment may not fall short, even by a miniscule amount, from that specified by the Torah. The *kalbon* is a hedge against either impurities which may not have been removed in the refining process [resulting in a coin of full weight but containing less than the required amount of silver] *(Korban HaEdah)*, or against the possibility that a particular coin may weigh less that the required amount *(Taklin Chadatin)*. In R' Meir's view the *kalbon* is an integral part of the half shekel payment in all cases [except for the voluntary contribution of one who is exempt *(Taklin Chadatin)*].

◆§ How was the Kalbon Used?

At least five different opinions as to the disbursement of the *kalbonos* are found in *Yerushalmi* (end of this chapter) and *Tosefta* (1:5):

(a) In accordance with his view that the premium is Scripturally ordained and is an integral part of the half shekel payment, R' Meir holds that these extra coins are used for the purchase of animals for the public offerings;

(b) R' Elazar would place this money into the chest marked נְדָבָה, *Donations* (see 6:5-6);

(c) R' Shimon Shezuri maintains that the coins were converted to gold which was used to plate the walls of the Holy of Holies;

(d) Ben Azzai says that the *kalbonos* paid the money-changers/collectors for their services; and

(e) an anonymous tanna holds that these monies paid the cost of transporting the collected shekalim to Jerusalem (Cf. 4:4; see also *Rambam, Hil. Shekalim* 3:7 and *Kessef Mishneh* there).

שְׁקָלִים לֹא כֹהֲנִים וְנָשִׁים וַעֲבָדִים וּקְטַנִּים.
א/ו הַשּׁוֹקֵל עַל־יְדֵי כֹהֵן, עַל־יְדֵי אִשָּׁה, עַל־יְדֵי
עֶבֶד, עַל־יְדֵי קָטָן פָּטוּר. וְאִם שָׁקַל עַל־יָדוֹ
וְעַל־יְדֵי חֲבֵרוֹ, חַיָּב בְּקָלְבּוֹן אֶחָד. רַבִּי מֵאִיר
אוֹמֵר: שְׁנֵי קָלְבּוֹנוֹת.
הַנּוֹתֵן סֶלַע וְנוֹטֵל שֶׁקֶל חַיָּב שְׁנֵי קָלְבּוֹנוֹת.

יד אברהם

וְנָשִׁים וַעֲבָדִים וּקְטַנִּים. — *women, slaves nor minors.*

[These persons are exempt from the half shekel payment, and are therefore not required to give a *kalbon* if they choose to contribute.]

הַשּׁוֹקֵל עַל־יְדֵי כֹהֵן, עַל־יְדֵי אִשָּׁה, עַל־יְדֵי עֶבֶד, עַל־יְדֵי קָטָן פָּטוּר. — *One who contributes for a Kohen, woman, slave, or minor is exempt.*

If someone lays out a half shekel on behalf of someone who is exempt from the *mitzvah* [or, in the case of a *Kohen*, who would not be coerced to contribute], he need not add the *kalbon*, even though he will be repaid. On the other hand, had he done so as a loan for an Israelite who will repay him the half shekel, a *kalbon* must be added. However, if someone contributed a half shekel as a gift on behalf of an Israelite who will *not* repay him, a *kalbon* need not be added (*Rav*).

וְאִם שָׁקַל עַל־יָדוֹ וְעַל־יְדֵי חֲבֵרוֹ, חַיָּב בְּקָלְבּוֹן אֶחָד. — *If one contributed for himself and for his colleague, he is obligated for [only] one kalbon.*

Even though both are obligated and the colleague will repay the donor, only one *kalbon* is required. This tanna holds that the standard contribution of a half shekel requires no additional *kalbon*; the surcharge is incurred only when a full shekel *(sela)* is given. Consequently, one *kalbon* suffices for both donors (*Rav*).

[*Rav* evidently accepts *Rambam's* view (see preface). According to the first view of *Rashi*, the *kalbon* is required primarily when a half shekel coin is given, but for reasons of

וְאֵלּוּ שֶׁחַיָּבִין בְּקָלְבּוֹן: — *The following are obligated to pay a kalbon:*

According to *Rambam* (see preface) and *Rav*, the *kalbon* is necessary only when two fully obligated people share in contributing a full shekel. Thus, if either one of the partners in the shekel is exempt, but gives only as a voluntary contribution, a *kalbon* is not required (*Hil. Shekalim* 3:2).

According to the two views expressed by *Rashi* and according to R' Meir, the mishnah refers to a half shekel payment. If, however, a full shekel is contributed jointly, the *kalbon* can be waived only if *both* contributors are exempt.

לְוִיִּם וְיִשְׂרְאֵלִים וְגֵרִים וַעֲבָדִים מְשֻׁחְרָרִים; — *Levites, Israelites, proselytes, and emancipated slaves;*

[All these persons are obligated to the half shekel (see mishnah 3), consequently they must also pay a *kalbon*.]

אֲבָל לֹא כֹהֲנִים — *but not Kohanim,*

[Although *Kohanim* are obligated to pay the half shekel (see mishnah 4), presumably the Sages absolved them from the *kalbon* premium for the same reason that *Kohanim* are not coerced — 'in the pursuit of peace' (see above mishnah 3). Alternatively, since as a practical matter even the half shekel contribution of the *Kohen* was given as an act of voluntary compliance with the *mitzvah*, it would be ludicrous to add a surcharge to the actual payment. According to either explanation, R' Meir who holds the *kalbon* to be an integral part of the half shekel payment would not agree to the exemption of the *Kohanim* (see *Tos. Yom Tov*).]

1
6

slaves; but not *Kohanim*, women, slaves nor minors.

One who contributes for a *Kohen*, woman, slave or minor is exempt.

If one contributed for himself and for his colleague, he is obligated for [only] one *kalbon*. R' Meir says: Two *kalbonos*.

One who gives a *sela* and takes back a shekel must pay two *kalbonos*.

uniformity (לֹא פְלוּג) the Sages required it of all contributions, hence one *kalbon* is sufficient when a full shekel is given.

According to *Rashi's* alternative view, one *kalbon* is enough because the money changer's service charge is the same for a shekel as for a half shekel. In either of *Rashi's* views, it matters not whether the third party contribution was a loan or a gift. However, in mishnah 7 (s.v. הַשׁוֹקֵל עַל יְדֵי עָנִי) where a half shekel coin is given, the distinction does apply. (See also *comm.* to mishnah 7, s.v. פְּטוּרִין מִן הקלבון.)

רַבִּי מֵאִיר אוֹמֵר: שְׁנֵי קַלְבּוֹנוֹת. — *R' Meir says:* [He must give] *two kalbonos.*

Since R' Meir maintains that even one who gives a half shekel piece must pay a *kalbon* (see preface), each of the two people contributing jointly must add a *kalbon* (*Rav*).

Rambam explains R' Meir's view differently: Had either of these two wished to give a shekel and receive change, he would have had to add a *kalbon* as the money changer's fee. In our case, since each is actually using a full shekel coin, the Sages ordained that rather than having them profit by avoiding the payment of a second *kalbon*, they should each contribute that amount to the Temple treasury. [This explanation is also compatible with the two views expressed by *Rashi*.]

הַנּוֹתֵן סֶלַע וְנוֹטֵל שֶׁקֶל — *One who gives a sela and takes back a shekel*

The Biblical shekel was known as a *sela* during the Second Temple era, thus the coin used for the half shekel payment was a half *sela*. However, because of its relationship to this *mitzvah*, the half *sela* coin was popularly called "shekel". Thus, in Mishnaic termino-

logy סֶלַע, *sela*, is a full shekel, while שֶׁקֶל, *shekel*, refers to a half shekel. The mishnah thus speaks of one who gave a *sela* in fulfillment of his obligation and received a shekel, i.e., half *sela* coin as change (*Rav; Tos. Yom Tov; Ramban* to *Exodus* 30:13).

חַיָּב שְׁנֵי קַלְבּוֹנוֹת. — *must pay two kalbonos.*

In this instance the *tanna kamma* concurs with R' Meir that a double *kalbon* is required; one as the premium paid whenever a *sela* coin is used for the head tax payment, a second one as the service charge [or, a hedge against possible short weight of the coin (*Rav*)] on the shekel coin received as change (*Rav; Rambam, Comm.* and *Hil. Shekalim* 3:6, but see *Emek HaMelech* there).

[According to *Rashi's* views (see preface) this exchange is presumably considered as two separate transactions. First, a *sela* is exchanged for two halves, incurring the usual charge of the money changers, this is the first *kalbon*. The second *kalbon* is that which is required with every payment of the head tax.]

The above interpretations, that the *tanna kamma* concurs with R' Meir in this case, are based on the amora Rav's understanding of the mishnah.

Yerushalmi (as understood by *Korban HaEdah*, *Vilna Gaon* and others; cf. *Pnei Moshe*) explains that the mishnah is in accordance with R' Meir and speaks of two people making their respective payments with a one *sela* coin held in partnership. Since every shekel

עַל־יְדֵי עָנִי וְעַל־יְדֵי שְׁכֵנוֹ [ז] **הַשּׁוֹקֵל**
וְעַל־יְדֵי בֶן עִירוֹ פָּטוּר; וְאִם
הִלְוָוּם, חַיָּב.

יד אברהם

payment must include a *kalbon*, the
double payment requires a double
kalbon.

Although *Rashi* (as understood by

Vilna Gaon) decides the halachah according to R' Meir, Rav and *Rambam*
(Hil. Shekalim 3:1) both accept the first
tanna's view as halachah.

7.

הַשּׁוֹקֵל עַל־יְדֵי עָנִי וְעַל־יְדֵי שְׁכֵנוֹ וְעַל־יְדֵי בֶּן־
עִירוֹ פָּטוּר; — *One who contributes for
a poor person, his neighbor or his
townsman is exempt [from a kalbon];*
Rambam, who maintains that a
kalbon is required only when a full *sela*
is used (see preface to mishnah 6), understands our mishnah as referring to a
person giving a *sela* on behalf of himself
and his colleague. However, unlike
mishnah 6 where the payment on his
colleague's behalf is a loan and requires
a *kalbon,* in our case a *kalbon* is not
needed because the money is a gift,
which will not be repaid. *Meiri* explains
that the person on whose behalf the
shekel is given is not present. Consequently, without the donor's generosity,
the Temple would not receive his payment. Since the donor's intention is to
increase the money available for the
purchase of sacrifices, he is not taxed
for the *kalbon* premium (*Rav; Rambam, Hil. Shekalim* 3:3; *Meiri*). According to *Rashi's* view (see preface to
mishnah 6), the mishnah speaks of one

who donated a half shekel coin for
someone else.

[It may be conjectured that the exemption
is granted here on the premise that the
kalbon is a Rabbinical obligation which was
waived by the Sages in this case. According
to R' Meir's view that the *kalbon* is mandated by the Torah (see mishnah 6, s.v. ר'
מאיר), however, a donor contributing a half
shekel without the *kalbon* would have failed
to pay the other person's debt in full.]

וְאִם הִלְוָוּם, חַיָּב. — *but if he lent [the half
shekel] to them* [i.e., the poor man, *et
al.*], *he is obligated [to pay a kalbon].*

[Since the contributor expects to be
repaid by the person for whom he
tendered the donation and since that
person is liable to pay the *kalbon,* it
must be given by the donor as well.]

[This point — that a half shekel donated
for another person must be accompanied by
a *kalbon* — has already been stated earlier
(mishnah 6, s.v. ואם שקל). This mishnah,
however, adds the distinction between a third
party donation given as a loan and one given
as a gift.]

⋖§ **Joint Ownership as it Relates to the Kalbon and Animal Tithes.**

In the following clause the mishnah discusses when the *kalbon* is applicable to
heirs and partners contributing from jointly held monies. The mishnah shows how
the *kalbon* is inversely related to animal tithes (מַעְשֵׂר בְּהֵמָה): Whenever partners are
obligated in one, they are exempt from the other. This mishnah reoccurs in *Chullin*
(1:7) and *Bechoros* (9:3).

Payments of the half shekel made by an estate on behalf of its heirs or from other jointly
held property on behalf of the partners are sometimes exempt from the *kalbon.* The same
holds true regarding the obligation to tithe animals — joint ownership and estate status can
cause exemptions.

וְכָל־מַעְשַׂר בָּקָר וָצֹאן כֹּל אֲשֶׁר־יַעֲבֹר תַּחַת הַשָּׁבֶט הָעֲשִׂירִי יִהְיֶה קֹדֶשׁ לַה', *Every tenth
cattle or sheep, whatever passes under the* [counter's] *rod, the tenth shall be consecrated to HASHEM (Leviticus 27:32).*

The Torah requires that one tithe the offspring of his kosher animals (goats,

7. **O**ne who contributes for a poor person, his neighbor or his townsman is exempt from a *kalbon;* but if he lent [the half-shekel to] them, he is obligated [to pay a *kalbon*].

YAD AVRAHAM

sheep, cattle). As the animals pass in single file through a narrow gate in their corral, the owner marks every tenth one and declares it קָדֵשׁ, *consecrated.* This animal is called מַעְשַׂר בְּהֵמָה, *animal tithe,* and must be brought as a sacrifice at the Temple. Certain portions of the sacrificial animal are place on the altar, the rest is eaten by the owner and his guests.

A) Heirs and Partners (Rashi's view)

An estate that has not yet been divided among the heirs is considered the property of the deceased and as such is not treated by the heirs as property jointly owned (שׁוּתָּפוּת). Half shekel payments made from the assets of such an estate (תְּפוּסַת הַבַּיִת, lit., *holdings of the house)* are subject to the same rules as the half shekel contributed by any father on behalf of his adult sons. They are categorized as הַשּׁוּקֵל עַל-יְדֵי עָנִי וְעַל-יְדֵי שְׁכֵנוֹ וכו', *one who contributes for a poor person, his neighbor, etc.,* and are exempt from the *kalbon.* [This rationale for the status of an undivided estate is suggested by the language of *Rashi* in *Bechoros* 56b, s.v. וכשחייבין.]

Partnerships, however, are considered as a collection of individual ownerships, and are subject to the *kalbon.* Thus, even in the case of property attained through divisions of an estate, if two or more of the heirs form a partnership by pooling their inheritances, the combined assets are no longer considered assets of the estate, but are treated like any other.

Since even a half shekel coin must be accompanied by a *kalbon* premium in Rashi's view (see preface to mishnah 6), a *kalbon* is required for each partner for whom the half shekel is given (*Rashi; Chullin* 25b; *Bechoros* 56b; *Beitzah* 39b). Only when a *sela* (full shekel) coin is contributed by a single donor on behalf of two people who will eventually repay their benefactor is one *kalbon* sufficient. [Cf. *Hon Ashir* and *M'lo HaRo'im* to *Beitzah* 39b.]

Regarding the animal tithes, the governing principle is that livestock owned in partnership is exempt according to this view (see *Bechoros* 56b). Consequently, an original, undivided estate — which is viewed as a single entity owned by one proprietor — is not exempt. But once the estate has been divided, if the brothers subsequently pool their resources, it is considered as a partnership and is exempt.

In summary, where an exemption to animal tithes exists in the above cases according to *Rashi,* it is because the property has the status of a partnership. Before division of an estate, therefore, there is no such exemption because the estate has the same status it had before the death.

Rambam has a different view, which will now be explained in detail.

B) Partners (Rambam's view)

Assets of a partnership fall under either of two categories: *Contributed capital* or *generated capital.* By contributed capital we refer to the assets that the respective people contributed to set up the partnership; in other words, the personal funds or animals that each of the partners invested in the partnership. By generated capital we refer to the profits or benefits that accrued to the partnership after it was set up; in other words, property purchased with the jointly owned funds, income that accrued to the newly formed partnership, or offspring born to the jointly owned

הָאַחִין הַשֻּׁתָּפִין שֶׁחַיָּבִין בְּקָלְבּוֹן פְּטוּרִין מִמַּעְשַׂר בְּהֵמָה; וּכְשֶׁחַיָּבִין בְּמַעְשַׂר בְּהֵמָה, פְּטוּרִין מִן־הַקָּלְבּוֹן.

יד אברהם

animals. The difference between the two is this: the contributed capital was once owned individually by the respective partners, while the generated capital was owned by the partnership from the start (לָקְחוּ מִמְּמוֹן הַשׁוּתָּפֹת אוֹ בִּרְשׁוּתָן).

Contributed capital is considered to have more than one owner, because the fact that the respective partners pool their assets does not diminish each one's individual ownership of the share he contributed to the partnership. If the half shekel payments are made with such funds a *kalbon* premium must be paid just as if two unrelated individuals jointly gave a *sela* in fulfillment of their obligation (see preface to mishnah 6).

Generated capital, on the other hand, is considered to have a single ownership, the partnership (see *comm.* below). Accordingly, half shekel payments made from these assets are treated as third-party payments, which are exempt from the *kalbon*. I.e., the partnership, which is viewed as a third party, distinct from the individual partners, is considered to have paid for the partners.

Regarding the animal tithe a different principle comes into play. Purchased livestock (לָקוּחַ) is exempt from the tithe (according to *Rambam's* interpretation of *Bechoros* 56b, see his *Comm.* there 9:3; *Lechem Mishnah* to *Hil. Bechoros* 6:10). Contributed capital is exempt from the animal tithe, because it is regarded as though each of the partners contributed his own assets to purchase a share in the contribution of his partner. Generated capital, however, is liable to animal tithes, because the newborn animals were never the property of an individual.

C) Heirs (Rambam's view)

In the case of estates, like other partnerships, a distinction is drawn between contributed capital and generated capital. Unlike other partnerships, however, the original, undivided estate has the status of generated capital, because it was never the private property of the individual brothers; from the moment they assumed title to it, it was a single entity, their father's estate. As long as the estate is intact, therefore, half shekel payments made from it are deemed third-party payments and are exempt from the *kalbon*.

If the heirs establish a partnership by combining their inheritances after the division of the estate, the assets are considered contributed capital like the formative assets of all partnerships, and the *kalbon* premuim must be paid.

Regarding the animal tithe, however, the original, undivided, estate is treated like any other partnership. The animals are considered as if they were purchased by the heirs and are exempt. Any livestock born before the estate is divided are obligated in the tithe; they are not seen as bought, but as the generated capital of the estate. But once the estate is divided, even if the brothers later repool their resources to form a partnership, the livestock involved in this transaction are now considered as if they were newly bought by the respective individual partners and are exempt (see *Rambam, Comm.* to *Bechoros* 9:3 and *Hil. Bechoros* 6:10).

הָאַחִין הַשֻּׁתָּפִין — *Brothers who are partners* [i.e., heirs sharing an estate] —
The section of our mishnah beginning הָאַחִין, *brothers*, and ending

פְּטוּרִין מִן־הַקָּלְבּוֹן, *are exempt from the kalbon* is also found in *Chullin* 1:7 and in *Bechoros* 9:3, and is quoted by the *Gemara Beitzah* 39b. In most editions of

Brothers who are partners — when they are obligated to pay a *kalbon*, they are exempt from the animal tithe; but when they are obligated to give the animal tithe, they are exempt from the *kalbon*.

YAD AVRAHAM

Mishnah, Talmud *Bavli* and Talmud *Yerushalmi* the words הָאַחִין, *brothers*, and הַשֻׁתָּפִין *partners*, are read together, *brothers who are partners*. In some editions the phrase appears as הָאַחִין וְהַשֻׁתָּפִין, *brothers or partners*,

Rashi (followed by *Rav*) adopts the former version, *brothers who are partners*. Hence the mishnah discusses the special case of brothers who become partners in the estate they have jointly inherited. According to the view presented in this version, regular partnerships have no special status exempting them from the *kalbon* premium.

Rambam adopts the latter version, *brothers or partners*, giving the mishnah a much broader range. To avoid confusion, we first offer the interpretation of *Rashi* and *Rav*. *Rambam's* interpretation follows.

הָאַחִין הַשֻׁתָּפִין שֶׁחַיָבִין בְּקָלְבּוֹן — *Brothers who are partners — when they are obligated to pay a kalbon,*
This refers to heirs who divided their inheritance and then pooled their

respective shares to form a new partnership. As noted in the prefatory remarks, their status is no different from any other partnership. Even when they pay their half shekels from the partnership, they are subject to the *kalbon.*

פְּטוּרִין מִמַּעְשַׂר בְּהֵמָה: — *they are exempt from the animal tithe;*
The fact that they are partners exempts their jointly owned livestock from the animal tithe which is incumbent only upon individually owned animals.

וּכְשֶׁחַיָבִין בְּמַעְשַׂר בְּהֵמָה, — *but when they are obligated to give the animal tithe,*
Before the estate has been divided, the estate is considered to be under individual ownership (as if the father were still alive), and is thus subject to the animal tithe.

פְּטוּרִין מִן־הַקָלְבּוֹן. — *they are exempt from the kalbon.*
Since the estate is viewed as still held by the father, shekalim given from it are like those contributed by a father for his

---

RAMBAM'S VERSION

הָאַחִין וְהַשֻׁתָּפִין שֶׁחַיָבִין בְּקָלְבּוֹן — *Brothers or partners who are obligated to pay a kalbon*
This refers to contributed capital (see prefatory remarks) used to pay the half shekels for the partners or brothers. Such property is subject to the *kalbon* premium.

פְּטוּרִין מִמַּעְשַׂר בְּהֵמָה: — *they are exempt from the animal tithe;*
Since these assets have dual ownership, they are exempt from the animal tithe.

וּכְשֶׁחַיָבִין בְּמַעְשַׂר בְּהֵמָה, — *but when they are obligated to give the animal tithe,*
This refers to generated capital (see prefatory remarks) which is considered to be under individual ownership (of the estate or partnership) and is thus subject to the tithe laws.

פְּטוּרִין מִן־הַקָלְבּוֹן. — *they are exempt from the kalbon.*
The partnership or estate is comparable to an individual who paid another's half shekel obligation and is exempt from the *kalbon* payment.

שְׁקָלִים   וְכַמָּה הוּא קָלְבּוֹן? מָעָה כֶּסֶף — דִּבְרֵי רַבִּי
ב/א   מֵאִיר. וַחֲכָמִים אוֹמְרִים: חֲצִי.

[א] מְצָרְפִין שְׁקָלִים לְדַרְכּוֹנוֹת מִפְּנֵי
מַשּׂוּי הַדֶּרֶךְ.
כְּשֵׁם שֶׁהָיוּ שׁוֹפָרוֹת בַּמִּקְדָּשׁ, כָּךְ הָיוּ
שׁוֹפָרוֹת בַּמְּדִינָה.

יד אברהם

children and are exempt from the kalbon.[1]

[The dispute between *Rashi* and *Rambam* does not involve the remainder of the mishnah.]

וְכַמָּה הוּא קָלְבּוֹן? מָעָה כֶּסֶף — דִּבְרֵי רַבִּי מֵאִיר. — *And how much is this kalbon? A silver ma'ah* — [These are] *the words of R' Meir.*

A *ma'ah* [מָעָה] is the Aramaic equivalent of the Scriptural גֵּרָה, *gerah*, which was one twentieth of a *sela* (שֶׁקֶל; *Exodus* 30:13 with *Onkelos*). However, since the Mishnaic *sela* contained

twenty percent more silver than the Scriptural *shekel*, (*Bechoros* 50a), the Mishnaic *ma'ah* is invariably referred to as one twenty-fourth of a *sela*. Thus the *kalbon* was worth one twelfth of the half shekel contribution. [See Appendix "The Shekel".]

וַחֲכָמִים אוֹמְרִים: חֲצִי. — *but the Sages say: half [a ma'ah].*

I.e., one twenty-fourth of the half shekel contribution.

The halachah follows the Sages (*Rav; Rambam, Hil. Shekalim* 3:7).

Chapter 2
1.

מְצָרְפִין שְׁקָלִים לְדַרְכּוֹנוֹת מִפְּנֵי מַשּׂוּי הַדֶּרֶךְ. — *They may convert* [lit. *combine*] *shekalim* [i.e., half shekels] *into darkons to lighten* [lit. *because of*] *the burden of the way.*

Once all the half shekels of the townspeople had been collected, the accumulated coins could be carried to Jerusalem only with great difficulty. To facilitate the task, the coins could be exchanged for gold coins known as *darkonos*. *Darkonos* were also called אֲדַרְכּוֹנִים, *adarkonim* (*I Chronicles* 29:7) and דַּרְכְּמוֹנִים, *darkemonim* (*Ezra* 2:69; *Rav*; see also *Rashbam, Bava Basra* 165b, s.v. דרכמונים).

[Aside from suggesting a pragmatic solution to a problem, the mishnah makes the statement that townspeople have the right to convert the shekels into gold despite the fact that gold might later go down in price relative to silver. Should that happen, the Temple treasury would suffer a loss of purchasing power. Because of such a fear of price fluctuation *Yerushalmi* rules that the shekalim may not be converted into precious stones. But because the price of gold, by virtue of its status as currency, does not fluctuate to the same degree as the price of gems, the conversion may be made (*Taklin Chadatin; Rashi* to

1. There is a question about the exemption from the *kalbon* both in the case of brothers contributing from the estate and of a father contributing for his sons. *Rashi* in *Chullin* (25b, s.v. וכשחייבין) maintains that no *kalbon* is paid, whereas in *Beitzah* (39b, s.v. כשחייבין) and *Bechoros* (56b, s.v. פוטירין), holds that only *one* of the two additional coins normally required in such a case is waived (see prefatory remarks); one *kalbon*, however, must still be paid.

2
1
And how much is this *kalbon*? A silver *ma'ah* — the words of R' Meir. But the Sages say: half [a *ma'ah*].

1. **T**hey may convert shekalim into *darkons* to lighten the burden of the way.
Just as there were collection chests in the Temple, so there were collection chests in the provinces.

YAD AVRAHAM

Bechoros 51a, s.v. מצרפין; cf. *Tif. Yis).*

Mossaf HeAruch (s.v. דרכון; see also *Tif. Yis.*) identifies the *darkon* with the *daric* struck by the Persian King Darius, bearing his portrait and available both in silver and gold.

Rambam (Comm.) records that this coin was equal to two *sela*. Since the purpose of the conversion was to lighten the weight to be carried to Jerusalem, it is puzzling why they did not convert into gold *dinars*, each of which was worth 25 silver *dinars* or 6¼ *sela* (*Bechoros* 50a; *Bava Metzia* 44b). *Rambam* himself (*Comm.* and *Hil. Shekalim* 2:4) indicates that in actual practice they converted the half shekels into gold dinars. The use by our mishnah of the word *darkon* seems to be another instance where an archaic term in use at the time of the formulation of this mishnah — the early years of the Second Temple — was preserved intact in the Mishnah, pointing to the authenticity and antiquity of the Mishnah. (See R' Yitzchak Isaac HaLevi, *Doros HaRishonim, vol. 2, pp. 206-292*). In later times even though other currencies came into use, the wording of the mishnah was left unchanged.[1]

כְּשֵׁם שֶׁהָיוּ שׁוֹפָרוֹת בַּמִקְדָּשׁ, — *Just as there were collection chests* [lit. *horns*] *in the Temple,*

In the Temple Courtyard there were thirteen collection chests, each labeled for its designated purpose (see 6:1,5) so that anyone who visited the Temple could then make his contributions. Two of them were set aside for the deposit of the half shekel (*ibid.*).

These chests were broad at the bottom and tapered to a narrow, funnel-like opening, so that their shape suggested a shofar (*Rav*).

Rav (6:1, based on *Yerushalmi*) adds that they (i.e., the funnel-like openings) also curved and totally resembled a *shofar*. They were so shaped to prevent a dishonest person from putting his hand through the opening and removing coins. [Because of the *shofar* shape of the openings, the entire chest was called a *shofar*.]

כָּךְ הָיוּ שׁוֹפָרוֹת בַּמְדִינָה. — *so there were collection chests in the provinces.*

According to *Rav*, the term מְדִינָה, *province,* refers to the parts of Jerusalem outside the Temple complex. According to *Rambam* this term refers to the cities outside of Jerusalem (see *comm.* and footnotes to 1:3, s.v. במקדש and בעשרים וחמשה; see also *Taklin Chadatin* and *Minchas Eliyahu* here).

Rambam (*Hil. Shekalim* 2:1) remarks that just as there were two collection chests for the half shekels — one for current and one for overdue half shekels (6:5) — in the Temple, so there were two chests at every collection point in the provinces. *Kessef Mishneh* suggests that this is derived from the use of the plural שׁוֹפָרוֹת, *collection chests.*

1. [I have not found a source (cf. R' *Shlomo Sirilio*) for *Rambam's* assertion that the *darkon* equalled two *sela*. Numismatic evidence indicates that the *daric* was 20 shekel or 10 *sela*. Due to the scarceness of coins from the Persian era, however, it is possible that a two-*sela* daric existed, but has not come down to us. Or, perhaps according to *Rambam*, the *darkon* is not synonymous with the *daric*.]

[31]   THE MISHNAH / SHEKALIM

בְּנֵי הָעִיר שֶׁשָּׁלְחוּ אֶת־שִׁקְלֵיהֶן וְנִגְנְבוּ אוֹ
שֶׁאָבְדוּ, אִם נִתְרְמָה הַתְּרוּמָה, נִשְׁבָּעִין
לַגִּזְבָּרִים; וְאִם לָאוּ, נִשְׁבָּעִין לִבְנֵי הָעִיר, וּבְנֵי
הָעִיר שׁוֹקְלִין תַּחְתֵּיהֶן.

יד אברהם

בְּנֵי הָעִיר שֶׁשָּׁלְחוּ אֶת־שִׁקְלֵיהֶן וְנִגְנְבוּ אוֹ
שֶׁאָבְדוּ,— If townspeople sent their half
shekels and they were stolen [from] or
lost [by the messengers],

The townspeople sent their shekalim
to Jerusalem with a messenger who was
not paid for guarding the money. Consequently, he was a שׁוֹמֵר חִנָּם, unpaid
watchman. Such a watchman is responsible to pay for loss or theft only if it
resulted from his negligence (פְּשִׁיעָה) or
if he made unauthorized personal use of
the object he was supposed to be
guarding (שְׁלִיחוּת יָד).

If an unpaid watchman claims that
the object in his charge was lost or
stolen, he must make three oaths in
order to absolve himself from liability:
That he was not negligent; that the object is not in his possession; and that he
had not used it [in which case he would
have become liable for even accidental
loss or damage] (Exodus 22:6-8 with
Rashi; Shevuos 8:1).

In the case of a שׁוֹמֵר שָׂכָר, paid
watchman, he is responsible for ordinary loss or theft, and is absolved
only in the case of circumstances
beyond his control (אוֹנֶס). Consequently, our mishnah, which tells of a messenger absolving himself by claiming —
and swearing — that a loss or theft had
taken place, could not apply to a paid
watchman, who would be responsible in
such cases. Yerushalmi (see also Bava
Metzia 58a) comments that our mishnah could refer to a paid messenger, if
the 'theft' was an armed robbery or the
'loss' was, for example, due to a ship
sinking at sea. Such cases constitute
אוֹנֶס, events beyond his control, and he
bears no responsibility.

[Having said that the messenger

makes a claim that frees him from
responsibility, the mishnah now turns
to the oath by means of which he must
establish the credibility of his claim.
The oath is made to the claimant who
seeks restitution for the missing shekalim. Who is the claimant — the Temple
treasury or the townspeople?]

אִם נִתְרְמָה הַתְּרוּמָה, — [then] if the
terumah had already been withdrawn
[lit. if the uplifted (funds) had been
lifted],

[The word terumah refers to the
withdrawal of funds, literally lifting,
from the collection chests for the
purchase of offerings.][1]

As related further (3:1), funds to
purchase offerings were not withdrawn
from the collection chests every day.
Instead this money was taken out of the
chests on three designated dates. Since
the purchase of the half shekel contribution was so that every Jew would
have a share in all the public offerings,
it is clear that whatever coins happened
to be withdrawn had to be regarded as
representing not only the donors of
those particular coins, but even the
donors of half shekels that were still in
the chest. Yerushalmi (also Bava Metzia
58a; Kesubos 108b; cf. Tosefta 2:5)
cites a baraisa which teaches that any
funds taken from the chests were
regarded as representing even those
whose half shekels had been lost in the
treasury before the withdrawal, those
whose contributions were still enroute
at the time of the withdrawal (even if
they would subsequently be lost before
reaching the Temple), and those who
had not yet contributed, but would do
so in the future. [Tosafos, Bava Metzia

---

1. See comm. to 3:4 for the different views of when the withdrawal of the terumah took place.

2
1

If townspeople sent their half shekels and they were stolen or lost, [then] if the *terumah* had already been withdrawn, they [the messengers] must swear in the presence of the treasurers; but if not, they must swear in the presence of the townspeople, and the townspeople must contribute other half shekels in their stead.

YAD AVRAHAM

58a s.v. נשבעין; *Rashi,* there, has a slightly different interpretation; cf. *Rambam, Hil. Shekalim* 2:9 and *Kessef Mishneh.*] Thus, in the case of the unpaid messenger of our mishnah, if the half shekels had been lost or stolen after a withdrawal from the Temple's collection chest, the donors would already have been represen.ted and have discharged their obligation. In such a case any loss would have to be borne by the Temple treasury, which consequently becomes the claimant to whom the messenger would make restitution if he were liable.

נשְׁבָּעִין לַגִּזְבָּרִים; — *they [the messengers] must swear in the presence of* [lit. *to*] *the treasurers;*

Since the Temple treasury is the injured party, it alone has a claim against the messengers. As always in such cases, the oath through which the messenger establishes his innocence must be imposed by the *Beis Din* in the presence of the claimant, in this case the treasurers representing the Temple.

Although Torah law excludes the Temple treasury from the right to demand an oath (*Bava Metzia* 4:9 and *Shavuos* 6:5), the Sages decreed that it have equal status with laymen to require oaths of accused watchmen. Their motive was to prevent people from holding their responsibility to protect consecrated money in contempt (*Bava Metzia* 8a).

וְאָם לָאו, — *but if not,*
[If the loss took place before funds had been withdrawn from the collection chests.]

In this case, when funds are withdrawn to purchase communal offerings these townspeople would not be represented, since their funds were neither in the collection chest nor enroute. They would be required to contribute another half shekel (*Rashi,* loc. cit., s.v. ואם לאו), and consequently they are the aggrieved parties to whom the messengers must swear to establish their innocence.

נשְׁבָּעִין לִבְנֵי הָעִיר, — *they [the messengers] must swear in the presence of* [lit. *to*] *the townspeople,*
[I.e. in their presence and at their request.]

Rambam (Hil. Shekalim 3:8-9) and *Meiri* arrive at a different conclusion based on this mishnah: The rule set forth here applies solely to a messenger who is paid to watch (שׁוֹמֵר שָׂכָר). Because the townspeople went to the expense of insuring reimbursement in the event of theft or loss, there is no negligence on their part. They are not held to be negligent for not insuring the Temple treasury against unavoidable loss (אוֹנֶס) because this type of damage is not common [i.e. otherwise they should have hired the messenger with the condition that he make good even unpreventable loss]. However, if the messenger was not paid to watch (שׁוֹמֵר חִנָּם) the townspeople are deemed to have been negligent in not protecting the Temple treasury even against (prevalent) theft or loss; consequently they must contribute new half shekels even if the loss occurred after the withdrawal was made [for the funds withdrawn in the *terumah* are intended to represent only those who are considered to have taken all reasonable precautions].

[This opinion is probably based on the versions of *Yerushalmi* printed together with the commentaries of *R' Meshullam* and *R' Shlomo Sirilio.*]

שקלים   נִמְצְאוּ, אוֹ שֶׁהֶחֱזִירוּם הַגַּנָּבִים, אֵלּוּ וָאֵלּוּ   ב/ב   שְׁקָלִים, וְאֵין עוֹלִין לַשָּׁנָה הַבָּאָה.

[ב] **הַנּוֹתֵן** שִׁקְלוֹ לַחֲבֵרוֹ לִשְׁקוֹל עַל־יָדוֹ,
וּשְׁקָלוֹ עַל־יְדֵי עַצְמוֹ, אִם
נִתְרְמָה תְרוּמָה, מָעַל.

יד אברהם

Rambam (based on *Yerushalmi*) adds that although the oath can be demanded only by the townspeople, they may nevertheless not waive their right to an oath by accepting the messenger's claim, even if they are willing to make a new half shekel payment. Since the Temple treasury is involved here, the Sages decreed that the oath must be taken [presumably to accentuate the gravity of negligence with consecrated funds]. (For elaborations on *Rambam's* view see *Kessef Mishneh*; *Binyan Shlomo* in the back of the regular editions; *Tumim* 66:67; *Korban HaEdah* and *Mishnas Eliyahu* here).

וּבְנֵי הָעִיר שׁוֹקְלִין תַּחְתֵּיהֶן. — *and the townspeople must contribute other half shekels in their stead.*

[Since the theft or loss took place before the withdrawal, the townspeople will not have discharged their duty unless they contribute another time.]

נִמְצְאוּ, אוֹ שֶׁהֶחֱזִירוּם הַגַּנָּבִים,—*If the missing half shekels* [lit. *they*] *were* [subsequently] *found, if if the thieves* [lit. *they*] *returned them* [after the replacement shekalim were collected],

אֵלּוּ וָאֵלּוּ שְׁקָלִים, — [*then*] *these* [the original half shekels] *and those* [the new half shekels] *are* [consecrated as] *half shekels*,

[I.e., both are קֹדֶשׁ, *consecrated property*. The second half shekels are not considered to have been consecrated erroneously (in which case they would be returned to the donors) because the information — concerning the loss — that necessitated the second contribution was correct at the time of the consecration. The subsequent discovery of the money does not retroactively render that information erroneous (cf. *Tif. Yis.*).]

Yerushalmi cites a *baraisa* (cf. *Tosefta* 1:6) stating that only one set of half shekels may be deposited in the chest marked שְׁקָלִין חֲדָתִין, *new shekels*, from which money is drawn for the public offerings of the new year. The other set is deposited in the chest marked שְׁקָלִין עַתִּיקִין, *old shekels* (see further 6:5), which is used for the purposes described in 4:2-3.

[The rationale behind this is that the Torah (*Exodus* 30:15) specifically forbids anyone to contribute more than the prescribed amount (see *Rambam, Hil. Shekalim* 1:1 and *Comm.* to *mishnah* 4). Which set is deposited with the *new shekels*? The amoraim disagree about this, one view maintaining that the original shekels retain the sanctity for which they were designated; another view holds whichever set reaches the Temple treasury first. *Rambam (Hil. Shekalim* 1:9) uncharacteristically cites both opinions without a ruling.]

וְאֵין עוֹלִין לָהֶם לַשָּׁנָה הַבָּאָה. — *but they are not credited to them for the following year.*

The townspeople may not hold over the second set to be credited toward the next year's collection of half shekels. The Talmud (Yoma 65a) explains that funds set aside for the public offerings of one year may not be used for the offerings of another year. R' Yehudah disagrees, maintaining that such funds may be laid over to the next year. *Rambam (Hil. Shekalim* 3:8 based on *Tosefta* 1:6 cited in *Yerushalmi*) rules that an individual who has consecrated a half shekel is responsible for it until it reaches the Temple treasurer; if it is lost he must contribute another. [The inference is that the periodic withdrawal does not represent an individual whose half shekel is subsequently lost and not replaced, even if this loss occurs after the withdrawal is made.]

If the missing half shekels were [subsequently] found, or if the thieves returned them, then these and those are [consecrated as] half shekels, but they are not credited to them for the following year.

2.One who gives his half shekel to his colleague to contribute for him, but [the colleague] contributed it for himself, if the *terumah* had already been withdrawn, he has misappropriated.

YAD AVRAHAM

2.

◄§ Me'ilah — Misappropriation of Consecrated Property

נֶפֶשׁ כִּי־תִמְעֹל מַעַל וְחָטְאָה בִּשְׁגָגָה מִקָּדְשֵׁי ה' וְהֵבִיא אֶת־אֲשָׁמוֹ לַה' אַיִל תָּמִים מִן־הַצֹּאן בְּעֶרְכְּךָ כֶּסֶף־שְׁקָלִים בְּשֶׁקֶל־הַקֹּדֶשׁ לְאָשָׁם. וְאֵת אֲשֶׁר חָטָא מִן־הַקֹּדֶשׁ יְשַׁלֵּם וְאֶת־חֲמִישִׁתוֹ יוֹסֵף עָלָיו וְנָתַן אֹתוֹ לַכֹּהֵן וְהַכֹּהֵן יְכַפֵּר עָלָיו בְּאֵיל הָאָשָׁם וְנִסְלַח לוֹ. — *If a person acts unfaithfully and sins inadvertently in the holies of HASHEM then he shall bring his guilt offering unto HASHEM; a ram without blemish out of the flock, according to your valuation in silver shekels, after the shekel of the Sanctuary for a guilt offering. And for that which he has sinned in the holy shall he pay, and he shall add its fifth part to it and give it to the kohen; and the kohen shall atone for him with the ram of the guilt offering, and he shall be forgiven (Leviticus 5:15-16).*

Scripture provides that for inadvertent (שׁוֹגֵג) private use of consecrated property a guilt offering for misappropriation (אָשָׁם מְעִילוֹת) be brought in addition to repayment to the Temple treasury twenty-five percent above the actual value used. [Although Scripture reads *he shall add its fifth part to it,* in actual practice the added payment equal one fourth of the consumed value. The Torah does not refer to one fifth of the value but to one fifth of the total repayment. Thus, one who ate four dollars worth of consecrated meat must repay five dollars. The extra dollar represents one fifth (20%) of the total payment, or one fourth (25%) of the consumed value.] The verb used by the Torah to describe this improper use is מָעַל [hence, the term מְעִילָה, *me'ilah*], therefore, wherever this root is used in the mishnah it indicates that the transgression is against Torah law (דְּאוֹרַיְיתָא) rather than a Rabbinic decree, and that the requisite sacrifice must be offered.

הַנּוֹתֵן שִׁקְלוֹ לַחֲבֵרוֹ לִשְׁקוֹל עַל־יָדוֹ, וּשְׁקָלוֹ עַל־יְדֵי עַצְמוֹ, — *One who gives his half shekel to his colleague to contribute for him, but the colleague* [lit. *he] contributed it for himself,*

Instead of using the money as the contribution of its true owner, the messenger gave the half shekel as his own contribution (Rav).

אִם נִתְרְמָה תְרוּמָה, מָעַל. — *if the terumah had already been withdrawn* [before the messenger misappropriated the half shekel], *he has misappropriated.*

The messenger is liable for having used consecrated funds for his own benefit, and must make restitution, pay the additional penalty, and bring a sin offering, as set forth above. The half shekel had become consecrated as soon as a withdrawal of funds had been made from the collection chests. Consequently, when the messenger discharges his own obligation with his colleague's half shekel he derives personal gain from consecrated property. Ordinarily, such a use of consecrated funds would not be considered *me'ilah* because the money

הַשׁוֹקֵל שְׁקָלוֹ מִמָּעוֹת הֶקְדֵּשׁ, אִם נִתְרְמָה
תְּרוּמָה וְקָרְבָה הַבְּהֵמָה, מָעַל.

יד אברהם

was put not to *personal* use, but for the performance of a *mitzvah*, and the rule is that מִצְוֹת לָאו לֵהָנוֹת נִתְּנוּ, *mitzvos were not given for personal enjoyment (Rosh HaShanah* 28a), i.e., the fulfill-ment of a *mitzvah* is regarded as a spiritual benefit that has no monetary value. In our case, however, the mes-senger is regarded as having derived a personal benefit aside from the fulfill-ment of the *mitzvah*, because he freed himself from the requirement of paying his tax, an obligation that would have been enforced by the seizing of his as-sets, as described in 1:3 *(Rav; Rambam; based on Yerushalmi).*

But if the *terumah* had not yet been withdrawn he is not liable for the *me'ilah* atonement. He need merely repay a half shekel to the original donor *(Rambam, Hil. Shekalim* 3:10). [The half shekel does not become consecrated property (הֶקְדֵּשׁ) until after the periodic withdrawal has been made. However, as pointed out by *Zafnas Pa'ane'ach (Mahadura Basra* p. 138), if the donor had explicitly pronounced the money 'Holy' (קוֹדֶשׁ), the coin became consecrated immediately, even before the withdrawal, and the *me'ilah* laws would apply. It is only in the absence of such a declaration that con-secration depends on the withdrawal.]

Rambam (Hil. Shekalim 3:10) implies that the dishonest messenger *has* discharged his personal obligation, even though the money was already consecrated *(Lechem Shamayim; Binyan Shlomo* to Rambam).

However *R' Shmuel* (p. 19) assumes that one cannot discharge his own obligation by misappropriating someone else's half shekel. Despite the fact that he remains obligated to pay his own half shekel, he is considered to have derived personal gain from consecrated funds, because, as a result of his fraud, the Temple officials will not compel payment (cf. *Ohr Sameach; Lechem Shamayim; Kol Sofer).*

הַשׁוֹקֵל שְׁקָלוֹ מִמָּעוֹת הֶקְדֵּשׁ, — *One who contributes his half shekel from con-secrated funds,*

He forgot that the money in his pos-session had previously been consecrated for use in purchasing supplies or paying for repairs to the Temple (בֶּדֶק הַבַּיִת) and now used it for his half shekel obliga-tion thinking was his own money *(Rav; Rosh).*

אִם נִתְרְמָה תְּרוּמָה וְקָרְבָה הַבְּהֵמָה, מָעַל. — *if the terumah [for public offerings] had already been withdrawn and the animal [bought with this money] had already been offered, he has misappropriated.*

Subsequently, when the withdrawal is made and the animals bought with this money are sacrificed,[1] he is liable to the laws of *me'ilah*. The sacrifice was performed on behalf of everyone who participated in the half shekel contribu-tion, including this individual who had mistakenly contributed consecrated funds. His share in the communal sacrifice, having been bought with money that had originally been con-secrated for a different sacred purpose, constitutes an improper misappropria-tion of such funds and is liable to the *me'ilah* laws. The actual transgression of *me'ilah* however, is not committed until the sacrificial service is performed; the mere *diversion* of funds from their designated sacred purpose to another use — although forbidden — does fall within the category of *me'ilah*. The *me'ilah* process comes into play only if the diverted sacred assets are used for secular (חוּלִּין) purposes (see *Me'ilah* 19a). In our mishnah, as noted above, in the first clause, a 'secular' benefit is in-volved because the donor has ostensibly fulfilled his half shekel obligation, thus, freeing himself from the danger that the

---

1. Specifically, the throwing of the blood on the altar (זְרִיקָה) has taken place *(Rambam, Hil. Me'ilah* 6:12, based on *Tosefta Shekalim* 1:6; *Me'ilah* 19a).

2
2

One who contributes his half shekel from consecrated funds, if the *terumah* had already been withdrawn and the animal [bought with this money] had already been offered, he has misappropriated.

YAD AVRAHAM

Beis Din will seize his assets. In the first clause too — where someone used another person's half shekel as his own contribution — the same rule applies: only after the offering has been sacrificed are the penalties for transgression applicable *(Rav based on Yer.)*.

[However, as implied by the mishnah, if the error had been discovered prior to the sacrificial service, a *me'ilah* liability would not be incurred. In that case, the sacrifice would not have been offered on behalf of this individual because he would have been known as a non-contributor, hence no improper use of consecrated funds would have taken place.]

Rambam (Comm. and Hil. Shekalim 3:10-11) apparently differentiates between the first passage of the mishnah — use of someone else's half shekel — where fraudulent contribution *per se* subjects the transgressor to *me'ilah*, and the second passage — inadvertent use of a consecrated half shekel — where sacrifice has to take place for *me'ilah* to be invoked. (See *Gaon* cited in *Taklin Chadatin; Lechem Shamayim; Tif. Yis.*, and *Ohr Sameach* for explanations of this view.)

◄§ Ma'aser Sheni

In the seven-year cycle which culminates in the Sabbatical year, one must tithe his produce in the following way:

(a) Each year (except the seventh) he must give a portion of his produce to a *Kohen*. This is called תְּרוּמָה, *terumah* [lit. *separated*] (see *Deuteronomy* 18:4).

(b) From the remainder, he must then give one-tenth to a *Levi* (again, each year with the exception of the seventh year). This is called מַעֲשֵׂר רִאשׁוֹן, *ma'aser rishon* [*first tithe*] (see *Numbers* 18:24).

(c) From the remainder of the original produce in the first, second, fourth, and fifth years of the cycle he must separate one-tenth which he must take to Jerusalem and eat there. This is called מַעֲשֵׂר שֵׁנִי, *ma'aser sheni* [*second tithe*] (see *Deuteronomy* 14:22).

(d) In the third and sixth years, instead of *ma'aser sheni* he must give one-tenth to the poor. This is called מַעֲשֵׂר עָנִי, *ma'aser ani* [*tithe for the poor*] (see *Deuteronomy* 14:28).

On the seventh (Sabbatical) year, all that the land produces is הֶפְקֵר, *ownerless*, and no tithes are given *(Exodus* 23:11).

Ma'aser sheni may be eaten only in Jerusalem under conditions of טַהֲרָה [*taharah*], *spiritual purity*. If, as is often the case, the owner is unable to transport all his *ma'aser sheni* to Jerusalem, he is permitted to redeem it for money. The funds, which acquire the restrictions of *ma'aser sheni*, must be taken to Jerusalem and used only for the purchase of food to be eaten in the Holy City. שְׁלָמִים, *peace offerings*, could be purchased because portions of these offerings are eaten by the *Kohanim* and the owner, but עוֹלוֹת, *burnt offerings*, because they are totally consumed on the altar, are not considered food and may not be purchased with דְּמֵי מַעֲשֵׂר שֵׁנִי, *ma'aser sheni funds (Deuteronomy* 14:22-27; *Sifrei).*

The Torah placed a further restriction on these funds: They are not to be used to purchase sacrifices for which one had obligated himself through a vow, for this is tantamount to using *ma'aser sheni* funds to settle personal accounts. The same restriction applies to the purchase with *ma'aser sheni* funds of any offering one is obligated to bring.

מִדְּמֵי מַעֲשֵׂר שֵׁנִי, מִדְּמֵי שְׁבִיעִית, יֹאכַל
כְּנֶגְדָּן.

[ג] הַמְּכַנֵּס מָעוֹת וְאָמַר, ,,הֲרֵי אֵלּוּ
לְשִׁקְלִי'' — בֵּית שַׁמַּאי
אוֹמְרִים: מוֹתָרָן נְדָבָה. וּבֵית הִלֵּל אוֹמְרִים:
מוֹתָרָן חוּלִּין.

יד אברהם

◆§ Shemittah — Sabbatical Year

וְשֵׁשׁ שָׁנִים תִּזְרַע אֶת־אַרְצֶךָ וְאָסַפְתָּ אֶת־תְּבוּאָתָהּ. וְהַשְּׁבִיעִת תִּשְׁמְטֶנָּה ..., *Six years you may seed your land and gather its crops; but on the seventh (שְׁבִיעִית) you shall leave it fallow ... (Exodus 23:10-11).*

During שְׁמִיטָה, *Shemittah,* the Sabbatical Year that concludes the recurring seven year cycle, certain restrictions are imposed on agricultural activities and commerce, as outlined in numerous references in the Torah *(Exodus* 23:10,11; 34:21; *Leviticus* 25:1-13; *Deuteronomy* 15:1-3). During the entire Sabbatical Year, also known as שַׁבַּת הָאָרֶץ, *the Sabbath of the land (Leviticus* 25:6), the land lies fallow; plowing, planting, sowing and harvesting are all forbidden *(Rambam, Shemittah V'Yovel* 1:1-3).

Produce which grew as a result of the previous year's cultivation, or which grew on its own accord during *Shemittah,* must be maintained in an ownerless state (הֶפְקֵר, *hefker)* and must be left accessible to all who wish to take it. Any display of ownership on the part of the farmer, such as fencing off the field or gathering large amounts of crops into his warehouse, is prohibited *(ibid.* 4:24), nor may one engage in commerce with large quantities of *Shemittah* produce, although one may purchase small amounts for meals *(ibid.* 6:1).

Money used to purchase *Shemittah* produce is called דְּמֵי שְׁבִיעִית, lit. *seventh year funds.* It has the sanctity of *Shemittah* produce itself and is thus subject to numerous restrictions. One may use it only to purchase food or products that will be used in accordance with the laws of *Shemittah,* but may not buy clothes or real estate, nor use it to pay for services or debts *(ibid.* 6:1; 10-11). [See below 4:1, s.v. *Shemittah.]*

מִדְּמֵי מַעֲשֵׂר שֵׁנִי, — *[If one paid his half shekel] with ma'aser sheni funds*

[Since the half shekels were used for the purchase of the תָּמִיד, *daily offering,* which consisted of עוֹלוֹת, *burnt offerings, ma'aser sheni* funds may not be used for the half shekel payments (see prefatory remarks). Moreover, in line with the Mishnaic dictum כָּל דָּבָר שֶׁבְּחוֹבָה, אֵינוֹ בָּא אֶלָּא מִן הַחֻלִּין, *any obligatory payments may be taken only from unconsecrated funds (Menachos* 7:6; see *Chagigah* 1:3 with *comm.),* half shekel payments must be made with money that has not been previously consecrated.]

מִדְּמֵי שְׁבִיעִית, — *or with Shemittah funds,*

[*Shemittah* funds may not be used for the half shekel payment for two reasons: the half shekels are used to purchase burnt offerings which are totally consumed by the altar fire, whereas *Shemittah* funds may only be used to purchase food for human consumption; and *Shemittah* money may not be used to redeem debts or other obligations.]

יֹאכַל כְּנֶגְדָּן. — *he must eat [food bought with other monies] of an equivalent value.*

2
3   [If one paid his half shekel] with *ma'aser sheni* funds or with *Shemittah* funds, he must eat [food bought with other monies] of an equivalent value.

3. If one collected coins and said, "Let these be for my half shekel" — Beis Shammai say: The remainder is [placed in the collection chest marked] "Donative Offering". But Beis Hillel say: The remainder is unconsecrated.

YAD AVRAHAM

He must take an unconsecrated half shekel and say: Let the *ma'aser sheni* or *Shemittah* funds, wherever they are, be redeemed with this half shekel. Thus the second half shekel assumes the *ma'aser sheni* or *Shemittah* status residual in the first, improperly used half shekel *(Rav based on Yer.).*

Even if the withdrawal had been made, and offerings sacrificed, the wrongfully contributed half shekel may still be in the collection chest, in which case it would be redeemed by the process described in the mishnah. Even if his shekel had been withdrawn and used, in which case redemption would not be possible because the animal purchased with it had already been slaughtered, the re-

quirement remains that he purchase and eat an equivalent value of food. The process would not redeem the misappropriated coin, but it would serve as an atonement for misuse of these funds (see a similar instance in *Tos. Succah* 39a, s.v. מעות, and *Kiddushin* 56a, s.v. מתקיף).

Rambam (Hil. Shekalim 3:11) uncharacteristically omits the provision that the one who made the improper donation must specify that his second shekel is intended to redeem the first. *Rambam's* failure to mention this implies that the second shekel serves only as an atonement, but not as redemption. Perhaps he holds, as does *Meiri,* that the provision specifying redemption, although cited by *Yerushalmi* from a *baraisa,* contradicts our mishnah, which makes no mention of it.

3.

הַמְכַנֵּס מָעוֹת וְאָמַר, "הֲרֵי אֵלּוּ לְשִׁקְלִי" — *If one collected* [lit. *gathered*] *coins and said* "Let these be for my half shekel"—
When he started to set these coins aside he stated explicitly that the accumulated monies were to be used for the half shekel tax. However he miscalculated and collected more than the required amount. What is the status of this surplus money? Does the original declaration consecrate the surplus, or does the declaration have no effect on the money that was contributed under the misconception that it was part of the half shekel? *(Rav).*

בֵּית שַׁמַּאי אוֹמְרִים: מוֹתָרָן נְדָבָה. — *Beis Shammai say: The remainder is [placed in the collection chest marked] "Donative Offering."*

Beis Shammai are consistent with their view *(Nazir* 5:1) that consecration made in error is valid (הֶקְדֵּשׁ בְּטָעוּת שְׁמֵיהּ הֶקְדֵּשׁ). Nevertheless, the excess may not be deposited in the collection chest set aside for half shekels, for the Torah *(Exodus* 30:15) forbids anyone to donate more than the required amount. Instead, the remainder is deposited in one of the six chests marked נְדָבָה, "Donative Offering." Those funds go toward supplying עוֹלוֹת, *burnt offerings,* for the altar in slack periods when no other offerings are ready to be brought *(Rav;* see further 6:5-6).

However, if he scooped up a handful of money and said, Let these be for my half shekel, Beis Shammai concur that any surplus is not consecrated. Here we have no reason to assume that he was under the con-

„שֶׁאָבִיא מֵהֶן לְשִׁקְלִי" — שָׁוִין שֶׁמּוֹתָרָן
חֻלִּין.

„אֵלּוּ לְחַטָּאת" — שָׁוִין שֶׁהַמּוֹתָר נְדָבָה.
„שֶׁאָבִיא מֵהֶן לְחַטָּאת" — שָׁוִין שֶׁהַמּוֹתָר
חֻלִּין.

[ד] אָמַר רַבִּי שִׁמְעוֹן: מַה־בֵּין שְׁקָלִים
לְחַטָּאת? שְׁקָלִים יֵשׁ־לָהֶם קִצְבָה,
וְחַטָּאת אֵין לָהּ קִצְבָה.
רַבִּי יְהוּדָה אוֹמֵר: אַף לִשְׁקָלִים אֵין לָהֶם

יד אברהם

ception that the full amount was exactly a half shekel; he meant only that the half shekel should be taken from these funds (this view in *Yer.* is accepted by *Rambam, Hil. Shekalim* 3:13; cf. his *Comm.*; see *P'nei Moshe*).

וּבֵית הִלֵּל אוֹמְרִים: מוֹתָרָן חֻלִּין. — *But Beis Hillel say: The remainder* [of the funds] *is unconsecrated.*

Beis Hillel hold that a consecration made on a false assumption (הֶקְדֵּשׁ בְּטָעוּת) does not take effect (see *Nazir* 5:1). In our mishnah, although the owner made an explicit statement consecrating the full amount, he did so under the misconception that all the money was needed for the half shekel; he had no intention of consecrating more than a half shekel (*Rav*).

„שֶׁאָבִיא מֵהֶן לְשִׁקְלִי" — שָׁוִין שֶׁמּוֹתָרָן חֻלִּין. — *If he said:] "I will bring my half shekel from these* [funds]" — *they* [Beis Shammai and Beis Hillel] *concur that the remainder is unconsecrated.*

Even according to Beis Shammai, since the donor specified that his payment would be made *from* this money,

his obvious intent was that no more than half a shekel was to be consecrated, with any excess remaining his own (*Rav*).

„אֵלּוּ לְחַטָּאת" — שָׁוִין שֶׁהַמּוֹתָר נְדָבָה. — [If he said:] *"These* [funds] *will go for* [the purchase of] *a sin offering"* — they [Beis Shammai and Beis Hillel] *concur that the remainder is* [placed in the collection chest marked] *"Donative Offering".*

[The next mishnah will explain the difference between this and the above passage concerning the half shekel.]

„שֶׁאָבִיא מֵהֶן לְחַטָּאת" — שָׁוִין שֶׁהַמּוֹתָר חֻלִּין. — [If he said:] *"I will bring* [an animal purchased] *from these* [funds] *for a sin offering"* — they [Beis Shammai and Beis Hillel] *concur that the remainder is unconsecrated.*

[See *comm.* above to parallel case concerning the half shekel.]

Here, too, this money is deposited in one of the chests marked נְדָבָה, *"Donative Offering"*, and is used to purchase burnt offerings. That such excess funds are used for burnt offerings is derived below at 6:6.

4.

— אָמַר רַבִּי שִׁמְעוֹן: מַה־בֵּין שְׁקָלִים לְחַטָּאת? *Says R' Shimon: What is* [the difference] *between half shekels and a sin offering?*

In the previous mishnah Beis Hillel hold that any surplus funds set aside for the half shekel remain unconsecrated, while surplus funds set aside for a sin

[If he said:] "I will bring my half shekel from these [funds]" — they concur that the remainder is unconsecrated.

[If he said:] "These [funds] will go for [the purchase of] a sin offering" — they concur that the remainder is [placed in the collection chest marked] "Donative Offering".

[If he said:] "I will bring [an animal purchased] from these [funds] for a sin offering" — they concur that the remainder is unconsecrated.

4. **S**ays R' Shimon: What is [the difference] between half shekels and a sin offering? Half shekels have a set limit, whereas a sin offering does not have a set limit.

R' Yehudah says: Even half shekels have no set

offering are sacred and must be used for voluntary offerings. R' Shimon now asks rhetorically for the rationale behind the differentiation between the two surpluses *(Rav)*.

שְׁקָלִים יֵשׁ לָהֶם קִצְבָה, — *Half shekels have a set limit,*

Scripture limits half shekel payments to the prescribed amount, as the verse states (*Exodus* 30:15): *The rich [man] shall not increase and the poor [man] shall not decrease from the half shekel ... (Rav).*

וְחַטָּאת אֵין לָה קִצְבָה. — *whereas a sin offering does not have a set limit.*

One may buy a sin offering for any amount he wishes. Therefore no matter how much money was set aside for a sin offering, it cannot be considered an erroneous contribution: whereas any amount above the sum of a half shekel must be considered to be given in error *(Rav).*

רַבִּי יְהוּדָה אוֹמֵר: אַף לִשְׁקָלִים אֵין לָהֶם קִצְבָה. — *R' Yehudah says: Even half shekels have no set limit.*

R' Yehudah disagrees with R'

Shimon's explanation and demonstrates that even the half shekel has no set limit as outlined below *(Rambam).*

Alternatively, R' Yehudah does not disagree with the substance of R' Shimon's explanation. He merely clarifies that R' Shimon's statement 'the half shekels have a set limit' means only that an individual may not exceed the limit prescribed by the community. The *community*, however, may designate a tax of more than a half shekel provided it applies to all people equally *(R' Shmuel p. 20).*

[Although R' Shimon later responds to R' Yehudah he does not dispute R' Yehudah's distinction. R' Shimon means only to stress that his explanation of Beis Hillel's view is not contradicted by R' Yehudah's point.]

Obviously *R' Shmuel* disagrees with *Rambam's* explanation because he considers it inconceivable that R' Yehudah could disagree with R' Shimon's basic premise that an individual may not contribute more than the prescribed amount. Consequently, although R' Yehudah cites instances where varying amounts were designated in place of the half shekel tax, he could not use them as a basis to disagree with R' Shimon who speaks only of an *individual* who has no right to give more than the required amount. (For an explanation of *Rambam's* view, see below, s.v. אבל חטאת.)

קְצָבָה. שֶׁכְּשֶׁעָלוּ יִשְׂרָאֵל מִן־הַגּוֹלָה הָיוּ
שׁוֹקְלִים דַּרְכּוֹנוֹת, חָזְרוּ לִשְׁקוֹל סְלָעִים, חָזְרוּ
לִשְׁקוֹל טְבָעִין וּבִקְּשׁוּ לִשְׁקוֹל דִּינָרִים.
אָמַר רַבִּי שִׁמְעוֹן: אַף עַל־פִּי כֵן, יַד כֻּלָּן
שָׁוָה; אֲבָל חַטָּאת, זֶה מֵבִיא בְסֶלַע, וְזֶה מֵבִיא
בִשְׁתַּיִם, וְזֶה מֵבִיא בְשָׁלֹשׁ.

יד אברהם

שֶׁכְּשֶׁעָלוּ יִשְׂרָאֵל מִן־הַגּוֹלָה הָיוּ שׁוֹקְלִים
דַּרְכּוֹנוֹת, חָזְרוּ לִשְׁקוֹל סְלָעִים, חָזְרוּ לִשְׁקוֹל
דִּינָרִים. טְבָעִין וּבִקְּשׁוּ לִשְׁקוֹל — *For when
Israel returned* [lit. *ascended*] *from the
[Babylonian] exile darkons were their
shekels* [lit. *they weighed out darkons*];
*later selaim were their shekels, [still]
later tevain* [half shekels] *were their
shekels and they* [i.e., some of the people] *wished to contribute dinars* [as their
half shekels].

Whatever coin was the standard currency of any particular era was considered as if it were the shekel, and half
of that coin was the half shekel payment. When the Temple was rebuilt by
those who returned from exile in the
Persian Empire, the standard currency
was the Persian *darkon* (see *comm.*
mishnah 1, s.v. מְצָרְפִין), which was
worth two *selaim*. Thus, the Temple tax
was half a *darkon* or one *sela* — double
the amount specified in the Torah (*Rav;
Rambam*).

With the collapse of the Persian Empire, the *darkon* was replaced by the
sela, which was the equivalent of the
shekel of the Sanctuary mentioned in
Exodus. Thereupon the half *sela* was
paid as the Temple tax. The half *sela*
coin was called 'shekel', but it was equal
to the *half* shekel of Scriptural time.

Eventually the half shekel coin

(טְבָעִין) gained ascendancy as the standard currency.[1] Following the rule of
paying half the prevalent standard,
some people sought to pay only half of
that coin — a *dinar* — which was only a
half of the Scriptural half shekel.
Although our mishnah does not relate
whether this proposal was ever adopted,
the term *they wished* clearly implies
that the proposal was rejected.[2] The
rule that the half shekel payment is
made with half the standard unit of currency applies only if the payment is at
least equal to the amount indicated in
the Torah — not if it is less.

The above interpretation of the mishnah is
based on two postulates: The half shekel
payment (a) is based on the standard currency unit; and (b) it may not be less than the
half shekel of the Torah. Many commentators, however, reject the view that the half
shekel amount can ever be affected by
changes in the standard currency (*Ravad,
Hil. Shekalim* 1:5; *Ramban, Exodus* 30:12;
R' Shmuel; Rivavan; Taklin Chadatin).
They understand the mishnah as follows:

Relatively few exiles returned to *Eretz
Yisrael* (42,360; *Ezra* 2:64). In addition to the
funds needed for the daily public offerings,
money was also needed for the reconstruction of the Temple. Due to the small number
of Jews in *Eretz Yisrael*, each of the returnees
had to contribute a full *darkon* to raise the required amount. As the need diminished, the
tax was reduced to a *sela*. Still later, the as-

---

1. This is not to imply that the *sela* was taken out of circulation, since numerous Mishnaic
references to it prove otherwise. The coin merely lost its popularity.

2. In explaining the rejection of this proposal, *Rambam (Comm.)* writes, the people did not
agree to this plan. This explanation is difficult, for *Rambam* himself (*Comm.* and in *Mishneh
Torah, Hil. Shekalim* 1:5) asserts that it is forbidden to give less than the amount set forth in
the Torah.

Tiferes Yisrael explains that it was the *Beis Din* that rejected the proposal of paying one
fourth shekel, based on the principle cited in *Mishneh Torah*.

2
4

limit. For when Israel returned from the [Babylonian] exile *darkons* were their shekels; later *selaim* were their shekels, [still] later *tevain* were their shekels and they wished to contribute *dinars* [as their half shekels].

Said R' Shimon [to R' Yehudah]: Nevertheless, they all gave a like amount; whereas [in the case of] a sin offering, this [person] brings one worth a *sela*, another brings one worth two [*selaim*], and yet another brings one worth three [*selaim*].

YAD AVRAHAM

sessment was reduced further to a half shekel. This is the era reflected by most, if not all, the mishnayos of this tractate. At some time during the Second Temple era, the population increased to such a degree that the half shekel tax yielded twice the necessary monies. Then, it was proposed to once again halve the payment, but the idea was rejected.

אָמַר רַבִּי שִׁמְעוֹן: אַף עַל־פִּי כֵן, יַד כֻּלָּן שָׁוָה; — *Said R' Shimon [to R' Yehudah]: Nevertheless, they all gave a like amount;*

No individual was permitted to give either more or less than the norm.

אֲבָל חַטָּאת, זֶה מֵבִיא בְסֶלַע, וְזֶה מֵבִיא בִשְׁתַּיִם, וְזֶה מֵבִיא בְשָׁלשׁ. — *whereas [in the case of] a sin offering, this [person] brings one worth a sela, another brings one worth two [selaim], and yet another brings one worth three [selaim].*

R' Shimon contends that a sin offering cannot be compared to a half shekel, notwithstanding R' Yehudah's argument that the half shekel tax may be increased. The half shekel tax may be increased only by the entire community in concert, and no individual may exceed

the designated amount. Consequently an individual's pronouncement: 'These coins are for my half shekel', must be considered an 'erroneous consecration' if they total more than the prescribed amount. In the case of a sacrifice, however, all the coins are holy even if their total exceeds the price of the animal *(Rav; Rambam)*.

The obvious inference from R' Yehudah is that one has the right to contribute more than the obligatory half shekel. This is puzzling in light of the verse *(Exodus 30:15): The rich [man] shall not exceed, and the poor [man] shall not diminish ...* (Rashash).

Apparently, R' Yehudah interprets the above cited verse as referring to something other than the annual head tax. Possibly it refers only to the one time contribution of silver that was melted down in the Wilderness to make the silver bases that supported the wall planks of the Tabernacle. The plain meaning [פְּשׁוּטוֹ שֶׁל מִקְרָא] of the passage supports this view (see *Sefer HaMitzvos* of R' Saadiah Gaon, v. 1, p. 297-8).[1] However, *Rambam* and most other authorities understand the verse to refer to the yearly Temple tax *(ibid.; see comm. above)*. Alternatively, R' Yehudah may hold

---

1. As noted in *Ramban's* commentary to *Exodus* 30:12, these contentions are supported by the fact that none of the early enumerators of the 613 commandments lists a prohibition against deviating from the prescribed amount. (However, the later commentator R' Shimon ben Zemach does list it in *Zohar HaRakia*.) Indeed, the alternative interpretation given above is indicated by *Ramban* in his commentary to Torah *(ibid.)*. Nowhere does *Rambam* indicate that any transgression is involved in an excessive payment (see *Hil. Shekalim* 1:5-6) although he uses this verse as a basis for ruling that no one, even the poorest, may give less than half a shekel tax *(op. cit. 1:1)*.

Since the *halachah* should follow R' Shimon (see *Rambam's Comm.* here), the omission of the verse, *the rich [man] shall not exceed ...* by the enumerators needs further explanation.

[43]   **THE MISHNAH / SHEKALIM**

שקלים [ה] **מוֹתַר** שְׁקָלִים חֻלִּין.
מוֹתַר עֲשִׂירִית הָאֵיפָה;
מוֹתַר קִנֵּי זָבִים, קִנֵּי זָבוֹת וְקִנֵּי יוֹלְדוֹת;
וְחַטָּאוֹת וַאֲשָׁמוֹת — מוֹתְרֵיהֶן נְדָבָה.
זֶה הַכְּלָל: כָּל־שֶׁהוּא בָא לְשֵׁם חַטָּאת וּלְשֵׁם

יד אברהם

that the verse should be rendered: *The rich man 'need not' exceed* and the *poor man 'should not' diminish* ... In this view, the verse is not meant to *prohibit* anyone from giving more should he so choose, but rather to dispel any notion that the half shekel is to be paid by someone of average means, and that the rich should pay more and the poor less.

R' Yehudah proves his contention from the fact that in previous generations the people *did* pay a greater tax. He advances the argument that if the verse cited above does refer to the Temple tax, that tax could not be increased even if the increase were applied uniformly or if the currency changed; for the verse refers to any payment in excess of the half shekel specified in the Torah.

R' Shimon's response to this is to draw a distinction between an *individual* paying more than the prescribed amount, which is *not* permitted, and the entire community being taxed at greater amounts, which *is* permitted.

According to R' Yehudah it should follow that the entire amount becomes consecrated

for public offerings, an opinion not heretofore found in the mishnah (Beis Shammai considers it only a donation, but not part of the regular fund). However, a reading of R' Yehudah's words indicates that he is not expounding a new halachic viewpoint. Rather he agrees with R' Shimon that the excess amount remains unconsecrated as stated by Beis Hillel, but he disagrees with R' Shimon's explanation of this rule. While R' Yehudah accepts the law on the basis of Beis Hillel's authority, he rejects R' Shimon's rationale for it, but cannot produce an alternative explanation. It is also possible that R' Yehudah had an explanation which was not recorded by the mishnah because the author of this mishnah agrees with R' Shimon's understanding of Beis Hillel. However, these interpretations cannot be reconciled with *Rambam* who states (*Comm.*) that even according to R' Yehudah the half shekel prescribed by the Torah refers to half the prevalent currency unit. Thus, none of the taxes paid in excess of the Torah half shekel were in excess of the minimum requirement — half the currency unit (see *Hil. Shekalim* 1:5).

5.

Having discussed the status of funds contributed in excess of the half shekel requirement, and its contrast with the disposition of an excess contribution for a sin offering (mishnah 3-4),the mishnah now goes on to list the rules of excess amounts in other cases. The mishnah introduces its listing by reiterating the law according to Beis Hillel, as given in mishnah 3 *(Rav; Rambam)*.

מוֹתַר שְׁקָלִים חֻלִּין. — *The remainder of [funds set aside for] the half shekels is unconsecrated.*

מוֹתַר עֲשִׂירִית הָאֵיפָה; — *the remainder of [funds set aside for the purchase of] the tenth of an ephah [meal offering];*

Since R' Shimon clearly prohibits any deviation from the set amount, it would seem to follow that he understands this verse as a prohibition.

Perhaps we can modify this interpretation. Even R' Shimon concurs that the verse is not a prohibition. He maintains, however, that in specifying an amount, the Torah sets forth that only a payment of exactly half a shekel — and no more — can become consecrated for this purpose. An excessive payment is indeed not a violation of a Scriptural prohibition, but is invalid in the sense that no sanctity devolves upon the amount in excess of half a shekel. R' Yehudah disagrees, maintaining on the basis of his proofs that voluntary consecration of greater amounts *are* valid.

5. **T**he remainder of [funds set aside for] the half
shekels is unconsecrated.

The remainder of [funds set aside for the purchase
of] the tenth of an *ephah* meal offering; the remainder
of [funds set aside for the purchase of] bird offerings
of *zavim, zavos* and women after childbirth; [the
remainder of funds set aside for the purchase of] sin
offerings and guilt offerings — these remainders are
[to be placed in the collection chest marked]
"Donative Offering".

This is the general rule: Whatever [money] has
been set aside for [the purchase of sacrifices to atone

YAD AVRAHAM

An amount of money was set aside
for the purchase of this offering, and
some money was in excess of the
amount needed.

The tenth of an *ephah* meal offering
referred to here is a sin offering (*Rav*
from *Yer.* and *Menachos* 108a) [as
shown by its placement with other sin
offerings].

Although a חַטָּאת, *sin offering*, must
be an animal in virtually all cases,
Leviticus 5:1-4 lists instances where an
indigent person may substitute a bird
sacrifice or a meal offering. The cases
are: (a) A witness swore falsely that he
had no information to offer in a litiga-
tion; (b) without knowing he was טָמֵא,
contaminated, someone entered the
Temple or ate sacrificial meat; (c)
someone knowingly swore falsely, or
violated his oath. Because the form of
the sin offering required for these
transgressions varies according to the
economic status of the sinner, it is
known as an adjustable sin offering
(קָרְבָּן עוֹלֶה וְיוֹרֵד, lit., *ascending and
descending offering*). In cases of extreme indigency, a meal offering consisting of one tenth of an *ephah* of flour
is sufficient (see *Leviticus* 5:1-14). [The
tenth of an *ephah* (or *omer*) has the
volume of 43.2 average eggs.]

מוֹתַר קִנֵּי זָבִים, קִנֵּי זָבוֹת וְקִנֵּי יוֹלְדוֹת;
וְחַטָּאוֹת וַאֲשָׁמוֹת— — *the remainder of*

[*funds set aside for the purchase of*]
bird offerings [lit. *nests*] *of zavim, zavos
and women after childbirth;* [*the
remainder of funds set aside for the
purchase of*] *sin offerings and guilt offerings—*

[Each of these terms is fully described above in 1:5.]

מוֹתְרֵיהֶן נְדָבָה. — *these remainders are* [*to
be placed in the collection chest marked*]
"*Donative Offering.*"

[Even though the leftover monies are
not needed for their originally designated purpose, they nevertheless remain
consecrated (see mishnah 4). However,
since sin and guilt offerings cannot be
brought at will — but only when the
Torah prescribes — this excess cannot
be used for an additional sin or guilt offering. The remainder is placed in one
of the six donation chests whose
proceeds were used to purchase animals
to be brought as burnt offerings
whenever the altar service slackened
(see 6:5-6).]

זֶה הַכְּלָל: כָּל־שֶׁהוּא בָא לְשֵׁם חַטָּאת וּלְשֵׁם
אָשְׁמָה—מוֹתָרָן נְדָבָה. — *This is the
general rule: Whatever* [*money*] *has
been set aside* [lit. *comes*] *for* [*the
purchase of sacrifices to atone for*] *a sin
or for guilt — its remainder is* [*to be
placed in the collection chest marked*]
"*Donative Offering.*"

As the mishnah relates further (6:6),

שקלים
ב/ה

אַשְׁמָה — מוֹתָרָן נְדָבָה.
מוֹתַר עוֹלָה לְעוֹלָה. מוֹתַר מִנְחָה לְמִנְחָה.
מוֹתַר שְׁלָמִים לִשְׁלָמִים. מוֹתַר פֶּסַח לִשְׁלָמִים.
מוֹתַר נְזִירִים לִנְזִירִים; מוֹתַר נָזִיר לִנְדָבָה.

יד אברהם

it was Yehoyada, who was *Kohen Gadol* during the reign of King Yeho'ash in the First Temple era, who taught that the use of these remainders for the purpose indicated in our mishnah could be derived from Scripture (*Rav*).

Although חַטָּאת is usually translated *sin offering* it must be rendered *sin* in this instance for two reasons: the parallel word אַשְׁמָה, *guilt*, of the next phrase is never used in place of אָשָׁם, *guilt offering*; and many texts have the variant reading חֵטְא, *sin*, for חַטָּאת (see *Shinuyei Nuschaos*). Indeed this is how a similar phrase is worded in 6:6.

The interpolations are based on *Rivavan* who writes: Whatever is because of a sin (חֵטְא) or because of a guilt (אַשְׁמָה) which necessitates a sin offering (חַטָּאת) or a guilt offering (אָשָׁם).

Thus far the mishnah has discussed cases where the excess funds cannot be used for their initially designated purposes. Now the mishnah will go on to cases where surplus funds should be used for their designated purpose wherever possible.

מוֹתַר עוֹלָה לְעוֹלָה. מוֹתַר מִנְחָה לְמִנְחָה. מוֹתַר שְׁלָמִים לִשְׁלָמִים. — *The remainder of [funds set aside for] a burnt offering is [to be used] for [the purchase of] a burnt offering. The remainder of [funds set aside for] a meal offering is [to be used] for [the purchase of] a meal offering. The remainder of [funds set aside for] a peace offering is [to be used] for [the purchase of] a peace offering.*

[These three offerings are discussed respectively in the first three chapters of *Leviticus*. Although the excess monies mentioned earlier in this mishnah are used for donations as are these, there is a basic difference between them. Those

of the first clause are placed in the "Donative Offering" chests to be administered by Temple officials who use it to purchase animals to be brought as burnt offerings when the altar is not being used.

Here, however, the individual who put the money aside uses the surplus to purchase a "private" offering in addition to the one for which the money was designated.]

מוֹתַר פֶּסַח לִשְׁלָמִים. — *The remainder of [funds set aside for] a Pesach offering is [to be used] for [the purchase of] a peace offering.*

That excess funds designated for the Pesach offering are used for peace offerings is derived from *Deuteronomy 16:2: And you shall slaughter the Pesach to HASHEM your God* (צֹאן וּבָקָר) *flocks and cattle.* But the Pesach may only come from צֹאן, *flocks* [i.e., sheep or goats], and not cattle (see *Exodus* 12:5, 21). The Talmud expounds that the verse in *Deuteronomy* refers not to the actual Pesach itself but to funds remaining after the purchase of the animal for the Pesach offering. Such excess funds should be used to purchase a type of offering that may be brought from either flocks or cattle. [Furthermore, since the verse does not specify gender, it must apply to an offering for which both male and female animals are valid (*Rashi*).] These criteria are met by the peace offering. Not only the funds but even the leftover animal itself (if for some reason the animal was not slaughtered on the eve of Pesach, e.g., its owner died) has the status of a peace offering (*Zevachim* 9a).

⋖§ **Nazirite**

One who has accepted upon him the status of נָזִיר, *nazirite*, is forbidden to eat or drink the produce of the grapevine, cut his hair or beard, or become contaminated

2
5

for] a sin or for guilt — its remainder is [to be placed in the collection chest marked] "Donative Offering".

The remainder of [funds set aside for] a burnt offering is [to be used] for [the purchase of] a burnt offering. The remainder of [funds set aside for] a meal offering is [to be used] for [the purchase of] a meal offering. The remainder of [funds set aside for] a peace offering is [to be used] for [the purchase of] a peace offering. The remainder of [funds set aside for] a Pesach offering is [to be used] for [the purchase of] a peace offering.

The remainder of [funds contributed for the offerings of] nazirites is [to be used] for nazirites; but the remainder of [funds contributed for the offerings of] a [specific] nazirite is [to be placed in the collection chest marked] "Donative Offering."

(טָמֵא) through a corpse, for the duration of his nazirite term. The term is ordinarily the minimum of thirty days unless the nazirite specifies a longer period (*Nazir* 1:3).

Should he become contaminated, he cuts off all his hair and brings two bird sacrifices, one a sin offering and the other a burnt offering, and a yearling lamb as a guilt offering (אֲשַׁם נָזִיר). Then he begins his term over again. This process is called תִּגְלַחַת הַטֻּמְאָה, *haircutting of the contaminated* (see *Nazir* 6:6).

Upon completion of the nazirite term, the *nazir* brings a group of sacrifices comprising male and female yearling lambs as a burnt offering and sin offering, respectively, a ram as a peace offering, ten each of two varieties of loaves, and the usual libations that accompany the burnt and peace offerings. The *nazir* cuts his hair and places it in the fire under the pot in which the peace offering is cooking. This process is called תִּגְלַחַת הַטָּהֳרָה, *haircutting of the pure* (see *Nazir* 6:7; *Numbers* 6:1-21).

מוֹתַר נְזִירִים לִנְזִירִים; מוֹתַר נָזִיר לִנְדָבָה. — *The remainder of [funds contributed for the offerings of] nazirites is [to be used] for nazirites; but the remainder of [funds contributed for the offerings of] a [specific] nazirite is [to be placed in the collection chest marked] "Donative Offering."*

If money had been collected to purchase animals for the offerings of indigent nazirites and there were leftover funds, it should be held until it is needed by other nazirites. However, if an individual *nazir* set aside his own money for the requisite sacrifices, any surplus is placed in the donation chests (*Rav*).

The distinction between funds for unspecified nazirites and funds for specified nazirites is quite simple. General funds collected for the benefit of indigent nazirites can be used for any future *nazir* who may be in need because the funds were designated for general use. Money designated for a specific individual or individuals however, cannot be used for the sin offering of different people. Consequently, if a group of nazirites pooled their personal funds for the purchase of offerings and there was leftover money, it must

שקלים מוֹתַר עֲנִיִּים לַעֲנִיִּים; מוֹתַר עָנִי לְאוֹתוֹ עָנִי.
מוֹתַר שְׁבוּיִים לִשְׁבוּיִים; מוֹתַר שָׁבוּי לְאוֹתוֹ
שָׁבוּי.
מוֹתַר הַמֵּתִים לְמֵתִים; מוֹתַר הַמֵּת לְיוֹרְשָׁיו.

יד אברהם

be used for donations, but not for other nazirites, because the pool consisted of private funds for designated people. Similarly if someone contributed funds to purchase offerings for a single *nazir*, any remainder may not be used for another *nazir* because the donor intended his gift for only one *nazir* (*Tos. Yom Tov* as explained by *Tif. Yis*; cf. *Hil. Nezirus* 9:1, *Tzofnas Pa'ane'ach* there; *Hil. Pessulei HaMukdashin* 5:9).

מוֹתַר עֲנִיִּים לַעֲנִיִּים; — *The remainder of [funds contributed for distribution to] poor people is [to be used] for poor people;*

If money was collected for a specific need of some poor people, and there were leftover funds, the remainder should be used to help other poor people (*Tif. Yis.*) [or to fill a different need of the same people].

מוֹתַר עָנִי לְאוֹתוֹ עָנִי. — *but the remainder of [funds contributed for the sake of] a [specific] poor man is [to be given] to that poor man.*

If money was collected to fill a specific need for a particular poor person, e.g., to buy him clothing, the remainder should be used to fill some other need for him (*Rav*).

[It should not be used even for another poor man. See *Yoreh Deah* 258:12 and sources cited by *R' Akiva Eiger* there.]

Although money set aside for the poor is not considered consecrated, it may nevertheless not be diverted from its designated purpose. Such money is classified as a vow that one must fulfill (see *Bava Kama* 36b and comm. there, esp. *Milchamos*; *Yoreh Deah* 258:6). A strong argument is made by some authorities that where someone designates

specific possessions for the poor, his intended gift transcends the obligation of an ordinary vow, the fulfillment of which is בֵּין אָדָם לַמָּקוֹם, *an obligation of man to God*. In the case of a vow to the poor, the ownership of the object is considered to have been transferred to the poor people; the mere vow serves as the legal formalization (קִנְיָן) of this transfer [אֲמִירָתוֹ לְגָבוֹהַּ כִּמְסִירָתוֹ לְהֶדְיוֹט, *an oral commitment to heaven is equivalent to the transfer of property to a layman*]. The argument is advanced that this should surely be so if the object (or money) is orally donated to a specific poor man (*Machaneh Efrayim, Hil. Tzedakah* ch. 2; cf. *Ketzos HaChoshen* 212:4 and 290:2 with *Teshuvos Panim Meiros* 2:134 [R' Meir Eisenstadt] cited there).

מוֹתַר שְׁבוּיִים לִשְׁבוּיִים; — *The remainder of [funds contributed for the ransom of] captives is [to be used] for [the ransom of] captives;*

מוֹתַר שָׁבוּי לְאוֹתוֹ שָׁבוּי. — *but the remainder of [funds contributed for the ransom of] a [specific] captive is [to be given] to that captive.*

Any surplus from funds collected to ransom a group of kidnapped people should be set aside for a similar need in the future. But if the money was collected for a specific person, he gains title to the money and any surplus is turned over to him (*Rav*).

Here too, *Tosefos Yom Tov* holds that if the money was collected for a *specific* group of captives, the remainder is theirs just as it is in the case of a single individual. Only where the money was collected for the general purpose of ransoming unspecified persons must the remainder be set aside for a similar use in the future.[1]

1. [It is difficult to understand the halachic justification for giving the remainder of the funds to 'that captive'. The donor's vow was to contribute toward a *ransom*, not to make a private gift to the victim if he does not need it to purchase his freedom. If the captive were poor, a vow to contribute for his benefit might be sufficient to give him possession of the money, as noted above (s.v. מותר עני). If the recipient is not poor, however, a mere vow should not constitute a transfer of ownership (קִנְיָן) that remains in force even if the intent of the vow — the ransom —

The remainder of [funds contributed for distribution to] poor people is [to be used] for poor people;
but the remainder of [funds contributed for the sake
of] a [specific] poor man is [to be given] to that poor
man.

The remainder of [funds contributed for the ransom of] captives is [to be used] for [the ransom of]
captives; but the remainder of [funds contributed for
the ransom of] a [specific] captive is [to be given] to
that captive.

The remainder of [funds contributed for the burial
of] the dead is [to be used] for [the burial of] the
dead; [but] the remainder of [funds contributed for
the burial of] a [specific] dead person is [to be given]

YAD AVRAHAM

מוֹתַר הַמֵּתִים לְמֵתִים; — *The remainder of*
[funds contributed for the burial of] the
dead is [to be used] for [the burial of]
the dead;
If money was collected for the burial
(or other needs, such as shrouds,
purchase of a plot) of deceased people,
the remainder of the money should be
used for burial of other dead *(Rav;*
probably based on a *baraisa* cited in
Sanhedrin 48b).

[*Rav's* words echo the view of *Tosefos
Yom Tov* (see above) that the use of the
plural form here indicates that the collection
is made for a cause without mentioning the
recipient of the funds. Money collected for a
group of specific individuals would go to
their heirs in accordance with the rule noted
above for money donated for individuals.]

מוֹתַר הַמֵּת לְיוֹרְשָׁיו. — *[but] the remainder*
of [funds contributed for the burial of] a
[specific] dead person is [to be given] to
his heirs.
If funds were collected for the burial

needs of a specific deceased person, any
surplus belongs to his heirs. That such a
collection had to be made to pay for a
burial is an intense humiliation to the
deceased. The *tanna kamma* maintains
that the dead person can be presumed to
forgive the slight to his honor only for
the sake of his children *(Rav* based on
the amora Rava's interpretation in
Sanhedrin 48a).

[The above cited passage needs explanation. How does the presumed humiliation of
the deceased obligate the holders of the
money to give it to the heirs. If these funds
are considered consecrated for the *mitzvah* of
burying the dead, then how is a *mitzvah* fulfilled by giving the money to the heirs, the
deceased's wishes notwithstanding?

Rashba (Teshuvos 1:375 cited by *Rama,
Choshen Mishpat* 210:3) maintains that the
principle implicit in this mishnah is that
money donated for the purpose of someone's
burial is legally considered the deceased's
money; it does not fall under the general rule
that the dead do not own property (see also

is no longer relevant. Perhaps this passage (unlike the preceding ones) does not refer to funds
merely designated but not yet handed over. If the donor still has the money and it is not
needed for the ransom, he may keep it. Our mishnah may refer only to cases where the money
has been given to a collector who will hold the money until it is used. In such instances, the
collector is considered to have taken possession on behalf of the captive (זְכִיָּה). It is an undisputed rule in Talmudic jurisprudence that if A gives B an object for C, by accepting it, B
takes possession as an implied agent of C, who becomes the owner.

רַבִּי מֵאִיר אוֹמֵר: מוֹתַר הַמֵּת יְהֵא מֻנָּח עַד
שֶׁיָּבֹא אֵלִיָּהוּ. רַבִּי נָתָן אוֹמֵר: מוֹתַר הַמֵּת
בּוֹנִין לוֹ נֶפֶשׁ עַל־קִבְרוֹ.

[א] **בִּשְׁלשָׁה** פְּרָקִים בַּשָּׁנָה תּוֹרְמִין אֶת־
הַלִּשְׁכָּה; בִּפְרוֹס הַפֶּסַח,

יד אברהם

sources cited in *Teshuvos Doveiv Meisharim* 3:95; *Teshuvos Tuv Ta'am Vada'as T'lissa'ah* 2:85. Accordingly, the reasoning of the Talmud can be understood as follows: all collected funds could have conceivably been used for the burial, but the deceased forgives this slight to his honor for the sake of his heirs (see *R' Chananel, Sanhedrin 48a*). Since it is our assessment that this is the will of the deceased — the rightful owner of this money — these funds are part of the estate, like all his other possessions (cf. *Machaneh Ephraim, Hil. Zechiyah UMatanah 31; Teshuvos Avnei Neizer, Choshen Mishpat 41*).

On the other hand, *Ramban (Sha'ar HaGemuel*, cited by *Bais Yosef, Yoreh Deah* 35b) and *Ran (Chidushei HaRan Sanhedrin* 48a), maintain that the deceased does not acquire these funds in a proprietary sense. The principle at issue here is that money designated for a specific *mitzvah* should not be diverted from that *mitzvah*. *Chazon Ish (Ohalos 22:31; Choshen Mishpat 22*) explains that people designating funds for charity can be assumed to wish that their money be put to the best possible use. In this case, because we assume that the deceased would want the remainder to go to his heirs, this is the best use of the money under the circumstances. *(Rashi to Sanhedrin* seems to have yet another approach; cf. *Levush Ateres Zahav 356*.)

רַבִּי מֵאִיר אוֹמֵר: מוֹתַר הַמֵּת יְהֵא מֻנָּח עַד שֶׁיָּבֹא אֵלִיָּהוּ. — *R' Meir says: The remainder of [funds contributed for the burial of] a [specific] dead person is to be held in escrow until Elijah shall come.*

[As is well known, the prophet Elijah will be the harbinger of the Messiah, and will pass judgment on all difficult points of law. In many cases where *Beis Din* lacks sufficient evidence to decide questions of ownership, the rule is that

the property in question be held in escrow until a decision is possible, even if it must await the coming of Elijah.]

R' Meir is not sure whether it can be assumed that the deceased forgives his indignity in favor of his heirs, therefore, in the absence of clear cut evidence of ownership, the money must remain in escrow *(Rav; Sanhedrin 48a).*

רַבִּי נָתָן אוֹמֵר: מוֹתַר הַמֵּת בּוֹנִין לוֹ נֶפֶשׁ עַל קִבְרוֹ. — *R' Nosson says: [With] the remainder of [funds contributed for the burial of] a [specific] dead person they build a monument for him on his grave.*

R' Nosson assumes that the deceased does *not* forgive his indignity in favor of his heirs, consequently the entire money must be used for his burial and related expenses *(ibid.).*

If there will be a remainder even after a monument has been set up, the money should be spent for perfuming the litter upon which the deceased is carried *(Tos. Yom Tov* from *Yer.).*

The halachah follows the first tanna *(Rav; Yoreh Deah 356).*

However, if the money had been collected because of a misunderstanding, e.g., they thought the deceased had left no money when in reality he had, the money does not belong to the heirs *(Rav* citing *Yer.),* but must be returned to the donors (cf. *Teshuvos HaRosh 32:6; Teshuvos HaRashba 1:375; Yoreh Deah 356).*

If the community where these funds had been collected is ruled by a body of communal officials, they may, if they so see fit, divert monies intended for one *mitzvah* to another *(Rav* from *Yer.; Yoreh Deah 253:6)* for it is assumed that the donors give the money to be used at the officials' discretion, even when the collection is designated for a different purpose *(Korban HaEidah).*

3
1

to his heirs. R' Meir says: The remainder of [funds contributed for the burial of] a [specific] dead person is to be held in escrow until Elijah shall come. R' Nosson says: [With] the remainder of [funds contributed for the burial of] a [specific] dead person they build a monument for him on his grave.

1. At three periods of the year they withdraw [funds] from the [treasury] chamber; fifteen days before Pesach, fifteen days before Shavuos, and

YAD AVRAHAM

Chapter 3

1.

בִּשְׁלשָׁה פְרָקִים בַּשָּׁנָה תּוֹרְמִין אֶת־הַלִּשְׁכָּה;
— At three periods of the year they withdraw [funds; lit., lift up] from the [treasury] chamber;

After the half shekels had been accumulated in the collection chests (see 2:1) the chests were brought to the Temple and deposited in a designated chamber (see Yerushalmi and Rambam cited in comm. to mishnah 2, s.v. בשלש). They did not withdraw an entire year's funds at one time, because the half shekels of the Jews living in distant places had not yet arrived, though they had no doubt been collected before the first of Nissan, as set forth earlier in 1:1 (Rav; Rambam based on his interpretation to Yer. 1:1; see Korban HaEidah and Shyarei Korban there; Rosh).[1]

Even those whose half shekels had not yet arrived had a share in the sacrifices purchased with the half shekels withdrawn on the first date (see mishnah 4, s.v. תרם את הראשונה below). Nonetheless, they withdrew funds three different times a year so

that everyone's half shekel should *actually* be among those from which the funds for the public offerings were taken (Tos. Yom Tov).

בִּפְרוֹס הַפֶּסַח, — fifteen days [lit. half] before Pesach,

The pre-Pesach season of study and preparation was thirty days. At its halfway mark (פְרוֹס) funds were withdrawn for the first time. The thirty days preceding Pesach are designated as the preparatory period for the festival; as the Talmud teaches: 'thirty days before Pesach they inquire and expound on the laws of Pesach' (Pesachim 6a; Tosefta 2:1; Rav and Rambam from Yer. and Bechoros 58a).

Whether the fifteen days are counted backwards from the first day of Pesach (15 Nissan) or from the day before Pesach (14 Nissan) is in dispute. Rashi (Bech. 58a, s.v. בן עזאי) and Rambam (Hil. Bechoros 7:8) give the date as 29 Adar, or fifteen days before the eve of Pesach. However, Rambam (Hil. Shekalim 2:5) lists Rosh Chodesh Nissan, apparently including the first day of Pesach

1. Alternatively, Jews in the Diaspora gave their half shekels much earlier than the fifteenth of Adar (see 1:1), so that their funds would arrive at the Temple in time for the first of Nissan withdrawal. If so, the practice of withdrawing funds three times a year was meant to publicize the fact that the Temple tax was indeed being used to purchase the public sacrifices (R' Meshullam; R' Eliyahu Fulda; P'nei Moshe; Taklin Chadatin to Yer.; cf. R' Shlomo Sirilio and R' Shmuel there).

שְׁקָלִים בִּפְרוֹס עֲצֶרֶת, בִּפְרוֹס הֶחָג, וְהֵן גְּרָנוֹת
ג/א לְמַעְשַׂר בְּהֵמָה — דִּבְרֵי רַבִּי עֲקִיבָא.
בֶּן־עַזַּאי אוֹמֵר: בָּעֶשְׂרִים וְתִשְׁעָה בַּאֲדָר,

יד אברהם

in the fifteen day period (see *Tos. Yom Tov,* s.v. בפרוס פסח).

[If it was 29 Adar, a full day was available for the purchase of animals for the next day's service. If it was Rosh Chodesh Nissan, the withdrawal was probably made at nightfall to allow as much time as possible for the purchase of the next morning's sacrifices.]

The reason R' Akiva uses the word פְּרוֹס, *half,* instead of stating the date explicitly, is discussed below, s.v. בֶּן־עַזַּאי.

בִּפְרוֹס עֲצֶרֶת, — *fifteen days before Shavuos,*

[The Shavuos festival is commonly referred to in the Talmud as *Atzeres* (lit. *a convocation;* see *Onkelos* and *Ibn Ezra* to *Leviticus* 23:36 and *Numbers* 29:35).]

The translation *'fifteen days before ... '* is based on *Rambam* (*Hil. Shekalim* 2:5 and *Hil. Bechoros* 7:8). *Tosefos* (*Kiddushin* 54a, s.v. מועלין) states that פְּרוֹס עֲצֶרֶת refers to the first of Sivan (cf. *Rashash*). This is compatible with *R' Shmuel's* comment here that the term פְּרוֹס (in its literal sense of *half* the thirty-day period) is used primarily for the pre-Pesach withdrawal of funds — but that the second and third 'periods' are closer in time to their respective festivals.

[According to *R' Shmuel's* comment, it may be that R' Akiva agrees with the later tannaim of our mishnah that the second

withdrawal is made on Rosh Chodesh Sivan. Support for this can be found in *Bechoros* 88a, which expounds on our mishnah. There the *Gemara* explains the reason for R' Akiva and Ben Azzai's disagreement concerning the *first* withdrawal date, but with regard to the second withdrawal date, the *Gemara* discusses only Ben Azzai's view, without mention of a disagreement. This is also consistent with the view that only before Pesach must there be a thirty-day inquiring and preparation period (see *Chok Yaakov* and *Beur HaGra* to *Orach Chaim* 429).]

However, *Tosefta* 2:1 states that each withdrawal period is fifteen days before its respective festival.

בִּפְרוֹס הֶחָג, — *and fifteen days before Succos* [lit. *the festival*].

[The Succos festival is consistently called 'the festival' in the Mishnah.]

Regarding the fifteen days before Succos, *Rambam* in *Hilchos Bechoros* 7:8 gives the date as 29 Elul; in *Hilchos Shekalim* 2:5 he identifies it as 'Rosh Chodesh Tishrei, either before [Rosh Hashanah] or after it'.

וְהֵן גְּרָנוֹת לְמַעְשַׂר בְּהֵמָה — דִּבְרֵי רַבִּי עֲקִיבָא. — *And these are also the designated dates* [lit. *gathering times*] *for the animal tithe* — [these are] *the words of R' Akiva.*

◈§ The Animal Tithe — Obligatory or Voluntary.

The Torah teaches that one should tithe the offspring of his kosher animals (goats, sheep, cattle). Each tenth animal is called מַעְשַׂר בְּהֵמָה, *animal tithe* and must be brought as a sacrifice at the Temple. Portions of the sacrificial meat are burned upon the altar and the rest is eaten by the owner and his guests (see *comm.* to 1:7).

The *mitzvah* of animal tithes differs from other tithes in that it is מִצְוָה בְּעָלְמָא, *a meritorious deed* [lit. *a general mitzvah*], in the sense that no commandment is violated if one sells or slaughters an untithed animal (*Rav; Bechoros* 57b-58a and *Rashi* there; *Meleches Shlomo*). In this, the commandment differs from the tithes of produce regarding which it is forbidden to make use of the crop once the tithing season has arrived, until the tithes have been separated.

The command to tithe animals could be fulfilled at any time and, as noted, the animals could be bought and sold without restriction before then. Nevertheless, most people refrained from engaging in such commerce before having tithed their animals. Consequently, shortages would result in the animal markets if tithing were

3
1
fifteen days before Succos. And these are also the designated dates for the animal tithe — [these are] the words of R' Akiva.

Ben Azzai says: [The three periods are] on the twenty-ninth of Adar, on the first of Sivan, and on

YAD AVRAHAM

delayed and surpluses would result after large numbers of people took their tithes.

To assure an ample supply of meat in Jerusalem during the pilgrimage festivals, Pesach, Shavuos and Succos, the Rabbis decreed that fifteen days before each of the holidays, no animals may be slaughtered unless they were tithed. The effect of this decree was that large numbers of animals would become available, at reasonable prices, in time for the pilgrims' needs.

Although those who wished to could evade the tithe, even after the Rabbinic decree, by selling or slaughtering their animals before the designated dates, there was no need to fear that many people would do so. The general maxim is: נִיחָא לֵיהּ לְאִינִישׁ דְּלִיעֲבֵיד מִצְוָה בְּמָמוֹנֵיהּ, *A person is gratified that a mitzvah be performed with his possessions* [especially when only a slight loss is involved — in this case the burden of taking the animal to Jerusalem to the Temple; the owner loses no meat, however, since all the meat belongs to him (*Rav; Bechoros* 57b-58a)]. Had the Rabbis not made tithing obligatory at these junctures, many people would have withheld animals from market until they found it convenient to separate the tithe. By assigning such firm dates, the Rabbis gave animals a status similar to that of produce which could not be used once their harvest and threshing had been completed. Because of this similarity, the animal deadline was named גְּרָנוֹת, *gathering times,* the same term applied to produce.

בֶּן־עַזַּאי אוֹמֵר: בְּעֶשְׂרִים וְתִשְׁעָה בַּאֲדָר, — *Ben Azzai says: [The three periods are] on the twenty-ninth of Adar,*

As noted above, the consensus of commentators is that R' Akiva, too, holds that the first withdrawal is on 29 Adar, even though he prefers to describe it as פְּרוֹס הַפֶּסַח. The difference between R' Akiva and Ben Azzai, however, is not merely semantic. R' Akiva holds that it would be inaccurate to set the date at 29 Adar, because the fifteen day period before Pesach can sometimes be 30 Adar. Since the proclamation of the new month depends on the sighting of the new moon by witnesses, a lunar month can be either twenty-nine or thirty days. Accordingly, the fifteenth day before Pesach can be either 29 or 30 Adar, depending on whether witnesses appeared before *Beis Din.* Ben Azzai, however, holds that the Adar before Pesach is *always* twenty-nine days; con-

sequently, he is justified in giving the date of the shekel withdrawal as precisely 29 Adar (*Bechoros* 58a with *Rashi*) [i.e., the disagreement is not over *when* the first withdrawal was made. The tannaim disagree only on *how* to *state* this date].

[Clearly, this controversy is relevant to the pre-calendar era in which these tannaim lived, when the length of months could vary depending on the visibility of the moon. (Since the institution of the permanent Jewish calendar by Hillel the Patriarch in 4118/358 C.E., the length of the Adar before Pesach is always twenty-nine days; see *Tos. Rosh HaShanah* 19b, s.v. אדר.) Consequently, we must assume that according to Ben Azzai, *Beis Din* would proclaim the thirtieth of Adar as Rosh Chodesh, even if no witnesses arrived to attest to a sighting of the new moon. Probably this unusual course was followed to dispel any doubt about the date of the Passover festival. For a more complete discussion of the Jewish calendar, see ArtScroll, *Rosh HaShanah* 1:3.]

שקלים וּבְאֶחָד בְּסִינָן, וּבְעֶשְׂרִים וְתִשְׁעָה בְּאָב.
ג/א רַבִּי אֶלְעָזָר וְרַבִּי שִׁמְעוֹן אוֹמְרִים: בְּאֶחָד
בְּנִיסָן, בְּאֶחָד בְּסִינָן, בְּעֶשְׂרִים וְתִשְׁעָה בֶּאֱלוּל.
מִפְּנֵי מָה אָמְרוּ ,,בְּעֶשְׂרִים וְתִשְׁעָה״, וְלֹא
אָמְרוּ ,,בְּאֶחָד בְּתִשְׁרֵי״? — מִפְּנֵי שֶׁהוּא יוֹם
טוֹב וְאִי אֶפְשָׁר לַעֲשֵׂר בְּיוֹם טוֹב. לְפִיכָךְ
הִקְדִּימוּהוּ לָעֶשְׂרִים וְתִשְׁעָה בֶּאֱלוּל.

יד אברהם

וּבְאֶחָד בְּסִינָן, — *(and) on the first of Sivan,*

Since the period between Pesach and Shavuos is only seven weeks, the Sages considered it disadvantageous to establish a tithing deadline of fifteen days before Shavuos as they did before Pesach. Were they to do so, the tithing date would be 20 Iyar and it would affect only the animals born from 29 Adar until that date — a relatively small number of animals. By delaying the tithing period until 1 Sivan, the Rabbis accomplished two goals. For one, this later date will include more animals; secondly there would be fewer days before the festival when animals can be slaughtered. Thus, a later date would assure a more ample meat supply for the עוֹלֵי רֶגֶל, *pilgrims,* on Shavuos *(Bechoros 58a).*[1]

This part of our mishnah is ambiguous: Does the dispute between the tannaim refer to the dates of the shekel withdrawals, or of the animal tithes, or of both?

Bechoros 9:6 quotes the dispute of our mishnah with reference only to animal tithes. Thus, the first possibility suggested above is inappropriate.

Rambam (Comm. ed Kafich) and *R' Shlomo Sirilio* seem to concur that all agree with R' Akiva regarding the withdrawal dates. Only the tithing dates are in dispute.

Tiferes Yisrael (4), on the other hand,

finds special significance in the fact that animal tithes are mentioned in a mishnah dealing with shekalim withdrawal; this juxtaposition implies that the two are related, as follows: the shekalim were withdrawn to purchase sacrificial animals, but since most breeders would not sell their animals before tithing, the availability of animals was greatest on the day of tithing. Thus, the shekalim withdrawal should always coincide with the tithe, and the dispute of the mishnah refers to the dates of both.

וּבְעֶשְׂרִים וְתִשְׁעָה בְּאָב. — *and on the twenty-ninth of Av.*

The Talmud *(Bechoros 53b)* derives from the Torah that animals born in one year cannot be counted together with those born in another year for the purpose of tithing. In other words, all the animals in the corral from among which every tenth one is consecrated must have been born during the same year.

The specific day that is considered the first day of the animal-tithing year is the subject of a tannaitic dispute. R' Meir maintains that it is the first of Elul. R' Elazar and R' Shimon hold the first of Tishrei. Ben Azzai is unsure which opinion is correct, so he must schedule the tithing in such a way that no violation can possibly take place. Consequently, he requires that animals born before Elul be tithed with the previous

---

1. [If both Nissan and Iyar are full, Shavuos will be on the fifth of Sivan; if both are deficient, it will fall on the seventh; if one is full and the other deficient (as happens under the calendar instituted by Hillel),the sixth of Sivan will be Shavuos.]

3 the twenty-ninth of Av.

1 R' Elazar and R' Shimon say: [The three periods are] on the first of Nissan, on the first of Sivan, and on the twenty-ninth of Elul. Why did they say "on the twenty-ninth [of Elul]" instead of saying "on the first of Tishrei"? — because that [day] is a festival and one may not tithe on a festival. Therefore they advanced it to the twenty-ninth of Elul.

year's; those born after Elul with the next year's; and those born during Elul as a separate group (Bechoros 9:5; see comm. to Rosh Hashanah 1:1 for the rationale of each opinion).

Here Ben Azzai follows his opinion that the animals born in Elul may not be tithed with animals born before or after that month. If the tithing date were any time after Rosh Chodesh Elul, this could result in Elul animals being used to tithe pre-Elul animals and vice-versa. Therefore, the third period must precede the first of Elul. Because Av could sometimes consist of only twenty-nine days in the pre-calendar period when months depended on the sighting of witnesses, the twenty-ninth day was fixed permanently as the day for the withdrawal (Bechoros 58a).

רַבִּי אֶלְעָזָר וְרַבִּי שִׁמְעוֹן אוֹמְרִים: בְּאֶחָד בְּנִיסָן, — R' Elazar and R' Shimon say: [The three periods are] on the first of Nissan,

They concur with R' Shimon ben Gamliel's view that the time designated to inquire and expound on the laws of the festival is not a full thirty days before Pesach (see above, s.v. בפרוס הפסח), but two weeks is sufficient. The tithing is fixed for Rosh Chodesh Nissan, to coincide with the beginning of this two week period (Bechoros 58a).

בְּאֶחָד בְּסִיוָן, — on the first of Sivan,
For the same reason given for this

date by Ben Azzai (ibid.).

בְּעֶשְׂרִים וְתִשְׁעָה בֶּאֱלוּל. — and on the twenty-ninth of Elul.

Were R' Elazar and R' Shimon to be consistent with their previously expressed opinion that the tithing precedes Pesach by two weeks, their date for the pre-Succos tithing should have been Rosh Chodesh Tishrei. The reason they advanced it by one day is now given by the mishnah (Bechoros 58a).

מִפְּנֵי מָה אָמְרוּ „בְּעֶשְׂרִים וְתִשְׁעָה,‟ וְלֹא אָמְרוּ „בְּאֶחָד בְּתִשְׁרֵי‟? — Why did they say "on the twenty-ninth [of Elul]" instead of saying "on the first of Tishrei"?
For as already mentioned this should be the date of the period.

מִפְּנֵי שֶׁהוּא יוֹם טוֹב וְאִי אֶפְשָׁר לַעֲשֵׂר בְּיוֹם טוֹב. — because that [day, i.e., the first of Tishrei] is a festival [Rosh HaShanah] and one may not [lit. it is impossible to] tithe on a festival.

When one tithes, the animals pass singly through an opening in the enclosure and each tenth one is marked with red paint. This marking falls into the category of צוֹבֵעַ, dyeing, one of the labors forbidden on a festival (אָבוֹת מְלָאכוֹת; Bechoros 58a).

— לְפִיכָךְ הִקְדִּימוּהוּ לַעֲשְׂרִים וְתִשְׁעָה בֶּאֱלוּל. Therefore they advanced it [the date for the period] to the twenty-ninth of Elul.

[ב] **בְּשָׁלֹשׁ** קֻפּוֹת שֶׁל שָׁלֹשׁ שָׁלֹשׁ סְאִין
תּוֹרְמִין אֶת־הַלִּשְׁכָּה; וְכָתוּב
בָּהֶן אָלֶ"ף בֵּי"ת גִימֶ"ל.
רַבִּי יִשְׁמָעֵאל אוֹמֵר: יְוָנִית כָּתוּב בָּהֶן
אַלְפָ"א בֵּיתָ"א גַמְלָ"א.
אֵין הַתּוֹרֵם נִכְנָס לֹא בְּפַרְגּוֹד חָפוּת, וְלֹא
בְמִנְעָל וְלֹא בְסַנְדָּל, וְלֹא בִתְפִילִין וְלֹא בְקָמֵיעַ,
שֶׁמָּא יֵעָנִי וְיֹאמְרוּ, ,,מֵעֲוֹן הַלִּשְׁכָּה הֶעֱנִי!" אוֹ
שֶׁמָּא יַעֲשִׁיר וְיֹאמְרוּ, ,,מִתְּרוּמַת הַלִּשְׁכָּה

יד אברהם

2.

בְּשָׁלֹשׁ קֻפּוֹת שֶׁל שָׁלֹשׁ שָׁלֹשׁ סְאִין תּוֹרְמִין
אֶת־הַלִּשְׁכָּה; — *With three baskets of three seah each* [lit. *of three three se'ah*], *they withdraw the terumah from* [*the funds in the treasury*] *chamber;*

The mishnah now describes how the periodic withdrawal was made. Three baskets, each with a three-*se'ah* volume, were filled with coins from money deposited in the chamber (*Rav*).

Rambam (based on a textual variance and alternate interpretation of *Yerushalmi*) maintains that first they filled three larger baskets (each with a capacity of nine *se'ah*) with the money in the chamber. At each periodic withdrawal they would fill three smaller (three-*se'ah*) baskets from the larger baskets. [Our version of *Yerushalmi* does not allow for *Rambam's* interpretation; based on our version *Rosh* objects vigorously to *Rambam's* view, as does *Rav*.]

וְכָתוּב בָּהֶן אָלֶ"ף בֵּי"ת גִימֶ"ל. — (*and*) *on them were written* [*the Hebrew letters*]

"aleph", "beis", "gimmel".

The baskets were numbered so that the funds would be used in the sequence in which they were withdrawn. Although a change of order would not invalidate the money it is, nevertheless, preferable (מִצְוָה) to use the first basket first (*Tosefta* 2:2 cited in *Yoma* 6:29).

רַבִּי יִשְׁמָעֵאל אוֹמֵר: יְוָנִית כָּתוּב בָּהֶן אַלְפָ"א בֵּיתָ"א גַמְלָ"א. — *R' Yishmael says: The Greek* [*letters*] *"alpha", "beta", "gamma" were written on them.*

The sequence of the baskets was indicated by the first three letters in the Greek alphabet. This alphabet was used in fulfillment of Noah's blessing (*Genesis* 9:27, interpreted according to *Megillah* 9b, see ArtScroll *comm.* to *Genesis*): *Let God beautify Japheth*[1] [i.e., Greek which is Japheth's language] *and it shall dwell in the tents of Shem*, i.e., the Greek language, which is the

---

1. Yavan, the progenitor of the Greek nations (see *Yoma* 10a; ArtScroll *comm.* to *Genesis* 10:2), was a son of Japheth (*Genesis* 10:2).

Tiferes Yisrael suggests that in the Second Temple era when Greek was an international language in the Orient, the Jews may have been more fluent in Greek than in Hebrew. However this seems improbable because: (a) The purchase of offerings was given over to the Temple officials who surely be familiar enough with Hebrew to identify baskets inscribed with Hebrew letters; (b) the discussion here is not which *language* was used, but which *alphabet* was employed; (c) during the Second Temple era (and for many centuries later until the Arabic conquest) the vernacular in *Eretz Yisrael* was Aramaic, as evidenced by the Aramaic translations of the Bible, and the language of contracts given in the mishnah (e.g., the *kesubah*); (d) the language of the Jerusalem Talmud is Hebrew. (Many other proofs can also be shown. Only the Egyptian Jews spoke Greek.) See also *comm.* to 5:3.

2. **W**ith three baskets of three *se'ah* each they withdraw the *terumah* from the [funds in the treasury] chamber; on them were written [the Hebrew letters] *"aleph"*, *"beis"*, *"gimmel."*

R' Yishmael says: The Greek [letters] *"alpha"*, *"beta"*, *"gamma"* were written on them.

The one who withdraws the *terumah* may not enter [the treasury chamber] wearing a hemmed garment, nor with a shoe or a sandal, nor with *tefillin* or an amulet, lest he become poor and people might say, "Because of the sin of [stealing from] the [treasury] chamber has he become impoverished!" Or, lest he become rich and people might say, "He has enriched himself with the *terumah* of the [treasury] chamber!"

YAD AVRAHAM

most beautiful of the Japhetic tongues, shall be used in the Holy Temple (*Rav*).

אֵין הַתּוֹרֵם נִכְנָס לֹא בְּפַרְגוֹד חָפוּת, — *The one who withdraws the terumah may not enter [the treasury chamber] wearing a hemmed garment,*

The translation *hemmed garment* follows *Rav* and *Rosh*. *Meiri* translates *a lined garment*. *Rambam* (*Comm.*, ed. Kafich) renders, *an enveloping cloak*, which would enable the wearer to conceal money under it. In his code (*Hil. Shekalim* 2:10) he states: 'He may not enter in a garment in which it is possible to conceal ... Any garment offering a possibility for concealment is prohibited.'

וְלֹא בְמִנְעָל וְלֹא בְסַנְדָּל, — *nor with a shoe or a sandal,*

That he may not be suspected of dropping coins into his shoe.

These terms have been translated according to *Mossaf HeAruch* (s.v. סנדל: see ArtScroll comm. to *Yoma* 8:1, s.v. וברחיצה). See the various opinions for the identification of סָנְדָּל and מִנְעָל in *Beis Yosef* to *Even HaEzer* 169.

The *Talmud* (*Yevamos* 102b) in a quotation very similar to our mishnah states: 'The one who withdraws does not enter ... and of course not with a shoe or sandal because one

may not enter the Temple Court wearing shoes or sandals' (see *Berachos* 9:5). *R' Shlomoh Sirilio's* version of our mishnah also reads this way. According to our version the quotation in *Yevamos* must be a *Baraisa*. *Tiferes Yisrael* suggests that our mishnah which apparently prohibits (leather) shoes and sandals because of suspicion, teaches us that, similar apparel made of cloth or the like (e.g., socks) is also prohibited.

וְלֹא בִתְפִילִין וְלֹא בְקָמֵיעַ, — *nor with tefillin or an amulet,*

[A קָמֵיעַ is an *amulet*, consisting of an inscribed piece of parchment or other object endowed with mystical powers to protect the wearer from illness or other danger. The amulet is placed in a leather pouch and worn around the neck. Suspicion could be raised that he had opened the leather pouch or *tefillin* and placed money in them.]

שֶׁמָּא יֵעָנִי וְיֹאמְרוּ, "מֵעֲוֹן הַלִּשְׁכָּה הֶעָנִי!" — *lest he become poor and people might say "Because of the sin of [stealing from] the [treasury] chamber has he become impoverished!"*

אוֹ שֶׁמָּא יַעֲשִׁיר וְיֹאמְרוּ, "מִתְּרוּמַת הַלִּשְׁכָּה הֶעֱשִׁיר!" — *Or, lest he become rich and people might say, "He has enriched himself with the terumah of the [treasury] chamber!"*

שקלים הֶעָשִׁיר!״ לְפִי שֶׁאָדָם צָרִיךְ לָצֵאת יְדֵי הַבְּרִיּוֹת
ג/ג כְּדֶרֶךְ שֶׁצָּרִיךְ לָצֵאת יְדֵי הַמָּקוֹם. שֶׁנֶּאֱמַר:
„וִהְיִיתֶם נְקִיִּם מֵה׳ וּמִיִּשְׂרָאֵל.״ וְאוֹמֵר:
„וּמְצָא־חֵן וְשֵׂכֶל־טוֹב בְּעֵינֵי אֱלֹהִים וְאָדָם.״

[ג] **שֶׁל** בֵּית רַבָּן גַּמְלִיאֵל הָיָה נִכְנָס וְשִׁקְלוֹ
בֵּין אֶצְבְּעוֹתָיו, וְזוֹרְקוֹ לִפְנֵי הַתּוֹרֵם.
וְהַתּוֹרֵם מִתְכַּוֵּין וְדוֹחֲפוֹ לַקֻּפָּה.

יד אברהם

לְפִי שֶׁאָדָם צָרִיךְ לָצֵאת יְדֵי הַבְּרִיּוֹת כְּדֶרֶךְ
שֶׁצָּרִיךְ לָצֵאת יְדֵי הַמָּקוֹם. — For a person
must please people in the same manner
that he must please the Omnipresent.[1]

שֶׁנֶּאֱמַר: ,,וִהְיִיתֶם נְקִיִּם מֵה׳ וּמִיִּשְׂרָאֵל.״ —
For it is said: And you shall be guiltless
[lit. clean] before HASHEM and before
Israel [Numbers 32:22].

[It is not sufficient to be guiltless in
fact before God. One must be above
suspicion as well — guiltless before
Israel. Acting in a way which may draw
suspicion upon oneself is in itself sinful.
The verse cited was said by Moses in
reply to the request by the tribes of
Reuven, Gad, and part of Menashe to
remain in Trans-Jordan. If they will
abide by their pledge to lead the fight of
their brethren to conquer the land Canaan their request would be granted and
they would be guiltless before HASHEM
and Israel.]

וְאוֹמֵר: ,,וּמְצָא־חֵן וְשֵׂכֶל־טוֹב בְּעֵינֵי אֱלֹהִים
וְאָדָם.״ — And it is also said [lit. and he

says]: And find favor and good understanding in the eyes of God and
mankind [Proverbs 3:4].

Here, too, Scripture teaches man to
find favor in the eyes of his fellow even
after he has attained perfection before
God. All the precautions mentioned in
this mishnah were taken, therefore, not
because of apprehension that money
would actually be stolen, but lest people
think it was.

The quotation from Proverbs goes further
than the verse from Numbers.[2] The verse
from Torah teaches us only to remove well
founded suspicion as in the case of these
tribes whose conduct suggested that they had
no yearning for Eretz Yisrael. [The command
וִהְיִיתֶם נְקִיִּם, lit. You shall be clean, indicates
that their reputation had truly been tar-
nished.] But the victim of groundless allega-
tions may think there is no need to clear his
reputation from aspersions cast by ignorant
or stubborn people. The verse from Proverbs
teaches us to find favor ... even in such cases
(R' Shlomo Sirilio cited by Meleches
Shlomo; cf. R' Shlomo Alkabetz cited there).

1. הַמָּקוֹם, lit. the Place, is an appellation frequently used in Talmudic literature for the Deity.
It signifies that God is larger than the universe and thus contains the world just as a place contains an object situated within it. הַקָּדוֹשׁ בָּרוּךְ הוּא מְקוֹמוֹ שֶׁל עוֹלָם וְאֵין הָעוֹלָם מְקוֹמוֹ The Holy,
One Blessed is He, is the place of the universe, but the universe is not His place (Bereishis Rabbah 68:9; cf. Shemos Rabbah 45:6).
Though vast beyond imagination, the entire universe is finite and as such cannot be the
receptacle of God, Who is Infinite, i.e., in referring to God as the Place, i.e., the ultimate receptacle, we conceptualize one of the cardinal attributes, as it were, of God, namely that He is אֵין
סוֹף, infinite.

2. In Talmudic usage, it is expected that an additional insight is implied whenever a second
Scriptural source is adduced. It is taken for granted that if the first citation were sufficient to
make the point, a second one would not be cited.
In a similar approach Kol Sofer explains that not only must one offer an explanation for his

For a person must please people in the same manner that he must please the Omnipresent. For it is said: *And you shall be guiltless before HASHEM and before Israel [Numbers 32: 22]*. And it is also said: *And find favor and good understanding in the eyes of God and mankind [Proverbs 3:4]*.

3. [Each member] of Rabban Gamliel's household would enter [the treasury chamber] with his half shekel between his fingers and throw it before the one withdrawing the *terumah*. The one withdrawing the *terumah* would purposely push it into the basket.

YAD AVRAHAM

3.

שֶׁל בֵּית רַבָּן גַּמְלִיאֵל הָיָה נִכְנָס וְשִׁקְלוֹ בֵּין אֶצְבְּעוֹתָיו, וְזוֹרְקוֹ לִפְנֵי הַתּוֹרֵם. — [*Each member*] *of Rabban Gamliel's household would enter* [*the treasury chamber*] *with his half shekel between his fingers and throw it before the one withdrawing the terumah.*

Rabban Gamliel and his household did not want their shekalim to be among those remaining after the withdrawal was made. They held their payment, therefore, until the date of the first withdrawal. When the appointed time arrived, they each entered (*Rambam*) [according to *Meiri* one emissary entered with all their shekalim] carrying a half shekel between their fingers [for they were not permitted to wear any garments in which a coin could be concealed · (see previous mishnah)]. When the Temple official began filling the first basket they would throw their

shekalim into it. *Meiri* offers a novel interpretation. The thrower held the half shekel between his fingers so that he could aim it more accurately when he threw it at the basket. This accounts for the terms לִפְנֵי הַתּוֹרֵם, [*he threw it*] *before the one withdrawing the terumah:* The emissary threw the coin into the basket that was in front of, *before*, the *Kohen* in charge of the withdrawal.

[Rabban Gamliel's manner of giving was not meant to imply that the contributors of shekalim leftover after the withdrawal had not fulfilled their obligation. Rather he felt that the donors of the shekalim actually used performed מִצְוָה מִן הַמּוּבְחָר, *a more meritorious act*. Because of his eminence as נָשִׂיא, *president of the Sanhedrin* (lit. *prince*), he was permitted to enter the treasury chamber and ensure the actual use of his coin.]

וְהַתּוֹרֵם מִתְכַּוֵּין וְדוֹחֲפוֹ לַקֻּפָּה. — (*And*) *the one withdrawing the terumah would*

ostensibly suspicious actions, as suggested by the verse from the Torah, but he must attempt to have his explanation understood and accepted by his fellows.

[It seems that both teachings are inherent in this verse, the former in חֵן, *favor*, and the latter in שֵׂכֶל טוֹב, *good understanding*.]

Tosefta (2:3 cited in *Yerushalmi*) states that the Temple officials kept the one making the withdrawal engaged in conversation for as long as he was in the treasury chamber. The *Yerushalmi* adds that this was done to preclude suspicion that the appointee had put money into his mouth. *Ramban (ibid.)* adds that in spite of these precautions, they appointed neither a poor man nor an avaricious one.

אֵין הַתּוֹרֵם תּוֹרֵם עַד שֶׁיֹּאמַר לָהֶם:
,,אֶתְרוֹם?'' — וְהֵן אוֹמְרִים לוֹ: ,,תְּרוֹם! תְּרוֹם!
תְּרוֹם!'' — שָׁלשׁ פְּעָמִים.

[ד] **תָּרַם** אֶת־הָרִאשׁוֹנָה וּמְחַפֶּה בַּקְטָבְלָאוֹת;
שְׁנִיָּה וּמְחַפֶּה בַּקְטָבְלָאוֹת; שְׁלִישִׁית
לֹא הָיָה מְחַפֶּה. שֶׁמָּא יִשְׁכַּח וְיִתְרֹם מִן־הַדָּבָר
הַתָּרוּם.
תָּרַם אֶת־הָרִאשׁוֹנָה לְשֵׁם אֶרֶץ יִשְׂרָאֵל;

יד אברהם

purposely push it into the basket.

Rabban Gamliel would throw his half
shekel onto the money pile directly in
front of the one making the withdrawal,
so that he could readily push it into the
basket he was filling. Especially since he
knew that the half shekel was being
thrown by so eminent a personage, the
official would make sure to push this
half shekel into his basket.

[According to *Meiri*, this cooperation was
necessary only if the throw missed the
basket.]

אֵין הַתּוֹרֵם תּוֹרֵם עַד שֶׁיֹּאמַר לָהֶם: ,,אֶתְרוֹם?''
— *The one making the withdrawal did
not withdraw the terumah until he had
inquired* [lit. *said;* i.e., to the administrators of the Temple or the
Sanhedrin], *"Shall I withdraw the
terumah?"*

וְהֵן אוֹמְרִים לוֹ: ,,תְּרוֹם! תְּרוֹם! תְּרוֹם!'' שָׁלשׁ
פְּעָמִים. — *and they had replied to him,
"Withdraw! Withdraw! Withdraw!"
three times.*

To underscore that an act was being
undertaken on behalf of the community, the Sages ordained that certain
acts be accompanied by a threefold
declaration *(Mishnah Acharonah* to
Parah 3:10). A similar instance may be
found in the command, קְצוֹר! קְצוֹר!
קְצוֹר!, *Harvest! Harvest! Harvest!* [and
the complete exchange between the *Beis
Din* and the one who harvested barley
for the *Omer* offering *(Menachos* 10:3]
(Rav).

Alternatively, the threefold repetition
is made whenever an act is done in
public view. Thus, the words חֲלוֹץ הַנַּעַל,
remove the shoe, were proclaimed three
times at the close of the *chalitzah*
ceremony *(Tos. Yom Tov* to *Parah* 3:10;
see *Deuteronomy* 25:5-10).

4.

תָּרַם אֶת־הָרִאשׁוֹנָה וּמְחַפֶּה בַּקְטָבְלָאוֹת;
— *[After]* he had made the first terumah
withdrawal. he covered *[the remaining
money]* with leather covers;

After the first of the three periodic
withdrawals — Rosh Chodesh Nissan
[or the twenty-ninth of Adar (see mishnah 1)] — they covered the money
remaining in the treasury chamber with
a leather cover. The half shekels arriv-
ing later from people living in distant

provinces, would be deposited atop the
leather cover. When the next withdrawal was made, the funds would be
appropriated from these new half
shekels *(Rav; Rosh).*

[*Rav's* comment here is in accordance with
his view in mishnah 1. *Rambam's* entirely
different interpretation is given at the end of
the commentary to this mishnah.]

שְׁנִיָּה וּמְחַפֶּה בַּקְטָבְלָאוֹת; — *[after]* the second *[withdrawal]* he covered *[the*

The one making the withdrawal did not withdraw the *terumah* until he had inquired, "Shall I withdraw the *terumah?*" — and they had replied to him, "Withdraw! Withdraw! Withdraw!" three times.

4. **[A**fter] he had made the first *terumah* withdrawal he covered [the remaining money] with leather covers; [after] the second [withdrawal] he covered [the remaining money] with leather covers; [but after] the third [withdrawal] he did not cover [the remaining money]. [The money is covered] lest he forget and withdraw from an accumulation from which [funds] had [already] been withdrawn.

He withdrew the first *terumah* on behalf of [the inhabitants of] *Eretz Yisrael;* the second, on behalf of

remaining money] with leather covers;
This was done to ensure that the funds given by those residing in Babylon and Media (or Persia) and other distant countries, whose taxes had not arrived in time for the second withdrawal, would be used for the third (*Rav; Rosh;* see below).

שְׁלִישִׁית לֹא הָיָה מְחַפֶּה. — *[but after] the third [withdrawal] he did not cover [the remaining money].*
After the third withdrawal there was no need to cover the remaining money. Those who had not yet given their Temple tax would not have funds withdrawn from their half shekels so there was no point in covering the remaining money now (*Rav; Rosh*).

After the third withdrawal had been made they removed the leather covering that had served as separations between the half shekels given in the different times. Now all would have the same status — שְׁיָרֵי הַלִּשְׁכָּה, *the remaining funds of the [treasury] chamber* (see 4:2), and the separation would serve no purpose *(Yer.)*

שֶׁמָּא יִשְׁכַּח וְיִתְרוֹם מִן־הַדָּבָר הַתָּרוּם. — *[The money is covered] lest he forget and withdraw from an accumulation*

[lit. *a thing] from which [funds] had [already] been withdrawn.*
The mishnah now explains why the 'remaining funds' were covered after the first and second withdrawals. If this were not done, the appointee might forget that it was necessary to withdraw from half shekels that had been received after the previous withdrawal (*Rav*).

[The expression *lest he forget* implies that it was feasible to withdraw from the new half shekel even without the device of leather covers. The appointee simply would take care to skim off only the uppermost coins (cf. *Tif. Yis.*).]

תֵּרַם אֶת־הָרִאשׁוֹנָה לְשֵׁם אֶרֶץ יִשְׂרָאֵל; — *He withdrew the first terumah on behalf of [the inhabitants of] Eretz Yisrael;*
I.e., he made the first withdrawal *from* the funds given by Jews residing in *Eretz Yisrael.* The designation of the money withdrawn, however, was on behalf of all Jews regardless of their residence, and the funds appropriated represented the entire Jewish community which would thus share in the public sacrifices (*Rav*).

Tosefta (2:4) states explicitly: He made the first withdrawal and said, 'This is from *Eretz Yisrael* for all of Israel.'

שְׁקָלִים וּשְׁנִיָּה לְשׁוּם כְּרַכִּים הַמַּקִּפִין לָהּ; וְהַשְּׁלִישִׁית
ד/א לְשׁוּם בָּבֶל וּלְשׁוּם מָדַי וּלְשׁוּם מְדִינוֹת
הָרְחוֹקוֹת.

[א] הַתְּרוּמָה מֶה הָיוּ עוֹשִׂין בָּהּ? לוֹקְחִין
בָּהּ תְּמִידִין וּמוּסָפִין
וְנִסְכֵּיהֶם; הָעֹמֶר וּשְׁתֵּי הַלֶּחֶם וְלֶחֶם הַפָּנִים;
וְכָל־קָרְבְּנוֹת הַצִּבּוּר.

יד אברהם

וּשְׁנִיָּה לְשׁוּם כְּרַכִּין הַמַּקִּפִין לָהּ; — *the se-cond, on behalf of [the inhabitants of] the cities surrounding it [i.e., Eretz Yisrael];*

The cities in the areas bordering *Eretz Yisrael*, e.g., Ammon and Moab, could not deliver their Temple tax before the first withdrawal was made (*Rav*).

וְהַשְּׁלִישִׁית לְשׁוּם בָּבֶל וּלְשׁוּם מָדַי וּלְשׁוּם מְדִינוֹת הָרְחוֹקוֹת. —*and the third on behalf of [the inhabitants of] Babylon, Media and the distant countries.*

[As explained above, s.v. שניה.]

Rambam has an entirely different interpretation of this mishnah. As already mentioned above (mishnah 1), he maintains that all regions, far or near, made sure that their Temple taxes reached the Temple before the first withdrawal, when all the monies were deposited in the treasury chamber. At the time of the first withdrawal three large (nine *se'ah*) baskets were filled

with coins enough for all the three periodic withdrawals (twenty-seven *se'ah*). Then the appointee transferred the coins from the three larger baskets into three smaller (three *se'ah*) baskets for the first appropriation. He filled one small basket from each of the large baskets. When he had filled the first basket he would cover the container that he had just taken from. The procedure was repeated when he filled the second basket. But the third of the large baskets was left uncovered to serve as a reminder that when making the second periodic withdrawal the first small basket be filled from this basket. Thus every big basket would have the first small basket filled from it once. The withdrawal of each of the small baskets was intended for a different region. The first basket was for *Eretz Yisrael*, etc. Accordingly, the translation would be as follows: *he withdrew terumah from the first* [*large basket*], וּמִחַפָּה, *and covered it* … The passage: *lest he forget* … explains the clause preceding it: *the third he did not cover lest he … He set aside the first* [of the small baskets] *for Eretz Yisrael* …

Chapter 4

1.

The monies for the treasuries of the Temple were classified into many different categories. Each of these categories was earmarked for a designated purpose as outlined in the first four mishnayos of this chapter.

As funds were withdrawn from the chamber and used for their designated purposes, it was inevitable that there would be surplus funds. The various surpluses, together with the *terumah* itself, fall into five categories. They are:

(a) תְּרוּמַת הַלִּשְׁכָּה, *funds withdrawn from* [lit. *the uplifting of*] *the* [*treasury*] *chamber* — the monies, referred to as the *terumah*, withdrawn from the treasury chamber at each of the three designated periods (mishnayos 1-2);

(b) שְׁיָרֵי הַלִּשְׁכָּה, *the remainder of the chamber* — the funds remaining in the

4
1
[the inhabitants of] the cities surrounding it; and the third, on behalf of [the inhabitants of] Babylon, Media and the distant countries.

1. What did they do with the *terumah?* — With it they would purchase daily offerings, additional offerings, and their *nesachim;* the Omer, the Two Loaves, and the *Panim* Bread; and all the public offerings.

chamber after the *terumah* has been withdrawn (mishnah 2);

(c) מוֹתַר שְׁיָרֵי הַלִּשְׁכָּה, *the surplus of the remainder of the chamber* — after the above remainder had gone for the designated uses, there may still be surplus funds left in the treasury chamber (mishnah 3);

(d) מוֹתַר הַתְּרוּמָה, *the surplus of the appropriated monies* — surplus money left from the *terumah* funds after the communal purchases had been made (mishnah 4);

(e) מוֹתַר הַפֵּרוֹת, *the profits* [lit. *surplus*] *of the fruits* — according to one tanna's view, certain surplus funds were invested in wine, oil, and flour, which were subsequently sold for use in meal offerings and libations. The profit generated by these sales is called *the surplus of the fruits* (mishnayos 3-4).

הַתְּרוּמָה מֶה הָיוּ עוֹשִׂין בָּהּ? — *What did they do with the terumah?*
How did they spend the money withdrawn in small baskets (see 3:1) from the treasury chamber? (*Rav*).

לוֹקְחִין בָּהּ תְּמִידִין — *With it they would purchase daily offerings,*
Every day two yearling sheep were sacrificed as burnt offerings, one in the morning, the second in the afternoon (*Numbers* 28:1-8).

וּמוּסָפִין — *(and) additional offerings,*
On the Sabbath, Rosh Chodesh, the three pilgrimage festivals (Pesach, Shavuos, and Succos), Rosh HaShanah and Yom Kippur, offerings are ordained in *addition* [*mussaf*] to the daily burnt offerings. The *mussafim* consist of burnt and sin offerings (except on the Sabbath, when no sin offering is sacrificed). The number of animals offered on each occasion is given in *Numbers* 28:9-29:38.

וְנִסְכֵּיהֶם; — *and their nesachim* [lit. *libations*];
Every burnt offering is accompanied by a meal offering and a wine libation.

[Although the literal meaning of נְסָכִים is *libations*, in mishnaic use the word connotes both the wine libations and meal offerings that accompany each burnt offering and peace offering.]

הָעֹמֶר, — *the Omer,*
On the second day of Pesach an offering, consisting of an *omer* (a measure equal to the volume of water displaced by 43.2 eggs) of crushed barley grains was brought (see *Leviticus* 2:14-16 and 23:9-11). As with other meal offerings, a fistful (קוֹמֶץ) of the flour was separated from the rest and offered upon the altar. The remaining flour was eaten by the *Kohanim* (see the verses cited above and *Rambam, Hil. T'midin U'Mussafin* 7:12). Presumably, the term Omer here includes the other offerings which accompanied the Omer meal offering (see *Leviticus* 23:12-13).

וּשְׁתֵּי הַלֶּחֶם — *(and) the Two Loaves,*
On the Shavuos festival, two leavened (חָמֵץ) bread loaves, made of flour from the 'new' crop of wheat (חָדָשׁ), were offered in the Temple (*Leviticus* 23:16-17). Since the loaves were leavened, no part of this offering was

שקלים שׁוֹמְרֵי סְפִיחִים בַּשְּׁבִיעִית נוֹטְלִין שְׂכָרָן
ד/א מִתְּרוּמַת הַלִּשְׁכָּה.
רַבִּי יוֹסֵי אוֹמֵר: אַף הָרוֹצֶה מִתְנַדֵּב שׁוֹמֵר
חִנָּם.
אָמְרוּ לוֹ: אַף אַתָּה אוֹמֵר שֶׁאֵינָן בָּאִין אֶלָּא
מִשֶּׁל צִבּוּר.

יד אברהם

placed upon the altar. The loaves were 'waved' (תְּנוּפָה), to the four points of the compass, and upward and downward (see *Leviticus* 2:12 with *Rashi; Succah* 34b; *Menachos* 62a with *Rashi*, s.v. מוֹלִיךְ מֵבִיא; cf. *Rambam, Hil. T'midin U'Mussafin* 17:2; *Siddur R' Saadiah Gaon* p. 237 and sources cited in footnote there). In conjunction with the Two Loaves two sheep were sacrificed as peace offerings (שַׁלְמֵי צִבּוּר) and a he-goat as a sin offering (*Lev.* 23:17-20). After the sacrifice the Two Loaves were given to the *Kohanim* to eat (one to the *Kohen Gadol* and one to be shared by all the other *Kohanim; Rambam, Hil. T'midin U'Mussafin* 8:11). Presumably, here too, the other offerings associated with the two loaves are included in this phrase.

וְלֶחֶם הַפָּנִים; — *and the Panim Bread;*
Every Sabbath twelve loaves, called *Panim* Bread, were arranged on the golden Table in the Temple in two tiers of six each. They remained there until the next Sabbath when they would be replaced with twelve fresh loaves. A spoonful of frankincense (לְבוֹנָה) was placed next to each tier. Upon removal of the loaves, the frankincense would be offered upon the altar. The loaves were then distributed among the *Kohanim* to be eaten (see *Succah* 5:7-8).

וְכָל־קָרְבְּנוֹת הַצִּבּוּר. — *and all the public offerings.*

This otherwise superfluous term is meant to include the incense offered daily and on Yom Kippur (*Rav; Rosh; Yer.* and *Kesubos* 106b). Also included are the special Yom Kippur offerings; the salt used to coat the offerings burned on the altar (see *Leviticus* 21:3), and wood, as needed for the altar fire (*Rambam, Hil. Shekalim* 4:1; *Menachos* 21b-22a).

◆§ **Shemittah — The Sabbatical Year.**

Just as the first six days of each week are designated for physical labor while the seventh day is the Sabbath, a day of rest (*Exodus* 20:8-11), so too are the first six years of each seven-year period designated for working the land while the seventh year is Sabbath, a year of abstention from such work (*Leviticus* 25:1-7). During that year — called שְׁבִיעִית [*Sheviis*], *seventh,* or שְׁמִיטָה [*Shemittah*], *release* — we are enjoined from cultivating and harvesting the fields, vineyards, and orchards of *Eretz Yisrael.*

Produce growing during the *Shemittah* year, either from seeds sown before the *Shemittah,* or from perennials, may be eaten. The סְפִיחִים, *aftergrowth,* i.e., the crops growing from seeds which fell inadvertently during the previous harvest and took root may, however, not be eaten; see *Pesachim* 51b; *Rambam Hil. Shemittah* 4:2. However, as long as this permitted produce is growing, it must be maintained in a state of הֶפְקֵר [*hefker*], *abandonment,* accessible to all who wish to take it. Any display of ownership on the part of the farmer, such as fencing off the field or gathering large amounts of crops into his warehouse, is prohibited (*Rambam, Hil. Shemittah V'Yovel* 4:24). [See above 2:2, s.v. Shemittah.]

4
1

Those who watch over the aftergrowth of the *Shemittah* year receive their wages from the funds withdrawn from the [treasury] chamber.

R' Yose says: Also, one wishing to, may volunteer as an unsalaried watchman.

They replied to him: You too admit that they must come from public assets.

שוֹמְרֵי סְפִיחִים בַּשְּׁבִיעִית נוֹטְלִין שְׂכָרָן מִתְרוּמַת הַלִּשְׁכָּה. — *Those who watch over the aftergrowth of the Shemittah year receive* [lit. *take*] *their wages from the funds withdrawn from the [treasury] chamber.*

Unlike other meal offerings, the *Omer* and the Two Loaves must come from the grain of the new crop *(Menachos* 8:1).

During the *Shemittah* year however, no new crops were sown, and these offerings were dependent on the availability of aftergrowth[1] (סְפִיחִים). To make the availability of such crops even more questionable, the Torah commanded that the fields be left unguarded during the *Shemittah* year *(Exodus* 3:11; *Leviticus* 25:6-7), so even the limited amount of aftergrowth was in danger of being consumed (although the overgrowth was forbidden for eating) before it could be reaped for use in the Temple offerings. To ensure an adequate supply of grain, the *Beis Din* hired watchmen to prevent animals from treading on the aftergrowth and to ask any would-be consumer to refrain from taking the grain because it had been reserved for the *Omer* and the Two Loaves (see *Tos. Bava Metzia* 58a, s.v. לשמור הזרעים; and *Yevamos* 122a, s.v. של עזיקה). The salaries of these watchmen is paid out of the *terumah* appropriation, because their work is indispensable to the offering. The rule is: צוֹרֶךְ קָרְבָּן כַּקָרְבָּן, *expenditures necessary for an offering have the status of funds for the offering itself (Rav; Rosh).*

Other preparatory services necessary for the public offerings were also paid for with funds from this appropriation: those who baked the *Panim* Breads (see above and *Yoma* 3:11) and those who prepared the daily incense *(Yoma* 3:11; see *Kesubos* 106a, *Tosefta* 2:6 and *Rambam, Hil. Shekalim* 4:1-7, for a list of others whose salaries are paid from the withdrawn appropriation).

ר' יוֹסֵי אוֹמֵר: אַף הָרוֹצֶה מִתְנַדֵּב שׁוֹמֵר חִנָּם. — *R' Yose says: Also, one wishing to, may volunteer as an unsalaried watchman.*

אָמְרוּ לוֹ: אַף אַתָּה אוֹמֵר שֶׁאֵינָן בָּאִין אֶלָּא מִשֶּׁל צִבּוּר. — *They* [the Sages] *replied* [lit. *said*] *to him: You too admit* [lit. *say*] *that they* [the *Omer* and the Two Loaves] *must come from public assets.*

The Talmud *(Bava Metzia* 118a,b) offers three possible interpretations of the dispute between R' Yose and the other Sages:

(a) The Sages maintain that the formal act of acquisition [קִנְיָן] of ownerless property is less stringent than that of acquiring property from a previous owner. Whereas, a transfer of ownership cannot be completed without a physical act of acquisition by the next owner, ownerless property can be acquired merely by watching it (הַבָּטָה בְּהֶפְקֵר קָנֵי; see *Tos. Bava Metzia* 2a, s.v. דבראיה). Accordingly, if the watchman were unsalaried, the aftergrowths would become his. Since public offerings may not come from private property, the watchman must be salaried, in which case he would not assume title [because one cannot take personal gain

---

1. Although this produce may not be eaten it may nevertheless be used by the owner. This offering is an exception to the rule barring materials prohibited for consumption from being offered in the Temple *(Tos. Menachos* 84a, s.v. שומרי).

יד אברהם

from something he is' paid to do]. R' Yose, on the other hand, maintains that ownerless property is not acquired merely through watching it, (וְהַבָּטָה בְהֶפְקֵר לֹא קָנֵי). Thus, the aftergrowth remains ownerless until the agents of *Beis Din* harvest it.

(b) All agree that ownerless property is acquired through watching. The debate centers on whether private property turned over to the public without reimbursement achieves the status of public property. The Sages are apprehensive lest watchmen not be sincere in turning over the grain.[1] In that case it would remain under private ownership and be invalid for a public offering. Thus, the aftergrowth acquired by the watchman may not be used for the *Omer* or the Two Loaves unless he is paid to guard it. R' Yose, on the other hand, is certain that anyone donating to the Temple will do so wholeheartedly. [This interpretation although followed by *Rav* and *Rambam (Comm.)*, is not in accord with the final halachah.]

(c) All agree that merely watching ownerless property is not sufficient for acquisition, so the aftergrowth remains ownerless until the agents of *Beis Din* harvest it. [This is the halachically adopted view *(Rambam, Hil. Nedarim* 2:19; *Choshen Mishpat* 273:11).] The difference of opinion between the Sages and R' Yose revolves around the question of unscrupulous people (בַּעֲלֵי זְרוֹעוֹת) who may disregard the watchman's admonitions and make off with the needed aftergrowth. The Sages feel that the use of public funds to pay a watchman will give him official status, thereby gaining him the respect of such people. A voluntary watchman, however, would be regarded as selfappointed and therefore ignored. R' Yose does not consider this a real threat.

According to this last interpretation, the Sages' response to R' Yose refers to the possibility that a watchman would reject the money halfheartedly and that money would subsequently be used to purchase public sacrifices. This would result in public sacrifices purchased with private assets. Therefore, the Sages insist that the watchman must accept the designated salary even if he wishes to return the payment *(Rashi)*.

2.

פָּרָה, — *The [Red] Cow,*
A red cow was burned and its ashes gathered and preserved. Anyone wishing to purge himself of טוּמְאָה, *contamination*, stemming from contact with a corpse, had to be sprinkled with a mixture of these ashes and well water, and then cleanse himself in a *mikveh* (see *Numbers* 19:1-22). Although this cow is *not* an offering and was not slaughtered in the Temple, the Torah nevertheless calls it חַטָּאת, *sin offering*, (ibid. v. 9; *Rav; Rosh).*

[Indeed the Talmud (*Yoma* 42a and

1. The Sages do not raise the question of wholehearted contributions with respect to voluntary half shekel donations (see 1:4-5), yet the possibility of halfheartedness would seem to exist there also.

Tosafos (to *Yoma* 35b, s.v. ניחוש) explains that since vast multitudes are giving their half shekels at the same time, their donation will be made in accordance with the public spirit. [See also *Meiri, Tos. Yom Tov* and *Tos. R' Akiva; Mishneh LaMelech* and *Sha'ar HaMelech, Hil. Shekalim* 4:6.]

[It may be that the problem exists only where someone is under an actual (or imagined) compulsion to turn over property, as in the case of the watchman who would be in a most awkward predicament if he were to insist on keeping the grain.]

2. The [Red] Cow, the he-goat which is sent [to Azazel] and the strip of red wool are purchased with funds withdrawn from the [treasury] chamber.

elsewhere) states that the Red Cow is not consecrated to the same degree as animals to be brought on the altar (קָדְשֵׁי מִזְבֵּחַ) but to the degree of those sanctified for upkeep of the Temple use (קָדְשֵׁי בֶּדֶק הַבַּיִת). Rosh's assertion that the Red Cow is considered an offering because the Torah calls it a sin offering — though it is tenable according to the rules developed by Tosafos (Chullin 11a, s.v. חטאת) — is nevertheless contradicted by Tosafos elsewhere (Bava Kamma 77b, s.v. אומר). Tosafos asserts the although the Red Cow is not to be considered an offering, it is nevertheless purchased with funds from the periodic withdrawal; for it is necessary for the Temple service (צוֹרֶךְ קָרְבָּן), because Kohanim who have become contaminated cannot perform the Temple service until they are cleansed. Thus, the Red Cow may be purchased with these funds for the same reason that the watchmen of the aftergrowth may be paid from this fund.]

וְשָׂעִיר הַמִּשְׁתַּלֵחַ — (and) the he-goat which is sent [to Azazel].

[In addition to the offerings sacrificed in the Temple on Yom Kippur, a he-goat specially designated by lot for this purpose, was sent to Azazel (i.e., a precipice in the desert; see Yoma 6:5), where it was hurled from a cliff (Leviticus 16:22).] It too is purchased with funds of the periodic withdrawal, for two he-goats are purchased toge-

ther, one of which will be designated by lot 'For HASHEM' (see Yoma 4:11) and offered on the altar (Rav; Rosh).

וְלָשׁוֹן שֶׁל זְהוֹרִית — and the strip of red wool

[When the Red Cow is burned, a bundle consisting of a piece of cedar wood, stalks of hyssop and a strip of red wool, which is used to tie the bundle together, is thrown into the blaze (Leviticus 16:6; Parah 3:11).] Although the cedar wood and hyssop stalks, too, are bought with these funds, the mishnah mentions only the wool to differentiate between the strip used for the Red Cow and the one tied to the he-goat that is sent to Azazel (Rav; Rosh; see Meiri's interpretation of this phrase below, s.v. (ולשון שבין קרניו.

בָּאִין מִתְּרוּמַת הַלִּשְׁכָּה — are purchased [lit. come] with funds withdrawn from the [treasury] chamber.

Thus far the mishnah has listed the primary use of the money appropriated at the periodic withdrawal. The disbursement of any surplus funds will be discussed in mishnah 4. Now the mishnah turns to the funds remaining in the treasury chamber after the periodic withdrawal.

✦§Unknown Grave and the Red Cow

Among the various ways in which one may become contaminated by the deceased is by passing directly over a buried corpse.

A corpse emits contamination upward and downward (בּוֹקַעַת וְעוֹלָה בּוֹקַעַת וְיוֹרֶד) from the depths of the earth to the highest heavens (i.e., any person, utensil or food stuff capable of being contaminated which passes either above or below this grave, becomes contaminated by it). However, should a tent (אֹהֶל) or any other roofed structure be constructed over the grave, and the tent has an opening of at least one handbreadth square, the contamination no longer ranges unchecked upward and downward, but is contained in the tent.

Those assigned to transport the Red Cow from the Temple Mount to the Mount of Olives, and subsequently slaughter and burn it, had to remain uncontaminated, and no expense was spared, no precaution overlooked, to assure their purity. Even the remote possibility of a hitherto unknown corpse lying buried beneath the road (קֶבֶר הַתְּהוֹם) was reckoned with. A ramp was constructed spanning the entire dis-

כֶּבֶשׁ פָּרָה וְכֶבֶשׁ שָׂעִיר הַמִּשְׁתַּלֵחַ וְלָשׁוֹן
שֶׁבֵּין קַרְנָיו וְאַמַּת הַמַּיִם וְחוֹמַת הָעִיר
וּמִגְדְּלוֹתֶיהָ וְכָל־צָרְכֵי הָעִיר בָּאִין מִשְׁיָרֵי
הַלִּשְׁכָּה.
אַבָּא שָׁאוּל אוֹמֵר: כֶּבֶשׁ פָּרָה כֹּהֲנִים גְּדוֹלִים
עוֹשִׂין אוֹתוֹ מִשֶּׁל עַצְמָן.

יד אברהם

tance to be traversed. Because the ramp was raised more than a handbreadth from the ground, and its sides were open, it served as a barrier preventing the contamination from rising above it. However, another unlikely possibility had to be considered. What if a corpse lay directly beneath the beam supporting the ramp? Since the beam had no opening, it would constitute a sealed grave and would contaminate anyone walking over the beam. To avoid this problem, a second ramp was built above the first in such a manner that the supporting columns of the second were not directly above those of the first (see *Parah* 3:6 with *Rav*).

כֶּבֶשׁ פָּרָה — *The ramp for [the transport of the [Red] Cow,*

Funding for the construction (and upkeep) for the special ramp used by those who transported the Red Cow from the Temple Mount to the Mount of Olives came from 'funds remaining in the treasury chamber' (*Rav; Rosh*).

וְכֶבֶשׁ שָׂעִיר הַמִּשְׁתַּלֵחַ — *(and) the ramp for [the transport of] the he-goat which is sent [to Azazel],*

A he-goat [see above] was conveyed from the Temple Mount to the outskirts of the city on a ramp built especially for that purpose to protect it from the Babylonian Jews who would tear at its hair saying: 'Take and leave! Take and leave! Do not let our sins tarry here any longer!' (*Rav from Yoma* 6:4 and 66b).

וְלָשׁוֹן שֶׁבֵּין קַרְנָיו, — *and the strip of wool [which is tied] between its [the he-goat's] horns,*

After the two he-goats had been designated, one 'For HASHEM' and the other 'For Azazel,' one strip of red wool was placed on the head of the he-goat 'For Azazel' and another on the neck of the one to be offered in the Temple (*Yoma* 4:2).Though the strip was on the head of the Azazel goat, the mishnah calls it a 'strip between its horns' be-

cause, immediately before he threw the he-goat off the precipice, the person in charge (אִישׁ עִתִּי) would divide the strip, tie half between the goat's horns and half to the rock (*Yoma* 6:6). The red strip, symbolizing sin, would turn white, representing cleansing, as *Isaiah* (1:18) prophesied: [Even] *if your sins will be as crimson threads, they will become white as snow.* Since this strip is not directly related to any altar offering, it could not be purchased with the *terumah* funds, but was bought with monies remaining in the treasury chamber (*Rav*).

Meiri understands that the 'strip of red wool' listed earlier among the things bought with the withdrawal appropriation refers to the strip between the goat's horns. It is apparent (as noted by *R' A. Sofer*) that *Meiri's* edition of the mishnah omitted the words: וְלָשׁוֹן שֶׁבֵּין קַרְנָיו, *and the strip between its horns,* from the list of items purchased with the 'remainder of the chamber' (see *Shinuyei Nuschaos*). *Rambam* too lists 'the strip between its horns' among the things bought from the withdrawal appropriation (*Hil. Shekalim* 4:1), although his version of the mishnah (see ed. Kafich) is identical to ours. *Mishneh LaMelech* suggests emendation of our versions of *Rambam* to agree with the mishnah (see *Shinuyei Nuschaos* in *Rambam* ed. Frankel).

A totally different approach is offered by

4
2

The ramp for [the transport of] the [Red] Cow, the ramp for [the transport of] the he-goat which is sent [to Azazel], and the strip of wool [which is tied] between its horns, the water canal, the walls of the city and its towers, and all the needs of the city are funded from the remainder of the [treasury] chamber.

Abba Shaul says: The *Kohanim Gedolim* built the ramp for [the transport of] the [Red] Cow from their own [funds].

YAD AVRAHAM

Semag *(Mitzvas Asseh* 45 and 209) and *Tos. Yeshanim (Yoma* 67a, s.v. לשון). Two strips of red wool were used in the Yom Kippur he-goat service: One strip was placed on the head of the goat chosen 'For *Azazel,*' and served to differentiate it from the goat chosen 'For *HASHEM' (Yoma* 4:2). This strip was removed when the goat left the Temple; for it was not to be carried by the goat on Yom Kippur. This is the strip our mishnah describes as 'the strip of red wool' purchased with funds from the withdrawal appropriation.

A second strip was deposited at the site of the precipice before Yom Kippur. One end was tied to the horns of the goat before it was hurled to its death, the other half was tied to the rock *(Yoma* 6:6). This strip was purchased from 'the remainder.' It is unlikely however that *Rambam* would agree with this interpretation.

All the above items, though used for the Temple service, are not essential to the offerings, and may therefore not be purchased with the withdrawal appropriation *(Rav; Rosh).*

וְאַמַּת הַמַּיִם — *(and) the water canal,*
[A water canal (or pipe) ran through the Temple Courtyard, to provide water for washing the Courtyard floor (see *Pesachim* 5:8; also *Yoma* 5:7).] Expenditures for its upkeep and repair came from the 'remainder' *(Rav; Rosh)*

Rambam (Hil. Shekalim 4:8) and *Meiri* interpret this to refer to the water canal(s) of Jerusalem.

וְחוֹמַת הָעִיר וּמִגְדְּלוֹתֶיהָ — *(and) the walls of the city and its towers,*
[The towers were part of the city's fortification.]

וְכָל־צָרְכֵי הָעִיר בָּאִין מִשְּׁיָרֵי הַלִּשְׁכָּה. — *and all the needs of the city are funded* [lit. come] *from the remainder of the [treasury] chamber.*

'All the needs of the city' refers to the digging of wells and ditches; upkeep and repair of streets and market places; and protection of the city *(Rav).*

[According to *Rambam's* view (see comm. to 3:1 and 4), as soon as the three big baskets were filled (on the first of Nissan), the rest of the money fell into the category of 'remainder.' According to the other view, which negates the existence of the three big baskets, the money in the chamber could not be categorized as remainder until the third withdrawal had been made.

The rationale for the use of the consecrated funds for the city is perhaps because the city Jerusalem is inexorably intertwined with the Temple, both halachically and socio-politically. Halachically, Jerusalem provided the consecrated periphery necessary for a Temple and corresponded to the מַחֲנֵה יִשְׂרָאֵל, *Camp of Israel,* surrounding the Tabernacle in the desert. Because offerings of a lesser magnitude of holiness (קָדָשִׁים קַלִּים) could be eaten in Jerusalem, it was regarded as an extension of the Temple for this purpose. Socio-politically it would not be feasible to situate the Temple in an isolated area. A city was needed to house the *Kohanim,* the Temple administration, and the pilgrims, and to sustain them. The surrounding city also provided needed protection.]

אַבָּא שָׁאוּל אוֹמֵר: כֶּבֶשׁ פָּרָה כֹּהֲנִים גְּדוֹלִים עוֹשִׂין אוֹתוֹ מִשֶּׁל עַצְמָן. —*Abba Shaul says: The Kohanim Gedolim built the ramp for* [the transport of] *the* [Red] *Cow from their own* [funds].

שקלים
ד/ג

[ג] מוֹתַר שְׁיָרֵי הַלִּשְׁכָּה מֶה הָיוּ עוֹשִׂין בָּהֶן? לוֹקְחִין בָּהֶן יֵינוֹת, שְׁמָנִים וּסְלָתוֹת, וְהַשָּׂכָר לַהֶקְדֵּשׁ — דִּבְרֵי רַבִּי יִשְׁמָעֵאל.

רַבִּי עֲקִיבָא אוֹמֵר: אֵין מִשְׂתַּכְּרִין מִשֶּׁל הֶקְדֵּשׁ וְלֹא מִשֶּׁל עֲנִיִּים.

ד/ד

[ד] מוֹתַר תְּרוּמָה מֶה הָיוּ עוֹשִׂין בָּהּ? רִקּוּעֵי זָהָב צִפּוּי לְבֵית קָדְשֵׁי הַקֳּדָשִׁים.

רַבִּי יִשְׁמָעֵאל אוֹמֵר: מוֹתַר הַפֵּרוֹת לְקַיִץ הַמִּזְבֵּחַ; וּמוֹתַר הַתְּרוּמָה לִכְלֵי שָׁרֵת.

יד אברהם

[Perhaps the *Kohanim Gedolim* funded this ramp because they were generally the ones who performed the service of the 'Red Cow' (see *Parah* 3:8).]

Yerushalmi (based on *Tosefta* 2:7) mentions that the *Kohanim Gedolim* would refuse to use the ramp erected by their predecessors; each *Kohen Gadol* would demolish the existing ramp and erect a new one at the extravagant cost of sixty gold talents (כִּכָּרוֹת = 90,000 *sela*). R' Chanina (*Yerushalmi*) comments that these *Kohanim Gedolim* were pompous and vainglorious

(שֶׁחֲצִית גְּדוֹלָה הָיְתָה: see *Yoma* 9a about the *Kohanim Gedolim* in the Second Temple era). However the *Yerushalmi* points out that even Shimon HaTzaddik ("the righteous"), *Kohen Gadol* of the Second Temple after the death of Ezra, who could surely not be accused of pomposity, built two of these ramps, one for each Red Cow which was burnt during his term. *Yerushalmi* concludes that this custom must have been in honor of the mitzvah and not for personal aggrandizement.

3.

מוֹתַר שְׁיָרֵי הַלִּשְׁכָּה מֶה הָיוּ עוֹשִׂין בָּהֶן? — **What did they do with the surplus of the remainder of the [treasury] chamber?**

I.e., any funds left in the treasury chamber after all the above needs have been attended to (*Rav, Rosh*) were used for the following:

לוֹקְחִין בָּהֶן יֵינוֹת, שְׁמָנִים וּסְלָתוֹת, וְהַשָּׂכָר לַהֶקְדֵּשׁ — דִּבְרֵי רַבִּי יִשְׁמָעֵאל. — **With it they would purchase wines, oils and fine flour [which they would subsequently resell], the profits accruing to the Temple — [these are] the words of R' Yishmael.**

These items would be sold to in-

dividuals for their meal offerings and libations (*Rav*).

רַבִּי עֲקִיבָא אוֹמֵר: אֵין מִשְׂתַּכְּרִין מִשֶּׁל הֶקְדֵּשׁ — **R' Akiva says: Investments may not be made with that which belongs to the Temple**

It is degrading (גְּנַאי) for the Temple treasury to engage in business; אֵין עֲנִיּוּת בִּמְקוֹם עֲשִׁירוּת, *there is no poverty in a place of affluence* (*Rav; Kesubos* 106b).

וְלֹא מִשֶּׁל עֲנִיִּים. — **nor with funds [collected] for the poor.**

Money donated for the poor may not be invested, but must be kept liquid, so that a needy person will not be refused assistance because money is temporarily

3.**W**hat did they do with the surplus of the remainder of the [treasury] chamber? — With it they would purchase wines, oils and fine flour [which they would subsequently resell], the profits accruing to the Temple — [these are] the words of R' Yishmael.

R' Akiva says: Investments may not be made with that which belongs to the Temple nor with funds [collected] for the poor.

4.**W**hat did they do with the remainder of the *terumah*? — [They made] gold sheets to plate the Holy of Holies.

R' Yishmael says: The profit of the fruits is [used to purchase animals which are] offered upon the altar [when it is idle]; and the remainder of the *terumah* is [used] for the utensils [needed] for the [Temple] service.

YAD AVRAHAM

unavailable (*Rav; Kesubos* 106b).

R' Akiva does not say what should be done with this money. *Rambam (Hil. Shekalim* 4:9) states that it was put to the same use as the remainder of the withdrawal appropriation in the next mishnah.

Meiri cites his teachers that it would be put to the same use as the remainder of the chamber funds (mishnah 2), and was put aside until needed for that purpose.

4.

מוֹתַר תְּרוּמָה מֶה הָיוּ עוֹשִׂין בָּהּ? — *What did they do with the remainder of the* terumah?

If the appropriation had not been entirely spent by Rosh Chodesh Nissan, the beginning of the new fiscal year, this money could no longer be used to purchase animals for public offerings. Such animals must now be bought with the newly withdrawn appropriation (*Rav*).

רִקּוּעֵי זָהָב צִפּוּי לְבֵית קָדְשֵׁי הַקֳּדָשִׁים. — [*They made*] *gold sheets to plate the Holy of Holies.*

To cover the walls and floor (*Rav*).

[This is the opinion of the first tanna. Divergent opinions are given later in the mishnah.]

רַבִּי יִשְׁמָעֵאל אוֹמֵר: מוֹתַר הַפֵּרוֹת — R' Yishmael says: The profits [lit. *remainder*] of the fruits

R' Yishmael had previously (mishnah 3) argued that the surplus of the remainder of the chamber was used to buy and sell the ingredients of meal offerings and libations. The profit realized from this enterprise is the subject of the first clause in R' Yishmael's statement (*Rav; Yer.*).

[See below, s.v. וּמוֹתַר נְסָכִים, for another interpretation of מוֹתַר פֵּירוֹת.]

לְקַיץ הַמִּזְבֵּחַ; — *is* [*used to purchase animals which are*] *offered upon* [lit. *dessert for*] *the altar* [*when it is idle*];

At times, when neither communal nor private sacrifices were being offered

רַבִּי עֲקִיבָא אוֹמֵר: מוֹתַר הַתְּרוּמָה לְקַיִץ הַמִּזְבֵּחַ, וּמוֹתַר נְסָכִים לִכְלֵי שָׁרֵת. רַבִּי חֲנַנְיָא סְגַן הַכֹּהֲנִים אוֹמֵר: מוֹתַר נְסָכִים לְקַיִץ הַמִּזְבֵּחַ, וּמוֹתַר הַתְּרוּמָה לִכְלֵי שָׁרֵת. זֶה וָזֶה לֹא הָיוּ מוֹדִים בַּפֵּרוֹת.

יד אברהם

and the altar was 'idle,' burnt offerings (עוֹלוֹת) were offered upon it. The funds for these offerings came from these profits.

The Talmud (Shevuos 12b with Rashi) explains that the term קַיִץ, lit. *dried figs,* which are eaten for dessert, is used here in the borrowed sense that these offerings are like a dessert for the altar after its main fare of the regular communal and private offerings.

וּמוֹתַר הַתְּרוּמָה לִכְלֵי שָׁרֵת. — *and the remainder of the terumah is [used] for the utensils [needed] for the [Temple] service.*

[R' Yishmael disagrees with the first tanna about the disbursement of the remainder of the *terumah.*]

The *Talmud (Kesubos 106b)* supports R' Yishmael's position from Scripture *(II Chronicles 24:14)* where it is told that the Temple tax collected in the time of King Yehoash was much in excess of the need. *They brought before the king and Yehoyada,* שְׁאָר הַכֶּסֶף, *the remainder of the money, and from it they made utensils for the House of HASHEM ...* The use of the definite article — *the* money — indicates that the reference is to the remainder of the distinctive 'appropriation'.[1]

The rationale for using the remainder of the terumah for the utensils is that these utensils are considered as appurtenances of the offerings rather than of the altar. They are, therefore, purchased from the same funds as the offerings and not from funds collected 'for repair of the House' *(Rivevan; Kesubos 106b).*

רַבִּי עֲקִיבָא אוֹמֵר: מוֹתַר הַתְּרוּמָה לְקַיִץ הַמִּזְבֵּחַ, — *R' Akiva says: The remainder of the terumah is [used to purchase animals which are] offered upon [lit. dessert for] the altar [when it is idle];*

וּמוֹתַר נְסָכִים לִכְלֵי שָׁרֵת. — *and the remainder of the nesachim is [used] for the utensils [needed] for the [Temple] service.*

[Nesachim, lit. *libations,* as used in the mishnah, includes the meal offerings which always accompany libations. See mishnah 1, s.v. וְנִסְכֵּיהֶם.]

This remainder of the *nesachim* could come about in two ways. Firstly, Temple officials would contract and pay purveyors of wine, flour and oil for a full year's supply of these items.[2] Although the contract fixed the price at the current rate, it also made provision for price fluctuation. If the market price rose, the agreed upon price stood. But if the market declined, the supplier would have to meet the lower price. Thus, if the contract

1. Although this verse seems to speak about money collected for upkeep and repair of the Temple (בֶּדֶק הַבַּיִת), the king's exhortation (v.6 and 9) spoke of מַשְׂאַת מֹשֶׁה, *the payment of Moses* (see *Rashi* and *Radak*), a clear reference to the half shekel tax first collected by Moses. In the parallel passage in *II Kings (12:5)* the words כֶּסֶף עוֹבֵר are rendered by *Yonasan* as כְּסַף תִּקְלַיָּא, *the money of the shekels* (see also *Rashi* and *Radak* there).

However it is apparent from our mishnah that the other tannaim may understand this 'rest of the money' to refer to other funds (cf. *Malbim* to Kings and Chronicles). Indeed the *Talmud (Kesubos* 106b) assumes as a matter of fact that the verse speaks of money collected for 'the repair of the House.'

2. It seems that these purveyors were given a lump sum advance upon contracting, but that this sum was not full payment. Also the final price was left open to float at the current price and was fixed every month for that particular month (see mishnah 9). Only at the end of the month, when the commodities had already been delivered and used, was full payment made (see *Tosefta* 2:13; *Tif. Yis,* to 4:9).

4
4
R' Akiva says: The remainder of the *terumah* is [used to purchase animals which are] offered upon the altar [when it is idle]; and the remainder of the *nesachim* is [used] for the utensils [needed] for the [Temple] service.

R' Chananyah, *S'gan* of the *Kohanim* says: The remainder of the *nesachim* is [used to purchase animals which are] offered upon the altar [when it is idle]; and the remainder of the *terumah* is [used] for the utensils [needed] for the [Temple] service.

Neither one nor the other admitted concerning [the permissibility of profiting from] the fruits.

price is three *se'ah* for the *sela*, but at the time of delivery a *sela* buys four *se'ah*, the Temple treasury gains a full *se'ah*, called here the 'remainder of the *nesachim*.'

Additionally, suppliers of the Temple needs are required to use a heaping measure, which would be leveled off by the Temple administrator. Since the original contract called for the exact number of measures needed for the Temple service, the amounts collected from the leveling off is a remainder of the *nesachim*.

Both of these surpluses were sold and it is to the profit of these sales that our mishnah refers (*Rav; Rosh; Menachos* 90a).

The above interpretation is cited in *Yerushalmi* as the view of R' Chiya bar Yosef. R' Yochanan (there) interprets the mishnah differently: The earlier mention of מוֹתַר הַפֵּרוֹת, *the profits of the fruits,* refers to the profits generated by the price fluctuations and those should be understood as the surplus resulting from the purchase of commodities (and should not be confused with the oil, flour, and fine flour purchased by the Temple treasury for resale to individuals according to R' Yishmael as stated in mishnah 3). The later mention of remainder of the *nesachim,* refers to those funds generated by the sale of the leveled off measures.

Selling the remainder of the *nesachim* is not regarded as 'commerce' with Temple funds, which R' Akiva frowns upon (see mishnah 3), since these commodities were bought expressly for use as communal *nesachim* (surely not an unseemly transaction) and *not* for resale. Only the unused excess is then sold. The commerce disallowed by R' Akiva is the purchase of commodities expressly for resale, albeit to individuals needing these items for their *nesachim* (*Ravad, Hil. K'lei HaMikdash* 7:9 cited by *Tos. Yom Tov*).

ר' חֲנַנְיָה סְגַן הַכֹּהֲנִים אוֹמֵר: מוֹתַר נְסָכִים — לְקַיִץ הַמִּזְבֵּחַ, וּמוֹתַר הַתְּרוּמָה לִכְלֵי שָׁרֵת. — R' *Chananyah, S'gan* [Deputy] *of the Kohanim says: The remainder of the nesachim is* [used to purchase animals which are] *offered upon* [lit. *dessert for*] *the altar* [*when it is idle*], *and the remainder of the terumah is* [used] *for the utensils* [*needed*] *for the* [*Temple*] *service.*

[This tanna is the R' Chanina (חֲנִינָא) *S'gan HaKohanim* cited in *Pesachim* 1:6; *Avos* 3:2 and *Ediyos* 2:1. Indeed some versions spell his name here too as Chanina (*Shinuyei Nuschaos*).]

זֶה וְזֶה לֹא הָיוּ מוֹדִים בַּפֵּרוֹת. — *Neither one nor the other* [i.e., neither R' Akiva nor R' Chananyah] *admitted* [to R' Yishmael] *concerning* [the permissibility of profiting from] *the fruits.*

[ה] מוֹתַר הַקְּטֹרֶת מֶה הָיוּ עוֹשִׂין בָּהּ?
מַפְרִישִׁין מִמֶּנָּה שְׂכַר הָאָמָּנִין, וּמְחַלְּלִין אוֹתָהּ
עַל־שְׂכַר הָאָמָּנִין, וְנוֹתְנִין אוֹתָהּ לָאָמָּנִין
בִּשְׂכָרָן, וְחוֹזְרִין וְלוֹקְחִין אוֹתָהּ מִתְּרוּמָה
חֲדָשָׁה.

יד אברהם

I.e., both tannaim concur that no commerce may be done with Temple property (as stated explicitly by R' Akiva in mishnah 3) and consequently disagree with R' Yishmael's ruling concerning the profit from these proceeds (Rav; Rosh; Rambam).

According to R' Yochanan (above s.v. מותר נסכים), these tannaim's view concerning produce cannot be based on R' Akiva's stand against commercial endeavors undertaken by the Temple treasury. Yerushalmi interprets this passage in the following manner: Neither one nor the other agree that the [profits resulting from the sale of] fruits should be used for burnt offerings when the altar is idle (as R' Yishmael holds). Rather this 'surplus' should be used for the purchase of utensils used in the Temple service

R' Shlomo Sirilio explains the disagreement between the tannaim concerning the 'remainder of the terumah' as follows: The mishnah assigns half shekalim to three categories: (a) The terumah appropriation; (b) the remainder of the terumah; and, (c) the remainder in the treasury chamber. Corresponding to this we find that Scripture

(Exodus 30:16) assigns three different purposes to the half shekels: (a) And it will be for the Children of Israel; (b) as a memorial; (c) to atone for your souls. The terumah, which is used to purchase animals for sacrifices, serves the third purpose, atonement. The remainder left in the treasury chamber is used for the Children of Israel, i.e., all the needs of the city. The tannaim disagree regarding how the 'remainder of the terumah' fulfills the remaining purpose — to serve as a memorial. The first tanna holds this can be achieved by using this money to plate the Holy of Holies. Similarly, we find the copper plating of the outer altar described as a memorial for the Children of Israel ... (Numbers 17:5). But ⸤he⸥ כְּלֵי שָׁרֵת, utensils used in the Temple service, are also referred to as a memorial (Numbers 31:54; see Ramban there) — hence R' Yishmael's opinion. R' Akiva finds that sacrifices, too, are a memorial as in the verse, a memorial meal offering (Numbers 5:15).

The halachah is that all these surpluses (that of the chamber, the terumah, and the nesachim) are all used for the purchase of burnt offerings when the altar is idle (Rav; Rambam, Comm.).

5.

מוֹתַר הַקְּטֹרֶת מֶה הָיוּ עוֹשִׂין בָּהּ? — What did they do with the remainder of the incense?

Incense must be offered twice daily on the inner altar of the Temple (Exodus 30:7-8). The formula used in blending this incense called for varying amounts of eleven spices with a total weight of 368 maneh.[1] A maneh was burnt on the altar each day, half in the morning, half in the afternoon. Reckoning by the solar year of 365 days, there would be

three extra maneh each year. From this the Kohen Gadol would remove two handfuls on Yom Kippur for the day's incense service in the Holy of Holies (see Yoma 5:1-2). Since the average handful holds only about a quarter-maneh (see Tos., Shavuos 10b, s.v. מותר הקטורת; and Shittah Mekubetzes, Kerisus 6b, note 1) there would always be leftover incense at the end of the year.

Additionally, there will be an eleven

---

1. A maneh is a weight equal to 100 dinar or 25 sela. Based on the accepted tradition of Rambam and the Geonim and the calculations of Chazon Ish [see appendix, "The Shekel"] the maneh weighed approximately 480 grams or 15.5 troy ounces.

5. **W**hat did they do with the remainder of the incense? — They would set aside from the *terumah* [an amount equal to] the artisans' wages, and would redeem the incense with the artisans' wages. Then they would give the incense to the artisans as their wages and repurchase it [from them] with [funds] from the new *terumah*.

YAD AVRAHAM

maneh excess in most years owing to the eleven days difference between the normal 354 day lunar year and the 365 day solar year (*Rav; Rosh;* see *Rashi* and *Tos., Shavuos* 10b, s.v. מותר הקטורת).[1]

The surplus accrued at the end of each year could not automatically be carried over into the next year, for as of the first of Nissan the incense must be bought with funds from the 'new shekalim.' The mishnah therefore describes the series of exchanges necessary to permit the use of this surplus in the following year (*Rav; Rosh*).

Why was the surplus incense not disposed of simply by having it redeemed [i.e., sold] for the use of individuals needing it for their personal offerings? In response to this question, *Ritva* (*Shevuos* 10b s.v. מפרישין ה"ג) infers from *Rashi* that it would be a זילול, *degradation*, of the Temple if incense prepared for communal use were sold to individuals. This objection does not apply to animals — only to incense, because the recipe for communal incense made it distinctive and easily recognizable.

מַפְרִישִׁין מִמֶּנָּה שְׂכַר הָאֻמָּנִין, — *They would set aside from the terumah* [*an amount equal to*] *the artisans' wages,*

The salaries of the artisans (the family Avtinas; *Yoma* 3:11) preparing the incense (cf. *Rashi* to *Kerisus* 6a, s.v. מפרישין) were paid from the *terumah* (*Kesubos* 106a). Though consecrated property (הֶקְדֵּשׁ) cannot as a rule be rendered unconsecrated (חולין) except

through חִילוּל, *redemption* [i.e., the substitution of another object for the redeemed article], a mere designation was sufficient to render the salaries unconsecrated (see *Tos. Shavuos* 10b, s.v. מפרישין; cf. *Rashi* there). *Beis Din* had the power to determine the final disposition of the collected shekalim, for as the Talmud (*Shavuos* 11a) teaches: לֵב בֵּית דִּין מַתְנֶה עֲלֵיהֶם, *the intent of Beis Din makes their consecration conditional,* i.e., when a half shekel was consecrated originally, it was done on the condition that *Beis Din* could appropriate it and even render it unconsecrated as needed (*Rav*).

וּמְחַלְּלִין אוֹתָהּ עַל-שְׂכַר הָאֻמָּנִין, — *and would redeem the incense with the artisans' wages.*

[The money appropriated for salaries was then used by the Temple officials to redeem the incense. As a result, the money became consecrated and the newly redeemed incense became unconsecrated.]

וְנוֹתְנִין אוֹתָהּ לָאֻמָּנִין בִּשְׂכָרָן, וְחוֹזְרִין וְלוֹקְחִין אוֹתָהּ מִתְּרוּמָה חֲדָשָׁה. — *Then they would give the incense to the artisans as their wages and repurchase it* [*from them*] *with* [*funds*] *from the new terumah.*

This course of action was adopted because it was so discreet. To have sold the incense on the open market and then repurchase it would have been demean-

1. Nineteen solar years will come to 209 days more than nineteen lunar years. However, the intercalation of an additional thirty-day month in seven of nineteen years equalizes the two calendars (see *Rambam, Hil. Kidush HaChodesh*, 6:10 and 10:6). Thus, any surplus incense will eventually disappear as the calendars equalize. But the annual three *maneh* surplus is not so easily disposed of.

[It could not be used to reduce the amount of incense prepared each year, for the spices had

שקלים אִם בָּא הֶחָדָשׁ בִּזְמַנּוֹ, לוֹקְחִין אוֹתָהּ
ד/ו מִתְּרוּמָה חֲדָשָׁה; וְאִם לָאו, מִן־הַיְשָׁנָה.

[ו] הַמַּקְדִּישׁ נְכָסָיו, וְהָיוּ בָהֶן דְּבָרִים
רְאוּיִין לְקָרְבְּנוֹת הַצִּבּוּר,

יד אברהם

ing [זִלְזוּל] to its holiness *(Rav; Rosh; Tos. Shevuos* 10b, s.v. מפרישין; cf. *Ritva* cited above, s.v. מותר הקטרת).

The above interpretation reflects the view of most commentators *(a) Rav; Rosh; Rambam; Rivevan; Meiri; Rashi; Tos.* and *Ritva* to *Shevuos* 10b and others). According to this view, the antecedent of the pronoun "it" [in the phrase מַפְרִישִׁין מִמֶּנָּה, *they would set aside from "it"*] is the treasury chamber. The grammatical difficulty with this interpretation is that the treasury chamber has not been mentioned in this mishnah. *(Tos. Shevuos* 10b, s.v. מפרישין, proposes that the word מִמֶּנָּה, *from it*, be deleted.) *Tiferes Yisrael* (anticipated by *Rashi, Me'ilah* 14b and *Tos., Kerisus* 6a) identifies the antecedent of "it" as the just mentioned remainder of the incense. Thus: *they would set aside from it* [the surplus incense] *the wages of the artisans*, i.e., an amount of incense equal in value to the artisans' wages. Then *they would redeem it with the wages of the artisans* — i.e., the incense is redeemed with the money set aside from the *terumah* for the wages of the artisans (thereby rendering the incense unconsecrated). They then *repurchase it* — the incense — *with funds from the new terumah.*

Rashi (Shevuos 10b, s.v. נפדין תמימין, cited by *Tos. Yom Tov)* explains that they could not simply redeem the incense with funds from the new appropriation without going

through the complicated process of first rendering it unconsecrated. Consecrated property cannot be redeemed with other consecrated property (see *Yer.* here).

אִם בָּא הֶחָדָשׁ בִּזְמַנּוֹ, לוֹקְחִין אוֹתָהּ מִתְּרוּמָה חֲדָשָׁה; — *If the new [shekalim] came in time, they purchase the incense with [funds from] the new terumah;*[1]

If the new half shekalim had arrived before Rosh Chodesh Nissan, then the appropriation was made and the incense bought from them *(Rav; Rosh).*

The punctuation הֶחָדָשׁ, literally, *the new one*, and the interpolation, *the new shekalim*, follows most commentators *(Rav; Rosh; Rambam, Hil. Shekalim* 4:12; *Meiri; Ravad* cited by *R' Shlomo Sirilio, Rivevan* and many others).

R' Shlomo Sirilio (cited by *Meleches Shlomo)* contends that the proper reading is not הֶחָדָשׁ, *the new*, but הַחֹדֶשׁ, *the new moon.* Thus: *If the new moon came* [i.e., witnesses testified before *Beis Din* that they saw the new moon] *at its [expected] time* [on the thirtieth of Adar] *then they purchase it* [the incense] *with funds from the new terumah* [for what has been *thought* of as the thirtieth of Adar became newly established as Rosh Chodesh Nissan]; *but if not* [i.e., no sighting of the moon was reported on the thirtieth and Rosh Chodesh is the thirty-first], *it is purchased with funds from the old*

to be blended either according to the full recipe of 368 *maneh* or a half recipe of 184 *maneh,* but not in any other quantity *(Kerisus* 6b).] Depending on the size of the *Kohen Gadol's* hands, this surplus will build up over the years until, after sixty or seventy years, a half year's supply of incense will have accumulated. At that time, only a half recipe will be blended which together with the accumulated excess will provide for the next year's supply.

1. Evidently *R' Meshullam* is attempting to resolve the obvious question: Was it possible that no half shekalim had been paid before Rosh Chodesh Nissan? *R' A. Sofer* (in his notes to *R' Meshullam)* comments that the question is still unresolved, for surely the people *inside* Jerusalem would pay this tax. Perhaps their contributions alone would be insufficient to fill the baskets in the Temple treasury in accord with the procedure outlined in 3:2. Our mishnah may mean that if there were not enough shekalim to carry out the full procedure, the offerings should be bought from the old appropriation.

Alternatively, one could apply *R' Meshullam's* resolution to a time when the Temple itself is under siege and *no* shekalim could be received (as related in *Bava Kamma* 82b).

If the new [shekalim] came in time, they purchase the incense with [funds from] the new *terumah;* if not, from the old.

6. If one consecrated his possessions and among them were things suitable for communal offer-

YAD AVRAHAM

terumah — for in such an eventuality the thirtieth of Adar belongs to the outgoing year. According to this interpretation, too, the mishnah applies also to offerings other than incense. [*Turei Even (Rosh HaShanah 7* cited by *Tos. R' Akiva* here) and *Tif. Yis.* independently arrive at this same interpretation.]

This interpretation is not without difficulty. Why does the mishnah have to teach the obvious fact that if *Beis Din* did not declare the thirtieth day Rosh Chodesh, then the old appropriation is still used? Since it is still the old year there is no reason to purchase the offerings with funds from the new *terumah (Turei Even loc. cit; Kol Sofer).*

Turei Even resolves this question by demonstrating that actually the offerings of the thirtieth of Adar should always be bought with the new appropriation because of the probability that witnesses may yet come and the *Beis Din* will declare this day Rosh Chodesh. For in the majority of instances witnesses did arrive on the thirtieth and an Adar comprised of thirty days was an anomaly. The mishnah informs us that in spite of this reasoning, the offerings brought on the thirtieth are purchased from the old appropriation until *Beis Din* actually confirms the designation of Rosh Chodesh. *Turei Even* believes that this ruling is alluded to in the Torah, for the provisions that the

offerings of Rosh Chodesh come from the new appropriation (*Rosh HaShanah* 7a) is found in the verse mandating the Rosh Chodesh *mussaf* offering (*Numbers* 28:14), indicating that it holds true (in all cases) only for this offering, but not for the daily offerings, which may be offered before the designation of Rosh Chodesh is known.

וְאִם לָאו, — *if not,*

The community had not yet paid their half shekalim *(Rav; Rosh).*

If, for example, Jerusalem was under siege[1] *(R' Meshullam).*

מִן הַיְשָׁנָה. — *from the old.*

If they had already redeemed the surplus incense, they repurchase it with funds from the old *terumah.* If the redemption had not yet taken place, they simply used the surplus incense for offerings in the new year *(Rav; Rosh).*

The same rule applies to all the public offerings; if the new funds have not yet arrived, offerings are bought with funds from the old *terumah* as set forth in *Rosh HaShanah* 7a and *Tosefta* 2:8. Indeed, R' Meshullam (cf. R. A. Sofer's emendation of the text) understands the pronoun אוֹתָה, lit. *it,* here to refer not exclusively to the incense, but to *all* public offerings.[1]

6.

Having digressed to describe the redemption of surplus incense, the mishnah now speaks of a similar redemption procedure. Indeed, according to the Talmud (*Kerisus* 6a) this mishnah too refers to incense.

הַמַּקְדִּישׁ נְכָסָיו, — *If one consecrated his possessions*

In general, *consecration* is defined as donating to the fund for בֶּדֶק הַבַּיִת, *upkeep of the Temple.*

Unless the donor specifies otherwise,

any consecrated objects or funds are assumed to be meant for upkeep of the Temple *(Rav, Rosh from Temurah 7:2).*

וְהָיוּ בָהֶן דְּבָרִים רְאוּיִין לְקָרְבְּנוֹת הַצִּבּוּר, — *and among them were things suitable for communal offerings,*

These 'suitable things' now belong to בֶּדֶק הַבַּיִת, *the fund for upkeep of the Temple,* and like all objects in this class, they may be returned to their secular

---

1. This interpretation raises a grammatical difficulty: אוֹתָה, *it* [lit. *her*], is feminine singular and ostensibly refers only to קְטֹרֶת, *incense.*

שקלים יִנָּתְנוּ לָאֻמָּנִין בִּשְׂכָרָן — דִּבְרֵי רַבִּי עֲקִיבָא.
ד/ו אָמַר לוֹ בֶּן־עַזַּאי: אֵינָהּ הִיא הַמִּדָּה. אֶלָּא
מַפְרִישִׁין מֵהֶן שְׂכַר הָאֻמָּנִין וּמְחַלְּלִין אוֹתָן

יד אברהם

status through redemption. Nevertheless, there is a rule that anything suitable for the altar [which has been consecrated to the upkeep of the Temple] must ultimately be offered upon the altar *(Terumah* 33b). [The mishnah now turns to the complex procedure of redemption and reconsecration to be followed before the 'suitable things' can actually be offered on the altar.]

'Things suitable for communal offerings' include animals, wine, oil, meal, and incense. Since animals are discussed in mishnah 7, and wine, oil, and meal are mentioned in mishnah 8 (see *comm.* there concerning the various textual readings), our mishnah must speak of incense *(Kerisus* 6a).

Additionally, since the mishnah specifies communal offerings, it must refer to that which can be brought by the community but not as a private offering. Only incense fits this description (see *Meleches Shlomo* citing *R' Suleiman).*

Rav and *Rosh* understand the 'things suitable for communal offerings' to include incense, wines, oils, and flour. Their view is questioned by *Tosefos Yom Tov,* however, who cites the passage from *Kerisus* cited above limiting this mishnah to the topic of incense. (See *Melechos Shlomo* who cites *R' Suleiman's* attempt to reconcile *Rav's* view with the Talmud.)

In his *Commentary, Rambam* includes animals in our mishnah's discussion, but he seems to have retracted this view in his *Code (Hil. Arachin* 5:10).

Tiferes Yisrael suggests that the mishnah means that, among *them* [i.e., the many articles he may have consecrated] *were things suitable* [only] *for public offerings,* i.e., incense.

The incense used on the Temple altar must be prepared within the Temple environs[1]

(Kerisus 6a based on *Exodus* 30:35-37). If so how can incense be found among the personal property which was consecrated to the Temple? The Talmud gives two possibilities. Either he was a Temple artisan who has received surplus incense as a part of his salary, and he consecrated it before it could be repurchased from him (see mishnah 5; *Yerushalmi* and *Kerisus, ibid.);* or the donation contained raw spices of the kind needed for the blending of incense *(Kerisus, ibid.). Rambam (Hil. Arachin* 5:10) mentions both these possibilities. [See *Tos. Yom Tov;* see also *Shittah Mekubetzes, Kerisus* 6a (36).]

יִנָּתְנוּ לָאֻמָּנִין בִּשְׂכָרָן — דִּבְרֵי רַבִּי עֲקִיבָא. — *these [things] should be given to the artisans* [i.e. the Avtinas family, which prepared the incense, *(Yer.)] for their wages* — *[these are] the words of R' Akiva.*

R' Akiva holds that consecrated property may be redeemed with an intangible object; in our case, the consecrated money is redeemed with the labor of the artisans. This is derived from *Exodus* 25:8: *They shall make* לִי, *for me, a Sanctuary.* The superflous pronoun לִי, *for me,* is understood to mean also מִשֶּׁלִי *from mine,* i.e., the Sanctuary is to be made, and the work paid for, from funds of the Temple treasury *(Rav, Rosh* from *Temurah* 31b).

The mishnah mentions only the beginning of the process. The later passage, *and repurchase them with the new terumah,* applies to R' Akiva as well as to Ben Azzai. The first mishnah describes the differing views of R' Akiva and Ben Azzai regarding the first step, then it returns to explain the undisputed second step *(Tos. Yom Tov;* see also *Rosh* and *comm.* below, s.v. וחוזרין).

As noted earlier, the mishnah refers to incense consecrated to the 'upkeep of

1. In actual practice, the preparation of spices for the incense was done in the Avtinas chamber [named for the family of master blenders charged with this duty (see *Yoma* 3:11)] atop the Water Gate in the southern wall of the Temple Courtyard (see *Middos* 1:4; *Rambam Comm.* to *Middos* 5:4).

4
6

ings, these [things] should be given to the artisans for their wages — [these are] the words of R' Akiva.

Said Ben Azzai to him: This is not the [same] method [described above]. Rather, they set aside from these [things an amount equal to] the artisans' wages and redeem them with [funds set aside] for the

YAD AVRAHAM

the Temple'. A special problem exists here which sets incense apart from the materials suitable for offering upon the altar. The latter may be sold to those needing them and the proceeds used for purchasing offerings, or the item itself could be offered upon the altar as outlined in mishnayos 7-8. This is impossible in the instance of incense, for incense may not be brought as a private offering, and the communal incense must be bought and the *terumah* appropriation. The mishnah describes the steps necessary to accomplish this.

אָמַר לוֹ בֶּן עַזַּאי: אֵינָה הִיא הַמִּדָּה. — *Said Ben Azzai to him: This is not the [same] method [described above].*

I.e., your method is different from the one given above (mishnah 5) for the surplus of incense. There the incense was not redeemed for the artisan's intangible work, but for tangible, unconsecrated money already set aside (Rav).

[The translation, *this is not the same method*, follows the interpretation of *Rav* and *Rambam*. The same expression אֵינָה הִיא הַמִּדָּה appears in *Pesachim* 1:7 where this rendition is not valid. There, *Rav* and *Rashi* render: *This is not indicated* ... Perhaps this is simply an idiomatic expression meaning: *This is not correct*.]

The mishnah leaves unexplained why R'Akiva in this case adopts a procedure different from the one given in mishnah 5 for surplus incense. *Rivevan* maintains that the anonymous mishnah 5 follows Ben Azzai, but that R' Akiva would rule that surplus incense, too, should be dealt with in the manner he describes in our mishnah. *Rambam (Comm.)* also decides the halachah according to Ben Azzai because the previous, anonymous, mishnah (סְתָם מִשְׁנָה) follows Ben Azzai's view.

However the mishnah in *Temurah* (7:2) draws a distinction between money designated for 'the upkeep of the House,' which may be redeemed for uncollected wages, and קָדְשֵׁי מִזְבֵּחַ, *funds designated for altar offerings*, which may not be so used. Accordingly, R' Akiva will admit that the 'surplus incense' — i.e., altar offerings — may not be redeemed in the manner he outlines here (see *R' Shmuel* p. 45, s.v. נותנין). *Tosafos* to *Shevuos* (10b, s.v. מפרישין שכר, and a parallel *Tosafos* in *Shittah Mekubetzes Temurah* 6a, note 34) should also be understood in this vein.

However *Rambam* (probably) understands the mishnah in *Temurah* to refer to an actual offering.

אֶלָּא מַפְרִישִׁין מֵהֶן שְׂכַר הָאָמְּנִין — *Rather, they set aside from these [things an amount equal to] the artisans' wages*

[The different interpretations regarding the use of funds for the surplus incense (mishnah 5) apply here as well. Our mishnah uses the plural מֵהֶן, *from them*, referring to the plural coins, whereas earlier the singular מִמֶּנָּה, *from it*, referred to the appropriation.]

Ben Azzai does not object to using uncollected pay to redeem money from the appropriation. Here, where the community pays its taxes to be used according to the best judgment of the administrators, the applicable principle is לֵב בֵּית דִּין מַתְנֶה עֲלֵיהֶן, *the intent of the Beis Din makes the consecration conditional* [upon the will and need of the Temple administration], so that this money may be spent for needs associated with public offerings (see *Rosh; Tos., Shevuos* 10b, s.v. קדושה: see also *Even HaAzel, Hil. Me'ilah* 8:3; *Rabbeinu Tam, Sefer HaYashar*, 480 old ed., 678 new ed.).

שקלים
ד/ז
עַל־מָעוֹת הָאָמָּנִין; וְנוֹתְנִין אוֹתָן לָאָמָּנִין בִּשְׂכָרָן וְחוֹזְרִין וְלוֹקְחִין אוֹתָן מִתְּרוּמָה חֲדָשָׁה.

[ז] הַמַּקְדִּישׁ נְכָסָיו, וְהָיְתָה בָהֶן בְּהֵמָה רְאוּיָה לְגַבֵּי הַמִּזְבֵּחַ, זְכָרִים וּנְקֵבוֹת — רַבִּי אֱלִיעֶזֶר אוֹמֵר: זְכָרִים יִמָּכְרוּ לְצָרְכֵי עוֹלוֹת וּנְקֵבוֹת יִמָּכְרוּ לְצָרְכֵי זִבְחֵי שְׁלָמִים; וּדְמֵיהֶן יִפְּלוּ עִם שְׁאָר נְכָסִים לְבֶדֶק הַבָּיִת.
רַבִּי יְהוֹשֻׁעַ אוֹמֵר: זְכָרִים עַצְמָן יִקְרְבוּ

יד אברהם

וּמְחַלְּלִין אוֹתָן עַל־מָעוֹת הָאָמָּנִין; וְנוֹתְנִין אוֹתָן לָאָמָּנִין בִּשְׂכָרָן — *and redeem them* [the 'suitable things'] *with [funds set aside] for the artisans' wages; then they give them* [i.e. the 'suitable things'] *to the artisans as their wages*
[As explained in mishnah 5]

וְחוֹזְרִין וְלוֹקְחִין אוֹתָן מִתְּרוּמָה חֲדָשָׁה. — *and repurchase them with [funds from] the new terumah.*

[This is so even according to the view (above s.v. יהיו) that the 'suitable things' are unprocessed herbs for the incense. These herbs could not be repurchased with funds from the old appropriation, because no spices would have been needed to replenish the incense supply of the outgoing year. Customarily the spices for an entire year's incense would be bought on Rosh Chodesh Nissan, thus eliminating the need for later purchases. Consequently they had to wait for the new appropriation and included these herbs in the supplies purchased for the new year.]

[We have already mentioned *Tosefos Yom Tov's* view that this clause, *They repurchase* ..., is a continuation of the words of both Ben

Azzai and R' Akiva. However, *R' Meshullam* (p. 45) assumes that this clause is part of Ben Azzai's position. R' Akiva disagrees, maintaining that not only may Temple property be redeemed with uncollected pay, but after being redeemed it need not be reconsecrated for altar use. This latter view is cited and subsequently rejected by a *Tosefos* in *Temurah* (see *Shittah Mekubetzes* 6a paragraphs 34 and 36; cf. 34 there).

[Presumably, R' Akiva permits this private use of previously consecrated incense only if it were tendered to the artisans as part of their salary, but outright sale of the incense would still be forbidden as degrading to the consecrated items. If so, R' Akiva would disagree with the next mishnayos as well, for the principle is the same in all three cases. In his view, therefore, it is probable that the items mentioned there could be used to pay the artisans.]

It is unclear whether (according to this view) R' Akiva also permits the transfer of the surplus incense to the artisans for their private use. Perhaps he will agree that incense which had already been designated for the altar service may not be used by individuals even after redemption (cf. comm. to mishnah 5, s.v. מה היו עושין).

7.

Having introduced the consecration of things suitable for public offering, the mishnah now discusses other facets of this topic.

הַמַּקְדִּישׁ נְכָסָיו, וְהָיְתָה בָהֶן בְּהֵמָה רְאוּיָה לְגַבֵּי הַמִּזְבֵּחַ, זְכָרִים וּנְקֵבוֹת — *If one* consecrated his possessions, and among them was an animal suitable for [offer-

artisans' wages; then they give them to the artisans as their wages and repurchase them with [funds from] the new *terumah.*

7. If one consecrated his possessions, and among them there was an animal suitable for the altar, either male or female — R' Eliezer says: The males should be sold to those needing burnt offerings and the females should be sold to those needing peace offerings; their proceeds should be used with the rest of the property for the upkeep of the Temple.

R' Yehoshua says: The males themselves should be brought as burnt offerings, but the females should

YAD AVRAHAM

ing upon] the altar, either male or female —

He consecrated his belongings to the fund for the upkeep of the Temple. The rule outlined above (*mishnah 6*, s.v. והיו בהן) that 'things fit for the altar must ultimately be offered upon the altar' applies here. However, as in mishnah 6, a consecration made for בֶּדֶק הַבַּיִת, *upkeep of the Temple,* is of insufficient sanctity to qualify for offering on the altar. Therefore our mishnah outlines the steps necessary to change the form of consecration. First it must be returned to its unconsecrated state and then specifically consecrated for the altar (*Rav*).

רַבִּי אֱלִיעֶזֶר אוֹמֵר: זְכָרִים יִמָּכְרוּ לְצָרְכֵי עוֹלוֹת — *R' Eliezer says: The males should be sold to those needing* [lit. *for needs of] burnt offerings*

[They should be used for the ultimate altar service — as burnt offerings — in which the entire offering is consumed upon the altar pyre.]

Only males are suitable for burnt offerings, as set forth in *Leviticus* (ch. 1).

וּנְקֵבוֹת יִמָּכְרוּ לְצָרְכֵי זִבְחֵי שְׁלָמִים; — *and the females should be sold to those needing* [lit. *for the needs of] peace offerings;*

[Peace offerings may be either male or

female (*Leviticus* ch. 3). Only specific parts of these offerings are burnt upon the altar — in general, fats and innards (see *Leviticus* 3:3-4) — and the rest of the meat is eaten by the *Kohanim,* the owner and his guests.]

וּדְמֵיהֶן יִפְּלוּ עִם שְׁאָר נְכָסִים לְבֶדֶק הַבָּיִת. — *(and) their proceeds should be used* [lit. *fall] with the rest of the property for the upkeep of the Temple.*

R' Eliezer maintains that even something suitable for a sacrifice is subject to the rule that anything consecrated but not designated for a specific fund, is placed in the fund for the upkeep of the Temple (סְתָם הֶקְדֵּשׁ לְבֶדֶק הַבָּיִת). When such items are redeemed, naturally the proceeds revert to their owner, namely, the 'fund for the upkeep' (*Rav; Rosh*).

רַבִּי יְהוֹשֻׁעַ אוֹמֵר: זְכָרִים עַצְמָן יִקָּרְבוּ עוֹלוֹת, — *R' Yehoshua says: The males themselves should be brought as burnt offerings,*

R' Yehoshua assumes that anything suitable for the altar must have been consecrated with the intent that it be offered on the altar [even if other property consecrated at the same time was specifically designated for the 'fund for the upkeep', such as here].

In the absence of any other designa-

שקלים עוֹלוֹת, וּנְקֵבוֹת יִמָּכְרוּ לְצָרְכֵי זִבְחֵי שְׁלָמִים,
ד/ח וְיָבִיא בִּדְמֵיהֶן עוֹלוֹת, וּשְׁאָר נְכָסִים יִפְּלוּ
לְבֶדֶק הַבַּיִת.

רַבִּי עֲקִיבָא אוֹמֵר: רוֹאֶה אֲנִי אֶת־דִּבְרֵי רַבִּי
אֱלִיעֶזֶר מִדִּבְרֵי רַבִּי יְהוֹשֻׁעַ, שֶׁרַבִּי אֱלִיעֶזֶר
הִשְׁוָה אֶת־מִדָּתוֹ וְרַבִּי יְהוֹשֻׁעַ חָלַק.

אָמַר רַבִּי פַּפְיַס: שָׁמַעְתִּי כְּדִבְרֵי שְׁנֵיהֶן.
שֶׁהַמַּקְדִּישׁ בְּפֵירוּשׁ, כְּדִבְרֵי רַבִּי אֱלִיעֶזֶר;
וְהַמַּקְדִּישׁ סְתָם, כְּדִבְרֵי רַבִּי יְהוֹשֻׁעַ.

[ח] **הַמַּקְדִּישׁ** נְכָסִים, וְהָיוּ בָהֶן דְּבָרִים
רְאוּיִין עַל־גַּבֵּי הַמִּזְבֵּחַ,
יֵינוֹת, שְׁמָנִים וְעוֹפוֹת — רַבִּי אֶלְעָזָר אוֹמֵר:

יד אברהם

tion, it is assumed that the owner meant the ultimate offering — burnt offerings. Thus consecrated male animals should themselves be brought as burnt offerings (Rav; Rosh).

וּנְקֵבוֹת יִמָּכְרוּ לְצָרְכֵי זִבְחֵי שְׁלָמִים, — but the females should be sold to those needing [lit. for the needs of] peace offerings,

[In order to satisfy the requirement that anything fit for the altar must ultimately be offered upon the altar (see above 6, s.v. וְהָיוּ בהן), the females must be sold to people who will use them as sacrifices.]

וְיָבִיא בִּדְמֵיהֶן עוֹלוֹת, — (and) burnt offerings should be brought with their proceeds,

The female animals are not suitable as burnt offerings, but they are eligible for use as peace offerings. Once an animal is suitable for sacrifice, it may not be used for another purpose — which is why the animal itself must be sold for use as a peace offering — but because the owner is assumed to have intended its use for the ultimate offering (see above) its value must be used to purchase a burnt offering (Rav; Rosh).

וּשְׁאָר נְכָסִים יִפְּלוּ לְבֶדֶק הַבָּיִת. — and the rest of the property should be used [lit. fall] for the upkeep of the Temple.

[Though part of the consecrated property is assumed to be designated as offerings, it does not follow that all the property be treated in the same fashion. Rather the rest of the belongings are subject to the rule of unspecified consecrations which are placed in the fund for the upkeep of the Temple.]

רַבִּי עֲקִיבָא אוֹמֵר: רוֹאֶה אֲנִי אֶת־דִּבְרֵי רַבִּי אֱלִיעֶזֶר מִדִּבְרֵי רַבִּי יְהוֹשֻׁעַ, שֶׁרַבִּי אֱלִיעֶזֶר הִשְׁוָה אֶת־מִדָּתוֹ וְרַבִּי יְהוֹשֻׁעַ חָלַק. — R' Akiva says: I prefer [lit. see] R' Eliezer's view over R' Yehoshua's, because R' Eliezer applies his [logical] method uniformly whereas R' Yehoshua differentiates.

[R' Akiva reasons that all the items in a single act of consecration are intended for the same purpose.]

אָמַר רַבִּי פַּפְיַס: שָׁמַעְתִּי כְּדִבְרֵי שְׁנֵיהֶן. — Said R' Papyas: I have been taught [lit. heard] that both views are correct [lit. according to both views].

שֶׁהַמַּקְדִּישׁ בְּפֵירוּשׁ, כְּדִבְרֵי רַבִּי אֱלִיעֶזֶר; — Regarding one who consecrates explicit-

4
8

be sold to those needing peace offerings, burnt offerings should be brought with their proceeds, and the rest of the property should be used for the upkeep of the Temple.

R' Akiva says: I prefer R' Eliezer's view over R' Yehoshua's, because R' Eliezer applies his [logical] method uniformly whereas R' Yehoshua differentiates.

Said R' Papyas: I have been taught that both views are correct. Regarding one who consecrates explicitly, [the halachah is] according to R' Eliezer; whereas regarding one who consecrates without explicit designation, [the halachah is] according to R' Yehoshua.

8. If one consecrated [his] possessions, and among them were things suitable for the altar, [such as] wines, oils or fowl — R' Elazar says: They should be

YAD AVRAHAM

ly, [the halachah is] according to R' Eliezer;

If he enumerated all the consecrated items individually, but did not specify that the animals should go for the altar, we must infer that even these items are intended for upkeep of the Temple. Had he intended any of them for the altar, he would have indicated this (Rav; Rosh citing R' Eliezer of Garmeisa).

וְהַמַּקְדִּישׁ סְתָם, כְּדִבְרֵי רַבִּי יְהוֹשֻׁעַ. — whereas regarding one who consecrates without explicit designation, [the halachah is] according to R' Yehoshua.

Since he did not bother to enumerate all the items, no inference can be drawn

from his silence concerning the consecration of the items suitable for the altar. Therefore, we can assume that his intent was to designate each item for its optimum holiness (ibid.).

Rambam (followed by Meiri and Rivevan) interprets R' Papyas as follows: The halachah would follow R' Eliezer (that all proceeds go for upkeep) if the donor specified that everything is for upkeep of the Temple; but if he merely consecrated without specifying any purpose, each part of the property goes for its respective optimum use.

The halachah is in accordance with R' Eliezer and R' Akiva (Rav; Rambam, Hil. Arachin 5:7).

8.

הַמַּקְדִּישׁ נְכָסִים, וְהָיוּ בָהֶן דְּבָרִים רְאוּיִין עַל־גַּבֵּי הַמִּזְבֵּחַ, יֵינוֹת, שְׁמָנִים וְעוֹפוֹת — If one consecrated [his] possessions, and among them were things suitable for [offering upon] the altar, [such as] wines, oils or fowl —

Wine is used in libations, oil is mixed

with the flour of meal offerings, and fowl, namely turtle doves and doves (תּוֹרִים וּבְנֵי יוֹנָה), are suitable for sin and burnt offerings (Rav).

Rav's version of the mishnah, as well as that of Rambam, Rosh, Meiri, and others (see Shinuyei Nuschaos) lists an additional item,

שקלים יִמָּכְרוּ לְצָרְכֵי הַמִּין וְיָבִיא בִּדְמֵיהֶן
ד/ט עוֹלוֹת, וּשְׁאָר נְכָסִים יִפְּלוּ לְבֶדֶק הַבָּיִת.

[ט] **אַחַת** לִשְׁלשִׁים יוֹם, מְשַׁעֲרִין אֶת־
הַלִּשְׁכָּה. כָּל־הַמְקַבֵּל עָלָיו לְסַפֵּק
סְלָתוֹת מֵאַרְבָּעָה, עָמְדוּ מִשָּׁלשׁ, יְסַפֵּק

יד אברהם

סְלָתוֹת, *flour*, which is used in meal offerings. This version also appears in the Talmud (*Temurah* 6a) in a quote from our mishnah.

רַבִּי אֶלְעָזָר אוֹמֵר: יִמָּכְרוּ לְצָרְכֵי הַמִּין — *R' Elazar says: They should be sold to those needing* [lit. *for the needs of*] *each particular item* [for an offering]

[For the same reason set forth earlier in mishnayos 6 and 7.]

וְיָבִיא בִּדְמֵיהֶן עוֹלוֹת, — *and their proceeds should be used for burnt offerings,*

In the verse (*Leviticus* 22:18) לְכָל נִדְרֵיהֶם וּלְכָל נִדְבוֹתָם אֲשֶׁר־יַקְרִיבוּ לַה' לְעֹלָה *all their vow-offerings and all of their donative offerings which they will offer to HASHEM for a burnt offering,* R' Elazar finds an illusion to the rule that anything consecrated should ultimately be used for burnt offerings if it is suitable for the altar. [Perhaps R' Elazar's perception of an additional meaning in the verse is based on the redundant use of כָּל, *all*, which appears twice in this verse. Thus even wines, etc.,

which cannot themselves be burnt offerings are sold and the proceeds go for the purchase of burnt offerings. From the fact that the following verse (*v.* 19) specifies only cattle and sheep, R' Elazar derives the further teaching that even fowl, which may themselves be offered as burnt offerings, nevertheless must be sold and their proceeds used to purchase animals for burnt offerings (*Rav, Rosh* from *Yer.*).[1]

[According to the above interpretation R' Elazar's view contradicts both R' Eliezer (who holds that the proceeds go for upkeep of the Temple) and R' Yehoshua (who would have the fowl themselves offered).[2] The mishnah presents R' Elazar's view regarding wines, etc., only to underscore that even the proceeds of items not suitable as burnt offerings go toward the purchase of these offerings. Also it teaches R' Elazar's view pertaining to fowl.]

Rambam followed by *Meiri* and based on *Yerushalmi*[3] understands R' Elazar not as a differing view, but rather a clarification of R' Eliezer's view concerning the items men-

1. The inference is that male animals suitable for burnt offerings may themselves be offered (females will naturally have to be sold like wines, etc.). In practice, therefore, R' Elazar's view in this case will be identical to R' Yehoshua's view in the previous mishnah. However, the rationale is totally different. R' Yehoshua understands that the donor intended to designate these animals as burnt offerings. According to this view, even fowl would be offered, like any other fowl designated as a burnt offering. As noted above, however, R' Elazar of our mishnah rules that even fowl should be sold and the proceeds used for animal burnt offerings. Clearly, therefore, R' Elazar interprets the donor's intent as does R' Eliezer (mishnah 6): the donor consecrated the birds for the upkeep of the Temple — but Scripture (see above in comm.) reassigns them to the altar.

2. A strong case may be made that the halachah should follow R' Elazar, inasmuch as his is the final view cited and it is stated unopposed (סְתָם), as if R' Elazar had the final say. *Rosh* makes no decision on this matter. *Rav* follows *Rambam* in deciding like R' Akiva. However since according to *Rambam* the position advanced in our mishnah does not contradict R' Akiva, his ruling cannot be a basis for *Rav*, who feels that R' Elazar is a third opinion.

3. It would appear on the surface that *Rosh* and *Rav's* view is a hypothetical interpretation, which is later repudiated by the *Yerushalmi*. However, there are other possible interpretations (see *Mareh HaPanim*).

sold to those needing each particular item and their proceeds should be used for burnt offerings, but the rest of the possessions should go to the upkeep of the Temple.

9. Once every thirty days they would set the price paid by the [treasury] chamber. Whoever undertook to supply fine flour at four [*se'ah* for a *sela*], and [the price subsequently] stood at [only] three [*se'ah* for a *sela*], must supply at four; [but if he un-

YAD AVRAHAM

tioned here. Indeed *Rambam's* version of our mishnah reads רַבִּי אֱלִיעֶזֶר, i.e., the same R' Eliezer whose view concerning 'an animal suitable for the altar' had been expressed in the previous mishnah. According to this reading, R' Elazar now draws a distinction between animals, whose proceeds go to the fund 'for the upkeep', and the items mentioned here, whose proceeds go for burnt offerings. *Rambam (Comm.* and *Hil. Arachin* 5:9 based on *Yer.)* explains the rationale for this difference as follows: 'If wines ... or

fowl were designated as an offering, they may not be redeemed under any circumstance, whereas animals may be redeemed, if they become blemished.' The commentators agree that this explanation still needs further elucidation (see *Ravad, Radbaz,* and *Ohr Same'ach* there).

וּשְׁאָר נְכָסִים יִפְּלוּ לְבֶדֶק הַבַּיִת. — *but the rest of the possessions should go to the upkeep of the Temple.*

9.

— אַחַת לִשְׁלֹשִׁים יוֹם, מְשַׁעֲרִין אֶת־הַלִּשְׁכָּה. *Once every thirty days they would set the price paid by the [treasury] chamber.*

They would set the price the treasury would pay for wine (libations) and flour (meal offerings) and this price would not be revised upward that month[1]. If the market price rose, the treasury would pay the lower, set, price; but if the price fell they would pay the lower price as set forth below (*Rav; Rosh; Rambam*).

As a service to people bringing meal offerings or libations — the ingredients of which must be prepared under rigid standards of טָהֳרָה, *purity* — two offices [each named for the first person to hold that position *(Rav* to 5:1)] were established. Tokens of varying denominations would be bought from the office of Yochanan and redeemed at the office of Achiyah for the proper amounts of

oil, flour, and wine needed for the particular offering. At day's end Yochanan and Achiyah would compare their records. At the end of each month the suppliers would be paid from the funds collected by Yochanan (*Tosefta* 2:13; see below 5:4).

כָּל־הַמְקַבֵּל עָלָיו לְסַפֵּק סְלָתוֹת מֵאַרְבָּעָה, עָמְדוּ מִשָּׁלֹשׁ, יְסַפֵּק מֵאַרְבָּעָה; — *Whoever undertook to supply fine flour at four [se'ah for a sela], and [the price subsequently] stood at [only] three [se'ah for a sela], must supply at four;*

He must honor his agreement with the Temple. *Rambam (Hil. K'lei HaMikdash* 7:13) seems to understand that agreement to a fixed price was sufficient to bind the supplier. *Rosh* and *Rav,* however, state that the Temple treasury (הֶקְדֵּשׁ) makes its transactions binding (קוֹנֶה) by an exchange of money, whereas private individuals re-

---

1. See note to s.v. ומותר נסכים in mishnah 4.

שקלים מֵאַרְבָּעָה; מְשַׁלֵּשׁ, וְעָמְדוּ מֵאַרְבָּעָה, יְסַפֵּק
ה/א מֵאַרְבָּעָה, שֶׁיַּד הֶקְדֵּשׁ עַל־הָעֶלְיוֹנָה. וְאִם
הִתְלִיעָה סֹלֶת, הִתְלִיעָה לוֹ; וְאִם הֶחְמִיץ יַיִן,
הֶחְמִיץ לוֹ. וְאֵינוֹ מְקַבֵּל אֶת־מָעוֹתָיו עַד שֶׁיְּהֵא
הַמִּזְבֵּחַ מְרַצֶּה.

[א] **אֵלּוּ** הֵן הַמְּמֻנִּין שֶׁהָיוּ בַמִּקְדָּשׁ: יוֹחָנָן
בֶּן־פִּינְחָס עַל־הַחוֹתָמוֹת; אֲחִיָּה
עַל־הַנְּסָכִים; מַתִּתְיָה בֶן־שְׁמוּאֵל עַל־הַפְּיָסוֹת;

יד אברהם

quire physical transference of goods (מְשִׁיכָה) to effect a change of ownership (see *Kiddushin* 29a; *Tos. R' Akiva* here).

מְשַׁלֵּשׁ, וְעָמְדוּ מֵאַרְבָּעָה, יְסַפֵּק מֵאַרְבָּעָה, — [*but if he undertook to supply at*] three [*se'ah for a sela*], and [*the price subsequently*] stood at four, he must supply at four,

Since his costs were down, the supplier stood to profit if the Temple treasury were constrained to honor its agreement and to buy at the higher price. Nevertheless the law is that the Temple is not bound by the agreement which binds the supplier. The treasury has the right to act as if it were a private individual, who is not bound by an oral agreement even if it was accompanied by an exchange of money (*Rav, Rosh*).

שֶׁיַּד הֶקְדֵּשׁ עַל־הָעֶלְיוֹנָה. — *for the Temple has the upper hand.*

Only to the advantage of the Temple do we apply the rule that transactions involving the Temple are binding even in instances where private business deals are not. Where the Temple would lose under such an arrangement, it is bound only by transactions that would bind private individuals as well. However though the price may be lowered, the agreement itself may not be canceled; the supplier must still provide what he has promised, albeit at a lower

price (see *Rambam, Hil. Mechirah* 9:1-2 with *Even HaAzel*).

וְאִם הִתְלִיעָה סֹלֶת, הִתְלִיעָה לוֹ; וְאִם הֶחְמִיץ יַיִן, הֶחְמִיץ לוֹ. — [*Likewise,*] *if the fine flour became wormy, the loss is his* [i.e., the supplier's] [lit. *it became wormy for him*]; *and if the wine soured, the loss is his* [lit. *it soured for him*].

[Wormy flour may not be used for meal offerings (*Menachos* 85b). Similarly sour wine may not be used for libations, for it is no longer wine but vinegar (see *Bava Basra* 97a).] This advantage to the Temple treasury exists even if the Temple had already transferred the goods to their premises (מְשִׁיכָה) and paid for them (*Rav; Rosh*). Unlimited warranty until the goods are used is another tacit understanding included in any sale to the Temple (*Tos. Yom Tov*).

וְאֵינוֹ מְקַבֵּל אֶת־מָעוֹתָיו עַד שֶׁיְּהֵא הַמִּזְבֵּחַ מְרַצֶּה. — *(And) he does not receive his money until the altar atones.*

I.e. even if the supplier had been paid, the money is not yet considered his 'until the altar atones'. Therefore if the wine soured he is still responsible (*Rav; Rosh*).

Rivevan sees this passage as a new statement and not just as explanation of the previous clause. Even if the wine spilled and could not be offered it is the supplier's loss (as stated in *Tosefta* 2:12).

dertook to supply at] three [se'ah for a sela], and [the price subsequently] stood at four, he must supply at four, for the Temple has the upper hand.

[Likewise,] if the fine flour became wormy, the loss is his; and if the wine soured, the loss is his. He does not receive his money until the altar atones.

1. These are the administrators who were in the Temple: Yochanan ben Pinchas over the tokens; Achiyah over the *nesachim;* Matisyah ben Shmuel

Chapter 5

1.

אֵלוּ הֵן הַמְמֻנִּין שֶׁהָיוּ בַּמִּקְדָּשׁ: — *These are the administrators* [lit. *appointees*] *who were in the Temple:*

The following is a list of officials who filled fifteen positions in the Temple. The mishnah enumerates the offices and gives the names of the administrators. Obviously during the 420 years of the Second Temple there were hundreds of such administrators; why then are only these fifteen named? The *Yerushalmi* cites two opinions. One view holds that the most pious and righteous men ever to hold these offices are named. Another holds that these were the names of the administrators at the time this mishnah was drafted.[1] *Rav* cites the view of his mentors (see *Rosh* and *Likutim* in ed. Vilna) that the mishnah lists only the first people to hold the respective offices [in the early Second Temple era]. He adds (see also *Tosafos, Menachos* 64b, s.v. אמר cited by *Tos. Yom Tov*) that successive ad-

ministrators actually assumed their predecessors' names upon entering their posts.

יוֹחָנָן בֶּן-פִּינְחָס עַל-הַחוֹתָמוֹת; אֲחִיָּה עַל-הַנְּסָכִים; — *Yochanan ben Pinchas over the tokens; Achiyah over the nesachim;*

Nesachim is used here not only in its literal sense, *libations*, but also to include the flour and oil of the meal offerings. Since libations are never poured without an accompanying meal offering, the entire libation service became known as *nesachim (Rambam,* intro. to *Menachos; Tos. Yom Tov;* see *comm.* to 4:4, s.v. ומותר נסכים). It was Achiyah's duty to assure the availability of wine, oil and flour which had been prepared under optimum conditions of purity (טָהֳרָה). A system of checks and balances separated the responsibilities of selling and stocking supplies. Thus Yochanan administered a cashier's office at which tokens (of four different

1. Since Mordechai (of *Megillas Esther*) is one of the administrators named here, it follows, according to this view, that our mishnah is part of the early body of *mishnayos* preceding R' Yehudah HaNassi's editorship of the Mishnah by some 500 years and points to a very early standardization of the mishnah text (as pointed out here by *Tiferes Yisrael*). For an elaboration of this subject see R' Y. Aisik HaLevi, *Doros HaRishonim,* v. 1, pp. 202-310; *Sefer HaZikaron* for R' Aisik HaLevi, pp. 119-128. Cf. *comm.* s.v. נחוניא and *Mishneh Lechem.*

פְּתַחְיָה עַל־הַקִּנִּין — פְּתַחְיָה זֶה מָרְדְּכָי (לָמָּה
נִקְרָא שְׁמוֹ פְּתַחְיָה? שֶׁהָיָה פּוֹתֵחַ בִּדְבָרִים
וְדוֹרְשָׁן וְיוֹדֵעַ שִׁבְעִים לָשׁוֹן); בֶּן־אֲחִיָה עַל־
חוֹלֵי מֵעַיִם; נְחוּנְיָא, חוֹפֵר שִׁיחִין; גְּבִינִי, כָּרוֹז;

יד אברהם

values) were sold to those obligated to bring *nesachim*. These tokens were redeemed at Achiyah's office where the supplies were actually kept (see below, mishnayos 3-5 for the exact procedure).

Rambam (Hil. Klei HaMikdash 7:9) identifies the administrators in charge of the various materials needed for offerings as the purveyors who would guarantee a maximum price every thirty days (see 4:9), i.e., they were merchants, not professional administrators.

Ravad disagrees and states that they were administrators who kept a supply of their items on hand and replenished their stocks from the aforementioned merchants.

מַתִּתְיָה בֶן־שְׁמוּאֵל עַל־הַפְּיָסוֹת; — *Matisyah ben Shmuel over the lots;*

[We find a Matisyah among those who stood with Ezra as he read the Torah to the assembled nation (*Nehemiah* 8:4). Matisyah ben Shmuel is also mentioned in *Yoma* 3:1.]

Because there were more *Kohanim* wishing to partake in the daily services of the Temple than there were services to perform, lots were used for the apportionment of the services. (See chapt. 2 of *Yoma* for a detailed description of the lots and duties assigned.)

פְּתַחְיָה עַל־הַקִּנִּין — — *Pesachyah over the bird offerings* [lit. *nests*] —

One obligated to bring a pair of birds as part of his cleansing (טָהֳרָה) process, e.g., a *zav*, a *zavah* or a woman after childbirth (see *comm.* to 1:5), did not actually have to bring these birds to the Temple. He could simply drop the needed amount of money into a collection chest (in the Temple) marked קִנִּין", *kinin* [*nests*]" and be certain that his offering would be offered that day; Pesachyah would make certain that by the end of that day, all the money in the

kinin chest had been used and that the birds were offered on the altar (see 6:5 and *Pesachim* 90b).

A great scholar was needed for this post, for complicated halachic problems were posed by mixups which were sure to occur [an entire tractate, *Kinin*, is devoted to resolving these mixups]. As the Mishnah (*Avos* 3:18) states: [*The laws of] fowl offerings ... are essentials of halachah ... (Rav; Rosh)*. *Rambam (Hil. K'lei HaMikdash* 7:10) adds that it was also Pesachyah's obligation to ensure an adequate supply of these birds and (in accordance with his view cited above, s.v. אחיה) to act as the supplier at a prefixed price.

פְּתַחְיָה זֶה מָרְדְּכָי (לָמָּה נִקְרָא שְׁמוֹ פְּתַחְיָה?—
this Pesachyah is Mordechai [*of Megillas Esther;*] *(so why is he called Pesachyah?*

שֶׁהָיָה פּוֹתֵחַ בִּדְבָרִים וְדוֹרְשָׁן — *because he was able to open up* [*mysterious*] *matters and investigate them,*

[פְּתַחְיָה is a compound word formed of the two words פְּתַח יָהּ, *YAH* (one of the Names of God) *has opened.* Mordechai's prowess at opening matters and investigating them transcended the point where it could be attributed merely to his superior mental acuity, it was patently a godly power.]

The Talmud (*Menachos* 64b; also *Yer.* here) relates that once the Pesach festival arrived and the *Beis Din* did not know where to obtain fresh uncut barley for the *Omer* offering [for there had been a blight in the crop (*Yer.;* cf. *Menachos loc. cit.*)]. A mute arrived and motioned by putting one hand upon a roof and the other upon a hut. Said Mordechai to them: Is there a place called, גַּגּוֹת צְרִיפִין, *Gagos Tz'rifin* (lit. *roofs of huts*), or צְרִיפִין גַּגּוֹת, *Tz'rifin Gagos*? They investigated and found [such a place and there they found the needed barley]. The Talmud (*ibid.*) also relates other instances where Mordechai demonstrated his penetrating powers of observation and investigation.

5
1
over the lots; Pesachyah over the bird offerings —
this Pesachyah is Mordechai [of *Megillas Esther;*] (so
why is he called Pesachyah? — because he was able to
open up [mysterious] matters and investigate them,
and he knew seventy languages); Ben Achiyah over
[the treatment of] stomach disorders; Nechunya, the

וְיוֹדֵעַ שִׁבְעִים לָשׁוֹן) — *and he knew seventy languages;*

Because the people purchasing pairs of birds for their offerings came from many countries and spoke many languages it was necessary that this official speak many languages and be very perceptive to prevent misunderstandings *(Taklin Chadatin).*

The phrase 'and he knew seventy languages,' is an additional reason why Mordechai is called Pesachyah. His facility in languages augmented his superior understanding and helped him uncover (i.e. to 'open' up) many a matter which would otherwise have remained sealed.

The Talmud *(Menachos* 65a) comments that it was not unusual for a member of the Sanhedrin[1] to be proficient in languages. Pesachyah's novelty lay in that he could combine many languages (בּוֹלֵל) at once. His mastery over languages was such that he was able to identify phrases and words from diverse languages in one person's speech. Ostensibly, this was a great aid in his position as administrator for thus he could communicate with individuals speaking in polyglot. The Talmud adds that Pesachyah/ Mordechai is the same Mordechai nicknamed בִּלְשָׁן, *Bilshan,* listed in *Ezra* 2:2 and *Nechemiah* 7:7 among the prominent returnees in the *Aliyah* leaded by Zerubavel (eighteen years before the rebuilding of the Second Temple and earlier than the miracle of Purim).[2] The nickname Bilshon is a contraction of בְּלַל לָשׁוֹן, lit. *he mixes languages,* and refers to Mordechai's linguistic prowess.

'Seventy languages' represents all (or most) languages. Before the הַפְלָגָה, *dispersion* of mankind throughout the world, they all had spoken one language *(Genesis* 11:1). At the time the ancients were dispersed and began speaking diverse languages, the Torah counts seventy nations (see *Genesis* ch. 10) speaking seventy languages. These tongues became the foundation for all spoken languages *(Tif. Yis.).*

[It is evident that these administrators were not necessarily *Kohanim,* for Mordechai was a Benjaminite (see *Esther* 2:5). See *Yuchasin Ma'amar* 2, s.v. מתיא; *Seder Hadoros (Seder Tannaim VaAmoraim,* s.v. מתיא). *Tosefta* 2:5 states this clearly, but *Rambam* does not mention this in his code (see especially *Hil. K'lei HaMikdash* 4:19) though he cites the rest of this *Tosefta (Hil. K'lei HaMikdash* 7:17-20).]

בֶּן־אֲחִיָּה עַל־חוֹלִי מֵעַיִם; — *Ben Achiyah over [the treatment of] stomach disorders;*

Kohanim serving in the Temple often suffered from stomach disorders for a variety of reasons:

— Shoes and other footwear may not be worn in either the Temple or the Courtyard. Constant contact with the cold stone floor chilled the *Kohanim* (see *Zevachim* 2:1).

— Only four garments could be worn during the performance of any service. Of the four only a light tunic protected the *Kohen's* body against cold or rain *(Rambam, Hil. K'lei HaMikdash* 7:14).

1. *Rambam* (preface to *Mishneh Torah)* mentions Mordechai as a member of Ezra's Sanhedrin called the 'Great Assembly'. This is also implicit in the comment of the Sages concerning Mordechai that some of his brethren [i.e., colleagues] (see *Esther* 10:3) — the Sanhedrin — disassociated themselves from him when he left the *beis hamidrash* to become a minister in Ahasuerus' cabinet.

2. *Ralbag (Ezra* 2:2) surmises that at first Mordechai remained in *Eretz Yisrael* when the new king ordered a halt to the construction of the Temple. He later left for Shushan in an attempt to persuade Ahasuerus to rescind his decree.

בֶּן־גֶּבֶר עַל־נְעִילַת שְׁעָרִים; בֶּן־בֵּבַי עַל־הַפָּקִיעַ;
בֶּן־אַרְזָה עַל־הַצִּלְצָל; הֻגְרוֹס, בֶּן־לֵוִי, עַל־
הַשִּׁיר; בֵּית גַּרְמוּ עַל־מַעֲשֵׂה לֶחֶם הַפָּנִים; בֵּית
אַבְטִינָס עַל־מַעֲשֵׂה הַקְּטֹרֶת; אֶלְעָזָר עַל־
הַפָּרֹכֶת; וּפִנְחָס עַל־הַמַּלְבּוּשׁ.

יד אברהם

בֶּן־גֶּבֶר עַל־נְעִילַת שְׁעָרִים — *Ben Gever over the locking of the gates;*

He would make sure that the gates were locked at night and opened in the morning (*Rav; Rosh;* cf. *Rambam*).

He oversaw the locking of the gates — at his command they would lock and at his command they would open. The trumpeters would not sound the three shofar blasts (*tekiah, teruah, tekiah*) which accompanied the opening of the gates until he gave permission (*Rambam, Hil. K'lei HaMikdash* 7:3; see *Succah* 5:5).

בֶּן־בֵּבַי עַל־הַפָּקִיעַ — *Ben Bevai over the whip;*

Kohanim and Levites would stand watch in twenty-four places in the Temple each night. *Ben Bevai* would make his rounds checking that the sentinels did not fall asleep on their watch. Any found sleeping would be awakened with a lashing. This administrator was also empowered to burn the blanket under which the watchmen was sleeping (*Middos* 1:1-2; see *Tif. Yis.* there; *Rav; Rosh; Rambam*). [In *Middos* this official is called אִישׁ הַר הַבַּיִת, *Master of the Temple Mount.*]

The above interpretation is based on the conclusion reached by *Yoma* 23a. The interpretation accepted by *Yerushalmi* (here) but rejected by the Talmud *Bavli* (ibid.) is that פָּקִיעַ refers to the making of wicks. *Ravad* (*Hil. K'lei HaMikdash* 7:1) apparently assumes that the Talmud does not totally reject that there was a wickmaker's office. *Tosefta* 2:14 mentions other administrators not found in our mishnah. *Tos. Yom Tov* suggests that according to *Ravad* this was part of the administrator 'over the whip'. *Tiferes Yisrael* explains according to *Rambam*, that since only seven wicks were

— A steady diet of sacrificial meats with only water to drink [wine may not be drunk in the Temple environs (*R' Shlomo Sirilio*) nor may certain sacrificial meat be removed from the Courtyard].

Ben Achiyah, who was knowledgeable in herbal medicine, was charged with treating these disorders (*Rav* from *Rosh* and *Yer.*; our editions have a slightly different version).

נְחוּנְיָא, חוֹפֵר שִׁיחִין — *Nechunya, the digger of pits;*

Nechunya administered the digging of reservoirs to ensure a plentiful water supply for the pilgrims (*Rav; Yer.*).

[Nechunya is mentioned twice in the Talmud (*Bava Kamma* 51b; *Yevamos* 121b) where it is indicated that he lived in the late Second Temple era (*Seder Tannaim Va-Amoraim* s.v. מתיא). However this does not contradict the view that the administrators mentioned here belong to the early Second Temple era because, as already pointed out, all the administrators would assume the first administrator's name. In the story related in the Talmud, Nechunya figures as the supplier of water, so he is mentioned by his official name.]

גְּבִינִי, כָּרוֹז — *Gevini, the crier;*

Every morning at daybreak Gevini would awaken the *Kohanim* with the call, "Arise to your services, you *Kohanim*." His voice was so powerful that it could be heard three *parsa* (24,000 cubits) away (*Yer.; Yoma* 20b).

Rambam (*Hil. K'lei HaMikdash* 7:2) describes this official as 'administrator over the schedule,' with the responsibility to announce at the proper time that such or such an offering should now be offered.

5
1

digger of pits; Gevini, the crier; Ben Gever over the locking of the gates; Ben Bevai over the whip; Ben Arzah over the cymbal; Hugros, a Levite, over the singing; the Garmu family over the preparation of the *Panim* Bread; the Avtinas family over the preparation of the incense; Elazar over the curtain; and Pinchas over the vestments.

YAD AVRAHAM

needed daily in the Temple, the job did not warrant the appointment of a separate administrator.

[The children (i.e., family or clan) of Bevai are mentioned among the returnees with Zerubavel *(Ezra* 2:11; *Nechemiah* 7:16).]

בֶּן־אַרְזָה עַל־הַצִּלְצָל; — *Ben Arzah over the cymbal;*

As related in *Tamid* (7:3), Ben Arzah would sound the cymbals as a signal for the Levites to begin singing *(Rav; Rosh* from *Yer.).*

He is the one who appointed the members of the orchestra which accompanied the Levites [who sing vocally] *(Hil. K'lei HaMikdash* 7:7).

הַגְרוֹס, בֶּן־לֵוִי, עַל־הַשִּׁיר; — *Hugros, a Levite, over the singing;*

[See *Yoma* 3:11] every day when the libation accompanying the daily offering (תָּמִיד) was poured, the Levites would sing to instrumental accompaniment. Hugros taught and conducted the choir of singers who stood on the *duchan* (a platform in the Temple court constructed for this purpose; *Rav; Rosh; Tif. Yis.*).

The shofar would be sounded at his command during the offering of the sacrifices (see *Succah* 5:5; *Rambam, Hil. K'lei HaMikdash* 7:5).

בֵּית גַּרְמוּ עַל־מַעֲשֵׂה לֶחֶם הַפָּנִים; — *the Garmu family over the preparation of the Panim Bread;*

[See *comm.* 4:1, s.v. לחם פנים, for a description of these breads and their place in the Temple service.] The Garmu family were privy to the recipe and manner of baking these breads, a very difficult process which no other

bakers were able to duplicate *(Rav;* see *Yoma* 3:11).

בֵּית אַבְטִינָס עַל־מַעֲשֵׂה הַקְּטֹרֶת; — *The Avtinas family over the preparation of the incense;*

Every day, morning and evening, incense was burned upon the inner altar. The incense had to be prepared according to the prescription set forth in Scripture *(Exodus* 30:34-38) and transmitted orally by the Sages. [See *comm.* beginning of 4:5.]

This family had the secret of a special herb, מַעֲלֶה עָשָׁן, *Ma'aleh Ashan* [lit. *raises smoke*], which, when blended with the incense, caused the smoke to rise in a straight column rather than spread in all directions *(Rav;* see *Yoma* 3:11).

אֶלְעָזָר עַל־הַפָּרֹכֶת; — *Elazar over the curtain;*

Elazar was responsible for the condition of the curtains in the Temple compound. He would remove and replace old, worn ones *(Rav; Rosh)* and supervise the weaving of new ones *(Rambam, Hil. K'lei HaMikdash* 7:16).

Thirteen curtains were used in the Temple: one for each of the seven gates of the Temple Courtyard (see *Middos* 1:4), one for that of the Ante-Chamber (אוּלָם), one for the gate of the Sanctuary (הֵיכָל), two between the Holy and the Holy of Holies (see *Yoma* 5:1), and another pair (see *Middos* 4:5 with *Tos. Yom Tov)* directly above these last two in the second story of the Temple *(Yoma* 54a).

The curtains between the Holy and the Holy of Holies would be replaced with new ones every year (see below 8:5).

וּפִנְחָס עַל־הַמַּלְבּוּשׁ. — *and Pinchas over the vestments.*

He was appointed to dress the *Kohen*

שקלים ה/ב **[ב] אֵין** פּוֹחֲתִין מִשְּׁלֹשָׁה גִזְבָּרִין וּמִשִּׁבְעָה
אֲמַרְכָּלִין. וְאֵין עוֹשִׂין שְׂרָרָה עַל־
הַצִּבּוּר בְּמָמוֹן פָּחוֹת מִשְּׁנַיִם, חוּץ מִבֶּן־אֲחִיָּה
שֶׁעַל־חוֹלֵי מֵעַיִם וְאֶלְעָזָר שֶׁעַל־הַפָּרֹכוֹת,
שֶׁאוֹתָן קִבְּלוּ רֹב הַצִּבּוּר עֲלֵיהֶן.

ה/ג **[ג] אַרְבָּעָה** חוֹתָמוֹת הָיוּ בַּמִּקְדָּשׁ. וְכָתוּב
עֲלֵיהֶן ,,עֵגֶל׳׳, ,,זָכָר׳׳, ,,גְּדִי׳׳,
,,חוֹטֵא׳׳.

יד אברהם

Gadol in his special vestments (בִּגְדֵי כְּהוּנָה) and to undress him after the service *(Yer.).* A special chamber was set aside for storing the vestments [לִשְׁכַּת פִּנְחָס הַמַּלְבִּישׁ; *Middos* 1:4] *(Rav; Rosh).*

Rambam (Comm.) adds that the manufacture of these vestments was also the responsibility of this administrator. In his code he lists this as his sole function. *R' Shlomo Sirilio* and *R' Meshullam* interpret the *Yerushalmi* in accord with *Rambam.*

2.

אֵין פּוֹחֲתִין מִשְּׁלֹשָׁה גִזְבָּרִין — *There may not be less than three treasurers [in the Temple]*

Most Temple funds were under the supervision of these treasurers. They collected all consecrated property, supervised the redemption of pledged materials, and designated the money for appropriate purposes *(Ramban, Hil. K'lei HaMikdash* 4:18; *Rav, Rosh,* from *Tosefta* 2:15).

וּמִשִּׁבְעָה אֲמַרְכָּלִין. — *nor [less than] seven superiors.*

These superiors were the supervisors of the treasurers. The seven keys to the Temple Courtyard [probably the treasury chambers; cf. *Tamid* 1:1 *and Mishneh LaMelech Hil. K'lei HaMikdash* 4:17] were in their possession. The locks could not be opened unless all the superiors were present. The superiors opened the doors and the treasurers entered to withdraw the needed amounts *(Rav; Rosh; Tosefta* 2:15; *Rambam, Hil. K'lei HaMikdash* 4:18).

Tosefta (2:16) states that אֲמַרְכָּל is a contraction of מַר עַל־הַכֹּל, lit. *master over*

everything. Similarly, the Talmud *(Horayos* 13a) says it is a contraction of אָמַר כֹּל, lit. *he says everything.*

To round out the Temple hierarchy, they appoint a *Kohen* called the סְגָן, *deputy,* who serves the *Kohen Gadol* as a viceroy serves the king; ... all the *Kohanim* are under the deputy's supervision. They also appoint not less than two *katholikin,* (overseers) who supervise the entire household, and are empowered to act according to their own judgment [*Mossaf HeAruch, s.v.* קתליכוס]. These latter serve the deputy as the deputy serves the *Kohen Gadol (Rambam, Hil. K'lei HaMikdash* 4:6-17 from *Yer.* and *Horayos* 13a).

Yerushalmi notes that the organization of the Temple hierarchy set forth here is patterned on that described in Scripture *(II Chronicles* 31:13) under the rule of King Hezekiah.

וְאֵין עוֹשִׂין שְׂרָרָה עַל־הַצִּבּוּר בְּמָמוֹן פָּחוֹת מִשְּׁנַיִם, — *Nor may financial authority be set up over the community with less than two [officers],*

[Any official body that has the authority to enforce compliance with its ruling must have at least two members to avoid capricious decisions by an individual.]

5
2

2. There may not be less than three treasurers [in the Temple] nor [less than] seven superiors. Nor may financial authority be set up over the community with less than two [officers], except for Achiyah who was in charge of [the treatment of] stomach disorders and Elazar who was in charge of the curtains, because most of the community accepted them over itself.

5
3

3. There were four [different] tokens in the Temple. Inscribed upon them were [the Hebrew words for] "calf", "ram", "kid", "sinner" [respectively].

YAD AVRAHAM

Yerushalmi (also Bava Basra 8b) derives this rule from the verse (in reference to the collection of materials for the building of the Sanctuary, Exodus 28:5): And they (plural) shall receive the gold and the silver ...
The Talmud (ibid.) explains that because these officers are empowered to resort to force when necessary (e.g., forcible collection of unredeemed pledges) they are considered to be controlling financial affairs.

חוּץ מִבֶּן־אֲחִיָּה שֶׁעַל־חוֹלֵי מֵעַיִם וְאֶלְעָזָר שֶׁעַל־הַפָּרכוֹת, — except for Achiyah who was in charge of [the treatment of] stomach disorders and Elazar who was in charge of the curtains,
[These officers, too, because they involved the expenditure of communal money are considered to be in control of financial affairs. Nevertheless one officer was sufficient to administer these functions.]

שֶׁאוֹתָן קִבְּלוּ רֹב הַצִּבּוּר עֲלֵיהֶן. — because most of the community accepted them over itself.
[But the others, though legally appointed by the Temple administration, were not as popular with the community.]
Tosefos Yom Tov points to the other financial jurisdictions, e.g., Pesachyah over the bird offerings and Nechunya, digger of pits, who operated singly without special approval by most of the community. Yesh Seder LaMishnah remarks (as does R' Shlomo Sirilio and Taklin Chadatin) that the other administrators were in compliance with this rule because they had assistants. This is attested to by Rambam (whose source may be our mishnah) who states (Hil. K'lei HaMikdash 7:2): Every one of these administrators had under him many people ... [See other resolutions of this question in Tif. Yis.; Hon Ashir; Teshuvos Sha'ar Ephrayim; and Mareh HaPanim.]

3.

אַרְבָּעָה חוֹתָמוֹת הָיוּ בַּמִּקְדָּשׁ. — There were four [different] tokens [lit. seals] in the Temple.
One obligated to bring nesachim (the meal offering and libation accompanying each burnt and peace offering, and the three animal offerings of a metzora) would purchase a token from Yochanan's office and bring it to Achiyah's office for redemption (see mishnah 4).
[Since the amounts of wine, oil and flour used for the nesachim varied with the animal they accompanied, four tokens were used, representing respectively each possible nesachim.]

— וְכָתוּב עֲלֵיהֶן ,,עֵגֶל'', ,,זָכָר'', ,,גְּדִי'', Inscribed upon them were [the Hebrew words for] "calf", "ram", "kid",
The עֵגֶל, calf, token was used to purchase the nesachim accompanying a cattle offering, and consisting of three

שקלים בֶּן־עַזַּאי אוֹמֵר: חֲמִשָּׁה הָיוּ; וַאֲרַמִּית כָּתוּב
ה/ג עֲלֵיהֶן ,,עֵגֶל'', ,,זָכָר'', ,,גְּדִי'', ,,חוֹטֵא דַל''
וְ,,חוֹטֵא עָשִׁיר''.
,,עֵגֶל'' מְשַׁמֵּשׁ עִם נִסְכֵּי בָקָר, גְּדוֹלִים
וּקְטַנִּים, זְכָרִים וּנְקֵבוֹת.

יד אברהם

esronim[1] of fine flour, half a hin[2] of oil and half a hin of wine.

The זָכָר, ram, [lit. male] token used for a ram offering, was redeemed for two esronim of fine flour, a third of a hin of oil and a third of a hin of wine. The Hebrew word זָכָר means male but is used here to represent דְּכַר, the Aramaic word for both male and ram (Rav; Rosh; Rambam). The same usage appears in Rosh Hashanah 3:5 (Tos. Yom Tov).

The גְּדִי, kid, token used for a goat or a sheep offering, bought one isaron of fine flour, a quarter hin of oil and a quarter hin of wine. [Although גְּדִי has been rendered kid it often is used to include all sheep, goats and sometimes even cows. See Genesis 38:17; Chullin 113b. See also chart at end of this mishnah.] The amounts listed above are given in Numbers 15:1-16.

These three nesachim would accompany all the burnt and peace offerings of the respective animals. However, bird offerings never require nesachim and sin and guilt offerings are not accompanied by nesachim except in the cleansing service of the metzora [see below, s.v. חוטא] (Rambam, Comm.).

⧉ Metzora

צָרַעַת, tzara'as, is an affliction mentioned in the Torah. The person stricken with this affliction is known as a מְצֹרָע, metzora, or צָרוּעַ tzarua. The symptoms of this ailment are white spots which appear on the skin (Leviticus 13:1-46). Although tzara'as is usually translated as leprosy, the symptoms described by Scripture are not those of leprosy. Moreover, the spontaneous cure mentioned in connection with tzara'as is unknown as a cure for leprosy.

From the case of the prophetess Miriam, who was stricken with tzara'as for speaking disrespectfully about her brother Moses, the Sages derive that this ailment is a punishment for לְשׁוֹן הָרָע, slander (see Numbers 12:1-16 and commentaries). The Torah exhorts us to remember what God did to Miriam and to beware of the plague of tzara'as (Deuteronomy 24:8,9). The metzora is called חוטא, sinner, because the Talmud (Arachim 16a) states that the affliction of tzara'as is visited upon people as punishment for seven sins (Rav; Rosh; Rambam).

,,חוטא'', — "sinner" [respectively].

This token was used by a well-to-do metzora (מְצֹרָע עָשִׁיר) whose cleansing included the sacrifice of three offerings — all lambs — accompanied by three nesachim. His total requirement was three esronim of fine flour, ten log of olive oil, (three to mix into each of the three flour offerings, and the tenth to be smeared on the metzora's right thumb and right big toe), and nine log of wine (see Leviticus 14:10-17; Rambam, Hil. Ma'asei HaKorbanos 2:6). [See also chart at end of this mishnah.]

1. The isaron, lit. tenth [of an ephah] (plural esronim) is a measure of the volume displaced by 43.2 average eggs [estimates of conversions range from 86 to 172 fluid ounces].

2. The hin, a liquid measure found in Scripture, contains twelve log. Each log displaces the volume of six average eggs. Thus half a hin equals six log or thirty-six eggs; a third of a hin, four log or twenty-four eggs; and a quarter hin, three log or eighteen eggs.

5
3

Ben Azzai says: There were five; and inscribed upon them were [the] Aramaic [words for] "calf", "ram", "kid", "indigent sinner", "wealthy sinner". [The] "calf" [token] serves for *nesachim* of cattle, adult or young, male or female.

Tiferes Yisrael maintains that the word חוטא here should be translated *cleansed one* as in וְחִטֵּא אֶת־הַבַּיִת, *he shall cleanse the house (Leviticus* 14:52). [See *Onkelos* there; see also *Numbers* 19:9,12 with *Rashi* and *Ibn Ezra.*]

בֶּן־עַזַּאי אוֹמֵר: חֲמִשָּׁה הָיוּ; — Ben Azzai says: *There were five* [tokens]; [As listed further.]

וַאֲרָמִית כָּתוּב עֲלֵיהֶן — *and inscribed upon them were* [the] *Aramaic* [words for]

Because Aramaic was the most commonly used language [in the Second Temple era] *(Rav, Rosh).*

To prevent mistakes or misunderstandings the tokens were imprinted in a language readily understood by the buyers *(Tos. Yom Tov).*

Ben Azzai does not necessarily disagree with R' Yishmael's view (above 3:2) that the withdrawal baskets were marked with Greek letters. The prevalent language was Aramaic and this was used in transactions with the masses. The withdrawal baskets were handled by the elite of the Temple administration, who could be expected to recognize the letters of the Greek alphabet although this was not the primary language of the country. *Rav* (there) says merely that 'they were proficient (רְגִילִין) in Greek', not that it was the common language *(Tos. Yom Tov).*

[Ben Azzai's view also does not contradict the first tanna in 3:2, who holds that the baskets were inscribed with Hebrew letters. Even the common people, whose spoken language was primarily Aramaic, wrote it with the Hebrew alphabet, just as Yiddish and Ladino are written in the Hebrew alphabet. Similarly *Rambam, R' Saadyah Gaon* and the other sages wrote Arabic works in the Hebrew alphabet; so, too, *Rashi's* translations into French. The Aramaic *Targumim,* as well as both Talmudim, the Babylonian and Yerushalmi, are testimony to this (cf. *Tos. Yom Tov*).]

„עֵגֶל״, „זָכָר״, „גְּדִי״, „חוֹטָא דַל״ וְ„חוֹטָא עָשִׁיר״. — *"calf", "ram", "kid", "indigent sinner", "wealthy sinner".*

Ben Azzai adds an additional token for the indigent *metzora* whose sacrifice differed in that he offered only one animal, a sheep guilt offering; — his burnt and sin offerings were birds, which do not require *nesachim*. Thus, the indigent *metzora* could not use the token "sinner" and an "indigent sinner" token was needed. The Sages disagree, holding that the "kid" token could serve the indigent *metzora* since it indicated the *nesachim* needed for a sheep *(Rav; Rosh; Rambam; Yer., Tosefta* 2:6).

Ben Azzai maintained that the *"kid"* token could not fulfill the requirements of the indigent *metzora,* for he needed an additional *log* of oil to be smeared upon his right ear lobe, etc. *(Yer.).*

According to the Sages the indigent *metzora* was permitted to supply this *log* from his own funds, thereby saving him the possible difference in price between oil produced at his home, and that for sale at the Temple *(Taklin Chadatin;* cf. *Tos. Yom Tov* and *comm.* to *Yer.* especially *Korban HaEdah).*

The halachah follows the first tanna *(Rav; Rambam, Hil. K'lei HaMikdash* 7:11).

[The mishnah now articulates the specific animals represented by each of these tokens. This section of the mishnah follows the view of the first tanna, and enumerates only four tokens.]

„עֵגֶל״ מְשַׁמֵּשׁ עִם נִסְכֵּי בָקָר, גְּדוֹלִים וּקְטַנִּים, זְכָרִים וּנְקֵבוֹת. — [The] *"calf"* [token] *serves for* [lit. *with*] *nesachim of cattle, adult or young, male or female.*

Unlike sheep, whose *nesachim* depend on the age and sex of the particular animal, all cattle require the same *nesachim*.

This differentiation is based on the verse

,,גְּדִי'' מְשַׁמֵּשׁ עִם נִסְכֵּי צֹאן, גְּדוֹלִים
וּקְטַנִּים, זְכָרִים וּנְקֵבוֹת, חוּץ מִשֶּׁל אֵילִים.
,,זָכָר'' מְשַׁמֵּשׁ עִם נִסְכֵּי אֵילִים בִּלְבָד.
,,חוֹטֵא'' מְשַׁמֵּשׁ עִם נִסְכֵּי שָׁלֹשׁ בְּהֵמוֹת שֶׁל
מְצֹרָעִין.

[ד] **מִי** שֶׁהוּא מְבַקֵּשׁ נְסָכִים הוֹלֵךְ לוֹ אֵצֶל
יוֹחָנָן, שֶׁהוּא מְמֻנֶּה עַל־הַחוֹתָמוֹת,
נוֹתֵן לוֹ מָעוֹת וּמְקַבֵּל מִמֶּנּוּ חוֹתָם. בָּא לוֹ אֵצֶל
אֲחִיָּה, שֶׁהוּא מְמֻנֶּה עַל־הַנְּסָכִים, וְנוֹתֵן לוֹ
חוֹתָם וּמְקַבֵּל מִמֶּנּוּ נְסָכִים.

יד אברהם

(Numbers 15:11): So shall be done with the one ox or with the one ram or with the young of the sheep or of the goats. From the words לְשׁוֹר הָאֶחָד, the one ox, is derived that, regarding nesachim, all members of the cattle family are the same, regardless of age or sex. אוֹ לָאַיִל הָאֶחָד, or with the one ram, teaches that all rams [i.e., male sheep] older than a year are the same. אוֹ־לַשֶּׂה כְבָשִׂים, or with the young of the sheep [plural], alludes to the fact that although male sheep are divided according to age, the nesachim of all female sheep are the same. Finally, אוֹ בָעִזִּים, or with the goats, means that although the nesachim of adult rams differs from that of ewes and lambs, nevertheless, adult billy goats, nanny goats and kids all require the same nesachim (Yer.; Bavli, Menachos 91b).

חוֹתָם TOKEN	מְשַׁמֵּשׁ SERVES	סֹלֶת FINE FLOUR	שֶׁמֶן OIL	יַיִן WINE
עֵגֶל CALF	BURNT AND PEACE OFFERINGS OF CATTLE	3 ESRONIM	½ HIN=6 LOG	½ HIN=6 LOG
זָכָר RAM	BURNT AND PEACE OFFERINGS OF ADULT RAMS	2 ESRONIM	⅓ HIN=4 LOG	⅓ HIN=4 LOG
גְּדִי KID	BURNT AND PEACE OFFERINGS OF GOATS, EWES, LAMBS	1 ISARON	¼ HIN=3 LOG	¼ HIN=3 LOG
חוֹטֵא SINNER	MALE LAMB (GUILT OFFERING)	1 ISARON	¼ HIN=3 LOG	¼ HIN=3 LOG
	FEMALE LAMB (SIN OFFERING)	1 ISARON	¼ HIN=3 LOG	¼ HIN=3 LOG
	MALE LAMB (BURNT OFFERING)	1 ISARON	¼ HIN=3 LOG	¼ HIN=3 LOG
	PLACED ON RIGHT EAR AND THUMB OF METZORA		1 LOG	
	TOTAL	3 ESRONIM	10 LOG	9 LOG

[The] "kid" [token] serves for *nesachim* of the flock, adult or young, male or female, except for adult rams.

[The] "ram" [token] serves for *nesachim* of rams only.

[The] "sinner" [token] serves for *nesachim* of the three animals [comprising the offering] of *metzoraim*.

4. Whoever required *nesachim* would go to Yochanan, administrator over the tokens, give him money and receive a token from him. [Then] he would come to Achiyah, administrator over the *nesachim*, give him the token and receive *nesachim* from him.

YAD AVRAHAM

„גְּדִי'' מְשַׁמֵּשׁ עִם נִסְכֵּי צֹאן, גְּדוֹלִים וּקְטַנִּים, זְכָרִים וּנְקֵבוֹת, חוּץ מִשֶּׁל אֵילִים. — [The] 'kid' [token] serves for [lit. with] nesachim of the flock, adult or young, male or female, except for adult rams.

[The term צֹאן, flock, includes sheep and goats. See above, s.v. עֵגֶל, for the Scriptural basis for the differentiation between adult rams and other animals of the flock.]

„זָכָר'' מְשַׁמֵּשׁ עִם נִסְכֵּי אֵילִים בִּלְבָד. — [The] "ram" [token] serves for [lit. with] nesachim of rams only.

[As described above, s.v. עֵגֶל.]

„חוֹטֵא'' מְשַׁמֵּשׁ עִם נִסְכֵּי שָׁלֹשׁ בְּהֵמוֹת שֶׁל מְצֹרָעִין. — [The] "sinner" [token] serves for [lit. with] nesachim of the three animals [comprising the offering] of metzoraim.

[See chart.]

4.

מִי שֶׁהוּא מְבַקֵּשׁ נְסָכִים הוֹלֵךְ לוֹ אֵצֶל יוֹחָנָן, שֶׁהוּא מְמֻנֶּה עַל-הַחוֹתָמוֹת, נוֹתֵן לוֹ מָעוֹת — Whoever required [lit. requested] nesachim would go to Yochanan, administrator over the tokens, give him money

The payment depended on the type of offering (sheep ram, or cattle) and number of nesachim it needed (Rav).

וּמְקַבֵּל מִמֶּנּוּ חוֹתָם. — and receive a token from him.

[I.e., he received a slip of parchment stamped with the information indicated (see Rambam cited below, s.v. ואחיה מוציא).]

בָּא לוֹ אֵצֶל אֲחִיָּה, שֶׁהוּא מְמֻנֶּה עַל-הַנְּסָכִים. — וְנוֹתֵן לוֹ חוֹתָם וּמְקַבֵּל מִמֶּנּוּ נְסָכִים. [Then] he would come to Achiyah, administrator over the nesachim [see mishnah 1, s.v. אחיה], give him the token, and receive [the materials for] nesachim from him.

This system was instituted to spare the people the difficult task of preparing these nesachim according to all the stringent safeguards against contamination, for even though the wine, oil and flour had not yet been consecrated, it would have been necessary to prepare them as if they were already sacred [עַל טָהֳרַת הַקֹּדֶשׁ] (Rav; Rosh).

וְלָעֶרֶב בָּאִין זֶה אֵצֶל זֶה; וַאֲחִיָּה מוֹצִיא אֶת־
הַחוֹתָמוֹת וּמְקַבֵּל כְּנֶגְדָּן מָעוֹת. וְאִם הוֹתִירוּ,
הוֹתִירוּ לַהֶקְדֵּשׁ; וְאִם פָּחֲתוּ, הָיָה מְשַׁלֵּם יוֹחָנָן
מִבֵּיתוֹ — שֶׁיַּד הֶקְדֵּשׁ עַל־הָעֶלְיוֹנָה.

יד אברהם

וְלָעֶרֶב בָּאִין זֶה אֵצֶל זֶה; וַאֲחִיָּה מוֹצִיא אֶת־
הַחוֹתָמוֹת — *In the evening they* [i.e., Yo-chanan and Achiyah] *would meet* [lit. *they come one to the other*]; *Achiyah would take out the tokens* [i.e., show them to Yochanan]

He would use the stamped slips as proof of the number of *nesachim* he had distributed, for these slips were in Yochanan's handwriting[1] (*Rambam*, ed. *Kafich*).

וּמְקַבֵּל כְּנֶגְדָּן מָעוֹת. — *and receive* [the] *corresponding* [amount of] *money.*

[He would receive payment for each token according to the price set every thirty days as mentioned previously (4:9).]

וְאִם הוֹתִירוּ,הוֹתִירוּ לַהֶקְדֵּשׁ; — *If they had anything left over, it belonged to the Temple* [treasury] [lit. *if they left over they left over to the Temple treasury*];

[If Yochanan found that he had taken in money in excess of the *nesachim* distributed by *Achiyah* the excess amount goes to the Temple treasury (i.e., it goes toward the purchase of burnt offerings; see below).] We do not assume that the surplus was Yochanan's private money which became mixed in with the money from the sale of tokens (*Rav; Rosh*).

Rather, the excess could be attributed to a number of reasons: Someone wishing to make an anonymous donation may have overpaid [or perhaps bought a token but left it unredeemed]

(Tos. Yom Tov); or someone may have mistakenly overpaid *(R' Meshullam)*; or lost his token *(Meiri).*[2]

Rambam, holding to his view (see above, s.v. אחיה) that the administrator over *nesachim* was actually a merchant supplying these materials to the Temple, and that it was with him that the price was fixed (4:9), understands that this 'remainder' is due to a difference between the pre-fixed price and the market price. As explained above, the supplier had to continue to supply at the fixed price even if the market price had risen at the time of delivery. Thus, in such a situation, though the person paying for a token would pay the prevailing price, Yochanan would pay Achiyah only the lower, pre-fixed price thus leaving a remainder of money. This is then another instance of 'remainder of *nesachim*' which the mishnah 4:4 previously designated for the purchase of burnt offerings (קִיץ הַמִּזְבֵּחַ).

According to *Ravad's* view, since Achiyah's function was only administrative — he merely delivered the materials needed for *nesachim* to the purchasers of the tokens and was not involved in their sale on a profit basis — the remainder discussed here cannot be the result of a change in price and must be explained as it is by *Rav* and *Rosh* (who seem to share *Ravad's* view). However, since this remainder is also used toward the purchase of burnt offerings, it may be included in the term 'remainder of *nesachim*' in 4:4 *(Tos. Yom Tov).*

וְאִם פָּחֲתוּ, — *but if there was a shortage,*

[If the money held by Yochanan was insufficient to redeem the tokens held by Achiyah, indicating that Yochanan

---

1. *Rambam's* comment does not necessarily mean that the stamped slips were actually signed by Yochanan. The reference to Yochanan's handwriting may refer to the date which was written on them as related in mishnah 5.

2. [*Tosefos Yom Tov* and *Meiri* do not attribute the surplus to a mistaken overpayment; if someone had indeed paid in error, they would presumably classify such money as belonging to its original owner, and it must be returned. *R' Meshullam*, on the other hand, assumes that upon discovering his mistake, the payer will relinquish his ownership (מִיְאֵשׁ וּמַחֲלִי) to the Temple treasury.]

In the evening they would meet; Achiyah would take out the tokens and receive [the] corresponding [amount of] money. If they had anything left over, it belonged to the Temple [treasury]; but if there was a shortage, Yochanan would pay [the difference] from his own funds — for the Temple [treasury] has the upper hand.

YAD AVRAHAM

had lost some of the money, had failed to collect the appropriate amount, or had been guilty of some other lapse.]

[In this situation, even *Rambam* will attribute the loss to error. If the price had fallen, the supplier would have to supply at the lower price as set forth in 4:5.]

הָיָה מְשַׁלֵּם יוֹחָנָן מִבֵּיתוֹ — *Yochanan would* [have to] *pay* [*the difference*] *from his own funds* [lit. *from his house*]

[Since the money had been given him for safekeeping, he was responsible for it like any other paid watchman (שׁוֹמֵר שָׂכָר) would be.]

[There is some difficulty with this rule: (a) Nowhere do we find that the administrators were paid (though probably they were); and a voluntary watchman not receiving pay (שׁוֹמֵר חִנָּם) is not responsible for loss or theft (*Shevuos* 8:1; see comm. to 2:1); (b) the laws pertaining to watchmen do not apply to Temple property (*Bava Metzia* 4:9; *Hil. Sechiros* 2:1); even a paid watchman need not pay the Temple for theft or loss.

Perhaps an explicit condition was made with the administrator that he be responsible for loss. Such an agreement, if formalized by a legalizing act (קִנְיָן; a piece of cloth or a utensil is given by the קוֹנֶה, *acquirer*, here the Temple treasury, to the giver; see *Ketzos HaChoshen* 66:47), is binding (*Choshen Mishpat* 304:4; see *Ketzos HaChoshen* and *Nesivos HaMisphat* there).

Moreover it is the opinion of *R' Aharon ibn Sasson* (*Teshuvos* 73 cited by *R' Akiva Eiger* in his glosses to *Choshen Mishpat* 6-6:40) and *R' Yonasan Eibeschutz* (*Tumim* there 67) that a Rabbinical statute (תַּקָּנָה) provides for payment to the Temple wherever such payment would be required in a civil case.

Another possibility is that the discovery of an unexplained discrepancy is considered a loss through negligence (פְּשִׁיעָה). If one gave an article to a watchman and when he asked

to return the article the watchman could not locate it, this is considered negligence (*Bava Metzia* 35a; *Choshen Mishpat* 291:7). *Rambam* (*Hil. Sechiros* 2:3; see *Ravad* there; *Choshen Mishpat* 66:40; *Shach* there 126) rules that a watchman is liable for negligence even to the Temple treasury.

Another avenue to be explored is the status of the money. Is it חֻלִּין *non-consecrated* (as suggested by *R' Meshullam's* comment, p. 55, s.v. ישלם) in the interim between reception of the token by the buyer and his purchase of *nesachim*, or is it consecrated forthwith? This seems to depend upon the status of the *nesachim* prior to the purchase. If they are consecrated they must be redeemed with nonconsecrated funds. According to *Ravad* the administrator bought the *nesachim* from the supplier with consecrated funds from the 'appropriation', thus they were consecrated in the transaction and had to be redeemed with nonconsecrated money. If, however, the administrator for *nesachim* was a merchant contracting to sell *nesachim* for the Temple, the *nesachim* were nonconsecrated, and could consequently be bought with consecrated or nonconsecrated funds, but the comment of the mishnah (here and 4:9) 'the Temple treasury has the upper hand' shows that the Temple treasury is involved in this transaction. If the money was nonconsecrated in the interim, the administrator would be viewed as a watchman for the buyer — an ordinary person — and would thus be subject to the laws involving civilians.]

שֶׁיַּד הֶקְדֵּשׁ עַל־הָעֶלְיוֹנָה. — *for the Temple* [*treasury*] *has the upper hand.*

If this were a transaction between two laymen, Yochanan would have to pay in the latter case. However, he would keep the excess in the former. Here because the Temple treasury is involved, he does not profit in the former case (*Tif. Yis.*).

מִי **[ה]** שֶׁאָבַד מִמֶּנּוּ חוֹתָמוֹ מַמְתִּינִין לוֹ עַד
הָעֶרֶב. אִם מָצְאוּ לוֹ כְּדֵי חוֹתָמוֹ,
נוֹתְנִין לוֹ; וְאִם לָאו, לֹא הָיָה לוֹ.
וְשֵׁם הַיּוֹם כָּתוּב עֲלֵיהֶן מִפְּנֵי הָרַמָּאִין.

[ו] שְׁתֵּי לְשָׁכוֹת הָיוּ בַּמִּקְדָּשׁ: אַחַת
"לִשְׁכַּת חֲשָׁאִים"; וְאַחַת "לִשְׁכַּת
הַכֵּלִים".

"לִשְׁכַּת חֲשָׁאִים" — יִרְאֵי חֵטְא נוֹתְנִים
לְתוֹכָהּ בַּחֲשַׁאי, וַעֲנִיִּים בְּנֵי טוֹבִים מִתְפַּרְנְסִים
מִתּוֹכָהּ בַּחֲשַׁאי.

יד אברהם

5.

מִי שֶׁאָבַד מִמֶּנּוּ חוֹתָמוֹ מַמְתִּינִין לוֹ עַד הָעֶרֶב.
— *If someone lost his token* [lit. *from him*] *they would have him wait until the evening.*

At evening Yochanan and Achiyah would meet [see previous mishnah] and see if Achiyah had received enough tokens to account for all the money received by Yochanan (*Rav; Rosh*).

אִם מָצְאוּ לוֹ כְּדֵי חוֹתָמוֹ, — *If they found [surplus funds] for him corresponding to his token,*

If Yochanan had extra money matching the value of the lost token (*Rav*).

נוֹתְנִין לוֹ; — *they would give him [his nesachim];*

[It is assumed that the excess money was paid for the lost unredeemed token.]

Rambam (*Comm.* and *Meiri*) stipulates that the excess amount must correspond exactly to the value of the token; it may be neither less nor more.

If the excess is greater than the cost of the token, we assume that it was someone else who erred or donated money (see above, s.v. ואם הותירו). Thus, while it is possible that the excess is due to the unredeemed token *plus* some other error or contribution, we cannot

know with surety that any part of it should belong to the loser of the token.]

וְאִם לָאו, לֹא הָיָה לוֹ. — *but if not* [i.e., if there was no remainder or the extra amount did not correspond to the worth of the token], *nothing was [given] to him* [lit. *there was not for him*].

[His allegation that he lost a token must be discounted.]

וְשֵׁם הַיּוֹם כָּתוּב עֲלֵיהֶן — *They were inscribed with the date* [lit. *the name of the day was written on them*]

The date, month and the year (*Rav; Rosh*; cf. *Gem.*). [The token could be used only on the date indicated.]

מִפְּנֵי הָרַמָּאִין. — *because of the deceptive ones.*

Someone may have found a token that had been lost by its purchaser, Yochanan, or Achiyah and used it illegally (*Rambam*).

[The date on the token helped avoid against this possibility, because a lost token could be used by the finder only if it was found and used on the day it was issued, an unlikely coincidence which cannot easily be avoided.][11]

Another interpretation is that the date was intended to prevent someone from buying *nesachim* (perhaps intentionally) at a

5. If someone lost his token they would have him wait until the evening. If they found [surplus funds] for him corresponding to his token, they would give him [his *nesachim*]; but if not, nothing was [given] to him.

They were inscribed with the date because of the deceptive ones.

6. There were two [collection] chambers in the Temple: One [was called] "the chamber of the discreet"; and the other [was called] "the utensil chamber".

[What purpose did] "the chamber of the discreet" [serve?] — the God-fearing would deposit [money] into it quietly, and the poor sons of good families supported themselves from it discreetly.

YAD AVRAHAM

time when the price is low and holding them as a hedge against a price rise *(Rav; Rosh; Rambam).* [Such a purchase would be deceitful; since the sale will take place at the later date, he should pay the price current on that day.]

Ravad (according to *Kessef Mishneh, Hil.*

Klei HaMikdash 7:12) suggests that one could buy a token, and falsely claim that he had lost it. Since he had indeed paid for it, the nightly reconciliation of account would show that he was entitled to *nesachim*. He could then defraud the treasury by producing his token at a later date.

6.

שְׁתֵּי לְשָׁכוֹת הָיוּ בַמִּקְדָּשׁ: — *There were two [collection] chambers in the Temple:*

[I.e., there were two chambers set aside for donations besides the thirteen collection chests listed below (6:1,4).]

אַחַת ,,לְשְׁכַּת חֲשָׁאִים"; — *One [was called] "the chamber of the discreet";*

This chest was for charity to be distributed to the poor. The name alludes to the contributors who would deposit anonymously and quietly, and to the recipients who would receive their por-

tion in a discreet manner, as described below *(Rav).*

חֲשָׁאי is the Aramaic word for whispering *(Tos. Yom Tov).*

וְאַחַת ,,לְשְׁכַּת הַכֵּלִים." — *and the other [lit. and one] [was called] "the utensil chamber."*

,,לְשְׁכַּת חֲשָׁאִים"—יִרְאֵי חֵטְא נוֹתְנִים לְתוֹכָה בַחֲשָׁאי; וַעֲנִיִּים בְּנֵי טוֹבִים מִתְפַּרְנְסִים מִתוֹכָה בַחֲשָׁאי. — *[What purpose did] "the chamber of the discreet" [serve?] — the God-fearing [lit. the sin fearing] would deposit [money] into it quietly, and the*

1. The above is the author's understanding of *Rambam.* It is also in *Meiri's* interpretation of the mishnah (and is probably his conception of *Rambam* as well). *Rav* (following *Rosh*) says that someone finding a token lost that day would wait and not use it forthwith for the owner would report the loss that day and be on the lookout for it. [It is not clear however, how the loser would identify the finder] (cf. *Tos. Yom Tov*).

„לְשְׁכַּת הַכֵּלִים" — כָּל־מִי שֶׁהוּא מִתְנַדֵּב
כְּלִי זוֹרְקוֹ לְתוֹכָהּ, וְאַחַת לִשְׁלֹשִׁים יוֹם גִּזְבָּרִין
פּוֹתְחִין אוֹתָהּ. וְכָל־כְּלִי שֶׁמָּצְאוּ בוֹ צֹרֶךְ לְבֶדֶק
הַבַּיִת מַנִּיחִין אוֹתוֹ. וְהַשְּׁאָר נִמְכָּרִין בִּדְמֵיהֶן,
וְנוֹפְלִין לְלִשְׁכַּת בֶּדֶק הַבַּיִת.

[א] **שְׁלֹשָׁה** עָשָׂר שׁוֹפָרוֹת, שְׁלֹשָׁה עָשָׂר
שֻׁלְחָנוֹת, שָׁלשׁ עֶשְׂרֵה
הִשְׁתַּחֲוָיוֹת הָיוּ בַּמִּקְדָּשׁ.
שֶׁל בֵּית רַבָּן גַּמְלִיאֵל וְשֶׁל בֵּית רַבִּי חֲנַנְיָה
סְגַן הַכֹּהֲנִים הָיוּ מִשְׁתַּחֲוִין אַרְבַּע עֶשְׂרֵה.
וְהֵיכָן הָיְתָה יְתֵרָה? — כְּנֶגֶד דִּיר הָעֵצִים, שֶׁכֵּן

יד אברהם

poor sons of good families supported themselves [with funds they withdrew] from it discreetly.

One of the highest forms of charity is to give in such a manner that the donor does not know the recipient's identity, nor does the recipient know his benefactor; this is a *mitzvah* performed for its own sake (לִשְׁמָהּ). An example of this is 'the chamber of the discreet' in the Temple (*Rambam, Comm.; Hil. Matnos Aniyim* 10:8).

„לְשְׁכַּת הַכֵּלִים" — כָּל־מִי שֶׁהוּא מִתְנַדֵּב כְּלִי זוֹרְקוֹ לְתוֹכָהּ, — [What purpose did] "the utensil chamber" [serve?] — whoever pledged a utensil [to the Temple] would

toss it into this chamber [lit. *into it*],

וְאַחַת לִשְׁלֹשִׁים יוֹם גִּזְבָּרִין פּוֹתְחִין אוֹתָהּ. וְכָל־ כְּלִי שֶׁמָּצְאוּ בוֹ צֹרֶךְ לְבֶדֶק הַבַּיִת מַנִּיחִין אוֹתוֹ. וְהַשְּׁאָר נִמְכָּרִין בִּדְמֵיהֶן, וְנוֹפְלִין לְלִשְׁכַּת בֶּדֶק הַבַּיִת. — *and once every thirty days the treasurers would open* [the chamber]. Any utensil for which they found a use towards the upkeep of the Temple they would leave [i.e. they would not sell it but would use it]. *The remainder* [those utensils not fit for use] *would be sold for their value, and the proceeds would go for the chamber* [holding the funds] *for the upkeep of the Temple.*

Chapter 6

1.

The main theme of this chapter is the enumeration and purposes of the thirteen collection chests, among which were two for the collection of the shekalim. Having mentioned two collection chambers at the end of the previous chapter the mishnah finds this place appropriate for a description of the thirteen collection chests. As is common in Mishnah, once a number is mentioned, other groupings of similar numbers are tangentially appended and discussed. In our case, upon mentioning the thirteen chests in the Temple, the Mishnah will discuss other groups of thirteen.

[What purpose did] "the utensil chamber" [serve?] — whoever pledged a utensil [to the Temple] would toss it into this chamber, and once every thirty days the treasurers would open [the chamber]. Any utensil for which they found a use towards the upkeep of the Temple they would leave. The remainder would be sold for their value, and the proceeds would go for the chamber [holding the funds] for the upkeep of the Temple.

1. There were thirteen collection chests, thirteen tables [and] thirteen prostrations in the Temple. [Members] of Rabban Gamliel's family and of R' Chananyah's family would prostrate themselves fourteen [times]. And where was the extra [prostration]? — Opposite the wood chamber; for

שְׁלֹשָׁה עָשָׂר שׁוֹפָרוֹת, — *There were thirteen collection chests,*

As related earlier (2:1) these collection chests were broad at the bottom, but had narrow curved shofar-like openings, and were therefore called *shofaros.*

They were so shaped to prevent people from putting their hands into these chests to steal, under the pretext of putting in money (*Rav; Yer.*).

[Mishnah 5 enumerates the different funds served by these chests.]

שְׁלֹשָׁה עָשָׂר שֻׁלְחָנוֹת, — *thirteen tables*

[Mishnah 4 will explain the purpose of these tables.]

שְׁלֹשׁ עֶשְׂרֵה הִשְׁתַּחֲוָיוֹת הָיוּ בַּמִּקְדָּשׁ. — [*and*] *thirteen prostrations in the Temple.*

Everyone entering the Temple compound would make a circuit of the whole area, circling to his right and exiting at the gate that was to the left of that through which he entered (*Middos* 2:2). During the circuit, he would

prostrate himself at each of the thirteen places enumerated in mishnah 3 (*Tif. Yis.*; cf. *R' Shmayah* to *Middos* 2:6).

שֶׁל בֵּית רַבָּן גַּמְלִיאֵל וְשֶׁל בֵּית רַבִּי חֲנַנְיָה — סְגַן הַכֹּהֲנִים הָיוּ מִשְׁתַּחֲוִין אַרְבַּע עֶשְׂרֵה. — [*Members*] *of Rabban Gamliel's family and of R' Chananyah's family would prostrate themselves fourteen* [*times*].

[As pointed out earlier (4:4), R' Chananyah is the same as R' Chanina. One version (see *Shinuyei Nuschaos*) has R' Chanina even here.]

וְהֵיכָן הָיְתָה יְתֵרָה? — *And where was the extra* [*prostration*]?

[I.e., at which spot did they perform the fourteenth prostration?]

כְּנֶגֶד דִּיר הָעֵצִים — *Opposite the wood chamber;*

Where the wood for the altar pyres (מַעֲרָכוֹת) was situated; in the northeastern corner of the Women's Courtyard (עֶזְרַת נָשִׁים: *Middos* 2:5; *Rav; Rosh*). [The Women's Courtyard faced the eastern side of the Temple Courtyard]

מָסֹרֶת בְּיָדָם מֵאֲבוֹתֵיהֶם שֶׁשָּׁם הָאָרוֹן נִגְנַז.

[ב] מַעֲשֶׂה בְּכֹהֵן אֶחָד שֶׁהָיָה מִתְעַסֵּק
וְרָאָה הָרִצְפָּה שֶׁהִיא מְשֻׁנָּה
מֵחֲבֵרוֹתֶיהָ. בָּא וְאָמַר לַחֲבֵרוֹ, לֹא הִסְפִּיק
לִגְמוֹר אֶת־הַדָּבָר עַד שֶׁיָּצְתָה נִשְׁמָתוֹ. וְיָדְעוּ
בְּיִחוּד שֶׁשָּׁם הָאָרוֹן נִגְנַז.

[ג] וְהֵיכָן הָיוּ מִשְׁתַּחֲוִים? אַרְבַּע בַּצָּפוֹן,
וְאַרְבַּע בַּדָּרוֹם, שָׁלֹשׁ בַּמִּזְרָח
וּשְׁתַּיִם בַּמַּעֲרָב — כְּנֶגֶד שְׁלֹשָׁה עָשָׂר שְׁעָרִים:

יד אברהם

שֶׁכֵן מָסֹרֶת בְּיָדָם מֵאֲבוֹתֵיהֶם שֶׁשָּׁם הָאָרוֹן
נִגְנַז. — *for they had a tradition (in their
hands) from their ancestors that the Ark
was hidden there.*

King Yoshiyahu hid the Ark there, in
the intricate underground labyrinth of
passageways and secret chambers built
by King Solomon when he erected the
Temple (*Rav; Yer.*; see also *Radak* to
II Chronicles 35:3). Yoshiyahu did so
because of the prophecies that the Temple would soon be destroyed (*Tif. Yis.*).

The verse (*II Chronicles* 35:3) telling of
Yoshiyahu's exhortation to the Levites and
the populace, *'Put the Holy Ark into the
House that Solomon the son of David, King
of Israel, built,'* refers to the secreting of the
Ark.[The sages could not take the above

verse literally for the Ark had *always* been in
the Temple. Thus the verse must refer to a
different "house" built by Solomon, i.e., the
labyrinth under the Temple complex.] When
the Holy Ark was hidden, the flask of manna
(see *Exodus* 16:33-34), the bottle of the
anointing oil (שֶׁמֶן הַמִּשְׁחָה: *ibid.* 30:31), and
Aaron's rod with its almonds and blossoms
(*Numbers* 17:25-26) were hidden with it
(*Rav; Yer.; Yoma* 52b, Tosefta Sotah 13:2).
[None of these items were returned to the Second Temple.]

Those who did not prostrate themselves at
this place were either of the opinion (see
ibid.) that the Holy Ark was taken to
Babylon with Nebuchadnezzar, or that it was
hidden in 'its' place, beneath the Holy of
Holies (*Shoshanim L'David;* see *Yer.; Tos.
Sotah* 13:2; *Rambam, Hil. Beis HaBechirah*
4:1).

2.

מַעֲשֶׂה בְּכֹהֵן אֶחָד שֶׁהָיָה מִתְעַסֵּק — *It once
happened that a Kohen who was oc-
cupied* [*at his task; lit. an occurrence
with one Kohen who was occupied*]

He had a disqualifying blemish [מוּם]
and was therefore given the job of pick-
ing out the wormy pieces of wood.
Wormy wood is unfit (*Middos* 2:5) for
burning upon the altar (*Rav; Yer.;
Yoma* 54a).

The mishnah uses the verb מִתְעַסֵּק, lit. oc-
cupying himself, instead of the usual עוֹבֵד,
he served, to allude to the nature of his work;

it did not have the status of a Temple 'service,' which can be performed only by a
qualified *Kohen* (Rambam).

וְרָאָה הָרִצְפָּה שֶׁהִיא מְשֻׁנָּה מֵחֲבֵרוֹתֶיהָ. —
(and) noticed [lit. *saw*] *that* [*a certain
stone of*] *the floor was different from
the others.*

He perceived that a certain floor-
stone was slightly higher than the rest,
and surmised that this stone had once
been removed [presumably to hide the
Ark] and then replaced (*Rav; Rosh*).

6
2

they had a tradition from their ancestors that the Ark was hidden there.

2. It once happened that a *Kohen* who was occupied [at his task] noticed that [a certain stone of] the floor was different from the others. He came to tell his colleague, but before he had concluded the matter his soul departed from him. Thus they knew with certainty that the Ark had been hidden there.

6
3

3. And where did they prostrate themselves [these thirteen times]? — Four in the north, four in the south, three in the east and two in the west — opposite [the] thirteen gates:

YAD AVRAHAM

Alternatively, he perceived that one of the slabs had a slightly different coloring, ostensibly because of its greater holiness (*R' Meshullam;* cf. *Kol Sofer*). The Talmud (*Yoma* 54a) relates that this *Kohen's* hatchet, which he used to test the wood for worminess, slipped his hand and while retrieving the hatchet he noticed this slab.

בָּא וְאָמַר לַחֲבֵרוֹ, — *He came to tell* [lit. *and told*] *his colleague,*

[He told his friend, who was occupied in the same work, what he had seen, and was about to show him the exact location.]

לֹא הִסְפִּיק לִגְמוֹר אֶת־הַדָּבָר עַד שֶׁיָּצְתָה נִשְׁמָתוֹ. — *but before he had concluded the matter* [lit. *he had no time to end the matter until*] *his soul departed from him.*

God did not wish the Ark's exact location to be revealed (*Tif. Yis*). The *Kohen* died because of his indiscretion

in revealing the secret, lest the Gentiles learn this information (*Rivevan*).

וְיָדְעוּ בְּיָחוּד שֶׁשָּׁם הָאָרוֹן נִגְנַז. — *Thus they knew with certainty that the Ark had been hidden there.*

The inference is that they drew this conclusion from the turn of events. *Meiri* suggests that the phrase וְיָדְעוּ בְּיָחוּד means that it was made known to them secretly, presumably through the agency of divinely inspired perception (רוּחַ הַקּוֹדֶשׁ).

The Talmud (*Yoma* 54a) states that this took place in the Second Temple era, implying clearly that when Nebuchadnezzar destroyed the Temple he left the pavement intact (cf. *R' Meshullam* cited above). Accordingly, the plowing under of Jerusalem on the Seventeenth of Tammuz (*Ta'anis* 4:6) must have occurred after the destruction of the Second Temple (*Tos. Yom Tov*).

3.

וְהֵיכָן הָיוּ מִשְׁתַּחֲוִים? — *And where did they prostrate themselves [these thirteen times]?*

The mishnah now enumerates the sites of the thirteen prostrations mentioned in mishnah 1.

אַרְבַּע בַּצָּפוֹן, וְאַרְבַּע בַּדָּרוֹם, שָׁלֹשׁ בְּמִזְרָח,

וּשְׁתַּיִם בַּמַּעֲרָב — כְּנֶגֶד שְׁלֹשָׁה עָשָׂר שְׁעָרִים: — *Four* [times] *in the north, (and) four* [times] *in the south, three* [times] *in the east and two* [times] *in the west — opposite* [the] *thirteen gates* [of the Temple Courtyard]:

They would prostrate themselves at these points to demonstrate their

שְׁעָרִים דְּרוֹמִיִּים, סְמוּכִין לַמַּעֲרָב — שַׁעַר
הָעֶלְיוֹן, שַׁעַר הַדֶּלֶק, שַׁעַר הַבְּכוֹרוֹת, שַׁעַר
הַמָּיִם.
וְלָמָּה נִקְרָא שְׁמוֹ שַׁעַר הַמָּיִם? — שֶׁבּוֹ
מַכְנִיסִין צְלוֹחִית שֶׁל מַיִם שֶׁל נִסּוּךְ בֶּחָג.

יד אברהם

gratitude to God for the beauty of the Temple (R' Shemayah to Middos 2:6 cited by Tos. Yom Tov here). At these points they could catch a glimpse of the beauty of the Temple by looking through the gates (see Tif. Yis. to Middos 2:6).

The mishnah will now enumerate these thirteen gates.]

שְׁעָרִים דְּרוֹמִיִּים, סְמוּכִין לַמַּעֲרָב — *The southern gates, adjacent to the west* [were the following] —

שַׁעַר הָעֶלְיוֹן, — *the Upper Gate,*
The Temple mount sloped upward going from the east to the west, so that the westernmost gate in the southern wall was the highest in elevation of all of the gates (Rav; Rosh).

The purpose served by this gate is not given (Tos. Yom Tov).

שַׁעַר הַדֶּלֶק, — *the Kindling Gate,*
The wood to be burned upon the pyres (מַעֲרָכוֹת) was brought in through this gate (Rav; Rosh).

Alternatively: The fire to light the pyre was brought through this gate (Ra'avyah cited by Tos. Yom Tov 1:4; Tosafos Yeshanim Yoma 19a, s.v. שער הדלק; cf. Lechem Shamayim there; Ravad to Tamid 25b, s.v. שער הניצוץ).

שַׁעַר הַבְּכוֹרוֹת, — *the Firstlings' Gate,*
The firstborn of cattle, sheep and goats [בְּכוֹרִים] which must be offered as sacrifices would be brought through this gate to be slaughtered in the area south of the altar, whereas קָדְשֵׁי קָדָשִׁים, *offerings of the greatest magnitude of holiness,* were slaughtered only in the

area north of the altar (Rav; see Tos. Yom Tov Middos 1:4).

Some versions in Middos 1:4 call this gate שַׁעַר הַקָּרְבָּן, *the Offering Gate* (see Shinuyei Nuschaos there; Yoma 19a with Hagahos HaBach, Rashi there, s.v. שער הדלקה).

Rashi (Yoma 19a, s.v. שער הדלקה) states he does not know the reason for the names of the two foregoing gates.

Rosh (here and Middos) explains that through this gate they would bring קָדָשִׁים קַלִּים, *offerings of a lesser magnitude of holiness.* These offerings were allowed to be slaughtered in the area south of the altar.

Alternatively, Rosh explains there was a tradition that Abraham led Isaac through this spot when he brought him to Mount Moriah to be sacrificed.

שַׁעַר הַמָּיִם. וְלָמָּה נִקְרָא שְׁמוֹ שַׁעַר הַמָּיִם? — שֶׁבּוֹ מַכְנִיסִין צְלוֹחִית שֶׁל מַיִם שֶׁל נִסּוּךְ בֶּחָג. — *the Water Gate. And why is it (its name) called the Water Gate? Because through it they would bring the flagon of water for the libation on Succos* [lit. *the festival*].

Since the other three gates were used daily, the derivations of their names were known to all. However, the infrequent use of this gate — according to the *tanna kamma* it was only used on the Succos festival — causes the mishnah to raise this question (Tif. Yis.).

On the Succos festival, a water libation was poured upon the altar. In addition to the regular wine libation, water drawn from the *Shilo'ach* spring would be placed in a gold flagon and brought to the altar via the Water Gate (Succah 4:9).

[Succos is often called הֶחָג, lit. *the festival,* in the Talmud. See 3:1, s.v., בפרוס החג.]

The southern gates, adjacent to the west — the Upper Gate, the Kindling Gate, the Firstlings' Gate, the Water Gate. And why is it called the Water Gate? — Because through it they would bring the flagon of water for the libation on Succos.

✑ The Thirteen Gates

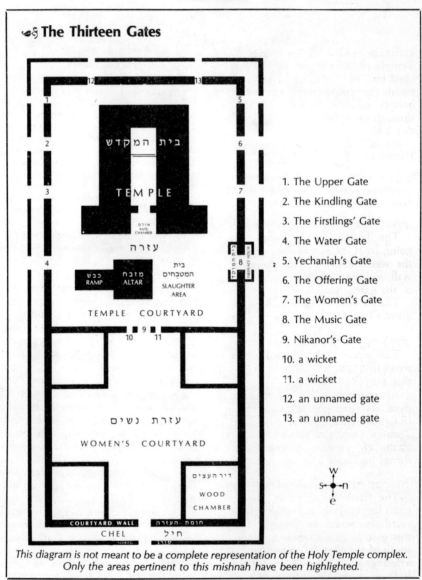

1. The Upper Gate
2. The Kindling Gate
3. The Firstlings' Gate
4. The Water Gate
5. Yechaniah's Gate
6. The Offering Gate
7. The Women's Gate
8. The Music Gate
9. Nikanor's Gate
10. a wicket
11. a wicket
12. an unnamed gate
13. an unnamed gate

This diagram is not meant to be a complete representation of the Holy Temple complex. Only the areas pertinent to this mishnah have been highlighted.

רַבִּי אֱלִיעֶזֶר בֶּן־יַעֲקֹב אוֹמֵר: בּוֹ הַמַּיִם
מְפַכִּים וַעֲתִידִין לִהְיוֹת יוֹצְאִין מִתַּחַת מִפְתַּן
הַבָּיִת.

לְעֻמָּתָן בַּצָּפוֹן סְמוּכִין לַמַּעֲרָב — שַׁעַר
יְכָנְיָה, שַׁעַר קָרְבָּן, שַׁעַר נָשִׁים, שַׁעַר הַשִּׁיר.
וְלָמָּה נִקְרָא שְׁמוֹ שַׁעַר יְכָנְיָה? — שֶׁבּוֹ יָצָא
יְכָנְיָה בְּגָלוּתוֹ.
בַּמִּזְרָח: שַׁעַר נִיקָנוֹר, וּשְׁתֵּי פִּשְׁפְּשִׁין הָיוּ לוֹ,
אֶחָד בִּימִינוֹ וְאֶחָד בִּשְׂמֹאלוֹ.
וּשְׁנַיִם בַּמַּעֲרָב שֶׁלֹּא הָיָה לָהֶן שֵׁם.

יד אברהם

רַבִּי אֱלִיעֶזֶר בֶּן־יַעֲקֹב אוֹמֵר: בּוֹ הַמַּיִם מְפַכִּים
— וַעֲתִידִין לִהְיוֹת יוֹצְאִין מִתַּחַת מִפְתַּן הַבָּיִת.
*R' Eliezer ben Yaakov says: Through it
the waters trickle and they are destined
to issue forth from beneath the
threshold of the Temple.*

This is a reference to *Ezekiel* 47:1-2:
*And the water was descending under
the right hand wall of the House ...
water trickles* (מְפַכִּים) *from the right
wall.* Right is used in Scripture to
denote the south as in (*Psalms* 89:13):
צָפוֹן וְיָמִין, *North and Right You have
erected them* (see *Rashi* to *Numbers*
34:15) — hence *Ezekiel* refers to the
southern wall. In Yechezkel's prophetic
vision, this stream issued from the Holy
of Holies (see there v. 1 ... *and behold!
Water was coming from under the
threshold of the House ...*) in a trickle
wide as locusts' antennae which
gradually widens to a streamlet wide as
a פַּךְ, *jug* (i.e., a stream as wide as that
poured out of a jug), hence the usage of
the verb מְפַכִּים (*Rav; Rosh* based on
Yoma 77b).

Vilna Gaon (to *Middos* 2:6) infers from
the present tense used here (*through it the
waters trickle*) that during the Second Tem-

ple era the water already had begun to trickle
through this gate. In contrast, the water
emanating from the Holy of Holies is said
only to be *destined* to issue. (For a lengthy
treatment of this subject and interpretation
of its significance see ArtScroll *comm.* to
Ezekiel 47).

לְעֻמָּתָן בַּצָּפוֹן סְמוּכִין לַמַּעֲרָב — שַׁעַר יְכָנְיָה,
— *Opposite these [southern gates], on
the north, adjacent to the west [were the
following gates]* — *Yechaniah's Gate,*

[The derivation of this name is given
below.]

שַׁעַר קָרְבָּן — *the Offering Gate,*
Through this gate they would bring
in all the קָדְשֵׁי קָדָשִׁים, *offerings of
greatest magnitude of holiness,* which
can be slaughtered only north of the
altar (*Rav; Rosh*).

An alternative explanation: All the
offerings would be brought through
this gate because the rings used to hold
the animals during slaughter were
situated north of the altar (*Rosh;* see
Middos 5:2).

שַׁעַר נָשִׁים — *the Women's Gate,*
Here women would enter to lean
(סְמִיכָה) on their offering, according to
R' Yose (*Rosh HaShanah* 33a)[1] who

---

1. Women are exempt from the obligation to lean on the offering. The question is now raised
whether they *may* do so voluntarily, inasmuch as one must lean on the animal with all his
might (*Chagigah* 16b), meaning that the animal supports the weight of the one who leans.
Unless the act is a *mitzvah* it can be considered prohibited work (עֲבוֹדָה) with a consecrated

R' Eliezer ben Yaakov says: Through it the waters trickle and they are destined to issue forth from beneath the threshold of the Temple.

Opposite these [southern gates],on the north, adjacent to the west — Yechaniah's Gate, the Offering Gate, the Women's Gate, the Music Gate.

And why was it called Yechaniah's Gate? — Because through it [King] Yechaniah went to his exile.

In the east — Nikanor's Gate which had two wickets, one to its right and one to its left.

And two [gates] in the west which were unnamed.

YAD AVRAHAM

permits women to perform this service voluntarily. Those who forbid women to lean on the offering (R' Yehudah, ibid.), nevertheless require women to be present at the sacrifice of their offerings for it is preferable that an offering not be sacrificed in its owner's absence (Ta'anis 27a; Rav; Rosh).

שַׁעַר הַשִּׁיר. — the Music Gate.

The instruments used to accompany the song of the Levites were brought in through this gate (Rav; Rosh).

וְלָמָּה נִקְרָא שְׁמוֹ שַׁעַר יְכָנְיָה? — שֶׁבּוֹ יָצָא יְכָנְיָה בְּגָלוּתוֹ. — And why was (its name) it called Yechaniah's Gate? — Because through it [King] Yechaniah went to his exile.

Because this gate's name was not related to its daily usage, the mishnah explains its source (Tif. Yis.).

When King Yechaniah was about to be taken into exile by Nebuchadnezzar (II Kings 24:12), he entered the Temple and prostrated himself as if to take leave (Rav).

בַּמִּזְרָח: שַׁעַר נִיקָנוֹר, — In the east — Nikanor's Gate

[Nikanor brought the two doors of this gate from Egypt and was instrumental in their miraculous deliverance

from a storm at sea en route (see Yoma 3:11 and 38a).]

וּשְׁתֵּי פִשְׁפְּשִׁין הָיוּ לוֹ, אֶחָד בִּימִינוֹ וְאֶחָד בִּשְׂמֹאלוֹ. — which had two wickets, one to its right and one to its left.

There were small doors in the great gates so that they could be opened easily at all times (Rav; Rambam). ['All the doorways that were there were twenty cubits high and ten cubits wide' (Middos 2:3). Small wonder then that these gates were very heavy and difficult to open. When the great gate was not open they would enter by way of these wickets.]

Rosh maintains that the פִשְׁפְּשִׁין were not wickets but small doors situated in the Temple Courtyard wall at a short distance from the Nikanor Gate.

Middos 1:7 mentions another wicket situated in the gate to the בֵּית הַמּוֹקֵד, Fireplace House, which was in the northern wall of the Courtyard. This wicket is not counted among these thirteen gates here, because it was smaller than even the wickets in the Nikanor Gate (Rav from Rosh). However, Rosh adds that the פִשְׁפְּשִׁין mentioned here differ also in that they were separate from the Nikanor Gate, whereas the one for the Fireplace House was in the gate itself, and included in it (see Middos ibid. with Rosh).

וּשְׁנַיִם בַּמַּעֲרָב שֶׁלֹּא הָיָה לָהֶן שֵׁם. — And

animal. R' Yose holds that though women are exempt, nevertheless they may perform leaning. R' Yehudah says they do not have this option, and consequently he prohibits leaning by women (Rav; Rosh).

שְׁלֹשָׁה [ד] עֶשָׂר שְׁלָחָנוֹת הָיוּ בַּמִּקְדָּשׁ: שְׁמֹנָה שֶׁל שַׁיִשׁ בְּבֵית

יד אברהם

two [gates] in the west which were un-named.

They were unnamed because they had very little use *(Meiri)*. *Tosefos Yom Tov* points out that there was relatively little space between the respective western walls of the Temple Courtyard and the Temple Mount, and that this area was not used much, as told in *Middos* 2:1. The view of R' Yitzchak Abarbanel (from his comm. to *Ezek.* 40) is that the Temple Courtyard of Yechezkel's prophetic vision did not have gates to the west, for if there were, then those who would enter there would have to prostrate themselves eastward toward the Temple. But this is un-desirable for that was the direction toward which sun worshipers were wont to bow.

Tosefos Yom Tov cites *Josephus Flavius'* comment in *Wars of the Jews* 5:14[1] that the western wall had no door at all and opines that in view of the fact that the Temple envisaged by *Ezekiel* also had no western door, Josephus may be correct. However, *Tosefos Yom Tov* concludes: We cannot depart from the tradition (accepted by) the Sages of the Mishnah [2] (see below).

Yerushalmi (cited by *Rav*) comments that our mishnah follows Abba Yose ben Chanan

(Middos 2:6), but the other Sages count only seven gates to the Temple Courtyard (see *Middos* 1:4). According to them, these thirteen prostrations were performed at the thirteen places where the סורג, *Soreg*, had been breached during the Syrian-Greek occupa-tion of Jerusalem.[3] The *Soreg* was a ten-cubit high lattice-work wall, ten cubits away from the Courtyard wall *(Middos* 2:3).

Following the successful revolt of the Hasmoneans, the *Soreg* was repaired, but the custom was adapted for Jews to prostrate themselves at these thirteen places to com-memorate and give thanks for the defect of the Greeks.

Tosafos (Kesubos 106, s.v. שבעה, cited by *Tos. Yom Tov)* suggests that there is no dis-agreement about the actual number of gates. There were seven great gates (10 x 20 cubits), and six smaller ones. Abba Yose uses the name 'gate' for all of them and believes that the thirteen prostrations were made opposite them. The Sages believe that only the seven larger gates are worthy of the name and con-sequently the thirteen prostrations were op-posite the breaches in the *Soreg*.

The gates eliminated by the Sages are the two small ones on the west, the two wickets in the east, and the Upper Gate on the south (see *Middos* 1:4). However, the gate eliminated in the north cannot readily be identified because *Middos* 1:5 where the Sages enumerate the seven gates, uses dif-ferent names for them.

1. In the English edition (Whiston) this is in Book 5, 5:2. Curiously, *Yossipon* (ch. 55) gives five gates for the western Courtyard. *Tosefos Yom Tov's* preference for Josephus' version warrants exploration. However, a close comparison of these two sources shows that what Yos-sipon calls the wall of the עֲזָרָה, *Courtyard*, is described by Josephus as the Temple Mount wall!

2. Josephus' description of the Temple differs from that of the Sages in very many details, so that it can hardly be credited. Interestingly, nowhere does Josephus mention (see his autobiography, *The Life of Josephus Flavius)* that he performed the service. By his own ac-count his youth to the age of 19 was spent in religious experimentation. At the age of 26 he was already in the midst of political and military intrigues. It is doubtful that he possessed more than a superficial knowledge of the Temple and its service.

3. *Tos. Yom Tov (Middos* 2:2) explains that the *Soreg* greatly irked the Greeks because Gen-tiles were forbidden to step beyond it *(Keilim* 1:8). Another purpose for the *Soreg* is adduced by *Rambam* and *Rosh (ibid.).*

4. Thirteen tables were in the Temple:
Eight of marble were in the slaughter area.

YAD AVRAHAM

4.

שְׁלֹשָׁה עָשָׂר שֻׁלְחָנוֹת הָיוּ בַּמִּקְדָּשׁ: שְׁמֹנָה שֶׁל שַׁיִשׁ בְּבֵית הַמִּטְבָּחַיִם. — **Thirteen tables were in the Temple: Eight of marble** *were in the slaughter area.*

The area near the altar's north was used for slaughtering. In it were both

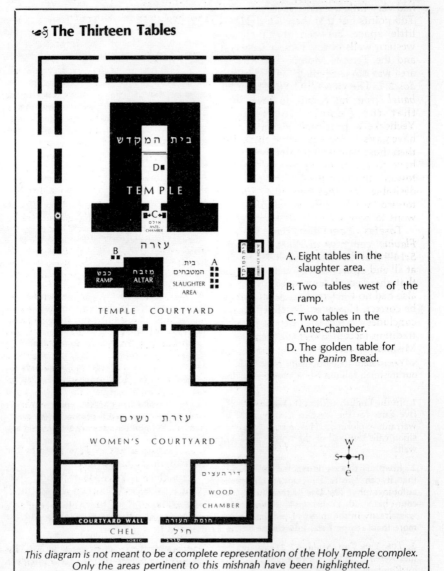

◄§ The Thirteen Tables

בית המקדש

D■

TEMPLE

◄■C►

אולם
ANTE-
CHAMBER

עזרה

B■

כבש
RAMP

מזבח
ALTAR

בית
המטבחים

SLAUGHTER
AREA

A ■■
   ■■
   ■■

TEMPLE COURTYARD

עזרת נשים

WOMEN'S COURTYARD

דיר העצים

WOOD

CHAMBER

COURTYARD WALL

CHEL

SOREG

חומת העזרה

חיל
סורג

A. Eight tables in the slaughter area.

B. Two tables west of the ramp.

C. Two tables in the Ante-chamber.

D. The golden table for the *Panim* Bread.

W
S — n
e

This diagram is not meant to be a complete representation of the Holy Temple complex. Only the areas pertinent to this mishnah have been highlighted.

הַמִּטְבְּחַיִם. שֶׁעֲלֵיהֶן מְדִיחִין אֶת־הַקְּרָבַיִם.
וּשְׁנַיִם בְּמַעֲרַב הַכֶּבֶשׁ — אֶחָד שֶׁל שַׁיִשׁ,
וְאֶחָד שֶׁל כֶּסֶף. עַל־שֶׁל שַׁיִשׁ הָיוּ נוֹתְנִים אֶת־
הָאֵבָרִים; עַל־שֶׁל כֶּסֶף, כְּלֵי שָׁרֵת.
וּשְׁנַיִם בָּאוּלָם מִבִּפְנִים עַל־פֶּתַח הַבַּיִת —
אֶחָד שֶׁל שַׁיִשׁ, וְאֶחָד שֶׁל זָהָב. עַל־שֶׁל שַׁיִשׁ
נוֹתְנִין לֶחֶם הַפָּנִים בִּכְנִיסָתוֹ; וְעַל־שֶׁל זָהָב

יד אברהם

the rings used to secure the animals during slaughter, and the tables upon
which the entrails were rinsed after
slaughter.

According to *Rambam* (*Hil. Beis
HaBechirah* 5:14) it seems that the
'slaughter area' was the place where the
intestines were rinsed, not where the
animals were slaughtered. Presumably it
was called 'slaughter area' by transference from the common practice of
rinsing at the place of slaughter. The
place where the slaughtering was done
was called 'the area of the rings' (see
Tif. Yis., Bo'az, to *Tamid* 3:5).

שֶׁעֲלֵיהֶן מְדִיחִין אֶת־הַקְּרָבַיִם. — *Upon these
they would rinse the entrails.*

Entrails had to be rinsed before offering upon the altar as set forth by the
Torah (*Leviticus* 1:9), *and the entrails
and the feet shall he wash with water* …
Tosafos (*Yoma* 19a, s.v. שׁשׁ) points out
that our mishnah contradicts *Middos* (5:3)
which states that there is a special 'Rinsing
Chamber.' *Tosafos* suggests that the tables
were used only for the rinsing of *meat*, not
intestines. As for the entrails, however, it
would have been unseemly to wash the intestines there, filled as they were with the
animals' feces; instead these were discreetly
rinsed in the privacy of the 'Rinsing
Chamber.' This view is refuted by *Tosefos
Yom Tov* (*Middos* 5:3), because our mishnah
clearly says 'they would rinse the *entrails*'. [It
seems likely that *Tosafos* version read:
שֶׁעֲלֵיהֶן מְדִיחִין אֶת־הַקֳּדָשִׁים, *for upon them
they would rinse the consecrated (offer-
ings)!*] *Tosefos Yom Tov* cites the view of the
commentator to *Tamid* 31a; see also *Ravad*
there and *Beur HaGra* to *Middos*, ibid.) that
only the stomach was washed in the 'Rinsing

Chamber', because of the great accumulation
of decayed matter in it. The rest of the
entrails (and the stomach after it had been
rinsed in the chamber) were rinsed on the
tables. *Rosh* (*Tamid* ibid.) adds another suggestion. The chamber was used only when
there were too many offerings for the tables.

Rambam (*Hil. Ma'aseh HaKarbonos* 6:6;
see *Mishneh LaMelech* and *Mirkeves Ha-
Mishneh* there) states that they would rinse
the stomach and entrails first in the chamber,
and a second time on the tables.
Nevertheless, in rephrasing our mishnah,
Rambam says (*Hil. Beis HaBechirah* 5:14)
merely: Next to it is the area of the tables …
upon which they would place the cuts (of
meat) and rinse הַבָּשָׂר, *the meat,* prior to
cooking (*Rambam's* version of our mishnah
has קְרָבִים *entrails*; see ed. Kafich).

These tables had yet another function.
When animals were hung upon the adjacent
hooks to be flayed, their carcasses rested on
these tables so that they would not lay on the
floor (*Rav* and *Tos. Yom Tov* to *Tamid* 3:5;
Rambam to *Middos* 3:5). *Tosafos* (*Yoma*
16b, s.v. מן; see *Tif. Yis.* to *Tamid* 3:5) assumes that the tables supporting the carcasses were not the ones used for rinsing. *Vilna
Gaon* (*Tamid* 4:2) remarks pithily that these
tables must have been the same, for the mishnah in *Shekalim* counts only thirteen tables.

וּשְׁנַיִם בְּמַעֲרַב הַכֶּבֶשׁ — *Two were to the
west of the [altar's] ramp*

[A sixteen cubit wide and thirty-two
cubit long access ramp on the southern
wall of the altar led to its top. These two
tables stood between the ramp and the
Temple.]

אֶחָד שֶׁל שַׁיִשׁ, וְאֶחָד שֶׁל כֶּסֶף. עַל־שֶׁל שַׁיִשׁ
הָיוּ נוֹתְנִים אֶת־הָאֵבָרִים; — *one of marble,
one of silver. Upon the marble one they*

6

Upon these they would rinse the entrails.

4 Two were to the west of the [altar's] ramp — one of marble, one of silver. Upon the marble one they would put the limbs [of the offerings]; upon the silver one, utensils for the service.

Two were inside the Ante-chamber near the Temple doorway — one of marble, one of gold. Upon the marble one they would put the *Panim* Bread when it was brought in; upon the golden one when it was

YAD AVRAHAM

would put the limbs [of the offerings];

[The burnt offerings had to be dissected into specified cuts and offered upon the altar.] In the interim they were placed upon this table. This table was not of gold or silver because metal has a tendency to become warm and this could cause the meat to spoil. On the other hand, marble stays cool and helps preserve the freshness of the offering. Otherwise, they would have preferred to make the tables of gold or silver, because אֵין עֲנִיּוּת בִּמְקוֹם עֲשִׁירוּת, *there should be no appearance of poverty in a place of wealth* (Shabbos 102b). One of the ten miracles that distinguished the Temple was that meat of offerings never spoiled (Avos 5:5), but they did not rely on this because (Pesachim 64b) אֵין סוֹמְכִין עַל־הַנֵּס, *one should not rely upon a miracle* (Rav; Rosh partly from Tamid 31b).

In articulating the entire daily service procedure, the mishnah in *Tamid* 4:3 mentions nothing about placing the limbs upon this table after dissection; rather it states that they were placed upon the lower half of the altar ramp. The anonymous commentator (מְפָרֵשׁ) to *Tamid* 31b feels that nevertheless, before bringing the limbs to the altar ramp, the *Kohanim* rested briefly, placing them upon the table during this short interval. *Rosh* (loc. cit.; also *Rivevan* here) holds that the limbs of the communal offerings were always placed directly upon the altar ramp without a stopover on the table. Limbs of private, burnt offerings (עוֹלוֹת יָחִיד), however, were placed upon the table when only one *Kohen* performed the whole service, so that he should be able to offer all the limbs one after the other. [If many *Kohanim* were

working together, there would have been no need to pause, because the limbs could be brought directly from the slaughter area to the altar; but if only one *Kohen* were available there would be an 'undue pause' (הֶפְסֵק) between the offering of one limb and the next. However, *Rosh* does not explain why the altar ramp could not be used as a holding area even for individual offerings. Perhaps since the ramp was considered part of the altar for many purposes (see *Menachos* 57b, *Tos.* there, s.v. אֵין), a pause between the placing of one limb and the bringing of the next would constitute an 'undue pause' and violate the rule governing correct procedure.

עַל־שֶׁל כֶּסֶף, כְּלֵי שָׁרֵת.—*upon the silver one, utensils for the service.*

Every morning, ninety-three utensils would be taken out for use in the service (*Tamid* 3:4). These were put this table (Rav; Rosh).

וּשְׁנַיִם בָּאוּלָם מִבִּפְנִים עַל־פֶּתַח הַבַּיִת — *Two were inside the Ante-chamber near the Temple doorway.*

[The Temple proper (whose exterior was seventy cubits wide) was faced by an antechamber measuring a hundred cubits from north to south, and fifteen cubits from east to west (*Middos* 4:7). It was separated from the Temple proper by the Temple wall, and connected to it by a door twenty cubits high and ten cubits wide (*Middos* 4:1).]

אֶחָד שֶׁל שִׁישׁ, וְאֶחָד שֶׁל זָהָב. עַל־שֶׁל שִׁישׁ נוֹתְנִין לֶחֶם הַפָּנִים בִּכְנִיסָתוֹ; — *one of marble, one of gold. Upon the marble one they would put the Panim Bread when it was brought in;*

שְׁקָלִים בִּיצִיאָתוֹ. שֶׁמַּעֲלִין בַּקֹּדֶשׁ וְלֹא מוֹרִידִין.
וְאֶחָד שֶׁל זָהָב מִבִּפְנִים שֶׁעָלָיו לֶחֶם הַפָּנִים
תָּמִיד.

[ה] **שְׁלשָׁה** עָשָׂר שׁוֹפָרוֹת הָיוּ בַּמִּקְדָּשׁ,
וְכָתוּב עֲלֵיהֶם: ,,תְּקָלִין
חַדְתִּין" וְ,,תִּקְלִין עַתִּיקִין", ,,קִנִּין" וְ,,גוֹזְלֵי
עוֹלָה", ,,עֵצִים" וְ,,לְבוֹנָה", ,,זָהָב לַכַּפּוֹרֶת".

יד אברהם

[See above 4:1, s.v. לחם הפנים, for a description of the *Panim* Breads and their service.] The *Panim* Breads were baked on Friday and held upon this table until the Sabbath day when they were brought into the Temple proper and placed upon their table in the Holy (*Rav; Rosh*).

Rashi (*Menachos* 100b) holds that the *Panim* Breads were placed upon this table only momentarily to demonstrate that 'one ascends in holiness but does not descend' (see below).

Tosafos (*Menachos*, ibid. s.v. שיש של) adduces versions which have here שֶׁל כֶּסֶף, *of silver*. A *baraisa* cited there (100b), has this version. *Tosafos* attributes to *Rashi* the opinion that there is a disagreement among tannaim whether it was of silver or marble. Our versions of *Rashi* reconciles these two versions. The color of the marble was silvery white. *Ravad* (to *Tamid* 31b, see p. 69 and *Meleches Shlomo* here) surmises that only the feet of this table were of marble; the table itself was of silver.

וְעַל־שֶׁל זָהָב בִּיצִיאָתוֹ. — *(and) upon the golden one when it was taken out.*

When the *Panim* Breads were taken off the golden table in the Holy where

they had lain since the previous Sabbath, they were placed on this table until they were apportioned among the *Kohanim* (*Rav*).

שֶׁמַּעֲלִין בַּקֹּדֶשׁ וְלֹא מוֹרִידִין. — *For regarding sanctified objects we ascend but do not descend.*

It would be considered a regression if breads that had lain upon the golden table in the Holy were to be put upon an inferior silver table (*Rav; Rosh*).

[According to *Rashi's* view cited above, this maxim also explains why a table was used at all when the breads were brought in: only by first laying them on a table of lesser value could their subsequent placement upon the golden table in the Holy be considered an 'ascent.']

וְאֶחָד שֶׁל זָהָב מִבִּפְנִים שֶׁעָלָיו לֶחֶם הַפָּנִים תָּמִיד. — *And one of gold on the inside* [of the Temple] *upon which the Panim Bread* [lay] *continually.*

[This was the golden table described in *Exodus* 25:23-30. The Torah requires that the *Panim* Breads be on the table *continually* (*Leviticus* 24:8). As soon as the old breads were removed, the new ones replaced them.]

5.

שְׁלשָׁה עָשָׂר שׁוֹפָרוֹת הָיוּ בַּמִּקְדָּשׁ, — *Thirteen collection chests were in the Temple,*

In the Courtyard (*R' Shlomo Sirilio; Tif. Yis.*)

[However it is logical to assume that these

chests were on the Temple Mount where they would be accessible to many people unable to enter the Courtyard (see *Keilim* 1:8), or at least in the Women's Courtyard where women could contribute. Besides, according to some authorities everyone entering the Temple Courtyard had to immerse himself in

6
5

taken out. For regarding sanctified objects we ascend but do not descend.

And one of gold on the inside [of the Temple] upon which the *Panim* Bread [lay] continually.

5. Thirteen collection chests were in the Temple, upon which were inscribed [respectively]: "New Shekalim", "Old Shekalim", "Nests", "Young Pigeon Burnt Offerings", "Wood", "Frankincense", "Gold for the Utensils", [the

YAD AVRAHAM

a *mikveh* (see ArtScroll *Yoma* 3:3, s.v. אֵין אָדָם), another imediment to contribution not present on the Temple Mount or even in the Women's Courtyard.]

All thirteen chests stood together, arranged in a circle (*Yerushalmi* cited by *Meleches Shlomo*).[See diagram in comm. to 7:1.]

וְכָתוּב עֲלֵיהֶם: ,,תִּקְלִין חַדְתִּין'' וְ,,תִּקְלִין עַתִּיקִין'', ,,קִנִּין'' וְ,,גוֹזְלֵי עוֹלָה'' — *upon which were inscribed [respectively]: "New Shekalim", (and) "Old Shekalim" "Nests", (and) "Young Pigeon Burnt Offerings",*

[The functions of these four chests are explained further in the mishnah.] Here everyone agrees that Aramaic (תִּקְלִין חַדְתִּין, תִּקְלִין עַתִּיקִין) was used (see above 5:3) because these inscriptions were meant to identify the chests for the general populace, some of whom did not understand Hebrew. Only regarding the tokens, which were handled by Temple administrators who could be expected to be conversant in Hebrew, is there any disagreement (*Tos. Yom Tov*).

,,עֵצִים'' — *"Wood",*

[This was the fifth chest.] Contributions to purchase wood for the altar

pyre were put into this chest (*Rav; Rosh; Rambam, Hil. Shekalim* 2:2).

If one wished he could donate wood to be offered upon the altar as a personal קָרְבָּן עֵצִים, *wood offering* (*Hil. Ma'aseh HaKorbonos* 14:1 and ArtScroll *Ta'anis* 4:4-5), but funds for such an offering could not be deposited in this chest. Money from the chest was used to buy wood if none was available (see *Hil. Shekalim* 4:1; cf. *Tosefta* 3:3).

,,וּ,,לְבוֹנָה'' — *(and) "Frankincense",*

[The sixth chest was for frankincense.] Whoever wished to make a donative offering of frankincense upon the altar (קָרְבַּן נְדָבָה) could do so by throwing money [or the incense itself (see mishnah 6)] into this chest. The administrators would buy frankincense with this money and give it to the *Kohanim* to offer (*Rav;* see *Tosefta* 3:4).

[The frankincense for the *Panim* Bread came from the remainder of the *Nesachim* (*Kesubos* 106b; see *Mishneh LaMelech* to *Hil. Shekalim* 4:2).]

,,זָהָב לַכַּפּוֹרֶת'' — *"Gold for the Utensils" [of the service],*

[This was the seventh chest.] If one donated gold[1] or money to this chest it

---

1. [The view that gold in addition to money was deposited in the chest is shared by *Rambam* (*Comm.; Hil. Shekalim* 2:2), *Rosh*, and *Rav.* This view is puzzling in the light of *Middos* 3:8, which relates that a vine-like golden figure stood at the gate of the Sanctuary [הֵיכָל], and anyone who donated a golden leaf, grape, or cluster would hang it on the figure. *Rambam's Commentary* (ed. Kafich) states that all donors of gold would shape it into these forms. If so, no gold coins were placed in the chest! It may be, however, that *Middos* 3:8 merely reports the prevalent custom to shape gold into forms, but not that there was a requirement to do so. If someone preferred to give coins, he would put them in the chest, whereupon they would be used for the same purpose as the money.]

שְׁקָלִים שִׁשָּׁה לִנְדָבָה.

ו/ה

,,תִּקְלִין חַדְתִּין'' שֶׁבְּכָל שָׁנָה וְשָׁנָה;
וְ,,עַתִּיקִין'', מִי שֶׁלֹּא שָׁקַל אֶשְׁתָּקַד שׁוֹקֵל
לְשָׁנָה הַבָּאָה.

,,קִנִּין'' הֵם תּוֹרִים; וְ,,גּוֹזְלֵי עוֹלָה'' הֵן בְּנֵי
יוֹנָה; וְכֻלָּן עוֹלוֹת — דִּבְרֵי רַבִּי יְהוּדָה.

יד אברהם

went for the purchase of utensils for the service (כְּלֵי שָׁרֵת).

The translation and punctuation follow *Rav, Rosh*, and *Rashi (Yoma 55b, s.v. כולן עולות)* who derive כפורת from בְּזוֹרֵי זָהָב, *golden utensils for service (I Chronicles 28:17; Ezra 1:10, 8:27).* The root of this word is the Aramaic כפר, *to wipe off* (see *Gittin 56b* וּבְעֵי לְכְפּוֹרֵי יָדֵיהּ) and is derived from the *Kohanim's* practice of wiping their fingers against the rims of the blood basin after the blood application had been made on the altar (see *Menachos 7b*). This practice arose in accord with the rule set forth in the Talmud *(Zevachim 93b)* that such remaining blood is invalid for subsequent applications.

Tosefta (3:5) says that the funds in this chest went for the purchase of gold to cover the walls of the Holy of Holies (see above 4:4), which is called בֵּית הַכַּפוֹרֶת, *the chamber of the cover*, because in it was the Holy Ark with its כַּפּוֹרֶת, *cover* (Riva in Tos. Yeshanim Yoma 55b s.v. זהב, Semag, Essin 45 cited by Meleches Shlomo). According to this view the punctuation should be לַכַּפוֹרֶת. *Rambam (comm.)* who comments tersely: 'Whoever donated gold to be used for the כַּפּוֹרֶת and the Holy of Holies put it there' obviously understood כַּפּוֹרֶת to refer to the Ark cover. The use of the gold to cover the walls is an additional use for these funds, and is based on *Tosefta*.

According to this view the inscription לַכַּפוֹרֶת, *for the Ark cover*, was an anachronism dating back to the First Temple era, for in the Second Temple there was no ark (see above mishnah 1, s.v. שׁם ארון).

Although the plain meaning of the mishnah indicates that the two words זָהָב לַכַּפוֹרֶת were inscribed upon this chest, as stated clearly by *Rambam (Comm.)*, this

view is not unanimous. *Rosh* says that the inscription read only זָהָב, *Gold*'', the word לַכַּפוֹרֶת [for utensils of service] is inserted by the mishnah to explain the use to which this gold was put. *Rosh's* view is indicated in *Tosefta* (3:5). Accordingly, the inscription on this chest was like those on the *wood* and *frankincense* chests: all identified only what would be bought with the funds, and not the purpose to which the purchases would be put. Nevertheless the mishnah specifies the purpose of the gold because it is not as evident as that of wood and incense. *Meiri* states that the inscription read only כפורת, indicating the purpose, but not naming the material. [Perhaps he reasons that the mere name of the other materials indicates their purpose as well, but such is not the case regarding gold]. According to *Rambam's* view (see below 6, s.v. זהב) an ordinary vow to contribute gold goes to the fund for the 'upkeep of the Temple'. Thus this chest had to state its intended purpose so that people who had vowed to donate gold not place it here.

שִׁשָּׁה לִנְדָבָה. — *[the remaining] six [were used] for [various] donative offerings.*

Burnt offerings were purchased with the money from each of these chests (*Rambam, Comm.*).

The inscriptions on these six chests were:

(a) מוֹתַר חַטָּאת, *remainder of sin offering* [see above 2:3-5];

(b) מוֹתַר אָשָׁם, *remainder of guilt offering* [see above 2:5];

(c) מוֹתַר קִינֵי זָבִין וְזָבוֹת וְיוֹלְדוֹת, *remainder of bird offerings of zavin, zavos and women after childbirth* [see above 1:5; 2:5];

(d) מוֹתַר קָרְבְּנוֹת נָזִיר, *remainder of a nazirite's offering* [see above 2:5];

(e) מוֹתַר אֲשַׁם מְצוֹרָע, *remainder of a*

6
5
remaining] six [were used] for [various] donative offerings.

"New Shekalim" [was for the shekalim] of each
year; "Old [Shekalim]" [was for] one who did not
pay his half shekel last year and pays it this year.

"Nests" refers to turtledoves; "Young Pigeon
Burnt Offerings" refers to young pigeons; and all are
burnt offerings — [these are] the words of R'
Yehudah.

metzora's guilt offering [see above 5:3];
and

(f) נְדָבָה, *donative offering*. Into this
chest, people put general contributions
to purchase burnt offering for times
when the altar was unoccupied (*Rav;
Rambam, Comm.* and *Hil. Shekalim*
2:2; based on *Tosefta* 3;6). [See
Menachos 107b-108a and *Yerushalmi*
for other views regarding these chests.]

,, תִּקְלִין חַדְתִּין" — *"New Shekalim"*
[The mishnah now returns to explain
the purpose of the first four chests.]

שֶׁבְּכָל שָׁנָה וְשָׁנָה; — *[was for the
shekalim] of each year;*
All those who would pay their tax in
the Temple would [themselves or
through the administrators (see *Tif.
Yis.*)] deposit their shekalim in these
boxes. When the time arrived for the
periodic withdrawals [see 3:1], the administrator would empty the contents
of the chest into the treasury chamber in
which all shekalim were held (*Rav;
Rosh*).

Tiferes Yisrael maintains that the chests
were emptied every evening.

Shekalim collected in the provinces would
not be deposited in these chests, but would
be put directly into the chamber (*Rambam,
Hil. Shekalim* 2:4). However it is *Rambam's*
view (*ibid.* 2:1) that in the province too, at
every collection point, there were two collection boxes, one for new shekalim, and the
other for old (see above 2:1).

[This is the purpose of the chest marked
"Old Shekalim"]:

וְ,,עַתִּיקִין", מִי שֶׁלֹּא שָׁקַל אִשְׁתָּקַד שׁוֹקֵל

לְשָׁנָה הַבָּאָה.—*(and) "Old [Shekalim]"
[was for] one who did not pay his half
shekel last year [and] pays it this year.*

The administrator would add these
monies to the 'remainder of the chamber' (see 4:2-3; *Rav; Rosh*).

Even before the third appropriation
(see 3:1) it was possible to recognize the
'remainder,' because anything left after
the first and second appropriations was
covered with leather covers (see 3:4).]

[It follows that after the third withdrawal, although the year was not over,
the remaining shekalim would be
deposited in the chest marked 'Old
Shekalim,' since it would now go into
the 'remainder of the chamber.']

,,קִנִּין" הֵם תּוֹרִים; וְ,,גּוֹזְלֵי עוֹלָה" הֵן בְּנֵי יוֹנָה;
— *"Nests" refers to turtledoves;
"Young Pigeon Burnt Offerings" refers
to young pigeons;*
The Torah lists two types of birds that
may be used as bird offerings: תֹּר (תֹּרִים), *tor*
(pl. *torim*), usually translated *turtledove, and*
בֶּן (בְּנֵי) יוֹנָה, *ben* (pl. *bnei*) *yonah*, usually
translated *pigeon* or *young dove.* [The
English words pigeon and dove are used interchangeably, although pigeon technically
refers to smaller and dove to larger species of
the same bird family.] Since Scripture invariably uses the adjective בֶּן, *young* [lit.,
son], when referring to the *yonah* as an offering, this species is fit for sacrifice only in
its pre-adolescent stage. Conversely, since
the words *tor* and *torim* are never preceded
by the qualifying "young," this species may
be offered only after reaching adulthood.
During their adolescent stage, neither of
these is valid (*Chullin* 22a,b).

וְכֻלָּן עוֹלוֹת — דִּבְרֵי רַבִּי יְהוּדָה. — *and all*

וַחֲכָמִים אוֹמְרִים: ,,קִנִּין" אֶחָד חַטָּאת וְאֶחָד
עוֹלָה; וְ,,גּוֹזְלֵי עוֹלָה" כֻּלָּן עוֹלוֹת.

[ו] הָאוֹמֵר: ,,הֲרֵי עָלַי עֵצִים," לֹא יִפְחוֹת
מִשְׁנֵי גְזִרִין; ,,לְבוֹנָה," לֹא

יד אברהם

are burnt offerings — [these are] the words of R' Yehudah.

[All birds purchased from funds in these two chests were sacrificed as burnt offerings.] Those required to offer a pair of fowl — a sin offering and a burnt offering (e.g., a *zav, zavah,* woman after childbirth, *metzora*) — could not discharge their obligation through putting money into these chests, because no sin offerings were purchased with these funds. *Yerushalmi* explains that R' Yehudah forbids such purchases because he is apprehensive lest someone requiring a sin offering dies. If so the money would be unusable, for a bird or animal consecrated as a sin offering whose owner died may not be offered on the altar but must be left to die (*Me'ilah* 3:1), nor may the money be used for any other purpose; it must be dropped into the Dead Sea (*ibid* 3:2). If so, *none* of the money in the chest could be used, because we have no way of determining which belonged to the deceased. Consequently, R' Yehudah rules, someone obligated to bring a sin offering must give either money or the appropriate bird directly to the *Kohen* (*Rav* from *Yer.* and *Yoma* 55b).

וַחֲכָמִים אוֹמְרִים: ,,קִנִּין" אֶחָד חַטָּאת וְאֶחָד עוֹלָה; — *But the [other] Sages say:* "Nests" [was used by one required to bring two birds], one a sin offering, one a burnt offering;

Money in this chest went for the purchase of pairs of fowl, of which one would be a sin offering and the other a burnt offering (*Rav*). [Thus people required to offer such sacrifices could simply deposit an adequate sum of money and be assured that their sacrifice had been offered on that day, for one can assume (חֲזָקָה) that the tribunal of the *Kohanim* would not leave for the day until all the sacrifices to be offered from the money in these chests had been offered (*Eruvin* 32a).]

The Sages hold that even in the event that one of the donors died, this would not cause the problem feared by R' Yehudah: that among the money in the chest are some funds designated for sin offering, the use of which is forbidden. The sages accept the principle of בְּרֵירָה, *Bereirah* [retroactive identification (see footnote)].[1] Following this rule, the *Kohanim* may set aside a sum of money (from the funds in the chest) sufficient for a fowl sin offering, and designate this money as the sum belonging to the deceased. The rule of *Bereirah* retroactively

1. A comprehensive exposition of *Bereirah*, the concept of retroactive identification, is beyond the scope of this work; but a few words of clarification are in order. This concept rests upon the maxim: הוּבְרַר הַדָּבָר לְמַפְרֵעַ, lit. *the matter is clarified retroactively,* i.e., matters in a state of סָפֵק, *uncertainty,* which will be resolved in the future, are, when such clarification takes place, judged to have been clarified retroactively. E.g., in the case of an estate that has not yet been divided among the heirs, the individual heir who will own any given item is not yet known. Only when the estate has been divided will ownership of each item have been established. According to the principle of *Bereirah*, the eventual owner of each portion of the estate is deemed to have become its owner the moment the death took place. The later distribution of the assets is deemed to have retroactively identified the owner, but not conferred title upon him. Similarly, here, when the money is set aside for the deceased, it is considered to have been his share of the pooled money from the very moment it was deposited in the chest. Thus, this is not in the category of admixture (תַּעֲרוֹבֶת) of prohibited and permitted substances where one cannot at random pick out one item and assume it to be the prohibited substance (see *Tos., Temurah* 30a, s.v. ואידך and *Sotah* 18a, s.v. חזר).

6
6 But the [other] Sages say: "Nests" [was used by one required to bring two birds], one a sin offering, one a burnt offering; but "Young Pigeon Burnt Offerings" was for burnt offerings only.

6. One who says: "I obligate myself [to offer] wood," may not bring less than two blocks; [if he says,] "Frankincense," he may not bring less than

YAD AVRAHAM

identifies that amount as the money intended for this person's sin offering. It is then disposed of in the appropriate manner (the money is thrown into the Dead Sea); the rest of the funds in the chest can then be used for burnt offerings, and the sin offering of living people (*Yoma* 55b). R' Yehudah does not accept the principle of *Bereirah (Eruvin* 36b).

,,וְגוֹזָלֵי עוֹלָה" כֻּלָּן עוֹלוֹת. — *but "Young Pigeon Burnt Offerings" was for burnt offerings only.*

Thus anyone wanting to donate a fowl burnt offering would deposit his donation in this chest.

According to the Sages, both turtledoves and pigeons may be purchased with money from this chest (*Rivevan*). [The term גּוֹזָל, *young pigeon,* is used inexactly, for turtledoves may be offered only in their mature state (*Chullin* 1:5). However there is no reason to suppose, according to the Sages, that a chest was assigned solely for pigeon burnt offerings, but that turtledoves could be offered only if the donor purchased them himself. Rather we assume (according to the Sages) that one chest was for those obligated to offer a pair (a sin offering and a burnt offering) and the other chest for voluntary burnt offerings.]

The translation of גּוֹזָל as *young pigeon* follows *Onkelos, Rashi* and *Ibn Ezra* to *Genesis* 15:9. *Radak (Shorashim,* s.v. גזל: comm. to *Gen., ibid.)* points out that גּוֹזָל technically includes the young of all fowl, but *Genesis* 15:9 is rendered as *young pigeon* because it is the only fowl whose young is suitable for sacrifice. Besides, since the verse uses this word in juxtaposition to תּוֹרִים, *turtledoves,* it must likewise refer to a species.

6.

The mishnah now sets the minimums which may be donated to redeem pledges of unspecified amounts.

הָאוֹמֵר: ,,הֲרֵי עָלַי עֵצִים," — *One who says: "I obligate myself* [*to offer*] *wood"* [lit. *wood is upon me*],

[I.e., he obligated himself to supply wood for the altar, but did not specify how much he wanted to offer. A promise to contribute to the Temple is considered a vow and must be fulfilled. The question is now, what is the minimum amount implied by the vow.]

לֹא יִפְחוֹת מִשְּׁנֵי גְזִרִין; — *may not bring less* [lit. *may not diminish from*] *than two blocks* [of wood];

[Because the Hebrew word עֵצִים, *wood,* is plural, it connotes at least two pieces of wood.]

These blocks should be of the type used upon the altar; a size that was known (*Rav; Rosh).*

Yerushalmi cites various opinions regarding the size of the wood used upon the altar. The view adopted by the Talmud (*Zevachim* 62b), and incorporated into *Rambam's* code (*Hil. Issurei Mizbe'ach* 7:3; see *Hil. Ma'aseh HaKarbonos* 16:13 and *Comm.* here), requires each piece to be 1 cubit (אַמָּה) square and of a thickness of the standard stick used to level the grain that was heaped on top of a *seah* measure.

If he used the singular form עֵץ, *wood,* in his vow, one block is sufficient (*Rav* from *Yerushalmi),* for even one block of wood is considered an offering. During the evening service, when the required two blocks (שְׁנֵי

שקלים יִפְחוֹת מִקֹּמֶץ; ,,זָהָב,'' לֹא יִפְחוֹת מִדִּינַר זָהָב.
שִׁשָּׁה לִנְדָבָה. נְדָבָה מֶה הָיוּ עוֹשִׂין בָּהּ?
לוֹקְחִין בָּהּ עוֹלוֹת; הַבָּשָׂר לַשֵּׁם, וְהָעוֹרוֹת
לַכֹּהֲנִים. זֶה מִדְרָשׁ דָּרַשׁ יְהוֹיָדָע כֹּהֵן גָּדוֹל:
,,אָשָׁם הוּא, אָשֹׁם אָשַׁם לַה'.'' זֶה הַכְּלָל: כָּל־
שֶׁהוּא בָא מִשּׁוּם חֵטְא וּמִשּׁוּם אַשְׁמָה, יִלָּקַח

יד אברהם

גִּזְרֵי עֵצִים) were added to the altar pyre, two *Kohanim* were chosen, each to carry a single block of wood (*Tos. Yom Tov*; see *Yoma* 2:5; cf. *Ramban* to *Menachos* 13:3).

If he wished he could contribute a sum of money adequate to buy two blocks of wood (*Hil. Ma'aseh HaKarabonos* 16:3).

,,לְבוֹנָה,'' לֹא יִפְחוֹת מִקֹּמֶץ; — [*if he says,*] *"Frankincense," he may not bring less* [lit. *diminish from*] *than a fistful;*

The Talmud (*Menachos* 106b) derives that the frankincense offered with (almost) all meal offerings must consist of a *kometz*. [A *kometz*, here translated *fistful*, is the amount held upon the palm of the hand by the index, middle and ring fingers.] Therefore a vow of an unspecified amount is assumed to refer to the minimum possibility — one fistful. However if one specified a vow to bring as little as one grain, he may do so[1] (*Rav*).

,,זָהָב,'' לֹא יִפְחוֹת מִדִּינַר זָהָב. — [*if he says,*] *"Gold," he may not bring less* [lit. *diminish from*] *than a gold dinar.*

[This is the smallest gold coin (see *Menachos* 107a). The silver dinar weighed as much as 96 barley grains, approximately 4.8 grams or 15 troy ounces. However there is a question whether the gold dinar, which was valued at 25 silver dinars (*Bava Metzia* 44b), was of the same weight as that of silver. *Rabbeinu Tam* (*Tos. Bechoros* 50a, s.v. רמזורבנא) supposes that it weighed about twice as much as the silver dinar.]

The rule enunciated here applies to one who vowed to contribute a gold coin. If he vowed to give 'gold' without indicating that he meant coins, he may give even a small amount of gold, enough to make a hook (*Rav* and *Rosh* based on *Yerushalmi*).

The Talmud (*Menachos* 107a), which mentions נְסָכָא, *nugget*, can be understood as agreeing with this. However *Rambam (Hil. Arachin* 2:10), obviously based on this passage of Talmud, rules that he must bring the maximum amount about which he cannot reasonably claim, 'I did not mean this much.'

The gold or gold coins contributed in this manner is assumed to have been earmarked for the fund 'for the upkeep of the Temple' (בֶּדֶק הַבַּיִת) (*Rambam, Comm.* to *Menachos* 13:3). Thus it is not placed in the chest marked "Gold".

However, *Tosefta* (3:5) states explicitly that 'one who says: "An obligation of gold is upon me" must bring a dinar's worth and put it in the collection chest … ' *Meleches Shlomo* derives from a quote in R' *Shlomo Sirilio's* commentary (not found in our edition) that the author's version of our mishnah reads לֹא יִפְחוֹת מִדִּינַר זָהָב לַכְּפוֹרֶת, meaning that the gold goes to the chest dedicated to the purchase of vessels for Temple use.

שִׁשָּׁה לִנְדָבָה. נְדָבָה מֶה הָיוּ עוֹשִׂין בָּהּ? — *What was done with the [funds in the] six chests [designated] for donative offerings?* [lit., *Six for donative offerings. What was done with donative offerings?*]

[See mishnah 5.]

---

1. *Rav* does not say explicitly that a single grain may be offered upon the altar. This would depend upon the conflicting views (*Menachos* 26b) whether less than כַּזַּיִת, *the volume of an olive*, may be burnt separately upon the altar. *Rambam (Hil. Pesulei HaMukdashin* 11:15) rules against the acceptability of such small quantities. Thus the single grain of frankincense must be held until such time as an amount equal to the volume of an olive has accumulated.

a fistful; [if he says,] "Gold," he may not bring less than a gold dinar.

What was done with the [funds in the] six chests [designated] for donative offerings? — They would buy burnt offerings; the meat for God, the hides for the *Kohanim*. This exposition was expounded by Yehoyada the *Kohen Gadol*: *It is a guilt offering, for he is guilty, a guilt offering to HASHEM* [*Leviticus* 5:19]. This is the general rule: Whatever comes because of sin or because of guilt, shall be used to

YAD AVRAHAM

לוֹקְחִין בָּה עוֹלוֹת; הַבָּשָׂר לַשֵׁם, וְהָעוֹרוֹת לַכֹּהֲנִים. — *They would buy burnt offerings; the meat for God* [lit. *the Name;* i.e., it is burnt upon the altar], *the hides for the Kohanim.*

[The hides of all burnt offerings (as well as those of all קָדְשֵׁי קָדָשִׁים (see *Zevachim* 12:3) go to the *Kohanim* of the family (בֵּית אָב) serving on that day (*Leviticus* 7:8; see *Bava Kamma* 110a).]

זֶה מִדְרָשׁ דָּרַשׁ יְהוֹיָדָע כֹּהֵן גָּדוֹל: — *This exposition was expounded by Yehoyada the Kohen Gadol:*

[Yehoyada was *Kohen Gadol* during the reign of King Yeho'ash (*II Kings* 11:4-12:17; *II Chronicles* 22:10-24:16). The exposition given here in Yehoyada's name is the source of the rule assigning the contents of the six chests for donative offerings to the purchase of burnt offerings. These funds (with the exception of the sixth chest) were remainders of monies set aside for sin and guilt offerings. Yehoyada showed that such remainders should be sacrificed as burnt offerings.]

"אָשָׁם הוּא, אָשֹׁם אָשַׁם לַה׳. — *It is a guilt offering, for he is guilty, a guilt offering to HASHEM* [*Leviticus* 5:19]. [The translation is literal and follows *Targum Onkelos.*]

Yehoyada sensed a contradiction: First we are told, *it is a guilt offering* which implies that all rules pertaining to guilt offerings are in effect [the whole statement seems superfluous: we

already know (from the previous verses) that it is a guilt offering (*Malbim*)], i.e., even after the guilt offering has been purchased the remaining money retains its status and is earmarked for the *Kohanim*. However, the final phrase indicates that the offering is completely consumed by the altar fire, i.e., it is to God, not to the *Kohanim* (*Rav; Rosh*).

Alternatively, Yehoyada does not base his exegesis on a contradiction within this verse, but upon another verse that contradicts the premise stated in this one, that the offering is completely '*to HASHEM*': Various such verses are adduced by the commentators:

Like the sin offering, so the guilt offering ... whichever Kohen atones with it to him shall it belong (*Leviticus* 7:7; *Rashi, Zevachim* 103a, s.v. אשם לה׳);

... According to its value as a guilt offering, to the Kohen (*Leviticus* 5:25; *Ravad* and *R' Shimshon of Sens,* to *Sifre* 5:19; see also *Malbim* there; cf. *Vilna Gaon's* emendation of *Sifre* which accords with *Rav* and *Rosh* cited above);

... the guilt offering (אָשָׁם: but this is not the simple meaning of the word here) *which is returned to HASHEM, is for the Kohen* (*Numbers* 5:8; *Rivevan*).

[The mishnah continues with Yehoyada's resolution of the contradiction.]

זֶה הַכְּלָל: כָּל-שֶׁהוּא בָא מִשּׁוּם חֵטְא וּמִשּׁוּם אַשְׁמָה, יִלָּקַח בּוֹ עוֹלוֹת; — *This is the general rule* [*derived from this verse*]: *Whatever comes because of sin or because of guilt, shall be used to purchase burnt offerings;*

שְׁקָלִים בּוֹ עוֹלוֹת; הַבָּשָׂר לַשֵּׁם, וְהָעוֹרוֹת לַכֹּהֲנִים.
נִמְצְאוּ שְׁנֵי כְתוּבִים קַיָּמִים; ,,אָשָׁם לַה' ''
וְ,,אָשָׁם לַכֹּהֲנִים''.
וְאוֹמֵר: ,,כֶּסֶף אָשָׁם וְכֶסֶף חַטָּאות לֹא יוּבָא
בֵּית ה'; לַכֹּהֲנִים יִהְיוּ.''

[א] **מָעוֹת** שֶׁנִּמְצְאוּ בֵּין הַשְּׁקָלִים לַנְּדָבָה
— קָרוֹב לַשְּׁקָלִים, יִפְּלוּ

יד אברהם

The words *"for he is guilty, a guilt offering to HASHEM"* are explained by Yehoyada: Any monies that come to the Temple coffers as a result of sin or guilt[1], i.e., the surplus of funds set aside for the purchase of such offerings, which is placed in one of the collection boxes, *is to HASHEM*, i.e., the surplus money is used to purchase offerings whose meat *Kohanim* may not eat — namely, burnt offerings (*Rav*).

הַבָּשָׂר לַשֵּׁם, וְהָעוֹרוֹת לַכֹּהֲנִים. — *the meat for God* [i.e., it is burned upon the altar], *the hides for the Kohanim.*

[As the hide of all burnt offerings.]

נִמְצְאוּ שְׁנֵי כְתוּבִים קַיָּמִים: ,,אָשָׁם לַה' ''
וְ,,אָשָׁם לַכֹּהֲנִים''. — *Thus the two verses are reconciled* [lit. *stand*]; [*it is a*] *guilt offering for HASHEM and a guilt offering for the Kohanim.*

[I.e., the two ostensibly contradictory segments of the verse, (or, according to the alternative views cited above, the two contradictory verses) are thus reconciled.]

וְאוֹמֵר: — *And it also says:*

The mishnah now adduces another verse that alludes to Yehoyada's exegesis (*Rav; Rosh*).

,,כֶּסֶף אָשָׁם וְכֶסֶף חַטָּאות לֹא יוּבָא בֵּית ה';
לַכֹּהֲנִים יִהְיוּ.'' — *The guilt offering*

money and the sin offerings money shall not be brought to the Temple of HASHEM; they shall be for the Kohanim [II Kings 12:17].

[The only possible interpretation (see below) is: *Guilt offering money and sin offerings money* — that had not been needed for the purchase of the offerings, i.e., מוֹתָר, *remainder* — *shall not be brought to the House of HASHEM* — i.e. it shall not be used for the 'upkeep of the Temple' (בֶּדֶק הַבַּיִת). Instead, *it shall be for the Kohanim* — i.e., burnt offerings should be purchased with this money, the hides of which are given to the *Kohen* (see *Rashi* and *comm.* to the verse; *Tos. Yom Tov*).]

The literal meaning of this verse is untenable. Surely money consecrated and designated for offerings may not be used for *Kohanim* (*Rav; Rosh*). Nor can it mean that this money should be used for guilt and sin offerings and the meat consumed by the *Kohanim*, because then the verse should have said 'they shall be for guilt-offerings and sin offerings.' (*Tos. Yom Tov*). Nor can it mean that the 'remainder' of this money be used for the purchase of these offerings, for once the owner has sacrificed his offerings, an unrequired sin or guilt offering may not be brought from his surplus funds (*Tif. Yis*).

[The intent can also not be that peace offerings be purchased and the meat be consumed partly by *Kohanim*, for this surely

---

1. The inclusion of חַטָּאת, *sin offering*, in the rule derived from this verse, which mentions only the אָשָׁם, *guilt offering*, is based on the redundancy of אָשָׁם אָשָׁם (*Sifre*). Also the word אשם in its verb form (אָשֵׁם) refers not to the guilt offering, but to *any* guilt or sin (see *Malbim* loc. cit. and *Ayeles HaShachar* 365).

purchase burnt offerings; the meat for God, the hides for the Kohanim. Thus the two verses are reconciled; [it is a] *guilt offering for HASHEM* and a *guilt offering for the Kohanim.*

And it also says: *The guilt offering money and the sin offerings money shall not be brought to the Temple of HASHEM; they shall be for the Kohanim* [*II Kings* 12:17].

1. **C**oins which are found between the shekalim [chests] and the donative offering [chests] — [if they are found] closer to the shekalim [chests] they

could not be termed 'it shall be for the *Kohanim,*' since most of such meat (and the hides) would go to the owner. Only burnt of- ferings (and guilt and sin offerings), where everything not offered upon the altar goes to the *Kohanim,* can be so termed.]

Chapter 7

1.

Having enumerated and described the thirteen collection chests (6:5-6), the tanna now discusses the status of money found between two of these chests (beginning of mishnah 1). Tangentially the status of various things found in the Temple environs or other parts of Jerusalem is discussed (through 8:3). In all cases, the object in doubt may have been consecrated, and we must determine its precise halachic status.

מָעוֹת שֶׁנִּמְצְאוּ בֵּין הַשְּׁקָלִים לַנְּדָבָה — *Coins which are found between the shekalim [chests] and the donative offering [chests] —*

Money was found between the two chests for new and old shekalim and the six chests for donative offering [נְדָבָה] (see above 6:5; *Tif. Yis.*).

Assuming that the thirteen collection chests of 6:5 were set in a straight line (*Korban HaEdah*), Yerushalmi wonders that the money was not found between the chests of shekalim and nests, which were adjacent to one another. Yerushalmi explains that the chests stood in a circle so that the first shekalim chest was next to the sixth donative offering chest [see diag. p. 125].

קָרוֹב לַשְּׁקָלִים, יִפְּלוּ לַשְּׁקָלִים; לַנְּדָבָה, יִפְּלוּ לַנְּדָבָה; — *[if they are found] closer to the shekalim [chests] they should fall to the*

shekalim [chests]; [if closer] to the donative offering [chests], they should fall to the donative offering [chests];

[If the money was found in the area nearer to the shekalim chest, it is assumed that it comes from that chest and vice versa.] The halachic principle states that items of unknown origin are assumed to have come from the nearest source (קָרוֹב). This principle is derived from the law of עֶגְלָה עֲרוּפָה, *the decapitated calf.* If the body of a murder victim is found between two cities, and the killer is unknown, the town nearest to the corpse must follow the procedure outlined in *Deuteronomy* 21:1-9. Included in the ritual is a declaration of the town elders that they are not responsible for the death, implying that

שְׁקָלִים לַשְּׁקָלִים; לַנְּדָבָה, יִפְּלוּ לַנְּדָבָה; מֶחֱצָה
לְמֶחֱצָה, יִפְּלוּ לַנְּדָבָה.
בֵּין ,,עֵצִים'' לְ,,לְבוֹנָה'' — קָרוֹב לְ,,עֵצִים'',
יִפְּלוּ לְ,,עֵצִים''; לְ,,לְבוֹנָה'', יִפְּלוּ לְ,,לְבוֹנָה'';
מֶחֱצָה לְמֶחֱצָה, יִפְּלוּ לְ,,לְבוֹנָה''.

יד אברהם

the murderer is presumed to have come from the nearest town.

There is, however, a second halachic principle which states that items of unknown origin are assumed to have come from the larger source (הָלַךְ אַחַר הָרוֹב). Which principle to follow, the greater numbers or the closer proximity when the nearer source is smaller, is debated in the Talmud (Bava Basra 23b): Our mishnah seems to follow the view that the test of proximity has greater validity than the test of numbers. To reconcile our mishnah with the opposite view, that numbers have more credence than proximity, we must interpret our mishnah as referring to a case where both chests contain an equal amount of money (Rav).

Alternatively, although one chest had a greater amount of money at the time the questionable coins were found, perhaps the balance was reversed since the time the money was lost. Thus, the principle of greater numbers cannot apply to our mishnah (Tif. Yis.; Soshanim L'David; cf. Rambam, Hil. Shekalim 3:14).

מֶחֱצָה לְמֶחֱצָה, יִפְּלוּ לַנְּדָבָה. — [if] equidistant from the two [lit. half to half], they should fall to the donative offering [chests].

Since the question of origin cannot be resolved by the principle of proximity, the questionable money should be put to the more stringent use [לְחוּמְרָא]. Funds for 'donative offerings' are used to purchase burnt offerings whose flesh is totally consumed on the altar fire, while shekalim funds are used partly for the sin offerings of Rosh Chodesh and Yom Tov and the peace offerings of

Shavuos whose flesh is eaten by the Kohanim. Thus the donative chest is considered a more stringent application (Rav; Rosh; Ramban). Also the surplus funds in the shekalim chest are used for the 'wall of the city and its towers' and the like, which are of a lesser holiness than the donative offerings (Rav; Yer.; see 4:2).

בֵּין ,,עֵצִים'' לְ,,לְבוֹנָה'' — [Coins which are found] between "Wood" and "Frankincense" —

[Money was found between the chest marked 'Wood' and the adjacent chest which was marked 'Frankincense'. See diagram.]

קָרוֹב לְ,,עֵצִים'', יִפְּלוּ לְ,,עֵצִים''; לְ,,לְבוֹנָה'', יִפְּלוּ לְ,,לְבוֹנָה''; מֶחֱצָה לְמֶחֱצָה, יִפְּלוּ לְ,,לְבוֹנָה''. — [if they are found] closer to "Wood", they should fall to "Wood"; [if closer] to "Frankincense", they should fall to "Frankincense"; [if] equidistant from the two [lit. half to half], they should fall to "Frankincense".

Frankincense is the more stringent purpose because it is itself an offering, whereas wood is only an accessory, albeit a necessary one, to an offering (מַכְשִׁירֵי קָרְבָּן; Rav; Rosh; Rambam).

[Presumably, this same logic, which is stated as a general rule at the end of this mishnah, applies to money found between the chests for donative offerings and gold; frankincense and gold; young pigeon burnt offerings and wood; nests and old shekalim; or new shekalim and old shekalim. In each of these cases the former item is the more stringent because it is offered on the altar while the latter is not. (See below, s.v. זה הכלל.) In the case of the six donative offering chests, however, since all are applied to the same purpose, it does not matter into which chest money found between two of them is

should fall to the shekalim [chests]; [if closer] to the donative offering [chests], they should fall to the donative offering [chests]; [if] equidistant from the two, they should fall to the donative offering [chests].

[Coins which are found] between "Wood" and "Frankincense" — [if they are found] closer to "Wood", they should fall to "Wood"; [if closer] to "Frankincense," they should fall to "Frankincense"; [if] equidistant from the two, they should fall to "Frankincense."

YAD AVRAHAM

placed. The only question remaining then is the status of money found between the nests and young pigeons chests, for both are used for altar sacrifices which differ, however, in their degree of stringency. The mishnah now takes up that case.]

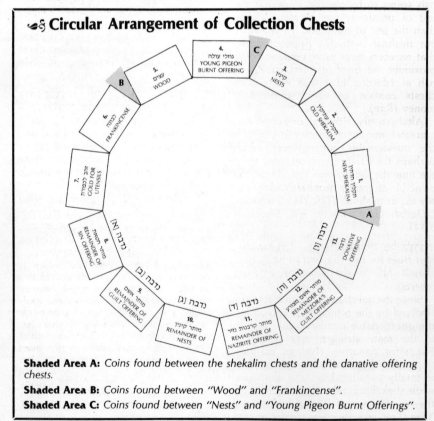

❧ Circular Arrangement of Collection Chests

Shaded Area A: *Coins found between the shekalim chests and the danative offering chests.*

Shaded Area B: *Coins found between "Wood" and "Frankincense".*

Shaded Area C: *Coins found between "Nests" and "Young Pigeon Burnt Offerings".*

בֵּין ,,קִנִּין'' לְ,,גּוֹזְלֵי עוֹלָה'' — קָרוֹב
לְ,,קִנִּין'', יִפְּלוּ לְ,,קִנִּין''; לְ,,גוֹזְלֵי עוֹלָה'', יִפְּלוּ
לְ,,גוֹזְלֵי עוֹלָה''; מֶחֱצָה לְמֶחֱצָה, יִפְּלוּ לְ,,גוֹזְלֵי
עוֹלָה''.

בֵּין חֻלִּין לְמַעֲשֵׂר שֵׁנִי —קָרוֹב לְחֻלִּין,
יִפְּלוּ לְחֻלִּין; לְמַעֲשֵׂר שֵׁנִי, יִפְּלוּ לְמַעֲשֵׂר שֵׁנִי;
מֶחֱצָה לְמֶחֱצָה, יִפְּלוּ לְמַעֲשֵׂר שֵׁנִי.
זֶה הַכְּלָל: הוֹלְכִין אַחַר הַקָּרוֹב לְהָקֵל,
מֶחֱצָה לְמֶחֱצָה לְהַחְמִיר.

[ב] מָעוֹת שֶׁנִּמְצְאוּ לִפְנֵי סוֹחֲרֵי בְהֵמָה
לְעוֹלָם מַעֲשֵׂר. בְּהַר הַבַּיִת
חֻלִּין.

יד אברהם

בֵּין ,,קִנִּין'' לְ,,גוֹזְלֵי עוֹלָה''— קָרוֹב לְ,,קִנִּין'',
יִפְּלוּ לְ,,קִנִּין''; לְ,,גוֹזְלֵי עוֹלָה'', יִפְּלוּ לְ,,גוֹזְלֵי
עוֹלָה''; מֶחֱצָה לְמֶחֱצָה, יִפְּלוּ לְ,,גוֹזְלֵי עוֹלָה''.
— [Coins which are found] between
"Nests" and "Young Pigeon Burnt Offerings" — [if they are found] closer to
"Nests", they should fall to "Nests"; [if
closer] to "Young Pigeon Burnt Offerings", they should fall to "Young
Pigeon Burnt Offerings"; [if] equidistant from the two [lit. half to half], they
should fall to "Young Pigeon Burnt Offerings".

The money in the pigeon chest is
used entirely for burnt offerings (Rambam; Rosh), whereas the funds in the
nests chest are used to purchase sin offerings as well, and such offerings are
not totally burnt upon the altar; some
portions are offered but the major part
of the meat is eaten by the Kohanim.
Thus, the expenditure for young pigeon
burnt offerings is the more stringent
one. Our mishnah follows the view of
the Sages (6:5) that the nests chest is
used for both sin and burnt offerings
(Tif. Yis.).

[According to R' Yehudah neither use is
more stringent than the other — the difference is only in the type of fowl purchased

— and in a case of equidistance, the money
could be deposited in either chest.]

By following the principle of placing the
found money into the chest used for offerings of more stringent sanctity, the mishnah
seemingly overlooks an important fact. Had
this money actually been intended for the
nests, it would have been used to complete
the cleansing process of a woman after childbirth (or the like). Thinking that her bird offerings were offered with this money she will
assume that her cleansing is complete and
proceed to enter the Temple Courtyard or eat
sacrificial meat, two acts which are prohibited before the birds have been offered. [This
objection is not valid if the money was found
nearer to one of the chests — for as derived
above (s.v. קרוב לשקלים) — proximity is a
Scripturally based ground for an assumption
of origin.] Yerushalmi resolves this situation
by having the Temple administration set
aside an equal amount of money and assign
its ownership to the loser who lost the
money, and then place it into the nests chest
on that person's behalf. However, since the
actual need for this offering is doubtful, the
sin offering so purchased may not be eaten
by the Kohanim (Rav; Rosh).

בֵּין חֻלִּין לְמַעֲשֵׂר שֵׁנִי — קָרוֹב לְחֻלִּין,
יִפְּלוּ לְחֻלִּין; לְמַעֲשֵׂר שֵׁנִי, יִפְּלוּ לְמַעֲשֵׂר
שֵׁנִי; מֶחֱצָה לְמֶחֱצָה, יִפְּלוּ לְמַעֲשֵׂר שֵׁנִי.
[Coins which are found] between non-

[Coins which are found] between "Nests" and "Young Pigeon Burnt Offerings" — [if they are found] closer to "Nests," they should fall to "Nests"; [if closer] to "Young Pigeon Burnt Offerings", they should fall to " Young Pigeon Burnt Offerings"; [if] equidistant from the two, they should fall to "Young Pigeon Burnt Offerings".

[Coins which are found] between nonconsecrated [funds] and second tithe [funds] — [if they are found] closer to nonconsecrated [funds], they should fall to nonconsecrated [funds]; [if closer] to second tithe [funds], they should fall to second tithe [funds]; [if] equidistant from the two, they should fall to second tithe [funds].

This is the general rule: We decide according to proximity [even] for leniency, but in a case of equidistance we decide for stringency.

2. **C**oins which are found before animal dealers [in Jerusalem] are always [assumed to be second] tithe [money]. [Coins found] on the Temple Mount [are assumed to be] nonconsecrated.

YAD AVRAHAM

consecrated [funds] and second tithe [funds] — [if they are found] closer to nonconsecrated [funds], they should fall to nonconsecrated [funds]; [if closer] to second tithe [funds], they should fall to second tithe [funds]; [if] equidistant from the two [lit. half to half], they should fall to second tithe [funds].

That this case, which does not refer to the collection chests, has been inserted by the tanna, indicates that the following general rule is not restricted to the collection chests, but has universal ap-

plicability (Taklin Chadatin).

זֶה הַכְּלָל: הוֹלְכִין אַחַר הַקָּרוֹב לְהָקֵל, מֶחֱצָה לְמֶחֱצָה לְהַחֲמִיר. — This is the general rule: We decide according to proximity [even] for leniency, but in a case of equidistance [lit. half to half] we decide for stringency.

Yerushalmi notes that the articulation of this general rule is needed for cases not mentioned in the mishnah, money found between wood and young pigeon burnt offerings and between frankincense and gold. (See above, s.v. מחצה למחצה יפלו ללבונה.)

2.

מָעוֹת שֶׁנִּמְצְאוּ לִפְנֵי סוֹחֲרֵי בְהֵמָה לְעוֹלָם מַעֲשֵׂר. — Coins which are found before animal dealers [in Jerusalem] are always

[assumed to be second] tithe [money].

'Always' means year round, as distinct from money found in other parts

בִּירוּשָׁלַיִם — בִּשְׁעַת הָרֶגֶל, מַעֲשֵׂר; וּבִשְׁאָר
כָּל-יְמוֹת הַשָּׁנָה, חוּלִּין.

[ג] **בָּשָׂר** שֶׁנִּמְצָא בָּעֲזָרָה — אֵבָרִין עוֹלוֹת,
וַחֲתִיכוֹת חַטָּאוֹת. בִּירוּשָׁלַיִם,

יד אברהם

of Jerusalem, whose status depends on the time of year it was found (see below).

This rule is based on the premise that the pilgrims who visited Jerusalem for only a limited period of time were not there long enough to consume all the goods they could purchase with their *ma'aser sheni* funds. They would leave the remaining funds with relatives and acquaintances in Jerusalem who would use it year round for the purchase of peace offerings. Throughout the year, therefore, most animals sold in Jerusalem were purchased with second tithe money. It follows that most of the money brought to the animal market had second tithe status. Consequently, in accord with the rule of following the majority (הָלַךְ אַחַר הָרוֹב), such funds are assumed to be second tithe money (*Rav*).

Majority rule, in this case, would seem to be inadequate to decide the status of the funds. Once second tithe money was used to buy food or an animal for slaughter, the consecrated status of the money passes to the purchased item and the money itself becomes nonconsecrated [חוּלִּין]. Since money found in the animal market may just as easily have fallen from a dealer after an animal was purchased, why should we assume that it was lost before a purchase was made? The resolution to this problem is found in another application of the majority principle: there are more buyers than sellers, therefore, it can be assumed that a buyer is more likely to have lost the money (*Rav; Rambam; Tos., Pesachim* 7a, s.v. לפני).

Alternatively, we apply the principle of taking the more stringent stand in unresolved halachic matters involving Scriptural prohibition [סְפֵיקָא דְאוֹרַיְיתָא לְחוּמְרָא] (*Rashi, Pesachim* 7a, s.v., רוב אוכלי: *Rambam, Comm.*).

בְּהַר הַבַּיִת חוּלִּין. — [*Coins found*] *on the Temple Mount* [*are assumed to be*] *nonconsecrated.*

Even during the festival season, when most monies in Jerusalem are of second tithe status, we do not assume that these funds are *ma'aser sheni*, because we cannot say that the money was lost during the festival period. The principle of majority dictates that because there is a preponderance of nonconsecrated money most of the year, any found money must be considered nonconsecrated, even during the festival period (*Rav; Rosh*).

Why do we assume that the money was lost by an ordinary person and consequently nonconsecrated? — This money could conceivably have come from the various consecrated funds in the Temple, and have been lost by a *Kohen* enroute to purchase an animal for Temple use. This conjecture is untenable, however, because of the rule that no money may be taken from any Temple fund unless it is instantly redeemed for an animal or other suitable item. Consequently, we adopt the presumption (חֲזָקָה) that this would have been observed (*Yer.* cited by *Rambam*).[1]

בִּירוּשָׁלַיִם — בִּשְׁעַת הָרֶגֶל, מַעֲשֵׂר; — [*Coins found elsewhere*] *in Jerusalem* [*if they are found*] *during the pilgrimage*

---

1. Another question is raised by *Tosafos* (*Pesachim* 7a, s.v. בהר, cited by *Tos. Yom Tov*) and *Rosh*. Since one is forbidden to enter the Temple Mount with money in his kerchief or money belt (*Berachos* 62b), the lost money must have been half shekels being delivered to the Temple. They advance the solution that only money carried in a conspicuous manner may not be carried into the Temple Mount. It is permitted, however, to carry money discreetly in a purse held under the clothing, for example. *Tos. Yom Tov* adds that even consecrated money may not be carried conspicuously.

[Coins found elsewhere] in Jerusalem [if they are found] during the pilgrimage festivals, [they are assumed to be second] tithe [money]; but during the rest of the year, [they are assumed to be] nonconsecrated.

3. If meat is found in the [Temple] Courtyard — limbs are [assumed to be] burnt offerings, but slices are [assumed to be] sin offerings. [If meat is

YAD AVRAHAM

festivals, [they are assumed to be second] tithe [money];

The disposition of money found anywhere in Jerusalem [with the exception of the animal market or the Temple Mount], varies with the time of year. During the pilgrimage festivals, we assume that the money was lost during the festival and it is consequently second tithe money, as is most of the money in Jerusalem during the festivals. In contrast to money found on the Temple Mount, we do not assume that it was lost before the festival, for the streets of

Jerusalem were carefully swept every day, so anything lost earlier would have been found and removed before the festival (*Rav, Rosh*, based on *Pesachim* 7a).

וּבִשְׁאָר כָּל-יְמוֹת הַשָּׁנָה, חוּלִּין. — *but during the rest of the year, [they are assumed to be] nonconsecrated.*

[Only in the animal market is there a preponderance of second tithe money even during the rest of the year, because the most common use of second tithe funds was for peace offerings.]

3.

◆§ Limits for Consumption of Sacrificial Meats

The following time and places limits for consumption of sacrificial meats are set forth in chapter 5 of *Zevachim*:

עוֹלָה, *burnt offering* — placed entirely on altar, ideally on day of slaughter before sunset, or until daybreak;

חַטָּאת, *sin offering, and* אָשָׁם, *guilt offering,* — eaten in the Temple Courtyard by male *Kohanim*, on day of slaughter until next morning at daybreak (until midnight by Rabbinic decree);

תּוֹדָה, *thanksgiving offering, and* אֵיל נָזִיר, *nazirite's ram* — eaten in Jerusalem, by all, on day of slaughter until next morning at daybreak (until midnight by Rabbinic decree);

שְׁלָמִים, *peace offering, and* מַעֲשֵׂר בְּהֵמָה — *animal tithe,* eaten in Jerusalem, by all, on day of slaughter until next day at sunset [two days and the included night];

בְּכוֹר, *first born* — eaten in Jerusalem by *Kohanim*, on day of slaughter until next day at sunset [two days and the included night];

פֶּסַח, *Pesach* — eaten by those 'counted on it', on night after slaughter until midnight.

Any part of an offering not consumed within its prescribed time becomes נוֹתָר, *leftover,* and is proscribed by Scripture. On the following day (after daybreak) it must be burned (see *Leviticus* 7:17).

בָּשָׂר שֶׁנִּמְצָא בָעֲזָרָה — *if meat is found in the [Temple] Courtyard —*

[Certainly this must be sacrificial meat, for otherwise it may not be

יד אברהם

brought into the Courtyard. The disposition of the meat (see below, s.v. זה וזה), however, is dependent on the type of sacrifice from which it came.]

אֵיבָרִין עוֹלוֹת, — *limbs are [assumed to be] burnt offerings,*

If the limbs were carved in the manner prescribed in *Tamid* (4:3; see *Yoma* 2:3) for the daily burnt offering, it can be assumed that they came from a burnt offering (*Rav; Rosh*). Because all the limbs of burnt offerings are offered upon the altar, they are not cut into smaller portions as would be done with meat for human consumption (*Rambam*, see ed. *Kafich*).

וַחֲתִיכוֹת חַטָּאוֹת. — *but slices are [assumed to be] sin offerings.*

Burnt offerings are left in the form of whole limbs (see above), so the slices must be from offerings that are eaten in the Courtyard, i.e., sin or guilt offerings (*Rav; Rosh*).

The mishnah mentions sin offerings because these are more prevalent — guilt offerings [אֲשָׁמוֹת] are required for only six specific sins — but the halachic status of the meat from sin and guilt offerings is the same. The eating of either is restricted to male *Kohanim*, in the Temple Courtyard, for a period of a day and a night (*Rivevan*). We do not conjecture that the meat may be from a peace offering [שְׁלָמִים], for it is improbable that such meat be left in the Temple Courtyard since it may be eaten in the rest of Jerusalem too (*Meiri*). [Possibly, this is another application of the majority principle. Most of the sliced meat in the Courtyard at any given time is from sin or guilt offerings.]

בִּירוּשָׁלַיִם, זִבְחֵי שְׁלָמִים. — *[If meat is found] in Jerusalem, it is [assumed to be] peace offerings.*

Since most of the meat eaten in Jerusalem (year-round) is from peace offerings, one cannot assume that this meat is חוּלִין, *nonconsecrated (Rav).*

It is also possible that this meat is from any other type of offering, e.g., animal tithe, which may be eaten in Jerusalem, but the mishnah singles out peace offerings because they are the most prevalent type of offering (*Rivevan*).

[Thanksgiving offerings (תּוֹדָה) differ from peace offerings, the former eaten for only a day and night but the latter for two days and the intervening night, so we must apply the majority principle to assume that the meat in question is from a peace offering.]

זֶה וָזֶה תְּעֻבַּר צוּרָתוֹ וְיֵצֵא לְבֵית הַשְּׂרֵפָה. — *In either case* [lit. *this and that*] *it must be left until it is unfit* [lit. *its appearance should pass*] *and then removed to the place of burning.*

Although the meat is assumed to be from offerings, it may not be eaten because the very fact that it was lost constitutes הֶיסַח הַדַּעַת, *a lapse in attention,* which renders offerings פָּסוּל, *unfit (Rav; Rosh* from *Yer.;* see *Pesachim* 34a). Nevertheless one may not burn this meat immediately because it is forbidden to destroy sacred meat before its eating time has elapsed. Therefore the mishnah requires עִיבּוּר צוּרָה, *leaving it until it is unfit.* For this purpose, the meat is set aside until its Scripturally assigned time of eating is over, then it becomes נוֹתָר, lit. *leftover,* [see preface] and *must* be burned by Torah law (see *Pesachim, ibid.*)[1]. In the case of peace

---

1. *Tosafos* (*Pesachim* 15a, s.v. ולד) holds that conceivably עִיבּוּר צוּרָה could refer simply to leaving the meat overnight, whether this renders it נוֹתָר or not.

Similarly R' *Chananel* (*Pesachim* 34b commenting on תעובר צורתו) and *Rambam* (Comm. here and to *Pesachim* 7:9, 82b; in his code, *Pisulei HaMukdashin* 19:2 and *Korban Pesach* 4:3, he does not clarify this) understand עִיבּוּר צוּרָה literally as *spoilage.* Even if the meat spoils before the prescribed period has elapsed, the unfit meat may nevertheless be burned immediately (see *Mikdash David, Kodashim* 17:4).

7
3
found] in Jerusalem, it is [assumed to be] peace offerings. In either case it must be left until it is unfit and then removed to the place of burning.

If [meat is] found in the province — limbs are [assumed to be] unslaughtered, [but] slices are permit-

offerings this is on the third day from its slaughter. In the first case of our mishnah this is on the day after its discovery [for possibly it was discovered on the same day that it was slaughtered] *Rav; Rosh).*

Alternatively, the disqualification of the meat for eating (or in the case of limbs, burning upon the altar) is based on the apprehension that it may already have become נוֹתָר, *leftover.* Nevertheless, it must not be burned immediately because it may yet be within its prescribed time *(Rambam, Comm., Hil. P'sulei HaMukdashin* 19:4; based on *Yer.* which he interprets differently from *Rav* and *Rosh;* see *Korban HaEdah* and *P'nei Moshe).*[1]

All kinds of sacrificial meat must be burned regardless of the final determination of the meat's origin. Why does the mishnah engage in a seemingly academic attempt to identify the pieces? However, there are practical halachic ramifications to this determination:

(a) Owing to the differing time periods after which sacrificial meats are rendered נוֹתָר, *leftover,* the day on which the found meat is burnt is dependent on its identification. For example, if we know it to be a sin offering, it will be burned the next day; if it is a peace offering, on the day after next *(Rivevan; Hon Ashir;* cf. *Shoshanim L'David).* [This view does not explain, however, why the mishnah differentiates between limbs and slices found in the Temple complex. In either case, the meat becomes leftover on the next day.]

(b) Burnt offerings are subject to the laws of מְעִילָה, *me'ilah,* [see above 2:2], whereas sin and peace offerings are not *(Ravad; Hil. P'sulei HaMukdashin* 19:4; however his

words are not clearcut and lend themselves to other interpretations; cf. *Kessef Mishneh, Mirkeves Hamishneh* and *Even HaAzel).*

(c) Identification of the found meat determines whether one violates a Scriptural prohibition if he eats it — e.g., if the meat is from a burnt offering, anyone eating it has sinned; if from a sin offering, a *Kohen* does not violate Torah law by eating it, but a Levite or Israelite does *(Rambam, Comm.* and *Hil. P'sulei HaMukdashin* 19:4). [In any case, it cannot be presumed that the proscription against eating נוֹתָר, *leftover,* has been violated, for the leftover status is only a possibility.]

נִמְצָא בַגְבוּלִין — אֲבָרִין נְבֵלוֹת, — *If [meat is] found in the province* [i.e., outside of Jerusalem] — *limbs are [assumed to be] unslaughtered,*

נְבֵילָה is a term used in Scripture for the carcass of an animal which died in any manner other than שְׁחִיטָה, *Torah prescribed slaughter.* The term does not refer to carrion, i.e., decaying meat, although it is often rendered that way erroneously (see *Chullin* 2:4 and *Rambam, Hil. Ma'achalos Assuros* 4:1).

It is customary to cut non-kosher carcasses into large chunks, to be fed to the dogs *(Rav; Rosh; Rambam).*

Rambam (Comm.) says, We must be apprehensive [נָחוּשׁ] lest it is unslaughtered. His use of the term 'apprehensive' implies that, unlike the earlier identification of types of sacred meat which are definitive, the identification of unslaughtered meat is not positive but rather only a possibility (סָפֵק).[2]

חֲתִיכוֹת מֻתָּרוֹת. — *but slices are permitted* [for consumption].

Unslaughtered meat is not usually cut

1. *Rambam* here is consistent with his view that lapse of attention does not result in disqualification (פְּסוּל; see *Mishneh LaMelech* and *Mirkeves HaMishneh, Hil. P'sulei HaMukdashin* 19:4; *Tzlach, Pesachim* 34a).

2. However, see *Yerushalmi* that R' Yose bar Chanina concludes that the designation of this meat as 'unslaughtered' is definitive and cites our mishnah as proof of his view. *(See R' Shlomo Sirilio; Mishnas Eliyahu; R' Meshullam.)*

שְׁקָלִים מֻתָּרוֹת. וּבִשְׁעַת הָרֶגֶל, שֶׁהַבָּשָׂר מְרֻבֶּה, אַף אֵבָרִין מֻתָּרִין.

[ד] **בְּהֵמָה** שֶׁנִּמְצֵאת מִירוּשָׁלַיִם וְעַד מִגְדַּל עֵדֶר וּכְמִדָּתָהּ לְכָל רוּחַ — זְכָרִים עוֹלוֹת, נְקֵבוֹת זִבְחֵי שְׁלָמִים.

יד אברהם

into slices (Rav; Rosh; Rambam). However, this rule applies only in a completely Jewish city, but if any Gentiles reside there, even slices are prohibited (Rav; Rambam).

This is due to Rav's (the Amora) rule that (Chullin 95a) meat without surveillance [נִתְעַלֵּם מִן הָעַיִן, meat that disappeared from view] is prohibited (Rambam, Comm.). However, in his code (Hil. Ma'acholos Assuros 8:12; cf. Yoreh Deah 63:2) Rambam decides that Rav's rule applies even to a city totally populated by Jews (Tos. Yom Tov).[1]

וּבִשְׁעַת הָרֶגֶל, שֶׁהַבָּשָׂר מְרֻבֶּה, — At the time of the pilgrimage festival, when meat is plentiful,

And large chunks of meat, i.e., limbs, are cooked before being sliced (Rav; Rambam).

אַף אֵבָרִין מֻתָּרִין. — even limbs are permitted.

[The sequence and language of the mishnah suggest that this rule refers to the provinces where the meat is definitely not sacred, and would consequently be permitted to be eaten. Even those who did not take part in the pilgrimage to the Temple, nevertheless ate meat in greater quantities than all year-round in honor of the festival.]

4.

בְּהֵמָה שֶׁנִּמְצֵאת מִירוּשָׁלַיִם וְעַד מִגְדַּל עֵדֶר וּכְמִדָּתָהּ לְכָל רוּחַ — An animal [of a species suitable for offering] that was found between Jerusalem and Migdal Eder or at a similar distance [from Jerusalem] in any direction —

Because of its proximity to Jerusalem we assume that the animal came from there and that it is an offering. The only problem is to identify the type (or types) of offering it may be (Meiri).

זְכָרִים עוֹלוֹת, — males are [assumed to be] burnt offerings,

Because most males animals in Jeru-

salem are burnt offerings (Rav; Rosh). [Burnt offerings must be males (Leviticus ch. 1); peace offerings, either male or female (ibid. ch. 3); and most sin offerings, female (ibid. ch.4). In addition, burnt offerings could be brought voluntarily and commonly were (so they were more numerous than involuntary male sin or guilt offerings). Thus, most males are burnt offerings.]

נְקֵבוֹת זִבְחֵי שְׁלָמִים. — females are [assumed to be] peace offerings.

Most females are peace offerings (Rav; Rosh). [Probably because peace

1. The Talmud (Chullin 95a) attempts to refute Rav's view (prohibiting 'meat which had been left without surveillance') because of our mishnah, which renders slices permissible. The Talmud however, cites Rav's opinion that the phrase 'they are permitted' refers only to Scriptural law [regarding the contamination conveyed by unslaughtered meat (Rashi)]; it does not preclude a rabbinical prohibition such as that proposed by Rav (this is Rambam's understanding of this passage; see Mirkeves HaMishneh; cf. Rashi there). In his commentary, Rambam originally took Rav as referring only to a town where some Gentiles reside, albeit as a minority, but later (in his code) adopted the view that this prohibition applies even in a town populated entirely by Jews. However many Poskim repudiate Rambam's and Rav's ruling and decide in accordance with Levi (Chullin 95a) who permits meat left without surveillance.

ted. At the time of the pilgrimage festival, when meat is plentiful, even limbs are permitted.

4. **A**n animal that was found between Jerusalem and Migdal Eder or at a similar distance [from Jerusalem] in any direction — males are [assumed to be] burnt offerings, females are [assumed to be] peace offerings.

YAD AVRAHAM

offerings express joy and thanksgiving, they are the most popular and therefore the most prevalent offerings. Furthermore, sin offerings are brought only as atonement for inadvertent transgression, and in many cases may be replaced with bird or meal offerings [.(קָרְבַּן עוֹלֶה וְיוֹרֵד)]

The *Talmud (Kiddushin 55a)* asks, in view of the fact that males may be used for peace offerings, why do we assume that any doubtful male animal is a burnt offering?

The Talmud concludes that indeed both of these possibilities *are* considered, but

regarding females, the mishnah makes a definitive statement: They are peace offerings, since a female cannot be a burnt offering. Regarding males, however, the mishnah must be understood to say that there is the *additional* possibility that they are burnt offerings; consequently the animal's status is in doubt and it cannot be offered at all.[1]

The Talmud (Kiddushin 55b) points out further that both males and females may be used for a variety of other offerings, and assumes that all possibilities must indeed be accounted for. Thus, the mishnah's statement 'females are considered peace-offerings' must be understood only in the negative sense that they are not burnt offerings.[2]

1. In light of its deviation from the Talmud's interpretation, the explanation given by *Rosh* and *Rav* requires clarification. They say that all males are burnt-offerings, because most males are brought for that purpose, but this seems to contradict the Talmud's explanation that the status of males remains in question. *Rosh's* view is even more puzzling, for he presents the Talmud's view as an alternative interpretation. It seems to this writer that the *Rosh's* version of *Yerushalmi* reads almost like that proposed by *Vilna Gaon* with a slight emendation. Where *Vilna Gaon* (and all our versions) have א׳׳ר יוחנן ... אלא הולכין בהן אחר הרוב אם רוב זכרים, עולות אם רוב נקבות שלמים, *R' Yochanon says we follow the majority, if most* [of the found animals] *are males, they are burnt offerings, and if most are females, they are peace offerings* (see comm.), *Rosh* deletes the word אם both times, leaving אלא הולכין בהן אחר הרוב, רוב זכרים עולות רוב נקבות שלמים *we follow the majority: most males are burnt offerings, most females are peace offerings.* This coincides exactly with *Rosh's* view. If so *Rosh's* interpretation is based on *Yerushalmi* and is adopted by *Rav* because of its simplicity. *Rambam's* commentary, too, seems to have adopted this view.

2. *Rambam (Hil. P'sulei HaMukdashin 6:18)* renders this law as follows: 'An animal found between Jerusalem and Migdal Eder or at a similar distance in any direction — if it is a yearling female it must be locked in a stall and left to die [because] it may be a sin offering (this is the procedure mandated by the oral tradition given to Moses on Sinai for any sin offering that cannot be used to atone for its owner's sins). If it is a female in its second year he should offer it as a peace offering and accompany it with (cf. *Tos.* loc. cit., s.v. דמייתי and *Kessef Mishneh*) breads [because] it may be a [תּוֹדָה] thanksgiving offering (*Leviticus* 7:12 prescribes that with every thanksgiving offering forty loaves of bread be brought). If he found a male in its second year its status cannot be determined [because] it may be a guilt offering (see *Leviticus* 5:15,18,25) and its owner has not yet been atoned for (a guilt offering whose owner *has* been atoned for with another animal may, after contracting a disqualifying blemish, be redeemed and its proceeds used to purchase a peace offering). If he found a yearling male he may leave it until it contracts a blemish. Then he brings two animals to redeem it and says: If it was a burnt offering let this one be a burnt offering in its stead, and if it was a peace offering let the other

רַבִּי יְהוּדָה אוֹמֵר: הָרָאוּי לִפְסָחִים פְּסָחִים,
קֹדֶם לָרֶגֶל שְׁלֹשִׁים יוֹם.

[ה] **בָּרִאשׁוֹנָה,** הָיוּ מְמַשְׁכְּנִין אֶת־
מוֹצְאֶיהָ עַד שֶׁהוּא
מֵבִיא נְסָכֶיהָ. חָזְרוּ לִהְיוֹת מַנִּיחִין אוֹתָהּ
וּבוֹרְחִין, הִתְקִינוּ בֵּית דִּין שֶׁיִּהוּ נְסָכֶיהָ בָּאִין
מִשֶׁל צִבּוּר.

[ו] **אָמַר** רַבִּי שִׁמְעוֹן: שִׁבְעָה דְבָרִים
הִתְקִינוּ בֵּית דִּין, וְזֶה אֶחָד מֵהֶן.
נָכְרִי שֶׁשִּׁלַּח עוֹלָתוֹ מִמְּדִינַת הַיָּם וְשִׁלַּח עִמָּהּ

יד אברהם

**רַבִּי יְהוּדָה אוֹמֵר: הָרָאוּי לִפְסָחִים — R'
Yehudah says: Those suitable for
Pesach offerings**
[Yearling males (*Rav;* see *Exodus*
12:5*).]*

**פְּסָחִים, — are [assumed to be] Pesach of-
ferings,**
Logic dictates that a pilgrim had consecrated it as a Pesach offering and lost
it en route to Jerusalem (*Rambam*). The
finder may offer it for his own Pesach
offering; but he must repay the original
owner if his identity is later discovered
(*Rav; Rambam*).
It stands to reason that according to the
view expounded by the Talmud in *Kiddushin* (see above) according to which all
possibilities are considered, we must wait for
the animal to contract a blemish. If it
becomes blemished before Pesach, it may
then be redeemed in the manner given by

Rambam (Hil. P'suei HaMukdashim 6:17,
as cited in footnote above). *Rivevan* (see also
R' Meshullam) indicates this clearly. Consequently *Rav's* view that we may assume it to
be a Pesach and act accordingly, is dependent
on his view throughout this mishnah that we
decide the status of the animal based on the
majority of similar animals.

**קֹדֶם לָרֶגֶל שְׁלֹשִׁים יוֹם. — during the thirty
days before Pesach.**
During this period one should start to
study the laws of Pesach (*Pesachim* 5b),
and as a result people commence to consecrate their Pesach offerings (*Rav;
Rosh*). The first tanna (who rules that
even yearling males are not regarded as
Pesach offerings) holds that people are
very careful with a Pesach offering so
we need not fear that they would have
lost it (*Kiddushim* 55b). The halachah
does not follow R' Yehudah (*Rav; Rambam*).

5.

**בָּרִאשׁוֹנָה, הָיוּ מְמַשְׁכְּנִין אֶת־מוֹצְאֶיהָ עַד
שֶׁהוּא מֵבִיא נְסָכֶיהָ. — Originally, they**
*would seize collateral from the finder
until he brought its [the found of-*

one be a peace offering in its place. Then he offers the first as a burnt offering and its [נְסָכִים]
libations are supplied from the public treasury (as set forth in mishnah 5), and the second as a
peace offering with the forty breads [because] it may have been a thanksgiving offering. What
should be done with this found [animal]? It should be eaten in its blemished state, for even if it
had been a first born or animal tithe [which cannot be *redeemed* even if blemished] it may be
eaten if blemished … '

R' Yehudah says: Those suitable for Pesach offerings are [assumed to be] Pesach offerings, during the
thirty days before Pesach.

5.**O**riginally, they would seize collateral from the
finder until he brought its *nesachim*. [But]
when they began abandoning it and fleeing, *Beis Din*
instituted that its *nesachim* should come from the
public [treasury].

6.**S**aid R' Shimon: *Beis Din* instituted seven
ordinances, and this is one of them. [The others
are:]
If a Gentile sent his burnt offering from a far away

YAD AVRAHAM

fering's] *nesachim.*

[The term *nesachim*, literally libations, includes both the meal offering and wine libation required for every burnt and peace offering as explained earlier (5:1, s.v. נסכים).]

The point of our mishnah is that the
finder who offers the animal is compel-
led to pay for the flour, oil, and wine
necessary for the *nesachim* (*Rav*).

The animal becomes the finder's possession since it has no identifying marks.
Because it is now his offering, he is obligated
to fulfill all requirements incumbent upon
one bringing such an offering (*R' Shlomo
Sirilio*).

חָזְרוּ לִהְיוֹת מַנִּיחִין אוֹתָהּ וּבוֹרְחִין, — [*But*]
when they [the finders] *began abandon-*

ing it and fleeing,

They would bring the animal to the
Temple for sacrifice, but leave immediately to avoid the additional expense of *nesachim* (*R' Shmuel*).

הִתְקִינוּ בֵּית דִּין שֶׁיְּהוּ נְסָכֶיהָ בָּאִין מִשֶּׁל
צִבּוּר. — *Beis Din instituted that its
nesachim should come from the public
[treasury].*

The term צִבּוּר, *public,* in this context
refers to the תְּרוּמַת הַלִּשְׁכָּה, *withdrawal
from the treasury chamber (*see above
3:1; *Rambam, Comm.* at end of this
chapter and *Hil. Shekalim* 4:3 cited by
Tos. Yom Tov here).

6.

אָמַר רַבִּי שִׁמְעוֹן: שִׁבְעָה דְבָרִים הִתְקִינוּ בֵּית
דִּין, וְזֶה אֶחָד מֵהֶן. — *Said R' Shimon: Beis
Din instituted seven ordinances* [lit.
matters], *and this* [the rule set forth in
mishnah 5] *is one of them.*

[The mishnah will now list the other
six ordinances, all of which involve expenditure of communal funds.]

נָכְרִי שֶׁשָּׁלַח עוֹלָתוֹ מִמְּדִינַת הַיָּם — [*The
others are:*] *If a Gentile sent his burnt
offering from a far away country* [lit.
the provinces of the sea]

[The term מְדִינַת הַיָּם is used elsewhere in
the Mishnah (*Gittin* 1:1) to denote all
provinces outside of *Eretz Yisrael.* Clearly
this is how *Rambam* (*Hil. Shekalim* 4:3) understood the term as it used here.]

That a Gentile may offer sacrifices is
derived (*Menachos* 73b) from *Leviticus*
22:18, אִישׁ אִישׁ, ... *a man, a man, who
will offer his sacrifice.* The repetitive
אִישׁ אִישׁ, teaches that any person, even a
Gentile, may offer sacrifices (*Rav*;
Rosh).

In stating עוֹלָתוֹ, *his burnt offering,* the

שְׁקָלִים נְסָכִים, קְרֵבִין מִשֶּׁלּוֹ; וְאִם לָאו, קְרֵבִין מִשֶּׁל ז/ו
צִבּוּר.

וְכֵן גֵּר שֶׁמֵּת וְהִנִּיחַ זְבָחִים — אִם יֶשׁ לוֹ
נְסָכִים קְרֵבִין מִשֶּׁלּוֹ; וְאִם לָאו, קְרֵבִין מִשֶּׁל
צִבּוּר.

וּתְנַאי בֵּית דִּין הוּא עַל־כֹּהֵן גָּדוֹל שֶׁמֵּת
שֶׁתְּהֵא מִנְחָתוֹ קְרֵבָה מִשֶּׁל צִבּוּר.

יד אברהם

mishnah here adapts R' Akiva's view (*Menachos* 73b) that a Gentile may offer only burnt offerings. According to R' Yose Ha-Glili (*ibid*) who holds that Gentiles may bring peace offerings too, the mishnah should have said: A Gentile who sent his offering [קָרְבָּנוֹ], without specifying the type (*Tos. Yom Tov*).

[Implied in the mishnah is that a Gentile's sacrifice is subject to all requirements incumbent upon an Israelite's, including the offering of *nesachim*.]

וְשָׁלַח עִמָּהּ נְסָכִים, קְרֵבִין מִשֶּׁלּוֹ; — *and sent nesachim with it, they are offered from his own;*

[I.e., he sent money to purchase *nesachim* (*Rashi Menachos* 51b, s.v. שלח). Had the Gentile sent *nesachim* rather than funds for their purchase, they would be judged contaminated (טָמֵא) and disqualified (*Tos. Chadashim; Tif. Yis.*).

It appears that according to *Rambam* (*Hil. Ma'aseh HaKarbonos* 3:5) a Gentile's *nesachim*, like his peace offerings, are refused by Torah law. Thus the mishnah's statement that 'they are offered from his' can refer only to *money* to purchase flour, oil, and wine, but not the materials themselves (according to *Mirkeves HaMishneh* and *Even HaAzel* there; cf. *Kessef Mishneh* and *Lechem Mishneh*).

וְאִם לָאו, קְרֵבִין מִשֶּׁל צִבּוּר. — *if not, they are offered from the public [treasury].*

From the periodic withdrawal of funds from the treasury chamber (*Ramban, Comm. end of this chapter*).

[This is the second of these seven institutions.]

By including the qualification 'from a far away county' in his paraphrase of this mishnah, *Rambam* indicates that public funds are used to purchase a Gentile's *nesachim* only if he lives outside of *Eretz Yisrael*. Had the Gentile resided in *Eretz Yisrael*, we would admonish him to pay for *nesachim* (*Tos. Yom Tov*).

[But only for a Gentile was this rule promulgated. A Jew, who should know better, must send money for *nesachim* or his offering is not accepted.]

וְכֵן גֵּר שֶׁמֵּת וְהִנִּיחַ זְבָחִים — *Similarly, a proselyte who died and left offerings* —

[The proselyte had consecrated animals as offerings that must now be sacrificed. The obligatory *nesachim* must be brought with them.]

אִם יֶשׁ לוֹ נְסָכִים קְרֵבִין מִשֶּׁלּוֹ; — *if he had nesachim, they are offered from his own;*

If he had set aside money and designated it for *nesachim*, it is used for that purpose. But if he had left only unconsecrated funds, they are הֶפְקֵר, *ownerless*, upon the proselyte's death, and become the property of the first person taking possession of them. Consequently this property cannot be used toward the purchase of the proselyte's *nesachim* (*Tos. Yom Tov.* citing *Tos., Menachos* 51b s.v. יש).[1]

[Upon his conversion, a proselyte

---

1. However it can be argued that since the requirement to bring an offering is considered a financial obligation that places a lien [שעבוד] on the obligant's real estate (see *Kinnim* 2:5; *Kiddushin* 13b; *Rambam, Hil. Mechusrei Kaparah* 1:13), such a lien should be equally applicable to *nesachim*. Thus if the proselyte had owned real estate, *nesachim* would be

7
6
country and sent *nesachim* with it, they are offered from his own; if not, they are offered from the public [treasury].

Similarly, a proselyte who dies and left offerings — if he had *nesachim*, they are offered from his own; if not, they are offered from the public [treasury].

It is a stipulation of *Beis Din* regarding a *Kohen Gadol* who died that his flour offering be brought from the public [treasury].

severs all legal connection with his previous relatives (בְּקָטָן שֶׁנּוֹלַד דָּמֵי). Thus, unless he married and had a family after his conversion, it is possible for him to die without leaving an heir to pay for his *nesachim*. If he did subsequently marry and bear children then his estate is inherited by his offspring.]

וְאִם לָאו, קְרֵבִין מִשֶּׁל צִבּוּר. — *if not, they are offered from the public [treasury]*.
[This is the third institution.]

This rule applies only to a proselyte without relatives; but if a Jew [or a proselyte] with relatives died and left offerings, the *nesachim* must be supplied from his estate by his heirs (*Tif. Yis.*).

[It stands to reason that where there was no money in the estate to pay for the *nesachim* the heirs need not defray the expense of the *nesachim* with their own money. In that case these *nesachim*, too, are purchased with communal funds (see *Tos. Yom Tov, Menachos 9:7* and here, s.v. קריבה; cf. *Mikdash David, Kodashim 10:4*).]

וּתְנַאי בֵּית דִּין הוּא עַל־כֹּהֵן גָּדוֹל שֶׁמֵּת שֶׁתְּהֵא מִנְחָתוֹ קְרֵבָה מִשֶּׁל צִבּוּר. — *It is a stipulation of Beis Din regarding a Kohen Gadol who died that his flour of-*

fering be brought from the public [treasury].

[This is the fourth institution.]

[Every day the *Kohen Gadol* brings a personal offering (מִנְחַת חֲבִיתִּין) consisting of one tenth *ephah* (i.e., an *omer*; the volume of 43.2 eggs) mixed with 3 *log* of olive oil. Half of it is brought during the morning service, and the other half in the afternoon (*Leviticus 6:12-16*). It is incumbent upon the *Kohen Gadol* to bring this offering at his own expense.]

Upon the *Kohen Gadol's* death, an obligation remains that the offering be brought even though a successor has not yet been chosen. Our mishnah teaches that the offering is brought at public expense until the new *Kohen Gadol* has been designated (Rav).

The Talmud (*Menachos 51b*) explains that this rule is of Scriptural origin and not Rabbinically ordained, for this offering is described as חָק עוֹלָם, *an eternal decree* (*Leviticus 6:15*), which is understood to mean, *it is a due from the public*[1] (in the event there is no *Kohen Gadol* to purchase the offering). Nevertheless, our mishnah describes

purchased from the proceeds from their sale. Moreover, regarding the estate of a proselyte who dies without heirs, it is the view of *Rashba* (*Chidushim Bava Kamma 49b*, s.v. משכונו: see *Choshen Mishpat 275:31* with *HaGahos R' Akiva Eiger, Ketzos HaChoshen 245:2-3* with *Gilyonos Baruch Ta'am*) that even מְטַלְטְלִים, *movable property*, is subject to a lien, and the demands of the lien holder must be satisfied before any claim arising from post-mortem possession is considered.

1. [The plain meaning of the phrase — that the *mitzvah* must be observed forever — is disregarded, probably because it is superfluous to say that any *mitzvah* is eternal. Instead, חָק is translated, *due*, as in חֹק לַכֹּהֲנִים, *the priest's due* (*Genesis 47:22*; see *Radak Shorashim*, s.v. חקק), and עוֹלָם is translated as *the public*, perhaps from עוֹלָם, *world*.]

רַבִּי יְהוּדָה אוֹמֵר: מִשֶּׁל יוֹרְשִׁין.
וּשְׁלֵמָה הָיְתָה קְרֵבָה.

[ז] **עַל־הַמֶּלַח** וְעַל־הָעֵצִים שֶׁיְּהוּ הַכֹּהֲנִים
נֵאוֹתִים בָּהֶן.
וְעַל־הַפָּרָה שֶׁלֹּא יְהוּ מוֹעֲלִין בְּאֶפְרָהּ.
וְעַל הַקִּנִּין הַפְּסוּלוֹת שֶׁיְּהוּ בָאוֹת מִשֶּׁל
צִבּוּר.

יד אברהם

this requirement as 'Rabbinical' because the Scripturally ordained course of action had been changed by the Sages. They had instituted an ordinance that the Kohen Gadol's heirs underwrite the cost of this meal offering. When they saw that the heirs occasionally neglected their duty to pay for the offering, the Rabbis promulgated a new edict that the responsibility be borne by the public treasury, as it had been under Scriptural law (Rav).

Tos. Yom Tov surmises that the apparently superfluous phrase 'it is a stipulation of Beis Din,' prefaces this ordinance to emphasize that the regulation is considered to be Rabbinic, even though the Rabbis did nothing more than abandon their earlier ordinance and revert to Scriptural law.

רַבִּי יְהוּדָה אוֹמֵר: מִשֶּׁל יוֹרְשִׁין. — R' Yehudah says: [It was purchased] with his heir's [money].

R' Yehudah holds this to be the Torah law and finds support for his

view (Menachos 51b) in Scripture: וְהַכֹּהֵן הַמָּשִׁיחַ, if the anointed Kohen [dies, the responsibility for the meal offerings falls] תַּחְתָּיו מִבָּנָיו, on his sons in place of him (Leviticus 6:15).

According to R' Yehudah, no 'stipulation of Beis Din' was needed or made regarding this flour offering (Rav). The halachah follows R' Yehudah (Rav; Rambam, Hil. Shekalim 4:4).

וּשְׁלֵמָה הָיְתָה קְרֵבָה. — [In this case] it was offered whole.

[Unlike the procedure followed by a living Kohen Gadol who offers half in the morning and half in the afternoon, when public funds are used, the entire meal offering is brought as a unit (Menachos 52a; see Rambam Hil. T'midim UMussafin 3:22).]

Although both R' Yehudah and R' Shimon agree with this ruling, they differ regarding its Scriptural derivation (Rav).

7.

This mishnah, a continuation of the previous one, contains the last three of the seven institutions mentioned by R' Shimon.

עַל־הַמֶּלַח וְעַל־הָעֵצִים שֶׁיְּהוּ הַכֹּהֲנִים נֵאוֹתִים בָּהֶן. — Regarding the salt and the wood [Beis Din instituted] that the Kohanim may make use [lit. enjoy] of them.

This [the fifth ordinance] is counted as a single institution (Tif. Yis.).

Since any consecrated substance may not be used for private purposes, wood for the altar pyre and salt for covering the portions of offerings that go on the altar may not be used for cooking or seasoning a private meal. Beis Din here instituted that such wood and salt purchased with communal funds may be used by Kohanim in the preparation of their portions of sacrificial meats. They may not use the wood and salt,

R' Yehudah says: [It was purchased] with his heir's [money].

[In this case] it was offered whole.

7. **R**egarding the salt and the wood [*Beis Din* instituted] that the *Kohanim* may make use of them.

Regarding the [Red] Cow [they instituted] that its ashes be exempt from [the laws of] me'ilah.

And regarding [replacements for] the disqualified bird offerings that they should come from the public [treasury].

however, in the preparation of the non-consecrated food that they customarily eat before the sacrificial meat. Although the eating of such is a *mitzvah*, because consecrated meat may not be eaten when one is ravenously hungry, it may not be prepared with consecrated wood and salt (*Rav* from *Menachos* 21b).

וְעַל-הַפָּרָה שֶׁלֹּא יְהוּ מוֹעֲלִין בְּאֶפְרָהּ. — *Regarding the [Red] Cow [they instituted] that its ashes be exempt from [the laws of] me'ilah.*

[This is the sixth institution.]

The Talmud (*Menachos* 51b-52a) teaches that the Torah exempts the ashes of the Red Cow [see above 4:2] from the laws of *me'ilah, secular use of consecrated property* [see above 2:2]. However, when the Sages saw that people took a casual attitude toward these ashes and used them for undignified purposes, they prohibited any secular use. As a result of this prohibition, people who had suffered a *possible* contamination — and *should* have cleansed themselves to remove the doubt — refrained from making use of the ashes. Seeing that the prohibition had resulted in unfortunate consequences, the sages instituted that the people revert to Torah law, under which use of the ashes is not forbidden.

Regarding the case of the *Kohen Gadol* who dies (mishnah 6), R' Shimon described the Sages' ordinance as 'a stipulation of *Beis Din*,' but here he omits this introductory phrase. In the former case R' Shimon's view is disputed by R' Yehudah, therefore he emphasizes his opinion by saying that *Beis Din* instituted the ordinance. In our mishnah, however, there is no dispute, so no emphasis is needed (*Tos. Yom Tov* to mishnah 6).

וְעַל-הַקִּנִּין הַפְּסוּלוֹת שֶׁיְּהוּ בָאוֹת מִשֶּׁל צִבּוּר. — *And regarding [replacements for] the disqualified bird offerings* [lit. *nests*] *that they should come from the public [treasury].*

[This was the seventh institution.]

People obligated to bring bird offerings would place an adequate amount of money in the chest marked 'Nests' and could safely assume that their offerings would be offered on that same day (see above 6:5, s.v. וחכמים אומרים).

Beis Din found it necessary to assure that each offering for which money was deposited would indeed be brought on the altar. If a bird flew away or became disqualified [i.e., its blood was placed on the wrong part of the altar (see *Zevachim* 7:1)], or some of the money was lost before it was used (see *Yer.* and mishnah 1 above, s.v. קרוב לקינין), a replacement would be purchased with communal funds [from the periodic withdrawal (*Rambam*)]. Ownership of the newly purchased bird would be transferred to the unknown owner of

[א] **כָּל־הָרְקִין** הַנִּמְצָאִים בִּירוּשַׁלַיִם
טְהוֹרִין, חוּץ מִשֶּׁל שׁוּק
הָעֶלְיוֹן — דִּבְרֵי רַבִּי מֵאִיר.

יד אברהם

the lost or disqualified offering and it would be brought on the altar (*Rav; Rosh*).

[Otherwise people could not assume that their deposit of the required sum had resulted in an actual sacrifice, for their offering might have been lost or disqualified.]

[*Rosh's* (and *R' Meshullam's*) version here reads, וְעַל־הַקִּנִּין וְעַל־הַפְּסוּלוֹת, *about the bird offerings and about the disqualified ones.* In this version the institution regarding 'bird offerings' is distinct from that concerning the 'disqualified ones.' First they instituted that it be incumbent upon the *Kohanim* to be sure that each day all the money in the chests reserved for bird offerings be used for its intended purpose. Thus the depositors are assured that their obligation has been discharged by day's end. Secondly, as a necessary adjunct of the first edict, they instituted a rule about 'the disqualified ones.' Probably *Rav*, whose commentary here is taken from *Rosh*, also had this version (cf. *Shinuyei Nuschaos*). However, since the institution 'about the disqualified ones' was necessitated by the institution about the fowl offering, they are considered in combination as one institution.]

Tos. Yom Tov points out that the owner of any offering was obligated to be present at its sacrifice. *Ta'anis* 4:2 states: How is it possible for a person's offering to be sacrificed without him being present? *Tos. Yom Tov* suggests that the institution of מַעֲמָדוֹת, Ma'amodos, established by the early proph-

ets (*ibid.*) to serve as representation for the public at the public service fulfilled this function for the individual offerer as well. *R' Shimshon Chasid* (cited in *Tosafos Chadashim*) distinguishes between offerings brought as part of the forgiveness process (מְחוּסְרֵי כַּפָּרָה) such as all obligatory bird offerings, which do not require their owner's presence, and other offerings, which *do* require their owner's presence.

רַבִּי יוֹסֵי אוֹמֵר: הַמְסַפֵּק אֶת־הַקִּנִּין — *R' Yose says: The one who supplies the birds* [lit. *nests*]

[See above 5:4.]

מְסַפֵּק אֶת־הַפְּסוּלוֹת. — *must supply* [*replacements for*] *the disqualified ones.*

Just as the supplier of *nesachim* must make up for spoilage and disqualification (above 4:9), so must the supplier of birds take these losses (*Rav, Rosh, Rambam,* from *Yer.*).

Rosh notes that this is so only for the designated supplier who had an agreement with the Temple administration for them to purchase from him for an extended period. Since his occasional losses would be made up through his profits, he could be required to make good on such losses. But someone who had sold birds for an offering on an individual basis is surely not required to pay for their replacement.

The halachah follow R' Yose (*Rav; Rambam*).

Chapter 8

The preceding chapter discussed the status of various unidentified items found in Jerusalem or its environs — money, meat and animals. Similarly, the next three mishnayos speak of unidentified items, with regard to *taharah* [purity] and *tumah* [contamination].

R' Yose says: The one who supplies the birds must supply [replacements for] the disqualified ones.

1. All spittle that is found in Jerusalem is [assumed to be] *tahor*, except for that [found] in the upper market — [these are] the words of R' Meir.

YAD AVRAHAM

1.

The spittle of a *zav*, *zavah*, woman after childbirth (seven days for a son, fourteen for a daughter) [see *comm.* to 1:5] or a *niddah* [menstruant] is *tamei* [contaminated] and contaminates any person or utensil with which it comes in contact (*Leviticus* 15:8; *Rambam, Hil. M'tamei Mishkav U'Moshav* 1:15). The Sages decreed that all unidentified spittle be considered as if it were from one of these four categories, thus rendering it *tamei*. A similar decree of contamination was promulgated regarding unidentified utensils (*Taharos* 4:5). However, as explained in the Talmud (*Pesachim* 19b), spittle or utensils found in Jerusalem are exempt from these decrees. Mishnah 1 discusses spittle found in Jerusalem, mishnayos 2-3 speak about utensils found there.

כָּל־הָרֻקִּין הַנִּמְצָאִים בִּירוּשָׁלַיִם טְהוֹרִין, — *Any spittle that is found in Jerusalem is [assumed to be] tahor [uncontaminated]*,

The rule set forth in *Taharos* (4:5) categorizing all spittle as *tamei* applies only to the provinces, but not to Jerusalem (*Pesachim* 19b; *Tos. Yom Tov*), because *zavim* and other types of contaminated people are not as prevalent in Jerusalem as in other places (*Rav; Rosh*).

[In Jerusalem there would be multitudes of pilgrims who had cleansed themselves of any contamination, so the incidence of *tumah* occurring among the year-round citizenry constituted a much smaller minority than elsewhere.][1]

Alternatively, in Jerusalem even those who were contaminated were careful to avoid contaminating people who were *tahor* (*Meiri*; cf. *Rashi* cited below, s.v.

חוץ). Or: In Jerusalem the Sages waived the decree relegating unidentified spittle to a status of contamination in order to avoid the destruction of consecrated objects (הֶפְסֵד קָדָשִׁים), because if this spittle were to be treated as contaminated, any sacrificial meat coming in contact with it would have to be burned — but there is an obligation to safeguard such meat from contamination or destruction (*R' Shmuel*).

חוץ מִשֶּׁל שׁוּק הָעֶלְיוֹן — דִּבְרֵי רַבִּי מֵאִיר. — *except for that [found] in the upper market — [these are] the words of R' Meir*.

Because Gentile laundrymen would frequent this market, and as promulgated by the Sages (*Niddah* 34a; *Shabbos* 17b), all Gentiles[2] are accorded the *tumah* status of a *zav* (*Rav; Rosh* from *Yer.*).

1. This is the writer's perception of *Rav* and *Rosh's* views. It is inconceivable that *t'meim* were actually in a majority anywhere.

2. According to Torah law, even the actual incidence of an emission does not contaminate a Gentile (*Niddah* 34a). Indeed, a Gentile is not subject to contamination under Torah law in any circumstance whatsoever.

רַבִּי יוֹסֵי אוֹמֵר: בִּשְׁאָר יְמוֹת הַשָּׁנָה,
שֶׁבָּאֶמְצַע טְמֵאִין, וְשֶׁבַּצְּדָדִין טְהוֹרִין. וּבִשְׁעַת
הָרֶגֶל, שֶׁבָּאֶמְצַע טְהוֹרִין, וְשֶׁבַּצְּדָדִין טְמֵאִין.
שֶׁמִּפְּנֵי שֶׁהֵן מֻעָטִין מִסְתַּלְּקִין לַצְּדָדִין.

[ב] **כָּל־הַכֵּלִים** הַנִּמְצָאִין בִּירוּשָׁלַיִם —
דֶּרֶךְ יְרִידָה לְבֵית
הַטְּבִילָה טְמֵאִין; דֶּרֶךְ עֲלִיָּה, טְהוֹרִין. שֶׁלֹּא
בְדֶרֶךְ יְרִידָתָן עֲלִיָּתָן — דִּבְרֵי רַבִּי מֵאִיר.

יד אברהם

Rashi (Pesachim 19b, s.v. שוק של) offers that *zavim* tended to congregate in this market place [which was avoided by most other people *(Rav)*] so as not to contaminate the others.

רַבִּי יוֹסֵי אוֹמֵר: בִּשְׁאָר יְמוֹת הַשָּׁנָה, שֶׁבָּאֶמְצַע טְמֵאִין, וְשֶׁבַּצְּדָדִין טְהוֹרִין. — *R' Yose says: At other times of the year* [i.e., all times except the pilgrimage festivals], *whatever [spittle] is in the middle [of the street] is [assumed to be] tamei, and whatever is on the sides, tahor.*

In Mishnaic and Talmudic times the place for pedestrian traffic was in the middle of the street. R' Yose holds that even in Jerusalem (see *Rambam, Hil. Avos HaTumah* 13:8 and *Meiri* here) contaminated persons constituted a significant enough minority to be reckoned with, so that the Rabbinical decree concerning doubtful spittle (see *Pesachim 19b*) must be as applicable there as elsewhere. Because people scrupulous about remaining *tahor* (חֲבֵרִים) would make it a point to walk at the sides of the street to avoid contact with the frequently contaminated multitudes, we may assume that the majority of those on the sides were not contaminated *(Rav; Rosh from Yer.).*

But even according to R' Yose, *all* spittle in the provinces is judged as contaminated whether found in the middle or the sides of the street *(Rambam, Hil. Avos HaTumah* 13:8; *Meiri).*

וּבִשְׁעַת הָרֶגֶל, שֶׁבָּאֶמְצַע טְהוֹרִין, וְשֶׁבַּצְּדָדִין טְמֵאִין. — *But at the time of the pilgrimage festival, whatever [spittle] is in the middle [of the street] is [assumed to be] tahor, and whatever is at the sides, tamei.*

At the time of the pilgrimage festivals all are considered חֲבֵרִים, scrupulous ones, in matters of *taharah (Rambam* from *Chagigah 26a)*, for a person is obligated to cleanse himself on the pilgrimage festivals *(Rosh HaShanah 16b).* Therefore the multitudes walking in the middle could be assumed to be uncontaminated. At those times, contaminated people would walk at the sides so as not to contaminate the multitudes *(Rav; Rosh from Yer.).*

שֶׁמִּפְּנֵי שֶׁהֵן מֻעָטִין מִסְתַּלְּקִין לַצְּדָדִין. — *Because, since they [the contaminated ones] are a minority [during the pilgrimage festival] they withdraw to the sides.*

The *halachah* follows R' Yose *(Rav; Rambam, Hil. Avos HaTumah* 13:8).

2.

כָּל־הַכֵּלִים הַנִּמְצָאִין בִּירוּשָׁלַיִם—דֶּרֶךְ יְרִידָה
לְבֵית הַטְּבִילָה טְמֵאִין; דֶּרֶךְ עֲלִיָּה, טְהוֹרִין. —

All the utensils that are found in Jerusalem — [those found] on the path

R' Yose says: At other times of the year, whatever [spittle] is in the middle [of the street] is [assumed to be] *tamei*, and whatever is on the sides, *tahor*. But at the time of the pilgrimage festival, whatever [spittle] is in the middle [of the street] is [assumed to be] *tahor*, whatever is at the sides, *tamei*. Because, since they are a minority they withdraw to the sides.

2. **A**ll the utensils that are found in Jerusalem — [those found] on the path leading down to the *mikveh* are [assumed to be] *tamei*; but [those found] on the path leading up [from the mikveh] are [assumed to be] *tahor*. For the path of their descent is not [the path] of their ascent — [these are] the words of R' Meir.

YAD AVRAHAM

leading down to the mikveh [lit. *place of immersion*] *are [assumed to be] tamei; but [those found] on the path leading up [from the mikveh] are [assumed to be] tahor.*

Two paths converged on each *mikveh*, one for those going there and the other for those coming back. Thus one bearing a contaminated utensil would not come into contact with those bearing cleansed ones. Utensils found on the way to the *mikveh* may be assumed to be contaminated utensils dropped on the way to being cleansed (*Rav; Rosh*).

Alternatively: The position of the utensil indicates whether it has already been immersed or not (*Rambam; Meiri*). [This interpretation renders דֶּרֶךְ as *manner*. Presumably, someone putting down the utensil before immersion would put it facing up, but after immersion he would put it face down to allow the water to drip off. (cf. *Pesachim* 19b, ולאפוקי גזייתא).]

שֶׁלֹּא בְּדֶרֶךְ יְרִידָתָן עֲלִיָּתָן — דִּבְרֵי רַבִּי מֵאִיר. — *For the path of their descent is not [the path] of their ascent — [these are] the words of R' Meir.*

[The translation follows the interpretation of *Rav* and *Rosh* above. According to *Ram-*

bam and *Meiri* the mishnah refers to the immersion, which is assumed to have taken place. Thus: *for not in the state of their descent* [which was a state of contamination] *is their ascent* [which is assumed to have occured after immersion]. Presumably, those utensils were brought there to be cleansed and had indeed been immersed (*Rav; Rosh*).

The *Talmud* (*Pesachim* 19b) concludes that utensils found elsewhere in Jerusalem (not in proximity to the *mikveh)* are judged to be uncontaminated, because the decree concerning utensils of doubtful origin (mentioned in the preface to this chapter) does not extend to Jerusalem. However utensils found near the *mikveh* were obviously contaminated, or they would not have been brought there, hence they must be judged as still in that status (חֲזָקָה) until the assumption that they had been immersed is proven. Therefore, utensils found on the way up are considered cleansed because of the assumption that 'not in the path of their descent is their ascent.' Where this cannot be assumed, e.g., side paths that are used both for ascent and descent, we cannot assume that the utensil has been cleansed. Regarding a utensil found elsewhere in Jerusalem, no supposition of contamination must be made, and since the decree regarding utensils of doubtful origin does not apply in Jerusalem, it is judged uncontaminated.]

רַבִּי יוֹסֵי אוֹמֵר: כֻּלָּן טְהוֹרִין חוּץ מִן הַסַּל
וְהַמַּגְרֵפָה וְהַמְרִצָה הַמְיֻחָדִין לַקְּבָרוֹת.

[ג] **סַכִּין** שֶׁנִּמְצֵאת בְּאַרְבָּעָה עָשָׂר שׁוֹחֵט
בָּהּ מִיָּד. בִּשְׁלֹשָׁה עָשָׂר, שׁוֹנֶה
וּמַטְבִּיל.
וְקוֹפִיץ, בֵּין בָּזֶה וּבֵין בָּזֶה, שׁוֹנֶה וּמַטְבִּיל;

יד אברהם

רַבִּי יוֹסֵי אוֹמֵר: כֻּלָּן טְהוֹרִין — *R' Yose says:*
All are [assumed to be] *tahor.*

[Even those found on the 'path
down.'] The decree regarding unidentified utensils does not apply anywhere
in Jerusalem, even to those utensils
found on the way to the *mikveh.*

חוּץ מִן הַסַּל וְהַמַּגְרֵפָה וְהַמְרִצָה הַמְיֻחָדִין
לַקְּבָרוֹת. — *except for the basket, the*
shovel and the spade that are reserved
for gravesites.

The translation of מְרִצָה follows *Rivevan*
and *R' Shmuel* based on *Yerushalmi.* An
alternative translation: a *hatchet (Rav; Ram-*
bam; Meiri; see Teshuvos Radbaz v. 2, 611).

The halachah follows *R' Yose (Rav; Ram-*
bam, Hil. Avos HaTumah 13:5).

3.

סַכִּין שֶׁנִּמְצֵאת בְּאַרְבָּעָה עָשָׂר שׁוֹחֵט בָּהּ מִיָּד.
— *A knife which was found on the*
fourteenth [of Nissan] may be used im-
mediately for slaughter [lit. one may
slaughter with it immediately].

[A contaminated utensil requiring immersion may not be used for consecrated objects
(קָדָשִׁים) until the nightfall after its immersion
(see *Leviticus* 12:4-7; *Negaim* 14:3). Therefore a knife found on the fourteenth of Nissan was presumably immersed on the
previous day, so that it could be used to
slaughter the Pesach offering on the afternoon of the fourteenth. In general, utensils
for the festivals were cleansed as close to that
festival as possible, to lessen the possibility
of recontamination. Therefore, if one finds a
knife on the fourteenth he need neither
cleanse it nor wait until nightfall (הָעֶרֶב שֶׁמֶשׁ)
before using it.] It can be assumed that its
owner had immersed it yesterday in preparation for the slaughter of his Passover offering
today *(Rav; Rosh).*

בִּשְׁלֹשָׁה עָשָׂר, שׁוֹנֶה וּמַטְבִּיל. — [*But if it*
was found] *on the thirteenth [of Nis-*
san], he must immerse it again.

Perhaps the owner had planned to
immerse it just before sundown, in time
to use it the next day. Although unidentified utensils found in Jerusalem are

not considered contaminated (see previous mishnah), this is so only
regarding unconsecrated items (חֻלִּין) or
Terumah, but concerning consecrated
items (קָדָשִׁים), *taharah* must be established. Thus, when in doubt, immersion must be performed *(Rav; Rosh;*
Rambam; Hil. Avos HaTumah 13:5; cf.
Ravad there).

Rambam (Comm. and *ibid.)* holds that
where contamination is suspected, even contact with corpses cannot be discounted, and
sprinkling of the Red Cow's ashes [see
comm. to 4:2] on the third and seventh day
of the cleansing process followed by immersion is necessary. Thus a knife being prepared for use with the Passover offering
would have received the first application of
these ashes before the thirteenth, but might
be lacking the second application and subsequent immersion, for these could be performed until sundown. Consequently the
phrase שׁוֹנֶה וּמַטְבִּיל refers to two separate
stages of the cleansing process which must
be adhered to, שׁוֹנֶה, *he performs the second*
application, וּמַטְבִּיל *and immerses. Kessef*
Mishneh finds support for *Rambam's* interpretation in the word שׁוֹנֶה, which means
he repeats [from שְׁנַיִם, *two].* This implies
something being done a second time, namely,
the sprinkling. According to *Ravad* (whose

8
3

R' Yose says: All are [assumed to be] *tahor* except for the basket, the shovel and the spade that are reserved for gravesites.

3. A knife which was found on the fourteenth [of Nissan] may be used immediately for slaughter. [But if it was found] on the thirteenth [of Nissan], he must immerse it again.

A meat cleaver, whether [found] on the thirteenth or on the fourteenth, he must immerse again___

YAD AVRAHAM

opinion is given anonymously by *Rosh* and *Rav*), only immersion is performed and this only once. Presumably he would translate שׁוֹנֶה וּמַטְבִּיל, *he immerses it again*, even though it might be reasonable to assume that an immersion had been performed already.

Rashi (*Pesachim* 70a, s.v. ואישנא) points out that we do not suspect that this knife had been lost before its cleansing began, since there was such a multitude in Jerusalem during the festivals that anything lost would surely be found the same day. [Additionally, the streets of Jerusalem were swept every day (see above 7:2, s.v. בשעת הרגל, and *Pesachim* 7a). But *Tos. R'Akiva Eiger* and *Shoshanim L'David* (in *Likutim* marginalia of *Mishnayos* ed. Vilna) point out that this latter reason does not suffice because it may be that only the busiest streets were swept, while our mishnah makes no distinctions where the knife was found; thus *Rashi's* reason is necessary.

וְקוֹפִיץ, — *(And) a meat cleaver*,

[A cleaver cannot be used with the Pesach offering because of the Scriptural injunction (*Exodus* 12:46) that no bone of the Pesach may be broken.]

בֵּין בָּזֶה וּבֵין בָּזֶה, שׁוֹנֶה וּמַטְבִּיל; — *whether [found] On the thirteenth or on the fourteenth* [lit. *on this or on this*], *he must immerse again* —

[Since there is no reason to cleanse this utensil for use with the Pesach offering, it cannot be assumed that it was cleansed prior to the festival. As far as using it for unconsecrated meat there is no question, for utensils of unknown origin found in Jerusalem are not considered contaminated.]

A second offering, the *chagigah*, sometimes accompanies the Pesach offering. Since at least part of the Pesach must be eaten עַל הַשּׂוֹבַע, *when one's hunger has been sated*, it is necessary to eat a considerable quantity of meat before performing this *mitzvah*. If a small group shares a Pesach, each person would receive a large enough portion to alleviate his hunger, and have enough left to fulfill the requirement of eating after he is no longer hungry. However, if a large group shares the offering, each member would receive only a minimum share of the meat. In such a case, a *chagigah* offering would be brought along with the Pesach, so that its meat can be eaten before the portion of the Pesach. But there is no prohibition against breaking a bone of the *chagigah*, so it would seem logical to assume that the meat cleaver had been cleansed for use on *chagigah* meat. If so, there should be no difference between a knife and a cleaver? This question is raised and resolved by the Talmud (*Pesachim* 70a): The mishnah's distinction between a knife and a cleaver is limited to an unusual case of a *nassi* [prince or president of the Jewish community in *Eretz Yisrael*] who is deathly ill on the thirteenth of Nissan, and probably will not survive the fourteenth. In the event of his death, all Israel would attend the funeral, and everyone would be contaminated. If so, the Pesach would be offered because in an instance where most of the people are contaminated, the commandment of Pesach supersedes the prohibition against making an offering in a state of contamination. The *chagigah*, however, would remain subject to all restrictions of contamination, and could not be offered. In case the *nassi* is hovering between life and death, there is no doubt that the Pesach will be sacrificed — either in a state of *taharah* (if the *nassi* re-

חָל אַרְבָּעָה עָשָׂר לִהְיוֹת בַּשַּׁבָּת, שׁוֹחֵט בָּה
מִיָּד. בַּחֲמִשָּׁה עָשָׂר, שׁוֹחֵט בָּה מִיָּד. נִמְצֵאת
קְשׁוּרָה לְסַכִּין, הֲרֵי זוֹ כַסַּכִּין.

[ד] **פָּרֹכֶת** שֶׁנִּטְמֵאת בִּוְלַד הַטֻּמְאָה,
מַטְבִּילִין אוֹתָהּ בִּפְנִים,

יד אברהם

mains alive), in which case the knife must be immersed on the thirteenth, or in a state of *tumah* (if the *nassi* dies), in which case the knife need not be immersed. Regarding the cleaver, however, the situation is different. If the *nassi* dies, the *chagigah* will not be offered. But even if the *nassi* remains alive, the Pesach portions of any given person may be sufficiently large to obviate the need for him to offer a *chagigah*. Thus, no one would hesitate to immerse the knife because its use is subject to only one unknown (the *nassi's* death). But he might not bother immersing a cleaver, whose use depends on two unknowns (the *nassi's* death and the size of his Pesach portions). Therefore, a knife may be assumed to have been immersed on the thirteenth while a cleaver may not be so considered.

חָל אַרְבָּעָה עָשָׂר לִהְיוֹת בַּשַּׁבָּת, שׁוֹחֵט בָּה מִיָּד. — [unless] *the fourteenth* [of Nissan] *fell on the Sabbath,* [in which case] *he may slaughter with it immediately.*

He may use even a cleaver without immersion, on the assumption that it had been cleansed before the Sabbath. Although the *chagigah* brought on every festival may be offered on any of the seven days of the festival, the preferable time to do so (לְכַתְּחִלָה) is the first day (see *Chagigah* 1:6). We may assume, therefore, that the cleaver's owner had planned to bring his *chagigah* on the first day of Yom Tov; accordingly he would surely want his cleaver to be cleansed for use with the offering. To do so in this instance, he must cleanse it on the thirteenth, for one is not permitted to immerse utensils on the Sabbath (*Beitzah* 2:2). When the fourteenth falls on a weekday, one can cleanse the cleaver on the fourteenth, so that it will be suitable for use on the next day. As explained above, the use of

a cleaver for the *Chagigah* which is offered together with the Pesach offering is of no concern (*Rav; Rosh*).

[Although a cleaver may be used for slaughter, (as stated by our mishnah) we still cannot assume that it had been cleansed on the thirteenth for the purpose of slaughtering the Pesach, — because slaughter is not the primary purpose of a cleaver. This explains the different rulings for a cleaver and a knife.]

Rambam (Comm., and *Hil. Avos HaTumah* 13:5) understands this passage to refer to a knife. Although the mishnah has already permitted the use of a knife found on the fourteenth that falls on a weekdays, that ruling is not adequate to cover the case of a knife found on Sabbath, the fourteenth, because the assumptions of the knife's purity are not as compelling on a Sabbath as on a weekday. On a weekday we might rely on an assumption of *taharah* because it effects only the valid slaughter of the offering. On the Sabbath, however, if the knife was not cleansed, the offering would be invalid, with the result that the Sabbath would have been desecrated. We might reason, therefore, that we dare not permit slaughter of the Pesach on the unsubstantiated assumption that the knife had been cleansed. Therefore, the mishnah must state that the assumption is accepted on the Sabbath as well.

R' Baruch Frankel (glosses to Mishnah ed. Vilna) demonstrates that according to *Rambam* only a consecrated knife (כְּלִי שָׁרֵת), but not a cleaver, may be used to slaughter an offering (cf. *Tos. Chullin* 3a s.v. כגון). Since our mishnah speaks of slaughter, we must assume that a knife is the item under discussion.

בַּחֲמִשָּׁה עָשָׂר, שׁוֹחֵט בָּה מִיָּד. — [But if it was found] *on the fifteenth* [of Nissan], *he may slaughter with it immediately.*

[For as explained earlier, it is assumed that even a cleaver has been purified at least on the fourteenth to make it fit for

8
4

[unless] the fourteenth fell on the Sabbath, [in which case] he may slaughter with it immediately. [But if it was found] on the fifteenth [of Nissan], he may slaughter with it immediately. If it was found tied to a knife, then it is [considered] as the knife.

4. If a curtain has been contaminated through [contact with] a secondary *tumah*, they immerse it within [the Temple complex], and they may bring it

YAD AVRAHAM

use on the *chagigah* offered on the fifteenth. Only when the cleaver is found on the fourteenth is this assumption not made, for the loser may have planned to defer the purification process to some time later in the day.]

Rambam (Comm.) remarks that cleansing (i.e., application of מֵי חַטָּאת, *purification water* and immersion) is prohibited on the festival (*Beitzah* 2:2), so that the utensil's owner could not have intended to cleanse it on the festival. [I.e., even if he had planned to use the cleaver only after nightfall, he would have to cleanse it before the festival (see *Tos. Yom Tov*).]

נִמְצֵאת קְשׁוּרָה לְסַכִּין, הֲרֵי זוֹ כַסַּכִּין. — *If it* [the cleaver] *was found tied to a knife, then it is [considered] as the knife.*

In a case where the knife is adjudged to have been cleansed, one can assume that the cleaver had been cleansed along with it (*Rav; Rosh*).

The above interpretation is based on *Rav* and *Rosh's* assumption, that the subject under discussion in the previous passage is a cleaver. Therefore the pronoun *it* is taken to refer to a cleaver. *Rambam*, however, understands that the previous discussion was about a knife. Thus here too, if *it*, meaning the knife whose status was unknown, *was found tied to a knife* whose status was known, both are assumed to have the same status: if the known knife was contaminated, the unknown knife is also assumed to have been contaminated even if found on Yom Tov, and if the known knife was uncontaminated the unknown knife is considered uncontaminated even if found on a weekday.

4.

After exhausting the tangential subject of substances whose status regarding *taharah* is unknown, the mishnah embarks upon another tangential subject, that of consecrated objects that have been contaminated. This discussion is probably prompted by the subject matter of the previous mishnah which spoke about the suitability of utensils for use in the Temple service.

פָּרֹכֶת שֶׁנִּטְמֵאת בְּוָלַד הַטֻּמְאָה — *If a curtain* [i.e., any of the thirteen curtains hanging in the Temple (see *Tos. Yom Tov*)] *has been contaminated through [contact with] a secondary tumah,*

The *tumos* in the Torah are classified as primary *tumos* (אֲבוֹת הַטֻּמְאָה, lit. *fathers of tumah*), and secondary *tumos* (וְלָדוֹת הַטֻּמְאָה: lit. *children of tumah*) With some exceptions, all basic *tumos* — such as corpses, *zav*, *zavah*, that are *tamei* of themselves, rather than

through contact with a contaminated substance — are considered primary *tumos*; *tumos* that are acquired through contact are usually considered secondary. A primary *tumah* can contaminate people and utensils, food and drink; a secondary *tumah* can contaminate only food or drink, but not people and utensils (*Parah* 8:5).

The only secondary *tumah* that can confer contamination upon a utensil is a liquid. By Rabbinic decree, a drink that

[147]   THE MISHNAH / SHEKALIM

וּמַכְנִיסִין אוֹתָהּ מִיָּד. וְאֶת־שֶׁנִּטְמֵאת בְּאַב
הַטֻּמְאָה, מַטְבִּילִין אוֹתָהּ בַּחוּץ, וְשׁוֹטְחִין
אוֹתָהּ בַּחֵיל. וְאִם הָיְתָה חֲדָשָׁה, שׁוֹטְחִין אוֹתָהּ
עַל־גַּג הָאִצְטַבָּא כְּדֵי שֶׁיִּרְאוּ הָעָם אֶת־
מְלַאכְתָּן שֶׁהִיא נָאָה.

‎[ה] **רַבָּן** שִׁמְעוֹן בֶּן־גַּמְלִיאֵל אוֹמֵר מִשּׁוּם
רַבִּי שִׁמְעוֹן בֶּן־הַסְּגָן: פָּרֹכֶת עָבְיָהּ
טֶפַח; וְעַל־שִׁבְעִים וּשְׁתַּיִם נִימִין נֶאֱרֶגֶת; וְעַל־

יד אברהם

is contaminated by a secondary *tumah* can contaminate a utensil (*ibid.*). Since the curtain of our mishnah is described as having been contaminated by a secondary *tumah*, it could only have occurred through a liquid (*Rav; Rosh; Rambam*).

מַטְבִּילִין אוֹתָהּ בִּפְנִים, — *they immerse it within* [*the Temple complex*],

The curtain need not be removed from the Temple Courtyard (unlike a utensil coming into contact with a corpse; see *Rambam, Hil. Bias HaMikdash* 3:16) since it was contaminated only by a secondary *tumah* (*Rav; Rosh*).[1]

[Of the three *mikvaos* that were in the Temple complex, only one (atop the *Parvah* Chamber) was halachically considered part of the Temple Courtyard. Others were the one above the Water Gate and the one beneath the בֵּית הַמּוֹקֵד, *Fire House*; see *Yoma* 3:2 and *Tamid* 1:1). The canal running through the Temple Courtyard could also serve as a *mikveh* (see *Rashbam, Pesachim* 109b, s.v. היכי מצי).]

וּמַכְנִיסִין אוֹתָהּ מִיָּד. — *and they may bring it in immediately.*

[I.e. even if it had become contaminated outside the Temple, and would not be allowed inside the Temple area for immersion, nevertheless, immediately after its outside immersion —

even before nightfall — it could be brought into the Temple.] The provision, that only with nightfall do contaminated objects attain sufficient purity for use in the Temple, does not apply to Rabbinically based contamination as stated in *Parah* (11:5). For such objects, immersion alone suffices (*Rambam; Rav; Rosh*).

וְאֶת־שֶׁנִּטְמֵאת בְּאַב הַטֻּמְאָה, — *But if it was contaminated through* [*contact with*] *a primary tumah,*

It became contaminated through contact with a Scripturally ordained primary *tumah*, such as a corpse or the carcass of an animal not slaughtered in the prescribed manner (*Rav*).

מַטְבִּילִין אוֹתָהּ בַּחוּץ, — *they immerse it outside* [*the Temple complex*],

[The object must be removed from the Temple Courtyard — and even outside of the Women's Courtyard and the *Chel* (see *Kelim* 1:88) — for immersion] because a contaminated utensil may not be left in any of these areas (*Rav*).

וְשׁוֹטְחִין אוֹתָהּ בַּחֵיל. — *and they spread it out* [*to dry*] *in the Chel.*

A wooden enclosure (סוֹרֵג) circled the Temple Courtyard (and the Women's Courtyard on the east side) at a distance of ten cubits from the outer wall. The

---

1. The reason the curtain need not be removed is because it contracted *tumah* only by Rabbinic decree, and the Rabbis did not go so far as to subject it to the further provision that all *tumah* be removed from the Temple. A utensil contaminated with a Torah-ordained secondary *tumah*, however, would be subject to removal (see *Rambam, Hil. Bias HaMikdash* 3:17).

in immediately. But if it was contaminated though [contact with] a primary *tumah*, they immerse it outside [the Temple complex], and they spread it out [to dry] in the *Chel.* If it was [a] new [curtain], they would spread it out upon the roof of the portico that the people may see their handicraft, for it was beautiful.

5. Rabban Shimon ben Gamliel says in the name of R' Shimon, son of the Deputy [*Kohen Gadol*]: The curtain was one handbreadth thick, woven upon seventy-two threads, each thread composed of

YAD AVRAHAM

area between the enclosure and the Courtyard walls was called the *Chel* (see *Middos* 2:3; cf. *Rambam, Hil. Beis HaBechirah* 5:2). If an object (or person) had been immersed but night had not yet fallen (טְבוּל יוֹם), it could remain in the *Chel* but not in the Women's Courtyard (and surely not in the Temple Courtyard itself).

וְאִם הָיְתָה חֲדָשָׁה, שׁוֹטְחִין אוֹתָהּ עַל־גַּג הָאִצְטַבָּא — *If it was [a] new [curtain], they would spread it out upon the roof of the portico.*

[The translation follows *R' Binyamin Mossafia* in *Aruch* (s.v. סטיו: see *Mossaf HeAruch*, s.v. אסטוה). *Rashi* (*Pesachim* 11b, s.v. על גב האאצטבא) adds that אִצְטַבָּא refers to

a portico set up to provide shade for benches underneath it.]

— כְּדֵי שֶׁיִּרְאוּ הָעָם אֶת־מְלַאכְתָּן שֶׁהִיא נָאָה. *that the people may see their handicraft, for it was beautiful.*

Because the curtain was draped over the portico, it could be seen even by people very far away (*Tif. Yis.*). [See *Pesachim* 1:5 that the roof of the portico was visible throughout Jerusalem.]

The purpose of this was to motivate the people to contribute toward the manufacture of the two new curtains that were made every year, as stated in the next mishnah (*R' Shlomo Sirilio* cited in *Meleches Shlomo*).

5.

רַבָּן שִׁמְעוֹן בֶּן־גַּמְלִיאֵל אוֹמֵר מִשׁוּם רַבִּי שִׁמְעוֹן בֶּן־הַסְּגָן: — *Rabban Shimon ben Gamliel says in the name of R' Shimon, son of the Deputy [Kohen Gadol]:*

The latter R' Shimon, who lived during the final years of the Second Temple, was the son of R' Chanina the *Deputy Kohen Gadol* (ר' חֲנִינָא סְגַן הַכֹּהֲנִים) and still saw the Temple (*Yuchasin, Ma'amar* 1, s.v. ר' שמעון בן הסגן, *Yuchasin HaShalem* p. 78; cf. *Shoshanim L'David*). *R' Yeshayah Pik* notes that in *Chullin* 90 and *Tamid* 29b he is called רַבִּי שִׁמְעוֹן הַסְּגָן, *R' Shimon the Deputy* (*Yesh Seder LaMishnah*).

פָּרֹכֶת עָבְיָהּ טֶפַח; — *The curtain was one handbreadth thick,*

[This refers to the curtain that divided the Holy from the Holy of Holies.]

וְעַל־שִׁבְעִים וּשְׁנַיִם נִימִין נֶאֱרֶגֶת; — (and it was) *woven upon seventy-two* [horizontal] *threads,*

[Presumably this fact was inserted to explain the thickness of the curtain. The threads were so arranged as to result in a fabric consisting of seventy-two layers (cf. *Tif. Yis. Bo'az* 2).]

Rambam (*Comm.* ed. Kafich and *Hil. K'lei HaMikdash* 7:16), *Rosh*, and probably also *Rav* (as well as *Aruch*, s.v. נר; *R' Meshullam, R' Shmuel* and *Meiri*; see also *Shinuyei*

כָּל נִימָא וְנִימָא עֶשְׂרִים וְאַרְבָּעָה חוּטִין; אָרְכָּה
אַרְבָּעִים אַמָּה וְרָחְבָּה עֶשְׂרִים אַמָּה;
וּמִשְׁמוֹנִים וּשְׁתֵּי רִבּוֹא נַעֲשֵׂית.
וּשְׁתַּיִם עוֹשִׂין בְּכָל־שָׁנָה. וְשָׁלֹשׁ מֵאוֹת
כֹּהֲנִים מַטְבִּילִין אוֹתָהּ.

יד אברהם

Nuschaos) had in their version: שִׁבְעִים וּשְׁנַיִם נִירִין, *seventy-two heddle shafts*, the devices used to lower and raise the looms horizontal threads. (See *Ravad* to *Tamid* 29b; see also *Shabbos* 13:2.) The version printed with *R' Meshullam's* commentary has וְשֶׁל שִׁבְעִים וּשְׁנַיִם נֶאֱרָגַת, *it was woven of seventy-two.*

וְעַל־כָּל נִימָא וְנִימָא[1] עֶשְׂרִים וְאַרְבָּעָה חוּטִין; — *each thread composed of* [lit. *and upon each thread were*] *twenty-four filaments;*

The filaments from which a thread was made were תְּכֵלֶת, *blue wool,*[2] אַרְגָּמָן, *purple wool,*[3] תּוֹלַעַת שָׁנִי, *wool dyed red,*[4] and שֵׁשׁ, *linen* (*Ex.* 26:31). Six filaments of each material were twisted into single threads (*Yoma* 71b), and then four of the different kinds of threads were twisted together to form one thick twenty-four-filament thread. Thus, each thick thread was made of four six-filament threads, one each of the three colors of wool and one of linen (*Rav*).

אָרְכָּה אַרְבָּעִים אַמָּה וְרָחְבָּה עֶשְׂרִים אַמָּה; — *forty cubits long and twenty cubits wide.*

[Corresponding to the height and width of the sanctuary (*Midos* 4:6-7; see *II Kings* 6:20 with *Rashi*).]

Rashi (*Chullin* 90b, s.v. ארכה) and *Rambam* (*Hil. K'lei HaMikdash* 7:16) understand our mishnah as referring to the curtain(s) separating the Holy from the Holy of Holies (see *Yoma* 5:1), as does *Rosh* (to *Tamid* 29b; see *Meleches Shlomoh* here and *Mefaresh* to *Tamid* 29b).

Rashi (ibid.) cites an opinion that our mishnah refers to the curtain that hung in the doorway leading into the אוּלָם, *Antechamber*, which measured 20 x 40 cubits (see *Midos* 3:7). *Rav* and *Rosh* (who cites this interpretation in *Tamid* as 'some interpret') also adopt this view. It may be that these commentators thought that since only a single cubit separated the Holy from the Holy of Holies (see *Yoma* 5:1, ArtScroll ed., footnote 1), it is improbable that each of the two curtains in that narrow area was a full handbreadth thick, for if so the space between them would have been narrowed to only four handbreadths. [The cubit used for the Temple building measured six handbreadths; *Keilim* 17:10.] That small space would have been too narrow for the *Kohen Gadol* to walk through en-route to the Holy of Holies as he had to do in the Yom Kippur service (cf. *Mefaresh* to *Tamid* 29b and glosses by *R' Yaakov Emden* there).

1. *Rosh's* version here is וְעַל־כָּל־נִירָא וְנִירָא, *upon* (or *in*) *each heddle shaft were.*

2. The blue wool, *techeles*, was dyed with the blood (or fluid) of a sea animal called חִלָּזוֹן. See *Rashi* to *Exodus* 25:4, *Menachos* 44a; cf. *Rambam*, *Hil. K'lei HaMikdash* 8:13 with *Mishneh LaMelech* there and *Mirkeves HaMishneh* to *Hil. Tzitzis* 2:1; *Tif. Yis.*, Preface to *Seder Mo'ed*, pp. 28-29; and *Ma'amar S'funei Tmunei Chol* by the *Radziner Rebbe*, pp. 14-17.

3. *Purple wool* is the traditional interpretation of אַרְגָּמָן (see *Tif. Yis.*, op. cit p. 29; *Shorashim* with notes, Berlin, 1847). However, *Rambam* (*Hil. K'lei HaMikdash* 8:10) holds that all reds are included in אַרְגָּמָן (see *Mishneh LaMelech* and *Or Same'ach* there). *Radak* (*Shorashim*, s.v. ארגמן) states: 'They say it is red called crimson (קרימזן).'

4. *Rambam* (*Comm.* to *Parah* 3:10) and *R' Sa'adyah Gaon* (cited in *Shorashim*, s.v. ארגמן) define תּוֹלַעַת שָׁנִי as *crimson*. Although the traditional view is that this wool was dyed with the blood or fluid of an insect, *Rambam* (*Hil. Parah* 3:2) explains that a type of seed (or berry containing this worm or insect) is used (see *Tif. Yis.*, loc. cit).

8
5

twenty-four filaments; forty cubits long and twenty cubits wide; and made of eighty-two times ten thousand.

They would make two [new curtains] every year. Three hundred *Kohanim* would immerse it.

וּמִשְׁמוֹנִים וּשְׁתֵּי רִבּוֹא נַעֲשֵׂית. — *and made of eighty-two times ten thousand.*

Rav (and *Rosh*) offer three interpretations: (a) It contained 820,000 threads (also in *Rashi Chullin* 90b); (b) it cost 820,000 dinars (a *dinar* is ¼ sela); and (c) the word רִבּוֹת, *young women*, is substituted for רִבּוֹא, i.e., eighty-two *young women* or *girls* were employed in its manufacture (see *Rashi ibid*). The second view is also found in *Rambam* (*Comm.*) and is adopted by *Vilna Gaon* (cited in *Taklin Chadatin*).

וּשְׁתַּיִם עוֹשִׂין בְּכָל-שָׁנָה. — *They would make two [new curtains] every year.*

The two curtains separating the Holy from the Holy of Holies would be changed every year (*Tif. Yis.; Mefaresh* to *Tamid* 29b).

[Those who feel that the curtain under discussion here is the one to the Antechamber, would hold that it was changed every half year.]

R' Shlomo Sirilio explains that this curtain

had to be changed twice every year, because the smoke from the incense would blacken it. [Consequently only the outer of the two curtains, which separated the Holy from the Holy of Holies, had to be changed, for it faced the inner altar where incense was burned twice every day (cf. *Tif. Yis., Bo'az* 3).]

וְשָׁלֹשׁ מֵאוֹת כֹּהֲנִים מַטְבִּילִין אוֹתָהּ. — *(And) three hundred Kohanim would immerse it.*

They would immerse every curtain upon completion, for even utensils completed in a state of *taharah* require immersion for consecrated use (*Chagigah* 3:2) (*Rav, Rosh*).

The Talmud (*Yer.* here; *Tamid* 29b; *Chullin* 90b) lists this as one of the three places where the Sages speak in hyperbole.[1] It is not clear, however, which part of the mishnah is meant. *Rav* (also *Rosh, Rashi* to *Chullin, Rivevan*, and the *Mefaresh* to *Tamid*) assumes that the statement that as many as three hundred *Kohanim* were needed to immerse the curtain is referred to. Such a large number of people was unneces-

---

1. *Meiri* adds that the intent of the mishnah is to illustrate the great size and worth of the curtain. *Aruch* (s.v. גוזמא) explains that when a speaker wants to impress upon his audience the great magnitude of some object or event, he will use an outlandish number as a figure of speech (cf. the often heard complaint: I have told you a *thousand* times!). He points out the verse in *Daniel* (5:1) where it is said about Belshazzar: *and corresponding to a thousand he drank wine* (see *Megillah* 11b). Clearly Belshazzar could not have consumed as much wine as a thousand people. Rather the verse means that he drank an immense amount — as much as is physically possible for any man, i.e., if one man could drink as much as a thousand so would Belshazzar have done in his drunken orgy (see there *Aruch's* interesting interpretation of *Deuteronomy* 1:28: *Great cities fortified to the sky*). In the case of our mishnah, so many *Kohanim* took part in the immersion that it seemed like three hundred. It seems that the number three hundred was a common figure of speech for a very great multitude (much as we use the numbers thousand and million).

Maharal MiPrague approaches this problem with typical originality. The Sages do not view objects and events in a physical manner. The numbers used by them, whether magnified or microscopic, are merely metaphors used to denote the spiritual dimensions of the topic under discussion. For example, the statement (*Pesachim* 94a): 'The world measures 6,000 *Parsah*,' conveys the message that the world was created to be self-sufficient and complete in itself; six represents completeness, for no object is complete without expansion toward six recognized points — the four directions, above and below (*Be'er HaGolah, Be'er* 6, p. 112 in ed. London; see a similar thought in *Tos. Beva Kama* 92b and *Bava Metzia* 107b, s.v. שתין).

קָדְשֵׁי קָדָשִׁים שֶׁנִּטְמָא, בֵּין בְּאַב [ו] **בְּשַׂר**
הַטֻּמְאָה בֵּין בְּוָלַד הַטֻּמְאָה, בֵּין
בִּפְנִים בֵּין בַּחוּץ — בֵּית שַׁמַּאי אוֹמְרִים: הַכֹּל
יִשָּׂרֵף בִּפְנִים, חוּץ מִשֶּׁנִּטְמָא בְּאַב הַטֻּמְאָה
בַּחוּץ.
וּבֵית הִלֵּל אוֹמְרִים: הַכֹּל יִשָּׂרֵף בַּחוּץ, חוּץ
מִשֶּׁנִּטְמָא בִּוְלַד הַטֻּמְאָה בִּפְנִים.

יד אברהם

sary.[1] However, *Rambam (Comm.)* comments tersely: Everything told here about

this curtain is hyperbolic — so has the
Talmud explained.

6.

Ravad (Comm. to *Sifra* 6:23 cited by *Meleches Shlomo)* provides the halachic
background for the controversy to be set forth in this mishnah. The rule is that
parts of offerings that become contaminated or disqualified in some way must be
burned (*Pesachim* 24a, 82b). In the case of קָדְשֵׁי קָדָשִׁים, *the most holy offerings*,
they must be burned in the Temple Courtyard, as derived by *Sifra* (6:23; cited partly in *Pesachim, ibid.*). Where the disqualification is due to contamination, this
Scriptural requirement of burning in the Temple Courtyard supersedes the prohibition against holding contaminated objects in the Temple area or, if the contamination occurred outside, bringing such objects into the Courtyard.

[That the prohibition is waived in the face of the *mitzvah* to burn these objects in
the Temple may be derived from the word כָּל, *all*, in *Leviticus* 6:23; see *Malbim*
there.] The Sages agreed, however, that in certain cases it would be demeaning
[מָאוּס] to burn contaminated objects in the Temple, and decreed against this practice. In our mishnah, Beis Shammai and Beis Hillel disagree regarding the cases
where this Rabbinical ban is applicable.

בְּשַׂר קָדְשֵׁי קָדָשִׁים שֶׁנִּטְמָא, — *Meat of the*
most holy offerings which became con-
taminated,

[Contaminated meat of offerings may

not be eaten but must be burned, as set
forth in *Leviticus* (7:19). Sin, guilt and
burnt offerings[2] are classified as the
most holy offerings, due to the fact that,

1. Nevertheless, *Vilna Gaon* (cited by *Tif. Yis. Bo'az* 4) gives a reason why the number three
hundred was picked. The curtain's circumference measured 120 cubits. If these cubits are each
five handbreadths wide (as are all cubits used to measure *utensils* in the Temple; *Keilim*
17:10), the circumference adds up to 600 handbreadths. Thus 600 hands (i.e., 300 *Kohanim*)
were the maximum that could hold the curtain. (See another explanation in *Hon Ashir*; cf.
Shoshanim L'David.)

2. Any parts of a sacrifice that are offered upon the altar [אֵמוּרִים] that became contaminated
— even from offerings of lesser sanctity [קָדָשִׁים קַלִּים] — must be treated the same way as meat
of the holiest offerings; such *emurim*, parts designated for the altar, are always classified as
the most holy of offerings, no matter their origin. That the mishnah specifies only the *meat* of
the most holy of offerings, is not to imply that *emurim* are different. Rather it is only because
meat happens to be under discussion that the qualification of the most 'holy of offerings' had
to be added because meat from lesser offerings is treated differently (see *Menachos* 104b with
Rashi, s.v. שם; *Sifra* to Lev. 6:23; below, s.v. בין בחוץ).

6. Meat of the most holy offerings which became contaminated, whether through [contact with] a primary *tumah*, or a secondary *tumah*, whether inside or outside [the Temple Courtyard] — Beis Shammai say: Everything should be burnt inside [the Courtyard], except that which was contaminated by a primary tumah outside.

Beis Hillel say: Everything should be burned outside, except that which was contaminated by a secondary *tumah* inside.

YAD AVRAHAM

unlike lesser offerings, they may not leave the Temple Courtyard. This mishnah will now discuss where the meat has to be burned.]

בֵּין בְּאַב הַטֻּמְאָה — *whether through [contact with] a primary tumah,*

[Such as a corpse (מֵת) or the carcass of an unslaughtered animal (וּבֵלָה) and the like.]

בֵּין בּוֹלַד הַטֻּמְאָה, — *or a secondary tumah,*

[The consecrated meat came into contact with a secondary *tumah*, i.e., a person, utensil, food, or drink that had been touched by a primary *tumah*. The meat, therefore, acquires the status of שֵׁנִי לַטֻּמְאָה, *a secondary tumah of the second degree,* (i.e., a tumah that is twice removed from the primary *tumah*).]

בֵּין בִּפְנִים בֵּין בַּחוּץ — *whether inside or outside [the Temple Courtyard]* —

[The latter case, if the burning takes place within, necessitates the introduction of a contaminated object into the confines of the Temple Courtyard, an act that would normally be forbidden (see above mishnah 4, s.v. מטבילין).]

בֵּית שַׁמַּאי אוֹמְרִים: הַכֹּל יִשָּׂרֵף בִּפְנִים, *Beis Shammai say: Everything should be burned inside [the Courtyard],*

[One of the three places of burning, the בֵּית הַדֶּשֶׁן הַגָּדוֹל, lit. *great place of ashes,* was in the Courtyard (*Zevachim* 104b).]

חוּץ מִשֶּׁנִּטְמָא בְּאַב הַטֻּמְאָה בַחוּץ. — *except that which was contaminated by a primary tumah outside.*

In this case two factors oppose bringing it into the Temple area for burning: (a) The severity of the contamination, and (b) burning in the Temple would involve introducing *tumah* into the Temple. In all other instances, where one or neither of these factors is present burning must be done in the Temple (*Rav; Rosh*).

וּבֵית הִלֵּל אוֹמְרִים: הַכֹּל יִשָּׂרֵף בַּחוּץ, — *Beis Hillel say: Everything should be burned outside,*

I.e., in the place designated on the Temple Mount, outside the Courtyard. This place was called בִּירָה, *Birah (Rosh* and R' *Yehudah* based on *Pesachim* 3:8; see *Zevachim* 104b; *Rashi* and *Tos.* to *Pesachim* 49a).

Actually such meat could be burned anywhere in Jerusalem. *Birah* was designated for the benefit of people with no domicile in Jerusalem where they could burn their disqualified meat, or for an entire (or most of an) offering that had become contaminated (see *Pesachim* 7:8 with comm.; *Gem.* there 81b-82a; *Rambam, Hil. P'sulei HaMukdashin* 19:18, *Hil. Ma'aseh HaKarbanos* 7:4).

חוּץ מִשֶּׁנִּטְמָא בוֹלַד הַטֻּמְאָה בִּפְנִים. — *except that which was contaminated by a secondary tumah inside [the Temple Courtyard].*

Beis Hillel hold that the Rabbis forbade burning of the meat inside the

שקלים [ז] **רַבִּי** אֱלִיעֶזֶר אוֹמֵר: אֶת־שֶׁנִּטְמָא בְּאַב
הַטֻּמְאָה, בֵּין בִּפְנִים בֵּין בַּחוּץ,
יִשָּׂרֵף בַּחוּץ; וְאֶת־שֶׁנִּטְמָא בִּוְלַד הַטֻּמְאָה, בֵּין
בִּפְנִים בֵּין בַּחוּץ, יִשָּׂרֵף בִּפְנִים.
רַבִּי עֲקִיבָא אוֹמֵר: מְקוֹם טֻמְאָתוֹ, שָׁם
שְׂרֵפָתוֹ.

[ח] **אֵבְרֵי** הַתָּמִיד נִתָּנִין מֵחֲצִי כֶבֶשׁ
וּלְמַטָּה בַּמַּעֲרָב; וְשֶׁל מוּסָפִין

יד אברהם

Courtyard unless neither of the two factors cited above (s.v. חוץ משנטמא) are present. Thus only where the contamination was contracted from a secondary *tumah* (thus eliminating the objection of bringing a severe *tumah* into the Courtyard) — and this occurred within the Temple Courtyard (so that no *tumah* whatever need be brought in, for it is there already)—may we burn the meat in the Temple Courtyard (*Rav, Rosh*).

Yerushalmi cites a disagreement regarding the definition of וְלַד הַטֻּמְאָה here and in mishnah 7. One view holds it refers only to a secondary Rabbinic *tumah;* accordingly, only objects not having a contaminated status under Torah Law may be burned inside. A secondary Torah-ordained *tumah*, for the purpose of our mishnah, is classified as a primary *tumah* and may not be burned inside.

The other view is that the term secondary *tumah* refers to every form of this genre, whether based on Torah law or Rabbinic decree. [Curiously, an identical controversy between the same Sages is found in *Pesachim* 15a concerning the definition 'secondary *tumah*' as it is used there (1:6).]

7.

Mishnah 7 is a continuation of the dispute begun in mishnah 6.

רַבִּי אֱלִיעֶזֶר אוֹמֵר: אֶת־שֶׁנִּטְמָא בְּאַב הַטֻּמְאָה, בֵּין בִּפְנִים בֵּין בַּחוּץ, יִשָּׂרֵף בַּחוּץ; — *R' Eliezer says: That which was contaminated by a primary tumah, whether inside or outside, should be burned outside;*

According to R' Eliezer, only one factor — the severity of the contamination — is crucial to the decision of whether the *tumah* may be burned in the Temple: If the *tumah* was severe, having been contracted from a primary *tumah*, the burning may not take place in the Temple (*Meiri; Rivevan; R' Shmuel; R' Meshullam* and others).

וְאֶת־שֶׁנִּטְמָא בִּוְלַד הַטֻּמְאָה, בֵּין בִּפְנִים בֵּין בַּחוּץ, יִשָּׂרֵף בִּפְנִים. — *but that which was* contaminated by a secondary tumah, whether inside or outside, should be burned inside.

R' Eliezer is unconcerned with the place where the *tumah* was contracted (ibid.).

According to *Rav*, R' Eliezer's ruling in this case is based on his holding that meat touched by a secondary *tumah* is completely uncontaminated under Torah law. As noted by *Mishnas Chachamim* cited in *Likutim (Vilna Mishnayos)* this interpretation is extremely difficult in that it is contrary to many sources and even Scriptural evidence that food *can* contract contamination from a secondary *tumah*.

The disagreement in *Yerushalmi* (cited in *comm.* to mishnah 6, s.v. חוץ משנטמא בולד הטומאה) regarding the definition of 'secondary *tumah*' concerns this passage as well.

7. R' Eliezer says: That which was contaminated by primary *tumah*, whether inside or outside, should be burned outside; but that which was contaminated by a secondary *tumah*, whether inside or outside, should be burned inside.

R' Akiva says: Wherever it became contaminated, there it is burned.

8. The limbs of the daily offering were placed on the lower half of the ramp on the western side;

YAD AVRAHAM

רִבִּי עֲקִיבָא אוֹמֵר: מְקוֹם טֻמְאָתוֹ, שָׁם שְׁרֵפָתוֹ. — R' Akiva says: Wherever it became contaminated, there it is burned [lit. *the place of its contamination, there is its burning*].

[R' Akiva takes into account only the consideration that contaminated items may not be brought into the Courtyard. The severity of *tumah* is of no concern to him.]

The foregoing two mishnayos discuss only meat of the 'most holy' offerings. Contaminated meat from offerings of lesser sanctity is always burned outside. Concerning such offerings, there is no provision to burn disqualified parts in the Temple. *Leviticus* 6:23, where the law of burning in the Temple area is given, specifies only sin offerings and, by extension [see *Sifra*], it is referred to all 'most holy offerings.' (See *Menachos* 104b, *Sifra* to *Leviticus* 6:23; *Rambam, Hil. Ma'aseh HaKarbanos* 7:4.) Whether lesser offerings must be burned only in the *Birah* or anywhere in Jerusalem has been discussed previously (end of mishnah 6, s.v. ובית הלל).

The halachah follows R' Akiva (*Rambam, Comm.; Hil. Ma'aseh HaKarbanos* 19:6).

8.

Mishnah 8 begins with a discussion of where the parts of various offerings were placed preparatory to being burned on the altar. Then the mishnah discusses new laws regarding *shekalim*. It would seem, therefore, that the first section of the mishnah has no relationship either to the subject of the preceding mishnayos or to the general theme of our tractate. *Tiferes Yisrael, R' Shmuel,* and *Shoshanim L'David* suggest that this segment of the mishnah is related to the central theme of chapters 7-8: the identification of unknown things that are found in the Temple. Since our mishnah will set forth that the limbs of various offering are left in specific parts of the ramp leading up to the altar, it follows that a question concerning the status of such limbs can be decided merely by noting on which part of the ramp they were found (see also *Ravad* to *Tamid* 31b).

אֵבְרֵי הַתָּמִיד נִתָּנִין מֵחֲצִי כֶבֶשׁ וּלְמַטָּה בַּמַּעֲרָב; — The limbs of the daily offering were placed on the lower half of the ramp on the western side;

[We follow the reading of most commentators that the limbs were placed on the *west*. Others read that they were placed on the *east*. Both versions will be explained in detail.]

On the altar's side was a ramp thirty-two cubits long and sixteen cubits wide (see diagram p. 157). After the daily offering has been slaughtered and its blood thrown upon the corners of the altar, the carcass was dissected and cut into the prescribed parts (see *Tamid* 4:3). The limbs were transported to the ramp of the altar where they remained

יד אברהם

while the *Kohanim* assembled in the לִשְׁכַּת הַגָּזִית, *Hewn-stone Chamber*, for prayer, and performed the services of incense and the *Menorah* (ibid. 4:3-5:2). Then they would return and bring the limbs up to the top of the altar to be offered on the pyre. The mishnah now informs us that the limbs were left on the lower western quarter of the ramp (*Rav*).

They were left on the lower half of the ramp so as to give the subsequent transport (הוֹלָכָה) of the limbs to the top of the altar more visibility and prominence (*Mefaresh* and *Rosh* to *Tamid* 31b).

The western side of the ramp was chosen because the Heavenly Presence (שְׁכִינָה) is in the west (*Bava Basra* 25a) [this is especially so in the Temple where the Holy of Holies was in the west] (*Rosh* and *Ravad* to *Tamid* 31b; *Rav* there 4:3[1]).

וְשֶׁל מוּסָפִין נִתָּנִין מֶחֱצִי כֶבֶשׁ וּלְמַטָּה בַּמִּזְרָח; — (and) those of the additional offerings were placed on the lower half of the ramp on the eastern side;

[The *mussaf* offerings are listed in Numbers 28:29 and are added to the daily offering on the Sabbath, festivals, and Rosh Chodesh.]

They were not placed near the limbs of the daily offering so that they would not become confused with them. If that were to happen, limbs of the *mussaf* might be offered on the altar before the limbs of the daily offering, in violation of the rule (see *Pesachim* 58b) that the daily morning offering must be the first offering placed on the altar (*Rashi* to *Succah* 54b, s.v. נותנין).

In adopting the reading that the daily limbs were placed on the west side of the ramp, we follow the version adopted by most commentators (*Rav; Rosh; Rivevan; Rambam, Comm.* ed. *Kafich* and *Hil. T'midin U'Mussafin* 6:3; *Ravad* to *Tamid* 31b; *R' Shmuel;* and *Tos., Succah* 54b, s.v. דתניא). It is also in our versions of *Tamid* 4:3 and 31b. The version in our editions of the mishnah, and adopted by *Rashi* in *Succah* 54b and *Yoma* 26a (s.v. היא מעלה), gives *east* as the place of the daily sacrifice and *west* for that of the *mussafin. Rosh* and *Mefaresh* (*Tamid* 31b) explain that this does not contradict *Tamid* 4:3 where all versions state that the limbs of the daily sacrifice were placed on the west side, the preferable side. Only when there were *mussafim* were they given precedence (according to this version) and placed upon the west side. Consequently, the limbs of the daily sacrifice had to be placed on the eastern side.

וְשֶׁל רָאשֵׁי חֳדָשִׁים נִתָּנִין מִתַּחַת כַּרְכֹּב הַמִּזְבֵּחַ מִלְמָטָה. — and those of [the additional offerings of] Rosh Chodesh were placed [on the ramp] below the karkov of the altar.

[The version upon which our interpretation is based is that of our editions and that of *Rashi* (*Succah* 54b, s.v. ושל ראשי חדשים). Other interpretations will be given further. We have not translated כַּרְכֹּב, *karkov*, because of the conflicting opinions as to its definition.]

The limbs of the Rosh Chodesh *mussafim* were placed in a higher, more prominent part of the ramp than other offerings in order to publicize the sanctification of that day as Rosh Chodesh (*Succah* 55a with *Rashi; Yer.*), because

1. *Ravad* to *Tamid* (4:3; also *Mefaresh* there 31b) offers that the east side of the ramp was left empty because *Kohanim* ascended on that side in order to throw the limbs upon the pyre, which was to the east of the ramp. However R' Yaakov Emden objects to this line of reasoning, because on days when there was an additional offering, both sides of the ramp held limbs without impeding the *Kohanim* (*Lechem Shamayim*).

He proposes (*ibid;* glosses to *Hil. Beis HaBechirah* 2:13) a solution based on the requirement (*Zevachim* 62b) that the limbs be thrown from the ramp upon the altar through an air space over the Temple Courtyard floor. The western part of the ramp stopped short of the altar's top. Thus the western side was used for the limbs because they would be thrown to the altar from that side of the ramp.

8
8
those of the additional offerings were placed on the lower half of the ramp on the eastern side; and those of [the additional offerings of] Rosh Chodesh were placed [on the ramp] below the *karkov* of the altar.

most people, not having seen the new moon, would not know it was Rosh Chodesh (*Tos. Yom Tov*). [Besides *Beis Din* had the right to defer Rosh Chodesh for the day after the new moon was sighted, if it saw fit. All versions and opinions agree with the above.] Unlike the altar described in *Exodus* 27:1-8 (see *Rashi* there), the walls of the Second Temple altar did not rise in a straight vertical line, but were indented by a cubit each in two places [see diagram in *comm.* to *Pesachim* 5:6]. The first indentation occurred one cubit above ground level, and was called the יְסוֹד, *foundation* or *base*, and the second indentation occurred six cubits above ground level and was called סוֹבֵב [*sovev*], *surround* or *encirclement* (see *Middos* 3:1). The limbs of the Rosh

Chodesh *mussafim* were placed on the upper half of the ramp (above the 4 1/2 cubit mark; the ramp rose to a height of nine cubits above ground) but below the *sovev*, to which our mishnah refers as *karkov* (*Rashi* to *Succah* 54b).

Lechem Shamayim points out that the use of *karkov* as a synonym for סוֹבֵב, *sovev*, also occurs in *Zevachim* 62a.

The version of *Rav*, *Tos. Succah* (54b s.v. דרתניא) and *Rambam* (*comm.* and *Hil. T'midim UMussafin* 6:3) reads נִתָּנִין עַל־ בְּרַכֹּב הַמִּזְבֵּחַ מִלְמַעְלָה — *they were placed atop the karkov of the altar*. Not all agree, however, on the definition of *karkov*. *Rav* explains that the limbs are not placed on the ramp, but upon the *sovev*. [The foregoing is *Lechem Shamayim*'s interpretation of *Rav* and *Tosafos*.]

Rambam holds that *karkov* refers to the walkway for the *Kohanim* atop the altar;

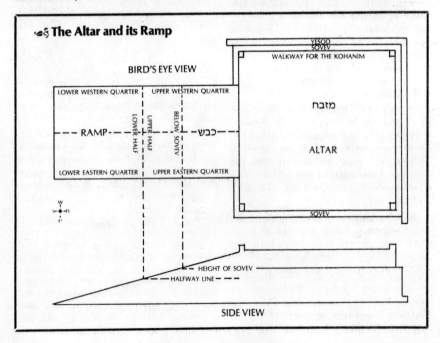

The Altar and its Ramp

BIRD'S EYE VIEW

LOWER WESTERN QUARTER | UPPER WESTERN QUARTER

RAMP

LOWER EASTERN QUARTER | UPPER EASTERN QUARTER

LOWER HALF | UPPER HALF | BELOW SOVEV

כבש

YESOD
SOVEV
WALKWAY FOR THE KOHANIM

מזבח

ALTAR

SOVEV

HEIGHT OF SOVEV
HALFWAY LINE

SIDE VIEW

הַשְּׁקָלִים וְהַבִּכּוּרִים אֵין נוֹהֲגִין אֶלָּא בִּפְנֵי
הַבַּיִת, אֲבָל מַעְשַׂר דָּגָן וּמַעְשַׂר בְּהֵמָה
וְהַבְּכוֹרוֹת נוֹהֲגִין בֵּין בִּפְנֵי הַבַּיִת בֵּין שֶׁלֹּא
בִּפְנֵי הַבָּיִת.

הַמַּקְדִּישׁ שְׁקָלִים וּבִכּוּרִים, הֲרֵי זֶה קֹדֶשׁ.
רַבִּי שִׁמְעוֹן אוֹמֵר: הָאוֹמֵר בִּכּוּרִים קֹדֶשׁ,
אֵינָן קֹדֶשׁ.

יד אברהם

thus the limbs were placed on the altar.

Mishneh LaMelech (*Hil. Ma'aseh HaKar-bonos* 6:4) and *Lechem Shamayim* point out, that this would circumvent the provision (*Zevachim* 62b) that the limbs be tossed upon the pyre through the air space between the ramp and the altar (see also *Mirkeves HaMishneh* and *Even HaAzel* there).

הַשְּׁקָלִים וְהַבִּכּוּרִים — *The [mitzvos of] shekalim and the first fruits*

[The Torah commands that one must set aside some of his first fruits from crops of the seven species for which *Eretz Yisrael* was prominent — wheat, barley, grapes, figs, pomegranates, olives and dates (*Deuteronomy* 8:8) — and bring them to the Temple. There he would recite the verses of thanksgiving found in *Deuteronomy* 26:5-10, put the fruits beside the altar, and give them to the *Kohen* (see *Deuteronomy* 26:1-11 with *Rashi*).]

אֵין נוֹהֲגִין אֶלָּא בִּפְנֵי הַבַּיִת, — *apply only in the Temple era* [lit. *before the House*],

Because the half shekel was needed to purchase offerings, and because the 'first fruits' must be brought to the Temple, these *mitzvos cannot* apply in the absence of the Temple (*Rav, Rosh*).

אֲבָל מַעְשַׂר דָּגָן — *but the grain tithe,*

[By Torah law, a tithe must be separated from the five types of grain (wheat, barley, rye, oats, and spelt) and given the Levites. See above 2:2.]

וּמַעְשַׂר בְּהֵמָה — *(and) the animal tithe*

[See above 3:1 for a description of this *mitzvah.*]

וְהַבְּכוֹרוֹת — *and [the laws regarding] the first born [animals]*

[The firstborn of cattle, sheep, and, goats are automatically consecrated. They must be given to the *Kohanim* and offered on the altar. If the firstborn animals contract a disqualifying blemish, they cannot be redeemed, but their use remains restricted, but they may be slaughtered and eaten. Also firstborn donkeys must be redeemed with a young goat or lamb, which is then given to the *Kohen* for his personal use.]

נוֹהֲגִין בֵּין בִּפְנֵי הַבַּיִת בֵּין שֶׁלֹּא בִּפְנֵי הַבַּיִת. — *apply both in the Temple era and in the post-Temple era* [lit. *both before the House and both not before the House*].

The grain tithe applies because even after the destruction of the Temple the land did not lose its holiness (קְדוּשַׁת הָאָרֶץ לֹא בָּטְלָה), so that all laws dependent upon the uniqueness of *Eretz Yisrael* still apply. He must also separate the animal tithe (*Rav*). The sanctification of the firstborn also applies because the animal is consecrated from the instant of its birth and is not dependent on the declaration of the owner. Once born, the animal is comparable to an animal consecrated for sacrifice in post-Temple times, consecration that is valid (from *R' Shmuel*).

[The continued applicability of the *mitzvah* of animal tithes seems difficult. In view of the law that one need not consecrate first fruit and half shekalim because their purpose no longer applies, why should animals be tithed when they cannot be offered? Perhaps this was so because, under Rabbinic law, the use of untithed animals was prohibited after a specific date (see above 3:1), and this prohibition was not automatically lifted with

The [*mitzvos* of] shekalim and the first fruits apply only in the Temple era, but the grain tithe, the
animal tithe and [the laws regarding] the first born
[animals] apply both in the Temple era and in the
post-Temple era.

If one consecrates shekalim or first fruits, they are
consecrated.

R' Shimon says: If one consecrates first fruits,
they are not consecrated.

YAD AVRAHAM

the destruction of the Temple. Thus one
must separate the animal tithe, not because
of the Scriptural *mitzvah* — it does not apply
just as that of first fruit does not — but in
order to permit the use of the rest of the
flock. *R' Shmuel* seems to hold that the
mishnah does not obligate anyone to tithe in
the post-Temple era; it is only when
someone *did* tithe that this *mitzvah* applied
after the Destruction.]

However at a later period the Sages
decreed that the animal tithe not be
separated because this would result in
the existence of a multitude of consecrated animals without the possibility
of sacrifice, a situation which would
lead to prohibited use of offerings
(*Bechoros* 53a).

Tos. Yom Tov (*Bechoros* 9:1) believes that
the Sages' decree not to tithe was based on
their power to suspend the practice of a
positive *mitzvah* (*Yevamos* 90a). According
to the view expounded earlier that the Scriptural *mitzvah* does not apply in the post-
Temple era because no sacrifices can be offered, all that the Sages had to do was to
revoke the prohibition against use of the
flock before tithing.

הַמַּקְדִּישׁ שְׁקָלִים וּבִכּוּרִים, הֲרֵי זֶה קֹדֶשׁ. — *If
one consecrates shekalim or first fruits,
they are consecrated.*

Though the *mitzvah* to consecrate
them does not apply in the post-Temple
era, nevertheless the consecration is
valid and all the relevant laws become
binding (*Rav*).

רַבִּי שִׁמְעוֹן אוֹמֵר: הָאוֹמֵר בִּכּוּרִים קֹדֶשׁ, אֵינָן
קֹדֶשׁ. — *R' Shimon says: If one con-
secrates first fruits* [lit. *one who*

pronounces first fruits consecrated],
they are not consecrated.

The Torah explicitly links the 'first
fruit' to the Temple, for it is said (*Exodus* 23:19) *The first fruit of your land
you shall bring to the House of
HASHEM your God*, teaching us that
only if there is a Temple can first fruit
be consecrated.

Rambam (*Comm.*) interprets this passage
of the mishnah in a totally different manner.
During the Temple era, one took coins
designated for the half shekel, or fruits
secrated for the first fruit offering, and
sought to divert them from their intended
purpose to בֶּדֶק הַבַּיִת, [the fund for the] *upkeep of the Temple.*

R' Shimon holds that the consecration is
valid for shekalim, but not so in the case of
first fruit, because they became the property
of the *Kohanim* from the moment of the
original designation (see *Rambam, Hil.
Arachin* 6:16, cited in *Tos. Yom Tov*). [The
first tanna holds, presumably, that as long as
the first fruits were not physically given to a
Kohen, the owner retains a share in them in
that he still holds the right to give them to
whichever *Kohen* he chooses (טוֹבַת הֲנָאָה
מְמוֹן; see *Kiddushin* 2:10 and there 58b).]

Tzofnas Pa'ane'ach (*Hil. Arachin* 6:16) explains that even though the shekalim have
already been designated as half shekel taxes,
the consecration is valid, *Rambam's* view is
that the half shekel is not actually consecrated until it reaches the treasurer's (גִזְבָּר)
hand (cf. *Yom Tov* here).

[It seems clear that the mitzvah of half
shekel has not been fulfilled in this case, and
the donor must still pay his half shekel tax
for the offerings.]

The halachah follows R' Shimon (*Rambam, Comm.* and *Hil. Arachin* 6:16).

APPENDIX I

◄§ The Shekel

The shekel mentioned in the Torah was, as were all coins until modern times, a fixed weight of metal, in this case silver. How much did this shekel weigh? From the Talmud *(Kiddushin* 12a) we can compute that the *ma'ah* (the Aramaic equivalent of the גֵּרָה, *gerah*, of Scripture) contained 32 פְּרוּטָה, *perutah* (a copper coin that was the smallest monetary unit). The Torah *(Exodus* 30:13) specifies that the shekel should be 20 *gerah* (i.e., 20 *ma'ah*; a total of 640 *perutah*). *Rambam (Comm.* to *Bechoros* 8:7) cites the tradition transmitted in his family that the minimum *perutah* is equal in value to pure silver weighing as much as half a grain of barley. *Rif* (to *Kiddushin* 12a) relates that the *perutah* equals one half *chakah* (חכה). In a note appended to his commentary (see Chavel edition) *Ramban* identifies the *chakah* (or חבה) mentioned in the responsa of the *Geonim* as a barley grain (see also *Ran* to *Rif* ibid.). Thus according to the *Geonim* (specifically *R' Yehudah*, *Rif* and *Rambam*), the shekel of the Torah, which contains 640 *perutah*, has a minimum value of a bar of silver weighing 320 barley grains, and the half *shekel* would be 160 barley grain weights.

Rashi (comm. to *Exodus* 21:32 and *Bechoros* 49b) states that the shekel is a weight equal to a half ounce (אונקיא) in the Cologne system of measurement (לְמִשְׁקַל הַיָּשָׁר שֶׁל קוֹלוֹנְיָא). *Ramban* (in the note mentioned earlier) informs us that *Rashi's* amount is one sixth less than the view attributed to the *Geonim*. Thus, according to *Rashi*, the shekel would be 266 2/3 barley grains of silver, and the half shekel 133 1/3 such weights. *Ramban* testifies that the evidence of shekel and half shekel coins dating back to the Temple period corroborates *Rashi's* view. *Abarbanel* (to *Exodus* 30:13) speculates that these old coins may have lost some weight due to abrasion.

However, *Shulchan Aruch (Yoreh Deah* 294:67 and 305:1; see *Beur HaGra* there) accepts *Rambam* and the *Geonim's* view.

Thus far we have discussed the shekel mentioned in the Torah. At some period [Ezra's era, according to *Ramban*, *Exodus* 30:12; according to *Rabbeinu Tam* in *Tos. Menachos* 77a, s.v. והשקל and *Rambam Hil. Shekalim* 1:2, it was the era of 'the Sages'] the amount of *gerah* or *ma'ah* in the shekel was increased from twenty to forty — an increase of one fifth.

So the *selah* (shekel) of the Second Temple era was increased, according to the first view, to 384 barley grain weights, and according to *Rashi* to 320 such weights. The half shekel would weigh, respectively, 192 or 160 barley weights of silver.

In contemporary weights, *Chazon Ish (Yoreh Deah* 182:19; see also *R' Yaakov Kanievski, Kuntres Sheurim shel Torah* 65) accepts the estimate of 1 gram=20 barley weights. Thus the shekel of the Torah would equal 16 grams [according to *Rambam*; or 13 1/3 according to *Rashi*] of silver. The half shekel would be 8 [or 6 2/3] grams of silver. In troy ounces (1 oz. troy=31.103 gram) this would be approximately .51 oz. troy [or .43 oz. troy] for the shekel and half that figure for the half shekel. Figuring the price of silver to be $12 per troy ounce (its approximate price on Purim of 1981), the shekel of the Torah would be the equivalent of $6.12 [or $5.16] in contemporary values, and the half shekel is $3.06 [or $2.58].

The mishnaic *sela* would be 19.2 gram (=.62 oz. troy) valued at $7.44 [or 16 gram (=.51 oz. troy) equivalent to $6.12]. For the half *sela* (shekel in mishnaic nomenclature) these figures would be halved, $3.72 according to *Rambam*, $3.06 according to *Rashi*.

APPENDIX II

◆§ Why must the half shekel be contributed in the month of Adar?

The Torah *(Numbers* 28:14) concludes the laws of the מוּסָף, *additional burnt offering,* of Rosh Chodesh with the statement: *This is the burnt offering of the month* [i.e., Rosh Chodesh] *in its month for the months of the year.* The Talmud *(Megillah* 29b) derives another requirement from the apparently redundant word בְּחָדְשׁוֹ, *in its month.* The Hebrew word used for *month —* חֹדֶשׁ — can also be vowelized חַדֵּשׁ, *renew;* this implies a requirement that the offering of one [unspecified] Rosh Chodesh be bought with money from a new contribution. By means of the hermeneutic rule of *gezerah shavah* the Talmud *(Rosh Hashanah* 7a) derives that the unidentified Rosh Chodesh is that of Nissan. *Yerushalmi (*1:1) gives yet another reason. The first date on which an offering purchased with the half shekel payments was brought was Rosh Chodesh Nissan, the day the Tabernacle was set up. Each subsequent year the new shekalim are also used first on the day (see *Exodus* 40:2, 17; *Shabbos* 87b with *Rashi,* s.v. ראשון לעבודה).

The assignment of the entire month of Adar for the collection of the *shekels* is also based on halachic considerations.

An analogy is found in the provision that the laws of Pesach should be studied for thirty days before that holiday. In the same manner a thirty-day period is set aside for the preparation of the *mitzvah* of the *shekel (Megillah* 29b).

Though the *mitzvah* of the half shekel does not apply in post-Temple days, (see 8:8) nevertheless the provision to 'proclaim about the shekalim' still finds expression in the reading of *Parashas Shekalim —* the portion of the Torah that is the basis of the *mitzvah* of the half *shekel, Exodus* 30:11-16 — as set forth in *Megillah* (3:4; see *Gemara* 29b there).

Yerushalmi (1:1, as understood by *Meiri* and *Taklin Chadatin; cf. Korban HaEdah)* explains that only for the Jews in *Eretz Yisrael* was the first of Adar the appropriate time for the proclamation about shekalim. For the Jews living far away (e.g., Babylon), however, thirty days would not suffice for the collection of the shekalim and their transportation to the Temple. For them, the proclamation to contribute shekalim would have to be made at the onset of winter. However, *Rambam (Hil. Shekalim* 1:9) seems to make no such distinction. It can be surmised (see *Taklin Chadatin)* that *Yerushalmi's* view is based on the premise that only those whose contributions had already reached the Temple by Rosh Chodesh Nissan — when money for the communal sacrifices (קָרְבְּנוֹת צִבּוּר) was taken from the shekel contributions (see 3:2) — were considered to have a share in the sacrifices. In order to make sure that they too would share in the sacrifices, therefore, the Jews in the Diaspora had to send their contributions earlier. *Rambam (Hil. Shekalim* 2:9) rules otherwise, however. He accepts the opinion expressed in *Kesubos* (108a) that money set aside for the sacrifices was considered to be the common property of those who had contributed as well as those whose shekalim had not yet been collected. Accordingly, there would be no need to collect shekalim earlier in the Diaspora than in *Eretz Yisrael.*